The Best Spas

THE
Best Spas

Theodore B. Van Itallie, M.D.,
and Leila Hadley

PERENNIAL LIBRARY

Harper & Row, Publishers, New York
Grand Rapids, Philadelphia, St. Louis, San Francisco
London, Singapore, Sydney, Tokyo, Toronto

A hardcover edition of this book is published by Harper & Row, Publishers, Inc.

THE BEST SPAS. Copyright © 1988 by Theodore B. Van Itallie and Leila Hadley.
All rights reserved. Printed in the United States of America. No part of this book
may be used or reproduced in any manner whatsoever without written permission
except in the case of brief quotations embodied in critical articles and reviews.
For information address Harper & Row, Publishers, Inc., 10 East 53rd Street,
New York, NY 10022.

First PERENNIAL LIBRARY edition published 1989

Designed by Patricia Girvin Dunbar

Library of Congress Cataloging-in-Publication Data

Van Itallie, Theodore B., 1919–
  The best spas.

  "Perennial Library."
  Includes index.
  1. Health resorts, watering-places, etc.—Guidebooks.   I. Hadley, Leila.   II.
Title.
RA794.V36   1988   613'.122'025   87-46177
ISBN 0-06-015994-4
ISBN 0-06-091596-X (pbk.)

89 90 91 92 93 CC/FG 10 9 8 7 6 5 4 3 2 1

For Caroline and Emily, with love from their
grandfather

For Carol Cohen, our editor, with gratitude for her
tireless efforts, expertise, and shared enthusiasm

CONTENTS

⌒ **Midwest** ⌒

⌒ **Southeast** ⌒

⌒ **Northeast** ⌒

European Spas

✌ England ✍

✌ Scotland ✍

✌ France ✍

⊘ **Germany** ⊘

⊘ **Italy** ⊘

⊘ **Spain** ⊘

Other Foreign Spas

Medical Weight Loss Programs

National Weight Loss Programs

Useful Information

INTRODUCTION

Improving your health and your appearance, and getting away from stresses to refresh and revitalize your body and your mind are the main reasons why people go to spas and why spas are becoming an increasingly important part of American life. The 7-day miracle, as some refer to a week's spa vacation, provides you with a necessary interlude to change your pace of life and your way of being, to lose weight, shape up, reduce stress, gain confidence, reassess your goals, recharge your vitality, learn new exercise and nutrition behaviors, reward yourself with time out for yourself—and to have a good time, a carefree holiday.

There are many spas in the United States and abroad, as well as physician-directed residential programs to choose from, and we hope that this book will help you make the choice that is best for you. We also provide information about nonresidential programs. The main differences among spas are in the quality of what they offer and provide—diet, exercise, training programs, beauty and grooming services, facilities, educational programs, individual and group counseling, recreational options, personalized programming, take-home benefits, follow-up assistance, as well as the location, ambience, comforts, and the clientele who are attracted to them. Roses or daisies, peaches or plums, it's a matter more of preference than cost. Health and well-being transcend price, but you'll find spas and programs here in a wide range of fees.

Centuries ago in Europe, Spau, or Spa as it is now written, a resort not far from Liège in what is now Belgium, gave its name as a generic term to mineral springs and the localities surrounding them where people could come to "cure" various ailments, renew and rejuvenate themselves, and offload stress, fatigue, and depression with baths drawn from hot springs and other forms of hydrother-apy. Spa-goers then, as now, also imbibed water from mineral springs and often felt benefited by the mud by-products found at these sources and utilized for cosmetic and therapeutic packs and baths. Seawater hydrotherapy and the use of seaweed and algae wraps, dating back, as do mineral springs, to the ancient days of the Greeks and the Romans, recently returned to vogue when Louison Bobet, a Tour de France bicycling champion and national hero, attributed his "miraculous recovery" from a motor accident to the time he spent at a seaside spa in northern Brittany. Linking the Greek words *thalasso* (sea) and *therapeia* (healing) to describe heated seawater treatments updated with modern technology, he did much to help France become a world leader in the development of thalassotherapy centers.

In the 18th and 19th centuries, European spa managers considered the essential attributes of a first-class spa to be a beautiful location, a large park, an agreeable climate, creature comforts, pleasant surroundings, plenty of music, a race track, a gambling casino, a qualified medical staff to prescribe treatments, and a list of the royal, the noble, the rich, and the celebrated who came there to be rejuvenated and to enjoy the good life. Today, modern health centers have added sports, beauty salons, recreational facilities, dietetic food (upgraded in some cases to the sublime), and many other refinements.

In Europe, the focus of spas is divided between "cures," or relief from a variety of problems and ailments of a specific nature, and the reduction of stress, through changing everyday routine and giving yourself over to the care of massage therapists and exquisitely skilled estheticians. Although exercise classes are available, they are optional, with a few exceptions. The "curative" waters you drink, the baths, and the spa facilities are usually, but not always, in one location, and you are a guest at whichever hotel you prefer. European spas usually, but not always, provide a rich buffet of cultural activities and tend to offer more spectator sports and cultural events than active recreational activities. Slimming is an objective to be found more in French spas than elsewhere in Europe.

In Europe, national health insurance systems enable almost anyone with a form signed by a physician to visit a spa for a cure and to be reimbursed wholly or in large part for their expenses. This is not the case in Britain, and it is only in Britain, with a few exceptions, that you find spas that resemble more closely the fully equipped and monitored spas of the United States, where exercise is considered as important a component of your program as nutrition.

Unlike British and European spas, where passive exercise machines outnumber by far the weight resistance units, treadmills, simulated cross-country skiing machines, and stationary bicycles you'll find in America, US spas give major attention to the benefits of active exercise in reducing stress, lifting depression, burning off excess calories for weight management, and improving your overall physical condition. Almost all spas in the US feature aerobic exercise, for example, which increases the body's ability to use oxygen efficiently. For older individuals, there is recent evidence that such training can enhance brain function and improve memory, mental flexibility, reasoning ability, and reaction time. This new research suggests that Juvenal's phrase *"mens sana in corpore sano"* is a more easily attainable goal than previously believed.

If you have a serious weight problem and possible weight-excess complications such as hypertension, heart disease, or diabetes, a physician-directed program may be best for you. Many corporations encourage their executives to go to Hilton Head, the Cooper Clinic Aerobics Center, Duke University Diet and Fitness Center, Pritikin, and other estimable programs. We have also included in this book university-affiliated and hospital programs that specialize in problems of excess weight.

You'll also find resort spas that are part of a sports and recreation complex and that offer you a range of activities to schedule as you choose; nonpermissive spas where you are assigned your own personal fitness instructor whose job it is to see that your program, prescribed after a medical check, is faithfully followed; spas for women, where beauty is given equal importance with exercise; no-frills retreats for women only; spas where the focus is on fitness, overall health, and nutrition, where you can do as much or as little as you please; spas combined with the amenities of hotels; health-conscious retreats for vegetarians; holistic spas, where the focus is on the unity and interaction of your mind, body, emotions, and spiritual being; spas where health and beauty treatments can be combined with skiing, tennis, golf, and hiking; spas where you can bring your children (with someone to look after them); spas where you can joyfully celebrate holidays on your own; spas where there are nearby boarding facilities for your pet dog or cat; and many spas and medical programs where you can reward yourself for lost weight and increased good health by shopping for unique bargains.

Because getting away from the source of stress is a major part of improving your well-being, there's no way you can truly duplicate the spa experience at home. Whatever the delightful extras, the basic advantages of a spa stay are monitored programs, fitness assessments, new information, increased motivation, a change of pace, a pocket of uncluttered time in which to concentrate on self, health, and life-enhancement. Being surrounded by the potential to refresh and regenerate yourself, in a community of people all seeking the highest level of well-being, is an experience that can return you to your family and workplace as a more vital and valuable influence, as a renewed self, energized, healthier, more capable, more productive, in better control of your own existence, better informed about good nutrition, which can add years to your life, and enable you to create a better way of being for yourself. So read on, and discover where you would like to go and which program suits you best.

Specialists in spa travel in the United States and throughout the world include:

Jeffrey Joseph's Spa Finders Travel Arrangements (784 Broadway, New York, New York 10003-4856; tel: [212] 475-1000, [800] ALL SPAS outside New York state) is a spa travel agency with a computerized data base and system for finding a spa to suit your specifics from a spa-going profile you supply when you request a questionnaire. *The Spa Finder,* a spa catalogue with photographs, costs $5, and the price includes the spa questionnaire and a telephone consultation.

Spa Trek International, Inc. (470 Park Avenue South, Suite 1404, New York, New York 10016; tel: [212] 779-3480) is a "one-stop travel advisory, booking and ticketing service" that helps to match clients to the spas best suited to their needs. Founder-owners Jenni Lipa and Deana Wemble have firsthand knowledge about many spas in Europe and the United States.

Naomi Wagman's Custom Spas Worldwide (1308 Beacon Street, Brookline, Massachusetts 02146; tel: [617] 566-5144 and [800] 443-SPAS) offers individual bookings and group tours to spas.

American Spas

West Coast

⊸ The Ashram Health Retreat ⊶
California

Located 30 minutes west of Los Angeles and 10 minutes inland from the Pacific Ocean in a secluded valley of the Santa Monica hills and mountains, the Ashram (from Sanskrit, "a place for religious exercise") accepts no more than 10 guests who share 5 bedrooms and 3 bathrooms.

The program is rugged. Meals are meager. But entertainers and Hollywood folk who need to get into good shape fast and achievers who make their living with their minds think the program is the greatest, and love Anne-Marie Bennstrom and Catharina Hedberg, the Swedish dynamos who run it. Some describe it as "Marine bootcamp without the food," which Bennstrom and Hedberg cheerfully confess it may be for couch potatoes and the languid. Except for a daily massage, the Ashram has no frills.

The program is one of physical challenge, a mind-body experience that demands total commitment and self-imposed discipline. The staff are caring and supportive. The setting is pure air and natural beauty. The goal is optimal physical, mental, and spiritual well-being. The philosophy is similar to Outward Bound's wilderness survival program: by subjecting yourself to physical demands and challenges you believed were beyond your capabilities, and by meeting these demands and challenges, you can experience a high of euphoric energy and can undergo a transcendent, positive change in attitude toward yourself, your life, and the world around you.

The Ashram is a unique program in the US. Nowhere else does such privacy and seclusion exist. You don't drive to the location; you are picked up at one of three locations and brought here by van. The same van later transports you to a dozen scenic sites for morning and evening hikes over trails, as a *Time* writer commented, "so steep and narrow that the only escape is to keep going up." When the Ashram is referred to as a "retreat," Bennstrom and Hedberg mean just that. They ask you to tell your business associates, family, and friends not to telephone or write to you during your stay, as this might be "a disruptive influence." Since few people know the precise location of the Ashram, there are no drop-in visitors, no paparazzi, no autograph seekers. All clothes are provided, and you are discouraged from bringing more than a small suitcase of belongings. The diet consists mostly of fresh fruits and vegetables, served "raw," uncooked. Mercifully, Guatemalan or south-of-the-border maids do your laundry and make your bed.

Swedish born (1930) and bred Anne-Marie Bennstrom, a chiropractor with years of experience in the field of preventive health medicine, and Catharina Hedberg, graduated cum laude from the University of Stockholm in Physical Medicine and Physical Education and 16 years younger than Bennstrom, call their place a "healthort," a neologism combining "health" and "resort," "but not really a resort." A last resort the Ashram may be for you if you have to shape up fast and are in good physical condition. For some, their stay is a punishing physical nightmare, but the majority who come here seem to cope, enjoy the camaraderie and closeness that develop among participants and staff, and emerge on such a "high" that re-entry into the world of air pollution, noise, and general hurly-burly comes as a momentary culture shock. Catharina Hedberg and Anne-Marie Bennstrom alternatively take time off to head an annual excursion to Sweden, Brazil, India, and elsewhere with former guests, and to supervise workshops in Palm Springs and other parts of California and the US.

The Ashram is a two-story stucco house built into a hillside and reached by an unpaved road that winds uphill through a rocky terrain of cactus and seasonal wild flowers on the edge of a nature preserve. The house is casual, simply and comfortably furnished. There's a fireplace in the living room and a great wall of books to delve into. The dining area is off the living room and opens onto a patio set about with chairs, chaises, and tables where you can rest in the sun or shade and watch the hummingbirds zip about and hover by the feeder. The gym occupies a glass-walled, covered porch on the second floor with a lovely view of the hills beyond. Close by is the hilltop wooden geodesic dome where yoga classes are held, a one-room cottage/shed also with a grand view and used as a massage room, and a small open-air, heated swimming pool. There are many repeat participants. The age range is between 20 and 55, about 60 percent women, 40 percent men. Although hiking is the highlight of the program, repeat guests say that it's the presence of Dr. Bennstrom, wonderful Anne-Marie, that makes a stay a peak experience.

Name: The Ashram Health Retreat
Mailing Address: P.O. Box 8009, Calabasas, California 91302
Telephone: (818) 888-0232
Established: 1974

Managing Director: Anne-Marie Bennstrom, Doctor of Chiropractic Medicine
Program Directors: Dr. Anne-Marie Bennstrom; Catharina Hedberg, Associate

Director, Ph.D., Physical Medicine and Physical Education

Owner: Dr. Anne-Marie Bennstrom

Gender and Age Restrictions: Co-ed; minimum age 16

Season: Year-round

Length of Stay Required: 7 days/6 nights. Pickup service Sunday at noon, 12:30 PM, 12:45 PM. Transportation from the Ashram provided for the following Saturday at noon.

Programs Offered: You discuss your goals and your physical condition with Catharina Hedberg. Minor adjustments may be made in the program, but it is taken for granted that you are in good physical condition and are motivated to undertake the program. You are weighed and measured for comparison with what your departure weight and measurements will be. A simplified stress test on an ergometer Monark bicycle is included. Except for the locale of your hike and the evening program, each day follows the same schedule. Wake up at 6:00 AM, dress, walk up the hill to the small geodesic wooden dome where you remove your shoes before entering and seat yourself on a Persian carpet for an hour of stretching and warm-up, yoga class, and "meditation."

You breakfast on orange juice and herbal tea. "Any more," says Hedberg, "and your energy is all concentrated in your stomach digesting food." So be it. At 8:00 AM, you set off in the van for a 10-minute ride to a different hike site each day and take a 2- to 2½-hour, 3- to 6-mile hike in the Santa Catalina or Santa Monica mountains near Malibu. Unspoiled, untrammeled, the trails are truly beautiful, pristine, and as arduous in places as negotiating a shepherd's pass in the Himalayan foothills.

By 11:00 AM you are back at the Ashram ready for your weights class with Maximilian Sikinger, 75 years old chronologically, but decades younger physically. The upstairs porch gym with its inspirational view is equipped with weights and 2 stationary bicycles. After a 60-minute weights class session, you have an hour of exercise in the 4½-foot-deep pool, which has rails along its interior sides for you to hold on to while you bend and kick. After your aqua-aerobic session, which is supervised by the 2 fitness instructors who are "on" for the day—there is a staff of 4 who alternate—and a water volleyball game, you have 30 minutes for your lunch break, followed by 90 minutes of rest and sun.

At 3:00 PM you have a 60-minute Swedish massage by either a male or a female massage therapist adept also in shiatsu, acupressure, and reflexology. There are 3 male and 3 female massage therapists who can massage you in your room, at the Dome, or in the cottage/shed. At 4:00 PM a fitness instructor leads you in a 30-minute jogging session before your aerobics class. After a 60-minute session of aerobics, you are warmed up for your evening hike of 3½ to 4 miles on a different site than your morning hike. Depending on the weather, maybe you'll have a 2-hour beach walk or a mountain climb. Then home again to gather around the big, rectangular dining room table for dinner at 7:30 PM.

At 8:00 PM, a lecture or discussion on a health topic may be scheduled in the living room, or perhaps a guest lecturer will come by to talk about a New Age topic such as channeling, past lives, or astrology. One night, perhaps, you and your fellow guests will watch television, another, you may just want to go upstairs and go to bed, or climb to the Dome to sit in silence and ponder Bennstrom's belief that the program "is a peeling-away process of both weight and the negative behavior which defeats self-love," and that "a physical challenge can make you receptive to what's really inside you." Some guests never get as far as the Dome and lounge instead in the little heated swimming pool, which converts at night to a large whirlpool. Very relaxing.

Diet and Weight Management: Calories are not counted, but it's safe to say that your daily intake is no more than 600 to 800 calories. Orange juice for breakfast, a fruit salad plate for lunch, with a small portion of cottage cheese and/or yogurt, an artichoke one night for dinner, a bowl of lentil soup another night, and the rest of your dinners may consist of steamed vegetables and/or salads with a small portion of cottage cheese, yogurt, or other low-cal dressing. No meat, fish, or poultry is served. No caffeine. No artificial sweeteners. A sliced hard-boiled egg might be served with your dinnertime salad of watercress and tomato. Garlic, onions, mung beans, alfalfa sprouts, lentils, parsley, and shredded carrots are typical components of your dinnertime salads. A typical luncheon fruit plate might include a slice of papaya, apple, orange, kiwi, banana, and a garnish of a few raisins or a strawberry. Dr. Bennstrom has said that "fat is stored when and where the emotions are blocked. Release the emotions . . . and the fat leaves too." The emphasis is on fresh raw fruit and fresh raw and steamed vegetables. "A chef?" chortles Catharina Hedberg. "Just myself and the Guatemalan girls chopping and slicing in the kitchen."

All the produce is wonderfully fresh. Herbal seasonings come from the Ashram's garden. Meals are invitingly set on the dining room table around which all guests seat themselves, joined by Bennstrom, Hedberg, and the fitness directors. Snacks are available morning and afternoon: choices of as many crudités—broccoli florets, carrot sticks, celery, zucchini slivers, and other raw vegetables—as you wish to eat. A blend of celery, zucchini, and parsley juice is also available twice a day. Herbal teas are always available.

Beauty Treatments and Welcome Indulgences: These include a daily 60-minute Swedish massage and choice of reflexology, acupressure, or shiatsu techniques if you wish these to be incorporated in your treatment.

Accommodations: There are 5 bedrooms for double occupancy, so you either come with a friend or share with a stranger of the same gender. Rooms are comfortably furnished with the necessities: beds, bureau, chairs, bedside table lamp. Nothing fancy, but tastefully arranged. You share 2 bathrooms upstairs and 1 bathroom downstairs with the other guests.

What to Bring: See USEFUL INFORMATION. You are provided with a sweatsuit, T-shirts, bathrobes, and caftans and in general "completely furnished" with the attire you'll need. You are given an "I Survived The Ashram" T-shirt when you leave. You are asked to bring walking shoes, "such as Adidas or Nikes," socks, bathing suit(s), shorts, and toilet articles. Except for books or personal hobby materials, Bennstrom and Hedberg "discourage your bringing any other clothing or belongings." Don't let this prevent you from bringing a bathing suit cover-up and a jacket or heavy sweater for those cool California evenings. Your gear-on-loan is laundered by the housemaids who will also take care of your socks-and-shorts washing for whatever gratuity you feel is appropriate.

Documentation from Your Physician: Neither requested nor required. You are expected to be relatively fit when you arrive.

The Use of Alcohol and Tobacco: Neither is permitted.

Fees, Method of Payment, Insurance Coverage: Your charge for the week is $1800. A deposit is required. Ask about the cancellation policy. Cash, personal checks, and travelers' checks are accepted in payment; no credit cards. Insurance reimbursement in whole or in part may be possible if your physician can substantiate your need for weight loss, exercise, and a holistic health program of "detoxification."

∽ Cal-à-Vie Health Resort ∾
California

Cal-à-Vie, c'est la vie splendide indeed of freedom from stress in a surprisingly charming enclave 50 miles northeast of San Diego, close enough to the ocean and high enough above sea level to assure clean air, constant breezes, and restful views of wooded hills you'll find yourself happily hiking up at dawn. Exclusive (24 maximum capacity in individual cottages), expensive, secluded on 130 acres of territory appropriately called Vista, with privacy secured by a TV-monitored electronic gate, Cal-à-Vie at first glance appears like a mirage—a mound at differing elevations of pale orange-pink one- and two-story houses, weather vanes perched on turrets, silvery-pink tiled roofs, a style of landscaping vaguely Andalusian, yet with sparkling colors in the courtyards and flower beds reminiscent of southern France. Actually, it's the fulfillment of "a dream to create an environment of peace and beauty where those interested in good health will be inspired to change their lifestyle," says founder and owner William F. Power, yachtsman, ocean racer, skier, avid fitness enthusiast, and leading developer of health-care institutions in the state of California. He believes that stress is the "number one health problem in the country" and that his spa "is the . . . antidote to the problem." New in 1986, Cal-à-Vie is acclaimed by America's top stressed-out executives (men and women), as well as by rising young affluent professionals and many celebrities who flock here to lose pounds and inches. Many also arrive in good shape. Overall director Susan Power, as avid a fitness enthusiast as her 60-year-old father, notes that many guests come for "maintenance and fine-tuning." With ages generally ranging from 30 to 60, guests enjoy state-of-the-art American fitness expertise harmoniously combined with European-style health and beauty-from-the-inside-out treatments.

No nail-wrapping, depilatory waxing, beard-tinting here. The focus, pure and fresh as the ornamental rock pool in the garden compound, is on the natural. Nature's own aromatic, tonic, healing extracts and essential oils are distilled from the sea and from the land's bounty of herbs and flowers. To bring mind and body into balance and harmony and help relax and "detoxify" the body, multisensual treatments—thalassotherapy, hydrotherapy, and aromatherapy, in conjunction with facials, body massages, modified acupressure, and scalp and hair conditioning—are performed with consummate skill and attention. The all-encompassing ambience soothes with the natural grace of light and space enhanced with the creature comforts of down-filled pillows, cushioned chaises, fires on cool nights set in stone fireplaces, furnishings attractively and comfortably styled, napkins furled beside service plates of good china, and similar niceties of detail. Fresh changes of exercise clothes are provided daily and with them the boon of noncompetitive spa dressing. Guaranteed is the total concentration of all staff members on your well-being, good health, relaxation, and comfort, with a courtesy of service remarkable for its thoughtfulness and attentive cosseting.

Name: Cal-à-Vie Health Resort

Mailing Address: 2249 Somerset Road, Vista, California 92084

Telephone: (619) 945-2055

Established: 1986

General Manager: Bruce Becker

Overall Director: Susan Power

Owner: William F. Power, founder and general partner

Gender and Age Restrictions: For men and women, minimum age 18. There are 16 women's weeks, including a mother-

and-daughter (not under 16 years) week; 26 co-ed weeks; 7 men's weeks; 3 weeks for couples.

Season: Year-round except for 14 days over Christmas and New Year's

Length of Stay Required: 8 days/7 nights; arrival between 1:00 and 4:00 PM Sunday and departure the following Sunday at 11:00 AM

Programs Offered: Stress reduction, body awareness, skin care, relaxation, weight loss, education in *cuisine fraîche,* fitness—an all-in-one package of personalized attention intended to balance and heal your mind, body, and spirit. You receive an individualized fitness program to follow at the spa and an exercise routine developed to fit into your lifestyle upon your return home. These are based on a personal assessment conducted the day you arrive, which incorporates testing of your areas of flexibility, cardiovascular capability, and upper and lower body strength. A computerized data-processing device that is informed about your bodily measurements, the ratio of your body fat to your lean body mass, and other personal statistics prints out an exercise program for you. It also tabulates how many calories must be eliminated from your food regimen to allow you to achieve your ideal weight based on your basal metabolic rate. If it is inches you wish to lose or gain, the exercise program is adapted to concentrate on the specific areas on which you need to work. Options are offered for all levels of fitness.

The basic fitness program includes hiking for overall toning and cardiovascular strengthening; classes in body awareness to put you in touch with your body's strengths and weaknesses as well as your posture, movements, and body alignment; body contouring to strengthen specific muscle groups; four 50-minute one-on-one training sessions to supplement body contouring classes with workouts on Nautilus and Keiser Cam II equipment, a NordicTrack treadmill, and Dynavit bicycles; swimming pool exercise that includes aqua-aerobics, volleyball, and swimming; classes in low-impact aerobics, stretching, yoga, and the ancient discipline of Tai Chi to promote flexibility, relaxation, and precise body alignment. "Physical endurance nourishes the spirit," says Susan Power. "The ability to challenge one's limits does wonders for the psyche." Built into the exercise regime she has developed, stress reduction is also a subject of evening discussions at which you will be gently hectored about topics relevant to your health and well-being. Your daily program, which begins with a 5:30 AM wake-up call, comprises a demanding, structured morning schedule offset with afternoons of sumptuous European spa–style treatments and services accorded you by deft and caring body and skin therapists. To relax you, help detoxify your body, and soothe your spirits, you are provided with these weekly panaceas:

· A 90-minute thalassotherapy treatment intended to help rebalance your body chemistry by eliminating excess water retention and stimulating "toxic waste" excretion through the skin (i.e., perspiration). You are wrapped in a paste of sea kelp and mineral-rich sea water imported from France, then cocooned in a plastic-coated heated blanket and gently roasted for 20 minutes, after which you shower, are rewrapped, shower again, and receive an application of cooling seaweed gel.

· Two 60-minute hydrotherapy treatments intended to slim, relax, and invigorate you. Immersed in a large tub imported from France and filled with a brew of minerals from the sea, you bask while strong multijets of water massage your stomach, back, and the soles of your feet. Simultaneously, a body therapist massages your back, neck, and shoulders with aromatic oils and essences of herbs and flowers.

· A 60-minute Body Glo (salt rub) treatment that sloughs away all your dead skin cells to reveal new layers of skin to be polished and buffed.

· A 60-minute aromatherapy massage with a blend of 25 oils to enhance your mood, whiff away your tensions, and detoxify your body.

· 5 body massages.

· A 60-minute reflexology foot massage to calm your mind and invigorate your body.

· Three 60-minute facials employing extracts from land and sea, essences of herbs and flowers, healing clays, and collagen fiber masques to cleanse, tone, and energize your relaxed and smiling visage.

· A 60-minute hair and scalp cleansing, massage, and conditioning treatment employing seaweed ingredients "to re-establish the hair's initial structure," so that one rises from the foam with the éclat of a Botticelli Primavera.

· Two 60-minute treatments which encase your hands and feet in paraffin molds to exfoliate, soften, and moisturize the skin of these extremities, to the nails of which polish, if you want, is applied the day of your departure, when your hair is coiffed and your face dramatized with a 60-minute makeup session, the only concessions to conventional "beauty treatments." Beauty at Cal-à-Vie is encouraged to develop from the inside outward.

To maximize the benefits of the fitness and skin care programs, Michel Stroot, the spa's master chef, and Linny Largent, the spa's nutritionist, present a well-balanced, slimming cuisine, utilizing the freshest of baby vegetables and herbs from the spa's own kitchen garden, and demonstrate the technique of his *cuisine fraîche* in a 60-minute weekly cooking class where the nutritional value of the spa menu is also discussed. There are evening lectures and counseling sessions on body therapy, stress management, and fitness.

Maximum Number of Guests: 24

Full-Time Health Professionals on Staff: 9, plus 14 certified body therapists, including a registered nurse, and 9 certified beauty therapists. For emergencies, Palomar Hospital in Escondido is within a 10-minute drive, and Scripps Memorial Hospital is in nearby San Diego; 15 staff members are trained in CPR.

Diet and Weight Management: Graduated with honors from the Hotel School Ceria in Brussels, French-speaking, Belgium-born Master Chef Michel Stroot, culinary consultant, teacher, lecturer, and co-author of *The Golden Door Cookbook,* during his 11 years at that world-famous spa created a low-calorie gourmet plan he calls *cuisine fraîche.* He and Linny Largent, former bread-baker, sous-chef, and nutritionist at the Golden Door, continue to work together in his new "dream kitchen" at Cal-à-Vie. Artfully, Stroot carves carrots and bell peppers into palm-tree shapes, sculpts segments of watermelon into whales with curving tails, fills pineapple boats with fresh fruit garnished with mint leaves, stuffs squash blossoms, arranges raspberries and slices of kiwi fruit on the surface of a gratin of apple and apricot, adds bright dashes of color to a salad of watercress and beansprouts garnished with toasted sunflower seeds, and to a paillard of turkey with grapefruit wedges and rosemary. His salads contain from 12 to 20 ingredients, "like miniature treasure chests," he says as he transforms fresh fruit, fresh herbs, and fresh vegetables from the spa's kitchen garden into beautifully presented menus—low in fat, salt-free, high in fiber and complex carbohydrates—allowing 800, 1200, or 2000 calories a day. On Wednesdays and Fridays a cleansing diet of fresh fruit and vegetable juices is optional. Stroot's sauces, a reduction of chives, garlic, and leeks, flavored with fresh cilantro, thyme, basil, marjoram, dill, and oregano picked at the peak of perfection, turn food that is good for you into delicious and crispy fare that comprises 50 to 60 percent fresh fruits and vegetables, 10 to 20 percent low-fat animal protein, and 10 to 20 percent fat. Herbal teas, Vittel mineral water, crudités and fruit slices, fresh fruit and vegetable juices, and fresh lemonade are always at hand to sip and nibble on throughout the day. Lunch is served on glass plates with white china cups for soup set on tables beneath large umbrellas on the patio in the garden compound. Dinner, presented on the finest Villaroy and Boch china, is served at the civilized hour of 7:15 PM in a French provincial–style dining room. Tables are set for four or six and centered with bowls of flowers, and napkins are folded and pleated in pretty shapes at each place setting. All meals are special, unhurried times to be savored by your eyes as well as your palate. "Starving yourself," Linny Largent cautions, "only slows down your metabolism. Your body's system goes into shock, shuts down, and your weight loss is not what it can be when you concentrate on consuming a diet rich in fiber and complex carbohydrates as we do at Cal-à-Vie." Although weight loss is one of the objectives of the spa, many women guests arrive who aim—generally successfully—to lose more inches than pounds. A nice parting touch is a picnic with appropriate menu provided for your trip home.

Exercise and Physical Therapy Facilities: The interior of the "beauty building," where you go for your facials, hair and scalp conditioning, and hands and feet treatments is as pink and peachy as the early morning sky you see on your hikes. The bathhouse is where you go for a dry or wet sauna, a Jacuzzi, or a whirlpool which seats six comfortably. Thalassotherapy, aromatherapy, and hydrotherapy treatments are performed here, and here also are the rooms with the weight machines, Nautilus, Keiser Cam II equipment, Dynavit bicycles, and treadmill. The bathhouse, like the building containing the low-impact aerobics class space, with its specially cushioned floor, and another space with traditional hardwood flooring where you do your stretch, Tai Chi, and yoga classes, are mostly beige in decor, with gray carpeting. All three buildings have great expanses of window glass or skylights and are wonderfully airy. Set about with bamboos and palms, with rooms that look out on rolling, wooded hills, the clinical aspects of the equipment are gentled by delicate bamboo screens placed here and there, by wheeled chaises and wicker furniture, by recordings of pleasant "environmental" music, by tonic fragrances of rosemary, geranium, citrus, cypress, almonds, apricots, seaweed, and meadowsweet wafting from aromatherapy treatment rooms, but most of all by the soothing virtuosity of the body and beauty therapists. The attentive expertise of the fitness instructors reveals physical potentials you did not know you had in exercise rooms that allow you plenty of space to move about in freely. And of course, at Cal-à-Vie there's never any waiting to make use of the equipment or facilities.

Opportunities for Recreational Exercise: Guests can enjoy an outdoor swimming pool; a tennis court complete with a super tennis pro to improve your game (60-minute private lessons, $30); complimentary access to an 18-hole golf course at the neighboring private Vista Valley Country Club (lessons extra); and hiking and walking trails.

Beauty Treatments and Welcome Indulgences: See Programs Offered. Phytomer seaweed products imported from France, Eve Taylor herbal and flower essences, Yonka and Avance products are employed for treatments.

Accommodations: The 24 guest cottages have roofs pleated like Fortuny silk with terra-cotta tiles, facades of pale pinky-orange stucco complemented with geranium-filled window boxes, wide-planked doors and shutters, and hand-forged iron door knockers. Each cottage has its own private deck, patio, or balcony for mountain or garden views. *All cottages for single adult occupancy.* If you arrive as a couple, you each have your own cottage to assure you of solitude to rest or nap. However, couples can do whatever they want at night, says Bruce Becker. Commodious interiors are peaceful and charming, decorated with flowered chintz covering plump down-filled pillows and comforter on a queen-sized bed, with matching curtains in pastel shades of rose, mint green, yellow, or blue at the wide windows and the French door that leads onto your balcony, patio, or sun deck. Beamed ceiling; large, hexagonal, mosaic-tiled bathroom; copper wall lanterns; a special mat thoughtfully laid out on the carpet on which to set your muddy hiking shoes; fresh flowers and plants and a carafe of Vittel water; hand-carved furniture in light and dark oak and pine, including a sturdy writing desk, roomy armoire, night tables for twin lamps, the bench at the foot of your downy bed, the frame of a cushioned chaise with a lamp standing behind it for comfortable feet-stretched-out reading—your cottage room is appointed with your comfort, serenity, and visual pleasure in mind. Air-conditioning and private telephone, of course, but no television. That you can watch if you like on a large screen in the main spa building where there is also a VCR hookup.

What to Bring: See USEFUL INFORMATION. You receive daily changes of exercise clothes: blue sweats for women, grey and blue ones for men; grey shorts and blue T-shirts for men, and peach-colored shorts and T-shirts for women; beige terry-cloth robes and jackets for cool mornings; and a pair of rubber thong slippers. This wardrobe, plus the exercise clothes that you bring, can get you through the entire week. No one wears anything dressier than shorts, leotards, or a robe and slippers most of the afternoon. Warm-ups are often worn at dinner. You are asked to leave fancy clothes and jewelry at home. There is a sports boutique in the main building and, if you have forgotten anything, your shopping can be done for you in nearby Escondido. If you are a reader, bring reading material with you.

Documentation from Your Physician: A letter of approval is requested if there is any doubt about your ability to take part in the spa's fitness program. Without a medical history and documentation of recent physical examination, you will be required to sign a medical release.

The Use of Alcohol and Tobacco: At your arrival day dinner, you get a glass of wine. Thereafter, no alcoholic beverages are available on the premises. No smoking in public areas, but there are, as of this writing, a few rooms in the main building where smoking is allowed.

Fees, Method of Payment, Insurance Coverage: Year-round rates for 8-day/7-night program: $3500 single, no doubles available. All prices are subject to change. Rates are subject to a $50.40 San Diego room tax (total fee). A 15 percent ($450) service charge is added, and no additional tips are expected. A deposit is required. Ask about the cancellation policy. Personal checks, travelers' checks, and Visa, American Express, and MasterCard are accepted. Depending on your health insurance carrier, partial reimbursement for your fees may be possible if you have a covering letter from your physician.

✆ Golden Door ✆
California

Created in 1959, now a $10 million complex on 177 acres in the foothills near Escondido in southern California, 40 miles north of San Diego, the Golden Door accommodates no more than 39 privileged guests in a style which its founder, Brooklyn-born Deborah Szekely (pronounced say-kay), models on that of the traditional *honjin* inns of Japan which have, since feudal times, restored and comforted noble travelers. With superlative service, your interior self and your outer body will be taken care of completely, your every preference and velleity attended to. What this celebrated arbiter of American fitness promises, you can be sure she will do her best to fulfill, on land as well as on sea—you can also enjoy the expertise of Golden Door personnel aboard Cunard's *Queen Elizabeth 2, Sagafjord,* and *Vistafjord.*

Deborah Szekely could be called the founding mother of American spas. Author, teacher, an advisor to the Council on Physical Fitness for three presidents (Nixon, Ford, Reagan), a member of the Board of Trustees of the Menninger Foundation, recipient of many citations and awards, Deborah Szekely is the only spa owner and founder to be honored by a listing in *Who's Who. Courvoisier's Book of the Best* recently acknowledged her sleekest of "health farms" (the British term for what we Americans refer to as "spas") as the best of the world's best.

Rancho La Puerta in Mexico (see OTHER FOREIGN SPAS: MEXICO), Mrs. Szekely's first-founded spa, throbs with energy. The leitmotif of the Golden Door is serenity, and your week here is based on a "Japanese transcendental experience." "The Golden Door," Szekely promises, "will point you on your way on your very personal life journey toward revitalization and perpetual renewal." The Golden Door successfully emulates the Japanese worship of nature as it follows art and tallies with elegance—a pinch of abstraction, a few touches of symbolism, carved stone lanterns, a Buddhist prayer rock, a lilting *torii* gate, and nature all around attuned to an aesthetic wavelength for your gratification and that of your fellow guests, who usually are involved in business, industry, banking, or law or married to spouses in those professions. Ages may range from 18 to 85, with the majority in their mid-40s. Often, there is a celebrity among them. Some want to lose 10 pounds. Others, slim as reeds, want to tone up and disencumber themselves of inches and stress by beneficial exercise.

One-story, weathered-wood-trimmed stuccoed buildings with silvery-green tiled roofs shelter you in bed-sitting rooms that are as comfortable and spacious as they are thoughtfully appointed. Each has its "moon-viewing" alcove and access to a private garden where hummingbirds feed and fuchsias bloom in profusion. These provide serenity and solitude, as do the abundance of tranquil walks and vistas offered by the spa's estate. To reach the spa's entrance, you cross a spring-fed stream that courses beneath a wooden footbridge portaled by a door with a tree-of-life motif hammered on its shining brass surface—the eponymous golden door. When you enter, the land of *shibui,* the quintessential Japanese word for the refinement of beauty, spreads before you. You hear a 17th-century temple bell, which summons you to meals that are a feast to your eyes and a skimp on calories. You inhale the scent of orange blossoms from your herbal body wrap, and the fragrance of gardenias at your window. You may meditate in a subtle Zen garden or in an exquisite tea house on a hillside. You walk on stepping-stone pathways through courtyards of camellias and azaleas and through a garden of boulders rising from a sea of raked and rippled waves of sand. You discover a garden of flowing streams, water basins, waterfalls, and a reflective pool, and a lake garden afloat with lilies and shimmering with the flash and glint of *koi* (carp). You walk among rugged hills, stands of bamboo, groves of century-old live oaks, black pines, and eucalyptus, and orchards of avocadoes, oranges, lemons, limes, grapefruit, and apricots. This is not just a super spa, but another world, in which you are encouraged to remain for a week of unflawed serenity, caring service, commodious accommodations, luxurious ambience, with delicious provisions for your body, eye, and mind from dawn until you pillow your head to sleep after a day of stimulating exercise. This stay can whittle away as much as 10 to 12 inches overall and at least half as many pounds.

Name: Golden Door
Mailing Address: P.O. Box 1567, Escondido, California 92025

Telephone: (619) 744-5777
Established: 1959, at present facility since 1975

Managing Director: Rachel Caldwell

Owner: Deborah Szekely

Gender and Age Restrictions: There are 35 women's weeks; 8 men's weeks (the first 2 weeks of March, June, September, and December); 7 weeks for couples (married) (the second 2 weeks of March and September and 3rd week in June). Minimum age 17.

Season: Year-round, except for 2 weeks (varying dates) in December

Length of Stay Required: 8 days/7 nights, Sunday afternoon after 2:00 PM to following Sunday noon. *N.B.:* To make all days count and not sacrifice Day One to upsets caused by time change, the Golden Door suggests that 10 to 14 days before your flight time you gradually change your sleeping hours to conform with Pacific Coast Standard (or Daylight Saving) time, and start eating your meals on Golden Door time. Invaluable reading material about how to beat jet lag, preliminary exercises you can do to prepare for your Golden Door week, and exercises you can do aboard the jet is sent to you when you request a brochure, a thoughtful service unique with the Golden Door.

Programs Offered: Your program is tailored to fit your needs and goals within a structured framework with many options. The program includes 2 hours weekly of consultations with the spa director, fitness supervisor, and professional fitness guides; 90 minutes of nutritional counseling and 2 hours of cooking classes and demonstrations with the chef in the spa kitchen; 60 minutes daily of training in stress management and relaxation techniques—up to 8 hours weekly in private sessions on request; and 7 hours daily of exercise counseling and supervision.

Fitness and knowledge of nutrition are the top priorities, followed by weight management by means of exercise, controlled calories, and behavior modification. Beginning with a brisk 1½- to 5½-mile hike at sunrise "before the dewdrops have dried," the exercise program continues with the Golden Door Da Vinci exercises, an aerobics session using hoops, Indian clubs, sticks, and towels, based on Leonardo's theories of movement, and climaxes in midafternoon with the Golden Door Special of the day, which may be one of the following: a walk-jog-run continuum with meticulous attention to prejogging warm-ups; a session on the parcours track; a class in tap-dancing or jazz or rhythm weights; a rapid workout on the aerobic circuit of stationary bicycles, the rowing machine, treadmills, free weights, rebounders, and Camstar's 14 pieces of specialized equipment; splash-dancing in the pool or water volleyball; or a Tai Chi session. The Golden Door introduced aquatic aerobics to spa life. Another first is the spa's analysis of your movement patterns with recommendations to give you increased awareness of your posture and habitual mistakes you might make while moving, doing exercises, or even carrying a briefcase or purse that could throw the proper alignment of your body out of kilter. On the last day, there's often a specially planned mountain hike, where a fitness instructor takes a photograph as a memento for each guest who makes it to the top. After the exercise crescendo of the day, you wind down at twilight with a quasiballetic stretch class in combination with progressive relaxation, using biofeedback techniques, guided imagery, and/or a Westernized form of yoga that demonstrates relaxation techniques for stretching out the body. Intermingled with your daily exercises, you receive a daily treatment in the bathhouse—a Kneipp herbal wrap, a sauna, a steam treatment, or a soak in the whirlpool, followed by a massage in your own room on a massage table unfolded from its hiding place in your room closet. Manicure, pedicure, scalp conditioning with an avocado oil pack massage, eyebrow waxing, and hair-do are once-a-week 60-minute treats. You receive a facial masque daily for that characteristic Golden Door "glow," with accompanying hand and foot massage. Skin care and makeup lessons, using specially formulated Golden Door cosmetics, are included in your program.

Dinner is followed by a short, brisk walk and by two sets of evening programs: The series for the first-time guest includes basics such as lectures on nutrition and stress management, a cooking class with the Golden Door chef in his kitchen, and an introduction to organic gardening illustrated with slides. The returning guest can sit in on discussions with a consulting physical therapist about back, posture, and neck problems, or touch on subjects such as time management, body language, stimulating the immunological system, left- and right-brain integration, and sports medicine. You can watch one of a hundred VCR films, play backgammon, attend an *ikebana* (Japanese flower-arranging) class, play old-fashioned parlor games, or learn a lot from Annharriet Buck's Inner Door course, which she developed to acquaint guests with the magic of the mind. This intensive course, limited to guests who are on their third or fourth visit, uses techniques of guided imagery, meditation, and autosuggestion; you conduct a week-long investigation of your whole self—"an in-depth interview of your inner being"—as a "prelude to creating your own script for your immediate future." At the end of the evening, guests troop to the bathhouse for a sauna, a steam, or a communal soak in a Japanese hot tub and a relaxing minimassage before they sleep. If, for any reason, you find it hard to sleep—few people do—a relaxation cassette player is attached to each bedside.

On arrival, you are interviewed to determine your fitness level, possible restrictions in diet or exercise, and your goals for the week. Sub-Max Stress testing to assess your physical performance is scheduled. On request, a caliper skinfold test to assess your body composition can also be scheduled. You are assigned a fitness instructor who will be your mentor and fitness confidant for the week. On your first day, he or she will discuss with you your movement assessment, which determines your range of motion and identifies where improvement is needed. You receive an orientation tour and a helpful orientation booklet and map. Announcements pertaining to the week's schedule of events are made at Sunday night dinner. You attend an orientation breakfast on Monday, and your Monday lunch is hosted in groups of 5 by a fitness guide with further program orientation. Your personal daily schedule is presented to you on your breakfast tray each morning—a small paper fan listing activities, which most guests pin on their T-shirts as a guide. The pace of each class is stepped up daily. If you wish some change in your schedule, your fitness advisor can offer alternatives such as lap swimming, tennis, or a workout in the vegetable garden. Lolling about is not encouraged, but no one is ever pushed to overexert. A qualified physical therapist checks you for possible back problems and flexibility. Sometime during the week, you'll be scheduled for an exercise session designed especially for you and put on a cassette tape—or a videotape if you prefer to pay extra—for you to take home as an aide-mémoire for fitness.

Maximum Number of Guests: 39

Full-Time Health Professionals on Staff: 19, plus 7 facialists, 8 masseuses, and 2 manicurist/pedicurists, a Kneipp-trained herbal therapist, hairdresser and staff. All fitness and hiking leaders are certified in CPR and trained in first aid. The night telephone operator is trained in emergency first aid. The Palomar hospital in Escondido is 5 miles away.

Diet and Weight Management: On the basis of individual height, weight, and fitness levels, and other information derived from a personal interview with each guest, individual calorie levels are determined by the nutritionist and spa director. Fewer than 900 calories a day are not encouraged, and the average caloric level is 1000. The daily menu is low in sodium, reduced in cholesterol, and high in fiber. Red meat is never served. The menu features fresh seafood and occasional poultry (the spa's own free-ranging fowl), plus legumes, yogurt, eggs, cheese, and milk as principal protein sources. The Golden Door provides 80 percent of its own table fare, fabled for its picked-that-day freshness, eye appeal, and delectable flavor combinations. Bread, pasta, herb vinegars, and yogurt are all freshly prepared in the spa kitchen. Vegetables and fruit unsullied by noxious chemicals, sulfites, and preservatives are a health and taste treat guaranteed to surprise your palate as piquantly as the palette of their fresh colors delights your eyes. Marine blue and cloud-white settings on trays and tables provide a pleasing contrast for crisp greens and the jewel tones of fruit. Every meal is presented with a different accent, a changed pattern or shape of china, another weave of cloth or napkin. Midmorning potassium-rich vegetable broth with minutely cut raw vegetables and cheese for nibbling is served by the swimming pool, and an afternoon break of pear juice or a fruit punch, also served poolside, plus low-calorie crudités, stuffed mushrooms, and appetizing dips served before dinner help to keep your appetite under control. No liquids are served with meals because Szekely believes they interfere with digestion. At the end of each meal, coffee, mineral water, and hot and cold herbal teas are offered. For those who opt to try it, a "virtue-making" day of juice fasting is available, more effective, Szekely says, for cleansing one's system than for weight loss.

Tracy Ritter, the executive chef, produces oat cuisine breakfast muesli with fruits, nuts, and spices, and prides herself on her French omelettes fluffy with the whipped whites of eggs and merely tinged with the rich color of the yolks. Her salsify soup is velvety smooth, even though she has "pulled out all the fats and oils from it." Her king salmon, aromatic with lemon thyme and basil, enveloped in flaky filo pastry, is astonishingly low in calories and handsomely presented with a julienne of spring vegetables or asparagus tied with a chive ribbon. Another of her specialties is pasta salad with wild mushrooms, basil, and smoked chicken. Individual orange soufflés with a base of ricotta cheese are among her innovative desserts, and vegetable pizza with a whole-wheat crust is one of her favorite luncheon dishes. Lacto-ovo and strictly vegetarian regimens as well as special menus for guests with allergies, diabetes, ulcers, or other diet requirements are prepared. When you leave, you depart with a super special low-cal boxed lunch for your journey.

Exercise and Physical Therapy Facilities: The Azalea, Bamboo, Camellia, and Dragon Tree gymnasia are each housed in buildings that are glassed in on three sides for unobstructed views of inspiring natural and planned landscaping; all feature off-white ceilings and indirect lighting. Used for exercise classes, A, B, and C are fully cushioned with aerobic flooring and supplemented by an outdoor gym, an unnamed pavilion where stretch classes are held on semipadded flooring. The Dragon Tree Gym contains Bosch stationary bicycles, Trotter treadmills, rowing machine, rebounders, free weight equipment, and Camstar body-building equipment comprising abdominal trunk curl, power leg press, seated thigh curl, seated thigh extension, outer thigh abductor, inner thigh abductor, bilateral chest, total triceps conditioner, shoulder press, bicep curl, heavy flat bench, incline bench, seated dorsi, and fixed double pulley. An outdoor lap pool and an exercise/volleyball pool, kept at 82 degrees in summer and 92 degrees in winter, and the outdoor Jacuzzi, which seats a maximum of 8 guests, are close to the Dragon Tree Gym and the bathhouse with its gleaming charcoal tiles where you'll find the steam room, sauna, crescent-shaped Japanese family hot tub, herbal wrap room, showers, and Swiss alternating hot-and-cold-jet shower. Up the hillside from the Dragon Tree Gym is a solarium. You receive personal supervision at all your exercise classes.

Opportunities for Recreational Exercise: Opportunities for hill climbing and hiking and walking (trails available) abound. Guests can use a lap-swimming pool and a heated exercise pool, both outdoors, and two concrete tennis courts, lit for evening play. Optional private tennis lessons with the pro are extra.

Beauty Treatments and Welcome Indulgences: The beauty rooms share a building with the Azalea Gym next to the administrative offices. Facials, skin cleansings, deep pore cleansings, paraffin masks, scalp treatments, a warm oil treatment with electric-blanketlike mittens and boots, manicures, and pedicures are all skillfully and caringly provided to you as part of your weekly fee, as are blissful massages—Swedish, shiatsu, and sports massages for muscles and tendons—in your room. The exclusive Golden Door hypoallergenic beauty products, available nowhere else, are employed for your treatments. Optional beauty treatments such as hair cuts, sets, and blow-drys, tints, highlighting, and permanents are extra.

Accommodations: Opening onto various courtyards and their own bamboo and flower gardens with hummingbird feeders, each of the 39 commodious guestrooms is a well-chosen East-West mix: queen-sized bed, surrounding decor of peaceful earth colors and light flower hues to complement museum-quality art objects—painted wooden and rice-paper screens, scrolls, triptychs, traditional *tokonoma* (Shinto altar niche) with a spare, fresh *ikebana* flower arrangement. You'll know this is your room because there's a plaque with your name lettered in gold on the door, and the white and gold writing paper supplied at your desk has your name printed on it. The large closet in the room's foyer contains almost all the gear you'll need for the week. Your personal laundry is whisked off in a laundry bag every morning and returned to you by 3 PM free of charge. An alcove with table and chairs and sliding glass doors which lead to your garden is your interior "moon-viewing" alcove. The majority of the bathrooms, all large and airy with pastel ceilings, also have sliding rice-paper or glass doors opening onto their room's garden. There's plenty of counter space and the cabinets are stocked with rich stores of complementary Golden Door skin care products. You have a telephone in your room with 24-hour switchboard service. No television except for the communal set in the lounge. Rooms are not locked, no keys to worry about. There is a safe for valuables at the reception facility.

What to Bring: See USEFUL INFORMATION. Supplied on arrival or waiting for you in your room closet, to be worn at the spa and left when you leave, are white plastic slippers; a blue-and-white lightweight cotton kimonolike robe called a "yukata" (fresh ones supplied as necessary); pink or lavender T-shirts for women, grey for men, as many as you need; unisex grey warm-up suits and running shorts, as many as you need; a windbreaker and a yellow knee-length rain slicker poncho. Men are asked to bring casual sportswear for evening, and women should bring a caftan or simple long skirt with a blouse or sweater for casual evenings. On Saturday's graduation night everyone dresses up a bit more. You are asked not to bring jewelry or formal clothes. The spa has its own small library. Magazines are available. Newspapers are supplied daily on request. Sundry items can be purchased by the spa's personal shopper three times a week. The Golden Door gift shop and clothing boutique is well stocked.

Documentation from Your Physician: A letter of approval is requested if you doubt your ability to undertake an active program, but not required. On arrival, a fitness questionnaire is filled in to determine your fitness level and physical limitations in order to plan your individualized schedule. You are asked to bring a supply of any medication you may be taking.

The Use of Alcohol and Tobacco: An alcoholic beverage is allowed for only one dinner a week and is "discouraged at all other times." Smoking is allowed only in guests' rooms and outdoors; no smoking in public areas or outdoor areas where guests congregate. The staff are all nonsmokers.

Fees, Method of Payment, Insurance Coverage: Year-round rates for the 8-day/7-night program: $3500 for all rooms. Price is subject to change, and the rate is subject to a San Diego room and food tax of $64.84. No tipping required. With the exception of purchases in the boutiques, no credit cards are accepted; payment is by check (including travelers' checks) or cash only. A deposit is required. Ask about the cancellation policy. Fees are not usually tax-deductible, but check with your doctor and tax advisor about insurance coverage.

Follow-up Assistance: Audio exercise cassettes individually taped for each guest are take-home maintenance aids, free of charge. Video cassettes of yourself can be made for an extra charge. Golden Door cookbooks are available as long as the supply lasts. Follow-up letters are sent in response to comments and suggestions, one along with the group photograph of your week. Most correspondence is "personal, individual."

La Costa Hotel and Spa
California

La Costa, in the foothills near the village of Carlsbad, about a 35-minute drive north of San Diego and 90 minutes south of Los Angeles, is often regarded as a California phenomenon akin to Disneyland—huge, packed with attractions, with architecture that is meant to impress. With its orange and raspberry-pink main building in post-modern Spanish traditional style, set on 1000 acres spreading back from the Pacific coast, La Costa easily encompasses 36 stunning holes of golf where Mutual of New York's (MONY) tournament of Champions tees off yearly; accommodation for 1000 guests or more in rooms and suites fresh from a $100 million renovation, as well as studio bungalows, rental villas, and "executive homes"; a private 180-seat cinema featuring first-run films nightly; and a 50,000-square-foot conference center. La Costa also claims baby-sitting services, a Children's Program Center operative during school holidays; tennis night and day taught by the venerable Pancho Segura, with 23 courts to play on; 7 restaurants, 4 snack bars; nighttime big-band and cabaret entertainment.

There is a seductive array of cosmetic services in its grooming and beauty salons and a multitude of exercise facilities and relaxation services in the men's and women's pavilions of its spa building, where everything is intended to appear as sumptuous as the Baths in the days of imperial Rome. (To loud-pedal this point, the spa is built around an atrium, you are robed in a "towel toga," and Jacuzzis are referred to as "Roman pools.") The ambience conjures the practiced professionalism and courtesies of a country club smoothly melded with the conviviality of a cruise ship chartered by people who are accustomed to expensive products and services—successful business owners, their spouses, senior executives, TV stars, and other people who do things that produce large incomes. The guests, whose average age is between 35 and 55, are evenly split between men and women, with about 40 percent visiting as couples. You may see a few guests who need to lose between 20 and 50 pounds, and a few have a medical problem such as diabetes, arthritis, or a cardiovascular ailment, but most of the time it's hard to tell the hotel guests from the spa guests, who comprise about 20 percent of the total guest roster.

Although La Costa offers little to those looking for tranquility or the sense of being part of a support- and goal-oriented group, and although it offers many temptations to stray from prescribed regimens of diet and exercise, nevertheless, you can lose weight and gain inches in all the right places and learn a great deal about nutrition and techniques for stress reduction, relaxation, and healthy repatterning of your mode of living if you enroll in La Costa's new *Life Fitness Program,* where a spirited sense of camaraderie among the participants obtains. It's a matter of setting your own goals and following them. Cautionary note: It takes a lot of self-discipline to confine yourself to the spa dining room when you could be enjoying "the sterling and crystal 5-star experience" of the expensive, candlelit Champagne Room to the tune of a violin's obbligato in another area of the clubhouse building, or flaked out in your room telephoning for room service.

Some guests never stir from La Costa's property. For those with wanderlust and without cars, a 6-passenger hotel van provides transport for a modest charge to La Jolla to shop for California crafts and clothes for the *vida alegre* and much more. Other opportunities for trips by hotel van, taxi, or rental car are: Tijuana across the Mexican border (jai-alai, bull fights, duty-free shopping); Del Mar racetrack in season; the San Diego Zoo, Sea World, Balboa Park with performances at the Shakespearean Old Globe Theater. Also in San Diego, the Maritime Museum, Natural History Museum, Aero-Space Museum, Hall of Science, Historical Society, and the Fine Arts Gallery with outstanding Oriental collections. From December through February, you can watch the white whales at their mating ground. Plus year-round quail-watching and horticultural displays at Quail Gardens; boat charters for deep-sea fishing at Oceanside Harbor, a marina at Seaport Village; and opportunities for 75-minute excursions northward to Disneyland, Knotts Berry Farm, and the Movieland Wax Museum.

Name: La Costa Hotel and Spa

Mailing Address: Costa del Mar Road, Carlsbad, California 92009

Telephone: (619) 438-9111; (800) 854-6564 in California; (800) 854-5000 outside California; *Life Fitness Program:* (800) 824-1264 in California, (800) 426-5483 outside California; telex 697-946

Established: 1965

Managing Director: Paul James; Gerald T. Gleason, General Manager

Program Directors: A. Gordon Reynolds, M.D., Medical Director and Executive Director of the Life Fitness Program; Jonelle Simpson, Director of the Life Fitness Program; Warde Hutton, Men's Spa Director; Anna Marie Smith, Women's Spa Director; Tony Ray, Director of Beauty

Owner: Sports Shinko Company Ltd. of Tokyo and Osaka, Japan; managed by the Global Hospitality Corporation of San Diego

Gender and Age Restrictions: None for the hotel. Co-ed; minimum age 18 for the spa and *Life Fitness Program*

Season: Year-round

Length of Stay Required: Introduction to the spa: 3 days/2 nights; the original *Spa Plan:* 5 days/4 nights; *Spa Plan Extension:* 8 days/7 nights; *Golf Holiday:* 4 days/3 nights; *Life Fitness Program:* 8 days/7 nights, arrival Sunday only.

Programs Offered: The *Minimum Spa Plan* begins with a medical evaluation. After an individual computerized nutritional analysis, you are assigned a specific diet, which gives you a choice of spa dining room or regular meals, within your per-meal allowance (breakfast, $10; lunch, $15; dinner, $35), at any of La Costa's 6 other restaurants. Besides nutritional counseling, you are provided with a basic exercise program, a skin analysis and review, and a schedule of cosmetic and body care services. For men and women, these services include daily exercise classes, massages, facials, herbal wraps, an oil conditioning for your scalp, a manicure and pedicure, a spot toning treatment, and a Sunbrella (sun lamp) tanning session. Complimentary greens fees and tennis court fees, the use of all spa facilities such as saunas, steam rooms, swimming and exercise pools, and gymnasium equipment, are also included. Before leaving, men get their hair styled and women have a shampoo, set, and comb-out and a makeup application. The 8-day/7-night *Spa Plan* includes all the above, plus a daily Sunbrella treatment, an Orthion treatment (described under Beauty Treatments), a special facial machine treatment, and an extra shampoo, set, and comb-out for women.

If you prefer total freedom, you can opt for the à la carte, pay-only-for-what-you-choose-to-enjoy plan, in which case, you have many other choices among beauty services and body treatments. If you prefer a structured and more educational program, you can opt for the *Life Fitness Program,* which focuses on nutrition, exercise, profound relaxation, and interpersonal relationships and "gives its participants a realistic, take-home program for longer life." Before you embark on the program, you receive an orientation, including a preliminary meeting with Dr. Reynolds, who is a member of the American College of Preventive Medicine and the American College of Sports Medicine. You also meet with Jonelle Simpson, M.A., its program director and an attitudinal lifestyle counselor, to establish your individual goals and to determine your perspectives and aspirations. You can request additional individual counseling with Dr. Reynolds and Miss Simpson, as well as a staff nutritionist and exercise physiologist, to supplement group behavioral therapy sessions concerning stress reduction, stress management, relaxation techniques, weight control, communication in work and personal relationships, health, and related topics.

You receive your medical evaluation from Dr. Reynolds, plus a report on the ratio of fat to lean body mass in your body composition. Your blood is tested for cholesterol, triglycerides, and sugar. You receive a nutritional analysis printout and consultation, and, if necessary, a vitamin/mineral supplement is recommended. *N.B.* Dr. Reynolds wrote *The La Costa Nutrition Encyclopedia* and the new *La Costa Book of Nutrition* and worked with La Costa Products International to develop the La Costa Spa's Daily Vitamin and Mineral Regimen, which is used in the *Life Fitness Program* and marketed worldwide. You also receive a treadmill endurance test, a strength evaluation, a flexibility test (using the same exercise system employed for training by the US Olympic team), a pulmonary function screening, and a posture evaluation. An individualized exercise regimen is then planned for you, supervised by an exercise physiologist who shows you how to monitor your own heart rate and keep within your targeted rate zone, and works with you during each exercise period.

Based upon your evaluation, realistic weight management goals are set for you. Nutritional guidance in the *Life Fitness Program* includes a regularly scheduled trip to a local supermarket to learn how to "shop healthy," lectures on how to "dine out healthy," cooking demonstrations and classes in the demonstration kitchen, and an analysis of dietary habits and nutritional deficiencies.

Your agenda allows you to spend time in the spa for a daily massage, 3 herbal wraps, a loofah massage, a skin analysis and review, 3 facials, and unlimited use of the sauna, whirlpool, and steambath facilities. The *Life Fitness Program* also includes a private makeup session, pedicure and manicure, shampoo and blow-dry for women; men get an oil conditioning scalp treatment and a manicure. Greens fees and court fees are waived for all participants.

No more than 20 participants take part in the program, and the majority eat their meals in La Costa's spa dining room, known for its varied and attractive presentations of delicious low-calorie, low-sodium, and low-fat meals, prepared by chef Helmut Leuck. Before you leave, laden with complimentary sweatsuit, T-shirt, textbook notebook and study materials, cookbook, relaxation audio tapes, and a meditation tape (if you request it), you have a final private consultation to discuss your nutrition, exercise, and lifestyle planning.

Maximum Number of Guests: 1000. The maximum capacity of the spa facility is 600, equally divided between the men's and women's pavilions of health, fitness, and beauty services.

Full-Time Health Professionals on Staff: 13, including 2 registered nurses and 2 registered dietitians; plus 11 exercise instructors in the men's spa, 6 exercise instructors in the women's spa, 36 masseuses in the women's spa, 29 masseurs in the men's spa, 30 technicians in the women's spa for herbal wraps, loofahs, steam, sauna, and whirlpool, and 12 technicians in the men's spa, plus 40 cosmetologists in the beauty salon.

Diet and Weight Management: If weight loss is your primary objective, your daily *Spa* or *Life Fitness* programs can be adapted to emphasize this requirement. Lacto-ovo diets, strict vegetarian diets, and other special diets can be accommodated. Caffeine-free beverages are optional. Although a specific recommendation is made by the medical director after a review of each guest's record, guests have a choice of 4 different calorie levels—600, 800, 1000, and 1200. The lower caloric levels are usually not recommended for more than a day or so.

For all La Costa programs, the recommended diet keeps the fat content to no more than 20 percent of the total caloric intake; the rest is comprised of 10 percent protein and 70 percent complex carbohydrates, and it is low in sodium. In the *Life Fitness Program,* guests are tutored about low-calorie foods, low-calorie cooking, and the nutritional values of foods. Registered dietitian Kathy Hall is on hand at mealtimes in the spa dining room to answer questions. Guests on *Spa* and *Life Fitness* programs receive cooking classes in the Life Fitness Center's demonstration kitchen.

Guests are offered a choice of selections on breakfast, lunch, and dinner menus, and they are provided with calorie levels of each selection and guidelines for calorie allowances for each meal. In a 2-week period, no lunch or dinner menu is repeated. "Calcium," "Iron," "Pre-Menstrual Syndrome," and "Menopause" are typical lecture titles in the weekly lecture program on women's nutrition. At weekly spa cocktail parties, guests can get together to meet each other while they sample alcohol-free beverages and low-fat appetizers.

The sky-blue spa dining room, with a seating capacity of 175, overlooks the resort's golf courses. Lunch includes pleasant low-calorie starters such as Swedish cold apple soup and chilled gazpacho. Typical entrées might be papaya stuffed with crabmeat, linguini with clam sauce, braised chicken in red wine, cheese blintzes, broiled swordfish, or zucchini cheese casserole, all under 200 calories. Dessert might be boysenberry parfait or vanilla custard, just 40 calories. A 4-course dinner of less than 300 calories could be asparagus soup, sliced tomatoes with herb dressing, roast leg of lamb with mint sauce, carrots with an orange juice glaze, and butterscotch mousse. Breakfasts offer pancakes, cereals, fruits, breads, egg-white and mushroom omelettes, jam, and raisins. The spa dining room coaches guests in portion control, and you are encouraged to select foods that comply with your nutritional programs when you eat out.

You can request a complimentary consultation with a dietetitian and then, armed with specific recommendations, sally forth to test your will power and selectivity at any of the other restaurants located in the clubhouse building— The Brasserie, José Wong, Le Figaro, The Gaucho Steak House and Rotisserie, and The Champagne Room—or at the Pisces restaurant near the market on La Costa Avenue, where wines, specialty foods, and groceries are sold. Room service is available day and night. Snack bars service the fairways, main swimming pool, and Racquet Club. Tea, coffee, and lemonade are served in the spa lounge.

Exercise and Physical Therapy Facilities: The 50,000-square-foot spa facility has a gymnasium with a Cybex Eagle Weight Circuit for body-building, Lifecycles, treadmills, rowing machines, free weights, individual minitrampolines, heart rate/EKG monitoring equipment, an Ariel computerized exerciser, and 2 exercise pools in the women's pavilion, 1 in the men's pavilion, each 20 meters long and 3 lanes wide, with water volleyball equipment and barres. There are separate exercise classes for men and women, which include stretching, toning, nonimpact aerobics, yoga, muscle strengthening, Aqua Thinics and Splash Dance in the exercise pool, and brisk early morning co-ed walks on the golf courses. Whirlpool baths, saunas, Roman pools, sun lamps, steam cabinets, Swiss showers alternating vigorous jets of hot and cold water, and massage rooms (shiatsu, Swedish, and reflexology practitioners) are at your disposal.

Opportunities for Recreational Exercise: Myriad opportunities await the guest at La Costa: 2 large outdoor heated swimming pools; a ¼-mile jogging track; walking paths (the Pacific Ocean beach is 2 miles distant); and 3-speed bicycles for nearby jaunts. Altogether, 23 tennis courts—2 grass, 4 clay, and 17 all-weather surfaces—are available. Court fees are complimentary for *Spa* and *Life Fitness* programs, but there is a modest surcharge for playing night tennis. Rental rackets and lessons are extra. La Costa also boasts two 18-hole tournament-level golf courses. Greens fees are complimentary for *Spa* and *Life Fitness* programs, but lessons, including a swing analysis videotape of the session, golf carts, caddy fees, buckets of practice balls, storage, and cleaning are extra. Special rates are available for *Golf Holidays.*

Beauty Treatments and Welcome Indulgences: The spa is open from 7:00 AM to 9:00 PM every day of the year, with maybe an hour or two earlier closing on holidays, for massages, facials, herbal wraps, loofah salt rubs, skin-smoothing milk baths (water to which dried milk products are added), spot toning therapy, and Orthion treatments (a 3-dimensional mechanical treatment with traction modes for "soothing, reflexive relaxation . . . to relieve aches and pains . . . good for arthritis and muscle spasms"). Skin analysis, cleansing and body treatments, tanning, wet and dry steam, and body wax depilation are all performed well, but facials with a European facial machine, and the La Costa special facial of complete care—cleansing, massage with a masque and masques or warm mittens and booties for your feet at the same time—are notable spa treatments.

The beauty salon services, available from 8:00 AM to 8:00 PM every day, offer facial wax depilation and everything for the hair. Men can have their beards trimmed or tinted. Women can have their hair highlighted or their eyelashes individually glued on for fullness and/or length. Everything for your toenails and fingernails—pedicures, manicures, repairs, wraps, extensions. Cosmetic and special services not included in the *Spa* and *Life Fitness* programs are extra.

Accommodations: Remarkably spacious guestrooms, with dressing rooms and separate shower and bath in each sumptuous marble bathroom, are available in the spa building, which has the additional assets of a courtyard swimming pool and a location most convenient to the spa facility and the Life Fitness Center. In the conference center vicinity, guestroom and suite accommodations, similarly decorated in shades of pink, orange, spring-leaf green, and écru, have more convenient access to the spa dining room, a pool, and guests resident in the nearby "executive home" complex. With the exception of the golf building, where all suites are furnished with a king-sized bed, all rooms are furnished with twin queen-sized beds. All accommodations have thermostatically controlled air-conditioning and heating, television sets with a Home Box Office channel, complimentary baskets of La Costa beauty and grooming products, and sun-shine-cheerful velour dressing gowns to use during your stay. A La Costa suite does not have an enclosed sitting area separate from the sleeping area as other suites do, nor is a La Costa suite equipped with a kitchenette and a refrigerator. Studio bungalows with kitchenette and refrigerator and twin pull-down beds cost slightly more than accommodations in the spa building and slightly less than La Costa suites available in the golf and tennis buildings. Rental villas with 2 to 3 bedrooms and "executive homes" with 2 to 5 bedrooms are other options.

What to Bring: See USEFUL INFORMATION. In case you were thinking of bringing your rubber-spiked golf shoes, DON'T. They are not allowed on the golf courses. For the *Life Fitness Program,* you receive and get to keep a sweatsuit and a T-shirt with the Life Fitness logo. The yellow bathrobe loaned to you during your stay is ideal as a bathing suit cover-up, but spa clothing (sweatsuit, towel toga, and slippers) furnished to you cannot be worn outside the spa facility.

Cotton and linen resort wear is favored by most of the guests. Nothing casual about La Costa. Everyone fancies up in the evenings. Women appear carefully made up to play golf and tennis. Everyone *dresses* for dinner. Clothing boutiques in the clubhouse building and in the spa pavilions carry everything from athletic footwear and simple and nonchalant pricey sportswear to designer fashions for day and night, along with a full line of La Costa cosmetics and skin care products. The gift shop in the main hotel building stocks chocolates, candies, cigarettes, stuffed animals, magazines, newspapers, film, sunglasses, health and beauty aids, paperback page-turners, and an array of gift items. The Sportique, the golf pro shop, carries top-name golf equipment and accessories as well as designer activewear for men and women. The Racquet Club pro shop carries designer tennis clothes and footwear.

Documentation from Your Physician: A medical history and documentation of recent physical examination are requested by the *Life Fitness Program* only. History and documentation should be no less recent than 6 months. Guests will be admitted without this documentation.

The Use of Alcohol and Tobacco: For *Spa* and *Life Fitness* programs, the use of alcohol is "totally discouraged." A smoking cessation program is available for interested guests. Smoking is prohibited during lectures and cooking demonstrations and discouraged in the spa dining room. Guests may smoke in any of the other 6 restaurants, in their rooms, and outside.

Fees, Method of Payment, Insurance Coverage: Year-round rates:

A la carte European plan: rooms, $180 to $255; La Costa suites, $295 to $640; 1- and 2-bedroom suites, $415 to $630

Spa Plans: $430 per person per night single occupancy; $310 per person per night double occupancy

Life Fitness Program: $460 per person per night single occupancy; $340 per person per night double occupancy

All rates are subject to an 8 percent room and sales tax and are subject to change. With proper ID, personal checks and travelers' checks, Visa, MasterCard, American Express, Diners Club, Carte Blanche, and Discover credit cards are accepted. Costs of enrollment in the *Spa* and *Life Fitness* program may be tax-deductible in part if you are referred by your physician for treatment of hypertension or other weight-related health problems. Health insurance forms consistent with eligibility will be completed with the assistance of A. Gordon Reynolds, M.D.

Follow-up Assistance: Participants in the *Life Fitness Program* receive take-home tapes, cassettes, work-study notebooks, and a cookbook.

⨾ The Oaks at Ojai ⨿
and The Palms at Palm Springs
California

"At age 50, I went to a spa and changed my life forever. I learned to make healthy choices and found myself brimming with energy. They call me a 'born-again fitness zealot.' " The smiling, bearded face of Mel Zuckerman, founder and owner of Canyon Ranch, gives you a look you can trust. The spa he went to was Sheila Cluff's The Oaks at Ojai, and Zuckerman credits his 4-week stay in 1979 with helping him to lose 30 pounds and to maintain an exercise program for the first time in his life. "I found a way of feeling that I wanted to experience for the rest of my life," he says, as he speaks of the stretch classes, the aerobic activities, and the muscle-strengthening classes, praising the "unstructured" program. "If you structure the spa experience too much," he adds, "who's going to structure it at home?" Zuckerman founded Canyon Ranch (see AMERICAN SPAS: WEST) in 1979, the same year Sheila Cluff founded The Palms, 190 miles southeast of The Oaks.

Five foot four, with eyes of blue, weighing in at 102, dynamic fitness buff Sheila Cluff was born in Canada, joined Sonja Henie's touring ice-skating show at the age of 16, acquired a teaching credential in Physical Education in New York, married, had four children (whose ages currently range from 18 to 30), and began her fitness empire selling fitness programming to parks and school districts, business and industry. In 1976, she set up Fitness, Inc., as the corporate headquarters for the affordable, low-key spa she established at Ojai, and later as the umbrella corporation for The Palms. Included in Fitness, Inc., are her radio, TV, and cassette exercise programs, and the health, fitness, beauty, and fashion holiday tours she organized in 1980 on cruise lines such as the *Pearl of Scandinavia* with Far Eastern cruise tours to Hong Kong, Manila, Singapore, Malacca, and Bangkok, plus Caribbean and Mediterranean cruises.

In 1987, Cluff wrote *Sheila Cluff's Aerobic Body Contouring* (Rodale Press). People can have trouble losing weight because they don't eat enough, she wrote. Get an exercise buddy and make exercise an integral part of your life, like eating, she advises. Never give up. Failure is not an option. Similar inspirational and sensible advice is offered in her "Fit for Life" column that appears in national and international publications. Fifty and fabulous, she considers Bonnie Prudden and Dr. Kenneth Cooper, who founded the Aerobics Center/Cooper Clinic in Dallas (see MEDICAL WEIGHT LOSS PROGRAMS), as her mentors.

Cluff developed the healthy eating and exercise programs she offers at the two spas she owns and operates, and they are as helpful to overweight penitents as they are to triathalon candidates. At each spa, you can choose among 16 fitness classes—18 in winter at The Palms and in summer at The Oaks—which include yoga, with all 45-minute sessions led by exceptionally well-qualified instructors and trainers who have had extensive teaching experience. At each spa, you eat well-prepared 500-, 750-, and 1000-calorie-level meals created by food consultant and nutritionist Eleanor Brown. You enjoy aqua-aerobics in an outdoor swimming pool and have free use of sauna and whirlpool. You can treat yourself to optional marvelous massages and facials, hairdos and nail care at additional cost (beauty services are not central to Cluff's spa programs). You can choose among a variety of easily reachable off-site recreational activities, and revel in low-cal lobster dinners on New Year's Eve. The core programs are almost identical. Both offer smoking cessation programs and cooking weeks, as well as off-season bargains in mother-daughter weeks (mama pays full price, daughter half), friendship weeks (bring a friend and get a 25 percent discount), and other specials and discounts off rates that are already bargains for the first-rate fitness programs you receive. Both spas are casual and relaxed in on-site ambience, but each has a distinctive setting and a different appeal.

THE OAKS

The Oaks is 750 feet up in the Ojai Valley of the Los Padres Mountains in a national forest area. Its site is in the center of an artists' colony township with a residential population of 7000 who acclaim the spiritual and meditative qualities of their sylvan environment. About 30 miles southeast of Santa Barbara, 12 miles inland from Ventura on the Pacific coast, with beaches a 20-minute drive away, and 75 miles northeast of Los Angeles, The Oaks at Ojai is a favorite California hideaway for successful businesspeople, writers, professionals, housewives, models, and a few TV and film stars from la-la land. Like The Palms, the clientele, 80 percent of whom are women, is aged from 18 to 80, the majority between 30 and 50.

The main lodge in the town center of Ojai is a Spanish mission–style landmark hotel of rough-hewn stone, rustic, comfortable, and unpretentious. The exercise rooms are decorated with murals of tropical jungles in the style of Haitian primitives. There is a spa shop, a fireplace in the lobby, and a gathering room called the Winners Circle. A brass-trimmed, old-fashioned, polished wood bar serving diet snacks and low-calorie fruit and vegetable juices spans the length of this comfortable room where evening lectures, discussions, and demonstrations are held. Massage and facial rooms, beauty salon, carpeted exercise rooms, whirlpool, and sauna are located in a wing off the lobby. Guestrooms with balconies are upstairs and in a block of 2- and 3-bedroom-with-sitting room cottage accommodations by the swimming pool, 50 yards away in a sunny grove of trees and flowers. All rooms have air-conditioning, telephones, color TVs, and private bathrooms, everything recently renovated and redecorated in a contemporary, functional manner, neat, as they say, but not gaudy.

The site, across the way from the Spanish-style arcades of a post office on Ojai's main street, hides, as all Spanish-style buildings do, its private garden area, just as the township does. Most guests enjoy strolling about town, which is pleasantly the same as it always was, yet upscale New Age intelligentsia in tenor, with a surprising mix of shops selling crystals, health foods, expensive European imports, good books, art supplies, the Oriental, the occult, and the organic everything in a Spanish mission-town setting. The bookseller feels free to leave books outside his shop for night-time readers to borrow or buy on the honor system.

Early morning nature walks and an 8-mile hike breathing in the mountain air and the scent of orange blossoms are part of the program, and opportunities for bowling, boating, fishing, roller-skating, and racquetball are all close by, as are golf, tennis, and riding stables. If you plan on any of these activities, just bring along the necessary gear and the spa receptionist can make all the arrangements. Bring bathing suit and cover-up, big towel for sunning on the lawn, shorts, T-shirts, warm-ups, and casual wear for meals and evenings and strolls around town, where the look is casual but well put together. Pack your jogging shoes, hiking boots, aerobic shoes, and flip-flop sandals. Bring a jacket or a sweater for cool mornings and evenings. The spa shop is stocked with casual sportswear and exercise gear. You'll find the same array of Sheila Cluff's video and cassette tapes, hand weights, recipes, vitamins, makeup, and skin care items available at the front desk here that you will at The Palms.

Name: The Oaks at Ojai
Mailing Address: 122 East Ojai Avenue, Ojai, California 93023
Telephone: (805) 646-5573

Managing Director: Mary T. Lins
Program Directors: Andrea Farr; Elizabeth Kinney, Fitness Director

(For more details about the program and its amenities, see below under The Palms.)

THE PALMS

Enclosed, Spanish style, in a compound with a wrought-iron gate, The Palms is not much more than a mile from the Palm Springs Airport, which means that a lot more out-of-state visitors wing in here than van in from Los Angeles to Ojai. Californians are usually outnumbered here by Easterners, Canadians, and guests flying in from Alaska and other states. In the off-season summertime, particularly in July, when you can stay for 2 weeks and get 1 week free, a slightly younger, less affluent group of visitors arrive. Mothers and daughters, who get a special rate at The Oaks in January, come here to get the same in July. This is desert country, and it can get baking, Bombay-hot in the summer. Low humidity makes the weather tolerable and, naturally, there's air-conditioning and Mt. San Jacinto as a getaway. But, no question about it, the cooler months are the time to come.

This is the land of Bob Hope Drive in Rancho Mirage, where the Betty Ford Clinic is, of dozens of golf courses with golf clubs and carts available for rentals, fabulous bicycle riding with many ramped curbs and well-marked trails and bicycles available to rent locally. There are several riding stables within a few minutes of The Palms, and numerous tennis courts, lighted for night play, also within easy walking distance. The shopping tends to be specialty larger-sized clothing as well as sables-and-designer-labels-trendy because, don't forget, Palm Springs is a resort. There are bus tours here to show you where Walter and Lee Annenberg live in *Architectural Digest*'s style of fabled splendor, and three-score homes and ten of celebrated notables and super-stars such as Frank Sinatra, Lucille Ball, and Bob Hope. At dawn and dusk, you can charter a hot air balloon in paint-box colors, piloted by a professional who will maneuver the balloon over sage brush, saguaro, and the whole desert panorama with memorable views of the Santa Rosa Mountains and Mt. San Jacinto. For much less, you can explore the wild animal park and botanical garden of the Living Desert, with all the color and diversity of desert flora and fauna, or visit the Palm Springs Desert Museum, or take in a film, concert, or dance production at the Annenberg Theater, or check out the Nelson Rockefeller Collection and other art galleries. Best of all, let the Palm Springs Aerial Tramway, the largest double reversible in the world, transport you from the desert floor to the pine-covered mountains, which are nearly 6000 feet above. During the stunning 15-minute ascent up the granite face of Mt. San Jacinto, up, up, and away to the Mt. San Jacinto State Park at the top, you'll pass in summertime through five separate life zones, from Sonoran Desert to Arctic Alpine, to 14,000 acres of hiking trails, picnic areas, and wilderness mule train rides—and a 40-degree drop in temperature. In the winter, you can throw snowballs and experience the best cross-country skiing in southern California. Tramway tickets are under $6, and you can bring a picnic lunch with you from The Palms, or dine (judiciously) once you reach this eagle's-eye eyrie. In Palm Springs, if you're not overcome with the scent of the mesquite-grill style of cuisine, you can dine in Moroccan, Thai, or *cuisine minceur* style, but meals at The Palms also include crispy, crunchy, creamy, sweet, and tart surprises minus salt, sugar, and chemical additives.

Name: The Palms at Palm Springs

Mailing Address: 572 North Indian Avenue, Palm Springs, California 92262

Telephone: (619) 325-1111

Established: 1979–1980

Managing Director: Barbara Nos

Program Directors: Jean Anne Kelser, Fitness Director, Marilu Rogers

Owner: Sheila Cluff

Gender and Age Restrictions: Co-ed; minimum age 16; exceptions and special arrangements made for nursing mothers

Season: Year-round

Length of Stay Required: 2-night minimum

Programs Offered: A permissive, nondemanding, structured-with-options program offers weight management/weight control/weight loss; stress reduction through exercise and good nutrition, with equal emphasis on diet, nutrition education, and behavior modification; and a dynamite fitness activity plan of stretch classes, hatha-yoga, aerobics and aqua-aerobics, brisk walking, low-impact aerobics, aerobic body conditioning, body dynamics, strength training, aquatoning, supervised workouts, and daily nature walks, plus a 6-mile walking tour of the super-star residential area.

There's a daily guest orientation at 5:30 in the Winners Circle sitting room. Each guest has a private consultation with a registered nurse on staff for a discussion of past medical problems, if any, and recording of weight, measurements, and blood pressure. You can discuss your physical limitations with the nurse for free, but if you want to consult with a trained fitness professional about exercises to strengthen, tone, develop, and shape up your arms, legs, or other specific body areas, it will cost you a well-spent $40. Body composition analysis with ultrasound equipment by either a registered nurse or a cardiac supervisor is also extra. A smoking cessation program is an optional extra available, like cooking class week and special discount programs, for a limited time period once a year at each spa. A sauna and whirlpool are available for unlimited free use. From 9:00 AM to 9:00 PM, you can make an appointment for a massage by a skilled massage therapist for $40 an hour. There are some 25 health professionals on hand at both spas as certified therapists, trained instructors, and registered nurses. A physician is on call at both spas, and a registered nurse is on duty from 8:00 AM to noon.

Diet and Weight Management: You have a choice of 500-, 750-, and 1000-calorie levels of low-fat, low-sodium, high-fiber meals. A 1500-calorie "athlete's portion" is available. Lacto-ovo, strictly vegetarian, Kosher, or special diets for medical reasons can be provided.

The nutritionally balanced menus, created by food consultant–nutritionist Eleanor Brown, are designed to help you lose up to a pound a day without hunger pangs. You get pancakes, lasagna, cheesecake. For these and other low-cal popular specials, recipes free for the asking are available for you to take home.

For breakfast, you might get cereal or oatmeal or a diet muffin, half a grapefruit, a wedge of cantaloupe, a packet of vitamin supplements, and a beverage. Not an iota of refined flour, sugar, or salt is added to menus featuring fruit, vegetables, homemade soups and salad dressings, low-cholesterol entrées of fish, seafood, and meat. Red snapper, veal loaf, ratatouille, chicken tostadas, vegetable quiches, and chicken and turkey with "cream" sauces are typical entrées, presented with vegetables, interesting seasonings, a daily baked potato, and always a dinnertime dessert. Coffee and hot and iced herbal teas and noncaffeinated beverages are available all day. The fruit and vegetable juices "straight" or in combination are delicious, and the homemade broths and soups excellent.

Beauty Treatments and Welcome Indulgences: Massages, facials, hair styling and care, depilatory waxing, and nail care (pedicure and manicure) cost extra. Sheila Cluff endorses the natural approach to skin care, and all skin care products are formulated by Vera Brown of Vera's Natural Beauty Retreat to eliminate irritants and allergens. Prices for services and skin care products are reasonable.

Accommodations: See earlier in this section for information about The Oaks. At The Palms, the hotel is set within a walled compound, entered off the street by an arched Spanish wrought-iron gate. With accommodation for 90 guests, the two-story hotel, with red-tiled roof and upper balcony blanketed with bougainvillea, is built around a courtyard with a large centerpiece pool. Ground-level guest bedrooms spread back on three sides from the courtyard in an area about the size of a city block. Most rooms are furnished with two double beds, double cupboards, and a bathroom, which can, for economy purposes, be shared with the adjoining double bedroom. Some rooms have balconies, porches, patios; others may have fireplaces. All rooms have maid service daily, a telephone, TV, and air-conditioning. Coin-operated laundry facilities are on the premises.

What to Bring: See USEFUL INFORMATION. Bring informal casual wear, dressier in Palm Springs than at Ojai, but casually chic at both spas, or anything you feel comfortable wearing around the spa if you don't plan on any outside activities. Leotards and tights for women, shorts or bathing trunks for men to wear for exercise; warm-up suits, bathing suits, bathrobe or pool cover-up, large beach towel for sunning and yoga, walking shoes, aerobic shoes. Pack warm clothing during winter months as early mornings and evenings are cool—and remember the 40-degree drop in temperature on the ascent to Mt. San Jacinto. Remember, also, that Palm Springs has a lot of ritzy restaurants and a lot of glitzy nightlife. Spa boutiques in both Ojai and Palm Springs carry the latest in exercise wear in small and large sizes. Since both spas, secret worlds to themselves, are entered from a town street with accessible shops, you can easily pick up anything you have forgotten to pack. You can rent tennis rackets, golf clubs, and cross-country skis. But you are advised to bring your own type of camera film.

Documentation from Your Physician: Requested only if problems exist. You will be asked to sign a medical release form.

The Use of Alcohol and Tobacco: No alcoholic beverages are served. Smoking is allowed only in the guestrooms and outdoors.

Fees, Method of Payment, Insurance Coverage: High-season (October to May) rates per night at The Palms:

For single: $160 to $185, depending on size

For double: $135 per person

For adjoining doubles (shared bathroom facilities): $105 per person

Summer (June to September 30) rates at The Palms are slightly less, and this is the time when the weekend specials (stay 2 nights, 3rd one free), bonus time (stay 2 weeks, 3rd week free), friendship time (bring a friend, each receives a 25 percent discount) are in effect.

Rates per night at The Oaks:

In the Lodge: $155 single, $105 to $118 per person double, depending on size

In the cottages: $165 single, $135 per person double, $118 per person triple (minimum stay 2 nights/3 days)

Rates are higher for deluxe accommodations, and all prices are subject to change. All rates are subject to a 9 percent tax and a 12 percent service charge. A deposit is required. Ask about the cancellation policy. Payment is acceptable by cash, personal check, or travelers' checks or by Visa or MasterCard. Insurance coverage may be possible; it is Sheila Cluff's experience that reimbursement varies with each individual and insurance company.

Follow-up Assistance: Newsletters are sent to former guests, who can buy take-home items such as video teaching tapes, cassettes, cookbooks, and Sheila Cluff's books.

～ Sonoma Mission Inn and Spa ～
California

A hour's drive north from San Francisco, in the heart of the California wine country, a team of well-qualified experts provides personalized programs for a maximum of 30 guests. Beauty and fitness packages of 1, 2, 5, and 7 days are offered in this Spanish mission–style inn the color of strawberry ice cream, a pink, posh, pampering palace with a bell tower and red-tiled roof. Sonoma Mission Inn's spa offers massage, herbal wraps, hydrotherapy, facials, hair and scalp treatments, complete salon services, hydrostatic weighing, fitness and nutrition evaluation, hikes, and a wide variety of fitness classes, including aerobics, low- and nonimpact exercise, relaxation, stretch and tone, and yoga. Facilities include sauna, steam, indoor and outdoor whirlpool, heated outdoor exercise pool, tennis courts and instruction, gym with Keiser Cam II equipment, lockers, lounge, and health bar. Some guestrooms have fireplaces. Daily menus of gourmet low-calorie, low-sodium spa cuisine start at 800 calories.

The Boyes Hot Spring site was originally used as a sacred healing ground by the indigenous Indians, who were attracted to the legendary healing powers of its waters. The concierge can arrange wine tours, hot air ballooning, and sightseeing in the area. Edward Safdie, spa developer par excellence and its former owner, maintains a 10 percent interest in this spa now owned by RAHN Properties. The Inn is a fine, first-class hotel with conference facilities and the best of California foods and wines in its Grille Restaurant beloved by Bay Area residents. A perfect romantic getaway where you can relax in luxury, enjoy spa fitness and beauty services, and eat delicious low-cal or gourmet food, irresistibly pictured in Edward Safdie's classic book, *Spa Food,* for $+$ \$350 a day, less with some spa packages.

Name: Sonoma Mission Inn and Spa
Mailing Address: P.O. Box 1447, Sonoma, California 95476

Telephone: (707) 938-9000; (800) 862-4945 in California; (800) 358-9022 or (800) 358-9027 outside California

West

✑ Canyon Ranch ✑
Arizona

The 60-acre Canyon Ranch, "America's first total vacation/fitness resort," at the foot of the Santa Catalina range of russet and violet-washed mountains near Tucson, basks in its desert setting of saguaro cacti, sunlight slanting sharply off adobe walls, wildflowers, mesquite trees. Mel Zuckerman, founder and president of Canyon Ranch, speaks of its ambience of "positive power and energy." Enid, his wife, speaks of the "caring and loving staff who have the talent and spirit to transmit healing powers to everyone." Satisfied guests tell Mel that he has given them new lives, transformed their inner and outer selves. They rejoice at quitting smoking, conquering a "sugar addiction," disencumbering themselves of stress and tension and experiencing "the perfect nurturing place."

Mel Zuckerman is pleased with the success of his Life Share ownership program (which provides annual medical/lifestyle evaluations, personal guidance, and significant savings on service and accommodations). In 1987, he invested $21 million to develop further accommodations and facilities designed to help others keep their energy flowering, stay on track, and be motivated to live well all year long, and not just during their brief sojourn at Canyon Ranch. In 1988, he invested more millions in the development of an east coast branch of the ranch to open in August 1989 a half mile from Tanglewood in the Berkshire Mountains (Bellefontaine, 81 Church Street, Route 7A, Lenox, MA 01240; tel: [800] 326-7100). William Day is Chief Operating Officer.

At 50, a successful real estate developer suffering from high blood pressure and asthma, and fat and round as an Apache olla, Mel checked into The Oaks at Ojai (see AMERICAN SPAS: WEST COAST) where Karma Kientzler, now the physical fitness guru at Canyon Ranch, helped him lose 30 pounds. He returned home a changed man. He no longer needed blood pressure medication, and he discovered the "natural high" which comes from good nutrition, physical activity, relaxation, and personal attention. "I want to feel this good forever!" he is widely quoted as having exclaimed. So he bought the old-time Double

U Dude Ranch, which he and Enid, with the help of Karma Kientzler, his first recruit, turned into the present-day Canyon Ranch. This super health and fitness resort, included in *Vogue*'s "Best Spas in the World," and *Money* magazine's top ten spas in the United States two years after it opened, is constantly expanding its programs and facilities, and its popularity seems to increase annually. The majority of the guests return and refer their friends. It averages 35 to 40 percent male guests year-round, and between 40 and 50 percent during most of the winter months. Couples visit together and bring teenage children. Many of the guests are single. The majority range in age from 35 to 55. Many are professionals, engaged in both business and the arts, with a broad spectrum of backgrounds and interests.

Canyon Ranch offers a wide range of exercise and learning programs, medical services, recreational activities, sports, and cosseting: tennis, racquetball, aerobics, fat-tire bicycling, 4- to 15-mile hikes in wilderness areas, weight-training classes, swimming, water classes in 3 of its 4 pools, 9 kinds of massage, including soothing massages with herbal oils, sensuous facials, stimulating lectures, and, yes, it's true, French body polishing with crushed pearls.

There are workshops in natural healing alternatives as well, sometimes referred to as "walks on the Weil side," because these sessions in Oriental medicine and naturopathy are supervised by Harvard graduate Andrew Weil, M.D. You'll find innovative programs for specialized needs, such as the *Arthritis Package,* along with workshops for pondering the significance and symbolism of dreams, insights about your astrological chart, analysis of colors most becoming to you. A popular activity is the morning walk along a sandy road you share with startled jackrabbits or a covey of quail whirring into the incredible freshness of the morning air or along the nature trail around the western boundary of the ranch where whiplike ocotillo and the stark sculptural beauty of prickly pear and saguaro are identified by their Latin names thoughtfully posted by the staff botanist.

With the exception of specialized 1- and 2-week sessions at the Life Enhancement Center, programs are unstructured. The staff focuses on educating guests in how to make healthy choices in all aspects of their lives, to make lasting positive changes for emotional and physical health and well-being.

Taxis and more economical rental cars are available for trips to Sabino Canyon State Park 2 miles away, with fern-fringed cascading pools, rock cliffs, and saguaros in profusion; to Saguaro Monument East, with walking, jogging, and driving trails providing panoramic mountain, pine forest, and desert vistas; or to Mount Lemmon's spectacular hiking trails for beginning and advanced hikers. The 1.8 million acre Coronado National Forest is at Tucson's doorstep, and Mission San Xavier del Bac, a dazzling white sanctuary, is an architectural reminder of the city's Spanish past you won't want to miss. The Arizona-Sonora

Desert Museum in Tucson's Mountain Park, contiguous with the Saguaro National Monument, displays 200 different animals and 300 kinds of plants alive in desert settings, with a walk-in aviary, earth sciences center, and under-water viewing, which compresses and intensifies the desert experience into a museum-zoo habitat unique in the world. For hot-air ballooning over fabulous scenery, then champagne breakfast, contact *A Balloon Experience* (7725 North Jensen Drive, Tucson 85741; telephone [602] 747-3866). For local crafts and jewelry, American Indian and Latin folk art, have a look at Old Town Artisans, an artisans' marketplace in historic El Presidio.

Name: Canyon Ranch

Mailing Address: 8600 East Rockcliff Road, Tucson, Arizona 85715

Telephone: (602) 749-9000 (call collect from Arizona, Alaska, Hawaii); (800) 742-9000 elsewhere in US; (800) 327-9090 in Canada

Established: 1979

Managing Director: Vince Watson, Hotel Operations

Program Directors: Karma Kientzler, Executive Fitness Director; Philip S. Eichling, M.D., Medical Director; Daniel Baker, Ph.D., Counseling Psychology, Behavioral and Special Programs Director

Owner: Mel Zuckerman, Founder and President

Gender and Age Restrictions: Co-ed; minimum age 14 (under 14, caretaker required, and must stay in casitas or haciendas. Not permitted in activities or dining room but, with supervision, permitted use of tennis courts and specified swimming pool)

Season: Year-round

Length of Stay Required: From September 16 to June 15, 4-night minimum; no minimum stay required June 16 to September 15. Plans available: *4-night package; 7-night package; 10-night package;* 8- and 15-day programs at The Life Enhancement Center.

Programs Offered: The core program is the mind-set: to think before you arrive about the specific improvements that are most important to you; then, during your stay, to work with health professionals to develop a long-lasting and well-balanced approach to healthful living. The activities are designed to exercise your heart (cardiovascular/aerobic activity); strengthen, tone, and/or build muscles; and improve flexibility, posture, and breathing. All levels of fitness are accommodated, with exercises ranging from stretching to the rigorous, vigorous Positive Power Hour, the most demanding of all exercise sessions in the program.

Spa packages include use of all spa and resort facilities: 30 co-ed indoor and outdoor fitness activities daily; miles of hiking, biking, and jogging trails; plus a choice, with the *7-night package,* of any 5 personal and sports services—full-body massage, 2 herbal wraps or steam baths, European facial, makeup consultation and application, haircut, shampoo and set, manicure and pedicure, private racquetball lesson, round of golf, riding; plus any 2 professional health consultations—life-change counselor, biofeedback therapist, hypnotherapist, natural healing therapist, exercise physiologist, body composition test, nutritional assessment, stress response test. The *10-night package* includes the choice of any 6 personal and sports services, plus any 2 professional health consultations.

For those who want more, you can push your body to its limit in a week-long fitness, testing, and training program called *Cross Training* which culminates in a minitriathalon: swimming a fast half-mile, cycling 15 miles up desert hillsides, sprinting 3½ miles to the finish line. This program is available at a surcharge above the 7-night package price, and is limited to a dozen physically fit participants each month from October through May. You can also enroll in a smoking cessation program or a smoking cessation diet plan. New in the summer of 1988, the Life Enhancement Center, in its own special building with exercise facilities, meeting and treatment rooms and separate kitchen and dining hall, offers 7- and 14-day structured programs for small groups of 25 to 35 spa-goers who have specific goals. These programs, rotating throughout the year, include *Thirty Plus* (pounds), a weight loss program ($3730, 14 days). Also new in 1988 is the wild and wonderful MindFitness training program (20 hours per week, $850) for electronically tuning in to and learning how to orchestrate the tones and rhythms of your brain waves to keep your beta waves pulsing *piano, piano,* and to augment the rich resonance of your alpha waves. (Prices given do not include 17 percent service charge and 5 percent sales tax.) The Personal Services directory at Canyon Ranch is packed with other opportunities to improve your way of life, your appearance, your sense of well-being, and your health. To make it easier for you to assimilate the variety of services available to you at Canyon Ranch, there is an orientation lecture, and the television set in your room has a 22-minute closed-circuit videotape presentation highlighting the essentials of the program. An orientation tour of the grounds is offered daily, mornings and afternoons.

If you are considering plastic or reconstructive surgery, Canyon Ranch works with a Tucson surgeon who performs facelifts, eyelid surgery, rhinoplasty, abdominoplasty, suction lipolysis ("tummy tucks"), and other contouring procedures. A 14-day stay at Canyon Ranch will give you time to get physically well and strong, complete the surgery, and recuperate.

The multidisciplinary emphasis for well-being at Canyon Ranch includes evaluation of a medical questionnaire you have filled in and mailed prior to your check-in, consultation with a registered nurse at check-in, and interviews or private consultations with health professionals at your request. The Medical

Department offers preventive health services—screening for high blood pressure, heart disease, mental stress factors, and other illnesses, and then helping you plan a healthier approach to life. The cost of these medical services is not included in the package price of your stay, but many guests take the opportunity to have their annual physical examination during their Canyon Ranch vacation break; they find it more convenient than taking time to do so from their time-crammed schedules at home.

There are three preventive medical programs: *Basic Prevention Evaluation* ($128) is a screening and education program for the prevention of heart disease which offers a treadmill test to monitor your heart rate and blood pressure. Individuals who are identified by this stress test as having potential cardiac problems are then evaluated and given specially prescribed exercise and nutrition programs to follow during their stay and at home. *The Comprehensive Evaluation* ($479) adds to the procedures above a series of pulmonary function tests; vision and hearing screenings; blood, urine, and stool analyses; and, if indicated or requested, a proctoscopic exam and optional chest X ray. You can also complete the 30-minute series of standardized mental and physiological challenges involved in the stress response test ($75) to determine if you are at risk for experiencing stress-related heart trouble, stroke, or other potentially fatal illnesses. These preventive health services and other special programs are part of a medical and behavioral service program that is continually being developed and expanded.

Maximum Number of Guests: 260

Full-Time Health Professionals on Staff: 33, including 2 M.D.s (Philip S. Eichling, the medical director is an internist; Andrew Weil is the specialist in alternative practices, such as hypnosis, acupuncture, and natural healing), 3 registered nurses, 4 licensed practical nurses, and 7 registered dieticians. Plus 40 fitness instructors trained and certified by Karma Kientzler, 50 certified massage therapists, 8 estheticians, and 20 cosmetologists. (Add in dining room and kitchen staffs, receptionists, and other personnel, and you come up with a staff of 450, or more than 2 staff members to serve every guest.)

Diet and Weight Management: Creative, imaginative, varied, delicious food is the hallmark of Canyon Ranch gourmet cuisine, which is prepared with whole grains, garden-fresh fruits and vegetables, no refined flour or sugar. The diet is high in carbohydrates (60 percent) and skimps on proteins (20 percent) and cholesterol. An optional menu provides 65 percent carbohydrates, 20 percent proteins, 15 percent fat. Salt is used sparingly, and fructose is substituted for sugar. No additives or preservatives are used, and vegetarian options are available at every meal. Brewed decaffeinated coffee and hot and cold herbal teas are served. Caffeinated teas and packets of instant caffeinated coffee are available, as are medical or "special request" diets and foods, although for these, there may be an additional charge based on specific requirements. You are encouraged to drink eight 8-ounce glasses of water daily.

In the dining room in the main house, you may sit alone or join some of the other guests at tables set with attractive china and vases of desert flowers. Large windows look out on a pool and gardens, and a skylight affords you a dazzling nighttime view of a star-spangled desert sky. You dine on such seductive fare as artichokes with dilled shrimp, cold orange soufflé, fettucine del mar, strawberries Romanoff, moussaka, bouillabaisse, barbecued chicken breast, blueberry cheesecake, 17-grain waffles with apple butter, fresh fruit blintzes, tamale pie, fruit shakes, and muffins. (Jeanne Jones, the menu consultant, is an author, syndicated newspaper columnist, and lecturer whose other clients include the Pritikin Longevity Center, Four Seasons Hotels, and Neiman-Marcus.) Calorie control is maintained through portion size, and calories for each item are listed on the menu. To help guests pinpoint portion size, dietitians use plastic cheese cubes, rubber chicken breasts, ornamental oranges, and measuring cups and spoons for demonstrations. No fewer than 1000 calories a day are recommended for women, 1200 calories a day for men. Optimal weight loss can be achieved by following a suggested menu at each meal. Dietitians and exercise physiologists help guests plan specific strategies to reach their goals during their stay and keep on the right track when they return home.

Exercise and Physical Therapy Facilities: The 40,000 square feet of white-tiled space colorfully splashed with graphics and murals in the spa building house five sunny mirrored gymnasiums and exercise rooms, a mirrored weight room, 4 racquetball courts, and separate locker and dressing rooms for men and women. Fitness staff offices are found on the second floor. The exercise rooms are carpeted with a cushiony, shock-absorbing material that gives you a floating-on-air feeling while you perform leg extensions, stretches, and what are called nonballistic aerobics (keeping one foot on the ground at all times). Below the Belt is a body-contouring intermediate class focusing on abdominals, legs, thighs, and buttocks, using wands, balls, V-bars, and a ballet barre; Stretch and Flex is designed to promote flexibility, enhance muscle tone, and prevent sore muscles. Activities are identified for beginner, intermediate, and advanced levels and further annotated as to categories: Introduction, Yoga, Aerobics/Cardiovascular, Strength, Meditation. In the morning, for example, you have a choice of race-walking, an invigorating hike for 3 or 4 hours on mountain trails, or a 30-minute 2-mile walk.

There's an Introduction to Weights class, a beginner's Circuit Weights class,

Aerobic Circuit Weight Training for those at advanced fitness levels, a Fitness First class in aerobics/cardiovascular exercise for beginners and an Aerobic Hi for intermediates, a Mini Power class and a Maxi Power class and Positive Power classes. Men's Stretch Energetics, weighted rope jumping for imagining yourself as a boxer in training, volleyball as well as classes to introduce you to creative movement/dance, classes in breathing and hatha-yoga, a meditation session, relaxation yoga, classes for lower back exercise. All classes are explained to you, and you are encouraged to do whatever makes you feel good.

Equipment in the weight room includes Precor 810, Tunturi, Schwinn, and Lifecycle stationary and recumbent bicycles, a Nautilus lower-back press, bench press, pull-up bar, dip bars, free weights, a NordicTrack cross-country ski machine, a Roman chair, treadmills, Concept II rowing machines, a K-300 Total Hip Press, a StairMaster stairclimber, an inclined bench, abdominal sit-up boards, heart rate/EKG monitoring equipment, Cam II and Cam III equipment, mini-trampolines. Whichever of the 30 daily scheduled fitness classes you opt for, from beginner to challenging advanced levels of fitness, trained instructors and spotters are there not only to help you perform every movement correctly and safely, but to assure that you gain the maximum benefit from your efforts.

Once you are inside the spa, assigned your clothes locker, and given a key, a terry-cloth robe and rubber thong sandals are provided for you. All comforts and sundries are available—suntan cream in two strengths (9 and 15), shampoo, conditioner, hair dryers, razors, skin creams, body lotions. Located in both the men's and women's pavilions are whirlpool baths, Jacuzzis, steam, sauna and inhalation rooms, and nude sunbathing areas.

You play water volleyball, or tone your muscles in water exercises with flugel flotation devices and kickboards in a shallow indoor heated pool in a separate building with a retractable roof across the way, next to one of the 3 heated outdoor pools. Aerobic water exercises are also held in the outdoor pools.

You can choose from 9 massage techniques for relaxation, greater mental alertness, increased body awareness, and relief from muscle soreness: Swedish, shiatsu, reflexology, cranial, lymph, polarity, Jin Shin Jyutso, and Reiki. Trager sessions, in which your arms and legs are rocked, are available on request and with advance notice.

Opportunities for Recreational Exercise: You can take advantage of the basketball court, jogging track, racquetball courts, and golf course (off the property; greens fees vary with course selected). You can also go bird-watching, hiking, riding (off the property; stable provides transportation), or bicycling, either on the Canyon Ranch property or with a group on daily excursions to nearby mountains and canyon areas.

Ordinary bicycles are free of charge, and 15-speed Mountain Bikes are also provided free of charge for 5-day bicycling tours. Additional use of 15-speed Mountain Bikes is $15 a day. The 3 outdoor (2 lap-swimming and 1 recreation) heated pools and 1 indoor heated exercise shallow pool make swimming readily accessible; private swimming lessons are available. There are also 6 tennis courts, lighted for night play; a curved backboard for practice; and private and semiprivate lessons, video lessons, and weekly tennis clinics. A 1-mile Exercourse with 12 exercise stations for complete cardiovascular conditioning is available for use any time. Brown-bag meals are available for off-property excursions, for lunches on the grounds, and for bicycle treks and hikes.

Beauty Treatments and Welcome Indulgences: Located in the spa building, the Gadabout Salon creates wash-and-wear hairstyles for active guests, cuts, tints, sparks, and highlights your hair for subtle or dramatic changes; manicures, pedicures, sculpts, and wraps nails with paper, linen, silk; shapes eyebrows; waxes your arms, legs, body; mixes, matches, charts, and coordinates the best colors in makeup, wardrobe, and even interior design for you. Leah Kovitz, believe it or not a former sergeant in the Israeli Army, whose New Image beauty products contain minerals from the Dead Sea, directs the makeup and skin care department with considerable panache. She uses the waxed-thread technique to eliminate unwanted facial hair quickly and painlessly, and makes use of sable brushes as a soothing method of facial massage in some of the many facial treatments incorporated in her inspired regimen. These include her unique Thermal Youth Masque, a 7-step treatment culminating in a thermal masque, which lifts off in a perfect rosy sculpture of your facial contours; a wonderfully relaxing paraffin facial; a breast treatment; aroma therapy wraps and baths; and the fabulous Parisian Body Polish, a French technique for buffing and polishing your body with a cream compounded of finely crushed pearls that leaves a lovely sheen on your skin—not to mention the glow the treatment imparts to your *amour propre!*

Accommodations: Canyon Ranch, formerly a working ranch and then a dude ranch, maintains some of its original buildings with their stone fireplaces and beamed ceilings, updated with modern bathrooms. Standard accommodations consist of 90 adobe guest cottages, each containing 2 or 3 double rooms with private baths and shaded porches and patios in a desert garden setting. All maid-serviced, air-conditioned rooms are furnished with twin double or king-sized beds, room telephone, chairs, bureau, table, and cable television, and, what is more important, the visible world outside is furnished with fan palms, mesquite and cottonwood trees filled with bird song, wild and cultivated flowers, spectacular vistas of the Catalina Mountains. For those who require more luxurious quarters and are willing to pay more for the privilege, there are

35 single-bedroom haciendas and 2-bedroom casitas—small, stuccoed houses with regional southwestern paintings and décor, each with its own sitting room and kitchen, accommodations required if you are accompanied by a child under the age of 14.

What to Bring: See USEFUL INFORMATION. The atmosphere is casual and relaxed, totally laid back. The Canyon Ranch Store carries the Canyon Ranch brand of clothing, cookbooks, exercise videotapes, vitamins, and herbal baths, and the Showcase Boutique, located in the Clubhouse, stocks sportswear, exercise clothes, magazines, some types of film, and sundries. There is a coin-operated laundry room on the premises; same-day cleaning and laundry services are available Monday through Friday. You are asked *not* to bring "dressy" clothing, jewelry, or large amounts of cash. If brought, valuables should be checked into a safety deposit box in the Clubhouse.

Documentation from Your Physician: Canyon Ranch sends out a medical and lifestyle questionnaire at the time you make your reservation. A staff physician reviews all returns and requests a personal meeting with those guests whose history indicates possible problems in participating fully in the programs offered. All other guests are referred to nurses. A medical history and documentation of recent physical examination are requested but not required. All guests are required to sign a medical release when they check in. Once a medical release is signed, you will be admitted without further medical documentation.

The Use of Alcohol and Tobacco: No alcohol is served or sold, and its use is discouraged. Guests are not permitted to smoke in any public areas, indoors or out. They are asked to smoke only on the patios of their rooms. No staff member may smoke on duty.

Fees, Method of Payment, Insurance Coverage: High-season (January to mid-June and mid-September to mid-December) rates:

For *4-night program:* $1330 single, $1070 double

For *7-night program:* $2330 single, $1910 double

For *10-night program:* $3230 single, $2630 double

Rates are higher for deluxe accommodations and lower in the off-season. All prices are subject to change, and all rates are subject to a 5 percent state tax and 17 percent service charge (which covers gratuities for *all* personnel, shuttle transportation to hiking and biking sites, round-trip airport transportation, evening programs and lectures, cable television, and local telephone calls). Additional tipping is not required or expected. Bills are presented weekly and at time of check-out. With proper ID, personal checks are honored, as are travelers' checks, Visa, MasterCard, and Discover credit cards. Canyon Ranch has no policy in regard to tax-deductible health-related expenses and recommends that guests consult their personal physician, their insurance carrier or their accountant concerning health insurance coverage.

Follow-up Assistance: The Round-Up, a bimonthly publication, is sent free of charge to all alumni/alumnae; *Lifeline,* a quarterly health digest, is sent to Life Share members, who can use the tollfree SPA-LINE to the Life Share office with any health or fitness questions they may have. Also available are series of "Fun and Fitness" videotapes (Mini/Maxi Power, Stretch and Flex, Body Contouring); cookbooks of menus and recipes; Jeanne Jones's books about eating strategies; multiple vitamins; packaged bread, cereal, and muffin mixes; herbal bath oils; skin care products; and fitness equipment. They can be ordered by check, Visa, or MasterCard from a fulfillment center at Canyon Ranch called Canyon Ranch Orders.

∾ The Cliff Lodge and Spa ∾
Utah

The Spa at the Cliff Lodge of Snowbird's Ski and Summer Resort, 31 miles (45 minutes) from the Salt Lake International Airport, is based in Little Cottonwood Canyon, a secluded alpine setting at an altitude of 8000 feet. The annual midmountain snowfall on the Wasatch Range is 550 inches, which provides Snowbird with winter, spring, and summer skiing from November to mid-June, the Rocky Mountains' longest ski season. During the summer, when the warm-weather temperature is a refreshing 70 degrees F, guests can swim, hike, play tennis, treat themselves to helicopter transport to mountain golf courses and champagne picnics in meadows that are a glorious tapestry of wildflowers, take classes in mountaineering and rock climbing and be entertained by Snowbird Institute's presentations of concerts, music and dance performances, and seasonal festivals.

Guest accommodations at Snowbird are available at 3 condominium facilities as well as at the Cliff Lodge and Spa, where a 900-person, 57,000-square-foot conference center and a child-care center are also located. The new Cliff Lodge, with its 11-story glassed atrium, art and book gallery, shops, restaurants, full-service salon, and spa (which includes a 54-foot rooftop lap-swimming pool), attracts a majority of young, affluent, fitness-oriented professionals who are enthusiastic skiers with a desire to work out and receive quality body and grooming/beauty treatments. The child-care center, the children's ski school, and baby facilities make it possible for many to bring their children with them. The child-care center, open in winter only, provides daily care for children 3 years or older and toilet trained. Children aged 4 and older enrolled in the children's ski school are also cared for when not in lessons. Children under 12 can ski free and stay free if they share their parents' room. Shared babysitting, in-room babysitting, and children's activities are available throughout the year.

Snowbird's adult ski school coaches beginners, intermediates, and advanced skiers, and both adult and children's schools have specially trained instructors to help the handicapped experience the thrill of skiing. Of Snowbird's 1900 acres of skiing terrain, about 20 percent is for beginners/novices, 30 percent for intermediates, and 50 percent for expert skiers. There's an aerial tram, one of the largest and fastest in the US, and 7 double chairlifts with a total capacity of 8810 passengers per hour.

Winter activities include ski movie nights, an adventure lecture series, Salt Lake historical tours, Western Barbecue Night, festivities with regional and international themes such as Italian Night and Cajun Night, and live entertainment. Christmas festivities include a torchlight parade, caroling, and candlight Christmas service, appearance by Santa Claus, and a children's Christmas party. The January Winterfest Celebration features professional and amateur skiing races, a snow sculpture contest, broomball (curling) competitions, and a costume parade. Easter begins with a sunrise service on Hidden Peak, followed by an Egg Hunt, Easter Bonnet contest, and a visit by the Easter Bunny. A Snowbird-based helicopter skiing and scenic flight service lifts you from Snowbird's high-rise construction across nature's high-rising mountains not only for golf, picnics, and hikes in the summer, but to 5 other ski resorts in the winter and spring for 200 days of superb powder skiing and 165 days of excursions during the summer and autumn festival season.

Name: The Cliff Lodge and Spa

Mailing Address: Snowbird, Utah 84092

Telephone: (801) 742-2222, ext. 5900; (800) 453-3000 for reservations and information

Established: 1987

Managing Director: Linda Walker

Program Directors: Linda Walker, Spa Director and Fitness Director; Pauline Wooten, Beauty Director

Owner: Richard D. Bass; Snowbird Corporation

Gender and Age Restrictions: Co-ed; minimum age 16

Season: Year-round

Length of Stay Required: 4-day/4-night and 5-day/7-night *Spa Plans* and *Ski and Spa Packages* (latter available January 3–May 3); ½-day Perk; 1-day *Revitalizer;* or Spa services offered à la carte

Programs Offered: Relaxation, health improvement, personal fitness, weight management; physically challenging full exercise program, full-service physical therapy treatments, and full-service salon services; selection of 1500-calorie per day spa meals. You receive a prearrival packet of information and are interviewed on arrival to schedule your spa treatments, exercise workout, beauty salon appointments, and skiing or hiking schedule, and to work out your nutritional plan. Therapeutic and fitness-oriented, the program is noncompulsory and structured according to your convenience and inclinations. All spa packages include the use of lockers, towels, sauna, steam room, whirlpool, sun deck, swimming pool, and exercise equipment. The 1-day *Revitalizer* includes 2 exercise classes, 1 herbal or parafango wrap, a massage, a basic skin care treatment, a shampoo/blow-dry, a manicure, and lunch at the Spa Café. The *4-day/4-night Spa Plan* includes as many exercise classes as you wish to take, 2 massages, 1 herbal or parafango wrap, 1 hydromassage, 1 skin care treatment; choice of manicure, pedicure, or shampoo/blow-dry; and a personal fitness consultation. The *6-day/7-night Spa Plan* includes the same services but extends your stay and the number of spa meals to which you are entitled. The *Ski and Spa Packages* do not include the price of meals but provide skiing privileges and the full use of the spa facilities with as many exercise classes as you wish to take. The *4-day/4-night Ski and Spa Package* includes 2 massages, 1 herbal or parafango wrap, 1 hydromassage, 1 skin care treatment, and a choice of manicure, pedicure, or shampoo/blow-dry. The *6-day/7-night Ski and Spa Package* includes a ski lesson, 3 massages, 2 herbal wraps, 2 hydromassages, a skin care treatment, and a choice of manicure, pedicure, or shampoo/blow-dry. Monitored exercise classes include low-impact aerobics, body sculpture, aqua-aerobics, stretch and flex, body alignment, body work/conditioning, controlled-impact and aerobic conditioning. Stress management lectures are offered in the evenings.

Maximum Number of Guests: 1064 in the Lodge; 30 to 40 full-time spa plan guests; plus 100 à la carte treatments per day

Full-Time Health Professionals on Staff: 5 fitness personnel, 20 massage therapists, plus 2 estheticians, and 7 salon personnel. From 10:00 AM to 6:00 PM daily, the Snowbird Clinic Emergency Room, staffed by the Alta View Hospital located 10 miles distant, is open in the resort's Plaza Building.

Diet and Weight Management: Spa meals include a recommended 400 calories for breakfast, 500 calories for lunch, and 600 calories for dinner, totaling 1500 calories a day. The Spa Café's menu lists calorie counts for all food choices offered. Guests can be seated at granite-topped tables or at the vegetable and fruit juice bar with spectacular mountain views always to gaze upon. A spa bran muffin, spa granola, blended fruit juices, and low-fat yogurt are breakfast offerings. On the menu for lunch and dinner, with seasonal variations, are specialties such as black pepper and parsley pasta tossed with grated Parmesan and Romano cheese, crabmeat salad, ratatouille, grilled Ahi tuna with lemon mayonnaise and dill, lobster ravioli, chicken paillard, peach melba, wholewheat shortcake with raspberry coulis, hazelnut mousse. Soups made from unsalted stock are delectable. Salmon soup in a broth of Nori seaweed is a happy surprise. The spa chef, Brophy Jones, former owner of a popular catering company in Milwaukee, and trained for a decade in food service, plans and supervises the preparation of all spa meal choices, which are served at Cliff Lodge's 4 restaurants as well as at the 9 additional restaurants in the Snowbird complex. The Aerie roof-top dining room features delightful low-fat, low-cholesterol dishes with no loss in flavor for "fine dining" as an alternative to the Spa Café, for spa guests as well as hotel guests. Children's menu available; live entertainment nightly. All 13 restaurants offer calorie-controlled food portions, high in fiber, low in sodium and cholesterol, and containing as little sugar as possible other than that which occurs naturally in the deliciously fresh vegetables and fruits presented. Fresh seafood is flown in daily from Massachusetts, Hawaii, Florida, and California. With advance notice, food choices can be accommodated to lacto-ovo, strictly vegetarian, food allergy, and other requirements.

Exercise and Physical Therapy Facilities: The 27,000-square-foot spa, on the top 2 floors of the 13-story Cliff Lodge, provides a high-tech ambience of natural wood and concrete with a rosy pink and dove-grey decor accented by potted trees and plants and enhanced by awesome views of the snow-crested or snow-mantled ridges and peaks of the Wasatch Mountains. Men's and women's locker/changing/shower rooms, bright with mirrors, convenient with hair dryers, bathing-suit dryers, and saunas, are on the first floor, along with the outdoor solarium, boutique (exercise clothes, bathing suits, beauty and skin care products), steam rooms, rooms for therapeutic massage in the Swedish-Esalen style as well as shiatsu and acupressure, rooms with imported German hydrotherapy tubs for underwater massage, Scotch hose equipment (alternating jets of hot and cold water), herbal wrap and skin care treatment rooms, and beauty salon. The Spa Café is on the second, or rooftop, floor, as well as a 54-foot-long, heated, lap-swimming pool; a 24-person Jacuzzi-style whirlpool hot tub; mirrored exercise and aerobic dance-and-exercise rooms; and a gym equipped with Keiser K300 pneumatic resistance exercise equipment, stationary bicycles and rowing machines. From 7:15 AM to 6:50 PM, classes are given in stretch and flex, aerobics and alignment, body work/conditioning, controlled-impact and aerobic conditioning—all on an à la carte basis. Snag for latecomers: they won't be allowed to participate.

Opportunities for Recreational Exercise: Skiing, skiing, skiing, from November to mid-June. Children's and adults' skis, boots, and poles can be rented on site. In the summer, guests enjoy swimming in the heated pool and playing on 5 Laykold outdoor tennis courts, open daily 9:00 AM to 8:00 PM. Rackets and ball machines can be rented, and tennis clinics, workshops, and private and semiprivate lessons are available at extra charge. High-altitude balls and accessories are on sale at Snowbird's tennis shop. Heli-golf—helicopter transport to a nearby mountain golf course (extra)—and heli-hiking—helicopter transport to a champagne picnic site, with a guided tour through a high-altitude meadow of alpine wildflowers (extra)—are other options. Hiking trails are on the property of the Snowbird complex, which is adjacent to the Wasatch National Park, so hiking possibilities are fabulous. Adventurous guests can also take advantage of Snowbird's off-site Mountaineering Center, which offers rock-climbing classes for beginners; full-day Peak Climbs to an elevation of 11,200 feet; half-day Ridge Climbs, beginning from 11,000 feet; guided sunrise hikes; backpack camping trips in the Wasatch Range, from 1 night to several days, with backpacks, sleeping bags, and tents available at Snowbird, and all meals prepared by a guide. Extra charges for these activities.

Beauty Treatments and Welcome Indulgences: Spa skin care and salon services include depilatory waxing, body massages and facials with Utah's own dermatological skin care products; hair styling, coloring, tinting, rinsing, highlighting. Salon manicures and pedicures are done plain or Hawaiian style with paraffin masques to soften the skin, and French manicures are given, which render the free edges of your nails as white as snow. Herbal foot baths and foot massages are another salon specialty. For sore or tired muscles, a European parafango treatment involves heated volcanic ash and paraffin wax applied to different parts of the body for deep heat and relaxation. Also for relaxation, in a cedar-lined, eucalyptus-scented room, your body can be wrapped in warm, herbal-soaked linens with the accompaniment of soft background music to soothe tired muscles and nerves.

Accommodations: Room corridors overlook an 11-story glass-paneled lobby lounge facing pines, peaks, and mountain slopes, and all 532 deluxe bedrooms and suites (some with balconies) have breath-catching mountain views. All rooms have private bath, cable TV with Movie Channel and ESPN Sports Network, telephone, a king-sized bed or twin queen-sized beds, checked ski storage, wake-up service, room service, bellman and valet service, air-conditioning. There is a coin-operated laundry on the premises. Dormitory accommodations (2 over-and-under bunk beds and 1 shared bathroom) and 1- and 2-bedroom suites with kitchenettes are also available.

What to Bring: See USEFUL INFORMATION. Robes and cover-ups are provided in the Spa. Most guests wear upscale sports clothing day and night. Bring your own boots, skis, poles, and tennis rackets if you don't want to rent or buy them, along with ski and tennis gear, at Snowbird Center's Breeze Ski and Sport, Powderhound Boutique, or SportStalker Ski Shop, which also has a service and repair shop. The Little Cottonwood Tailor Shop in Snowbird Center does alterations and repairs. The Norsk Leather Shop has specialty leather apparel and furs, including fur-lined leather moccasins. T-shirts, running gear, shorts, children's wear, hand-made items for children and grown-ups, photography equipment, and film are all available in shops at the Snowbird Center, plus a full-service pharmacy for prescriptions, health and beauty aids, and magazines, and a post office. Gift items and accessories galore at both Snowbird Center and Cliff Lodge, plus a grocery-delicatessen and package liquor store and small book store and art gallery. What to bring? Money!

Documentation from Your Physician: A letter of approval, medical history, and documentation of recent medical examination are requested. You are asked to consult with your physician if you have any doubt about your ability to take part in the spa or skiing programs. Snowbird is based at 8000 feet. Those with heart or respiratory problems are requested to "take precautions to allow for the altitude." In cases of high blood pressure, recent surgery, varicosities, or other obvious health issues, guests are asked to sign release forms or not work out at the spa.

The Use of Alcohol and Tobacco: To comply with Utah's liquor laws, if you want to buy wine, mixed drinks, beer, or liquor, you are required to pay a $5 fee for a temporary membership in all club facilities at Cliff Lodge; or to buy minibottles or tenths of wine and pay set-up and corkage fees at designated restaurants at Snowbird; or to buy your bottle at the package agency at the Snowbird Center and bring it with you into any Snowbird restaurant or lounge. No smoking is permitted in the spa, and 38 smoke-free guest rooms are available on level 9 of the Cliff Lodge.

Fees, Method of Payment, Insurance Coverage: High-season (November 22 to April 4) rates:

For the *Perk,* ½-day Spa package: $80

For the *Revitalizer,* 1-day Spa package: $160

For the *4-day/4-night Spa Plan:* $975 single, $775 per person double

For the *6-day/7-night Spa Plan:* $1525 single, $1200 per person double

For the *4-day/4-night Ski and Spa Package* (no meals included): $775 single, $575 per person double

For the *6-day/7-night Ski and Spa Package* (no meals included): $1225 single, $900 per person double

Rates are higher for deluxe accommodations and lower in the off-season. All prices are subject to change, and all rates are subject to 6 percent state tax plus gratuities at your discretion. During the high season, nightly rates per double room range from $130, with discounts during the spring, April 4 to May 3, and summer. Special rates for ski packages, which include lift tickets. Condominium rates and packages also available at Snowbird, The Inn, and Iron Blosam Lodge, downhill from Cliff Lodge.

Fees for supervising children before and after classes at the ski school, plus cost of lunch is extra; hourly child-care and in-room baby-sitting fees are modest. For à la carte services, you are requested to call at least 2 weeks prior to your arrival to make appointments. All prices are subject to change. A deposit is required. Ask about the cancellation policy. Visa, MasterCard, American Express, and Diners Club credit cards are accepted. The spa program is not tax-deductible.

∽ The Greenhouse ∾

Texas

Inarguably, The Greenhouse is unique. The stated goal of The Greenhouse is "to help each woman develop a heightened sense of self in nurturing, caring, elegant surroundings." In an environment totally weatherproof, with controlled temperature, humidity, and light, in a glass-domed, latticed sanctuary that is a blend of exclusive women's club, super-deluxe small hotel, and highly struc-tured program, you are committed to only as much as you would like to be. If wilted plants thrive when well tended in a hothouse, wilted ladies emerge after a week in an ambience of tranquil privacy, of undivided attention by masseuses, estheticians, and fitness instructors assigned to them, with new-found energy and vitality, feeling so revivified and beautiful that at least 75 percent of the guests return for other visits made all the more agreeable because they find on returning that they are happily remembered and their every preference catered to. To grow younger as one grows older is another dream to which The Greenhouse addresses itself, and it is a rare spa that is as attentive as The Greenhouse to one's happy child self. Your exercise/play clothes are freshly placed in your room every evening. Everything you need in the spa is handed to you, arranged for you. You'll find yourself surrounded by the rich, the famous, and the celebrated. You can invite friends over to have lunch or to dine with you or you can enjoy your meals in solitude in your room while you listen to your room's radio or watch television, knowing at the same time you never have to be alone. The Greenhouse has its own chauffeured station wagons to transport you safely to and from a few destinations with no charge, and anywhere else you would like to go for an extra fee.

The three-story, airy, lattice-vaulted solarium-atrium is the core of the spa. Cusped latticed arches are pendant with plants and, set along the second-floor balcony, flowering plants repeat in miniature the plant motifs of palms, ferns, topiary trees, and seasonally flowering shrubs ranged about the white marble-floored pavilions beneath. The symmetry throughout the spa is manifest in the decor of your comfortable guestroom and in the precise and balanced arrangement of the French provincial–style furnishings. Greenery everywhere silently replenishes oxygen to the air you breathe. Everything has been arranged and ordered and created so that once in the heart of the spa's centerpiece atrium, you never have to leave to go outside. For guests who feel claustrophobic in such calm, ordered perfection, there is an adjacent golf course, plus an outdoor pool, outdoor tennis courts, and a walking path for a morning brisk.

For those who adore shopping but hate the inconveniences, The Greenhouse is a dream come true. A Neiman-Marcus credit card with your name on it is in your room when you arrive. Evening fashion shows present the latest in seasonal wear, casual wear for the *sportif* look, as well as furs and precious jewels. A weekly shopping trip is scheduled with complimentary transportation into Dallas provided in stretch limousines. You are met at Neiman-Marcus by attendants who escort you to whichever department is of interest to you and assist you in a manner usually reserved only for visiting royalty. If fashion shows and shopping appeal to you less than they do to the majority of guests, the Arlington Fine Arts Council (P.O. Box 13741, Arlington, Texas 76013; telephone [817] 429-7272) can supply you with a year-round calendar of cultural events; or the Dallas Arboretum on White Rock Lake may delight you with its spectacular gardens; or you might even feel like a frisk at Six Flags Over Texas if you are feeling rambunctious and have time to spare before you go back home and impress everyone with your newfound sylphlike figure and the life enhancement of your newfound self.

Name: The Greenhouse

Mailing Address: P.O. Box 1144, Arlington, Texas 76010

Telephone: (817) 640-4000

Established: 1965

Managing/Executive Director: Lori Horvath

Program Directors: Betty Godfrey, R.N.,

Medical Supervisor; Shirley Ogle, Beauty Manager; Eura Oster, Facial Manager; Lori Horvath, Director of Fitness; Elsa Pouch, M.T., Director of Treatment; Laureen Mody, R.D., Nutritionist; Toni Beck, Consultant
Owner: Edward J. Safdie

Gender and Age Restrictions: Women only; minimum age 19
Season: Year-round except for 2 weeks in July and 4 weeks in December/January
Length of Stay Required: 8 days/7 nights, Sunday 1:00–6:00 PM to following Sunday noon

Programs Offered: With variations, such as *The Active Woman's Week, The Executive Woman's Week, Mother-and-Daughter Week,* and *Festive Italian Week,* when The Greenhouse's food, fashion shows, lectures, beauty department, and exercise classes are specifically themed to special interests, the core program of The Greenhouse is *Total Wellness* (nutrition, beauty, health, and fitness) *for the Total Woman.* Postnatal exercises are offered year-round, available on request.

On admission, after you are armed with sturdy pasteboard map in hand so that you can easily find your bearings with The Greenhouse's interior garden and solarium-atrium pool as your lodestar, you receive a physical examination by The Greenhouse's exercise physiologist and attending registered nurse, who will check your heart, lungs, and blood pressure. You are then assigned a personal fitness instructor for your entire visit. Before your first exercise class, she will assess your body's alignment, cardiovascular training zone, ratio of lean to fat with the skin-fold caliper technique, and your current and future fitness goals. With Dr. Almand's report, her assessment, and your inclinations as a guide, she will then diagram your schedule to include what you get in the package: 4½ hours daily of instructor-supervised and monitored exercise, cardiovascular conditioning, and exercises to relax you; six 60-minute massages a week; five 60-minute facials; 6 hours of beauty school, with a facialist, hairdresser, masseuse, and manicurist/pedicurist assigned to tutor you in the revelation of your personal beauty style and its enhancement with facial masques, cleansing, the removal of facial hair or stray eyebrow hair by waxing as the foundation for further enhancement with becoming new colors, makeup techniques, and the ritziest of Charles of the Ritz creams, potions, and other products; 30 minutes daily devoted to the care of your fingernails and toenails, including 2 Therafin treatments (heated wax masques) to soften and silken the skin of your hands and feet; 30 minutes daily devoted to conditioning treatments for your hair and scalp with oils and rinses to add shine and the fresh luster of health to each and every strand; and a loofah bath to improve your skin's texture. For tutelage in the nurturing of your body, you are offered 105 minutes of nutritional counseling, plus an hour's group cooking class demonstration performed by Spa Chef Michele Tezak. Diagnostic treatment, supervised by an exercise physiologist, such as an electrocardiograph or a full lab chemistry workup, is available for an additional fee for the medically minded. Private instruction for a particular exercise class, written instructions and tapes, and testing your endurance, heart rate, and other responses to a treadmill test are all included as an optional part of your exercise program at no extra charge.

Your individual exercise program, with your own fitness instructor (trained, as all the fitness instructors are, under the tutelage of Dr. Kenneth Cooper's world-acclaimed Aerobics Center in nearby Dallas) offers a daily morning walk; 30-minute classes of wake-up stretching, flexibility, and alignment exercises; 40-minute classes of flex and stretch and its gentler companion, "E-Z" flex and stretch; 30-minute interval training classes, using 3-, 5-, and 8-pound hand weights and rubber tubing you stretch like giant elastic bands; water classes in the spectacular heated-to-94-degrees swimming pool, using inflated floating balls to cling to while practising leg kicks; (splashing childhood bathtub play raised to physiologically beneficial grown-up pleasure); 45-minute classes of high-energy, low-impact aerobics (cardiovascular conditioning); and a 30-minute relaxation class designed to teach the body to release stress and tension, as well as to concentrate on body alignment and breathing. One-on-one instruction may also include aerobic circuit training with Nautilus equipment; the use of stationary bicycles and rowing machines in the exercise room; or using the exercise path to sample the 4 stations of the parcours for leg lifts, push-ups, sit-ups, and pull-ups. Whenever you have an elective period in your schedule, the wet and dry sauna and the Jacuzzi whirlpool are there for your pleasure, as are attendants to monitor you and attend to your every need or velleity while you are relaxing in the steam room. In your elective free time you can go outside to swim or play golf or tennis, or stay inside where the climate is always perfect to browse in the ever-charming boutique with its array of jewelry and clothes and exercise tapes. You can also view the tapes in The Greenhouse's videotape library as well as checking out all the other videotapes you might wish to see of an evening. Your week's package also includes a quiet night on Wednesdays, when your dinner tray is served to you in your room and a video film is shown later in the drawing room. There is generally a game night with prizes, and there are usually beauty and fitness lectures as well as poolside lunchtime fashion shows, dance lessons and other playtime, fun things to entertain you in your free time.

Maximum Number of Guests: 40

Full-Time Health Professionals on Staff: 11, including 1 doctor, 3 registered nurses, and a registered dietitian, plus 7 fitness instructors, 6 massage therapists, 3 cosmeticians, 5 hairdressers, 4 manicurist/pedicurists, and 6 facialists. The Greenhouse physician is always on call. A nurse is on duty each day from 8:30

AM to 4:30 PM and on call after office hours. All the fitness staff are trained in CPR.

Diet and Weight Management: Levels of 850, 1200, and 1500 calories a day are prescribed in consultation with The Greenhouse's physician, nutritionist/dietitian, R.N., and exercise director on the basis of your medical history, height, weight, body build, and body's need, and in conformance with your preferences. Your session of individual nutritional counseling and the group cooking demonstration class in The Greenhouse kitchen will clue you in to the mindset and practicalities of following similar healthy guidelines at home for weight loss, weight maintenance, or weight gain. The Greenhouse accommodates guests with any diet they may require for medical reasons. Kosher meals, lacto-ovo, or strictly vegetarian meals are provided. You can have your coffee and tea with or without caffeine. Otherwise, as you might expect, the diet is low in saturated fat/cholesterol, low in sodium, high in fiber, low in calories, and nutrient-rich.

The presentation of the food, and the ambience in which it is set before you and served, is as much a treat to your eyes as the varied selection of the daily menu is to your palate. Your breakfast, brought to your room by a crisply uniformed maid, is served to you on a wicker tray covered with a voile or embroidered linen tray cloth. It is set with a bud vase containing a yellow rose (for Texas, naturally), Ainsley china prettily patterned with pink roses, silver plate (the sterling silver forks, knives, and spoons are reserved for dinner time's formality). Your personalized schedule is there, together with the newspaper of your choice. Hot broth or fresh fruit smoothies, juices, or frappes are served midmorning and midafternoon. You may ask for tea, coffee, mineral water, or fresh lemonade to be served to you at any time. Carbonated beverages are a no-no. If you would like your lunch or dinner served on a tray in your room, you can have it, if you alert the kitchen in advance. Otherwise, lunch is served poolside, indoors or out, on round glass-topped tables set with pastel linen placemats and Herend, Limoges, or Rosenthal china, all the better for you to enjoy such goodies as crabmeat and almond soufflé and broiled pineapple fingers delicately flavored with curry, or hot pasta primavera with basil sauce, or California minestrone soup and Jack's Caesar salad. Dinner is served in grand style in the chandeliered dining room with its celadon-green walls and carpet, antique furniture, and 10 round tables seating 4 to 6 spa guests and guests they may invite (at an additional charge) any time *except* Wednesday evening (quiet night), Sunday lunch, and Sunday evening. Male guests can only be invited for dinner on Saturday night, when a pianist also entertains during the dinner hour.

Spa Chef Michele Tezak, graduate of La Varenne Ecole de Cuisine in Paris, produces delicious recipes from Edward J. Safdie's *Spa Food* as well as legendary favorites from *The Greenhouse Cookbook,* both books available at The Green-house boutique. Weekly cooking demonstrations. You are scheduled to be weighed and measured before lunch on Monday and Saturday mornings—and if you are hopping up and down on one toe with curiosity, you can also be weighed on Thursday morning—to find out just how much weight you can lose on such delectable fare. Most guests shed at least 3 to 5 pounds, and sometimes twice that number of inches overall if they have done the exercises scheduled for them.

Exercise and Physical Therapy Facilities: Nautilus equipment, a StairMaster, sta-tionary bicycles, a recumbent bicycle, and ergometrically monitored equipment, including treadmills, are located in 2 rooms on the first floor of the solarium-atrium, separated by a corridor from 2 exercise rooms, 4 treatment rooms, wet and dry saunas, the whirlpool, the steam room (which, for the amount of cosseting they receive there, is often referred to by guests as "the dream room"), and the loofah bath. The centerpiece of the solarium-atrium is the heated swimming pool, 60 feet long and 4 feet deep. Scalloped at each end, the pool reflects the symmetry of the arches above, and is centered with a ballet barre for you to hold on to while you perform your underwater leg movements in the pool. A ceramic tile bench runs the length of the pool for exercises you do in a seated position. Outdoors, there is a ¼-mile jogging track and 4 parcours stations along the walking/exercise path that winds around the live oaks and oleanders of the property.

Opportunities for Recreational Exercise: The Great Southwest Golf Course, an 18-hole lovely sward adjacent to the spa property, is a favorite of golf champion Arnold Palmer, who often uses it. No greens fees for Greenhouse guests. Golf carts and clubs can be rented. There is an outdoor swimming pool. There are 2 daytime tennis courts with a backboard for practice. Tennis and swimming lessons are extra.

Beauty Treatments and Welcome Indulgences: In the beauty department, you are treated like a queen and, like royalty, no detail pertaining to your grooming and exterior self is left unattended. Facial waxing, lip and brow waxing, and underarm waxing are included in your fee. There is a charge for other waxing depilation. Since you have the same technicians throughout the week assigned to take care of your hands, feet, fingernails, toenails, your face, your hair, and your body, in progressive conditioning daily treatments, each technician can really get to know your exterior self and work with you to see which treatments are best to "assist in creating the new YOU!"—and which products suit you best—Charles of the Ritz, Yves St. Laurent, or other delights. At the beauty school, personal, group, and individual classes in makeup for special occasion techniques and other innovative ideas guide you in experimenting with a variety of new looks for your newfound self. Services in addition to the regular program, such as frosting your hair, or henna, tints, toners, or permanents, are available at additional charge. A shampoo, set, and blow-dry is scheduled for you on departure day and special makeup for the occasion if you so desire and schedule an appointment for it. For those who like to be indulged and pampered—and who, when one gets down to it, does not?—The Greenhouse is paradise on earth.

Accommodations: Either located off the ground floor of the solarium-atrium or opening off its second-floor balcony, each of the 40 spacious guestrooms is decorator perfect with Texas-rose yellow, pink, peach, celadon-green, or floral patterns for the matching or complementary-hued curtain, headboard valance-canopy, and quilted bedspread covering your queen-sized, dust-ruffled bed. There is no dust, of course. Everything is immaculate. The wall-to-wall carpet is plush and soft. The bathroom is separate from the dressing room and contains a sumptuous sunken bathtub, a bidet, and a "commode," as they say at The Greenhouse. The dressing area has 4 full-length mirrored doors, a large and well-lit closet, a dressing table with a huge lighted mirror and a lavish supply of Charles of the Ritz and Yves St. Laurent goodies to greet you on your arrival. Two suites are available with the added convenience of a sitting room with a fireplace. Two single rooms, #219 and #220, each have a balcony overlooking a courtyard with a fountain, trees, and flowers on the opposite side of the house from the outdoor swimming pool.

What to Bring: See USEFUL INFORMATION. Navy-blue tights, leotards, shorts, headbands, and a fluffy yellow terry-cloth bathrobe are provided for you to use during your stay. Fresh exercise clothing is placed in your room every evening. You'll need a suit or dress for your Neiman-Marcus shopping excursion. You'll need casual evening wear for dinners; that is, casual evening wear such as Mary McFadden evening pajamas or pajama-tunic-surcoat designer wear or designer caftans. Covered-up elegance is *de rigueur* for dinner. You can always find what you need in the boutique to fill in if you can't wait for the Neiman-Marcus shopping trip on Thursday. Pick-up and delivery service for pressing, dry cleaning, and laundry is provided for clothes left at the office before 8:00 AM on Monday, Wednesday, or Friday, and the cost will be charged to your room. There is an in-house dispensary for toothbrushes and other little essentials; a library; available stationery, film, and writing materials. Newspapers, local, national, or from your own hometown, can be supplied on request at no additional charge.

Documentation from Your Physician: A letter of approval is requested and required if a guest has medical problems, allergies, or dietary restrictions that limit or alter participation in the regular diet, exercise, or beauty treatments. All guests receive a physical examination by the Greenhouse physician. Guests will be asked to sign a medical release form only if warranted by the medical examination.

The Use of Alcohol and Tobacco: Alcoholic beverages are prohibited at The Greenhouse. Smoking is not allowed in the dining room, but coffee is served after dinner in the drawing room or poolside in consideration of those who wish to smoke. No smoking is allowed in the solarium-atrium from 8:30 AM to 1:00 PM or from 2:00 to 4:00 PM, these being the hours when exercise classes are held. Smoking is allowed in your room, outdoors, and in designated areas.

Fees, Method of Payment, Insurance Coverage: Year-round rates for the 8-day/7-night program:

For single: $2850

For double: $2825 per person (suite)

Rates are higher for deluxe accommodations. All prices are subject to change. A service charge is included in these rates, and additional gratuities are optional. A deposit is required. Ask about the cancellation policy. Personal checks, travelers' checks, Visa, MasterCard, American Express, and Neiman-Marcus credit cards are accepted. Fees are not tax-deductible as medical expenses or health institute fees.

Follow-up Assistance: Your personal fitness instructor keeps in touch with you, as does the managing director with private correspondence. Video teaching tapes, cassettes, a cookbook, and Edward J. Safdie's *Spa Food* are splendid take-home items as aides-mémoire for following The Greenhouse program. Each guest receives a take-home sourcebook filled with easy-to-follow tips, advice, and procedures for diet and nutrition, exercise, beauty care, and makeup.

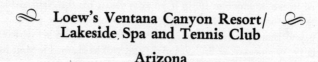

Loew's Ventana Canyon Resort/ Lakeside Spa and Tennis Club
Arizona

A double-width bathtub, telephone, and television set in every bathroom. Luxuriously appointed guestrooms and computerized lighting in the lobby that dims with twilight for memorable sunset watching. Golf, tennis, swimming, and other recreational delights along with state-of-the-art facilities rated 4 diamonds by AAA and 4 stars by Mobil. A 90-acre super-resort at an altitude of 3000 + feet tucked into Arizona's Catalina Mountains, with a natural water course that flows from the mountains, highlighted by an 80-foot cascade, to a lake and a tiered waterfall at its dramatic entrance. All this PLUS a gemlike little spa with personalized exercise/fitness programs for no more than a dozen participants with room plus hotel guests who care to join in à la carte. What's more, the spa is under the direction of Bill McGrath, resident tennis pro, who designed the world's largest resort at Sea Pines Plantation, Hilton Head, South Carolina, and who has coordinated the Lakeside Spa's exercise and diet program to comply with recommendations of the 6-physician member group of Tucson's Heart Institute.

Another asset is the Sonora Desert environment (enjoyed also by Canyon Ranch) where you can burn off a lot of calories and learn a lot at the same time walking or bicycling along well-documented nature trails. And there are the attractions of Tucson, a 30-minute drive away, and its environs. In addition to Tucson's annual rodeo, La Fiesta de los Vaqueros, plus its annual festival and gem and mineral show, other unique attractions are its Sonora Desert Museum with underwater viewing, walk-in aviary, earth sciences center, and outdoor display; the San Xavier del Bac Mission on the outskirts of the Papago Indian Reservation, one of the finest examples of colonial period baroque architecture in the US; the Old Tucson movie set and tourist trappings; Sabino Canyon in Coronado National Forest; Saguaro National Monument; Eastertime ceremonials of the Yaqui Indians; Tubac Village's arts shops and artists' center; Colossal Cave, one of the world's largest dry caverns; and hot-air balloon rides at reasonable rates.

Name: Loew's Ventana Canyon Resort/ Lakeside Spa and Tennis Club

Mailing Address: 7000 North Resort Drive, Tucson, Arizona 85715

Telephone: (602) 299-2020

Established: 1985 (hotel and spa facility); 1987 (spa program)

Managing Director: Bill McGrath, Director of the Lakeside Spa and Tennis Club; John Thacker, General Manager of Loew's Ventana Canyon Resort Hotel

Program Director: Mary Ann Santander

Owner: Ester Company in syndication with Catalina Properties, managed by Loew's Corporation

Gender and Age Restrictions: None in hotel; for Lakeside Spa, co-ed, minimum age 16

Season: Year-round

Length of Stay Required: 4 days/3 nights; 7 days/6 nights, Monday to Sunday; also à la carte use by hotel guests by appointment

Programs Offered: Your stay begins with a caliper skin-fold test to determine your percentage of body fat, and an individual physical fitness evaluation to test your flexibility, strength, and endurance. If indicated, you have blood workups and a stress test supervised by physicians at Tucson's Heart Institute, an independent, privately owned and operated organization with access to, but not affiliated with, local hospitals.

Open Monday through Sunday from 7:00 AM to 10:00 PM, the 3000-square-foot spa, with 6 skylights and floor-to-ceiling glass windows, provides Exercycles, motorized treadmills, Versa-Climbers, a rowing machine, 12 separate Universal exercise stations, and free weights; a mirrored room with aerobic flooring and ballet barre for classes in stretching, toning, conditioning, low-impact aerobics, and body contouring; separate men's and women's locker rooms and sauna; a steam room and heated whirlpool; an outdoor heated 50-foot lap-swimming pool with kickboards and pull paddles; the hotel's heated swimming pool with adjacent hot tubs and cold plunge is also available for your use.

McGrath and Mary Ann Santander, certified by the International Dance Education Association as a qualified instructor of aerobic exercise, with a staff of 2 full-time health professionals, design a program of exercise suited to your individual needs, and help you establish personal fitness goals. They see that you know your way around the 2.5-mile, 18-exercise-station fitness par course trail, so beautiful a window on the desert and its wildlife that it's guaranteed to take away your breath as it takes away your breadth. A morning power walk, a 60-minute brisk on the par course track, is scheduled daily. McGrath and his staff encourage you to rent a bicycle for $6 an hour to explore the Sonora Desert terrain on a mapped tour, or to make use of trails easily accessible from the hotel lobby.

For relaxation at the spa, there are massage therapists skilled in Swedish, shiatsu, and reflexology techniques and, for an extra charge, you can have massages in your room. The *3-night program* includes 1 massage, the *7-night program* includes 2 massages.

You have playing privileges at the 36-hole PGA Ventana Golf and Racquet Club, with rental golfclubs, driving range, putting practice green, and the option of private golf instruction at $30 per half-hour. Bill McGrath presents a superb tennis bill of fare. You can rent rackets, shoes, and a ball machine and enjoy private tennis lessons, tennis game evaluations, and tennis-playing lessons at reasonable rates as well as court reservations on 10 championship Plexi-Pave courts (at an hourly fee), all lit for night play. There's a croquet court at the hotel and game room billiards. Reddington Riding Stables are a 15-minute drive away for trail rides available at extra charge.

Diet and Weight Management: Tucson's Heart Institute, in collaboration with the sous-chef, have come up with high-fiber, low-sodium, low-fat, delicious light spa cuisine. Avoid the temptations of all those complimentary hors d'oeuvres and the clotted cream and scones and pastries served with high tea in the hotel's Cascade Lounge. Stay away from the hotel's poolside snack and beverage station with its mesquite grill and chili burgers. If you can trust yourself to exercise restraint and portion control and sample only the fresh fruit from the dessert cart, the Ventana, one of the 100 best restaurants in Arizona, features new American cuisine with venison, quail, and fresh fish entrées. And 24-hour room service can provide you with low-calorie fare if you request it.

Beauty Treatments and Welcome Indulgences: The spa's Great Waves Beauty Salon provides full-service treatment for men and women: nail, hair, skin care, and facials. Massages and reflexology treatments at extra cost in your room or in the spa in this desert paradise should be considered your just desserts!

Accommodations: 366 guest rooms and 26 suites, each with minibar, refrigerator, private terrace, remote control television, 2 telephones in the bedroom, 1 in the bathroom, along with bathroom television and sumptuous double-width bathtubs.

What to Bring: See USEFUL INFORMATION. Sportswear is available at the spa's pro shop, and the hotel's gift shop carries sports accessories and some items of wearing apparel. Evenings? Simple dresses for women, blazers and ties for men. Mornings and evenings are noticeably cooler than noon and afternoon, so for women, a shawl or sweater is always useful to have on hand. There is no dress code other than comfortable simplicity, which guests generally interpret at designer levels or reasonable facsimiles thereof. Check the hotel for seasonal temperatures and plan to layer your clothing accordingly. Sundries, stationery, newspapers, paperbacks, and gifts are all available at the hotel, which has its own minishopping center.

Documentation from Your Physician: A letter of approval, medical history, and documentation of recent physical examination are requested. If there is any doubt about your ability to participate in the spa's exercise programs or recreational activities, you will receive a physical examination at Tucson's Heart Institute, including a physician-supervised stress test and blood analysis.

The Use of Alcohol and Tobacco: Neither is allowed in the spa facility.

Fees, Method of Payment, Insurance Coverage: High-season rates, mid-January to last week in April, and from the first week in September to mid-January:

4-day/3-night spa program: $695 single, $765 double

8-day/7-night spa program: $1600 single, $1755 double

Summer, or low-season, rates:

4-day/3-night spa program: $285 single, $350 double
8-day/7-night spa program: $655 single, $795 double

Suites (1- and 2-bedroom) are available at extra cost. Ask about the cancellation policy. Visa, MasterCard, American Express, Diners Club, and Carte Blanche credit cards, as well as personal checks, travelers' checks, and cash are accepted in payment. (Except for an automatic 10 percent service charge on room service orders, gratuities are at the guests' discretion.) Spa fees may be tax-deductible in part as a medical expense providing you have a letter from your physician prescribing your stay as a recommended or necessary health procedure.

Follow-up Assistance: On request, video cassettes can be made of you performing exercises, demonstrating learned techniques of aerobic exercise, improving your golf swing or your tennis serve.

❧ Maine Chance ❧
Arizona

Your grandmama, your mother, or—can it be possible?—even you may remember the original Maine Chance in the north woods of Maine, in Mt. Vernon, near Augusta, where your night maid turned down the bed and drew a bubblebath for you before dinner, where the cream of American society's womanhood did warm-up exercises on a platform floating in the middle of an idyllic lake fringed with a forest and a mountain view. You walked on Aubusson carpets beneath crystal chandeliers, went to sleep on hand-embroidered linen sheets, enjoyed Elizabeth Arden's light and airy lemon meringue pie dessert, and dined with a different, exquisite setting of china and sterling silver for each of the 14 days you spent at this retreat where quality was the watchword. Anything chemical or artificial was shunned in both the food you ate and the creams with which your body or face were massaged as sedulously as the grooms massaged the hocks of Miss Arden's prizewinning Maine Chance racehorses.

The original Maine Chance closed in 1970 after two devastating fires, but by then, Phoenix Maine Chance had been operating for 24 years, and the Arden cachet was in evidence there as it had been in Maine: monogrammed silver and linens, paintings by Magritte, Chagall, and Mary Cassatt, plus the southwestern genius of Georgia O'Keeffe. There was a Savonnerie carpet in the drawing room. Venetian mirrors, crystal-and-mirrored dressing tables, armoires, one-of-a-kind antiques, flowers, and books could be found in each of the bedrooms and suites. With an 83 percent repeat record, why should anything change much more than that, even after Miss Arden's death, the subsequent takeover of the spa by Eli Lilly Pharmaceuticals, and then its acquisition in 1987 by Fabergé, Inc., and its new ownership by Unilever in 1989? Nothing much has.

For some, Maine Chance may be ho-hum, snooze, yawn, zzzzz, but for others, Maine Chance remains the all-women's queen of the pampering retreat and relaxation spas, never advertised (nothing vulgar like that!), super-private, exclusive, and with maid service "the way it used to be." The maximum number of guests is 52, and the staff-to-guest ratio, as in Miss Arden's day, is never permitted to drop below 2 to 1. (The staff at present numbers 130.) Old Guard, Socially Registered, to-the-manner-born ladies feel right at home here. The stark, white, fortresslike contemporary building and 14 outbuildings shelter the beauty service areas and new-in-1987 indoor swimming pool, and include 7 residential "cottages," each with 5 to 7 rooms, some with cathedral ceilings. Surrounded by 110 acres of manicured lawns, citrus groves, palms, and stretches of saguaro cactus, this haven is nestled against the landmark Camelback Mountain. Garden Club members are ecstatic about the plantings—more than 89,000—of pink peace roses (the late Miss Arden's favorites), pink petunias, white asters, larkspur, snapdragons, calla lilies, and the blankets of shocking-pink bougainvillea thrown over white adobe walls.

Indulgent grandmothers bring their granddaughters, mothers bring their daughters, and if the crowd at Maine Chance seems younger these days, it's because, as Mr. Quirk, that proper and charming Bostonian who has been associated with Maine Chance "forever," says: "We're on our third generation, now. The wonderful old families keep on coming back to us." Women who work in a man's world may welcome the camaraderie of all women being together, finding it a relief to talk about personal issues and themselves in the company solely of other women. Some women may find the ambience here—a sedate, ladylike refuge—a bit repressive, like staying with a rich aunt who spoils you, but expects you always to be on your best behavior.

Taxis and rental cars are made easily available for shopping excursions to, and cultural events in, Scottsdale and Phoenix, or for sight-seeing excursions to the Pima Indian reservation, nearby Phoenix's fine arts museum, and naturally occurring scenic pleasures in the vicinity. The program is structured, however, and most ladies staying at Maine Chance have neither the time nor the inclination to stir from the property during their stay.

Name: Maine Chance
Mailing Address: 5830 East Jean Avenue,

Phoenix, Arizona 85018
Telephone: (602) 947-6365

Established: 1932 in Mt. Vernon, Maine (closed 1970); 1946 in Phoenix, Arizona

Managing Director: Frederick Quirk

Program Directors: Mrs. Emily Alvarez, Beauty Service Manager; Françoise Kraus, Cosmetic Manager; Darlene Gregory, Reservations Manager

Owner: Unilever (British-Dutch company), parent company of Lever Brothers

Gender and Age Restrictions: Women only; minimum age 16

Season: Open from the last Sunday in September until the end of May

Length of Stay Required: 8 days/7 nights, Sunday to Sunday

Programs Offered: Relaxation, weight loss, weight gain, beauty, and fitness are components of the daily program's activities, which are scheduled from 7:30 AM to 5:00 PM. Your daily agenda includes 4 classes in exercise, many developed by the legendary Marjorie Craig, as well as slendercises and dance exercise, low-impact aerobics classes, yoga, calisthenics, and water exercises in a turquoise pool evocative of those in Long Island's great 1930s country estates.

You ascend to the 75-foot-long pool by double stairways, walled with thick adobe, white as snow, through Roman arches, into an area of greenery (natural and Astroturf wall-to-wall) brilliant with the deep pink of bougainvillea, potted pink hydrangeas, and petunias. The new 55-foot-long indoor pool for nonheliotropic ladies is adjacent to the body-building building and connected with it by a hallway.

You receive 2 each of these heat treatments—steam cabinet, sauna, Ardena paraffin wax bath—weekly, plus Scotch hose sessions. Daily massage, face treatment, skin care and makeup classes, scalp and nail treatments, and, at week's end, to set the seal on the new and beautiful you, a shampoo, hairstyling, manicure, and pedicure. Electives are offered in Tai Chi and advanced dance exercise.

During your free time, you can play tennis on the property's well-maintained court; shop and browse in the enticing boutique, or stroll around the grounds enjoying vistas of Camelback Mountain and the lovely gardens. Evening programs may include guest speakers, a game of bridge or backgammon, a VCR film, a recorded concert, or a rousing game of bingo, followed by lights out at 10:00 PM. A doctor is on call and a registered nurse is on staff for your preliminary health consultation and for any emergency that might arise. There are 8 fitness/exercise instructors, 8 estheticians, and 8 massage therapists.

Diet and Weight Management: Dieters can expect to lose an average of 3 pounds a week on the Maine Chance food regimen of 950 daily calories, which includes garden-fresh vegetables and fruits, lean meats and fish with natural seasonings. At 7:30 AM, a maid trained in traditional courtesy brings you your breakfast tray set with a rose in a bud vase, the morning paper, your appointment schedule for the day, which you can later pin to your terry-cloth dressing gown as an aide-mémoire. Fruit or fruit juice, coffee or tea, whole-grain bread or cereal, and skim milk are arrayed before you on and in bone china prettily patterned with flowers.

Weather permitting, your lunch, and often dinner, will be served outside on the main house terrace with its yellow umbrella-ed tables. Mixed salads of endive, shredded beets, shredded raw carrots, water chestnuts, raw spinach, bean sprouts, watercress, and Bibb, Boston, and romaine lettuce with delicious dressings; cheese soufflés and dessert soufflés; bran muffins; Elizabeth Arden–pink shrimp, angelhair pasta served with pesto sauce, cactus pear ice milk sorbet, a découpage of vegetables and veal, lean and fork-cuttable filet mignon—Maine Chance is known for these delightful, time-tested, low-calorie num-nums. Count on pineapple and lemon desserts, lots of eggplant, asparagus, and artichokes. Those who want to gain weight receive additional portions, and such pleasant items as cornbread with their breakfast, or an avocado pear with their salad. There's always a midmorning broth break and a late-afternoon tea beautifully presented poolside or indoors.

Beauty Treatments and Welcome Indulgences: In a makeup classroom with individual makeup tables, you learn step-by-step proper skin care and makeup techniques for contouring and doing celestial things to your eyes, brows, and mouth. Hot emulsion manicures, warm wax treatments for your hands and feet, depilatory waxing, reflexology massages for your feet, wonderful facials, treatments to make your hair shine and feel lustrous and silky, acupressure massages for your body—you feel pampered and indulged, soothed and prettified with every treatment.

Accommodations: All guestrooms and suites in the 7 "cottages" are individually furnished with distinctive 18th- and 19th-century antique furniture and accessories and contemporary furnishings of first-rate quality. You'll find a Venetian mirror in one room, a carved Italian or French armoire and a marble-topped table in another, swagged and pouffed draperies, crystal decanters for decoration, marble and travertine floors, crystal and vermeil candelabra on your dressing table—presumably, just as you would at home. You can expect lots of fresh flowers charmingly arranged; comfort; little luxuries such as a bedside thermos; attractive bed linen, blankets, and bed coverings, and, in some rooms, matching upholstered bed-head or a four-poster bed. Your marble bathroom and dressing-room table are stocked with Elizabeth Arden goodies. Nicely uniformed maids are at your beck and call to take care of your laundry and do any mending or pressing you require. All rooms are equipped with air-conditioning, heating, telephone, color TV. VCR units can be rented.

What to Bring: See USEFUL INFORMATION. A royal blue tanksuit, for exercise and swimming, and a fluffy pink terry-cloth bathrobe, for between spa and beauty treatments, are hanging in your cupboard when you arrive. This is the daily uniform everyone wears. Bring flip-flops for around-the-pool wear and getting from the beauty salon to the sauna; aerobic shoes; tennis shoes if you play; and dress-and-sweater ensembles for excursions or shopping in Scottsdale and Phoenix. For dinner, at-home-style caftans, pajamas (one-piece or with overblouses and tunics), long skirts and light sweater or blouse tops, and long dinner dresses are worn by the majority of the guests. Unobtrusive little towel turbans may be worn at dinner if you feel your hair is "a mess," which it well may seem to be to ladies used to having their hair "done" every other day. Bring your Kenny Lane faux baubles for the festive formality of dinnertime. The desert resort's daily temperatures range from 65 to 85 degrees F.

Documentation from Your Physician: If you have a special medical problem, allergy, or any question about participating in the Maine Chance program, by all means bring a letter from your doctor about what you can or can't do. You are given a brief physical check-up on arrival.

The Use of Alcohol and Tobacco: No alcohol. No smoking except outside if you are still in the process of cutting back or giving it up.

Fees, Method of Payment, Insurance Coverage: Year-round rates per week:

For single: about $2500 to $3200

For double: about $2400 to $3000 per person

Rates are higher for deluxe accommodations. All prices are subject to change, and all rates are subject to a 9.25 percent state room tax and a 15 percent charge for gratuities. A deposit is requested. Ask about the cancellation policy. Cash, personal checks, and travelers' checks in dollars are the only acceptable form of payment. No credit cards are accepted. Insurance coverage reimbursement in whole or in part is unlikely unless your physician can substantiate your need for rest and relaxation and low-calorie nutrition as therapeutic for a medical problem, in which case your travel expenses may also be deductible.

The Phoenix Fitness Resort
Texas

The Phoenix in Houston promises "renewal," "a permanent lifestyle change and weight-control program in one week," "the best way to become a better you," and "much more than a great vacation; it will be an investment for life." Kathleen Hargiss, its director, newly installed in the summer of 1988, is a private pilot, a professional gymnast, and a lecturer who earned her black belt in karate and authored *The Womanly Art of Self-Defense.*

The spa's brochure describes the spa as "nestled on a 22-acre wooded former private estate" with grounds shared by the "nationally known and exclusive Houstonian Health and Fitness Club and the Houstonian Medical Center," the latter now known as the Houstonian Medical Specialists. It goes on to say, "Your private accommodations are located in the club's intimate Ambassador House Hotel," a landmark Art Deco mansion backed by a circular pool pictured in the brochure and advertisements. Of the 50 rooms actually located in the Houstonian Hotel but managed by the Ambassador House, 13 rooms, accessible by a separate entrance, are allocated to spa guests, although more will be made available when plans for doubling the number of guests in the program are completed. At present, a maximum of 15 women guests, with an average age range from 30 to 55, usually business-oriented or in the banking or legal professions, stay, eat, and attend classes in a four-flight walk-up area in an east wing of the Houstonian Hotel, thereby using up seven times more calories than they would have had they taken an elevator to reach their pleasant rooms with private baths, and the attractive facilities, which day guests enrolled from the ranks of Houston's fitness-minded women also share.

The surrounding property, watered by a major bayou, forested with oaks, pines, and magnolias, and well landscaped with seasonal flowers and flowering bushes, is shared not only by the $39 million Houstonian Fitness Center, with offices of the Houstonian Medical Specialists and much else incorporated within its 120,000 square feet of glass and brick; but also by the 246-room Houstonian Hotel and conference center next to it, and the historic, but not lived-in Ambassador House; the Manor House, the private dining facility of club members; Josey House, where office space is located; and half a block away, by a 29-story highrise with 174 condominium apartments and its own pool and exercise facility. Off-site, but conveniently close, is the Galleria, which houses Neiman-Marcus, Lord & Taylor, and Tiffany & Co.; museums; and a variety of varying seasonal attractions.

Name: The Phoenix Fitness Resort

Mailing Address: 111 North Post Oak Lane, Houston, Texas 77024

Telephone: (713) 680-1601; (800) 548-4701 in Texas, (800) 548-4700 outside Texas

Established: 1980

Managing Director: Vicki Bailey, certified by the American College of Sports Medicine and by the Institute for Aerobics Research

Program Director: Sarah Brightman, Executive Coordinator

Owner: H-Fund Corporation

Gender and Age Restrictions: Women only except for couples weeks twice yearly in May and October; minimum age 18

Season: Year-round except for 2 weeks over Christmas and New Year's

Length of Stay Required: 6 days/6 nights, Sunday to Saturday, 4:00 PM check-in, noon check-out, or 1 nonresidential day

Programs Offered: Highly structured. On arrival, you receive a caliper skinfold test to determine ratio of body fat to lean, a test of basal metabolic rate, and a computerized personal exercise prescription. There are 3 full-time fitness instructors, one of whom is assigned as a personal fitness counselor to each guest. A medical technician from the Breast Center of Houston teaches guests methods of breast self-examination. In the adjacent Houstonian Health and Fitness Club, John C. Matocha, M.D., a family practice and sports physician, heads the Houstonian Medical Specialists, where, at additional charges, you can receive such services as a comprehensive physical examination; treatment for sports injuries of body, ankle, and foot; podiatry and analysis of your gait; treatment of hand and wrist; plastic and reconstructive surgery; cosmetic surgery; individual and family counseling in eating disorders and substance abuse; physical therapy rehabilitation; exercise consultation; nutritional counseling and weight control programs; a blood profile analysis; a coronary risk profile. Some guests arrange with Neal R. Reisman, M.D., F.A.C.S., for nips, tucks, and face-lifts. The physicians are all on call 24 hours a day to serve guests and resident Houstonians. There is also a dentist and a beauty salon on the premises.

The facilities include a basketball court with adjoining salad and snack bar, 8 racquetball, handball, and volleyball courts, and an 8-mile cushioned indoor track programmed by a computer with track lights to pace your progress as you jog around the weights room on the third floor. The top floor is spectacularly equipped with such state-of-the-art equipment as Powercize computerized equipment that *talks* with you as you work out on its 6 stations; the new Finnish David-500 power chair; Nautilus, Dynamic, Keiser Cam, and Universal equipment; 25 Lifecycle and Schwinn Air-Dyne stationary bicycles; Trotter treadmills; and more, more, more. Elsewhere in this vast blue, white, and red facility are steam rooms, Swedish/Swiss showers, saunas, whirlpools (to be found on the second floor near the massage rooms and rooms for herbal wrap treatments), exercise rooms, and a boutique on the first floor. The center is open from 7:00 AM to 10:00 PM. Outdoors, there are 3 heated swimming pools, 5 Laykold tennis courts, and a mile-long track cushioned and carpeted with green "Super-Turf" that circles the property's rustic, woodsy areas.

The exercise schedule for Phoenix guests is designed to produce overall strength, toning, coordination, and cardiovascular fitness, and includes "soft" aerobics, aerobic dance, comprehensive stretching, toning up with weights, water exercise, and brisk walks. An *Ultimate Week* program offers 5 massages, 2 facials, 1 manicure, 1 pedicure, 1 skin consultation, 2 hair appointments, and 2 makeup applications. *An Ultimate Day* includes exercise, meals, self-help lectures, beauty and massage treatments, sauna, steam, Jacuzzi, and à la carte services at the Houstonian Fitness Center, until 9:00 PM.

Several evenings a week, experts from various fields give informal talks. A registered nurse might speak on behavioral eating disorders, the Phoenix chef on streamlining recipes and nutrition, a fashion expert on organizing your clothes closet, and a guest speaker on lifestyle and balancing and fitness. Optional consultations are available on negative addictions, personal skills mapping, and fashion. Toward the week's end, a fitness counselor meets with each guest to help her organize a take-home health plan. The recently expanded Phoenix boutique in the Fitness Center offers a cookbook, activewear, accessories, and exercise shoes, in addition to the offerings of the center's Pro Shop and exercise audio and video cassettes.

Diet and Weight Management: The eating plan provides mainly fruits, vegetables, and whole grains; skinned chicken or fish prepared without oils or sauces; and further protein from nuts, seeds, skim or low-fat dairy products; minimal fat intake; and lots of water, herb teas, fresh fruit juice, no caffeine. The diet is based on 1000 calories a day, with no added salt or artificial sweeteners used, and everything served as fresh as possible. Breakfast might be Shredded Wheat or Nutri-Grain with half a cup of skim milk, with raisins, sliced peaches, or bananas, or half a papaya with half a cup of low-fat yogurt. Salads for lunch. For dinner, possibly a chicken breast with steamed vegetables, brown rice, spinach, or whole-wheat noodles, and a salad and fresh fruit dessert. Nutritionist Nancy Fong, R.D., has worked out low-cal recipes that include tangy lemon cheesecake, seven-vegetable broth, guacamole-stuffed cherry tomatoes, pickled shrimp, asparagus in a blanket, cold cucumber soup, marinated mushrooms, fish en papillote, and herbed Neufchatel cheese rounds for delicious spa cuisine that has tempted the palates of celebrities, locals and guests at the spa's dining room.

Beauty Treatments and Welcome Indulgences: See Programs Offered.

Accommodations: Pleasant, comfortable, air-conditioned, private rooms have telephones, television, and queen beds. There are 2 rooms for "shares" with 2 queen-sized beds, and may be more when the program expands and rooms on other than the fourth floor are available in 1988–89. Rooms are rosy-carpeted with a floral decor and bamboo accents for a light and pretty look. Bathrooms are stocked with sample Christine Valmy cosmetics.

What to Bring: See USEFUL INFORMATION. Terry-cloth robes in assorted colors, light blue, navy blue, burgundy, and taupe, as well as bright pink caftans to wear in the evenings, are provided. Bring open-toed sandals with nonslip soles for use in wet areas and for after pedicures; tennis and racquetball gear if you play; hostess skirts or your own caftan or lounge wear to wear instead of the caftan provided for evening wear; and resort wear if you plan on shopping or socializing in the Houstonian Hotel's public areas.

Documentation from Your Physician: A letter of approval, medical history, and documentation of recent physical examination are requested but not required. If indicated, all testing can be performed for a fee by the Houstonian Medical Specialists.

The Use of Alcohol and Tobacco: Alcohol is not allowed in the spa program. Smoking is not allowed in the Houstonian Fitness Center facility.

Fees, Method of Payment, Insurance Coverage: High-season (October to May) rates, for single room:

For *Ultimate Day:* $400

For *Ultimate Week:* $2800

Rate for *Ultimate Week* does not include a 7.25 percent state tax and 11 percent room tax. *Ultimate Day* does not include state tax. Lower rates are available for Share Room/Share Program, Share Room/Full Program, and summer time. Special 10-day rates and other rates are also offered. All prices are subject to change. A deposit is required.

Ask about the cancellation policy. All major credit cards, checks, and money orders are accepted. Fees may be tax-deductible in part if this is supported by a letter from your physician or by consulting physicians for services performed by the Houstonian Medical Specialists.

❧ Rocky Mountain ❧
Wellness Spa and Institute
Colorado

A former automotive wheeler–dealer sales executive and his wife, who both have experienced overweight, stress burnout, and a variety of physical ailments, founded, own, and direct the Rocky Mountain Wellness Spa and Institute in Steamboat Springs, a popular ski and summertime resort. At an altitude of 7000 feet in the foothills of the Rockies, the resort is surrounded by extensive national and regional parklands, forests, rivers, lakes, mineral springs, summertime wildflowers, and wintertime "champagne powder" snow for exceptionally fine downhill and cross-country skiing. The majority of the guests who attend the spa's nutritional and stress reduction programs are in their late 30s or early 40s with an average of 20 pounds to lose. About one-third of the guests don't need to lose weight and come to tone up. A maximum of 15 people participate in the individualized programs, which are the foundation of a workable life plan for a "more energized, efficient, and ultimately more happy, healthy, and successful lifestyle." You can sail and windsurf on Catamount Lake 15 minutes away by car, or rent rafts for river rafting on the Yampa River, a 5-minute walk away. If you feel like fishing for trout, equipment can be rented at Steamboat Lake, a scenic 45-minute drive from the spa. There are weekly rodeos in Steamboat Springs during the summer, within easy walking distance of the spa. In winter, Steamboat Springs is a rollicking ski resort town with options for ice-skating, sleigh rides, chariot races, powder cat skiing (access and pickup to virgin snow in the back country), downhill skiing competitions, and all the fixings of ski rentals, lifts, ski schools, and nursery child-care for children not old enough to attend ski schools or ski nurseries or to join the Kids Ski Free programs. Hot-air balloon rides at reasonable rates are offered over the resort and the Rockies. To take full advantage of the region's celebrated champagne powder snow, ski instructors at the Rocky Mountain Wellness Spa and Institute choose cross-country skiing terrain to suit each guest's ability level. Terrain includes flat tracking as well as challenging trails in the 150,000 acres of the neighboring Routt National Forest.

Name: Rocky Mountain Wellness Spa and Institute

Mailing Address: Box 777, Steamboat Springs, Colorado 80477

Telephone: (303) 879-7772, (800) 345-7771 in Colorado; (800) 345-7770 outside Colorado

Established: 1982

Managing Director: Larry Allingham, B.S. Nutrition

Program Directors: Larry and Dorothy Allingham; Debbie Allingham, Administrative Director

Owners: Larry and Dorothy Allingham

Gender and Age Restrictions: Co-ed; minimum age 18

Season: Year-round

Length of Stay Required: 5 days/4 nights; 7 days/6 nights for *Total Wellness program,* from Sunday afternoon to the following Saturday morning; 3-week, 4-week, and 2-month sessions arranged and discounted up to 15 percent; shorter packages available.

Programs Offered: The *Total Wellness Program* is a health and fitness program that focuses on stress reduction, nutrition, weight loss, and exercise to raise energy levels, productivity, and quality of life. A prearrival nutritional questionnaire, an on-site preliminary medical checkup by a registered nurse, a urine test, "a saliva test, a bionutritional analysis of your blood chemistry, an analysis of your hair for the levels of 22 minerals and toxic heavy metals it may contain," an electrocardiograph if called for, and/or a treadmill stress test if indicated, under the supervision of the spa's physician, are the basis for your personal 39-page computerized nutritional program, your dietary analysis, an assessment of your metabolism, a 29-vitamin-and-mineral analysis, and an assessment of your body's chemical balance.

Spa guests who complain of being unable to lose weight no matter what their diet are placed on a simple regimen of 20- to 30-minute walks after each meal, brisk rambles usually to and from the Routt National Forest or on the many walking paths around the Steamboat Springs ski resort a few blocks away, or along the paths on the 3-acre spa site. Even with the same caloric intake, Allingham reports that these problem dieters begin to lose 4 to 10 pounds a week as their basic metabolisms respond to this post-meal activity. Fast aerobic fitness walking ("wogging") and hiking, as well as nature walks and rambles, are an integral part of the program in this Rocky Mountain area of pines and aspens, elk and deer, and weasels you may occasionally glimpse, which are transformed, white coated, into wintertime ermine.

Living close to nature, learning self-relaxation techniques, personal instruction in stress release, plus 3 massages weekly are helpful in relieving high irritability and anger levels caused by stress. Other alleged causes of stress, such as low calcium levels and low sugar levels, are treated in your eating regimen. Stress is further eased by members of a staff "hired to give hugs, support, and love," and by evening seminars on stress control, lifestyle modification, nutrition, and ways to maintain "peak performance" psychologically. Optional analyses and stress-reducing services are available at bargain rates, such as a smoking cessation program (16 hours) for $50, a relationship readiness analysis, a career compatibility analysis, an adjustment analysis measuring 19 psychological and personality traits that affect your physical health, a motivation analysis, a personality profile, a test of your perception awareness, an analysis of your reactions to criticism, an analysis of your "irrational beliefs," a test of your situation satisfaction, and an analysis of your body type.

To take further advantage of the healing potential of the pine-scented mountain air—nature's own aromatherapy—as much time as possible is spent outdoors, swimming in an outdoor heated lap pool, open year-round, 5 minutes away off-site; bicycling (bicycles supplied at no charge); playing tennis on the spa's two courts; hill climbing; mountaineering. The program includes 3 outings: to the Continental Divide, 15 miles distant; to the natural hot mineral sulphur springs in Steamboat, 8 miles away; and to the Fish Creek Falls, with a drop equivalent to 20 stories, 7 miles away. In-house transportation is provided. Box lunches are provided for biking and hiking excursions. Horses with Western-style saddles are available for hire.

Year-round, the Rocky Mountain Wellness Spa and Institute offers an on-site heated outdoor pool for water aerobics, an exercise room/gymnasium with free weights, rubber bands, slant board, and stationary bicycle. Low-impact aerobics, water aerobics, and yoga are taught; instruction is given in fast walking, or "wogging," cross-country skiing, and, at extra cost, in tennis and swimming, by fully qualified instructors certified in CPR and advanced first aid. There is a sauna and an indoor and an outdoor Jacuzzi. Two follow-up newsletters are sent annually.

Diet and Weight Management: Allingham believes that "allergic reactions" to certain foods "promote tremendous weight gain." Guests are introduced to this philosophy when they sit down to their first meal, which contains no wheat, corn, salt, sugar, chocolate, or dairy products—with the exception of breakfast yogurt—or caffeine of any kind. After 5 days of abstinence from these foods, the items are reintroduced one at a time in moderate amounts. The person being tested takes his or her pulse before eating certain items and again at 15-minute intervals for 1 hour after eating. If the pulse rate increases by 1 to 12 or more beats per minute over that period, there is a possibility that an allergy exists, Allingham believes. In this way, Allingham encourages his guests to eliminate specific foods "which are causing them to experience allergic weight gain, and in most cases to realize weight reduction without altering their normal caloric intake."

The diet is vegetarian, with seafood served once a week; a fruit or vegetable juice break before lunch and before dinner; and lemon slices in water served at lunches and dinners in a daily regimen that consists of 65 percent complex carbohydrates, 20 percent protein, and 10 to 15 percent fat. Lunch usually consists of a salad and a filling soup; dinner might be bell peppers stuffed with wild rice, plus a fresh carrot-pineapple salad, and strawberry and banana freeze for dessert. Breakfasts usually include a fruit shake, yogurt, an oat bran muffin, and additional fresh fruit. Guests are enthusiastic about this low-cal, "high-energy" regime, which can be adjusted as required for problems of arthritis, hypoglycemia, high blood pressure, diabetes, and cardiovascular ailments. Cooking classes, demonstrations, nutritional instruction, and counseling are provided in both group and one-on-one sessions, and a spa cookbook is included.

Beauty Treatments and Welcome Indulgences: The services of off-site hairdressing salons and barbershops are available. On-site facials, manicures, pedicures, a marvelous masque by Fanie International that tightens neck and facial skin, and inches-off body contouring application are all included in the fee.

Accommodations: Adjacent to the chocolate-brown stucco building housing the spa offices, dining room, and exercise facilities is a 3-story matching chocolate-brown stucco building housing 34 condominium suites where the accommodations are comfortable, pleasant, functional. Each guest has a private bedroom with a queen-sized bed and private bath. From 2 to 6 guests have access to each suite's kitchenette and central living room, which has a a wood-burning fireplace (logs supplied free of charge), a telephone, a television set, and a small balcony with unobstructed Rocky Mountain and national forest views. Air-conditioning is nature's own. Each suite has its own thermostat for cosy wintertime warmth and comfort on summer nights; summer temperatures can reach 80 degrees F in the daytime but can drop to 40 degrees when the sun goes down.

What to Bring: See USEFUL INFORMATION. Dress is casual. You are asked to bring a canteen water bottle for hikes and picnics, back pack, alarm clock, camera and film. You are also asked to bring a natural bristle skin brush or loofah sponge, as well as a tennis racket if you play, although a few tennis rackets may be available at the spa. There is an on-site library, and a dispensary for sundries and stationery a block away. Winter days average 30 degrees F, perfect for the snow, and summer days' heat is always breeze cooled.

Documentation from Your Physician: Neither requested nor required. You will be required to sign a medical release at the spa after you have received a physical checkup by the registered nurse in charge. The spa does request that you bring with you a recent blood cholesterol analysis.

The Use of Alcohol and Tobacco: No alcohol is permitted while attending the program. Smoking is not allowed in suites or in areas common to the facility.

Fees, Method of Payment, Insurance Coverage: Year-round rates:

For 5-day/4-night package: $860 single, $760 per person double occupancy

For 7-day/6-night *Total Wellness Program:* $1285 single, $1140 per person double occupancy

These fees do not include a 7.1 percent lodging tax and 15 percent service charge. All prices subject to change. Ask about the cancellation policy. Cash, personal/business checks, travelers' checks, American Express, MasterCard, and Visa are accepted in payment. Fees may be deductible in part as a medical expense if this is confirmed by a letter from your physician.

◌ The Spa at the Crescent ◌
Texas

Just north of downtown Dallas, the 10½-acre, $250 million Crescent complex designed in French chateau–style by Philip Johnson and John Burgee has been likened to bringing Versailles to the Great Plains. On the top three levels of the sumptuous five-story, 240-room Crescent Court Hotel are shops and galleries stacked on interior balconies, a flower-filled conservatory adjoining the hotel's restaurant, the Beau Nash, where everything you nosh has a nouvelle spin, and guest rooms with a Sun King's opulence where you'll find armoires instead of chests of drawers, dimmers on your lamps. On the two lower levels, in an airy, radiant marble grotto, exquisitely decorated with mirrors, wood, and marble and flowing with a variety of the world's mineral waters to drink and to bathe in, is the spa, offering "the best of American fitness, the finest of European treatments." Consultant Toni Beck (one of the great names in exercise) and a cadre of personal trainers assess and evaluate needs, set goals, and monitor the progress of Crescent Club and spa members in individually tailored programs of exercise, nutritional counseling, skin care, and beauty available only to members and not to hotel guests. Individual, life, corporate, and out-of-town memberships in the Crescent Club are available. Billionaire Caroline Rose Hunt, the wealthiest woman in America, is chairman of the board, and governors include Texas oil and cattle barons; actors Bob Hope, Arnold Schwarzenegger, and Larry Hagman, who plays J. R. Ewing in "Dallas"; designer Jack Lenor Larsen and champagne tycoon Claude Taittinger. So, join the club, you'll be in good company. If you're a frequent Dallas visitor, the investment of $1000 and yearly dues of $550 may provide you with invaluable dividends of health and fitness.

Your membership includes access to one-on-one trainers for use of the stretching area to tone muscles prior to strenuous exercise; the flexibility area to acquire control, elasticity, strength; the cardiovascular area complete with stationary bicycles, jump ropes, minitrampoline, and treadmill; the weight-resistance area with 52 pieces of Cam III equipment, the latest Nautilus equipment, and free weight systems; hot and regular mineral tubs, whirlpool, cold plunge, pulsating hot and cold Swiss showers; the steam room with tiers of benches swirled around with eucalyptus-scented vapors; the sauna with imported Finnish rocks. The double-insulated "quiet rooms" are for body massages, reflexology treatments, herbal wraps, facials. Swiss water massages and relaxing and stimulating inhalations are offered in the Treatment Center, which uses both Chanel products and Yon Ka treatments with their fragrant ingredients of plant extracts such as carob and ivy, and essential oils of sweet almond, lavender, geranium, rosemary, thyme, cypress, black currant, raspberry, orange, lemon, grapefruit, and sweet lime.

The spa, open from 6:30 AM to 8:30 PM Monday to Friday, from 8:30 AM to 5:00 PM Saturday, from 11:00 AM to 5:00 PM Sunday, provides dove-grey logo-ed shirts, shorts, warm-up suits, full-length cotton hooded robes, and slippers. All you have to do is bring footwear. The locker rooms are stocked with shampoos, conditioners, soaps, body lotions, sponges, cotton towels, and hair dryers. Manicures, pedicures, depilatory waxing, everything for the hair in the beauty salon. Just around the corner from the locker rooms through French doors is the "Fruit and Juice Bar," a deceptively modest name for ivory marble largesse, grouped with lettuce-leaf-green cushioned rattan chairs and round taupe and ivory checkerboard tables set with exotic flowers culled from 26 countries that are a feast for your eyes. Selected by the spa's nutritionists and a registered dietitian as a calorie-conscious feast for your palate are such yummies as a wicker basket filled with steamed vegetables, some wrapped like dim sum in whole-wheat pasta with a watercress dip (155 calories); slivers of grilled lamb fillet with tangerine-tarragon dressing, tomatoes, zucchini, and yellow squash (290 calories); grilled free-range chicken breast with spicy mozzarella and Jicama relish, grilled corn, whole-wheat grain, and roasted bell pepper (394 calories), marvelous muffins, frozen fruit and yogurt desserts, with prices as low as the calories you consume (under $12). Room prices at the Crescent Court Hotel from $200. Hourly rate at the spa for nonmember hotel guests for a personal trainer $45, facials $60, use of wet area $25. Members get wet area and workout free, and facials, pedicures, makeovers, manicures, and massages at discounted member rate.

A *first-time* weekend spa package, including club initiation fee and annual dues, is $2175 ($1000 initiation fee + $550 dues + $625 weekend package price) for a single. If you share double accommodations with your spouse or a family member listed as a dependent on your tax return, your total first-time price is $2480, including single initiation fee and dues which entitle a club member to share membership privileges with a spouse or a "dependent." *When you are a member and have paid your dues,* prices for a weekend spa package are $625 single, $465 per person double.

Name: The Spa at the Crescent

Mailing Address: 400 Crescent Court, Suite 100, Dallas, Texas 75201

Telephone: (214) 871-3232; (800) 828-4772 outside Texas

Established: 1986

Managing Director: William Mills, Executive Director

Owner: Rosewood Hotels

Gender and Age Restrictions: Co-ed; minimum age 18

Season: Year-round

Midwest

∽ **Bluegrass Spa** ∼
Kentucky

Nancy and Charles Rutherford's Bluegrass Spa beckons from central Kentucky's lush and tranquil bluegrass pasturelands, where the rich raise their thoroughbred horses to race at the Derby and southern hospitality abounds. The hub of the spa is an antebellum brick mansion, circa 1813, with a Greek Revival pediment supported by a double colonnade, its formality gentled by a pair of cushioned porch swings. Two hours flying time from New York, a 30-minute courtesy pick-up drive from Lexington Airport, and you reach this peaceful 52-acre estate for fitness and good old-fashioned pampering. "Ten guests a week are my ideal, says Nancy Rutherford, although the Manor House and its Lodge and cabana, which opens onto the pool area, can accommodate up to a score of guests, which at present are more women than men. Accommodations are airy, light and bright, distinctively decorated with white wicker furniture, polished brass bedsteads with lots of down pillows, antiques selected with a discerning eye, thick, fluffy towels in the bathrooms, and no room telephones or television sets to detract from the serenity of this getaway retreat.

The emphasis here is on holistic living—"Body, mind, spirit equally involved in optimum wellness"—with plenty of massages, body and beauty treatments (including a nonsurgical face-lift facial), and exercise. Charles Rutherford, a graduate of Annapolis, is a triathalon athlete—swimming, running, and bicycling are his specialties, so you can bet your Reeboks that the bicycles here include 3- to 18-speeders. The 4 fitness instructors, the 3 massage therapists, and the registered nurse on staff are all fully qualified, capable, and devoted to your comfort and well-being. Nancy Rutherford is in charge of meal-planning and preparation. She presents a low-cal, high-carb diet, and guests lose from 3 to 12 pounds, and often more inches, on this delectable fare, plus exercise.

In winter, the Bluegrass program will be offered aboard an Epirotiki liner which cruises out of Fort Lauderdale, Florida, to destinations in the Caribbean and the Amazon. In January and February the spa moves to Akumal, Mexico, and accommodations in villas on the Caribbean beach. From April to November, the program returns to its old Kentucky home for guests "who are interested in lifestyle changes and learning more about metaphysics, alternative health care, and holism but are not ready for total immersion in any particular discipline." "We offer a potpourri of new thoughts," Nancy Rutherford says, "exciting alternatives to mainstream thinking in as many areas as we can comfortably present. It should be stressed that we are not promoters of any discipline, but offer all that we believe to be enlightening, thought-provoking, and of interest to New Age participants and investigators." Workshops range from approaches to handling stress, "America's deadliest pre-disease," or an introduction to meditation and guided imagery, or a metaphysical journey of consciousness expansion, to private readings in astrology, numerology, Tarot, and palmistry for an additional fee.

Arrangements can be made for guests to ride, play golf and tennis, to attend free meetings of Alcoholics Anonymous or Overeaters Anonymous, or one of Kentucky's thoroughbred racing meets, or the Headley-Whitney Museum with its fabulous collection of jeweled assemblages unique in the world, or the Kentucky Horse Park, an equine showplace that is a horse lover's paradise, or the restored Shaker village at Pleasant Hill, or to embark on a foray of antique seeking and buying. There is a variety of reading material here as well as a VCR and a library of films. Guests come from all over, Mrs. Rutherford says, "for all sorts of reasons, but mostly to feel better when they leave. Many are veteran spa aficionados, and some don't even ask for the weight-loss menu." Many do, however. "No two people are exactly alike," says Nancy Rutherford. "At Bluegrass, we recognize and celebrate your individuality, and your step toward a healthier, more joyous lifestyle in a caring, supportive environment."

Name: Bluegrass Spa

Mailing Address: 901 Galloway Road, Stamping Ground, Kentucky 40379

Telephone: (502) 535-6261

Established: 1985

Managing Director: Nancy Rutherford

Program Directors: Nancy Rutherford, Spa Director; Cindy Hutchison, Fitness Director

Owners: Charles and Nancy Rutherford

Gender and Age Restrictions: Co-ed; minimum age 16

Season: Mid-April to mid-November; program available aboard Epirotiki cruise liners and in Mexico, December through mid-March

Length of Stay Required: By the day or longer. Package rates for 3-day weekends, Friday to Sunday; 6 days/5 nights, Sunday to Friday; 8 days/7 nights, Friday afternoon to following Friday noon

Programs Offered: The program is structured but noncompulsory and highly personalized. If weight loss is your goal, that will be the focus of your schedule. At the same time, "much is offered to broaden the focus to a more holistic approach." Under the supervision of a registered nurse on staff, all guests receive a routine physical, an assessment of body-fat content, heart rate, blood pressure, and training heart rate for aerobic exercise. A physician's examination is required and will be arranged for guests with physical problems that indicate an inability to participate in exercise classes.

Small, personalized classes emphasizing individual instruction and attention are held outdoors or in a former carriage house converted into an exercise studio with a windowed wall. Instruction is offered in yoga, body movement and awareness, limber and stretch exercises, body contouring and toning, aerobics, trampolinelike rebounders, free dance, Tai Chi, and aqua-aerobics in the 30- by 60-foot outdoor pool where you can also swim laps or join in a water volleyball game at the shallow end. Fitness Director Cindy Hutchison received her high-energy–low-impact style of training at the Molly Fox Studio in New York, a studio highly commended by *Shape* magazine. Besides your individualized spa workout schedule, each day includes brisk walking, power walking, jogging, and bicycling, either on your own or as part of a group. Always on the agenda are swimming, basketball, badminton, croquet, and tennis on a Har-Tru court. You can work out in the gym with hand-held weights, pedal a stationary bicycle, steam in a sauna, loll in the Jacuzzi. You can opt for 5 to 8 hours daily of physical activity, or snooze in the hammock and dream away your stay listening to your Walkman. Some guests get exercise helping weed the pesticide-free organic garden where marigolds are nature's own herbicide. Some wander off to explore country lanes with vistas of farmland, and a nearby lake. There's a local golf course with nine holes, inexpensive greens fees, and rental golf clubs; also a next-door stable which offers trail rides, a jumping ring, English or Western-style saddles, and mounts for affordable hourly rates. Additional tennis courts are available within a mile's radius.

You have a choice of reflexology, Swedish, shiatsu, Trager, polarity, Esalen or the "Ultimate" 90-minute massage performed by 4 highly qualified massage therapists on staff, 2 men, 2 women. The evening programs comprise workshops by Lea Schultz or by Karen Thompson, as well as other speakers concerned with stress and de-stressing, energy, exercise, nutrition, food labeling, "positive wellness," "living in the Now," "expanding consciousness," beauty, and similar topics. These are interspersed with low-fat cooking classes, parlor games, sing-alongs around the grand piano, chamber music concerts, or an occasional talk by Sally Richardson, a graduate of Dr. Kenneth Cooper's Fitness Instructor certification course, who is one of Nancy Rutherford's daughters. Quarterly newsletters. Purchasable audio and video cassettes; cookbooks available.

Diet and Weight Management: Nancy Rutherford prepares low-fat, high-fiber meals using all natural foods without salt, sugar, or chemical additives, and calorie-counted for weight maintenance or gradual weight loss. You can expect baked cinnamon grapefruit with fresh-from-the-oven blueberry bran muffins or pancakes and mixed berry syrup, or cornbread with fruit preserves for breakfast; a midmorning tangerine or apple mix snack; a shrimp and grapefruit salad with fresh horseradish dressing or salmon burgers on whole-grain sunflower buns with lettuce, tomato, and onion for lunch; frozen grapes or a banana popsicle as a midafternoon snack; and a three-course, candlelit dinner in a dining room remarkable for its chandelier and fireplace, with 4 tables set with pretty china and crystal glasses. You might start with a Scandinavian peach soup or a cheese potato soup, followed by baked stuffed squash or eggplant parmesan or chicken with orange dressing and wild rice, and cheesecake topped with fruit sauce as one of Nancy's "licentious" desserts; and a cup of tea before you go to bed. Diets for allergies, hypoglycemia, diabetes, and other problems can be accommodated. With portion control and exercise, guests lose from 3 to 12 pounds on Bluegrass fare, a fact that bears repeating because the food is both filling and exceptionally tasty. Recipes for mock sour cream made with cottage cheese, for stir fry veggies, whole-grain breads, divine desserts, and much more, with an emphasis on herbs for flavoring, are on sale at the spa's small boutique.

Beauty Treatments and Welcome Indulgences: Astonishing in this intimate family setting to find a full-service beauty salon offering (at additional charge if not included in your package) such niceties as herbal wraps, Salt-Glo loofah scrubs, manicures, pedicures, makeup and color analysis, scalp treatments, facials, eyebrow waxing and lash/brow tinting, paraffin wax hand and foot treatments, hair coloring and permanents, deep cleansing facials and an aromatherapy facial, plus a facial styled "a nonsurgical face-lift" that is truly special, as is Katheen Bailey, the cosmetologist and facialist who performs this and other treatments with care and flair. The spa's own oatmeal-and-honey scrub is a pleasure to use.

Accommodations: The two-story Lodge by the swimming pool has a downstairs room with a fireplace and private bath; upstairs, a 4-bedded room with access to a shared large bathroom with 2 of everything, a twin-bedded room with private bath, a double with private bath. The Cabana, also by the pool, has 2 guestrooms with private baths that can be single or double accommodations; and there are 2 splendid guestrooms in the Manor, one with a fireplace. Each room is distinctively decorated with light, bright colors and floral prints. Lots of plants, white wicker, wrought iron, antiques, space, air, and pleasant window views of trees, lawn, and, from the Lodge, farmland vistas, provide a comfortable and inviting ambience. A few rooms have a terrace, a porch, a patio. None have telephones or television. All have air-conditioning, as well as down comforters. On request to your room maid, your laundry will be done for you for a small fee.

What to Bring: See USEFUL INFORMATION. Robes are provided for you to wear to beauty treatments and exercise sessions. The spa provides tennis rackets and golf clubs free of charge, and you can also rent golf clubs at the golf course. Bring your riding gear. Jodhpur boots and breeches are preferable to blue jeans and sneakers. Although comfort is the key here, you might want to bring a seasonally suitable outfit for excursions or antiquing. For evening, slacks and shirt, or blouse, or caftan. Be prepared for both warm and cool weather. Sundries, film, and stationery supplies are available on the premises. Portable television sets or radios are allowed only if you plan to room alone. You have unlimited use of library, tapes, and videos.

Documentation from Your Physician: A letter of approval is requested if you have a health problem. If necessary, guests can consult with a physician when they arrive. A medical history and documentation of recent physical examination are requested but not required. You will be required to answer a brief health history questionnaire and sign a medical release form. Guests who have serious health, drug, or alcohol problems are not accepted.

The Use of Alcohol and Tobacco: Neither is permitted on the spa grounds.

Fees, Method of Payment, Insurance Coverage: Rates, depending on accommodations:

> *Day of Fitness:* $125
>
> *Friday-to-Sunday weekend package:* $310 to $418
>
> *Sunday-to-Friday package:* $790 to $1085
>
> *Friday-to-Friday package:* $1115 to $1495

All rates are subject to a 5 percent Kentucky tax, and all rates are subject to change. Gratuities are at guests' discretion. There are discounts for returning guests; repeater discounts for repeat visits during any one year; mother/daughter discounts; father/son discounts; incentive discounts for bringing new guests; group rates for 4 or more. A deposit is required. Ask about the cancellation policy. Personal checks, travelers' checks, cash, Visa, and MasterCard are accepted. At publication date, fees were not tax-deductible as a medical expense, but it is possible they may be in the future.

⚲ The Heartland Health ⚲
and Fitness Retreat/Spa
Illinois

Cited in December 1986 by *Shape* magazine as one of the top 10 spas in America, the Heartland is purely and refreshingly secluded in the center of Illinois on a 31-acre wooded estate. The 3-acre lake ripples peacefully before a large white colonial-style house connected by an airy underground passageway to a large white hip-roofed barn, which contains the latest in high-tech exercise equipment plus an indoor lap-swimming and exercise pool. This is not the only welcome surprise. In your bright, small, band-box-fresh room, you'll find almost all the clothes you'll need laid out for you—sweatsuits, shorts, T-shirts, socks, slippers, bathrobes, jackets and rainwear, wool hats and gloves, evening lounging outfits, plus a bathroom stocked with shampoo, hair conditioners, and skin lotions, and a library stocked with books.

In this oasis bordered by fields of soybeans and corn, you will find yourself doing surprising things—in an exercise class, where you throw imaginary feathers, glass bowls, or even a fantasied train at your fellow guests who are supposed to catch the objects as they would if they were real; in the main house, where you remove your shoes and put on slippers before you tread on polished floors or carpets as plush and lush as the azure blue one you sink into in the yoga room; in the serenity of the estate, where you may find yourself race walking, an exercise not commonly taught in spa-dom, or enrolled in fitness classes that range from the gentlest of pre-aerobic sessions to whatever level of wellness or attitude change you may desire being coaxed into. This may include challenging yourself to the *Challenge Program,* which requires scaling a 40-foot telephone pole and walking with guidelines across highwires. Many confirmed acrophobics slough off their phobias, dissolve self-imposed boundaries, and change their opinions of themselves and their former lifestyles at the Heartland. You can water-bicycle on the placid lake, or swim in it. You can have the pores of your back cleansed and the skin of your back conditioned to the texture of satin. You can bask in the gentle peace of an estate where all you are likely to hear is bird song, the plop of rising fish, the hum of cicadas, and the voices of your 26 fellow guests. Guests' general ages range from 25 to 55 and they are likely to be interested in losing between 5 and 15 pounds—a few may want to lose 40 pounds or more. The majority of them are business-oriented. There's a fairly even distribution between younger and older professionals, between the married, who sometimes attend together, sometimes arrive on their own, and the single. In its short history, the Heartland has welcomed guests from 37 states as well as Canada, Mexico, and Ireland, who experience encouraging weight loss, point themselves in the direction of a new regime of healthy eating and exercise, offload stress, and rediscover the joy of well-being. Although the emphasis is on developing a blueprint for long-lasting, lifestyle-oriented results—whatever your goal— guests are free to attend as many or as few classes as desired and can choose among different levels of difficulty. The setting is homelike. There are a few eclectic and ectopic touches such as *lassi,* a classic thirst-quencher of India (which is, after all, nothing more than a buttermilk frappé), and classes in relaxation and yoga and healing from Darjeeling, but midwestern hospitality and courtesy are what confer an authentic quality of serenity to this retreat. The only excursion you'll want to make is a flight into Heartland's peaceful sense of healthy well-being.

Name: The Heartland Health and Fitness Retreat/Spa

Mailing Address: 18 East Chestnut, Chicago, Illinois 60611; address of the Retreat, Rural Route #1, Box 181, Gilman, Illinois 60938

Telephone: (312) 266-2050 for information and reservations; (815) 683-2182 (the Retreat)

Established: 1983

Managing Director: Earl W. Cowell

Program Directors: Earl W. Cowell, B.S. Psychology, M.S. Physical Education, specializing in corporate and adult fitness

Owner: Gerald S. Kaufman

Gender and Age Restrictions: Co-ed; minimum age 18

Season: Year-round

Length of Stay Required: Minimum 2 days; 5- and 7-day programs

Programs Offered: Education and motivation for establishing your personal long-term health-care habits for total health and fitness in a get-away-from-it-all, no worry, no strain, no pain ambience; permanent weight loss; stress reduction and management by monitoring stress, managing it, and utilizing it in a positive, creative way; classes and lectures on positive thinking, calming imagery, and communication strategies; gourmet vegetarian cuisine supplemented with fish, whole grains, and low-calorie dairy foods (higher or lower calorie levels on request); indoor and seasonal outdoor exercise from aerobics and Keiser Cam II pneumatic resistance machines to race walking, water bicycling on the lake when weather permits, or cross-country skiing; a focus on body awareness as a component of a three-part approach to stress management through education, exercise, and nutrition, with special care given to protecting vulnerable body parts and safeguarding against injuries; cardiovascular training; body care and beauty services; nutritional counseling sessions.

Guests usually come to the Heartland either for a *weekend (2-day) stay,* from Friday afternoon through Sunday afternoon, for a *5-day* Sunday-through-Friday *stay,* or for a full week *(7 days),* Friday to Friday or Sunday to Sunday. Guests can also be accepted midweek. After you have been transported by the Heartland's complimentary van from downtown Chicago to the lakeside spa (a 110-minute drive to health and fitness), you are given a brief medical questionnaire to fill in, are weighed in, your measurements taken, and a caliper skin-fold test performed to assess the ratio of your body fat to your lean mass. You put on a spa-provided velours lounging outfit and are led through a 15-minute relaxation class before dinner and a body awareness class after dinner. Your dinner dessert, which might be apple crisp or a fruit sorbet, is served at the evening's end. *Weekend* guests receive 1 massage; *5-day* guests receive 4 massages and a facial; *7-day* guests get 5 massages and a facial. Director Earl W. Cowell describes his program as permissive, nondemanding, moderately structured with options. The nutrition and fitness assessment you receive on arrival reveals your ideal weight, an estimate of the number of pounds you need either to lose or to gain, and the calories required to achieve or maintain your ideal body weight. This information plus your replies to a brief medical questionnaire together indicate your level of capability for your activities program, which is tailored for you in order for you to take home a regimen suitable for your lifestyle or, better, your newfound *healthstyle.* You choose from a schedule operative from 7:00 AM to 6:00 PM of up to 10 different supervised exercise classes. These might include All the Fun Moves, a series of "getting to know yourself" games and challenges; All the Right Moves, an introductory class that demonstrates how to exercise safely; Bodyworks, a pre-aerobics conditioning class for beginners or previously inactive guests; Apparatus Muscle Training, an instruction session in using various pieces of small equipment designed to develop strength and endurance; Free Weights, strengthening and shaping muscles while learning the proper techniques for using free weights; Gotta Dance, a simple choreographed routine; Heartbeat, a low-impact aerobic exercise session; Major Motion, a more advanced low-impact aerobic workout; Resistance Conditioning, techniques of weight training and the use of weight-training machines; Waterworks, a muscle and cardiovascular workout in the pool; Yoga, "stretching and energizing the body, calming and focusing the mind, uplifting and nourishing the spirit" with breathing, relaxing, and body work techniques; Parcours, a jogging track outdoors with a variety of obstacles for improving flexibility, balance, agility, strength, and body awareness; and for the advanced, a Challenge Course, "as a method for providing outcomes . . . needed in businesses—teamwork, trust-building, cooperation, solving problems in dynamic ways, and helping change patterns in the workplace," a program that starts off with "easy games and fun challenges" and works up gradually to scaling a 40-foot telephone pole and then completing a series of 3 different highwire walks 30 feet in the air, walking a tightrope between telephone poles, hooking a small line onto a wire, and then gliding back to the ground. In addition to these exercise classes and fitness activities, you can hike in the surrounding countryside, with the pace and distance a matter of your choice, walk or race-walk, or attend massage workshops. Educational programs in the areas of fitness/exercise physiology, stress management, and nutrition, plus access to a print and video library covering a wide range of health-care information as well as entertainment are at your disposal. Nutritional and exercise counseling is also available by request for private sessions. After swimming, water bicycling, cross-country skiing, playing tennis or croquet, you can relax in the steam room, whirlpools, or saunas or enjoy at extra cost pedicures, manicures, depilatory waxings, cosmetic makeovers, hairstyling, or additional massages and facials. After the evening lecture, you are free to play Trivial Pursuit, backgammon, or other card or board games, to watch television or a video film, or to curl up in a comfortable armchair in the wood-paneled living room and read a book—your own, or one borrowed from the Heartland's own eclectic library.

Maximum Number of Guests: 27

Full-Time Health Professionals on Staff: 4, plus 2 massage therapists, an esthetician, a part-time fitness instructor, 2 part-time massage therapists, and a part-time associate professor of physical education as a consultant and lecturer. All the staff are trained in CPR. Watseka Hospital, Illinois, is 10 miles distant.

Diet and Weight Management: Vegetarian meals, supplemented with fish, cheese, and eggs add up to 1200 calories a day for women, 1500 to 1600 calories for men. Guests are fed every 2½ hours to ward off hunger pangs. Extra food is available upon request. The nutrition regimen emphasizes the importance of nutritional education concerning "proper" nutrition (low cholesterol, low sodium, low fat, high fiber and complex carbohydrates, moderate protein). Susan Witz, R.D., prescribes the calorie levels and does not recommend intake of fewer than 1000 calories. Regular coffee and tea are available at breakfast. Decaffeinated coffee and herbal teas are available all day and during the evening. Special diets for allergies or medical reasons are accommodated. Midmorning and afternoon snacks may consist of uncooked fruits and vegetables, *lassi,* or fresh seasonal berries, low-fat cheese and high-fiber crackers, blueberry/banana shakes. A typical luncheon entrée is vegetarian lasagna or salmon and spinach salad. A dinner entrée might be eggplant casserole or stuffed baked fish. From the windows of the colonial-style dining room, you have seasonal views of the estate lake. Chef Karen Kroson frequently serves soups—egg drop, minestrone, onion, cream of broccoli, mulligatawny, clear mushroom, gazpacho, bouillabaisse, and egg lemon are some of her specialties, and you can enjoy these year-round. Her "mock cream cheese"—ricotta, honey, and lemon juice—is a healthy substitute for the more fattening version. Dinner desserts are served at 9:00 PM to sweeten dreams and fend off midnight snack attacks. Weight management is one of the major program objectives, and the program offers education and on-site experience concerning nutrition and exercise as well as stress management for guests whose weight is influenced by stress.

Exercise and Physical Therapy Facilities: An underground tunnel connects the living quarters to a three-story barn converted into a complex of exercise studios, massage and facial facilities, and a mirrored aerobics studio. In the high-tech studio, there are 12 pieces of Keiser Cam II weight equipment (which uses adjustable air pressure for resistance); Cybex and Tunturi exercycles; Amerec rowing machines, a StairMaster, a NordicTrack cross-country ski machine, soft joggers, free weights, and spring-loaded V-bars. There are pulse monitors and EKG monitoring equipment on some of the equipment. The attractive barn-spa also houses a 44-foot-long lap-swimming and exercise pool beneath a plastic roof which lets in the light and sunshine. For arm toning, you may try to keep a rubber ball submerged in the pool. Hard to do! There are also whirlpool baths, steam rooms, and rock saunas for men and women. In the dimly lit massage rooms, your combination Swedish and Oriental massage, with pressure applied to aching or tense muscles, is expertly performed to the accompaniment of Gregorian chants as yet another measure to transport you further away from the fast-paced life you left behind.

Opportunities for Recreational Exercise: The spa has hiking and walking trails, a ¼-mile jogging track, and facilities for croquet and for bicycling on land or water. Guests can enjoy cross-country skiing—all equipment is provided free of charge—as well as swimming in the indoor heated pool or in the 3-acre private estate lake, where you can skate during the winter months. Two outdoor courts are available for tennis players.

Beauty Treatments and Welcome Indulgences: Facials combine the benisons of a cucumber facial bath, an aloe vera facial scrub, and a sulphur masque skillfully applied to the harmonies of classical music. Hairstyling (after you have washed your own hair), manicures, pedicures, makeup consultations, and depilatory waxings are available for an extra charge, as are a half- or full-back deep pore cleansing and conditioning, a splendid service not common among other spas.

Accommodations: In the 50-year-old colonial-style white clapboard house, there are 14 twin-bedded guestrooms, small, cozy, each with a window looking out on the lake, and simply furnished with nightstand, reading lamp, chair, and bureau; beige walls, soft pink carpet, beige dust ruffles, and soft pink comforters; beige, blue, and pink flower-sprigged curtains at the windows; everything country fresh. No television, no telephone, but each room is equipped with an intercom for you to call the office if you wish and for you to receive your morning wake-up call. Each room with a private bath and shower. Air-conditioning. When you leave your room in the morning, you leave your room key in the lock.

What to Bring: See USEFUL INFORMATION. During your visit, you are supplied with sweat suits, shorts, T-shirts, evening leisurewear, socks and slippers, bathrobes, jackets and rainwear, wool hats and gloves, hairdryers, shampoo, hair conditioner, skin lotion. Whenever you deposit outside your doors the clothes you have worn, fresh ones will appear laid out on your bed. There is a boutique on the premises for small gifts, activewear, and Heartland's own brand of cosmetics, but do remember to bring your own camera film and your own writing materials and books. If you have forgotten your chapstick or sunblock, the staff will shop for you. You are asked *not* to bring a portable TV, radio, or your Walkman and cassettes "to preserve a feeling of retreat."

Documentation from Your Physician: A letter of approval is requested only if a medical condition warrants it. A medical history and documentation of recent physical examination are neither requested nor required. A brief physical examination is given on arrival.

The Use of Alcohol and Tobacco: No alcohol served. No smoking in any indoor facilities.

Fees, Method of Payment, Insurance Coverage: Year-round rates:

For *2-day program:* $660 single, $440 per person double

For *5-day program:* $1650 single, $1100 per person double

For *7-day program:* $2175 single, $1450 per person double

All prices are subject to change, and all rates include tax and gratuities. There is a policy of no tipping. If you prefer double occupancy and arrive alone, the Heartland staff will arrange for you to share with another single if possible. A deposit is required. Ask about the cancellation policy. Cash, personal checks, travelers' checks, Visa, MasterCard, and American Express are accepted. Few clients have health problems related to being overweight that could qualify their attendance for medical reasons and insurance coverage.

Follow-up Assistance: The *Heartland Health News,* an exceptionally good newsletter filled with excellent health tips and advice, is sent 4 times a year to past guests. Previous guests are offered reduced rates during specified periods or free stays if they bring new guests. Video teaching tapes, cassettes, and cookbooks are offered for sale.

✑ The Kerr House ✑
Ohio

The Kerr House, clublike in its ambience of intimacy, accepts no more than 8 women (or, during designated weeks, men, couples, or families) at a time, and for those who require the privilege and privacy of royalty and celebrities, the entire spa can be rented for a week. The ratio is more than 2 staff members, health professionals, specialized consultants, and massage therapists/estheticians for each guest. Laurie Hostetler, the developer, director, and owner of what may be the most unusual private health retreat in America, states that the aim of Kerr House is to help guests to relax, renew and rejuvenate themselves, and to achieve harmonious balance of mind, body, and spirit by combining the practices of hatha-yoga, polarity therapy, healthful nutrition, aerobic exercise, skilled facial and body treatments, and massage with an environment of Old World serenity and civility.

Hatha-yoga, the core of the fitness regimen, is an ancient Oriental system of physical, mental, and spiritual development with the purpose of self-realization. The yoga postures involve stretching but not straining. Done slowly, they consist of deep breathing, excellent stretching exercises, and techniques of relaxation and control. Combined with proper diet, the postures are credited with streamlining your body; retarding the aging process; benefiting your nervous system by releasing tension and increasing relaxation; improving circulation, flexibility, muscle tone, metabolism, and respiration; and transforming physical, mental, and emotional problems into good health. Laurie Hostetler, who studied hatha-yoga in India and France, has taught its practice to many groups in courses, workshops, and seminars.

The practice of hatha-yoga is supplemented by polarity therapy, which also works to enhance the beneficial interaction between mind and body. Weight loss is considered a fringe benefit, but guests' average weekly weight loss is at least 3 pounds, with a gain of firming and muscle toning. The program is both permissive and structured. Nothing is mandatory, everything is suggested. You can do pretty much what you please, but somehow not going along with the program of breathing, exercise, and diet is not even considered. Whims and preferences are indulged at Kerr House, not forbidden. Casual modes of appearance and personal idiosyncrasies are accepted; no makeup, oiled scalps covered with turbans, and dressing gowns may be found side by side with elegant dresses in the formal dining room, where dinner is served to the accompaniment of classical harp and violin music. Guests at Kerr House, a varied spectrum of business women, owners of companies, teachers, housewives, editors, and doctors, whose ages range from 19 to 83, appear united in their enthusiasm for the benefits of hatha-yoga.

Kerr House, built in the 1880s, renovated with authentic Victoriana and reproductions of period wallpapers and fabrics, is listed in the National Register of Historic Places. The 10,000-square-foot, 35-room house offers many surprises, not only with its carved and gilded cherry and oak antique furnishings, well-polished silver, touches of lace, and bouquets of fresh flowers, but also with its old-fashioned pleasures of breakfast in bed, naps after lunch, nice touches of the contemporary world dovetailed neatly with the traditional (a guest speaker seated in what looks like a Belter horsehair upholstered armchair chats about applied kinesiology; a NordicTrack cross-country skiing machine can be found in the carpeted exercise quarters of the attic loft); and afternoon walks and excursions that are revels of nostalgia for a bygone era charmingly revivified.

Only 20 minutes southwest of Toledo by car, Kerr House, perched on a hilltop, overlooks the Maumee River and the minuscule working village of Grand Rapids, where shops and businesses have been restored to their turn-of-the-century appearance. The entertainment and crafts demonstrations at the Apple Butter Festival in October draw 35,000 people to this community with a residential population of only 950. The little town fascinates with its antique and curio shops, its canal houses, its historic houses sheltered in large parks, and its herbary where soap-making and other homely arts are taught and demonstrated. In July, the festivities of River Rally days are a major attraction. The wall-eye and white bass run in April, a fisherman's delight. In warm weather, you may hike to a scenic destination where a table is appointed for a picnic with a lace tablecloth, pretty china, and flowers; visit English-style country gardens; delight in the *anatidae*—200 rare swans, geese, and ducks to be seen on a nearby farm for endangered species. Laurie Hostetler often charters the *Shawnee Princess* for a paddleboat cruise down the Maumee, or accompanies her guests on an historic train ride aboard the Bluebird Special, or goes with them to visit Fort Meigs, a reconstructed fort of 1812, the largest renovation of its kind in the US, which features lantern-lit tours of *tableaux vivants* amd skits of historic incidents. Christmas is celebrated in Victorian style. Since there is a great volume of return business, the programs vary somewhat, and substitutions are offered for those who return frequently.

Name: The Kerr House

Mailing Address: P.O. Box 363, 17777 Beaver Street, Grand Rapids, Ohio 43522

Telephone: (419) 832-1733

Established: 1980

Managing Director: Barbara Zilbu

Program Director: Laurie Hostetler

Owner: Laurie Hostetler

Gender and Age Restrictions: Women only except during specified weeks for men and co-ed occupancy. Guests under 18 accepted only if a group (family,

friends) has reserved the entire facility, or for special programs, such as mother-daughter. All guests must be capable of climbing the flight of stairs from the basement to the ground, or first, floor to the second-floor sleeping quarters, to the attic exercise facilities.

Season: Year-round

Length of Stay Required: The main program is 5 days—Sunday evening through the following Friday. Day, weekend (Friday evening to Sunday afternoon), and 2-week programs are also available.

Programs Offered: The program is as permissive, nondemanding, or highly structured as you wish it to be. On Sunday evening, there is a house tour and an orientation session where guests talk about themselves and their goals, which they review again before they leave to discuss progress and achievement. With so few guests, much individual counseling is woven into the program at scheduled times and informally during walks and exercise programs. Consultations are also possible with psychologists and a variety of therapists, counselors, graphologists, and nutritionists who are guest speakers for evening programs.

Every morning, you descend for a beauty treatment to the house's former cellar, attractively altered with white-painted stone walls and wicker furniture, plants, and flowers to contain the kitchen, an informal lunchtime café; a "wet area" comprising whirlpool, sauna, mineral water hot tub, and herbal wrap; massage rooms; a beauty salon for skin, hair, and nail care; a gift shop. If you prefer, a masseuse can massage you in your bedroom. The 5-day program includes 2 massages, a herbal wrap, a cellophane wrap, a "finger facial," a deep-cleansing facial, a reflexology treatment, use of the hot tub, sauna, and whirlpool at any time, and a kinesiological treatment. Paraffin wax masques to soften the skin or your hands and feet; manicures; pedicures; scalp treatments; and facial-hair depilation by means of the Oriental thread-lassoing of each hair method are other treatments *all included* in the program.

Beneath the soaring peaks of the Queen Anne–style Victorian rooftop, the attic loft has been transformed into 2500 square feet of exercise space carpeted in robin's egg blue to match the painted ceiling. Laurie Hostetler guides you in the morning in the various *asanas* (postures) of hatha-yoga. There are aerobic workouts twice daily using 8 individual rebounders (minitrampolines). There are also oscillating backswings on which, with supervision, you can be suspended with your feet up, head down, for a few minutes at a time to release tensions and improve circulation. A NordicTrack cross-country ski machine is at your disposal for use any time.

Following your exercise class, your morning massage, facial, and body treatments are scheduled. Optional lessons in judo, Tai Chi, and fencing are available. Depending on the weather, you can also play badminton, croquet, or volleyball, enjoy afternoon walks, hikes, and outings, and wintertime cross-country skiing.

Diet and Weight Management: Weight loss is seldom discussed, but most guests lose up to a pound a day. For those who wish to gain weight or to maintain their weight but tone up with exercise, larger portions of food are provided. Dean Hostetler, B.A.C., Laurie's son and the resident chef, prepares all fresh, natural foods with no refined flour, no processed sugar, no salt, no additives, no preservatives, no food dyes. Varied and delicious meals are low in calories, sodium, and saturated fat/cholesterol, high in fiber. Lacto-ovo vegetarian or strictly vegetarian requirements can be accommodated, as can requests for Kosher meals and any special diets for medical reasons. Herbal teas and caffeine-free beverages are served. Guests are advised to chew their food well, drink plenty of water, eat lots of fiber, and, when they return home, to be sparing in their use of processed and franchised food products.

The daily intake of food at Kerr House varies between 750 and 1000 calories. A breakfast of fruit juice, bran muffins, fresh fruit, and yogurt with granola is served to you on a wicker tray bright with a fresh flower to begin your morning at 7. Lunch, perhaps a cup of carrot soup, fresh red leaf lettuce, whole-wheat pita bread with its pocket stuffed with chicken and couscous, is served to you at the small round tables in the basement café where guests gather at half-past 12 dressed in their treatment attire of leotards or bathrobes. The player piano is usually turned on as a lively accompaniment. Dinner is as elegant as lunch is informal. In the formal ground-floor dining room, the French-polished table is set with antique lace or embroidered linens, crystal stemware, Haviland or Heisey china, and silver candelabras. For background music, a performer in evening dress plays classical selections on the violin or a great carved and gilded harp. Typical dinner fare might be tomato soup, baked chicken breast with sweet basil or eggplant parmesan with tomato sauce, wild rice, brussels sprouts with lemon sauce, and baked apple with strawberry sauce, fare that leaves few guests hungry, in spite of small portions. If you want more food, or feel you must have salt, or a pear as a morning or afternoon snack instead of an orange, or whatever, no need to feel deprived, you can have it. Nutritional counseling is available, and nutritional subjects are taught in cooking classes in the attractive kitchen with its array of glass containers, copper and porcelain cooking ware, and herbs growing in terracotta pots.

Beauty Treatments and Welcome Indulgences: Remarkable among many skillful, caring treatments is the "finger facial," a head-and-neck massage and cleansing, with heated booties and mittens to soften your creamed hands and feet, or paraffin wax masques for your hands and feet. You can be wrapped with linen sheets impregnated with herbs while you rest and steam in the sauna. You can be wrapped with creams and cellophane to reduce (temporarily) the circumference of your thighs. *All treatments offered are included in your program.* All-natural skin products are selected for your skin type. The European facials, performed partly with a vibrating machine and partly by hand, and the other cleansing, toning, moisturizing, and refining skin treatments are done with gentle, caring expertise. The reflexology massages, polarity massages with gentle pressure point manipulation, and body massages are all outstanding. More attention is given to conditioning your scalp than to having your hair coiffed; more attention is given to the perfection of your interior makeup than to cosmetic applications. Except on the day you leave. Then you are treated to a hairdo and makeup, and to polish applied to your manicured hands and pedicured toes.

Accommodations: Clifford's Room, the former nursery, with its quaint collection of dollhouse china and teddy bears; the B. F. Kerr Room, with an antique sewing machine in working condition serving as a bedside table; the Hat Room, with its collection of antique hats and a fireplace—each of the 4 guestrooms is a spacious Victorian charmer, comfortable, serene, fascinating in its furnishings and memorabilia. The Hat Room is the only single available and is considerably pricier than the other guestrooms, which are all doubles. Unless you bring a friend with you, you share your room with someone Laurie has decided will be a companion with similar tastes and background. There are jacks in each room into which you can plug a telephone. There are no radios or television sets in your room; remember, this is a fantasy getaway place, made comfortable with Victorian grace and latterday air-conditioning and heating. The bathroom on your floor is furnished with 2 private toilets, 2 bidets, 2 showers, 2 sinks. There are bathrooms on each floor, so that there is no waiting. On the main floor, you can use the sizable copper bathtub if you prefer tub baths to showers.

What to Bring: See USEFUL INFORMATION. Laurie Hostetler provides white terry-cloth bathrobes for wear in the spa treatment area, maillot tank bathing suits for wear in the hot tub and whirlpool, Birkenstock "noppy" sandals, soaps, shampoos, and body creams. You should bring a sweatsuit or other exercise clothes and walking shoes. It's customary to dress for dinner in a caftan, long skirt, or pretty dress, but if you don't want to, it's not required. Be sure to bring your camera to capture romantic images of the town and site. In summer, bring insect repellent to ward off midges and mosquitoes that abound along canal towpaths. Guests are *not* encouraged to bring Walkmans, radios, or portable television sets. A cassette player to record seminars and talks, while not suggested, is a worthwhile item to bring. Notions, sundries, stationery, and some types of film are available in the village of Grand Rapids.

Documentation from Your Physician: If guests are "under a doctor's care," a letter is required for permission to use the sauna and whirlpool and to exercise. Since most of the guests are "basically healthy," a letter of approval from a physician is not required. A medical history and documentation of recent physical examination are requested. Guests will be admitted without this documentation but will be asked to sign a medical release. Guests should be able to go up and down steps.

The Use of Alcohol and Tobacco: If a group requests wine with dinner, it is served on occasion, but generally no alcohol is available on the premises. There are 2 areas where guests can smoke. If guests desire to give up smoking, a stop smoking program is available, for a modest fee.

Fees, Method of Payment, Insurance Coverage: For the 5-day program year-round rates:

$2350 single

$1950 double occupancy

For the weekend:

$675 single

$575 double occupancy

All services, outings, treatments, and transport to and from the Toledo Airport are included in your fee. With proper ID, personal checks are honored, as are travelers' checks, Visa, MasterCard, and American Express. No provisions are made for deductibility of fees by your health insurance carrier. If you leave a deposit of $100 for a future visit within the year, you receive a 10 percent discount on your next visit.

Follow-up Assistance: Video and audio teaching cassettes and cookbooks are purchasable as take-home items, available in the basement boutique, where you'll also find cosmetics, Birkenstock sandals, and exercise accessories. Delightfully well-written quarterly newsletters filled with low-cal, high-fiber recipes, wit, and wisdom are sent to former guests.

The Wooden Door
Wisconsin

The Wooden Door is an all-woman's get-away back-to-nature retreat located on 54 acres of wooded lakefront property beside Lake Geneva, 90 miles north of Chicago. Founded in 1979 by Shirley McAlear, Jill Adzia, and Naomi Stark, this all-season rustic camp, open during designated weeks in January, April, May, June, August, September, and October, offers a 6-day/5-night weight loss program based on a low-salt, low-fat, high-fiber, high-carbohydrate diet of 900 or more calories a day, with well-balanced meals of fresh fruit and veggies, chicken, fish, pasta, and no red meat. The operative philosophy is to help a woman develop her full potential, mentally and physically, and to create a take-home program.

Activities include seasonal cross-country skiing, waterskiing, boating, fishing, windsurfing, sunrise yoga, jogging, walking, hiking, stretch and warm-up classes, aerobics, weight training, calisthenics, dance movements—ballet, modern, jazz—and tennis on nearby courts. (If you like to play, bring your own racket and tennis balls.) Live entertainment; films; workshops on nutrition, self-awareness, stress-relief, self-defense; and speakers for evening discussions are part of a full day's program.

For some, "rustic" is a euphemism for a lack of amenities and comforts, no pampering. For others, it means a change of pace, adventure, and for them, hiking along pinewood trails, the view of Covenant Harbor, the peace and quiet of woods and lake are more than compensation for having to lug your own sheets, pillowcases, and towels with you when you come, do your own laundry in a coin-operated laundromat, and make your own bed. There's room for about 90 women in modern cabin accommodations with heating and plumbing, private shower and lavatory facilities. You share a cabin with 1 to 3 other women, minimum age 18. There's a pleasant main lodge with a fireplace, an air-conditioned gymnasium, a sweet lake-front gazebo, a small store where you can buy sundries, leotards, exercise gear.

Young mothers who have parked their children elsewhere, retired housewives, elder hostelers on an athletic spree, teachers, professional women of all ages are on the guest roster. Dress is casual: blue jeans, exercise clothes, bathing suits and cover-ups, warm-ups, comfortable gear to exercise and slop about in. Bring walking shoes, aerobic shoes, insect repellent for summertime mosquitoes, no-see-ums, gnats. A physician is on call. A medical release is required before you visit. If you want frills, there's a charge of $30 for a 60-minute massage, $18.50 for a pedicure, $8.50 for a manicure, $30 for a facial. The price is about $100 a day, $500 per person for 5 nights in a shared cabin in June and August; less in January, April, May, September, and October. Prices for Geneva Bay Center accommodation are under $600 for a 4½ day program. *N.B.* Rates are subject to change and not inclusive of taxes and gratuities.

NEW! With management, service, and catering provided by the Marriott Hotel chain, a multimillion-dollar, 2-story country inn, the Geneva Bay Center, provides 32 double rooms as alternative accommodation. Linens and maid service are provided, and all rooms come with private bathrooms. In addition to exercise rooms, meeting rooms, and dining room, the new facility also features a 15 foot by 20 foot "swim-resistant" whirlpool for fun and fitness aquacize.

Name: The Wooden Door
Mailing Address: P.O. Box 830, Barrington, Illinois 60010

Telephone: (312) 382-2888
Owner: Covenant Harbor Swedish Evangelical Church

Southeast

∽ **Sheraton Bonaventure Resort & Spa** ∼
Florida

A 25-minute drive inland from Fort Lauderdale's Atlantic-lapped beaches, the Bonaventure Spa shares 1250 manicured acres with the Bonaventure Resort Hotel, its award-winning conference center, extensive recreational facilities, and the Bonaventure community of villas, houses, and apartments, which are serviced by a convenient town center. The glittering spa, the 9 four-story buildings where guests have their sleeping quarters, the conference center, a choice of restaurants, and an evening *boîte* with entertainment and dancing are clustered in a 20-acre section embracing 3 azure-clear swimming pools. Reflecting pools, flowering hedges, waterfalls, fountains, and imaginative landscaping create pockets of serenity and seclusion that are a complementary environment for stress-management programs designed to fit into conference schedules and spa packages. The exterior architecture and interior settings confronting you— expanses of polished wood, tile, shining brass, sun sparkling on glass and chrome, white lounge chairs for you to bask on, lots of rattan furniture, the pewter grey and burgundy decor of the spa, and the matching work-out clothes given to you to wear—are functional, substantial, immaculate. The wide range of Bonaventure's health, fitness, pampering, beautifying, educational, and recreational opportunities appeals to singles, couples, groups of friends, and business colleagues who want to be rested, revitalized, redirected in their exercise and nutrition habits, and to have a good and comfortable time while they are exercising and learning. Celebrities as well as weary Miami housewives and families with toddlers and teenagers are here.

On holidays, and from Thanksgiving until New Year's, Bonaventure offers free of charge an innovative child-care and daytime entertainment program, *For Kids Only.* Supervision for children up to 4 years of age is provided in a pleasant playroom. From 9:00 AM to 5:00 PM counselors give swimming, basketball, tennis, and soccer lessons, supervise field trips to the Miami Planetarium, the *Miami Herald* newspaper offices, the Miami Zoo, Ocean World, the beach, and the Everglades for airboat rides and the spectacle of a husky Seminole Indian wrestling with a temperamental alligator. Children can enjoy pony rides, crafts, aerobics, cooking lessons, puppet shows, sing-a-longs, video games, videotapes of themselves, kite flying, volleyball, bowling and roller-skating, poolside barbecues, mother-and-daughter tennis tournaments, father-and-son golf tournaments. Field trips and dinner programs are extras, available for nominal fees. Children under 5 are cared for from 10:00 AM to noon and from 2:00 to 4:00 PM. Families who prefer to play together will find bicycles equipped with tot-carriers, canoes, sailboats, and a heated outdoor pool designated only for the use of families.

Guests who come for the spa package discover not only one of the largest and best-equipped facilities in the US, but a racquet club (tennis, squash, racquetball), saddle club (show jumpers, thoroughbreds, Arabian horses, and ponies for stabling and rental mounts), and golf club (with 2 courses) which are each first-rate attractions on their own. There is also the town center—more like a minivillage than a proper town—a neat little aggregate of full-service bank, insurance agency, travel agency, dry cleaner, dentist, attorney, and community center with multilane bowling alley, sizable roller-skating rink, and reading rooms for the benefit of the Bonaventure residential community (presently being developed for the potential housing of 10,000 occupants) but accessible also to hotel and spa guests.

Hotel shuttle van transport whisks you from the spa area to golf, racquet, and saddle clubs. Taxis are also available, as are limousines and Hertz rental cars for the excursion-minded. The *Jungle Queen,* which resembles a wedding cake afloat, departs daily on sight-seeing cruises of the Everglades from Fort Lauderdale, and daily airboat tours are also operative in the Everglades Holiday Park. You can ask at the bellman's desk at the hotel for information about nearby jai-alai games, recommended restaurants in Fort Lauderdale, admission times for Six Flags Atlantis aquatic amusement park, and diverse attractions in Miami and environs for adults and children. If you have children with you, don't miss the Discovery Center in Fort Lauderdale, a museum with hands-on exhibits and workshops, nature, art, optical illusions, computers, history, crafts.

Name: Sheraton Bonaventure Resort & Spa

Mailing Address: 250 Racquet Club Road, Fort Lauderdale, Florida 33326

Telephone: (305) 389-3300; (800) 327-8090

Established: 1982

Managing Director: John Van Ordstrand

Program Directors: Josefina Feria, Spa Director; Gilles Avellana, Men's Spa Director; Robert Dollinger, M.D., Medical Director

Owners: Herbert Sadkin, Thomas Ireland and the Continental Companies

Gender and Age Restrictions: None for hotel. Co-ed; minimum age 18 for the spa

Season: Year-round; sometimes closed in August for repairs and renovation

Length of Stay Required: No minimum stay required at the hotel. Plans available: 2-day/2-night Spa Sampler; 2-day/2-night Tennis package; 3-day/3-night Golf Package; 4-day/4-night Executive Spa Experience; 7-day/7-night Complete Spa Retreat; 10-day/10-night Lifestyle Enhancer

Programs Offered: Training in stress management and relaxation, nutritionally controlled meals, individualized exercise for fitness, cooking classes, lectures on health and well-being, full-service spa, beauty salons, skin care treatments, wide range of recreational facilities. Emphasized at Bonaventure is the philosophy that basics must not merely be learned but continually be relearned and made a part of your life for continuing years of good health. Exercise classes cater to all levels of fitness, progressing from walks, stretches, and basic calisthenics to water volleyball and weight training. Spa guests receive a 20-minute consultation with a physician, including a brief physical examination (blood pressure, pulse, weight), and their medical history (medical problems, surgery, medications) is noted. On request and at additional cost, you can determine your percentage of body fat with the RJL Body Composition Analyser, determine your fitness level, receive a nutrition profile. The RJL computer, said to be accurate within 2 percent, sends an imperceptible charge of electricity through your body to measure total body water and, based upon age, sex, weight, height, and activity levels, determines your lean and fat tissue. It then prints out your desired weight loss, graphs a plan to lose weight, recommends exercises for you, and calculates the number of calories, based upon your predicted metabolic rate, that you will burn off while doing them. The RJL analysis is included in an optional Fitness Profile, which evaluates your cardiovascular system by your performance on a stationary bicycle and your ability to perform stretching and reaching exercises. Your results are compared to the norm for your age group and exercises are then prescribed for you. A caliper test to measure body fat is available at extra cost. Before you head off to the gym or the outdoor Jacuzzi, the whirlpools and massage rooms of the separate men's and women's pavilions in one of the largest spa facilities in the US, you may want to have your Nutritional Profile tabulated. This is done in an optional personal consultation with a registered dietitian who will develop a weight loss or weight maintenance program featuring the ideal caloric intake required to reach your goal along with menu ideas and recipes to follow at home.

The Bonaventure Spa plans are structured to give you a well-rounded workout of four basic types of exercise: stretching warm-ups and cool-downs, aerobics, resistance, and toning. After your individual orientation tour of the spa, you are assigned your locker and workout wardrobe of warm-up suit, leotard, slippers, and terry-cloth robe and receive your regimen of exercise from a programmer. This provides you with a suitable level of exercise and treatment sequence. As part of a daily lecture and evening program, you receive 3 hours a week of training in stress management and relaxation techniques, 2 hours of cooking classes, lectures every other evening on massage, wellness, skin care, goal-setting, positive mental attitudes, and physiology. Group sessions are limited to 15 participants, and individual counseling is always available. With the *4-day/4-night Executive Spa Experience* you receive fitness classes, 3 massages, a whirlpool bath, 2 herbal wraps, a loofah body buff, thermal back treatment, scalp massage, a manicure and pedicure, a facial, a shampoo and set for women, a shampoo, cut, and blow-dry for men.

New Wave news: Holland America offers a *Bonaventure Spa at Sea* program aboard cruise ships *Westerdam, Noordam* and *Nieuw Amsterdam* sailing to Caribbean ports. The comprehensive spa package includes massages, a salon makeover, and special menus. Prices begin at $2335 a person, and a 2-night, pre- or postcruise package at the spa's home base is also available.

Maximum Number of Guests: The maximum number of guests accommodated by the spa facility is 200, about 20 percent of the average total Bonaventure guest roster. At full capacity, Bonaventure can accommodate over 1000 guests. Within the Bonaventure community of villas and town houses, there are 3356 occupied residences, scheduled to be increased to 5000 residences for lease or rental. The current population is approximately 8400.

Full-Time Health Professionals on Staff: 7, including 1 doctor, 2 registered nurses, and 1 registered dietitian; plus 22 massage therapists, 12 exercise instructors, 8 estheticians, 7 exercise programmers, and 16 attendants. Add in the spa salon, dining room, and kitchen staffs plus 22 massage therapists, 12 exercise instructors, 8 estheticians, 7 exercise programmers, and 16 attendants. Add in the spa salon, dining room, and kitchen staffs plus receptionists and personnel in the spa boutique and you come up with a total spa staff of 110 for a maximum number of 200 guests.

Diet and Weight Management: Weight management shares first priority with fitness in the spa programs. Spa guests have their meals in a separate spa dining room serving low-sodium, low-fat, low-cholesterol foods. Guests who do not wish to lose weight may have larger portions or dine in one of the hotel's other restaurants. The spa weight loss plan is based on a 900- to 1200-calorie diet. A registered dietitian is on hand at mealtimes to answer questions and give advice (adequate for some guests, less satisfactory to others who may prefer an individual, custom-caloried nutrition program for weight management or for any therapeutic requirements, which can be provided by the dietitian in an optional private consultation). Features of the spa menu are at least 2 quarts of Evian water daily, minimal amounts of saturated fats and cholesterol, decaffeinated tea and coffee, high quantities of complex carbohydrates—fresh fruits, vegetables, and grains—relatively low protein with emphasis on fresh seafoods, no red meat, no added sodium, one egg yolk per week, polyunsaturated oils only, limited amounts of pure fructose as the only sweetener, emphasis on ethnic foods to maintain variety and interest, some vegetarian entrées. Strictly vegetarian and lacto-ovo diets can be accommodated as can special diets for medical reasons. Menus are provided with calorie counts so that you can tally your choices for the ideal 300- to 400-calorie meal. All pasta served is half pasta and half tofu. Certain spa recipes call for acidophilus milk, a cultured low-fat milk that lends a creamy quality to foods and for which 1 percent butterfat milk may be substituted. Dieters are advised to fill up on salad with a reduced calorie dressing to make it easier to eat less of the entrée, which is usually the calorie culprit, and to drink 2 quarts of filtered, deionized water a day to help curb the appetite as well as "flush out the body." Thai chicken salad and baked red snapper "almondine" are favorite main dish recipes, and there are many palatable surprises in high-quality carbohydrates—cellophane noodles, kasha, wild rice, a variety of flavorful pasta. High-bulk selections, such as carrot-raisin bran muffins, eight-grain French toast with warm fruit conserves, and whole-wheat cottage cheese zucchini pancakes with hot apple sauce, are some of the specials appearing on the breakfast menu. You can practice calorie control and portion control when dining out at Bonaventure's Terrace Bar, Sunspot, Garden Restaurant, and the attractive Renaissance Seafood Grill (rated 5 stars by the Chaîne des Rotisseurs), which features mesquite-grilled seafood, fresh Florida stone crabs, fresh Florida alligator tail, individual soufflés, and other haute cuisine supervised by Debbie Daley, R.D., a young chef who is a graduate of the Culinary Institute of America.

Exercise and Physical Therapy Facilities: Encompassing 43,000 square feet, with separate men's and women's pavilions, the Bonaventure Spa features aerobic exercise programs developed specifically for men and for women in rooms carpeted with Everflex carpeting, which provides three layers of shock-absorbing cushioning; nonskid surfaces around its pools and the "wet" areas of its Finnish saunas, Turkish steam baths, Swiss showers, Jacuzzis, whirlpools, hot and cold plunge pools, and water exercise pools (each 3 lanes wide and 60 feet long, with facilities for volleyball). The 2500 square feet of the shared gymnasium facility is outfitted with a Paramount multistation body builder, free weights, Precor 9.5 treadmills, Precor 8.6 stationary bicycles, Lifecycles, individual trampolines, an ergometrically monitored Bodyguard, an ergometrically monitored Concept II rowing machine, and heart rate/EKG monitoring equipment. There are individual rooms for massage, herbal wraps, and loofah scrubs, and private solariums. With skylights, walls, and floors in "wet" areas of imported Italian tile, and mirrored exercise rooms, the spa is airy, immaculately maintained, sparkling with points of light. Sports boutique available.

Opportunities for Recreational Exercise: There are 3 swimming pools by the hotel, 1 children's and family pool at the town center; a 73-stall stable with thorough-bred and Arabian horses and ponies for children at the saddle club, which offers riding lessons, trail riding, 2 equestrian rings with brush, rail, and water jumps (horse rental, lessons, and use of rings extra); 24 tennis courts, 17 Har-Tru, 7 Fast-Dri (clay), all lit for night play at the racquet club, which also has 5 indoor air-conditioned racquetball courts and an air-conditioned squash court (court fees, lessons, rackets, and shoe rental extra); a 4-lane bowling alley; a 1200-square-foot roller-skating rink at the town center (shoe and skate rental extra, free use of bowling alleys and rink); two PGA-managed 18-hole championship golf courses at the golf club—the par 72 East Course, cited by *Golf Magazine* as one of Florida's top 10 (with a spectacular waterfall at the base of the green on the third hole) and the par 70 West Course (greens fees, lessons, and equipment rental extra); bicycle rentals with a selection of children's bicycles and tot-carriers available (extra); canoe, sailboat, and paddleboat rentals (extra); walking paths and trails; bird-watching; waterskiing and windsurfing at Fort Lauderdale beaches. *N.B.* The golf club has a bar, dining room, locker rooms and showers, and a Pro Shop that carries a complete line of golf equipment and clothing. The saddle club has a restaurant and bar, but no locker rooms or showers. Reasonably priced jodhpurs, boots, and riding caps are for sale at Karen's Tack in nearby Davie, with free transport provided there and back. The racquet club has a Tennis Pro Shop stocked with rackets, balls, and tennis gear. Free round-trip shuttle van service from the hotel is furnished to all three clubs.

Beauty Treatments and Welcome Indulgences: Judith Jackson, author of *Scentual Touch, A Personal Guide to Aromatherapy* and a certified aromatherapist, has trained spa personnel to give men's and women's massages using her techniques and botanical-oil products for their beneficial physiological and psychological effects. The fragrances that make up the heart of her line of scented skin care products, massage essences, and room fragrances include lavender as a calming influence, camomile as a soporific, ylang-ylang as a stimulus, basil for its invigorating effect, and fragrances that encourage detoxification and deconges-tion. Her products are available at the spa for you to buy and take home with you, plus her book of instructions. Another exclusive at Bonaventure is Kerstin Florian, whose live-cell therapy and skin care line is used by the spa's estheticians to emphasize Florian's Beauty Point System, based on the acupressure theory, to increase circulation and beautify facial skin, another system you can learn at the spa and take home. The salon at the spa also furnishes full-service waxing depilation; nail care, which includes nail designs for the trendy; hair, beard, and mustache care; as well as the aromatherapy massages, shiatsu, and Swedish body massages. Computerized Body Analysis Composition, Individualized Fitness Profile, Individualized Nutrition Profile, and cosmetic and fitness services not included in your spa program are extra.

Accommodations: Guestrooms have king-sized beds or twin double beds; 1- and 2-bedroom suites come with refrigerators and wet bars. All suites have balconies. Ground floor rooms have enclosed patio areas. Most bathrooms are equipped with bidets. All guestrooms have air-conditioning, television sets with cable TV and pay-movie Spectravision, and are expediently situated in 9 four-story buildings grouped about the conference center; the lounges, restaurants, gift shop, and boutiques are in the hotel building, along with the 3 swimming pools and the spa facility. Rooms are functionally furnished in candy-box hues of vanilla, caramel, chocolate, and pecan with much rattan furniture in evidence. Laundry, valet, secretarial, and late night room service at your beck and call. Everything well organized and efficiently planned for your convenience, comfort, and well-being in a stress-free atmosphere.

What to Bring: See USEFUL INFORMATION. Although men and women are provided warm-ups, bathing suits, and workout gear for use in the spa facility, these clothes are for use only in the spa. Bring extra tops and shorts, T-shirts, bathing suits, and a cover-up or robe to get you decently dressed to and from your room to a pool. You can buy sportswear, bathing suits, Reeboks, and exercise clothes at the spa boutique. Boutiques in the hotel building promise that women can buy "everything" from underwear to beaded cocktail dresses and accessories, but don't count on "everything" being to your taste or in your size. Relaxed, easy, what's-in-fashion clothes are worn by guests in the evening. No need for women to bring "dressy" evening or cocktail dresses. The gift shop in the main hotel building carries magazines, cosmetics, and drugstore items, but you are advised to bring your own camera supplies.

Documentation from Your Physician: A letter of approval is requested but not required. A medical history and documentation of recent physical examination are neither requested nor required. A physical examination will be done at the spa.

The Use of Alcohol and Tobacco: Alcohol is not served in the spa dining room but is freely available elsewhere on the premises. The use of alcohol is discouraged, but not prohibited in the spa programs. No smoking is allowed in the spa facility. Smoking areas are provided in the spa dining room. You are free to smoke in your room or outside and in many designated areas.

Fees, Method of Payment, Insurance Coverage: High-season (January 1 to April 16) rates:

Per night: $195 single, $225 for a double room

2-day/2-night Spa Sampler: $549 single, $439 per person double occupancy

2-day/2-night tennis package: $300 single, $251 per person double

3-day/3-night golf package: $411 single, $200 per person double

4-day/4-night Executive Spa Experience: $1349 single, $1075 per person double

7-day/7-night Complete Spa Retreat: $2250 single, $1795 per person double

10-day/10-night Lifestyle Enhancer: $3495 single, $2695 per person double

Rates are higher for deluxe accommodations and lower in the off-season. All prices are subject to change. All rates are subject to a 9 percent hotel tax and an 18 percent gratuity charge.

The spa charges extra for meals and excursions for children enrolled in *For Kids Only* program. A deposit is required. Ask about the cancellation policy. With proper identification, personal checks are honored as are travelers' checks. Visa, MasterCard, American Express, Diners Club, and Choice credit cards. Guests enrolled in the *Spa Fitness* programs make payments to the medical director, who will assist in insurance billing.

Follow-up Assistance: Body Talk, a complimentary quarterly 8-page newsletter is sent to all former hotel and spa guests. Video teaching tapes for exercise and relaxation, cookbooks, and exercise books are available at the spa and hotel boutiques.

✑ Doral Saturnia ✑
International Spa Resort
Florida

In 1962 Alfred Kaskel created his dream of a golfer's and tennis enthusiast's paradise, located a 7-mile drive from Miami's International Airport and named the Doral (Doris and Alfred) Hotel and Country Club. In 1987 his son Howard, together with other members of the family, teamed up with Leandro Gaultieri, owner of the Terme di Saturnia spa near Rome, to create the Doral Saturnia. This luxurious spa combines old world grace and European water and mud therapies with a top-flight American fitness program of aerobic stretching and strengthening exercises, high-tech Scandinavian and American weight-resistance machines and other elegant fitness equipment.

The complex cost over $30 million and an investment of thoughtful detail and style that gives Doral Saturnia the look of both elegance and comfort. The exquisitely appointed 48-suite, U-shaped "villa" hotel is built around a garden courtyard of trellises and brilliant beds of flowers and is surrounded by topiary trees priested by dark candleflame cypresses in the Roman tradition, with reflecting pools, grottos, fountains, and ornamental sculpture. Etched glass panels, orange-pink, symmetrically laid clay-tiled hotel and spa rooftops, Roman arches, pale pink balustrades, beige and cream travertine floors, terra-cotta tiles, a free-form swimming pool, and 4 pools with cascades, 99 holes of golf, 15 tennis courts, the four-story Spa Centre—it's all an immaculate, delightful other world in which even the outdoor pool's border of smooth coral rock mined from the Florida Keys never heats up.

Several executive directors have come and gone. Beth Figueroa, who helped launch Terme di Saturnia cosmetic products, and whose 20 years in the cosmetic industry have blessed her with leadership qualities, maintains smooth transitions. Handsome young Executive Chef Michael McVay has been lured from the Golden Door to work with nutritionist Cheryl Hartsough, R.D., on a full menu of spa cuisine based on "a breakthrough Fat Point System nutritionally computerized that allows for a diet pattern of 20 percent fat, 20 percent protein, and 60 percent carbohydrates." (See Diet and Weight Management.)

If you need some well-deserved R&R, want to get in shape, shed a few inches and pounds, disencumber yourself of stress, enjoy sensational treatments, luxuries, and impeccable beauty services and sports facilities, you can happily join the literati, glitterati, and prosperati who spring for this fabulous new candidate on the spa scene. Pricey, but what quality, what value. Four months after it opened, Doral Saturnia had a 40 percent repeat guest roster.

Name: Doral Saturnia International Spa Resort

Mailing Address: 8755 Northwest 36th Street, Miami, Florida 33178-2401

Telephone: (305) 593-6030; (800) 247-8901 in Florida, (800) 331-7768 outside Florida

Established: 1987

Managing Director: Unknown at press time

Program Directors: Beth Figueroa, Personal Services and Beauty and Spa Treatments; Kathy Sanders, certified with International Dance Exercise Association (IDEA) and Aerobics and Fitness Association of America; Cheryl Hartsough, R.D., Nutrition Director; Michael

McVay, Executive Chef
Owners: Howard Kaskel and other members of the Kaskel family
Gender and Age Restrictions: Co-ed; minimum age 18
Season: Year-round

Length of Stay Required: Nonresidential *Ultimate Spa Day* (available daily 9:30 AM to 6:00 PM); 3-day/2-night *Grand Getaway;* *4-night* and *7-night Spa Plans*

Programs Offered: You have your choice of *Health, Sports,* or *Total Image* programs. Both the 4-night and the 7-night programs begin with a fitness assessment and an exercise prescription, and include four 1-hour massages. After you have checked into your glorious suite, a resident R.N. does your medical screening, recording your weight, measurements, and blood pressure and doing a finger-prick blood cholesterol test that takes 90 seconds to complete. You fill out a health questionnaire and then meet with one of 15 counselors to schedule your program and prebook some services. Orientation tours are scheduled every hour from 9:00 AM to 5:00 PM 7 days a week. At the end of your program, you will have another medical screening to check out the results and to prepare a take-home program for continuing fitness maintenance.

If you choose the *Health Emphasis,* besides your four 1-hour massages, you get a total body fango (mud) pack or a Doral Saturnia facial, hydrotherapy with hydromassage (an operator hoses your body at close range while you relax in a special hydrotherapy tub imported from France), a computerized health-risk assessment, a nutrition consultation with a registered dietitian, with a dietary computer analysis, plus 4 additional choices from the Personal, Professional, and Sports Service list if you are on the *7-day program,* or 2 choices if you are on the *4-day program.*

If you choose the *Sports Emphasis* program, besides your four 1-hour massages, you get 4 rounds of golf with golf cart, a 1-hour golf or tennis lesson, unlimited tennis court time (as available), 3 buckets of golf balls or 1 hour of tennis ball machine practice, plus 4 additional choices from the Personal, Professional, and Sports Service list if you are on the *7-day program,* or two 60-minute massages, a facial and additional choice of three 30-minute services if you are on the 4-day program.

If you choose the *Total Image Emphasis,* besides your four 1-hour massages, you get a back "facial" with fango mud or total body fango, a Doral Saturnia facial, a total image consultation or a makeup application, a shampoo and blow-dry, a manicure and pedicure, plus 4 additional choices from the Personal, Professional, and Sports Service list if you are on the *7-day program,* or 2 choices if you are on the *4-day program.*

The Personal, Professional, and Sports Services list comprises: 1 full body massage; 2 herbal wraps with choice of camomile, marigold, horse chestnut, lime, mallow, cucumber, linden, or other essences; 2 hydrotherapy treatments; a body polish with sea salt plus a herbal wrap; a Doral Saturnia facial; a back "facial" with fango mud; a total image consultation; 1 makeup application and instruction; a haircut, shampoo, and set or blow-dry; a manicure and pedicure; color analysis of colors most becoming to you; a computerized health-risk assessment; a nutrition consultation; a one-on-one exercise workout; a golf lesson; a tennis lesson; a round of golf with golf cart.

A smoking cessation program is offered. If stress management is your interest, you have a broad range of options for classes in biofeedback, guided imagery, and other techniques for identifying and relieving "hot spots," or places where stress is stored, supplemented by physical therapy—fango treatments, mineral baths, massages, and hydromassages. Exercise is part of all programs. From the many offerings, you're sure to find the activity that fits your level and one you will really enjoy. Lectures, seminars, films, and other entertainments are also offered.

Maximum Number of Guests: 96

Full-Time Health Professionals on Staff: 15 fitness instructors, 1 registered dietitian, 2 registered nurses; consulting and referral arrangement with Doctors Hospital in Miami; 50 massage therapists, 15 cosmetologists, tennis and golf trainers; 15 "guest specialists." Add in kitchen and dining room staff and other staff personnel, and you get a carefully selected staff of 300.

Diet and Weight Management: The Doral Saturnia Fat Point System (1 gram of fat is equivalent to 1 fat point) is a diet that is nutritionally analyzed by computer to assure a balance of 20 percent fat, 20 percent protein, and 60 percent carbohydrates. The Fat Point System features food rich in fiber, vitamins, and minerals: grains, legumes, fruits, vegetables, lean meat, poultry, fish, and low-fat dairy foods recommended by the American Heart Association and the American Cancer Society. By keeping track of fat points and total calories, your diet is nutritionally balanced for easily controlled weight management.

Guests committed to losing weight are limited the first 4 days to 1000 calories daily for women, 1300 calories for men. From the 5th day on, this is increased to 1300 calories for women and 1700 calories for men. This allows for a continued weight loss at a recommended 1 to 2 pounds a week. The Fat Point System diet plan and booklet goes home with you. While you are at the spa, you can go to two 90-minute cooking demonstrations. The quarterly spa newsletter contains follow-up recipes for you to try at home.

The Villa Montepaldi Restaurant, exclusively for hotel guests, seats 30 and is located in the courtyard of the hotel. You eat here beneath a trompe l'oeil ceiling painted with sky and clouds and hung with a real silver and crystal chandelier. Tables, with white linen cloths, are set with English bone china with moss green and silver banding, crystal goblets, and Christofle cutlery. As you dine, you have a view of Italianate gardens ornamented with trellises that repeat the lattice design of the beige and green restaurant carpeting—everything is that well planned and designed.

You enjoy your lunch at the Ristorante di Saturnia, seating 70, on the Spa Centre's lobby level where day guests and people from the country club are also welcome. The restaurant's floor is tiled with Italian terra-cotta and its glass cupola 100 feet above your head is supported with pale mauve columns. Glass paneling, etched with Roman arches, separates the restaurant from the indoor aerobic exercise pool, and an art nouveau wrought-iron-and-glass stairway leads from the restaurant to the Spa Centre's upper levels. Tables are set with white china and gold-banded silver cutlery. In these entrancing settings you are served zucchini-corn soup or lemon chicken consommé or a garden salad for starters; followed by a choice of pizza topped with sliced mushrooms, bell peppers, and part-skim-milk mozzarella cheese, or Gulf red snapper grilled with herbs served with steamed vegetables and brown rice, or an open-faced sandwich of breast of turkey with tomato, sprouts, asparagus spears and Ranch dressing. Dessert might be fresh berries, or sliced kiwi fruit, or a sorbet. For those who want to eat more, lunch may be supplemented with an apple, a wedge of juicy canta-loupe, ½ cup of low-fat yogurt, additional portions of steamed vegetables, a portion of carrot cake. You are provided with a choice of options and extras, such as an additional baked potato, a spa roll, a portion of margarine or butter, extra salad dressing. At dinnertime only, guests at both restaurants are offered a choice of wine or champagne. Menus list the calories and fat content of each item and calculators are provided so that you can keep accurate score.

For breakfast, you get buckwheat waffles or pancakes with a fruit topping, a choice of omelettes (whole egg plus an egg white), or just plain egg boiled or poached, plus a choice of fresh fruit, plus a choice of cereal with skim milk, or ¼ cup yogurt or cottage cheese, or a slice of wholewheat toast with jam. A choice of coffee or herbal tea. Meals can be served in your room for an additional charge.

When you arrive, the minirefrigerator in your room discloses a bottle of Carolina mountain water from North Carolina, a bottle of San Pellegrino water, and a cornucopia of fruits. In the hotel's reading room, stocked with a wide variety of books, magazines, and international newspapers, plus backgammon boards and a billiard table, you can have fruit juice, vegetable juice, herbal tea, coffee, and crudités throughout the day and evening.

Exercise and Physical Therapy Facilities: A 2-mile morning hike is scheduled daily at 6:30 AM, but no guilt should obtain if you don't feel like joining that pleasant brisk across the holes of 5 golf courses next door at the Doral Country Club. Every day, from 9:00 AM to 5:00 PM, 3 or 4 choices are available each hour of 50 different aerobic, stretching, and strengthening exercises, including jogging, swimming, golf, tennis, riding, and bicycling. There are 4 fully equipped exercise studios, all with mirrored walls, 2 featuring spring-loaded floors for aerobic workouts. Aerobic classes feature low-impact aerobics and aqua-aerobics, aimed at shaping abdomen, buttocks, and thighs through natural water resistance. Flexibility classes include yoga, stretch and tone, posture, and lower back strengthening. The mirrored fitness studio features Scandinavian David Fitness resistance weight-training equipment, high-tech, light, easy to use and quiet, as parts are rubber-coated; also rubber-coated free weights, leg extension machines, stationary bicycles, StairMasters, rowing machines, and treadmills.

For jogging, there's an indoor banked track with its own hi-fi stereo system and a shock-absorbent surface. The outdoor ¼-mile exercise trail, the Exercourse, also equipped with a shock-absorbent surface and handsomely landscaped with palms and shrubs, consists of 3 clusters of exercise stations, each offering a choice of 5 sit-ups, stretches, and see-if-you-can-do-this exercise challenges. The free-form pool and attractive outdoor lounging area by the Spa Centre face the 4 warm-water cascades dropping from a height of 12 feet over you as you sit on 1 of 4 separate blue-and-white-tiled benches, waist deep in water, with 2 jets of water massaging your lower back, a celestial experience free of the reek of sulphur which this experience carries at the place of its origin at the Terme di Saturnia in Italy. There's also an outdoor whirlpool; plus separate facilities for men's and women's saunas, private men's and women's sundecks, 2 Swiss showers needling hot and cold at you, separate indoor Jacuzzis for men and for women. Using European hydrotherapy tubs, you can soak in Terme di Saturnia's mineral water reconstituted in Florida, or you can be enfolded in linen sheets soaked in herbal extracts for a relaxing herbal wrap. There are 26 massage rooms with individual lighting and sound systems for your massage treatments.

Opportunities for Recreational Exercise: If you like to go it alone, you can pick up a complimentary all-terrain bicycle for cycling around trails by the golf course. There's a tennis court on site on which you can play without charge, or you can make use of the 15 Har-cor courts at the Doral Country Club ($22.50 for 30 minutes, $50 an hour; rental rackets available), or play on any of the 5 Doral golf courses (greens fees and golf cart for 18 holes about $65). Scheduled group activities include volleyball, water volleyball, basketball, aerobic golf, croquet, and lawn bowling (boccie). There are 2 outdoor recreational and lap pools. Private arrangements may be made for riding and instruction at Doral Country Club's excellent Equestrian Center.

Beauty Treatments and Welcome Indulgences: Optional consultations are available to learn how to maximize strengths and minimize any weaknesses. Services include makeup instruction, wardrobe consultation, hair analysis, scalp treatment and styling tips, and other services guaranteed to have you feeling great. You can choose to have your skin buffed to a fine polish with mineral salt, paraffin face and body masques, manicures, pedicures, depilatory waxing, and hairdos, all admirably performed by skilled estheticians. The fango mud applications, to soothe muscle and joint pain, cleanse and tone the skin, and reduce stress, are imported magic from Italy's Terme di Saturnia. The charcoal gray mud, imported in 55-gallon drums, smells of sulphur, but it is one of the few renowned Italian muds that are free of radioactivity, you'll be delighted to know, and it's rich in mineral salts and plankton, said to be an antiaging treatment and therapeutic for the skin. You can see and feel for yourself how smooth and nice your face and body feel after a treatment. Cosmetic thermal-spa formulae imported from Terme di Saturnia include cleansing, toning, nourishing, soothing thermal-plankton serums, creams, and muds for facials and body care. Whether or not they do more than temporarily firm, contour, reduce cellulite, or plumpen-out wrinkles, the treatments feel great and make you look wonderful, and who could ask for more than that? Makeup treatments aren't just a matter of the application of cosmetics, but amount to "face design." And there are "facials" not only for your back but for your elbows, and elbow massages that seem to rival the beneficial effects of reflexology massage for your feet. Everything is included for your comfort: men's and women's full-sized personal lockers in pleasant locker rooms with hot and cold plunges, showers, toiletries and amenities for your grooming needs, and big, thick silver-gray towels.

Accommodations: There are 42 "luxe" suites with 12-foot ceilings, including living room, a wet bar, and a minirefrigerator. Each luxe suite has 2 marble bathrooms and dressing areas. Each bathroom has a marble Jacuzzi bath, bidet, glassed-in shower, heated towel racks for sumptuous peach and gray towels, gold-plated fixtures, knobs to show you the exact temperature of your bath and shower water, plenty of mirrors, and 3 hand basins with lots of counter space. Each suite has a balcony or a patio with a view of gardens and golf course, telephones in the living room and in the bathroom, tape decks, remote control TV, VCRs (movies are supplied free by the concierge), creamy beige travertine floors covered with soft rugs, room cupboards with a private safe, and a decor designed by Sarah Tomerlin Lee. For friends traveling together, some suites are designed with 2 large beds in separate sleeping alcoves. Then there are 6 "supreme" suites, designed by Piero Pinto, with 3 bathrooms each, with all the features of "luxe" suites, plus a fabulous decor, different for each suite. All the supreme suites have wraparound terraces.

What to Bring: See USEFUL INFORMATION. The ambience is casual elegance and comfort. Some guests slop in for dinner at the Villa Montepaldi in their spa-provided peach-colored dressing gowns. Others arrive all jacketed-and-tied, or dressed in flowing silk caftans. Both in your room and in the Spa Centre, you are provided with gray-and-white shorts, T-shirts, women's leotards, men's and women's shorts, warm-up sweats, peach-colored bathrobes, and flip-flop sandals with nonskid soles. You can wear these or bring your own. Women are asked to bring tights. Men and women should bring swim wear, cover-ups, aerobic shoes, tennis and golf gear, if they play, or riding gear if they intend to ride. Don't forget to bring your running shoes. Bring money. There's a designer boutique, which carries activewear, sportswear, and designer evening clothes and accessories.

Documentation from Your Physician: Neither requested nor required.

The Use of Alcohol and Tobacco: A 3-ounce portion of fine wine or champagne is proffered at dinner. No smoking is allowed in public places, but it is permitted in your suite.

Fees, Method of Payment, Insurance Coverage: High-season (October 1 to May 1) rates:

For *Ultimate Spa Day* (nonresidential): $185

For suite, per night: $500 single, $375 double occupancy

For *2-night getaway:* $1035 single, $775 per person double occupancy

For *4-night Spa Plan:* $2221 single, $1735 per person double occupancy

For *7-night Spa Plan:* $3500 single, $2840 per person double occupancy

New *Tennis, Golf,* and *Cellulitis* packages

Rates are higher for deluxe accommodations and lower in the off-season. All prices are subject to change, and all rates are subject to a 6 percent tax and a 17 percent service charge. A deposit is required. Ask about the cancellation policy. Travelers' checks in dollar amounts are accepted, as well as Diners Club, American Express, Visa, MasterCard, and Carte Blanche. Insurance reimbursement may be possible for smoking cessation and stress management courses, including travel costs.

◌ Palm-Aire Spa Resort ◌
& Country Club
Florida

The Spa at Palm-Aire, located in a lush 1500-acre resort, condominium, and conference center complex, about 20 minutes from Fort Lauderdale and Pompano Beach, has acquired status as the spa where celebrities and *Fortune 500* executives come when their clothes feel snug and their waistbands don't button, to lose weight on the spa's get-thin/eat-rich diet. Guests from all walks of life discover muscles they didn't know they had in body conditioning classes, exercise classes, working out with weights, or getting in shape for tennis, golf, and skiing in the spa's sports conditioning program. Guests aged from their late 20s to their late 60s talk about the bliss of Palm-Aire's 700 acres, 5 golf courses, its 37 tennis courts, its pleasant country clubs, swimming pools, and tropical gardens. They speak of their equally enjoyable massages with almond oil, or their heavenly mummification in steaming linen sheets scented with rosemary in the inner sanctum of the newly renovated spa where all the ladies literally are "in the pink," swathed in that color of toweling as they tone their bodies. Women outnumber men 3 or 4 to 1 at the spa, and Carol Upper, Director of the Ladies' Spa, reports that some 42,000 women, guests as well as nonresident members of the spa, make use of the facilities annually. However, no one is lost in the shuffle. The staff is well trained in courteous and attentive service to each and every guest.

The University Health Center at Palm-Aire is a "personalized wellness program." The program comprises weight management, a personalized eating plan, nutrition information, individualized and group exercise programs, relaxation methods to relieve stress and tension, techniques for improving lifestyle, and personal counseling regarding nutrition, behavior, and exercise. The 2-week program takes no more than 12 participants at a session. This program is noteworthy, but more remarkable is the *esprit de corps* that has become characteristic of Palm-Aire's spa. Guests really do have a good time.

Many guests make the spa part of a longer vacation experience in order to take advantage of deep-sea fishing trips, which are easily arranged out of Fort Lauderdale and Pompano Beach, or spectator sports such as harness racing, thoroughbred horse racing, greyhound racing, and jai-alai. Some prospective spa guests will be delighted to know that, besides the excellent tennis, golf, and swimming offered at the spa, excellent shopping is available at Loehmann's Plaza next door.

Name: Palm-Aire Spa Resort & Country Club

Mailing Address: 2501 Palm-Aire Drive North, Pompano Beach, Florida 33069

Telephone: (305) 972-3300; (800) 327-4960

Established: 1971

Managing Director: Marc Mastrangelo, for hotel and spa

Program Directors: Carol Upper, Director of the Ladies' Spa

Owner: Katzoff Development Corporation, Inc., Philadelphia

Gender and Age Restrictions: Co-ed; minimum age 16

Season: Year-round

Length of Stay Required: For spa programs, a 2-night minimum in summer, 3 nights in winter; for hotel, 1-night minimum. Packages include a 2-day/3-night Mini Spa Program, a 6-day/7-night Full Spa Program, a 13-day/14-night University Health Center Program starting on Saturday, a 4-day/3-night Golf Fitness Program, and a 1-day/2-night Tennis Program

Programs Offered: All spa programs begin with a medical screening (blood pressure, pulse, weight and general history) by the spa's licensed physician. The *Mini Spa Program* includes a fitness interview, 15 exercise classes, 2 body massages, 2 scented whirlpool treatments, 2 herbal wraps, a facial, use of all spa facilities, unlimited use of 5 golf courses and 37 tennis courts. With the *Full Spa Program,* you receive a fitness evaluation test, which includes testing for your body's ratio of fat to lean tissue and the capabilities of your strength and flexibility. The results are fed into a computer, along with your weight, to help plan the appropriate activities and diet for you. With this program, you receive 35 exercise classes; 6 body massages; 3 whirlpool sessions; a skin analysis; two 30-minute facials; 3 herbal wraps; a Salt-Glo loofah scrub; a program of custom-tailored exercise to use at the spa and at home; a Spa Beauty Package comprising a shampoo and set, makeup consultation and application, manicure and pedicure; and lectures in behavior modification, stress management, nutrition, cardiovascular conditioning, and other health-related topics, including nutritional counseling conducted in group seminars as well as on an individual basis if requested, at extra charge. All spa programs are structured with options.

The *University Health Center (UHC) Program,* for 2–12 participants, was developed by a team of medical experts from leading universities. By means of one-on-one counseling and group seminars, as well as personalized diet and exercise plans, this 2-week program offers instruction in weight control and stress management for "a happier, more energetic, healthier lifestyle" for you and freedom from "the weight loss and gain syndrome for good." You are asked to complete 3 in-depth questionnaires that assess when and how you eat, your health risks, and your level of stress. The morning after your arrival, you meet with the resident physician for a private consultation and testing. Your body's fat content is measured and your blood tested for triglycerides, cholesterol, and hemoglobin content. Your tolerance for exercise and your flexibility and strength are assessed. Based on your medical evaluation, the staff helps you set your goals for the next 2 weeks and designs a nutrition and exercise plan to help you achieve your fitness objectives. You receive 4 exercise classes daily; unlimited use of all spa facilities; individual daily sessions on nutrition, lifestyle, or exercise in addition to group seminars on these topics; a daily body massage or facial; a daily session in the whirlpool; as much swimming, tennis, or golf as you desire, along with free use also of the racquetball and squash courts and jogging track. You receive a personal health, exercise, and eating manual for take-home use as well as a videotape for home reference of you performing an exercise routine. "This is not a magical program," caution the directors. "It takes a real commitment on your part. But the rewards are well worth the effort." Spouses, urged to accompany their mates through this program, may opt for Tennis or Golf packages or spa packages.

The spa fitness staff help you ease into exercise classes appropriate to your individual level of fitness—Beginner, Intermediate, and Advanced levels for women, Beginner and High Levels for men, including both low-impact and high-impact aerobics. Optional for women, who can make use of the equipment but for whom there is no organized class as there is for men, is the Circuit Class in the co-ed gym. Four different types of water exercise are offered for both men and women. The women's stretch and relaxation class styles itself yoga, whereas the men's S & R class styles itself stretching and "deep breathing," an indication, perhaps, that CEOs and other corporate types who want to de-stress and unwind would prefer to sound more macho than mystical while doing so.

For both men and women, there are warm-up exercises before morning walks around the lushly landscaped ribboning loops of the ½-mile parcours track. Other options are competitive volleyball in the spa pool, squash and racquetball. Fitness programs are supplemented with the soothing and sybaritic pleasures of being swathed in linen sheets steamed in eucalyptus, mint, rosemary, and camomile oils; Swiss needle showers, saunas, steam baths, whirlpool baths, hot and cold contrasting pools, Salt-Glo loofah scrubs, a variety of facials and massages, thalassotherapy treatments, and the services of a complete beauty salon. Guests can also incorporate Palm-Aire's extensive recreational facilities in their spa program.

Evening programs for both spa guests and *UHC* participants offer cooking classes and demonstrations. For *UHC* participants, there are group discussions on Exercise and Weight Control, Exercise and Health Benefits, Effective Communications, Stress Reduction, *UHC* offers group and individual training in stress management and relaxation techniques, and individual counseling is included in the fee. Movies and field trips are also included in the evening activities of the *University Health Center Program*. For spa guests, there are no group discussions of any of the above topics, and individual counseling is available only at extra charge.

Maximum Number of Guests: The 166-room four-story Palm-Aire Spa Resort, with its conference center, can accommodate approximately 388 guests; the adjacent 18-suite Renaissance Club can accommodate approximately 50 guests. The Ladies' Spa can accommodate 80 women; the Men's Spa can accommodate 40 men. The University Health Center accepts a minimum of 2 and a maximum of 12 participants in its program. On the basis of space availability, hotel guests and nonresident members with paid-up membership in the spa also can use the facility and the services of the beauty salon.

Full-Time Health Professionals on Staff: 30, including 1 M.D., 1 R.N., and 1 R.D./nutritionist; in the Ladies' Spa, 15 fitness instructors, plus 22 massage therapists, 15 facialists, 6 manicurist/pedicurists, 2 makeup artists, 4 hairdressers, and 18 herbal wrap/Salt-Glo loofah/whirlpool attendants; in the Men's Spa, 6 fitness instructors, plus 14 massage therapists, 4 facialists, and 9 herbal wrap/Salt-Glo loofah/whirlpool attendants.

Diet and Weight Management: From 800 to 1000 calories are offered daily for significant weight loss, 1200 calories for those participating in the *University Health Center Program,* and 2200 for those who wish to add a few pounds in the right places. The spa dining room, open daily for breakfast, lunch, and dinner is shared with other guests who enjoy delicious, nutritious, calorie-conscious meals, but guests may also dine in the Peninsula Room, The Palms, and The Oaks restaurants. Spa guests serious about losing weight follow the high-carbohydrate, low-fat diet plan, which is based on an exchange system that lets you orchestrate your own meal from a selection of foods up to your calorie limit. The regimen includes no snacking between meals; omitting added fats and oils; limiting white sugar, honey, and syrup; increasing fresh vegetables and fruit; drinking 5 to 8 cups of water daily and preferably between meals; avoiding caffeine; limiting beef to 3 portions weekly; omitting high-fat luncheon meats; controlling portion sizes; and not using salt.

Breakfast specials (200-calorie portions) include French toast with apples, buckwheat pancakes with blueberries, strawberry crêpes with mock sour cream, bagel melt, and egg Palm-Aire. Spa light wine (50 calories) is served at lunch or dinner; take it or leave it or treat yourself instead to a bonus dessert of fluffy chocolate mocha mousse. Menus are on a 21-day cycle to avoid repetition. Lunch selections include an appetizer, salad, a sandwich or entrée special, and a dessert, plus beverage or a selection of hot and cold items from the buffet, with the server doling out calorie-controlled portions to you. For dinner entrées, choices include poached salmon with dill sauce, beef brochettes, broiled chicken breast, catch-of-the-day fish with lemon and herbs, and seafood diablo. Dinners always include an appetizer, salad, either an entrée and vegetable or a dinner special, and a dessert plus a beverage. The element of choice gives you a sense of control.

The *UHC* participants get to eat more of the lobster pernod and shrimp Rockefeller and vegetable lasagna and stuffed mushrooms than spa goers, while still on a diet consistent with guidelines from the American Heart Association and National Cancer Institute, which provides no more than 30 percent of calories from fat, a cholesterol intake of no more than 100 mg/1000 calories, a fiber intake of 20 to 25 grams daily, and 50 to 55 percent of calories a day from complex carbohydrates. Each participant in the *UHC* program is scheduled to meet privately with the nutritionist for 4 half-hour sessions during his/her 2-week stay plus mandatory daily group nutrition sessions each lasting close to an hour to learn not only "what" to eat but "how" to eat for good health and weight control. For *UHC* participants, cooking demonstrations are presented at night, and sessions in label reading, estimating portion sizes of food, and reading menus are included during group nutrition sessions. For *UHC* participants who don't need to lose weight, or require a higher number of calories, provisions are made. Both *UHC* participants and spa guests on different calorie levels are encouraged to achieve a Personal Eating Plan, or a food regimen for long-term, personal, realistic use.

Exercise and Physical Therapy Facilities: The twin spa pavilions for men and women, with an area of 35,000 square feet, are under one roof, and include a full-service beauty salon. If you include the looping, winding ½-mile parcourse track (green Har-Tru surface) with 8 stationary exercise stations, bounded by the three perimeter walls of the spa, which screen off the 25-yard co-ed pool, co-ed area, and outdoor Jacuzzis, the spa area is 42,000 square feet. The spa is attractively landscaped with tropical vegetation. Past the courtyard, beneath a covered walkway, you enter the huge reception area with its impressive marble desk and reception area, with the Men's Spa facilities on your left, the Women's Spa on your right, and the beauty salon, with public access. The spa facilities, renovated in 1987, contain circular pools, 3 feet deep, for exercise classes, one for the men, one for the ladies; Swiss showers on the men's side; hot and cold contrast "pools"—tubs, actually—for hydrotherapy in both spas; separate but equal steam rooms, solariums for sunbathing clad or unclad, saunas, individual whirlpools (often referred to as "Roman Tubs") and rooms for loofah scrubs, herbal wraps and hydrotherapy treatments. The co-ed gym includes 12 different stations of Body Masters equipment, as well as computerized stationary bicycles, Lifecycle and Heartmate bicycles, elevated Trotter treadmills, a StairMaster, a Marcy recumbent bicycle you operate with your legs straight out in front of you, and rowing machines to pump up muscle strength. New in 1988! Sports conditioning for toning and strengthening muscles used in golf, tennis, and skiing for both men and women is an additional feature of the fitness classes offered.

Opportunities for Recreational Exercise: Guests can use the swimming pool by the hotel area and the swimming pool at the Renaissance Club, as well as the spa's co-ed swimming pool outdoors (admissions charge). The spa and hotel boast 37 tennis courts, 6 lighted for night play. Computer evaluation of your moves and patterns of performance and/or video analysis of yourself in action, frame by frame, are available for moderate fees, as well as individual or group instruction with resident pro and tennis staff (extra). Tennis rackets can be rented. Racquet-ball and squash are also available (admission, lessons and rental equipment are extra). Five golf courses are available for use: The Palms and The Pines have hosted the Florida Open, US Open qualifying matches, and the Florida PGA; and The Sabals is a par-60 circuit. The Cypress and The Oaks are also good for exercise and perfecting your short game. All 94 holes are superbly manicured. Moderate fee for the required use of golf carts; clubs can be rented. Private instruction with resident golf pro is available.

Beauty Treatments and Welcome Indulgences: In addition to the massages, facials, herbal wraps and whirlpools, Salt-Glo loofah scrub, manicure, pedicure, and hair treatment included in your package, women may also opt for a makeup consul-tation, plus assorted à la carte waxing, hair and nail services, as well as additional spa personal services for both men and women.

Accommodations: Of the 191 generously scaled guestrooms, 155 are furnished with 2 double beds (the others are furnished with king-sized beds) and come with seating areas, separate dressing alcoves with ample mirrors and good lighting, room telephone and television set, air-conditioning, and your own private terrace. Both 1- and 2-bedroom suites are available; some rooms with kitchenettes; all with plenty of closet space; soft or firm bed pillows provided, depending on your preference; large bathrooms; valet service.

What to Bring: See USEFUL INFORMATION. Men are provided with robe, slippers, warm-up suit, shorts, and T-shirts. Women are provided with robe, slippers, warm-up suit, leotards. Spa clothing is not to be worn outside of the spa. So, bring bathing suits, bathrobes or cover-ups, leotards, shorts, and T-shirts. There are 3 tennis and golf pro shops on site, as well as boutiques for sportswear and casual wear. A dispensary for sundries in the hotel carries most small necessities as well as a selection of stationery items and film. From December to April, men are requested to wear jackets in the dining room. Simple, casual, comfortable day and evening wear is the choice of most guests.

Documentation from Your Physician: Neither requested nor required.

The Use of Alcohol and Tobacco: Spa wine is served at lunch and dinner. The University Health Center's policy is to discourage the use of alcohol. Participants in the *UHC Program* are taught that a moderate use of alcohol is fine if their calorie level is not exceeded and their diets are well balanced. Alcoholic beverages are not allowed inside the spa building, but are available at the hotel. No smoking is allowed in the spa building except in the beauty salon. Smoking is permitted only in the à la carte section of the spa dining room, where guests enrolled in the spa program may arrange to be seated.

Fees, Method of Payment, Insurance Coverage: High-season (mid-December to mid-April) rates:

For 4–day/3–night *Mini Spa Program:* $1557 single, $1241 per person double

For 8–day/7–night *Full Spa Program:* $3612 single, $2875 per person double

For 13–day/14–night *University Health Center Program:* $7623 single, $6148 per person double

For *Golf Vacation,* 4 day/3 night: $968 single; $641 per person double

For *Golf Fitness,* 4 day/3 night: $1108; $791 per person double

For *Tennis Program,* 3 day/2 night: $728 single; $523 per person double

Rates are higher for deluxe accommodations and lower in the off-season. All prices are subject to change, and all rates are subject to a 6 percent state tax, 2 percent room tax, and 17 percent service charge. A deposit is required. Ask about the cancellation policy. Personal checks, travelers' checks, Visa, MasterCard, American Express, and Diners Club are accepted. Fees for the *University Health Center Program* may be covered by your insurance policy or may be considered as medical expenses on your tax return. Check with your physician and with your insurance carrier.

Follow-up Assistance: Cassettes and cookbooks are available for take-home use. UHC provides a videotape of you performing an exercise routine for home reference; also a pantry food list (low-fat exchange-food regimen system) and a fat/calorie counter.

❧ Safety Harbor Spa & Fitness Center ❧
Florida

If you want to drink, soak in, swim in, or be showered by the blend of mineral spring waters proclaimed in 1539 by Hernando de Soto as the Fountain of Youth of Espiritu Santo, you can enjoy the experience many have found tonic, cosmetic, and healing at Florida's Safety Harbor Spa & Fitness Center, a 35-acre site fronted by palm-fringed Tampa Bay. The spa has recently increased the scope of its programs, decreased the average age of its clientele from golden oldies to fitness-minded 40s, added more and better accommodations, and gussied up the premises with the help of designer-decorator Michaele Vollbracht. At present, the 20- to 65-year-old clientele comprises 60 percent women, 40 percent men, but the percentages are expected to even out in the months to come. Most of the guests are married, but many women come on their own or with a chum to lose weight, restyle their bodies and their eating habits, or to improve their tennis game. A Lancôme Skin Care Institute is installed here to perform delicious miracles on your face as well as on your body, which you can exercise to your heart's content with an array of classes and state-of-the-art equipment that caters to all levels and goals of physical fitness. You can play golf on the spa's minicourse or on 18-holers PGA-approved in the neighborhood.

The staff is friendly. The atmosphere is low-keyed and relaxed. Recreational and sight-seeing opportunities abound. The spa provides off-site afternoon shopping and nightly movie theater transportation. The local bus service is well run and extensive. Taxis are available, as are rental cars. There are pick-up minibus services operated by Sunlift and DART (Dial-A-Ride Transit) operating out of nearby St. Petersburg for the wheelchair-bound. Attractions? The Salvador Dali Museum and the Sunken Gardens, both in St. Petersburg; Tampa Downs Race Track for thoroughbred racing (December to end of March); waterfront shopping at the Boatyard Village in Clearwater; Harbour Island Market's specialty shops and entertainments (everything from mime, jazz, and circus acts to waterside symphonic concerts). You can reach them in minutes from downtown Tampa by car or on foot by the People Mover operative from an upper floor of the Fort Brooke Garage. You are surrounded by the "Real Florida" preserved in state parklands which offer natural, cultural, historic, and entertainment attractions, plus many surprises, such as a fine Rubens collection in the Ringling Museum in Sarasota, an excursion well worth the taking. You can sail or cruise on Tampa Bay or flake out on Clearwater's popular beach, where you can also fish or collect seashells. For information about music, film, dance, and the visual arts, check out *Good Times,* a monthly guide to the arts and entertainment in the Tampa Bay area, obtainable from the Arts Council of Tampa-Hillsborough County, 1420 Tampa Street, Tampa, Florida 33602; or from the Pinellas County Arts Council, 400 Pierce Boulevard, Clearwater, Florida 33516.

Name: Safety Harbor Spa & Fitness Center

Mailing Address: 105 North Bayshore Drive, Safety Harbor, Florida 33572

Telephone: (813) 726-1161 (from Canada, call collect); (800) 237-0155

Established: 1926

Managing Director: Alan Helfman

Program Directors: Richard Gubner, M.D., Medical Director; Fred Banke, M.S., Executive Spa Director; Dawnne Micket, M.S., Fitness Director; Susan Swanson, R.D., Director of Nutrition; Anick Fuchs, Director of Beauty Services

Owner: Bright Star Holding Corporation

Gender and Age Restrictions: None

Season: Year-round

Length of Stay Required: Plans vary: 5-day/4-night, 8-day/7-night *Total Fitness Plan,* weekend, and other packages are available, as are à la carte spa and beauty salon services.

Programs Offered: The *Total Fitness Plan* offers a medical examination, blood chemistry analysis, fitness profile, daily massage, 1 loofah scrub, 2 facials, 2 herbal wraps, 1 manicure and pedicure; for women, 1 Lancôme makeup and consultation, 1 shampoo and blow-dry; for men, 1 scalp treatment, 1 styling haircut and blow-dry. *5-day program* includes 4 massages, 1 loofah scrub, 1 facial, 1 herbal wrap, 1 manicure; for men, 1 styling haircut and blow-dry, 1 pedicure. The *Fitness Plan* (minimum 4 nights) emphasizes exercise. You receive a full medical screening, a daily massage, and unlimited classes, which include aerobics, dancercize, water exercise, yoga, and basic flexibility.

All package programs entitle guests on a first-come-first-served basis to complimentary use of recreational bicycles, shuffleboard courts, and the outdoor lap-swimming pool when not in use for classes; Nautilus, Paramount, aerobic, and free weight machines; relaxation in whirlpool, sauna, or steam room; an opportunity to join team sports such as water volleyball or water basketball in the indoor pool; and, on an availability or appointment basis, unlimited complimentary use of tennis courts, exercise classes, golf course, and driving range. Offered also: optional nutritional counseling with a registered dietitian to develop a personalized program for continued weight loss/weight maintenance;

smoking cessation through medical hypnosis conducted by a member of the American Society of Clinical Hypnosis (extra); a weekly program of evening activities including a 90-minute cooking demonstration with nutritional guidelines, a fitness lecture, a fashion show, films, music for dancing, fun and games.

Maximum Number of Guests: The hotel can accommodate 460 guests; the spa can accommodate 400 program participants.

Full-Time Health Professionals on Staff: 13, including 1 full-time M.D. specializing in cardiology, 1 full-time M.D. specializing in internal medicine, 2 registered nurses, and a consulting exercise physiologist, plus 8 fitness instructors, 50 licensed massage therapists, 12 estheticians, and 15 cosmetologists.

Diet and Weight Management: Instead of diets, which "people go on and go off," Nutrition Director Susan Swanson works to change eating patterns by preparing meal plans that will become food lifestyles. She believes in basic, fresh foods with an emphasis on complex carbohydrates, low sodium, low cholesterol, and no added sugars. Chilled Gazpacho Andalucia, poached salmon with mustard sauce, mandarin spinach salad, ratatouille, fresh fruit desserts, and low-calorie mousses are specialties of Cordon Bleu–trained chef Drew Kasley. A limited selection of Kosher foods is available (no Kosher kitchen). Lacto-ovo vegetarian, strictly vegetarian, and special diets for particular medical reasons are accommodated. Weight management is a principal objective, inclusive of weight loss, weight maintenance, and weight gain; and Safety Harbor's program is individualized with options at each meal and the caloric content provided. Dishes are attractively herbed, spiced, and garnished for regimens requiring 900 or more calories a day. "Light international food, with a touch of nouvelle and a spark of northern Italian," everything fresh, is served in the Terrace Dining Room with its peach and green carpeting, peach tablecloths, and lattice-webbed center dome. Edible fresh flowers are one of chef Kasley's specialties. Hotel and spa guests alike eat here in one continuous seating for breakfast, and in two seatings, from 55 to 75 minutes apart, for lunch and dinner, which is served with the pleasant accompaniment of piano music. Complimentary refreshments of juices and fresh Florida fruit are served in a lower lobby juice bar in the afternoon and evenings.

Exercise and Physical Therapy Facilities: The fitness center was recently expanded to add a 3rd aerobic gymnasium and a 2nd machine room, and now comprises 100,000 square feet of air-conditioned space. Each 7500-square-foot gymnasium is equipped with Super-Gym aerobic flooring. Equipment includes a full complement of Nautilus, Paramount, Hydra-Fitness, and free weights; Precor M-8.5, Monark 868, Tunturi, Schwinn Air-Dyne, and Heartmate color TV stationary bicycles; a dozen Precor M-9.5 treadmills; upper body ergometer; Versa-Climber; Concept II and Precor rowers; boxing speed and heavy bags; dumbbells, elastic for exercising, ballet barres, and gymnastic benches. An indoor 3½-foot-deep, 20- by 40-foot exercise pool is complemented by an outdoor 4-foot-deep, 25-meter lap pool. There are separate men's and women's steam rooms, men's and women's saunas, men's and women's whirlpools (4 each), separate men's and women's locker rooms, 2 Jacuzzis for co-ed groups of 8 to 10, and 35 individual treatment cubicles for massages, herbal wraps, and loofah scrubs provided as you recline on a thickly padded ceramic pedestal covered in fluffy toweling. An oval pool is encircled by smaller elevated tubs of heated water from Safety Harbor's renowned mineral springs for you to soak in after an exercise session or before your massage or other treatments, in itself a procedure restorative and tranquilizing. (All water used at the spa comes from the mineral springs, and when heated, its effect seems extraordinarily beneficial.) Classic, Swedish, or Japanese shiatsu massages are available. Towels from small to outsize, but not robes, are provided, as well as paper slippers, soaps and toiletries, hair dryers. For heliotropes who wish to tan all over, comfortable sunbathing in the nude on royal blue–cushioned adjustable lounge chairs is there for the basking, along with men's and women's locker rooms, showers, saunas, at the men's and women's solaria 50 yards away by the tennis department.

Opportunities for Recreational Exercise: Facilities at Safety Harbor include a ¼-mile jogging track and hiking and walking trails. Guests can enjoy tennis on 9 courts—2 Har-Tru and 7 clay—during the day and on the court lit for night play. A ball machine permanently set up for practice on one of the courts is complimentary for lessons and available for a small fee for half-hour practice sessions. Golfers can choose between a 4-hole course and a 250-yard driving range on site or among 3 nearby PGA-approved courses—Lansbrooke, Tarpon Woods, and Nine Eagles—where greens fees are waived for all guests on package vacations. Golf carts and golf club rental are reasonably priced extras. In addition, 7 bicycles are available for complimentary use, excellent pelican and other water-bird watching sites can be found within walking distance, and fishing spots (rental equipment available) are within 200 yards. Those wishing to venture further afield can find commercial bowling alleys in Clearwater; waterskiing and windsurfing at Clearwater Beach; and boating and sailing—both bare boats and crews available—at Old Tampa Bay.

Beauty Treatments and Welcome Indulgencies: The full-service salon provides everything for your nails and hair, including coloring and highlighting beards and foil-frosting, as well as eyebrow tweezing and depilatory waxing. The spa's Lancôme Skin Care Institute treatments are fabulous, and the cosmetics can always be relied upon for exquisite quality. Truly special is the Lancôme facial with its stroking *effleurage,* kneading *petrissage,* percussion *tapotement,* friction, pressures, and vibrations guaranteed to reveal your facial skin at its softest, most radiant, and healthiest best. Salon services, skin care treatments, health and fitness classes in addition to those included in your package are extra.

Accommodations: Guestrooms, deluxe guestrooms, suites with kitchenettes—some with terraces, balconies and patios—and all with air-conditioning, room telephones, television, private baths, have recently been supplemented with 30 additional luxury apartments (spacious 1-bedrooms, commodious studios), a few with private terraces, and many overlooking Old Tampa Bay, in a three-story apartment building, Safety Harbor House, adjacent to the spa. These are available by the day, week, month, or year. Deluxe rooms have terraces overlooking the bay and are larger than the guestrooms.

What to Bring: See USEFUL INFORMATION. Bring a cover-up to wear in the dining room for breakfast and lunch, and a robe for the bathhouse. No clothing articles are provided by the spa. For evenings, many men wear blazers, ties, white or bright colored trousers; women wear caftans, dressy tops and trousers, pretty sportswear. Toiletries, sundries, stationery, newspapers, and some types of camera film are available at a hotel shop. The Tennis Pro Shop carries a wide variety of sports and exercise clothing and footwear. Georgette's Boutique in the hotel carries other sports clothes as well as women's resort wear, office wear fashions, and accessories.

Documentation from Your Physician: A letter of approval, medical history, and documentation of recent physical examination are requested but not required. A medical examination is available without charge to guests.

The Use of Alcohol and Tobacco: No alcoholic beverages are allowed in the spa or the salon. Alcoholic beverages are served in the hotel lounge. If weight loss is desired, the use of alcohol is discouraged. Smoking is strongly discouraged, and no smoking is permitted in the spa or salon. A smoking cessation program is offered at extra cost.

Fees, Method of Payment, Insurance Coverage: High-season (January to April) rates:

For weekend program: $400 single guestroom, $320 per person double

For 5-day/4-night *Total Fitness Program:* $1080 single guestroom, $880 per person double

For 8-day/7-night *Total Fitness Plan:* $1820 single guestroom, $1470 per person double

Rates are higher for deluxe accommodations and lower in the off-season. All prices are subject to change, and all rates are subject to a 6 percent state tax, a 3 percent room tax, and a 16 percent service charge. A deposit is required. Ask about the cancellation policy. All major credit cards, personal checks and travelers' checks are accepted.

Follow-up Assistance: A newsletter, *Harbor Lights,* is sent 4 times a year to all guests.

ᘇ The Spa at Turnberry Isle ᘒ
Florida

Turnberry Isle, an island in the Intercoastal Waterway opposite Miami, comprises 300 acres encompassing the amenities of a marina and helipad, two 18-hole golf courses designed by Robert Trent Jones, 24 tennis courts with 18 lit for night play, 4 apartment buildings, which no one calls anything but "residence towers," meeting rooms and audio-visual equipment for conferences in a 13,000-square-foot facility, the Country Club Inn, the Yacht and Racquet Club, the Country Club for the golf courses, an off-site Ocean Club, the Marina Hotel, and the extraordinary spa. The maximum number of guests at the spa is 24. Fitness training is provided with superb equipment, 12 highly skilled instructors, and 8 massage therapists; there's a dazzling beauty salon, and diets are monitored through a gourmet kitchen. The image throughout is space, quality, luxury, comfort, privilege, and extravagance.

Privacy is the watchword here, and a minimum of fanfare and publicity. The emphasis is a combination of relaxation, exercise, healthy nutrition, and time for oneself for a rewarding and enjoyable experience. This is opulence on a grand scale for those mostly between 30 and 45 who have worked hard for their money and want some time to relax in style and have their needs accommodated by skilled professionals.

The 8-day/7-night *Spa Nutrition and Fitness Plan* features accommodation in a regally large room in the Marina Hotel with 2 queen-sized beds and a circular terrace for outlooks on the Intercoastal Waterway; a private Jacuzzi bathtub and a bidet in the bathroom; personalized diet/nutrition consultation with a staff nutritionist who is a registered dietitian; and 3 well-planned, delicious meals nicely classified not only as to calories and types but also as to "calcium counters" and "muscle retainers." At breakfast you are advised to have a Jarlsberg cheese omelette or a double eggwhite mushroom omelette as a "muscle retainer," and low-fat cottage cheese or melon-flavored yogurt or skim milk as a "calcium counter," along with your choices of fresh fruit and juices, breads and cereals. For lunch, your appetizer might be a spinach and mushroom salad, your entrée might be pasta primavera, dilled salmon salad, cold shrimp plate, or grilled swordfish, and your dessert might be hot bananas and berries, vanilla custard, fruit cup, melon wedge, or half a broiled grapefruit with cinnamon. Dinner offers such goodies as snow peas and onions served on a bed of radicchio, fresh steamed artichoke, or iced cucumber soup for starters; steamed lobster tail with dill sauce, broiled lamb chop with thyme and rosemary, or eggplant parmesan for entrées; potato skins, pineapple rice, broiled tomato, and braised seasonal vegetables *pour légumes;* and minted pear, fresh seasonal fruit, or apricot crème for dessert.

Medical examination by a staff physician in an hour's consultation, with other services, such as blood chemistry workups and an EKG, are available on request at additional charge. There is unlimited use of the Swedish sauna, Turkish steam bath, 15-station Nautilus equipment, free weights, stationary bicycles, Treadmaster, StairMasters, rowing machines, whirlpools, outdoor swimming pool, 2 championship racquetball courts, and jogging or running Vitacourse track with exercise stations. Also included are 6 half-hour massages, two 60-minute facials, 4 herbal wraps, a loofah/Salt-Glo treatment to slough off your dry skin's flakiness, a wash/set or blow-dry at the hair salon, a pedicure, and a manicure.

Your spa attire is provided—warm-up suits, exercise clothing, bathrobes, slippers, towels. All you need are appropriate shoes to wear for jogging and your 5 personal exercise classes—just you and the instructor. And there is, of course, a spa boutique.

In the high season (January 1 through April 30), price for 5-day/4-night *Spa Nutrition and Fitness Plan* for single or per person double accommodations is $1373; for 8-day/7-night Spa Nutrition and Fitness Plan for single or double accommodations is $2381, *including* 11 percent tax and 20 percent service charge to cover gratuities. Less at other times of the year.

Name: The Spa at Turnberry Isle

Mailing Address: 19735 Turnberry Way, Miami, Florida 33180

Telephone: (305) 932-6200 (hotel); (800) 932-6200 in Florida, (800) 327-7028 outside Florida

Established: 1980

Managing Director: Karl Heinz Zimmerman, for hotel

Spa Director: Hugh Jones

Owner: Don Soffer and Rafael Resorts

Gender and Age Restrictions: Co-ed; minimum age 16

Season: Year-round

Length of Stay Required: 5-day/4-night and 8-day/7-night Spa Nutrition and Fitness Plans

Northeast

∽ Deerfield Manor ∾
Pennsylvania

Little more than 90 minutes from New York by car or bus, in the uplands of the Pocono Mountains of northeastern Pennsylvania, close to the Delaware Water Gap, is a commodious white clapboard house set on 12 wooded acres, which provides an intimate country setting for an excellent exercise program, including calisthenics in a heated outdoor swimming pool, intelligent and personalized attention, and a quick start on weight loss at bargain rates. In 1987 *Shape* magazine cited Deerfield Manor as one of a dozen "best new spas ... excellent for first-time spa vacationers, with warm atmosphere provided by owner Frieda Eisenkraft." Don't expect high-tech equipment, saunas, whirlpools, or lavish beauty treatments. None are provided, and you receive only one full-body massage in the program, although you may pay for as many more massages or reflexology treatments as you would like at refreshingly low rates. What Deerfield Manor does provide in clean-as-a-whistle, fresh-as-a-daisy surroundings are the basics of well-motivated weight loss: exercises that you can follow at home and a supportive, friendly, and stress-free environment where you can change your eating patterns with a choice of low-calorie foods and closely supervised fasting regimens, which should not be embarked upon without first consulting your physician or health-care specialist. "People cannot live this way all the time," says Eisenkraft, a former high school teacher with a master's degree in English and a passion for obesity research. She states unequivocally that for long-term results there is no substitute for eating properly and exercising moderately. "But if a guest opts for fasting, 3 to 5 days of fasting is all that I allow, and only with daily blood pressure checks. Even guests who are eating 3 meals a day are closely watched."

No more than 33 guests, mostly women, with a sprinkling of couples and single men, with ages ranging from 18 to 80, are accommodated in 23 rooms in the main house or recently constructed annex. Each crisp and country-fresh room is differently decorated, but each has individually controlled air-conditioning, a private bath, and peaceful views of birch trees, red maples, lawns, and woods from tied-back-curtained windows. No room telephones; you may receive person-to-person calls on the lobby telephone. There are communal television sets for viewing films from an extensive video library, but no room televisions or radios. No objection if you bring your own Walkman or portables if they are played "softly." The gymnasium and exercise room are housed in a cathedral-ceilinged, mirror-walled, converted barn. The outdoor heated swimming pool is invitingly ranged about with lounge chairs.

Most guests have their own cars, but taxis and rental cars are available to take advantage of an area filled with antique shops, antique fairs, and antique markets; summertime playhouse theaters; factory discount outlet shops for candles, clothing, pottery, ribbons, and much more in and around the Stroudsburg area; plus Bushkill Falls ("The Niagara of Pennsylvania") with lots to see and do including renting a paddleboat, fishing without a license for bass, and playing miniature golf; no-license-required trout fishing at Paradise Trout Preserve; riding on guided trail rides offered by the Shawnee Stables; a chairlift ride up Camelback ski mountain and a sit-upon ride down the Alpine slide; canoe rentals and guided, outfitted Delaware River canoe trips; many golf courses; indoor and outdoor tennis; the Pocono Indian Museum.

Name: Deerfield Manor
Mailing Address: R.D. 1 (Route 402), East Stroudsburg, Pennsylvania 18301
Telephone: (717) 223-0160
Established: 1981
Managing Director: Frieda Eisenkraft
Program Director: Frieda Eisenkraft
Owner: Frieda Eisenkraft

Gender and Age Restrictions: Co-ed; minimum age 18
Season: Mid-April to mid-November
Length of Stay Required: A week's stay is recommended, Sunday to Sunday, check-in time 2:00 PM, check-out time 11:00 AM; weekends and shorter stays can be arranged.

Programs Offered: On arrival, you have a personal conference with Mrs. Eisenkraft. You discuss and fill in a form concerning your state of health, medical problems, medication taken, allergies, eating habits, attitudes on dieting and exercise, and goals. On your arrival evening, there is a complete orientation for guests to meet each other and be informed about the program and social activities available. Highly structured, the program is not compulsory, and guests have 2 scheduled midweek consultations with Eisenkraft, as well as consultations whenever desired, to discuss their progress and to make modifications to the program to suit their needs.

The day's 5 exercise classes in the airy gymnasium in the barn or in the 20-by 40-foot swimming pool in which everyone can stand comfortably are supplemented with a prebreakfast walk and another brisk walk after lunch around the country roads and over the fields that surround the property. Basic warm-up and stretch classes, advanced calisthenics, low-impact aerobics exercise, water aerobics followed by water volleyball, and yoga classes are included in your daily program. You have the free use of 2 outdoor tennis courts adjacent to the property and, if you wish, you can always put in extra time with the weights or add on extra mileage on the stationary bicycles in the gym. Guests on a fasting regimen may opt for aerobic shopping or sightseeing in lieu of more active exercise, and are encouraged to pair up on a "buddy system" for excursions. Some fasters prefer just to rest.

In the evenings, guests gather to sit on the pleasant side porch with its potted geraniums and greenery and cool breezes; convene in either of 2 lounges before or after dinner for television, viewing video films, and playing parlor games; listen to music or play the piano in the music room; read and have time to think in the well-stocked library. The shining clean kitchen is always open to guests for informal cooking demonstrations or to ask for anything they need, and there are also scheduled cooking demonstrations. Brief seminars and talks focus on the art of flower arranging, buying and selling antiques, makeup and ways to improve one's appearance, film critiques. There are group discussions led by a psychologist and lectures on topics concerning dieting, nutrition, and exercise.

Eisenkraft is assisted by a registered nurse on duty daily; a licensed massage therapist who also qualifies as an R.N.; 3 highly qualified fitness instructors, whose training includes hatha-yoga, dance therapy, and exercise physiology. On a monthly basis for varying periods of time, other health professionals visit to augment the exercise program and instruct in new techniques such as self-massage you can use at home.

Diet and Weight Management: Fasting is accommodated as an option by Frieda Eisenkraft for a few guests. Those eager to try can fast by drinking only mountain water drawn from Deerfield Manor's own well, water and lemon with honey, or freshly squeezed vegetable and fruit juices (approximately 350 calories a day). No one leaves Deerfield without first having broken his/her fast with foods selected with "the utmost care." Eisenkraft acknowledges that the effectiveness of the fast is temporary, but believes that it is a helpful beginning to changing unhealthy eating habits and forming new patterns of healthier nutrition. Guests select meals according to their individual caloric requirements.

High-fiber, low-salt diets consisting of fresh fruits and vegetables, eggs, cottage cheese, fish, and chicken, averaging 700 to 1100 calories, are provided with herbal tea and other caffeine-free beverages available all day, plus an afternoon snack of raw vegetables. Everyone eats in a pleasant dining room where tables are set with pink linen cloths and napkins with fresh flowers to contemplate at breakfast and lunch, silk flower arrangements at suppertime. Breakfasts are usually a combination of yogurt, fruit, cereal, one egg with yolk, or egg whites whipped into an omelette. Lunches are usually a choice of salads and fruit plates. At dinner, main dish portions never look skimpy. Zucchini soup, turkey quiche, fish salad, French chicken, and vegetable soup are admirably presented. You are served a dessert such as "orange almond delite" or other gelatine–fruit–cottage cheese low-cal combos, or a deliciously spiced baked apple. Other diets can be accommodated on request.

Beauty Treatments and Welcome Indulgences: Appointments can be made for massages and reflexology treatments at about $30 an hour, $15 a half-hour. Barber, hairdressing, and manicure services are available in Stroudsburg.

Accommodations: You have a choice of 4 double-bedded rooms and 2 singles with king-sized beds in the annex or a dozen twin-bedded or double-bedded rooms in the main house, each with private bath, individually controlled air-conditioning, and a variety of styles of dust-ruffled beds, some with wicker or brass headboards, simple or canopied, with good reading light and comfortable bedroom chairs. Overall decor is simple, tasteful, restful, fresh, and clean. If you come alone and wish to have company to share a room, Frieda Eisenkraft will try to find you a roommate as close in age and interests as possible for double occupancy rates.

What to Bring: See USEFUL INFORMATION. Walking shoes and a cover-up are necessary, because you aren't allowed in the dining room in bare feet or a bathing suit without a cover-up. At supper time, some women prefer to slip into a caftan or something wearable to a local movie. For both men and women, slacks and shirts will see you through most leisure time activities during the week. You can pick up anything you forgot to pack at local stores, and if getting your own newspaper is important to you, you can make arrangements for delivery at the A-OK store about ¼ mile up Route 402. Otherwise, guests share one local newspaper and one copy of the *New York Times,* which may not be removed from the Red Room. There are laundry and dry cleaning facilities in Stroudsburg. Bring a tennis racket and tennis balls if you play.

Documentation from Your Physician: Without a physician's letter of approval and documentation verifying your good health, you will be required to sign a medical release.

The Use of Alcohol and Tobacco: No alcohol is allowed on the premises. No smoking is permitted inside the main house, the annex, or the gymnasium or exercise rooms.

f Payment, Insurance Coverage: Rates for mid-April to mid-No-

nd: $257 to $290 single, $213 to $243 per person double
For 7 nights: $715 to $810 single, $595 to $675 per person double
Additional days are approximately pro-rated.

A deposit is required. Ask about the cancellation policy. Fees do not include a 6 percent state tax, but are inclusive of gratuities. Cash, personal checks, travelers' checks, Visa, MasterCard, and American Express are accepted. Although your visit is not covered by Blue Cross/Blue Shield as a medical expense, it may be tax-deductible if you have a letter from your physician prescribing your visit as a necessary or strongly recommended medical expense.

✥ Evernew ✥
Massachusetts

Barbara Slater, an attorney, former television producer, and member of the Massachusetts Bar Association who served on the Governor's Commission on the Status of Women in Massachusetts, founded this summer spa camp exclusively for women to provide them with an affordable opportunity to relax, energize, and renew their lives in a casual ambience, and, at the same time, provide a "persuasive nudge" toward a healthier lifestyle. Barbara Slater believes that "it shouldn't have to cost a lot to feel like a million." Her first year was a great success. Women went home "having lost up to 8 pounds and 5 inches and gained new strengths and new resolve."

A healthier lifestyle and weight management are the principal objectives of her carefully planned Sunday-to-Friday program for 40 to 50 women, aged from 20 to 70, the majority business and professional women, who come with friends, sisters, mothers, daughters, or on their own. Evernew convenes on the campus of the all-women's private liberal arts college of Mount Holyoke in South Hadley, Massachusetts, during the last week of June through mid-August. Each guest and up to 20 exceptionally versatile, interesting, and skilled staff members, aged from the late 20s to the vigorous early 60s, has her own single room, or shares, on request, a double room, in a dormitory building. Large, multishower, multibath bathroom facilities are shared. Program cost is kept to $650 for a 6-day/5-night program, while guests enjoy the sports and recreational benefits of one of the most beautiful college campuses in New England, stretching over 800 acres of rolling lawns, wooded areas, brooks, and canoeing lakes. There are Japanese meditation gardens, a bird sanctuary, bicycle paths, trails for running, hiking, and power walking, an art museum, summer theater, four museum buildings filled with historical objects, a college library, a solar greenhouse, an equestrian center, and an 18-hole golf course either on site or within walking distance. There are 18 tennis courts outdoors and indoors. Squash courts, racquetball courts, a sauna, and an indoor 8-lane, 25-meter pool supplement Evernew's program of power walking, aerobics, jazz dancing, water exercise, and instruction in body alignment and injury prevention.

There are unpretentious, informal, and informational workshops on subjects such as stress management, the mind-body connection, nutrition, sharpening communication skills, wardrobe planning, positive visualization, improving self-perception, and self-defense. Evening entertainment may focus on music, story-telling, color analysis, or handwriting analysis discussions led by Jean Caya Bancroft, an expert in the field. Evernew's all-women staff, which includes a nutritionist/dietitian, a menu consultant, fitness instructors skilled in yoga, dance, aerobics, and calisthenics, a nail care practitioner, massage therapists, and estheticians, take an active part in all the spa activities and join with guests in meals and entertainment, a practice which assures a companionable, sharing, caring, nurturing ambience. There is no dressing up. Everyone is encouraged to feel comfortable and to be themselves.

Attractions in the South Hadley area include unique crafts shops, charming architecture, farmers' markets, antique shops, county and town fairs, historic sites and residences, nearby co-ed Amherst College, and the Berkshire Music Festival a 90-minute drive to the west.

Name: Evernew

Mailing Address: 67 Temple Street, West Newton, MA 02165 (Barbara Slater); Mount Holyoke College, South Hadley, Massachusetts 01075 (the spa)

Telephone: (617) 332-8010

Established: 1985

Managing Director: Barbara Slater, J.D. (Doctor of Jurisprudence)

Program Directors: Barbara Slater; Nancy Tulowiecki, Fitness Manager

Owner: Barbara Slater

Gender and Age Restrictions: Women only; 18 to 70

Season: From last week in June to mid-August

Length of Stay Required: Miniweek, Sunday through Tuesday; 6 days/5 nights, Sunday through Friday

Programs Offered: The highly structured but permissive, optional program is designed to improve physical and emotional health for a healthier lifestyle. Weight management focuses on healthy, nutritional eating habits and the incorporation of regular exercise into daily life. In the initial group orientation upon arrival of guests, Barbara Slater and Assistant Director Samantha Koumanelis, who has attained black belt proficiency in the martial arts and who teaches a college course on crime prevention, show each guest the personal attention for which Evernew is notable. "We choose to stay away from the 'group therapy' approach," Slater says. Together, in a stress-free, nonjudgmental atmosphere, the guests create their own beneficial ambience in which they can "get away," tone up, relax, have fun, lose weight, exercise, and learn how to change their eating habits.

Exercise classes comprise sunrise yoga, power walking, cardiovascular conditioning, exercise and conditioning classes for all levels, stretch and relaxation classes, aqua-aerobics in the 8-lane, 25-meter college pool, and low- and high-impact aerobics. If guests want to make use of the Hydra-Fitness workout room equipped with stationary bicycles and free weights, or make use of the sauna, they are free to do so. They can play squash, tennis, handball, racquetball, use the college's trails for running, jogging, or walking, hire a horse for $12 an hour, play golf, or hire a bicycle in South Hadley. Golf clubs are rentable for $5 at the golf course, where balls can be bought. Greens fees are $12. Rackets for all ball games are rentable for a pittance at the Kendall Sports Complex where the exercise rooms, dance studios, courts, and pool are housed.

Sandy Hagen, a professional dancer, choreographer, and teacher to whom surgeons and physical therapists regularly send their patients for her conditioning program, evaluates each woman's fitness and flexibility the first day to determine which strengthening exercises she needs. Hagen then works on the way each woman moves, sits, stands, and walks and makes each guest aware of her body alignment and aware also of how improper alignment can cause muscle fatigue and pain. She designs a conditioning program that takes into account, for each guest, areas in need of stretching and toning.

After lunch, guests can relax, sit in the sun or in the sauna, go canoeing on the lake, swim, sightsee, or, for an additional charge, have a massage, facial, manicure or pedicure. Or they can attend workshops on skin care, nutrition, massage basics, gardening, or on subjects previously mentioned in the introduction. After dinner, and before the evening programs, most guests join together for a leisurely twilight stroll. Bedtime is early—9:00 PM—but since wake-up is at 6:30 AM, there are few objections.

Diet and Weight Management: Slater's philosophy is that changes in eating habits work and that diets don't. Slater and Nancy Anderson, Nutritionist/Dietitian, believe that "When you enjoy what you are doing in life, when you are happy about yourself and the choices you are making, when your life is filled with friends, interesting activities, and self-trust, you won't need to fill yourself up with food. So, instead of thinking, 'I need to feed myself, I need to eat,' think

'I need nourishment.' " Fueled with physical and mental nourishment, guests enjoy 1200-calorie daily allowances, 3 meals and a morning and afternoon snack, of caffeine-free beverages (required) and low-fat, low-sodium, high-fiber food. Breakfast: orange slices, French toast with apple-cinnamon syrup. Lunch: vegetable-cheese quiche, mixed green salad, honeydew melon with lime. Dinner: chicken Tandoori, herbed rice, cucumber raita (a yogurt, cucumber, well-seasoned combination), a watermelon wedge for dessert.

Guests are encouraged to reduce their intake of caffeine, simple sugars, refined food products, and fatty meats for a week before they arrive, and to continue to do so when they go home. (Recipes are included in the quarterly newsletters.) Juice breaks include such low-cal energizers as cranberry spritzer, grapefruit/ tangerine, vegetable broth, and California citrus. Snacks midafternoon might be half a frozen banana, popcorn, a mélange of grapes, a mixture of melon slices, a cocoa beverage. Herbed teas, decaffeinated coffee, and water are available at every meal, and guests are encouraged to drink eight 8-ounce containers of water daily.

Beauty Treatments and Welcome Indulgences: Manicures, pedicures, facials, makeup applications are available at extra cost, reasonably priced. The massages, under $40 an hour for a full body massage, are exceptional. Deep-tissue body work that mobilizes energy, enhances joint movement, and releases muscle tension provides the basis for assessment of individual needs or programs for chronic tension-related conditions, such as PMS, headaches, and insomnia; weight management; perineal support; fitness goal-setting; athletic massage; and massage-generated energy. Reflexology, shiatsu, and Swedish massage are combined with acupressure, general massage, relaxing imagery and healing visualization, and deep-muscle work. Self-massage and stretching techniques guests can use on their own are also taught. Super massage therapists and super massages.

Accommodations: Private singles or private doubles, if you request to share a room with a friend or relative, in the relaxed atmosphere of college dormitory life. Bedding, linen, towels are provided. No telephone, no radio, no television unless you bring your own. Dormitory bathrooms have multiple washbasins, toilets, showers, bathtubs. There are public telephones. There are laundry facilities. And the good news is that there is daily maid service. Your bed is made for you.

What to Bring: See USEFUL INFORMATION. Bring whatever is comfortable, casual, informal. No dressing up. Slacks, blue jeans, shorts, exercise clothes are the norm. Bring a bathing suit, light rain gear. You can bring your own tennis balls or golf balls if you plan to play, or buy them in South Hadley. Other sports equipment is readily rentable. If you are coming by car, you might want to toss in a folding beach chair or back-support chair for sitting by the lake. If you are planning on going to the summer theater, fairs, making an excursion to the Berkshire Festival, sight-seeing, bring appropriate informal cottons and a sweater. Otherwise, "This is no fashion show. Everything is supposed to be fun, stress-free. So relax and be comfortable," advises Barbara Slater. If you want to bring a radio or your Walkman, you are free to do so. Keep your jewelry at home. Don't bring any work to do. All sundries, writing materials, and clothing necessities are at hand across the campus in South Hadley.

Documentation from Your Physician: A letter of approval and health profile are required. On arrival, all guests must sign a standard release form.

The Use of Alcohol and Tobacco: No alcohol is allowed on the premises. Smoking is not allowed in any building and permitted outdoors only.

Fees, Method of Payment, Insurance Coverage: The 6-day/5-night program, Sunday to Friday, is $675 per person. Miniweek (Sunday morning through Tuesday, leaving Wednesday morning) is $425. No taxes, no service charge. A deposit is required. Ask about the cancellation policy. No credit cards are accepted. You can pay by personal check, money order, travelers' check, or cash. Gratuities to the member of the housekeeping staff who takes care of your room are welcome. You pay what you wish directly to the service provider. Check with your physician and/or accountant to determine whether your fees are wholly deductible or deductible in part as a medical expense or health maintenance organization fee. It is likely that they may be under section 23(x) of the Internal Revenue Code, under Revenue Ruling 55-261.

Follow-up Assistance: Slater keeps in touch with staff and former guests by monthly postcards recording health facts and inspirational quotations and through a quarterly newsletter.

There is a women's networking alliance open year-round, with meetings every 6 weeks to promote shared information and experience for furthering a healthy women's lifestyle. Cost for membership, $60 annually. At present operating only in Massachusetts, but planned to operate nationwide within a few years.

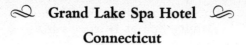 Grand Lake Spa Hotel
Connecticut

Definitely not luxurious, but a good place to go with a friend to lose weight and ease back into exercising without spending a fortune, for those in the New Jersey, Connecticut, New York area, Grand Lake is frequented mostly by older women who prefer the 7-night spa package for $650 and up and by professional women in their 30s who go for the 3-night weekend package for $400 and up. The weight loss program is the focus here, with the promise that you can lose up to 10 pounds or more in a week. Owned and supervised by Natalie Skolnik, a nutritionist and diet counselor, the spa offers a safe, effective weight loss program on a 650-, 900-, 1200-calorie diet. The food is varied, attractively presented, and satisfying. A registered nurse on staff weighs you and checks your blood pressure daily. A 30-minute daily massage is included in your spa package, as well as the use of indoor and outdoor swimming pools, sauna, whirlpool. Optional services include facials and an on-site beauty salon. Cooking classes, health and beauty talks and demonstrations, nutritional seminars, and stress management lectures are included in the evening entertainment programs. Beginner and intermediate level exercise classes are offered in a mirrored exercise room with mats, a barre, and, alas, a carpeted, concrete floor. Fishing on a private lake; 2 tennis courts with free tennis instruction. Bring your own equipment. In the wintertime, there are free cross-country skiing lessons.

The white colonial-style hotel in a 75-acre estate setting offers small, motel-type rooms with single bed, color TV, telephone, individually controlled air-conditioning and heating, private bath. A changing room, but no lockers, so most people change in their own rooms for all activities. A terry-cloth bathrobe is a must here for getting to and from pools, massages, sauna. Lebanon is southeast of Hartford.

Name: Grand Lake Spa Hotel
Mailing Address: Route 207, Lebanon, Connecticut 06249
Telephone: (203) 642-6696; (800) 237-2772 in Connecticut (800) 232-2772 outside Connecticut

Season: Year-round
Gender and Age Restrictions: Co-ed; minimum age 18

The International Health and
Beauty Spa at Gurney's Inn

New York

Nick and Joyce Monte have expanded the original Gurney's Inn, built in 1926, accommodating 24 guests when they bought it in 1956, to a 108-room hostelry. Gurney's offers motel-like accommodations, from studios and suites to cottages, each with 1 or more bedrooms, for use by inn guests and for time-share vacation ownership, as well as for guests at oceanfront conference facilities whose participants repair here for conventions and postmeeting enjoyment of the health and beauty spa. Since the spa was opened in 1979, under the leadership of Baroness von Mengersen, its "international" aspect has been loud-pedaled. Treatments offered include French and German thalassotherapies, Italian fango (mud) therapies, Swedish and Japanese massage techniques, Finnish rock saunas, Swiss showers, Roman baths, Scandinavian Tanfit sunbathing lounges.

Although in recent years Gurney's has frequently been cited as one of the top 10 spas in the world, and it is frequented by celebrities, many guests complain about the food, the service, the caliber of the inn's staff, accommodations with a view of the sea, as promised, but also overlooking a parking lot. Yet few would honestly deny that the buildings, a cluster of green-roofed two- and three-story constructions plus 4 renovated old-time beach cottages not far from the tidemark, are placed in a beautiful setting: the Atlantic Ocean, with its great waves rolling onto miles of white sand beach, the benison of sea air and sand to buff the calluses from your feet in summer or to scrunch against your boots in winter, dunes to clamber across, clam and scallop shells to pick up, a marina, Montauk's landmark lighthouse nearby, and excellent opportunities for sports fishing—blue fin tuna, flounders, mako sharks, marlin, bluefish, striped bass, and more. If you like riding, you can gallop along the beach. You're on the Atlantic flyway for bird-watching. You're close to a state-run public golf links course similar to St. Andrew's in Scotland and Pebble Beach in California, designed by Robert Trent Jones. And, in the summertime, there is the treat of an *al fresco* moonlight massage.

With a maximum capacity of 216 time-share owners and residential guests, plus a daily flow of nonresident health spa and beauty salon visitors and convention attendees, Gurney's permissive spa program allows each guest to determine as active or as relaxing a schedule as desired. At mealtimes, guests scatter to picnic, to snack at the beach restaurant, to eat indoors or outside or in their rooms, reappearing to rest supine on cushioned beach chaises or to involve themselves in the exceptional range and diversity of physical therapy, beauty, and pampering services Gurney's twin men's and women's spa facilities provide. With such a mill of services, treatments, and classes, guests are cautioned to be flexible about their schedules and not to expect that any class or appointment will begin or end precisely at the minute planned.

Name: The International Health and Beauty Spa at Gurney's Inn

Mailing Address: Montauk, Long Island, New York 11954

Telephone: (516) 668-2345

Established: The inn dates back to 1926 and was acquired by Nick and Joyce Monte in 1956; the spa was established in 1979.

Managing Directors: Nick and Joyce Monte, keepers of the inn; Angelo and Gladys Monte, General Managers

Program Directors: Baroness von Mengersen, Director of Spa and Spa Operations; Margaret McNeill, Associate Spa Director; Nesha Tibbits, Fitness Director; Nancy Latorre, Director of the Salon de Beauté

Owners: Nick and Joyce Monte

Gender and Age Restrictions: None at the inn. Co-ed; minimum age 18 for the spa. No facilities for children, and guests under age 18 can use the indoor pool only between 1 and 2 PM and after 6 PM when the pool is also available for nonresidents. "Especially not recommended for children under 14!"

Season: Year-round

Length of Stay Required: Day of Beauty for women, *Day of Vitality* for men, any weekday, including spa cuisine lunch, not available on weekends or holidays; *4-Day Health and Beauty Plan* (5 days/4 nights), *4-Day Marine Renewal Plan* (5 days/4 nights), starting Sunday or Monday, ending Thursday or Friday; *5-Day Executive Longevity Program* (6 days/5 nights), starting Sunday, ending Friday, or Friday ending Wednesday; *7-Day Rejuvenation Plan* (8 days/7 nights), starting any day of the week, check in 3 PM, check out noon. Spa available also for nonresident guests on a daily facility fee basis; services and treatments à la carte. Minimum stay of a week is requested for peak season between June 5 and September 7. A 4-day minimum stay is requested for Memorial Day, 3 days for Columbus Day, Easter, Passover, and Rosh Hashanah.

Programs Offered: After completing a health questionnaire, reviewed by a registered nurse in attendance, you are given a blood pressure check and a nutrition consultation and your measurements and weight are recorded. The staff gives advice for an individualized program of exercise classes, beauty treatments, and therapies. The twin spa pavilions, one for men and one for women, are open from 8:00 AM to 10:00 PM. All resident spa plans include use of the 35- by 60-foot indoor seawater co-ed pool with south-facing ceiling-to-floor windows for ocean views; rock saunas; steam rooms; Swiss showers; Roman baths (Jacuzzi-type pools with sides shaped to form benches and water heated to 101 degrees F in the ladies' pool and 105 degrees F in the men's pool) with the diffused spray also serving to turn this room into an inhalation room. Locker rooms and siesta rooms with cots and blankets are provided. The gyms each contain 2 Monark stationary bicycles, a Concept II rowing machine, a 15-station Universal and a 6-station Nautilus weight-training machine. Before you start on the 14-station parcours, which combines aerobic, strengthening, and stretching exercises, you are advised to make an appointment with one of the 6 licensed fitness instructors on staff who will conduct a guided tour to demonstrate heart checks, pacing, and exercises appropriate to your fitness level.

Group exercise classes include a beach walk at the beginning of the day; stretching; calisthenics; cardiovascular and isometric exercises; supervised parcours; hatha-yoga; aerobic exercises and dance; body contour; weight-training instruction; hydro-calisthenics; beginner's aerobic advanced, and aerobic lap swimming; swimming stroke improvement (private swimming lessons are also available); and aquatic conditioning. A few classes may convene on the beach or on the Astroturf of the spa's sun roof.

You can select from *8 "massotherapies"* administered by the spa's licensed massage therapists: Swedish massage; athletic massage, concentrating primarily on the muscles used in your sport; cosmetic lymph drainage, to reduce puffy or swollen tissues; shiatsu; deep fascia manipulation to relieve tension and pain; polarity, a relaxation treatment; reflexology, Trager Psychophysical Integration, a technique using rocking movements for relief of tension. Aromatherapy massage, using aromatic herbal oils, is also available, as are herbal wraps. "Thermotherapy" to release tension, good for achy joints and arthritis, is fango (Italian for mud) therapy. Not just any old mud, but mud from the hot springs of Battaglia in northern Italy, heated to 116 degrees and mixed with paraffin, applied as a therapist massages your feet and calves with warm almond oil.

Hydrotherapies include the Swiss shower, and the Vichy treatment (overhead hot and cold fresh water needle showers of varying velocity raining down on you) followed by an exfoliating rub with Dead Sea salt mixed into a paste with almond oil, or a loofah scrub with tingling mint soap. All treatments end with a fresh-water spray.

What the spa is best known for are the thalasso (sea water) therapies, or marinotherapies, in a bath (balneotherapy) or in thalasso-seaweed combinations, such as the Seaweed Cell Fluid Wrap where you are lathered in an extract of seaweed imported from St. Malo in France's Brittany, then loosely wrapped in Irish linen sheets soaked in seaweed cell liquid while heat packs are applied. After the treatment, your skin will feel smooth and soft, although few dermatologists would agree with the long-term benefits claimed. Other treatments are the German thalassomassage where underwater jets massage your body, which is immersed in a private tub heated to an invitingly warm temperature, while a therapist massages you with a special underwater hose; and the Hydro Relaxation treatment, which surrounds you with bubbles and "floats" you with the gentle pressure of underwater jets.

The spa also offers hypnotherapy on a one-session basis for smoking and overeating, and individually designed cardiovascular programs. The therapists, technicians, and estheticians are competent and capable, many highly skilled, but with so many people coming and going, personal attention is not a strong point here. The spa locker rooms can be crowded, and there are often as many as 35 to 40 people splashing about at the same time in the indoor sea-water pool. Exercise classes, commendably, are limited to groups of 5 to 15 men or women.

Entertainment includes such regularly scheduled events as a palm and tarot card reader, an astrologer, a movie of the week, a makeup demonstration, bingo games, bridge games, art exhibits by local artists, hospitality receptions, a spa cocktail party offering low-cal spa wine and crudités with a low-cal vegetable dip, talks on nutrition and health and fitness.

An Exercise Physiology Unit administered by certified specialists of the American College of Sports Medicine supervises a resident/nonresident *Adult Fitness testing program,* and offers a comprehensive health/fitness profile with these components: an evaluation of your current health/fitness status; a cardiovascular assessment using a bicycle ergometer; caliper skinfold measurements to determine the ratio of your lean to fat tissue; a pulmonary assessment of your lung volume and expiratory flow rates; an anaerobic isometric strength assessment to determine your overall body strength; a torso stability evaluation, which encompasses abdominal muscular endurance and hip/hamstring flexibility; a musculoskeletal health assessment to examine your range of motion, posture, gaits, flexibility, and skeletal alignment to determine possible weak or problem areas for special exercise prescriptions; and exercise prescriptions for short- and long-term goals. Reasonable rates.

A Physical Therapy Center makes it possible for the spa to treat specific complaints of its resident and nonresident guests.

The *5-day Executive Longevity Program* focuses on exercise, stress reduction, and nutrition. You receive a comprehensive health/fitness profile supervised by certified exercise physiologists. At the end of the program, you get an information packet containing the results of your health assessment and your personal fitness prescription as well as other useful information concerning the maintenance of your future well-being.

With the *7-day Rejuvenation Plan,* besides the use of all spa facilities, you get 2 German thalassotherapies, 2 Italian fango packs, 2 herbal wraps, unlimited use of sea water Roman baths, 2 choices of brush and tone therapies or French Vichy treatments with either Salt-Glo loofah, 6 half-hour Swedish massages, one 30-minute aromatherapy massage, 7 aerobic morning beach walks, 21 conditioning and exercise classes as prescribed, 1 health/fitness profile with musculoskeletal health assessment, 1 private exercise class based on health assessments, 1 half-hour facial treatment, 1 hour-long facial, 1 shampoo and styling set (cut, shampoo, and styling for men), 1 hair conditioning oil treatment, 1 manicure, 1 nail polish change, 1 pedicure, 1 makeup application (treatment of choice for men).

There are special programs on Thanksgiving, Easter, Passover, Christmas, New Year's, Rosh Hashanah, and Chanakah. The outdoor patio becomes an ice-skating rink from Thanksgiving to Easter.

Diet and Weight Management: Spa meals are designed to provide an average of 800, 1000, or 1200 calories daily, depending on the entrées or additions you choose. Nutritionally well-balanced meals, with fresh, natural ingredients, are high in fiber, low in fat, cholesterol, sugar, salt, and calories. With advance notice, special arrangements can be made for vegetarians or guests on special diets. It is suggested that vegetarians, smokers, pregnant women, heavy drinkers, lactating women, people "with frequent illnesses," and long-term antibiotic users take vitamin-mineral supplements. Meals are planned on an 8-day rotation basis so that you never get the same lunch or dinner menu if you stay for a week, and low-cal meals are provided for holiday festivities as well. A New Year's Eve low-cal dinner might include lobster, shrimp, salad, and a wee nip of champagne.

The spa dining room is small, light, bright, and airy, with picture windows overlooking the beach. Dietitians come to each table during lunch to answer questions and share menus and recipes. Spa meals can also be enjoyed in the main resort dining room, but don't look for the portion control here that you get in the spa dining room. Let's hope that by the time you try either dining room the service will have improved.

What do you get for breakfast? A soft-boiled egg and a slice of whole-grain bread, or a serving of hot cereal with ½ cup of skim milk, or a small bran muffin, half a fresh grapefruit or 4 ounces of orange or grapefruit juice, also choices of egg white omelettes with herbs or low-fat cottage cheese, low-fat cottage cheese and herbs with mushrooms, yogurts, breads, fresh fruit in season. The calories of each item are marked on the menu. Mineral water is available at extra cost.

Lunch? A choice of appetizers, such as breaded eggplant sticks, wedge of melon with lemon, potato leek soup; a choice of salads; a choice of entrées: mushroom stuffed fish rolls, vegetables au gratin, broiled Peconic Bay scallops served on a bed of spinach; a choice of desserts, such as orange whip, fresh fruit cup, frozen banana, chiffon cake. A light Chablis is available at extra cost.

Dinner might have for starters Gazpacho Andalusian or artichoke vinaigrette; a choice of carrot and cabbage, spinach and mushroom, or cucumber yogurt salad; followed by veal Marsala with fresh mushrooms and herbs, seafood paella Valencia with spicy tomato sauce served over a bed of brown rice; vegetable lasagna. For dessert, a choice of custard, pineapple-lemon whip, ginger apples, or fresh fruit with Amaretto.

If you must have between-meal snacks, stay away from Gurney's new pastry showcase but choose juices and crudités with low-fat cottage cheese or yogurt dip, available in both the men's and women's spa quarters. You can picnic on the beach—box lunches and picnic baskets are available on request for all-day outings—or dine informally, if you wish, at the Riviera Patio.

Beauty Treatments and Welcome Indulgences: Marino Vital seaweed products imported from France's Brittany coast and Milopa skin care and cosmetic products from Switzerland are for sale as well as gift baskets of beauty products in the spa. The full-service Salon de Beauté, which accommodates both men and women, is open from 10:00 AM to 6:00 PM 7 days a week. Manicures and pedicures with heated mittens and booties are a specialty. This is where you come for body, lip, eyebrow, and chin waxing; permanent waves, hair coloring, shampoos, styling, haircuts, skin and hair analysis, a variety of facials, including one called Ocean Breeze that could become addictive for its zippy, tingling, alive, alive-oh! effect.

Accommodations: Overlooking the main parking lot and furthest from the ocean are the Flying Bridge, Promenade Deck, Forecastle, and Chart House buildings with double rooms and suites including refrigerator. The Forward Watch, the Foredeck, and the 4 cottages—Lookout, Crow's Nest, Quarterdeck, and Bridge—have unobstructed beach and ocean views. Each cottage has a living room with a fireplace, from 1 to 3 bedrooms, kitchen pantry with refrigerator, sun porch, and private decks with lounge chairs for sunning. The majority of the units have time-share owners with about 25 percent of the units regularly available on a rental basis to spa-goers and vacationers. What you get depends on what accommodations are available. Most of the accommodations are decorated in brown in motel-room style. The welcome exception is the new Foredeck, where the decor is rose, grey, and white. All have private ceramic tile bath and shower, dressing room, color TV, direct dial telephone, coffee maker, heat and air-conditioning, queen- or king-sized beds, and most have private terraces.

Corner rooms on the beachfront Forward Watch have 50-foot wraparound terraces for private entertaining, and the top deck of the Forward Watch, called the Lido, is available for private parties. Lovers of peace, quiet, and solitude should request accommodations away from these areas.

What to Bring: See USEFUL INFORMATION. Bring sweaters for cool early mornings and evenings even in the summertime; waterproof ponchos for boating and/or rain gear; warmies, woolies, and thermals for wintertime. Bring appropriate gear if you plan to play golf. Blue jeans and jodhpur boots or even sneakers will do if you plan to ride. Sunglasses are a must, and cotton turbans or beach hats come in handy. Day wear is casual. For evenings, women will want to bring dresses, caftans, skirts, tops; evening shawls, capes, sweaters; dressy pants outfits. Men are expected to wear a jacket and tie or the Southampton regimentals of navy blue blazer and white trousers if they really want to look classy. Sports apparel is available at the on-site boutique. Towels and terry-cloth robes are provided at the spa. Camera, film, your Walkman, reading and writing materials, and a totebag for seashell collectors may be necessities for some, pleasant extras for others.

Documentation from Your Physician: Neither requested nor required unless you have a medical problem.

The Use of Alcohol and Tobacco: No smoking or drinking allowed in the spa. No smoking allowed in the spa dining room. No restrictions elsewhere.

Fees, Method of Payment, Insurance Coverage: Pricing is complicated. Everything not covered in your spa package price is available à la carte, as it is to those guests at the inn who may want treatments and classes without signing on for a full spa stay.

Year-round rates:

7-day Rejuvenation Spa Plan: $775 PLUS room rate of your choice
5-day Executive Longevity Program: $628 PLUS room rate of your choice
4-day Health and Beauty Plan: $495 PLUS room rate of your choice
4-day Marine Renewal Plan: $339 PLUS room rate of your choice
Day of Beauty/Vitality: $127
Adult Fitness testing program: $150

Nonresident spa plans:

7-day Rejuvenation Plan: $915 with all meals; $810 with lunch only
5-day Executive Longevity Program: $753 with all meals; $678 with lunch only

4-day Health and Beauty/Marine Renewal Plan: $439 to $550 with all meals; $379 to $490 with lunch only

In the high season (mid-June to mid-September), rooms range from $115 to $150 per person (double occupancy) per night, depending on location, view, and furnishings. Rates are higher for deluxe accommodations. The 4 beach cottages, with occupancy by 2, 4, or 6 persons, at peak-season rates, cost from $150 to $160 per person per night. All prices are subject to change, and all rates are subject to a 15 percent service charge and sales tax of 7.5 percent where applicable. (The service charge is subject to sales tax.) A deposit is required. Ask about the cancellation policy. Payment is accepted in cash or by personal check (with driver's license and major credit card ID), Optima, Discover, American Express, Diners, Visa, MasterCard or travelers' checks. Fees may be tax-deductible in part as a medical expense if this is confirmed by a letter from your physician.

Follow-up Assistance: Varies according to plan. On the *7-day Rejuvenation Plan* you receive recipes and recommendations for diet and exercise, and you may telephone the spa director or the exercise physiologist for advice and recommendations at any time.

✑ Kripalu Center for Yoga and Health ✑
Massachusetts

Situated in the beautiful Berkshires, next door to the summertime Tanglewood Music Festival, close to Stockbridge, Kripalu has an inspiring setting of 350 acres of forests, meadows, meditation gardens, miles of woodland trails, a private beach on Lake Mahkeenac for swimming, fishing, and boating. Andrew Carnegie, the legendary philanthropist, once owned the estate with its scenic forest and lake views. Formerly a Jesuit Novitiate, the huge brick building houses a staff of 250, plus tuition-free work-study residents, plus a maximum of 225 guests in private, semiprivate, and dormitory accommodations, institution-formidable on the exterior but attractive, cheerful, airy, and bright inside. No television, no private telephones, no daily newspapers, Kripalu is a true retreat. This haven is for all who seek physical, mental, and spiritual well-being through the practice of yoga, comprehensive training programs, innovative personal growth workshops, aerobic exercise, vegetarian cuisine, and the option of a *Health for Life* program as well as superb individual health services.

The founder and guiding force of Kripalu is Yogi Amrit Desai, born in 1934, married, father of three children, and often referred to by his disciples as

Gurudev (beloved teacher). All the staff at Kripalu have alternate Sanskrit names and are remarkably caring, healthy, cheerful, and friendly. The center attracts men and women with an average age of around 35 for many of its programs, men and women with an average age between 50 and 65 for its *Health for Life* program, and parents with children, for whom there is no charge up to the age of 3 and for whom, aged 4 to 12, there is an excellent summer day camp.

Kripalu is about as far removed as you can get from Hare Krishna cults, aberrated Buddhist and Tantric groups given to sex orgies, and phony-baloney "Oriental" groups big on peacock feathers and incense. The ambience here for programs of yoga, self-discovery, relaxing, unwinding, and unfolding draws as much on Christian-Judeo themes as it does on the practice of *pranayama* (a form of breathing that quiets the mind for meditation). "Your body is the most sacred place of pilgrimage to which you'll ever come," the charismatic Desai has written. "It is the dwelling place of the divine spirit, it is the true temple of God. Go within and experience the glory of God within you. . . . When you love the body, know that you are not the body but the soul."

The supportive environment at Kripalu in which people can make the change to a more healthful, stress-free way of being is enhanced by a peaceful atmosphere where vegetarian meals are eaten in silence, and by the security of a full staff of medical personnel, which allows guests with a wide range of stress-related and other medical problems to improve their personal well-being, while others who are fit and healthy learn techniques for continuing good health.

Because Kripalu is a nonprofit organization, costs are kept down, and prices are refreshingly affordable. At these prices, people don't mind being asked to bring their own blanket or mat for yoga exercises, or make their own bed. Summer, winter, spring, or autumn, Kripalu is a unique environment for personal development, greater health, and lasting take-home benefits.

Name: Kripalu Center for Yoga and Health

Mailing Address: P.O. Box 793, Lenox, Massachusetts 01240

Telephone: (413) 637-3280 (Monday through Saturday, 8:30 AM to 5:00 PM)

Established: 1971

Managing Director: 5-member board of directors headed by Sandra Healy

Program Directors: Sandra Healy, Chief Administrator; *Health for Life* program: Jo Ann Levitt, R.N., Program Director, Ron Dushkin, M.D., Medical Director

Owner: Kripalu Yoga Fellowship, a nonprofit corporation

Gender and Age Restrictions: Co-ed. Infants to children through age 12 are welcome any time of year as long as adult supervision is provided. From the end of June through the end of August, a summer day camp at Kripalu serves children 4 through 12. No program is provided for ages 13 through 16, and you are asked not to bring youngsters 13 through 15. Young adults 16 and older can attend adult programs at adult rates. No upper age limit.

Season: Year-round except for 1 week each in September, January, and April;

inquire for exact dates. Arrival time 2:00 to 5:00 PM, departure 2:00 PM

Length of Stay Required: 2 nights minimum; 3 nights minimum during Christmas holidays and July to mid-August

Programs Offered: All programs are aimed at discovering your inner capacity for greater health and happiness, abundant energy, long-lasting contentment, and limitless ability to love.

The *Rest and Renewal* program is basically unstructured, with the option of combining any of these activities: yoga classes, danskinetics (a special Kripalu blend of yoga, aerobics, and dance), toning and conditioning classes, aerobic hikes and nature walks, morning and evening meditation, relaxation training, nutrition lectures and cooking classes, workshops on such topics as communication and stress management, tennis clinics, sauna and whirlpool, individual health services at additional cost.

There are programs for a weekend or a week on self-discovery (the art of communication, a workshop for married couples, a workshop on relationships, a workshop on inner quest, self-esteem). There are programs for a weekend, a week, or a month on health (transform stress/learn to relax, holistic health training, and the *Health for Life* program). There are weekend, week-long, and month-long programs in yoga, dance, and fitness and a tuition-free (free for US residents only) work/study program in spiritual lifestyle training.

The 21-day/20-night program of *Health for Life* for no more than 22 participants, addresses weight management among other aspects of health and healing in a holistic approach that encompasses diet, nutrition education, behavior modification, and exercise. It includes a 60-minute physical examination and evaluation by a resident physician, both at the beginning and at the end of the program, daily monitoring, education, and counseling support. (The program is directed and staffed by 2 M.D.s and 2 R.N.s.) The initial consultation includes a stress test, optional blood chemistry workup and laboratory tests as required, and body measurements including ratio of fat to lean tissue, with twice-a-week check-ups for the remainder of the program. This is supplemented by daily consultations with registered nurses and class teachers, 6 hours of nutrition counseling, daily relaxation training, 4 hours a week of personal behavior modification counseling by registered nurses and psychologists, 5 hours a week of training in stress management and relaxation techniques, and 6 cooking classes and demonstrations. Scheduled for completion in 1990, the new *Health for Life Building* will feature its own guestrooms, work-out rooms and dining room with lakeside views.

A highlight of the program is a series of 7 individualized bodywork sessions. A skilled therapist helps you release feelings and attitudes that may have caused chronic tension and muscular stress, with therapeutic massage, acupressure, reflexology, and yoga. Daily therapeutic yoga classes focus on repatterning postural imbalances in order to strengthen your body's weak areas. Specialized stretching movements increase your flexibility, and breath training improves your capacity to exercise. Walking, hiking, and dancing are included for aerobic fitness. All exercise programs are tailored to your individual needs and capacities.

For relaxation, you receive practical training in guided visualizations and meditation. The program offers more than 80 hours of seminars and practical experience to teach you how to maintain your health for life at home. At the end of the program, you meet with staff members, medical doctors, bodywork therapist, nurses, trained health counselors, and yoga therapists, to discuss your specific health challenges and how to respond to them.

In the summer, there is lake swimming supervised by a lifeguard. In winter, there is cross-country skiing and ice-skating if you bring your own equipment. If you bring your own racket and tennis balls, you can play on Kripalu's 6 tennis courts—usable, but not in great condition—or have tennis lessons. If you bring your own fishing gear or collapsible boat and paddle, you can make use of Lake Mahkeenac for fishing (no license required) or paddling about within view of the lifeguard.

Days begin at 5:45 AM. Evening programs, every evening, include dancing, chanting, workshops, and, in season, wonderfully convenient, the concerts at Tanglewood not more than a 10-minute walk away offer the pleasure of the Boston Symphony's best outdoor music. There are men's and women's saunas, men's and women's whirlpools, as well as a flotation tank for deep relaxation (see Beauty Treatments and Welcome Indulgences).

Diet and Weight Management: The menu is lacto-vegetarian with dairy and nondairy food choices; that is, fruit, vegetables, whole grains, legumes, lots of fiber and protein, very few fats and sweeteners, no red meat, no fish, no eggs, no salt, no caffeine, no alcohol. Whole milk, low-fat milk, and yogurt are available as well as a variety of low-calorie soft cheeses for salads, salad dressings, and spreads. Meals are eaten at rectangular tables seating 8 in a large, carpeted room with windows looking out on mountains. Silence is observed at meals. This practice gives you an awareness of chewing and of food—conscious eating—so that you are likely to eat less, feel more satisfied with what you are eating, and be more aware of the taste and texture of food. With a chance to sit quietly and simply think, each meal is a sort of meditation in itself. You serve yourself from a buffet. There is no calorie counting. You can eat as much as you want or as little.

Here's what you get for breakfast: oranges, bananas, apples; a choice of cold or hot cereals; vegetable soup, brown rice, miso (soy bean paste), honey, maple syrup, tahini (sesame seed paste), scallions, corn, oat milk, raisins, sunflower seeds, herbal tea, hot or cold whole milk, or low-fat milk.

For lunch, there's soup—lentil, split pea, black bean, and vegetable mine-strone are typical. The main entrée may be pizza or pasta, a dairy lasagna with cheese, a nondairy lasagna with tofu. At the salad bar, there are dairy dressings (blue cheese or thousand island) or nonoil, nondairy dressings made with beets or carrots, garlic, tahini, and spice, or Greek tamari (a sort of soy sauce). Rice, millet, or other whole grains are served. You have steamed vegetables—carrots, broccoli, kale, collards, Chinese cabbage. There are also sea vegetables—hijiki, arame, wakame—good sources of minerals, rich in plankton, cultivated sea-weeds, actually. Baked potatoes are usually on the menu, as well as stone-ground whole-wheat or sourdough bread from Kripalu's bakery. Fresh bread is made every other day.

Lunch is the main meal of the day. Dinner is a simpler version of lunch, less of an extravaganza of choices. Desserts are served once a week. Fresh fruit, whole milk, or low-fat milk are available at every meal. Bancha, a twig tea made from parts of the tea bush that have low or no caffeine, hot or cold, with a taste somewhat like carob or chocolate, is always available in carafes throughout the center. Halvah, a confection made with honey and nuts, can be bought at the Kripalu store. Through conscious eating, many participants lose as much as 4 pounds a week, both at the center and at home, and are able to maintain weight loss.

Beauty Treatments and Welcome Indulgences: Hour-long sessions of individual health services are available by appointment Monday from 10:00 to 11:00 AM and 2:00 to 4:30 PM, Tuesday through Saturday from 8:30 to 11:00 AM and 2:00 to 4:30 PM. A great many people who experience these health services speak of "rejuvenation," "transformation," therapists' hands that "radiate love." To en-sure receiving the service of your choice, Kripalu recommends that *you make reservations at least 3 weeks in advance* by calling the Health Services Scheduling Office, (413) 637-3280, for the following 60-minutes sessions, which are also obtainable at a reduced rate for a series of 6: foot care/reflexology; polarity therapy, which consists of gentle contacts and rocking manipulations to "con-nect, stimulate, and balance your body's polar energies," to redirect your energy "beyond a physical level to an experience of mental and emotional balance"; shiatsu therapy "to bring balance to your body's energy, relax your internal organs, release your healing potential"; Kripalu bodywork "to facilitate the release of muscular tension, increase circulation, improve recovery from physical fatigue," with the therapist drawing from a wide range of skills that may combine acupressure, trigger point stimulation, polarity, and soft-tissue manipulation; advanced bodywork, which employs the same techniques as Kripalu bodywork in combination with dialogue, creative visualization, and affirmation, which "assist in understanding how your mental attitudes and emotions affect your body"; yoga therapy for repatterning muscles and improving postural alignment. All these sessions cost between $35 and $40 for 60 minutes. A 1¾-hour session for facial skin care, including heat treatments and gentle bodywork to relax your hands and feet, may be just about the best facial you have ever had for $60. An hour's session in a flotation tank—a back-to-the-womb experience—costs $30 including guidance by a trained staff member during "the resulting physical relaxation which draws your mind into a profound state of stillness." A comprehensive health service package, including 2 Kripalu bodywork sessions (advanced bodywork $10 extra per session), facial skin care, foot care/reflexology, polarity therapy, and yoga therapy costs $200. Private counseling sessions are available for $35 an hour.

Accommodations: Standard, doubles, and deluxe. Standard are dormitory rooms for 10 to 22 people furnished with substantial maple bunk beds for which you provide your own blankets, sheets, pillow and case, or a sleeping bag. (You can also rent sheets and towels for a minimal charge when you arrive.) These accommodations, thickly carpeted, furnished with wardrobe units, are light, bright, with mountain views, share large hall bathroom(s) with multiple tubs, showers, basins. Doubles are small rooms for 2, carpeted, furnished with platform beds, wardrobe unit, also light and bright with mountain views, also share a hall bathroom. With deluxe rooms, sheets, blankets, and towels are provided, and you have a choice of double or twin beds and of a hall or private bathroom. These rooms are carpeted, furnished with a bureau, wicker settee, or chairs. Your sheets are changed twice a week by a staff member. There is no maid service at the center. All cleaning and maintenance work is done by staff members.

What to Bring: See USEFUL INFORMATION. Bring loose-fitting sports clothes, shorts, slacks, warm-ups for easy body movement; lightweight shoes or slippers for house wear; "modest one-piece swimsuit" for whirlpool or lake; required cover-up for swimsuit or leotard except in the spa areas or in dance classes; tennis racket or other outdoor gear of your choice (fishing gear, ice skates, cross-country skis, paddle boat); warm clothing for cool evenings and mornings; rainwear. The dress code is "modest dress appropriate to a spiritual institution." There is an on-site library, and an off-site neighborhood store where sundries and items of personal hygiene can be bought. You are asked not to bring your Walkman, portable radio, or TV. Bring your own writing materials. Bring yoga mat, extra blanket, and/or meditation cushion to sit on.

Documentation from Your Physician: The *Health for Life Program* requires documentation of as recent a physical examination as possible be sent with... ɔ weeks of the start of the program.

The Use of Alcohol and Tobacco: Alcohol is forbidden on the premises. No smoking is allowed inside the building. Smoking is discouraged, but permitted outside the building.

Fees, Method of Payment, Insurance Coverage: Year-round rates:

For *Rest and Renewal* program, depending on choice of accommodations and view: from $50 to $115 per day

For *Health for Life* program: $2800 (plus Medical Option: $450)

For each child 4 to 12: $20 per day; $30 during July and August

Midweek winter packages offer reduced daily rates on *Rest and Renewal* program. Infants through 3 years of age are free of charge, but must be supervised at all times, which may mean bringing along a babysitter or sharing supervision. A deposit is required. Ask about the cancellation policy. Fees are payable by cash, personal check, travelers' checks, Visa, or MasterCard. They may be tax-deductible in part if programs taken are used to maintain or improve skills required in your work, or as a medical expense (*Health for Life* program). Consult your tax advisor.

⊰ New Life Spa ⊱
Vermont

Ritzy and glitzy it isn't, but if you appreciate value and quality at affordable prices, Jimmy LeSage's New Life Spa in the foothills of Vermont's Stratton Mountain may be the best possible place to come to celebrate the birthday of a lifetime of nutritional, physical, and mental well-being. Jimmy LeSage is New Life's owner, founder, and resident guru, and the author of the *New Life Guide to Healthy Eating.* Men and women, from 18 to 80, single, married, couples, young professionals and senior citizens, some involved with legal, financial, sales, and business professions, some involved in the arts, some performing artists, representatives of widely ranging income brackets, some with 5 pounds to lose, some with 20 or more to shed, some who simply want to enjoy a fitness vacation and/or disencumber themselves of stress—all have gone on record to praise New Life's diet, exercise, and behavior modification benefits. Jimmy LeSage is appreciated also by fellow spa owners and founders such as Mel Zuckerman, of Canyon Ranch Resort (see AMERICAN SPAS: WEST), who describes New Life's assets as "integrity of programming, good food, a comfortable atmosphere, and people who care about you." New Life Spa is his "summer getaway." From a fellow of Zuckerman's experience and exacting criteria, this is hard-won, well-earned praise, but Jimmy LeSage, with his attractive and comfortable New Life Spa, and his philosophy of life beyond spa-dom in the real world, deserves all the encomiums he receives.

New Life Spa is not an all-in-one physical plant. It makes use of the estate and facilities of Liftline Lodge, the adjacent Glockenhof chalet, and the Stratton Sports Center, with springtime and summer golf a mile distant at the championship Stratton Mountain golf course, to come up with a thoughtfully planned spa program, health retreat, and fitness vacation. You're in the heart of southern Vermont's Green Mountain National Forest area and you'll do best if you bring your own car for nonscheduled nature trips, historic sight-seeing, and shopping at the many discount outlet stores located in and around the old village of Manchester, where the streets are still paved with the original Dorset marble. In barns and boutiques around Route 7 you'll find a shopper's heaven where you can save enough to pay for your week at New Life while you indulge in the virtuous exercise of aerobic bargain-hunting, sprinting from closeouts of Christian Diors and Polo/Ralph Lauren to classic buys at Orvis, Anne Klein, Purdy's, Johnny Appleseed, and regional wood, glass, and wool specialties. (A smidgin of Vermont maple sugar or maple syrup? "If you want maple taste, always use the real thing instead of commercial brands mostly made of corn syrup and artificial flavorings," says Jimmy LeSage.) For Stratton area trail maps, mountain information, children's ski school programs, call (802) 297-2200. For weather conditions, call (802) 297-2211.

Name: New Life Spa
Mailing Address: Liftline Lodge, Stratton Mountain, Vermont 05155
Telephone: (802) 297-2534
Established: 1978
Managing Director: James T. LeSage
Program Director: James T. LeSage
Owner: James T. LeSage

Gender and Age Restrictions: Co-ed; minimum age 14
Season: Mid-March to mid-September; closed October and for 2 weeks over Christmas and New Year's
Length of Stay Required: 7 days/6 nights

Programs Offered: Here are realistic, sensible, straightforward approaches to lifestyle changes with emphasis on weight loss through a good-to-eat, low-cal, high-fiber eating regimen; physical activity with exercise classes that balance cardiovascular fitness with stretching and strengthening supervised by certified instructors; behavior modification, nutrition education, and stress reduction. Guests have full use of the Stratton Sports Center complex which includes free indoor tennis, indoor swimming, racquetball, fully equipped Nautilus exercise room, steam room, Jacuzzi, in addition to the rowing machine, NordicTrack, stationary bicycles, rebounders, and stairs (real ones!) at the Glockenhof Lodge, where you also sleep, are massaged, enjoy manicures and facials, soak in a hot tub, and steam in a sauna. The number of participants in the *New Life Program* is limited to 40 a week to ensure individual attention. Flexible scheduling for all programs includes time for swimming, hiking, tennis indoors or outside, racquetball, excursions, evening entertainment programs. Workouts for all fitness levels are provided, and however much time you wish can be allotted for body and beauty treatments (at extra cost) in addition to the 2 hour-long full body massages included in your program.

The program begins on Sunday afternoon. On arrival, you are measured and weighed; your blood pressure is recorded; your body's ratio of fat to lean tissue is ascertained with skin calipers; your responses to a health questionnaire you have filled out in advance are discussed. Jimmy LeSage, a bespectacled dynamo of energy and enthusiasm, hosts your arrival evening with get-acquainted name games, orientation information, and familiarization with the types of exercise you'll be doing. You'll begin the next day at 9:00 AM (after wake-up at 7:00, breakfast at 8) with gentle stretches to loosen your body for a half-hour walk, and you'll spend a few more minutes with these energizer stretches after your walk. Body Awareness is a 45-minute stretch class to explain and demonstrate proper body alignment and its relationship to the way you move. Body Conditioning is a briskly paced class to exercise your upper body, abdominals, thighs, and arms (using small hand weights) in an hour-long total fitness workout that incorporates some aerobic movement. Aerobics focuses on your cardiovascular endurance with warm-up, workout, and wind-down routines. Body Works is an optional class for those who feel they need more of a workout, integrating the three components of the morning classes in a fast-paced session. If you are interested in jumping rope, speed walking, water calisthenics, or hiking, you can opt for classes in these as well. To fine-tune and tone your system, yoga, aerobic dance, and a variety of other body movement activities are offered. Interspersed in the program are cooking classes and demonstrations as well as tips on the fine art of reading food labels; group training in stress management and relaxation techniques; lectures on preventing and managing sports injuries; a demonstration of guided imagery and visualization techniques to achieve holistic fitness goals. It all adds up to a workable approach to integrating health and fitness techniques into your life in the "real world."

Maximum Number of Guests: 40

Full-Time Health Professionals on Staff: 7; plus 4 massage therapists at New Life Spa and a part-time qualified esthetician; plus the members of the staff at the Stratton Sports Center, racquetball pro, tennis pro, and Nautilus instructor. All the massage therapists have their certification, and everyone on staff is trained in first aid and CPR. Medical services are available at the Otis Clinic, on the mountain 5 minutes distant, and the Mountain Valley Clinic in Londonderry, 15 to 20 minutes away by car.

Diet and Weight Management: Jimmy LeSage describes the diet at the New Life Spa as 800 to 1000 calories a day, modified Pritikin. Neither a health-food purist nor a fanatic, he has worked out a low-sodium, low–saturated fat/cholesterol, high-fiber diet accompanied by caffeine-free beverages (with both lacto-ovo and strictly vegetarian regimens accommodated if desired) that is astonishingly tasty with its moderate use of protein and abundance of complex carbohydrates. His *New Life Guide to Healthy Eating* is a refreshingly honest, practical, and realistic book about good food—how to buy it, order it, prepare it, and pig out on it without gaining weight. From gazpacho and crabmeat salad, cold melon soup, corn chowder, and country vegetable soup to moussaka, pasta primavera, whole-wheat lasagna, and veal with hearts of artichokes, to hot fudge sundaes, banana bread, and strawberries Romanoff, the food recipes included in LeSage's cookbook bespeak his experience as a professional chef. Cleverly low-calorie (20 percent protein, 15 percent fat, 5 percent simple sugar, 60 percent complex carbohydrate), the fare is appetizing in texture, flavor, and color, satisfying even when doled out in sparing servings. Even if you eat large helpings at home, you will maintain your new weight and probably keep on shedding pounds until you reach your ideal weight. Most guests lose from 4 to 6 pounds during their week's stay, tone up, and vow they will trade in their former eating habits for the workable New Life way. The spa's dining room, as *gemütlich* as an Austrian café, which it resembles, is located at the Liftline Lodge and maintained exclusively for spa guests.

Exercise and Physical Therapy Facilities: This is not your conventional spa facility. Instead of a Versa-Climber, Jimmy LeSage uses a flight of real stairs as a workout component. These are in the Glockenhof building, where the workout room contains rebounders, a NordicTrack cross-country skiing machine, a Concept II rowing machine and 2 other rowing machines, weights, 3 stationary bicycles, a yoga studio, massage rooms, and a room for facials, plus a dry sauna and a hot tub. For your aerobic classes, you hie yourself to the Liftline Lodge next door where the main aerobic studio has an advanced spring floor. Outside, there's a heated swimming pool for water sports, plus a clay tennis court. At the Stratton Sports Center, a 5-minute brisk walk away, there's a steam room, a Jacuzzi, a fully equipped Nautilus exercise room, treadmills, indoor tennis courts, and racquetball courts, plus a handsome, palm-fringed pool for indoor lap swimming, all for your pleasure, all at no extra charge.

Opportunites for Recreational Exercise: In addition to those mentioned above, guests can enjoy hiking and walking trails, as well as bird-watching and hill climbing. Golf can be found a mile away at the Stratton Mountain 36-hole golf course (greens fees and club rentals at moderate charges).

Beauty Treatments and Welcome Indulgences: There's an extra charge if you want more than the 1 or 2 massages allotted to you in your program. Manicures, soothing facials, and makeup skilfully administered by the resident esthetician will also cost you extra, as will getting your hair done in the hairdressing salon across the road.

Accommodations: Each of the 23 guestrooms in the two-story Austrian-style Glockenhof chalet, adjacent to the Liftline Lodge, is bright and airy, with built-in storage space, 2 double beds covered with dark blue comforters. Cheerful red curtains are at the windows, a telephone is at your bedside. There's no need for air-conditioning. The bathrooms are standard, but immaculate. You have a TV set, but you would be wise, if you have some must-see program in mind, to record it back home on your VCR. Vermont mountain reception is not the greatest.

What to Bring: See USEFUL INFORMATION. High-top walking shoes are *required* for the hiking program; optional golf and tennis gear, which are available, but you may prefer to bring your own. Dress is casual for meals. Film, writing materials, reading materials, and sundries are all available, and there's an activewear boutique on the premises.

Documentation from Your Physician: A letter of approval, medical history, and documentation of recent physical examination are requested but not required. If you don't bring along this documentation, you will be admitted to the program but will be required to sign a medical release.

The Use of Alcohol and Tobacco: No alcoholic beverages are allowed, and smoking is permitted only inside a guest's room.

Fees, Method of Payment, Insurance Coverage:

New Life Program (7 days/6 nights, mid-March to mid-September): $1280 single, $1095 per person double

Rates are higher for deluxe accommodations and lower in the off-season. All prices are subject to change, and all rates are subject to a 6 percent state tax and a 15 percent service charge. (Any additional tipping is at your own discretion.) A deposit is required. Ask about the cancellation policy. Payment can be made in cash or by personal check, travelers' checks, Visa, or MasterCard. Your accountant or insurance carrier can advise you if your fees and travel expenses are tax-deductible in part on your physician's recommendation.

Follow-up Assistance: A quarterly newsletter advertises seasonal discounts to past guests, video teaching tapes, exercise cassettes, and Jimmy LeSage's *New Life Guide to Healthy Eating* ($13.50 postpaid mail order).

◇ The Norwich Inn Spa & Villas ◇
Connecticut

The Norwich Inn, offering an intimate conference center, rental villas, and a world-class spa, is a quiet, romantic, high-gloss, country-style retreat. It promises the best of two contradictory worlds: a regimen of physical virtue in a "structured, demanding, health and fitness program," according to its spa director, as well as "the nurturing philosophy of spa life—pure, unadulterated pampering," according to its creator, Edward J. Safdie, progenitor of the Sonoma Mission Inn & Spa in California, and The Greenhouse in Texas (see AMERICAN SPAS: WEST COAST and WEST). Renovated and restored at a cost of $3.5 million by Safdie, the 66-room, 3-story, ivy-covered red brick inn, which once attracted Edward, Prince of Wales, and George Bernard Shaw as favored guests, now attracts young professionals, business-oriented spa-goers, and those in the art, entertainment, and fashion worlds with from 5 to 20 pounds to lose. Spa-goers comprise about 40 percent of the inn's guest roster. Adjacent to a 200-acre, PGA-rated 18-hole golf course, the hilltop inn commands a 40-acre parklike estate wooded with oaks, elms, and maples. Among the trees at the forest's outer fringe are 160 light blue clapboard villa buildings with a private clubhouse containing a minispa and an outdoor heated swimming pool available only to villa owners and renters and their guests. Both the villas and the inn are furnished in New England elegance, complete with wood-burning fireplaces, flowered chintz a-bloom on sofas and wing chairs, and gentle Colonial colors. A notable accent of whimsy in the inn's lobby is the towering but lacily delicate white birdcage which houses a pair of Mexican fan-tailed doves. Guestrooms, seductively comfortable, feature country-print wallpaper, scrubbed pine floors, ruffled drawback curtains, fresh flowers and plants, wicker and blanched-wood furniture, antique sleigh beds and four-posters, and floral-sheeted queen-sized lovelies you can sink into. Restrained yet extravagant country-club plushness envelops you in the peach-colored Sun Room, the Hunt Room, the Grill restaurant with its terrace for summertime meals, the ballroom and banquet rooms, and the cozy Pub. The facilities in the sophisticated 1-story spa building a few steps from the inn include everything from aromatherapy and thalassotherapy to Keiser Cam II weight-resistance equipment and a Liferower with a fellow oarsman on a computer screen you can beat if you try hard. The Spa cuisine is as attractive as the pages of Safdie's illustrated book on spa food. If you're looking for additional recreational entertainment, there are seasonal tennis, ice skating, cross-country skiing, trail walking on site, golf next door, and nearby beaches.

If there is free time in your schedule, there's Mystic Seaport, one of America's leading maritime museums, and out-of-Mystic schooner cruises on whalers and clippers beckoning within 20 minutes' motoring from the inn, plus the Mystic Marinelife Aquarium, steamboat cruises, art gallery, Olde Mistick Village's Memory Lane and Doll Museum, antique shops for browsing, and fishing vessels to tour. New London, with its US Coast Guard Academy as well as its Ocean Beach Amusement Park, is only 15 minutes away. You can reach the beach in 20 minutes and Gillette Castle State Park, Goodspeed Opera House, Ivoryton Playhouse, and the Essex Valley Railroad in 30 minutes. New London, East Lyme, Stonington, Groton, Waterford, Norwich—the neighboring areas abound in Indian museums and burial grounds, historic houses, fabulous little museums, opportunities for antique and mall shopping, summertime barbershop quartet and jazz cruises, lobster and chowder fests, charter fishing, and garden tours. And what about the historical Caprilands Herb Farm in Coventry near New London, with year-round attractions and celebrations? The Southeastern Connecticut Tourism District, located in New London, (800) 222-6783 or (203) 444-2206, can supply you with packets of information. Taxis are available, but you'll have more fun if you bring your own wheels to explore the area.

Name: The Norwich Inn Spa & Villas

Mailing Address: 607 West Thames Street, Route 32, Norwich, Connecticut 06360

Telephone: (203) 886-2401; (800) 892-5692

Established: the inn, 1929; the spa, 1987; the villas, 1988

Managing Director: Beth Kucharski

Program Directors: Rigo Brueck, Spa Manager; Diane Kent, Fitness Supervisor;

Paula Upton, Body Skin Supervisor

Owner: Edward J. Safdie Group

Gender and Age Restrictions: None for the inn. Co-ed; minimum age 18 for the spa.

Season: Year-round

Length of Stay Required: 1-day Revitalizer; 1½ day/2 night Norwich Revitalizer; 5-day Spa Program; spa services and meals à la carte on weekends

Programs Offered: Individualized health, beauty, and fitness programs are offered for weight management, stress control, fitness, skin care, and a "revitalization for mind and body." The *1-day Revitalizer* program, from 8:30 AM to 5:30 PM Monday through Friday, includes a choice of 4 body and skin care treatments and 2 fitness classes. For the *48-hour Revitalizer,* check in Monday at 4:00 PM, check out Wednesday at 1:00 PM, or check in Wednesday at 4:00 PM, check out Friday at 1:00 PM, and enjoy a Swedish massage; a honey and almond body scrub, or loofah skin polish, or thalassotherapy treatment; a hand treatment or foot massage-and-masque treatment; a facial; and 3 fitness classes. For the *1½ day Norwich Revitalizer* and the *5-day Spa Program,* check in Sunday at 4:00 PM, check out Friday at 1:00 PM. With the 5 day program, receive 2 full-body Swedish massages; an aromatherapy treatment with a massage of calming mandarin blossom oil or energizing lemon grass oils; 1 hydrotherapy treatment; 1 thalassotherapy treatment; a body scrub or loofah polish; a 4-layer facial; a deep-cleansing facial; a hand treatment (nail shaping and cuticle removal followed by a seaweed or paraffin skin-softening masque); a foot massage and softening, smoothing paraffin foot masque; a scalp and hair treatment; a complete fitness program of aerobics, aqua-aerobics, gym, fitness classes; evening seminars on nutrition, fitness, stress management; and a cooking class and demonstration of spa cuisine preparation. The 5-day program is compulsory, highly structured, and demanding (days begin at 6:45 AM with a 3- to 6-mile hike on hilly terrain along the Atlantic bluffs), but it includes as lagniappe luxurious body and skin care treatments which you generally pay whopping extra fees for elsewhere. The program begins with a private discussion of your goals and your nutritional preferences with Spa Manager Vicki Poth and Fitness Supervisor Vicki Bailey, who will review the medical fitness questionnaire you filled out in advance to determine your level of fitness. A personal tour of the spa facilities follows, then a get-together with other guests over hors d'oeuvres and a 4-ounce toast of wine with an after-dinner guest orientation.

The standard fitness classes comprise limber-and-tone stretching exercises to improve flexibility; a body awareness class to focus on correct body posture and to improve body alignment; a beginner's approach to the movements and deep-breathing techniques of yoga to increase relaxation and inner awareness; a low-impact, high-energy workout to condition and strengthen your cardiovascular system; a pool workout that utilizes the natural resistance of water to strengthen and tone your muscles; a class that focuses on toning, strengthening, and sculpting your lower and upper body; and a monitored workout to strengthen, tone, and contour your body with resistance equipment, free weights, and sessions on machines such as the StairMaster, treadmill, cross-country skier, Lifecycle, and Liferower. On an à la carte basis, and with 24-hour advance notification, an evaluation of your cardiovascular system, body composition, flexibility, and strength and endurance levels makes it possible for an individual program to be tailored to meet your specific fitness needs. Also on an à la carte basis, you can meet with the nutritionist to define your nutritional goals and needs.

Maximum Number of Guests: 120 at the inn; 60 at the spa; 320 in the villas.

Full-Time Health Professionals on Staff: 20 (including 6 exercise instructors and a nutritionist), plus 30 certified body and skin care therapists and 6 estheticians. A doctor is always on call.

Diet and Weight Management: Menus, based on the US Dietary Guidelines and the latest findings of the American Heart Association and the American Cancer Society, emphasize a diet high in complex carbohydrates and low in fat, sugar, and sodium that incorporates delectable New England specialties with pleasing, fresh tastes. The expertise of chef Daniel Kucharski and sous-chef Bernice Veckerelli is evident in dishes such as a salad of arugula and radicchio with hazelnut vinaigrette; a brochette of jumbo shrimp and scallops on a bed of wild rice; spa pizza with goat cheese, fresh tomatoes, mushrooms, and basil; poached pears in a cobweb of multicolored fruit sauces; and a spa tart of cut fresh fruit mounded on honeydew purée and sprinkled with mint leaves, wheat germ, coconut, and slivered almonds. For breakfast, Kucharski whips up hot apple-cinnamon muffins and yogurt and granola ramekins fanned with fruit slices. The morning brioche and crusty whole-wheat rolls studded with currants testify to his baking skills. Outstanding spa presentations are also listed daily on the menus of the Grill, the inn's main restaurant, said to be one of the best in Connecticut. Spa meals are served in the rose-and-green Spa Dining Room, where cooking and food preparation demonstrations are also presented and where game tables and handcrafted checkerboards are invitingly displayed. Lacto-ovo and strictly vegetarian diets and Kosher, lactose-intolerant, and food allergy requirements are accommodated. Calories are not severely restricted: 1200 to 1500 calories for women and 1800 to 2000 calories for men. The spa's philosophy is that this, combined with a daily workout, will promote permanent weight loss rather than the rebound effect of stringent dieting.

Exercise and Physical Therapy Facilities: The Georgian-style whitewashed brick spa building, separated from the inn by a shallow stone stairway, is 20,000 handsome square feet, centered by a ceramic-tiled exercise and water volleyball pool canopied by a 25-foot-high cathedral ceiling evocative of traditional Roman bathhouse architecture. Flanking the pool are the glass-walled aerobics exercise and dance studio and the monitored gymnasium equipped with Keiser

Cam II equipment, StairMaster machine, Lifecycles, Liferowers, Trotter tread-mills, free weights, and CPR equipment. There are separate men's and women's whirlpools, saunas, and steam rooms (1 each), about which, as an admirable safety precaution, two typewritten pages of tips and cautionary advice are supplied to each guest. Separate men's and women's locker rooms are lavishly outfitted with white terry robes and rubber thongs for each guest, soaps, shampoos, hand and body creams, and pyramids of rolled white towels. In combination with the natural lighting, bleached woods, sponge-painted pink, blue, and gray walls, and the cheerful, caring competence of the spa staff, the soundproofed treatment rooms for massage, herbal wraps, hydrotherapy, loofah scrubs, and facials are blissfully relaxing. Adjacent to the lodgelike reception area, with its great fieldstone fireplace, the spa boutique offers a tempting array of activewear, sportswear, accessories (no footwear), bathing caps, eye goggles, cosmetics, skin care products, and tennis balls. A fruit juice bar offers refresh-ment.

Opportunities for Recreational Exercise: Guests can enjoy 2 Har-tru tennis courts, open day and night. (Court fees are complimentary, but lessons with the pro are extra.) A 4-foot-deep indoor exercise pool as well as a heated indoor-outdoor pool for spa guests and guests of the inn is available as is a similar pool for villa owners and renters for use in 1989. In season, badminton, croquet lawn, a 5-acre pond stocked with bass for fishing (tackle and rowboats available), cross-country skiing trails, and 5 kilometers of hiking and walking trails are there to be enjoyed. Guests have access to the adjacent 18-hole Norwich Golf Course (greens fees, cart, and club rental extra) and to indoor tennis and racquetball at the Norwich Health and Racquetball Club, located 10 minutes from the inn. Transportation from the inn available. Within 10 to 15 miles, guests can find beaches, bowling, canoeing, fishing (equipment can be rented), riding (at modest hourly costs), and boating, with a choice of bare boat or crewed sailing (81-foot and 95-foot schooners and 34-foot Tartans available), priced depending on type and length of cruise.

Beauty Treatments and Welcome Indulgences: Personal instruction in makeup techniques are available on an à la carte basis only. A *5-day Spa Program* provides, in addition to Country Suite accommodation, a few more cosseting services than the *5-day Total Energizer.* Whichever you opt for, you'll receive luxurious pampering, warmth, glorious aromas, and services guaranteed to make you feel revitalized.

Accommodations: All 66 spacious, quiet, comfortable rooms are individually decorated in soft Colonial colors with charming appointments and country motifs, chintz-upholstered sofas and armchairs, stripped-pine and wicker furniture, and ceiling fans. Some have Chippendale mirrors, many have four-poster or sleigh beds. Types of guestrooms include queen, double, or twin beds (standard/regular); queen bed with window seat or bay window sitting rooms (deluxe); queen, double, or twin beds with shared bath (family suite); Country and Garden Rooms (larger in size, with sleeping and living areas distinctly set apart); and a luxurious Master Suite. All rooms have telephones, color television, air-conditioning, and nouvelle England distinction. Housing in a villa building, comprising 8 units—6 Country Room villas and 2 Villa Duplexes—is a short stroll from the tennis courts. A villa Country Room is a spacious room with a sitting area, convertible sofa bed, clock-radio, color television, bathroom, wood-burning fireplace (logs at extra charge), and full kitchen including garbage disposal, icemaker, coffeemaker, utensils, and stoneware crockery, as well as a balcony or a terrace with larger suites. The Villa Duplex comes with an extra bathroom, an additional television set for a sleeping loft, with a convertible sofa bed, and an upper-level deck. Villa owners and renters have access to a club house with a minispa facility and an outdoor swimming pool as well as access to the inn and the major spa on an à la carte basis. Maid service and room service are available.

What to Bring: See USEFUL INFORMATION. Bring your exercise clothes, a tote bag to carry them between inn and spa, and tennis racket, golf clubs, or cross-country skis if you so desire. Remember, you can rent golf clubs from the neighboring golf course. Spa guests wear sweatsuits or exercise gear for lunch, but for dinner, informal dress—*not* spa attire—is requested. If you forget anything, the spa boutique has a selection of wardrobe and personal items for your convenience. A small selection of toiletries, sundries, and film is available at the front desk of the inn, and there are drugstores nearby. One-day valet service will take care of your laundry, cleaning, and pressing.

Documentation from Your Physician: A letter of approval, medical history, and documentation of recent physical examination are requested but not required. If you answer yes to any of certain questions on the medical questionnaire, you must receive a physician's consent before you can begin the spa program. If you do not bring documentation with you, you will be asked to sign a medical release and be examined by the spa's physician.

The Use of Alcohol and Tobacco: On your first orientation night, you are offered 4 ounces of wine, but no alcohol is served to spa guests thereafter. No smoking is permitted in the spa or the spa dining room.

Fees, Method of Payment, Insurance Coverage: High-season (April through November) rates:

For *1-day Revitalizer:* $195

For *1½ day/2 night Norwich Revitalizer:* $598 single, $510 per person double

For *5-day Spa Program:* $1675 single, $1455 per person double

Daily rates for standard rooms $125, Country Rooms $160, Villa Country Suites $170, Villa Duplex $195

Accommodation in a Villa Suite, including the *5-day Spa Program:* $1855 single, $1545 per person double; in Villa Duplex, $1990 single, $1613 per person double. Rates are lower in the off-season. All prices are subject to change, and all rates are subject to a 7.5 percent state tax, not inclusive of gratuities. A deposit is required. Ask about the cancellation policy. Payment can be made by check, Visa, MasterCard, American Express, Diners Club, or Discover.

Follow-up Assistance: Edward J. Safdie's spa cuisine cookbooks *Spa Food* and *Hearty Spa Food* are available in the spa boutique.

European Spas

England

Brooklands Country House Health Farm
Lancashire

Open year-round, with only 12 guestrooms for single or double occupancy, most with adjoining bathrooms, some with shared bathroom facilities, this century-old Georgian-style red brick house—its chimneypots bespeaking plenty of fireplaces, supplanted now by central heating—with a recent bedroom wing addition and a separate spa building, offers a simple, relaxed, unpretentious family atmosphere and warm personal attention. Established in the late 1970s, the first health farm of its kind in the northwest of England, Brooklands, in the red-rose county of Lancashire, is owned and operated by Mrs. Judith M. Brown, who has passed the British Association of Beauty Therapists examination and has international accreditation from the Comité International d'Esthétique et de Cosmetologie. It has a staff of 11 health and beauty and massage therapists, along with several cooks, reception personnel, and a domestic staff. Guests include housewives and businessmen, and range in age from 40 to 60.

Fresh flowers from the garden in season decorate the comfortable, pleasant rooms, all of which have a color TV and private telephone, and a daily British newspaper of your choice is supplied free of charge. Under 10 acres, Brooklands' property includes 2 tennis courts, well-maintained flower gardens and lawns, old trees, orchards, and a flourishing kitchen garden. Plenty of freshly picked fruit and vegetables are included in your daily food regimen, high in fiber, low in fat, with no red meat served.

Calorie content and other preferences are subjects you can discuss in your initial personal consultation, when an appropriate course of services and treatments is planned for you. A physician in general medical practice is available for consultation on short notice if necessary. Offered at Brooklands are daytime lunch and beauty treatments, a *weekend break* (£152 for standard accommodations, £175 for deluxe),or a *5-day stay,* which includes 6 treatments by a well-qualified staff for £425 to £475. Additional services and treatments are à la carte. Treatments encompass Swedish and G5 massage, faradism, aromatherapy, infrared, paraffin wax bath, cathiodermie, biopeel, electrolysis, reflexology, manicures, pedicures, masques for your hands and feet and face, facials, hairdressing, and other cosmetic services. Facilities include a 20- by 40-foot heated indoor pool, sauna, solarium, whirlpool, individual steam cabinets, steam room, hydrotherapy bath, and gymnasium with minimal but adequate equipment. "The place is done up real loverly," they say in the pub of the Royal Oak in nearby Garstang.

A deposit is required. Ask about the cancellation policy. Remember to bring a warm dressing gown and slippers since you have to go outside to gain entrance to the spa building. If you're ever going to catch up on your correspondence and reading list, this is a likely spot to do it in. For recreational exercise, your best bet is exploring the woodland paths of the nearby Forest of Bowland.

Name: Brooklands Country House Health Farm.

Mailing Address: Calder House Lane, Garstang, Lancashire PR3 1QB, England

Telephone: Garstang (09952) 5162; from US, 011 44 (9952) 5162

⨳ Cedar Falls Health Farm ⨳
Somerset

In the foothills of the Quantock Hills, ideal for walking, and close to the Exmoor National Park in Somerset on the southwest coast of England, Cedar Falls is an 18th-century landmark Georgian mansion of locally quarried rose-colored sandstone with 33 rooms, from budget-basic to luxurious lovelies, accommodating 55 guests. Promising to relax your body, refresh your mind, and improve your general health with stress- and weight-reduction, body treatments, and beauty and grooming sessions for pleasurable indulgence, Cedar Falls is within 3 hours' motoring distance from London, or reachable in 2 hours from London by train. Carefully restored and modernized, albeit without room telephones or central heating, the spa's living quarters and public rooms are well furnished in a timeless, traditional, comfortable English style. Sir Winston Churchill and Lord Baden-Powell once were honored guests in the handsome paneled dining room, where present guests—the majority British, with a regular contingent of weekly arrivals from Canada, France, Germany, and the US—enjoy both calorie-controlled and full diet meals. Spa facilities—the basement's heated indoor pool, sauna, whirlpool, exercise rooms, well-equipped gymnasium, beauty and hairdressing salon, and treatment rooms—are well planned, freshly decorated, and immaculately maintained.

Recreational pleasures to be found on the tranquil 40-acre estate encompassing woods, lakes, lawns, landscaped gardens, and a flagstone garden terrace, include a challenging 9-hole golf course with the necessary clubs to play on it supplied, badminton, croquet, walking and jogging trails. Bicycles are provided for exploring the property and the surrounding countryside. For under $15, you can hire a suitable mount from the Quantock Riding Centre, 3 miles away, or a pony and high-wheeled trap for an hour's drive clip-clopping through trim, rolling farmland along tree-lined country lanes. Vivary Park, 5½ miles away in Taunton, has tennis courts you can reserve. The Wellington Sports Centre, 8 miles distant, offers squash and the fun of a ski-slope covered year-round with a plastic surface for schussing. If you're game for a flight in a glider and the prospect of soaring silently above high hills, dramatic gorges, and the unspoiled expanse of Exmoor Forest, the Devon and Somerset Gliding Club is only 10 miles away, and charges under $50 for a heavenly ride. Taxis are easily arranged.

Name: Cedar Falls Health Farm

Mailing Address: Bishops Lydeard, Taunton, Somerset TA4 3HR, England

Telephone: (0823) 433233; from the US, 011 44 (823) 433233

Established: 1982

Managing Director: Terry Yeadon

Program Directors: Terry Yeadon; Jennifer Robinson

Owner: Ray Smith

Gender and Age Restrictions: Co-ed; minimum age 16

Season: Year-round

Length of Stay Required: Stays of 3, 4, and 7 nights are suggested but not mandatory. For *3-night stay* (extended weekend), arrive before 3:00 PM Thursday and depart after lunch on Sunday; for *4-night stay,* arrive before 3:00 PM on Sunday and depart after lunch on Thursday; for *7-night stay,* arrive before 3:00 PM on Sunday or Thursday and depart after lunch the following Sunday or Thursday.

Programs Offered: Every stay includes unlimited use of the heated indoor swimming pool, whirlpool, gymnasium (outfitted with 3 stationary bicycles, rowing machine, 8-station multigym Power Sport equipment, and free weights), 9-hole golf course (clubs provided), free use of 1 of 6 bicycles, croquet lawn (mallets and balls provided), garden tennis court (half regulation size, rackets and soft ball provided), badminton court (racquets and shuttlecock provided), walking and jogging trails. Tackle is supplied for fishing estate lakes well stocked with trout.

With a *7-night stay,* your program includes conducted walks, aqua-aerobic classes in the indoor pool, relaxation classes, yoga classes, dance and body-shaping classes, calisthenics and other exercise classes, 3 sauna sessions, 3 sessions in an individual steam cabinet, 3 Swedish body massages, 3 hydrotherapy baths to which aromatherapy oils are added, 3 G5 vibratory massages, 1 hydrotherapy bath to which oil of peat essence is added, and talks on health-related and general interest subjects. Specialist treatments—acupuncture, osteopathy, reflexology, iridology—are available. A local doctor is on call. No registered nurses are on staff, but the fitness instructors are trained in safety precautions and first aid. *N.B.* No beauty treatments and no massages, hydrotherapy, or specialist treatments on Sunday.

Diet and Weight Management: Emphasis is placed on raw and natural foods, many of which are grown in Cedar Falls' extensive kitchen garden. A registered dietitian is on hand to discuss "constructive fasting . . . to rest the digestive system" at the commencement of your stay if you so desire. You have your choice of a 600- to 700-calorie daily regimen (the low-cal diet), a calorie-controlled diet, which allows you 1000 calories daily, or a full diet—as many helpings or as much of the healthful, wholesome food as you wish. An à la carte menu is also offered.

On the Spa diets, both the low-cal and calorie-controlled (by portion sizes), you have yogurt, whole-meal toast, muesli, fruit, and tea or coffee for breakfast. For lunch, there is a salad buffet in the green-carpeted, mahogany-paneled dining room, set with tables for 4. Among the 15 to 20 salads presented, you'll find some that include pasta, fish, chicken, and many unusual combinations, such as bean shoots and strawberries. Your evening meal has a homemade soup for a starter, a meat dish such as chicken baked in cider for an entrée, or the option of a vegetarian platter, and a fruit dessert. If you would like wine with your meals, you may have it à la carte.

Beauty Treatments and Welcome Indulgences: A stylist and beauticians offer a "Top to Toe" service. The highly qualified co-ed staff of estheticians and therapists are expert in the Paris method facial, a regenerative facial, and a desensitizing facial; paraffin waxing for face, feet, and hands; depilatory waxing; makeup; electrolysis; manicures and pedicures; aromatherapy baths and massages; Slendertone exercise; Clarins Bust treatment and body massage; mud packs and other treatments, including complete hair care, all available à la carte. The hairdressing salon is closed on Sunday.

Accommodations: There are 33 rooms: 7 with bathtubs; 8 with showers; 10 with washbasins, sharing facilities; and 8 sharing all facilities. The latter accommodations are in the budget category, simply furnished, but obviously not to compare with the 2 luxury suites, named after Sir Winston Churchill and Lord Baden-Powell, or the Executive rooms, which also have baths. Premier rooms have showers. Standard rooms have handbasins. The luxury suites and Executive rooms, spacious, airy, charmingly furnished, have panoramic views of the Quantock Hills and the beautiful lawns, lakes, and trees surrounding Cedar Falls. All rooms have color television. But remember: *no private room telephones, no central heating.*

What to Bring: See USEFUL INFORMATION. Bring your thermal underwear and sheepskin-lined bedroom slippers. Bring your bathing suit(s), rubber thongs for wear around the pool, and a terry robe for a cover-up and for in between treatment times. Bring a raincoat. Dress for the informal ambience. No special dress required for mealtimes. There is an on-site boutique stocked with leisurewear and gift items, but bring your own reading and writing material as it is simpler to have them on hand than to have to shop for them in Taunton.

Documentation from Your Physician: Neither requested nor required. Guests are expected to be in good health when they arrive.

The Use of Alcohol and Tobacco: Wine is sold for mealtime consumption. Smoking is not encouraged, but is allowed in your room or outdoors.

Fees, Method of Payment, Insurance Coverage: Daily rates:

Budget accommodations: £54 single, £43 per person twin or double

Standard accommodations: £76 single, £65 per person twin or double

Premier accommodations: £98 single, £81 per person twin or double

Executive accommodations: £105 single, £87 person twin or double

Rates are higher for suites. All prices are subject to change, and all rates are subject to 15 percent VAT. No service charge. No gratuities expected. A deposit is required. Ask about the cancellation policy. Leading credit cards, cash, and checks on UK banks are accepted in payment.

∽ Champneys at Tring ∾
Hertfordshire

The latest additions to Champneys, Britain's best-known and very popular spa, are an exotic co-ed Japanese aromatherapy suite, an interior waterfall in the spiffy atrium complex housing this and other commendable facilities, and a giant outdoor chessboard. As a test of skill and for recreational exercise, you can jump, shove, and slide outsize plastic pawns, knights, and bishops weighted with sand across a board of paving stones reminiscent of a Mogul ruler's playground at

Fatehpur Sikri. Champneys, which has licensed health and leisure clubs in London's Meridien Hotel, Cumbria's Whitewater Hotel in the Lake District, and Scotland's Gleneagles Hotel, is about as holistically upscale as you can get, yet manages to avoid glitziness and to retain many easily affordable features. It began more than six decades ago as Champneys Nature Cure Resort, a rather austere health hydro near tiny Tring, 33 miles north of London, nicely situated amid the greenery of Hertfordshire's beechwood forests. It was a health retreat mostly favored by elderly Oxford dons, members of the royal staff at Windsor Castle, and weary Londoners who needed to recuperate from excessive partying. Today, this premier health spa, with separate men's and women's pavilions and a co-ed gym, attracts clients from all over the world.

The first British health establishment to be operated under full medical supervision, Champneys emphasizes preventing health problems and promoting "positive health." Obviously, the program is successful and many guests are return visitors. Most of them are in their late 30s, early 40s and wish to lose from 5 to 10 pounds. The labyrinthine red-brick mansion, formerly owned by a Rothschild, and its conveniently linked and dovetailed contemporary installations are surrounded by 170 acres of lush parkland. Champneys even has its own vocational training college of health and beauty near the main house, and guests staying for 5 days or more can participate in a course of massage techniques, including aromatherapy and reflexology, during their stay. Fitness instructor John Brickell assures you that the refurbished gym has "user-friendly," adaptable equipment. Al Murray, former national coaching advisor to the British Olympic team and director of the London City Gym, has designed a notable exercise program to promote cardiovascular fitness. Other exercise classes range from gentle tone-ups to a fast-paced, strenuous, challenging session referred to as Body Blitz. But exercise is only part of the program.

Whether you are strolling through lovely gardens or among topiary bushes of boxwood on lawns rolled and mowed to bowling green perfection in summer, or sitting in comfort around a crackling log fire in winter, you'll always find an enormous choice of activities, pastimes, and options open to you. What shall it be—aerobics, the use of a complimentary 3-speed bicycle, or an art class? A Clarins or a René Guinot facial? Trout fishing or a flower-arranging demonstration? Tennis or tap dancing? Vibro massage, volleyball, or yoga? Scrabble, a sauna, billiards, or a Salt-Glo treatment? Swimming in a heated pool or beginners' squash on either of 2 glass-backed squash courts? Or would you rather learn the essentials of gliding with a newfound chum? There is a small practice golf area on the estate plus 3 good golf courses nearby (no golf club rentals but greens fees in the $10 range) as well as a riding stable. But maybe you would rather shop at the boutique, play backgammon, badminton, croquet, indoor or outdoor chess, learn how to dye fabrics, or listen to a concert in the new music room. Champneys is nothing if not eclectic, as are the excursions you can make from it.

If you want to get away on your own or with a friend, you can explore the 16th-century village of Aldbury 3 miles away, or Tring, even older, with an interesting museum 4 miles away. You can taxi out to the renowned Whipsnade Zoo, 11 miles away, or make a day of it at the whopping attraction of Woburn Abbey, its safari park and garden center, which is twice the distance but possibly double the fun. You don't have to be a roads scholar to find your way 30 miles west to Oxford's handsome and beautiful colleges and Bodleian Library, or to Blenheim Palace, 8 miles north of Oxford and sometimes called "England's Versailles." Some guests venture no further than a snuggle with their pusscat or doggums, which they have parked in kennels close to Champneys, while others hie away on the 61-mile day trip to Stratford-on-Avon in Warwickshire for the April-through-November Shakespeare Festival. There are caves and a picturesque village at West Wycombe, and Roman excavations at St. Albans Abbey, both within 15 miles of Champneys; the London Gliding Club is 12 miles away at Dunstale Downs.

The shy are encouraged to come out of their shells and "socialize" at Champneys, which makes it an excellent place for a single person to go on holiday, combined with a trip to London or a sightseeing tour. The friendliness of the staff and guests is such that a fair number of clients choose to spend Christmas and New Year's here, when it's like a jolly house party for a maximum number of 110 to 120 residential guests. Even though there are health and beauty programs for nonresidential men and women, and the constant come-and-go of regular members of the Champneys Country Club (those living within reasonable driving distance use the spa facilities as a health club), there is a remarkable feeling of relaxation and shared endeavor among both guests and health club members alike.

Name: Champneys at Tring

Mailing Address: Tring, Hertfordshire, HP23 6HY, England

Telephone: (04427) 3351; from the US, 011 44 (4427) 3351; for reservations, (04427) 73155/6

Established: 1925

Managing Directors: Allan Wheway, Managing Director of Champneys Group; Tanya Wheway, Operations Director of Champneys Group; Derek Goss, Managing Director of Champneys at Tring

Program Director: Susan Sims

Owner: Guinness, PLC

Gender and Age Restrictions: Co-ed; minimum age 16. No children under 16 are allowed to stay or visit at any time.

Season: Year-round

Length of Stay Required: 2-, 5-, and 7-day programs. The *2-day weekend* program begins Friday afternoon and you leave before noon on Sunday. The 5- and 7-day programs begin on Sunday. Other arrangements can be made.

Programs Offered: The programs, permissive, highly structured, and educational, emphasize supervised physical activity and nutrition education. On arrival, you begin with a compulsory consultation with a registered nurse. Depending on your reasons for visiting, a personal program is mapped out appropriate to your level of fitness and general health condition. Candace Johnston, a skilled and professional counselor in lifestyle planning, is available to you for an initial 15-minute consultation at no extra charge. "Healthy living doesn't just 'happen.' It takes a decision from within yourself to make it a priority." If appropriate to your needs, you can schedule a further 45-minute session (for about $35) to help you devise strategies for taking charge of your particular stress areas. A free Monday evening lecture is also offered, which focuses on practical solutions to real life stress situations, at which you are given the opportunity to identify your own stresses and your responses to them. There is a free introduction to a self-hypnosis workshop, and private consultations are available at an extra charge.

For reasonable fees, a full range of treatments is available by a qualified chiropodist as well as by an acupuncture specialist. Optional consultations and treatments by an osteopath for musculoskeletal aches and pains, sciatica, migraine, arthritic problems, and tension headaches are also available at extra charge. "Well Woman" talks given by one of the Champneys nursing staff to update you on the latest developments in the field of women's health are free, but if you would like a consultation with a gynecologist, a breast examination, cervical smear, or other examinations and treatments, this will cost you a modest additional sum. For £25 (under $50), you can have a Fitness Assessment, a 45-minute check-up that includes a test of your body's fat-to-lean ratio by skin calipers, monitoring of your heart rate to test its aerobic capacity, and measurement of your lung power, blood pressure, and other vital statistics under the supervision of highly qualified instructors who will discuss the results with you.

In the *Health and Fitness Program,* a talk given by Champneys' medical advisor, an orthopedic physician, covers health, fitness, and exercise during your stay at Champneys and after you leave. General medical consultations and additional consultations and treatments with Champneys' orthopedic physician are costs which, in Britain, can be claimed through private health insurance plans, as can the cost of treatments at Champneys' comprehensively equipped physiotherapy department run by a team of physiotherapists. Treatments include "infrared, pulsed shortwave, shortwave diathermy, ultrasound, faradism, interferential pain-relieving therapy, hydrotherapy, Maitlands manipulation, mobilization, and exercise." Champneys' *Medi-Check* for men and women—about £25 more for women than for men as it includes mammography—is a comprehensive medical screening that comprises a full physical examination, X rays, blood tests, and a detailed medical report for £185.

Individual or group swimming and tennis lessons are available, also a short massage course at Champneys training college of health and beauty, and a smoking cessation program for which you pay only if you feel the program has been successful. Individual counseling appointments at an extra charge are available for other behavior therapies.

All dieters, often referred to as "reducers," and those on special food regimens are encouraged to have an optional appointment with a nutritionist. Once you have decided which, if any, of these optional treatments and consultations at extra charge may be appropriate for you, you can relax and enjoy your dinner in the Trellis dining room or the adjacent Sundial Room exclusively for reducers, followed by a reception and a slide lecture to welcome you to Champneys and familiarize you with the current weekly activities listed in a 5-page booklet you receive at your initial consultation.

From 8:00 AM, when you meet for a group walk in woods and parkland, until 8:45 PM, when the last exercise class of the day is scheduled, what's offered in the way of exercise includes a body-conditioning circuit with multigym equipment; water exercises in the indoor swimming pool, which features a tile mosaic of butterflies; morning stretch exercises; gymnasium instruction and advice (you'll find user-friendly 14-station David Cam range equipment, developed in Finland for a wide range of exercise programs; Power Jog treadmill; Monark, Schwinn, and Tunturi stationary bicycles; free weights in this 1000 square feet of airy space); jogging on a ¼-mile track; yoga; the fast-paced Body Blitz session for advanced level exercise; tone-up to music; the once-a-week fun-and-games exercise class; back-care exercises; and relaxation classes. Squash and tennis classes are included as are leisure craft pottery, painting, and drawing activities. *N.B.* Guests' visitors are not allowed to use the leisure facilities. A demonstration of makeup techniques and beauty tips by a beauty therapist; a lecture on nutrition by the Champneys registered dietitian; a demonstration by Chef Mark Hickman about meal preparation and attractive presentation of food; a flower-arranging demonstration; a talk on the attitudes, priorities, and aspects of positive thinking by Tanya Wheway; talks on health and fitness and stress management are scheduled at different hours throughout the week. In the regular 2-, 5-, and 7-day programs you get—except on the day you arrive, and on the day you leave, when only the heat treatment is included—a daily 30-minute body massage and a 15-minute heat treatment.

There's a fully equipped games room with everything available—table tennis, bridge tables at the ready, chess, backgammon, cards, word and board games galore. You can practice putting or smacking golf balls (your own) into a net. Private lessons in European languages and in English are available by appointment with local qualified teachers.

There are 4 fitness instructors, 2 men and 2 women; 25 beauty therapists; 9

masseurs and masseuses; 4 hairdressers on the spa staff and in the beauty salon of the Atrium spa facility. The medical section in the same handsome building includes the services of 16 registered nurses, 6 physiotherapists, a chiropodist, and other specialized health practitioners. Dr. John Tanner, Champneys' medical advisor and orthopedic physician, covers health, fitness, and exercise fields and can advise you about continuing or improving your level of fitness once you are back home. Pamela Wells, a registered nurse, is the expert on the Well Woman Program.

Diet and Weight Management: You eat light in the white Sundial Room with its cheerful accents of peach and jade. Only calorie-controlled and portion-controlled food is served here. In the adjacent Trellis Room, its high ceilings conferring a more baronial feeling, but identical in decor, guests are served in larger portions, a healthy regimen of tender venison, delectable Scottish salmon, and trout fresh from a local trout farm. The walled, organically cultivated kitchen garden supplies fresh produce, and more exotic fruits and vegetables come from London's famous Spitalfields market. Champneys bakes its own whole-meal bread, makes its own low-cal yogurt, and offers these and other "take-away" food products, such as natural honey, for sale.

You have a choice of fasting, and calorie levels of 500, 1000, or 1000 plus of low-cholesterol, high-fiber food, with lacto-ovo or strictly vegetarian options. Salt is added in cooking. Protein and carbohydrate are served at each meal, and foods are prepared from fresh produce in season. The registered dietitian, Helena Champion, prescribes a calorie level appropriate to your needs, and one of the nursing sisters assigns you to the appropriate dining room on your arrival. Helena Champion checks on each guest's progress during their stay and is available for consultations.

Breakfasts are hearty, and include yogurt and a small jug of honey, whole-meal toast, grilled tomatoes, 4 rounded dessertspoonfuls of muesli or 3 of bran or porridge made with water or 1 portion of shredded wheat, plus a variety of chilled fruit juices, and a choice of teas or decaffeinated coffee.

Prawns with a yogurt dip, Parma ham with figs, melon, and chilled fruit juices are "starters" on a typical luncheon menu. A variety of omelettes, salads, seasonal vegetables, and potatoes are offered at both lunch and dinner as entreés along with main dishes of chicken, salmon or other fish, and delicious lean venison. There's always a platter of cheeses and a fruit dessert, which may be a fruit compote or an apple tart. In the Trellis Room, you can split a half bottle of wine between lunch and dinner or drink it at dinner. In the Sundial Room, no wine is allowed.

Beauty Treatments and Welcome Indulgences: Packaged health and beauty programs by the day include a facial, heat treatment, full body massage, Salt-Glow treatment, for men a sun-bed treatment, for women a beauty makeup, a manicure, a pedicure, and a shampoo and set or blow-dry with conditioner. Additional use of the sauna, individual steam cabinets, steam room and showers, spa hydrotherapy treatments with seaweed or pine essence or Epsom salts, and aromatherapy massages are all extras.

Over 100 à la carte treatments and services are offered, using Clarins, René Guinot, RoC Hypo Allergenic, Charles of the Ritz, and other products. All facial treatments include a skin analysis, cleansing, toning, and approximately 20 minutes of facial, neck, and shoulder massage. All facials are approximately 55 minutes, with the exception of cathiodermie, which takes 85 minutes and is equally relaxing and soothing when used as a back massage. Aromatherapy massages, Slendertone faradic treatments, underwater massage, paraffin wax body treatments, paraffin wax masques for your hands and feet, depilatory waxing and body hair bleaching, and sun tanning serve to relax, tauten, smooth, and prime your body. Sixtus, an extended pedicure, includes a foot-to-knee massage using essential oils of plants and flowers, an introduction to aromatherapy and reflexology combined in a single treatment recommended to help you to unwind, relax, and get rid of the blahs or tensions. Beauty may come from within, but often how a woman feels depends very much on how she looks, and a makeup lesson or application by a Champneys-trained specialist is another recommendation. "Rest rooms" are provided for resting and relaxing between a soak in a spa bath, let's say, and a massage—rooms with stretch-out cots and blankets. The warm pulsating glow of indoor and outdoor hot tubs imported from California can be enjoyed "under the sun, stars, or even surrounded by snow."

Accommodations: The best suite is the Rothschild suite in the Mansion, which features a silk-tented boudoir that converts into a tented dining area; a high-ceilinged drawing room; and a bathroom with a double, sunken, Jacuzzi bath guaranteed to raise your spirits. Warm shades of peach predominate and include a chaise longue with a fruitwood frame upholstered in peach fabric piped in navy. This set of rooms connects with the Emily Anne room, which features a separate lobby, a beautifully appointed bathroom, fruitwood furniture, a canopied and curtained four-poster bed, a chaise longue, and a decor in peach, jade, and ivory—a room that can be booked separately or linked up with the Rothschild suite for the pleasure of super-rich guests who don't care what they spend. There's also the Noel Coward room, decorated in rose and pewtery shades, with a canopied bed, carved furnishings, and a mirrored bathroom done in soft pink tiles with a lush, plush carpet, a double Jacuzzi bath, and twin washbasins. In all, there are 37 rooms in the Mansion, ranging from singles without a private bathroom to premier twins/doubles with sumptuous bathrooms. All rooms, no matter what the price, are centrally heated, have color television, radio, and telephone. In the East Wing, there are 50 rooms, the majority individually furnished as are all the rooms in the Mansion. All the East Wing rooms, constructed at a later date than the Mansion's accommodations, are pleasant and share touches of the Mansion's gracious ambience of old world living. Luxury suites in the East Wing include garden suites with a patio. The new ground-floor rooms have sliding French doors opening out onto the lawn, and are larger than the new East Wing first-floor rooms and the old East Wing rooms.

What to Bring: See USEFUL INFORMATION. Remember to bring bathrobes and slippers for wearing to spa treatments, and a cover-up for your bathing suit. Casual sports dress for lunch and dinner is *de rigueur.* Be sure to bring a raincoat, waterproof shoes or Wellington boots, and a head covering for walks in the country when sun alternates with gentle rain. Tennis, squash, and badminton rackets are available, as is a putter for putting green practice, but it is recommended that you bring your own rackets, as well as golf clubs and fishing gear. Gifts, sportswear, athletic footgear, and other clothing are for sale in the boutique. Film is not sold in the boutique, and only a limited range of toiletries are available from the spa reception desk.

Documentation from Your Physician: A letter of approval is neither requested nor required. If you have a known medical problem, your medical history and documentation of a physical examination within the last year are requested. In your initial consultation with Champneys' medical staff, you will be advised about the suitability of all facilities, programs, and diets for your needs and preferences. If you wish to have services and treatments that are not advised, you will be asked to sign a waiver of responsibility.

The Use of Alcohol and Tobacco: Wine is available in the Trellis dining room only. Not permitted if you are following a low-calorie diet. Smoking is allowed only in the smoking room or in a guest's bedroom.

Fees, Method of Payment, Insurance Coverage: Year-round rates per day run from £92 (sharing bathroom; showers instead of bathtubs) to £156 for single accommodations and £107 to £182 per person for double occupancy. Suites per day are £462 for single accommodations and £275 per person for double occupancy. Rates are higher for deluxe accommodations, and all prices are subject to change.

The cost depends on the type and location of accommodation, length of your stay, and the number of optional medical and beauty treatments taken. The scale of charges for these treatments is about the same as or often less than what you might expect to pay in the US. Rate sheets are sent on request. Daily fees do not include a 15 percent VAT or gratuities, which are entirely at your discretion. You may wish to contribute on an individual basis; if you would like to give a collective tip, envelopes are provided at the guest accounts office for the General Staff Fund. A deposit is required. Ask about the cancellation policy. Personal checks, travelers' checks, American Express, Diners Club, Access, Visa, and MasterCard are accepted. Depending on your insurance carrier, medical programs and consultations may be tax-deductible as medical expenses.

Follow-up Assistance: Newsletters, providing 8 pages of tips about losing weight, maintaining fitness, beauty, general health, and news notes, are sent to guests several times a year. Audio and video exercise tapes and Champneys cookbooks are for sale.

Champneys Health and Leisure Club at the Hotel Meridien, Piccadilly, London, W.1; telephone (01) 734-8000, from the US, 011 44 (1734) 8000

Champneys Health and Leisure Club at the Meridien Hotel in London occupies an acre of space in what used to be areas allocated to a Grand Ballroom and a Masonic Temple. Old world elegance has not been sacrificed for New Wave technology. Expect high, hand-painted ceilings, vast expanses of marble, crystal chandeliers and other Edwardian accoutrements for your visual pleasure. Spa restaurant; exercise classes; use of drawing room and library; massages; sun bed; Nautilus-equipped gym with treadmills, free weights, rowing machine, stationary bicycles; indoor swimming pool, sauna, Jacuzzis; billiard and snooker facilities.

Champneys Health and Leisure Club at the Whitewater Hotel, Windermere Lake, Newby Bridge, Ulverston, Cumbria LA12 8PX; telephone (0448) 31144, from the US, 011 44 (448) 31144

This facility is set up at Lakeland Village, a time-share vacation resort on the hotel property. In the heart of Wordsworth country, you can enjoy all the body, skin, and beauty programs, plus exercise facilities and a well-equipped gymnasium, and all the heat treatments offered by a Champneys' licensee, as well as low-cal or other special diets, for a *weekend, 5-day,* or *7-day program.* You probably don't need to be told how lovely and attraction-filled England's Lake District is, and your base here on the banks of Lake Windermere is ideally situated for touring and sight-seeing convenience.

~ Forest Mere ~

Hampshire

What do jockeys, actresses, businessmen, American socialites, sedentary scholars, and plump matrons of many nationalities have in common? They all come to Forest Mere to lose weight, wind down, tone up—and return, as though to a beloved camp or boarding school, year after year. If you're counting pounds—sterling or avoirdupois—Forest Mere is a great value. Guests, average age 40ish, speak happily about how "immaculate" everything is, how well run, about the excellence of the twice-daily maid service that keeps their beds unruffled and their pillows plumped up and their sheets turned down neatly over the electric blanket with which each comfortable bed is provided.

Most guests thank heaven that Forest Mere isn't a chichi place, that smart clothes don't matter here, that they can get by with a dressing gown, slippers, a raincoat and Wellies, and not much else. Some guests complain that the massages aren't the "coddling variety." Others are delighted with the series of no-nonsense massages designed to tone and relax, and to make any muscle mass loosen up, with the use of lanolin and verbena cream rather than oil because it leaves one's skin feeling silky and soft and seems to allow the 5 masseurs and 8 masseuses to give a deeper massage. Your once-a-week underwater massage in a bathtub where a strong stream of water is directed at various muscles penetrates so deeply that Julie Hughes, the manager, says "the client feels as if he or she has just run 5 miles."

Forest Mere, a large and handsome house, stands in 250 acres of wooded grounds and gardens and overlooks a lovely lake, or mere, on which you can go boating in a canoe or row boat. Close to the border of Surrey, 48 miles southwest of London, it is situated in lovely Hampshire countryside which offers good hacking terrain for riders, and pleasant paths for bicycling, for which the spa provides a little fleet of about twenty 3-speeders for its guests' use. In addition to an all-weather tennis court, indoor and outdoor swimming pools, and easy access to a riding school (less than a mile away) and an 18-hole golf course at the foot of its drive, Forest Mere is approximately an hour's drive from Chichester and Goodwood to the south, Winchester to the northwest, and the delightful cathedral city of Guildford to the northeast. Winchester is probably the most riveting, one of the loveliest and most unspoiled of English cities, crammed full of history, with its famous Norman cathedral; the burial place of Jane Austen and Izaak Walton; The Great Hall, which is all that remains of its castle, where you can see King Arthur's Round Table.

Because of its no-nonsense massages and the attitude of its attentive staff that "a bit of discipline" is good for you, Forest Mere has the reputation of being a somewhat spartan spa. True, its programs are well-structured. True, there are showers but no bathtubs. Your accommodations in 65 rooms located in the Main House and its wings, in the charming Clock House across the courtyard, or in the garden chalets, which provide extra privacy with a view of the swimming pool and the lake in the background, are all comfortable and attractively furnished. Most have access to private lavatory facilities, some with, some without showers, and a few share lavatory facilities. True, no coffee is served. But spartan? With a lake-view indoor swimming pool, direct dial telephones, maids who take away your laundry at night and return it the next morning all done so that you never have to rinse out so much as a pair of socks if you don't feel like it? With video films, concerts, and flower-arranging classes in the evening, a choice of more than 20 different salads, Dover sole, venison, or duck for those not on a light diet at lunch in the tall-windowed dining room? With breakfast served in your room, ample servings of low-calorie cake at afternoon tea for those who are on a light diet? Spartan, with all those heavenly vistas of woods, smoothly rolled lawns dipping gently toward the lake past a mass of pink roses and rhododendrons? Not so, and despite no bathtubs to sink into and no coffee to gulp, no swank, no glitz, pure subtle luxury in restorative surroundings.

Name: Forest Mere

Mailing Address: Liphook, Hampshire, GU30 7JQ, England

Telephone: Liphook (0428) 722051; from the US, 011 44 (428) 722051 telex 858336

Established: 1962

Managing Director: Julie Hughes

Program Director: Dr. John Meehan

Owner: Savoy Hotels, Ltd.

Gender and Age Restrictions: Co-ed; minimum age 16. No one is accepted who is not "fully mobile." *No first-time guests 70 or over accepted,* a policy necessary to assure accommodation of returning septuagenarian guests as well as young folk to maintain a median age of 40+.

Season: Year-round

Length of Stay Required: Stays of 3, 4, 7, 10, 11, and 14 days (maximum). Recommended length of stay, from 7 to 10 days for maximum benefit. Arrival and departure on Sunday and Wednesday only. Arrivals between 2:00 and 4:30 PM, departures immediately after lunch.

Programs Offered: The program emphasizes stress reduction and/or weight loss, weight maintenance. Physiotherapy, at an extra charge of about £13 a session, includes interferential therapy, rhythmic traction, infrared, ultrasonics, short-wave diathermy, wax baths. Osteopathic treatments, if desired, are included in your program at no extra charge. Included in your fee are daily treatments which are part of the Forest Mere routine and which take place mainly in the morning: a daily massage, sauna, or session in an individual steam bath, and a once-a-week hydrotherapy treatment of water massage. Also included are voluntary afternoon classes in movement to music, yoga classes remarked upon by many guests for their excellence, fitness and aquatic exercises in the indoor heated swimming pool, rest and relaxation classes, and calisthenics and supervised workouts using the multigym equipment, rowing machine, stationary bicycles, dumbbells, and free weights in what is called the recreational room. Since no treatments are given on Sunday, guests who arrive right after lunch on Wednesday for a 4-day stay begin treatments the same afternoon.

Indoors, you have a choice of billiards and snooker, table tennis, a card room, a sun lounge with a view of the mere, an airy space where guests often gather to read or socialize. What can you do outdoors? The attractive outdoor heated pool, operational all year round, has a walkway area squaring its perimeter, and a raised terrace set back for reclining and sunning yourself in canvas lounge chairs among flowering shrubs, deciduous and evergreen trees. Nearby is an all-weather tennis court, and a canoe and rowboat are available for boating on the mere. You'll need a letter signed by your club secretary stating that you are a member of a golf club and indicating your handicap in order to play on the Liphook Golf Course at the foot of the driveway, and for which greens fees are far from exorbitant. There's a golf practice range and a net you can thwack balls into on Forest Mere's property, and a few rather clunky clubs you can borrow to do so. Beyond the golf practice range, there are lovely rambling possibilities in the hills, suitable also for hacking about with good horses available by the hour for solo or accompanied rides from a riding school and stable less than a mile away. *Helpful hint:* In summer, when you set off for a country walk, remember to tuck a plastic bag into your pocket. You're bound to spy bramble berries or raspberries growing along the hedgerows by the roadside.

In the evenings, light classical piano concerts are given in the drawing room, which also serves as a pleasant place to read, settled into a chintz-covered chair by its tall windows, or to write letters at its roll-top desk. After dinner, there might be a flower-arranging demonstration, a talk about antiques, a video film, a talk on health by the resident physician, all of which diversions are entirely voluntary. Supervised by Dr. Meehan, Forest Mere's resident physician, members of the fitness, massage, and physiotherapy staff are highly qualified. Qualified state-registered nurses are on duty around the clock.

Diet and Weight Management: Fasting, to provide physiological rest and to suit individual needs, can be prescribed if desired. Guests are then given a balanced diet that will maintain health. Food for guests in the Light Diet Room and in the regular dining room for nondieters is fresh and of the highest quality. Forest Mere produces its own yogurt, a special treat when served with wheat germ and honey. "We do not believe in 'crash' dieting," says the registered dietitian, "but rather in a regime to point you in the right direction and start you on your way to healthier habits on a basis which you will be more inclined to maintain after you leave Forest Mere." Before guests leave, they are given advice on health and food regimens to follow at home. For those who wish to lose weight, the diet at Forest Mere will depend on the weight loss desired and realistically achievable.

Usually, the light diet consists of fresh fruit, soups, and homemade yogurt served with wheat germ and honey. Some guests, who want to lose the greatest possible amount of weight during their stay, will opt for an orange for breakfast, half a grapefruit for lunch, and half a grapefruit for dinner, with lots of water to drink, a fasting program that does not meet the approval of the residential nutrition consultants who are strongly opposed to the fasting and starvation diets some guests like to practice. Most guests start off in the Light Diet Room for both lunch and supper, and then spend part of the time in the dining room before they leave Forest Mere, through a graduated return to a normal regime, a procedure recommended and generally practiced at Forest Mere.

The breakfast you decide upon with the nutritional consultant is always served to you between 7:30 and 8:00 AM in your room. For those not dieting, Forest Mere is renowned for its selection of more than a score of luncheon salads, oatcakes, cheeses and fruits, and for its 3-course suppers with duck, venison, chicken, and fish entrées. Tea is available throughout the day, and afternoon tea, often taken on the broad terrace set with umbrella-ed tables, overlooking the lovely lake, is graced with goodies for both dieters and nondieters. You eat at separate tables for 4 in the dining room—which like all the public rooms has tall windows opening onto views of lawns and trees. The Light Diet Room, lake-facing, next to the sun lounge, lends itself to reading in a pour of sun after lunch.

Beauty Treatments and Welcome Indulgences: A variety of beauty and skin treatments are available to both male and female guests—facials, biopeeling, depilatory waxing, cathiodermie, eyelash and eyebrow dying, pedicure and manicure, chiropody, and faradism, all extras. A facial with subsequent makeup may run you about £17; biopeeling is about £14. (Prices are subject to 15 percent VAT.) A visiting color analyst and a hypnotherapist are available by appointment each week at additional charge. The hairdressing salon is leased as a concession on the premises, with full service. Forest Mere's manicurist and pedicurists will attend to you while your hair is being set or blown dry. Massages are truly therapeutic and a special treat for those who prefer their bodies massaged with a cream rather than with oil.

Accommodations: There are 65 single and twin rooms, all centrally heated, half the rooms facing south and open-fronted to permit sunbathing in your room, in the Main House, its Main Wing and West Wing, in the Clockhouse across the courtyard from the Main House, and in the single-occupancy chalets, which afford privacy without a feeling of isolation. Each room is provided with color TV, direct dial telephone, electric blanket, washbasin, and private toilet, with the exception of a few rooms on the ground floor of the Clockhouse with shared lavatory facilities. More expensive rooms have an additional bidet and shower, as do each of the 11 rooms in the recently built West Wing Extension linked to the Main House. All rooms are attractively decorated in a comfortable, traditional style—lots of polished dark wood, and tables and chairs where you want them. Twice-daily maid service keeps your room ever fresh, ever tidy. On arrangement, maids will take away your laundry in the evening and return it to you the next day for a modest fee. Fresh garden flowers and a good reading light enhance the comfort of all wall-to-wall-carpeted rooms. Whether your room's windows face the lake in front or the forested hills in back, and its location, determine the price. There is 1 suite available in the Main House for single or double occupancy.

What to Bring: See USEFUL INFORMATION. Bring a presentable dressing gown and comfortable slippers to wear between treatments; bathing suits(s), cover-up, and nonskid rubber thong sandals; jodhpur boots if you plan to ride, golf shoes if you plan to golf; comfortable, informal country clothes to wear off-site for sight-seeing; low-key, get-you-through-anything clothes to wear if you decide to go to a race meet or to the theater or to a local event when you don't know from one day to the next if it's going to be warm, chilly, or rainy. Think layering, and bring extra sweaters, cardigans, sweater-coats, raincoat and Wellington boots or other waterproof footwear. What you wear in the evening at Forest Mere is optional. Women will find a caftan easy and comfortable to slip into. Forest Mere is centrally heated, but something on the order of a warm stole, cape, or shawl is useful for a summer evening stroll. The spa boutique has a wide selection of athletic clothes, sunglasses, accessories, gifts.

Documentation from Your Physician: A letter of approval is requested but not required. However, if you think you will be needing physiotherapy or other treatments that could be claimed on your insurance for medical reasons, it would be helpful and advisable if your doctor could confirm this by letter to the resident physician, with any relevant information, prior to or upon your arrival. All guests receive a brief health consultation on arrival and are provided with a short medical form to answer when they send in their written reservation form.

The Use of Alcohol and Tobacco: No alcohol is served on the premises, and you are expected to refrain from alcohol altogether for the entire length of your stay. You are encouraged to stop or to reduce smoking during your stay, and to smoke, if you must, only in designated areas.

Fees, Method of Payment, Insurance Coverage: Year-round rates per week:

For single accommodations: £385 to £567; in a suite £891

For double accommodations: £385 to £660 per person

Prices depend on view and bathroom facilities (shared or private), and rates are higher for deluxe accommodations. All rates include a 15 percent VAT, but not gratuities, which are at the discretion of guests. A deposit is required from first-time visitors. Ask about the cancellation policy. Payment is accepted in cash, by personal check, or by travelers' checks in pounds. No credit cards are accepted. Insurance coverage? See Documentation from Your Physician above.

Follow-up Assistance: A health-promotion guidebook is given to all clients.

◌ Grayshott Hall Health ◌
and Leisure Centre
Surrey

Mulled wine is poured into crystal cups at Christmas time, and champagne corks pop on New Year's Eve—the rest of the time, no alcohol is served and guests socialize instead over morning coffee, afternoon tea served in the Light Diet Room, and nonalcoholic punch served in the drawing room before dinner. Alfred, Lord Tennyson, was inspired to write some of his finest poetry in the peace and tranquility of Grayshott Hall's beautifully landscaped 47 acres of Surrey greenery and adjacent 700 acres of unspoiled woodland preserved by the National Trust. About half of a maximum number of 100 guests with a general age range from 16 to 60 come here to shed weight on a program individually structured to suit their objectives, and the others come to relax, have a good time, tone up and slough off stress while "educating their minds and bodies into a healthier lifestyle through exercise and diet and a healthy regime."

If you have been searching for a no-strain health and fitness spa with up-to-date beauty and fitness facilities in romantic Old World surroundings with a variety of cultural, social, and recreational/spectator sports to choose from, you need look no further than Grayshott Hall, 43 miles southwest of London, an hour's drive from Heathrow, Gatwick, or the channel ports of Dover and Portsmouth, the latter with its wondrous array of sailing ships and marine museum stocked with figureheads. A favorite retreat of power brokers, the social, and the celebrated who want to get away from it all in the blessed disguise of anonymity to power jog, play snooker, walk in the woods, and have their pressure points fragrantly soothed with aromatherapy oils blended to their custom, Grayshott Hall also attracts young mothers for its stretch mark treatment, as well as business professionals of all ages from Britain and America's eastern seaboard states. There's a new 3-day stress course for high flyers, and brand-new 900-square-foot gymnasium featuring Hydra-Fitness omnikinetic equipment.

Grayshott Hall itself, a Victorian mansion with some 50 new rooms added since Tennyson lived there more than a century ago, is a curious architectural mix. From the front, there's an impression of a formal York-stone gray-buff castle with towers and mullioned bay windows. From the back, there's an impression of cheerful cottage, a rosy-red tiled facade beneath half-timbered eaves, the ground-floor walls covered with a luxuriant growth of wisteria. In the early morning, down by the kitchen garden from which the ingredients for an array of luncheon salads are being picked, you may see red deer or a fox, and geese swimming among the lilies on an ornamental lake. You are surrounded by areas of natural beauty both on and off the property. Waggoners Wells, with woodlands and scenic lakes, is within walking distance. Winkworth Arboretum, with woodlands and flower gardens and 60 lovely acres to explore, is 20 minutes by car. The Royal Horticultural Society's gardens at Wisley are half an hour's drive away. Frensham Ponds' woodland and lakes are 10 minutes by car, and there are good kennels here in case you don't know what to do with your dog while you are away. Race meetings at Goodwood, Sandown Park, Kempton Park, and Ascot throughout the year are all within easy reach by chauffeur-driven or self-drive hired car, which the reception staff can arrange for you. If stately homes and historic houses are one of your interests, you'll find many within 30 minutes' motoring distance. Guildford, on the river Wey, the county town of Sussex, has many interesting old churches. Lewis Carroll (Charles Lutwidge Dodgson) is buried there in the Mount Cemetery. There's also a good theater. And the Festival Theatre in Chichester might be just the ticket after a rewarding afternoon of sightseeing.

For those who prefer to stay put, Grayshott has a splendid leisure and activities program: indoor heated pool, golf, tennis, badminton, croquet, woodland trails, and bicycles all available on site; nearby riding stables at Headley Down, local squash courts on which you can play; therapies and treatments in skilled abundance; physiotherapy; osteopathy; excellent evening video presentations; a Christmas and New Year's program; evening entertainment of exceptional interest and quality, not only on health, fitness, nutrition, beauty, and fashion topics, but on antiques, gardens, handwriting analysis, memory, magic, stargazing, flower arranging, art, and sports as well, plus light classical harp and piano concerts and musical sing-along evenings. Among Grayshott Hall's many assets, you can come and go and stay as briefly or as long as you please. Indulgences? From breakfast in your room to security locks provided for your bicycle, everything is simplified for you; your favorite newspapers delivered to your room each morning, cars ordered, appointments booked, everything you ask for seemingly effortlessly arranged.

Name: Grayshott Hall Health and Leisure Centre

Mailing Address: Grayshott, near Hindhead, Surrey GU26 6JJ England

Telephone: Hindhead (042 873) 4331; from the US, 011 44 (42873) 4331

Established: 1966

Managing Director: Anthony Stalbow

Program Directors: Peter Abbott, M.D., Medical Director; Moya Myers, Director of Leisure and Treatments

Owner: G. R. Holdings, PLC

Gender and Age Restrictions: Co-ed; minimum age 16

Season: Year-round

Length of Stay Required: None. With advance notice, guests may arrive on any day convenient for them and leave when they wish. Check-out time is 11:30 AM. A stay of at least 5 days is recommended.

Programs Offered: All programs are specifically tailored to suit your individual requirements. When you arrive, you are given a guided tour of the facilities and accompanied by a consultant with whom you have an initial interview, a midweek check, and a final consultation before you leave. A physician in general practice, a psychiatrist, a dietitian, a nutritionist, an osteopath, a physiotherapist, a state-qualified registered nurse, a stress specialist, sports coordinators, and beauty therapists are all available for consultation. There are 8 state-qualified registered nurses rotating duties around the clock, and all 43 members of the fitness, health, and beauty staffs, as well as their part-time colleagues, are eminently qualified in their fields of expertise.

Guided by a fitness assessment (a recommended £17 option), and your initial 30-minute discussion with a consultant (supplemented with 2 additional 20-minute consultations), a program is devised and adapted to suit your special requirements. Each evening, an appointment card is sent to your room detailing your schedule for the next day. For a fee of £220, a *3-day training course in stress management* created by Dr. Audrey Livingstone-Booth, Director of London's Stress Syndrome Foundation, is available. Chiropody and physiotherapy treatments at reasonable prices are other extras you might wish to consider. Included in your daily charge are a choice of either sauna, individual steam cabinet, or, for those who prefer dry heat, a swaddling in heated blankets before you have your daily Swedish massage; or a session in an Impulse shower (alternating hot and cold jets of water), or a sitz bath (stimulating for your circulation!).

You receive daily nutritional advice, daily organized walks and jogs, and your choice of daily exercise classes and body workouts. These include a stamina-developing class in the gym and introduction to the Hydra-Fitness equipment, a wake-up and stretch class, aerobics, yoga, body toning with light weights and dumbbells, a total leg workout, a "pop mobility class" (45-minute body tone-up orchestrated to music), a continuous circuit of exercises using the Hydra-Fitness equipment to improve muscle tone and stamina and "boost your metabolic rate," a 30-minute aqua-aerobic session, a particularly effective "tummy trimmer" session with simple exercises that can easily be continued at home, and a stretch and relaxation class.

A 30-minute informal discussion gives you a chance to discuss which exercises you should or should not do if you suffer from back, neck, or any other physical problems. Suitable for everyone is a 40-minute morning walk and the 60-minute afternoon National Trust stroll encompassing lakes, rivers, and woodlands.

Besides the Hydra-Fitness equipment, you'll find "bouncers" (individual trampolines), a rowing machine, a power jog treadmill, an abdomen-toning machine, 3 computerized Universal stationary bicycles, and other equipment in the gym, where exercises can be designed for first-timers as well as for highly trained athletes. You have unlimited use of the 12½-meter indoor heated swimming pool and an attractive Jacuzzi, both open from 6:00 AM to 10:00 PM; a 9-hole golf course and putting green for which golf clubs are available on request from the reception desk; a year-round hard-surface tennis court, with available rackets; a grass badminton court, with racquets and shuttlecock yours for the asking from the reception desk; a full-size croquet pitch, mallets and balls also available on request; a bowling green and lawn bowls. Swimming and tennis lessons are available for a reasonable extra charge. Excellent local facilities are available for riding (horses can be brought to the Hall) and for squash. The men's and women's saunas are open daily from 8:00 AM (Sunday, 9:00 AM) and under constant supervision, with cold plunge pools.

As an alternative to your daily Swedish massage, you can have an underwater massage, with jets of water used to stimulate your muscles. Less of a workout is a G5 vibratory massage, for all-over deep toning. Optional body treatments also include reflexology foot massage; aromatherapy with a choice of 100 essential oils extracted from herbs, flowers, fruits, and grasses; a blissful combination of reflexology and aromatherapy; passive exercise with a Slendertone machine (faradism); Clarins and Cleor bust treatments; Cleor Toni Lastil stretch mark treatments; infrared treatments under the supervision of a state-registered nurse; and suntanning. Hairdressing and other beauty and grooming treatments are other options. No massages are given on Sundays.

To give you an opportunity to relax at the end of the day and meet other guests, there is a 6:00 PM nonalcoholic cocktail/mocktail gathering in the cosy drawing room. There is a nightly video film on the in-house system, which you can view in the privacy of your room or in the drawing room, and a variety of evening entertainments: music, flower arranging, chef's demonstrations, crafts, and talks on antiques, poetry, alternative medicine, art, nutrition, textiles, horticulture, and sports. Attendance is voluntary, and some guests repair instead to the billiard room, play bridge, backgammon, or other board games, or opt for a game of table tennis in the gym.

For £30 inclusive of VAT you can spend a *Health and Beauty Day* at Grayshott, which includes a choice of sauna or steam cabinet; Swedish or G5 vibratory massage; exercise classes/workout in the gym; unlimited use of the indoor heated pool and the Jacuzzi; lunch in the dining room; use of the golf, tennis, and badminton courts, croquet pitch, putting greens, billiard and snooker tables, and bicycles; and optional treatments in the beauty salon. Bookings for this memorable day can be made between 9:00 AM and 4:00 PM, 7 days a week, and must be paid for in full prior to your appointment day.

Diet and Weight Management: You have a choice of calorie level, which you work out with the dietitian. Special diets for medical reasons, Kosher food preparation, "any feasible diet" can be worked out for you. If you would rather stay away from the temptation of a table d'hôte choice, you are assigned to the Light Diet Room, a light airy room set with cloth-covered tables and rattan chairs overlooking the gardens. Portion-controlled meals are individually prepared for you and served to you here. No menu. Each guest has his or her own separate diet.

If you have come more to gain fitness than to lose weight, you are assigned to the regular dining room where buffet lunch and dinner are served. For all guests, breakfast is served in your room, morning coffee and afternoon tea are served in the Light Diet Room. Nonalcoholic punch is served in the drawing room before dinner. Some guests may prefer to have lunch in the Light Diet Room and dinner in the main dining room. The 3-course table d'hôte dinner menu in the main dining room is marked with calories per portion. For a 60-calorie starter you might have fresh mushroom soup, purée of cauliflower soup, French onion soup, with parmesan and croutons, or purée of vegetable soup. For 100 calories, you might have a choice of poached egg served on a bed of ratatouille, prawn salad, or strips of chicken breast marinated in yogurt and spices, served hot with a twist of lemon. For under 200 calories, you can opt for such delights as grilled sardines, a light creamy mousse of rainbow trout, crabmeat and mango salad, or smoked salmon, quails' eggs, and a tomato basket filled with cottage cheese. Main courses feature either vegetarian plates—mushrooms in a paprika sauce, vegetable curry, and other imaginative fare—or such entrées as boned spring chicken layered with pâté and laced with a chestnut sauce; grilled swordfish with a cucumber, mint, and yogurt dressing; marinated haunch of venison served with a red currant sauce and parsnips seasoned with nutmeg; chicken Tandoori-style. Desserts might be an apricot-flavored cheesecake with a ginger biscuit base (210 calories), fruit basket (15 calories), selection of cheeses (85 to 115 calories), almond baskets of fresh fruit served on a bed of raspberry sauce (160 calories), a concoction of honey, yogurt, oats, and apples (140 calories). Recipes are available on request. The chef gives a weekly demonstration of his techniques in the pleasant kitchen. At Christmastime, traditional English fare is served with all the trimmings—on request, you can have a light diet or a fish menu—and guests are invited to guess the weight of the Christmas fruitcake, which is more fruit than cake; the nearest guess wins a bottle of champagne.

Beauty Treatments and Welcome Indulgences: The hairdressing salon is open daily except Sunday. The beauty salon, open daily from 8:15 AM to 4:15 PM, offers a Clarins Regenerative Facial, a Clarins Paris Method Facial, a DeCleor Firming Facial, a Geloide Facial, and a cathiodermie facial designed to make your skin look and feel fresh, vital, and a decade younger; biopeeling; eyebrow and eyelash tinting, eyebrow trimming and reshaping; makeups and cosmetic prescriptions; manicures, pedicures, and Sixtus cosmetic foot treatments, the ultimate in luxury; and depilatory waxing. A complete range of "100 percent natural" beauty products is for sale. Reflexology and aromatherapy combined is a £35 treatment that will make you feel like a million, truly a special therapeutic treat.

Accommodations: The 10 suites in the Main House have bathtubs. All other accommodations have showers. All rooms have private loos. The 8 luxury double rooms in the original Main House, each individually decorated, open off the minstrels' gallery. Twin, double, and single rooms on the ground floor of the Main wing have French doors opening onto a patio with chairs you can stretch out on to catch the sun. All the single-room accommodations in the Century wing have either a private patio or a balcony with sun loungers. All amenities are reachable without having to go outside.

All rooms are centrally heated, with a color TV and a video channel for the nightly film, a wall safe, and an operator-assisted telephone service available from 8:00 AM to 10:00 PM (charges are considerably more than for direct dial telephones). The furnishing and general decor of the guestrooms is hotel-like functional with the use of a lot of pink and beige, and a retro impression of the 1920s. Interior decor is not a strong point at Grayshott Hall, but all rooms are light and bright, quiet, and supplied with fresh flowers.

What to Bring: See USEFUL INFORMATION. Bring bathing suits, cover-up terry-cloth bathrobe or dressing gown, rubber thong sandals to wear in the pool area and between treatments; jodhpur boots and riding gear if you plan to ride; informal country clothes and clothes suitable for optional excursions to race meets, historic houses, the theater in nearby towns. Some guests change for dinner, some don't. Valet service is available from Monday to Friday, with collections between 8:00 and 8:30 AM and returns the same day between 4:00 and 5:00 PM The shop on the ground floor across from the appointments desk and hairdresser offers a wide range of sports and leisurewear and accessories, also handmade toys and gifts. Tennis, golf, badminton, and croquet equipment is provided for on-site facilities, but many guests prefer to bring their own tennis rackets and squash racquets if they plan to make use of off-site facilities. There is a small library on the premises, a selection of health and fitness books for sale, and newspapers and magazines can be ordered daily. There is a dispensary for sundries in the Hall and a good pharmacy in the local village. Although film is available, it is advisable to bring your own supply.

Documentation from Your Physician: A medical history and documentation of recent physical examination are requested. Your medical history is checked at the time of your initial consultation.

The Use of Alcohol and Tobacco: No alcohol is served on the premises. Wine is used in some recipes for flavor. Smoking is not encouraged, but there is a smoking room, and guests can also smoke in the billiard room and in their own rooms.

Fees, Method of Payment, Insurance Coverage: Year-round rates per day:

For single accommodations: £99 to £149

For double accommodations: £88 to £127 per person

Daily fees include service, but not 15 percent VAT. Rates are higher for deluxe accommodations, and all prices are subject to change. A deposit is required from each new guest. Ask about the cancellation policy. After payment by cash or by English check for initial deposit, credit cards are accepted: American Express, Access, Barclaycard, Diners Club, Visa; also travelers' checks in pounds. Depending on your insurance policy, physiotherapy treatments may be deductible as medical expenses.

Follow-up Assistance: Exercise cassettes and Grayshott recipes are available.

∾ Henlow Grange Health Farm ∾
Bedfordshire

By a winding river in Bedfordshire, in the eastern Midlands, 40 miles north of London, family-owned Henlow Grange is a serviceable and egalitarian fitness and health spa based in a red brick Georgian-style house with a recently constructed additional guestroom wing. A total of 62 rooms with pleasantly functional decor provides accommodation for a maximum 101 guests, usually in a ratio of 75 percent women to 25 percent men, with an average age range between 35 and 50. Guests, as described by Director Stephen Purdew, are "everyone from everywhere—America, Australia, Israel, Saudi Arabia, Zambia—from secretaries who save up all year for a visit, to lords and ladies." Many come with 10 or 12 pounds to lose and want "maximum results with minimum effort or discomfort." Henlow Grange does its best to oblige with an extensive exercise program, a Nautilus-equipped gymnasium, an indoor heated swimming pool, archery, bicycling, boating on the river, and more, plus beauty and hairdressing services, and all the traditional and trendy body treatments you love or want to try—aromatherapy, reflexology, paraffin wax body masques, parafango volcanic mud baths, a seaweed bath, a panthermal ionized vapor bath, faradism, body buffing, bust firming, sauna and massage, steam cabinet, cathiodermie, biopeeling, facials, and other enticing possibilities.

You can come for a day, a weekend, several days, or a week for package plans. Woburn Abbey and its safari park, Hatfield House's Tudor magnificence across the county border in Hertfordshire, and the art treasures housed in Luton Hoo are all within easy reach by village taxi. Nearby riding stables and kennels for boarding your pet are additional recreational and convenient amenities. Winter reductions and specials.

Name: Henlow Grange Health Farm
Mailing Address: Henlow, Bedfordshire, England SG16 6DP
Telephone: (0462) 811111; from the US 011 44 (462) 811111
Established: 1962
Managing Director: Stephen Purdew
Program Directors: S. Purdew, K. Holland, C. Wood
Owner: Mrs. D. R. Purdew

Gender and Age Restrictions: Co-ed; minimum age 16
Season: Year-round
Length of Stay Required: Nonresidential day, 2–day/1–night, and 3-, 4-, and 7-day packages offered. Arrival Saturday, Sunday, Wednesday, from 2:00 to 4:00 PM. Departures Wednesday, Saturday, Sunday, 11:00 AM.

Programs Offered: Programs are unstructured, with options varied to suit individual preferences. Emphasis is on diet with nutrition education, and on physical activity and exercise. When you arrive, you have an individual consultation and are weighed and measured; your body and figure are analyzed and your medical history noted. A fitness program is then worked out for you. Types of exercise offered are: jazz ballet, yoga, gym instruction, aerobics, water exercises in the swimming pool, freestyle toning, relaxation classes, men's gym workouts, jogging, body alignment, bottom line exercises to trim your derrière, top line exercises for your upper body, water volleyball, breathing exercises, exercises syncopated to jazz and rock. The new gymnasium contains Nautilus equipment, stationary bicycles, individual trampoline rebounders, free weights, and other equipment. On Saturday and Sunday, fewer classes are offered, leaving more time for body and beauty treatments or excursions. The heated indoor swimming and exercise pool is the same depth throughout so that nonswimmers can safely participate in all aqua-gym exercises. On-site recreational exercise opportunities include archery, badminton, bicycling, bird-watching, boating (row boats for river use), croquet, golf practice net, hiking and walking trails, swimming in the indoor exercise pool when it is not in use for classes, and tennis on Henlow Grange's court, which is floodlit for night use. Golf can be arranged on nearby courses. Well-schooled horses are available from local riding stables.

A week's package program (arrival Sunday afternoon, departure the following Saturday morning) includes 5 full body massages; 5 facials (or neck and shoulder massage); 6 saunas or steam baths in individual cabinet; 5 infrared sessions; complete exercise and relaxation program; use of swimming pool, gymnasium, golf practice net, bicycles, boats, and tennis court. Evening lectures and demonstrations on health, beauty and such topics as self-defense and reflexology are offered as voluntary diversions.

If you can squeeze a *Minibreak* into your busy calendar (arrival Saturday at 11:00 AM, vacating your room Sunday at 11:00 AM—although you can stay on the premises after your complimentary Sunday lunch until 4:00 PM), you get a full body massage, a facial or a neck and shoulder massage, 2 sauna treatments, 1 infrared session, and either an exercise class of your choice or a supervised jogging trek around and about Hitchin Village or other nearby areas of interest. You are also entitled to free use of the exercise pool, bicycles, boats, gymnasium, golf practice net, and tennis court.

Diet and Weight Management: Depending on individual weight goals, a 600-calorie or 1000-calorie diet is suggested. Usually, a "sensible eating plan" of 1000 calories a day is recommended. The carbohydrate diet advocated by the Weightguard Slimming Club is an alternative recommendation. Individual diet and nutrition consultations are available at extra charge. High-fiber, low-fat meals are served.

Incorporating high-quality fresh produce, fish, and meat with no salt added, your wholesome meal might include a sharp, bright, and vinegary seafood salad with scallops appearing like ivory buttons among julienned vegetables, or a fruit salad with a mist of mint. Other choices might be free range chicken with an aromatic sauce, a variety of soups, poached salmon, or super pasta. Homemade whole-wheat bread is freshly made daily in the main kitchen where cooking demonstrations are staged during the week. Decaffeinated coffee is served. Diets and food regimens can be arranged to suit all requirements.

You have your meals buffet-style, assisted by waiters and waitresses, in the Main House dining room, with fireplace, brass chandelier, tall windows, and tables set at lunchtime with individual cork-backed mats and coasters. At lunch and dinner, you are allowed to have a glass or two of champagne or wine of your choice if you are not on a strict weight loss diet. There is a coffee bar. White wrought-iron tables are ranged by the swimming pool for guests' fruit juice, tea, or coffee breaks, and you can also use the bright-green-carpeted, arcaded solarium with its settings of white wrought-iron tables and chairs for light refreshments and magazine reading.

Beauty Treatments and Welcome Indulgences: You can have René Guinot face, eye, and neck cathiodermie treatments, biopeeling and acne treatment, a De Cleor deep cleansing and regenerative facial, a Clarins steam cleansing, double serum or pick-me-up facial, or a face masque and makeup applications and lessons. There's a full-service hairdressing salon for men and women; and you can have your ears pierced, your nails wrapped with silk to strengthen them, your eyebrows tinted, depilatory waxing, electrolysis, manicures, and luxurious Sixtus pedicures. Body treatments include applications of volcanic mud and paraffin, a seaweed bath, the Italian treatment of a panthermal ionised vapor bath, G5 massage, a vacuum suction massage, faradic muscle tone exercise, aromatherapy combined with reflexology, aromatic baths, bust firming and body exfoliating treatments, and wax baths for your hands, feet, and body. Approximately 40 beauty therapists full time, and 10 part time are at your service. Henlow Grange operates its own beauty school where trainees come to be taught by Henlow Grange's staff of estheticians.

Accommodations: There are 50 rooms with private bathrooms, a dozen with shared facilities. All rooms have color TV and direct dial telephone. Economy, Standard, Savile (with bath and shower), and Premier Main House (luxury) accommodations are offered in single, twin, or double rooms, some with patio doors leading to a terrace overlooking the river. Rooms are functionally, comfortably appointed with restful simplicity.

What to Bring: See USEFUL INFORMATION. Bring bathing suit(s), bathing slippers or sandals, bathrobes to wear in between beauty treatments and for cover-ups at the swimming pool. For dinner, guests are expected to wear regular clothes— skirts and blouses/sweaters, dresses for women. Jackets and ties for men. No warm-ups or exercise clothes or dressing gowns permitted in the dining room in the evening. There is an activewear boutique on the premises which also stocks sundries. Newspapers are available in the public rooms. Bring your own film.

Documentation from Your Physician: Only if a medical problem makes this relevant. Clients fill in a brief medical history form and attest to its accuracy on arrival.

The Use of Alcohol and Tobacco: Champagne and wine in small amounts are permitted only at mealtime. Smoking is restricted to the coffee bar and to guests' bedrooms.

Fees, Method of Payment, Insurance Coverage: Year-round rates for the *7-day/6-night exercise, fitness, and relaxation program:*

Single accommodations: £319 to £413

Shared accommodations: £297 to £352 per person

Rates are higher for luxury accommodations (£501 single or £457 per person shared, inclusive of the spa program, from Sunday through Saturday, leaving Saturday AM), and special reductions are available during the winter. All prices are subject to change. All prices include 15 percent VAT. A deposit is required. Ask about the cancellation policy. Payment is accepted in cash, by travelers' checks, or by personal check accompanied by Barclaycard, Access, Diners Club, Visa, or American Express. Since Henlow Grange is not a medical center and does not have a resident physician, fees are not deductible as medical expenses.

Follow-up Assistance: Newsletters are sent several times a year to guests.

ꙅ Inglewood Health Hydro ꙅ
Berkshire

Tall Inglewood, mentioned in the Domesday Book as one of the great 12th-century houses of the Knights Templar, the site of the Royal Falconry during the reign of Henry VIII, was converted to a health spa in 1975. It is set on 50 acres of gardens and parkland in Berkshire, in one of England's green and pleasant rural areas, an hour from London by train or by car.

For mothers of infants and children under the age of 6, Inglewood has an arrangement with the famous Norland Nursery, just 2 miles away in Hungerford, where infant and child care is provided by qualified staff. There each precious little angel is assigned his or her own nanny who never leaves her charge's side as long as he or she is at Norland, while devoted mama is benefiting from her exercise classes at Inglewood. Nowhere else in Britain, possibly nowhere else in the world, is a similar arrangement possible for mothers with young children who need to get away to exercise and be pampered but who don't want to be separated from their babies for more than a few hours or by more than a walkable distance when doing so. Norland-trained nannies are often said to be the best to be found anywhere.

For guests who require or would like seclusion and special security while enjoying Inglewood's health and fitness regime—royalty and film stars with their entourages, movers and shakers and sheikhs of the world, politicians, lovers of luxury and privacy—Inglewood maintains Falcon Lodge, a centrally heated brick house with gabled windows, a thatched roof, and its own permanent domestic staff. Several patios open onto a rose garden and a private apple orchard. Inside, along with a sophisticated security system, television and video in the drawing room, plus a Jacuzzi, you'll find 5 bedrooms, 4 marble bathrooms, entrance hall, dining room, drawing room, playroom, and study nicely arranged with substantial furniture of contemporary design.

Inglewood's major drawing power is that it provides an extensive range of clinical and medical facilities, a dietary and weight management program, nutrition education, chiropody, physiotherapy, beauty and body treatments galore, hairdressing facilities, an attractive and serene ambience, and a pleasing choice of diversions, entertainment, and recreational facilities for its co-ed clientele, of whom 50 percent are business-oriented, 30 percent are involved in the arts, and 20 percent are spouses of successful men. Their general age range is from 25 to 60. About 50 percent are married, half of this group often visiting with their spouses. Meals for friends and visitors can be arranged at any time and charged to your account.

On site, there are two hard courts for tennis open all year and a heated indoor swimming pool with a double-glazed, teak-framed roof for visibility of the sky. Guests gather on the patio by the pool to read, sun, swim. Bicycles are available at no charge, and there are scenic routes for bicyclists, walkers, and joggers to try around the estate, either individually or in organized, supervised groups. Inglewood's indoor games room is equipped with good billiards, snooker, and Ping-Pong tables. On Friday evenings, the Cellar Bar becomes a live music disco. Riding on well-schooled mounts can be arranged at a local stable. Golf and fishing can also be arranged if you can scrounge up your own equipment—there don't seem to be any local facilities for rental golf clubs or tackle.

The environment Inglewood provides for guests who come here to relax, exercise, and recuperate, find health, fitness, and vitality, and slough off pounds, inches, and stress is attractive, pleasurable, refreshing, and restorative.

In the summer, when clock golf and croquet are played on the lawn, and the Inglewood cricket pitch is the venue for local village matches, guests can also take in performances at the Watermill Theatre in nearby Newbury. The Kennet and Avon Canal offers barge trips. Hungerford, within walking distance, is an antique collector's shopping delight. Windsor is to the east, Bath to the west, Oxford to the north, and Salisbury and Stonehenge to the south. No local rental cars, but there are plenty of taxis to help you get around.

Name: Inglewood Health Hydro

Mailing Address: Kintbury, Berkshire, RG15 0SW, England

Telephone: (04888) 2022; from the US, 011 44 (4888) 2022

Established: 1975

Managing Director: Mrs. Maxine Metcalfe

Program Director: Dr. James Walker

Owner: Jonathan Aitken, M.P., chairman of Inglewood and member of a private investment consortium

Gender and Age Restrictions: Co-ed; minimum age 18

Season: Year-round

Length of Stay Required: Minimum residential stay 3 days. Arrival between 2:00 and 4:00 PM Sunday or between noon and 2:00 PM Wednesday, Thursday. Rooms must be vacated by 11:00 AM Monday through Saturday and by 10:00 AM Sunday.

Programs Offered: After check-in, you have a consultation with one of the medical staff to establish a dietetic and treatment program for your stay. Guided tours of the Hydro are held on Sunday between 3:00 and 5:00 PM and at varying times to suit your convenience throughout the week. Dr. Walker gives an introductory talk to new arrivals every Sunday evening at 6:00 PM, and Tini Carson, a state-qualified registered nurse, talks to midweek arrivals on Thursday evening at 7:00 PM. Gail Pollard, also a registered nurse, will see you soon after your arrival to help you decide what diet to follow during your stay.

Rest, relaxation, healthy living guidance, and weight management are components of a permissive, nondemanding, structured-with-options program concerned with diet, nutrition education, behavior modification, physical activity, and exercise programs, for which in-depth individual counseling is available. Stress management and smoking cessation programs are offered. Full medical check-ups can be arranged on request. A wide range of clinical investigations are available, including a cardiac profile assessment, stress EKG tests, full biochemical and blood analyses, X-ray facilities, physiotherapy, and osteopathy.

Inglewood is also equipped to cater for the care of postoperative patients and general medical convalescence.

An individual program of diet, treatment, and exercise is prescribed to suit your needs. You normally receive 4 treatments each day—Sundays excepted. You select treatments from sauna or steam cabinet, peat bath hydrotherapy, massage or G5 vibratory massage, Slendertone passive exercise, physiotherapy, or osteopathy. Exercise classes and individual exercise programs are given daily by qualified instructors under the supervision of Mrs. Debbie Jenkins, the gymnasium manager. These classes include yoga, swimming, water exercises, calisthenics, and workouts on the gymnasium's treadmills, stationary bicycles, weight machines, and free weights. Additional activities for which there is no charge include bicycling, jogging, walking through Inglewood's beautiful gardens and woodland or the surrounding country, tennis, croquet, clock golf, lawn bowling, table tennis, billiards, snooker, and swimming. Bird-watching opportunities abound, and you have options of off-site riding and, if you can round up the equipment, fishing and golf. You can combine barge trips on the Kennet and Avon Canal with bicycle picnics.

Diet and Weight Management: If you wish to fast you may do so for the first 24 hours, taking only lemon or orange water, and from there progress to fruit or a light diet. Fruit only can be used as a first or intermediate stage, with each main meal consisting of 2 to 3 pieces of fruit (100 calories) with a piece of fruit for breakfast for a total of 250 calories a day. The Light Diet (500 calories daily) consists of a piece of fruit for breakfast and 2 main meals between 200 and 250 calories. Breakfast, served in your room between 7:30 and 8:30 AM (except Sundays if you are leaving, when it is served in the main dining room between 8:30 and 10:00 AM) offers you a choice of tea, coffee, decaffeinated coffee, herb tea, hot water and lemon and grapefruit, melon, or other piece of fruit. If you are on a full diet, you have a choice of bran flakes, All Bran, or muesli served with semiskimmed milk, as well as whole-meal toast with honey, marmalade, Marmite, or fruit spread. Coffee, tea, and fruit juice are served in the Light Diet Room mornings, afternoons, and evenings. Lunch and dinner are served in both the Light Diet Room and the dining room. The main dining room offers a selection of salad dishes with cold meats, fish, and seafood for lunch. In the evening, potatoes boiled in their jackets and 1 hot dish are added. Fresh fruit is served at lunch, and dessert varies each evening. All food is calorie-labeled. Your calorie intake depends on what is prescribed for you to select, or what you choose to select.

The paneled main dining room, hung with tapestries, with rosy-red curtains brightening its bay windows, is set with tables for 4. You can carry your own food to eat alone and read, if you like, or join a group of convivial guests. The

Light Diet Room, as its name suggests, is light and bright, contemporary in design. All food served at Inglewood is fresh, delicious, low in fat, low in sodium, high in fiber. Special diets for medical reasons or allergies can be accommodated. There is usually a short, optional demonstration given of low-calorie food preparation.

Beauty Treatments and Welcome Indulgences: The Cedars hair and beauty care salon at Inglewood promises that "a structured course at Cedars can achieve more in a week than six months of regular visits to a beauty parlour, because with the Inglewood regime your body will be far more receptive to treatment." Available are such treatments as Kabuki, a recontouring face mask that "uplifts tissue and recontours the face by pushing out the surface skin cells"; Kwik Slim, a treatment in which "a warm herbal gel is placed on the body and the client is wrapped in bandages for 90 minutes. This treatment causes a temporary loss of inches as it tightens skin tissue, and is usually taken as an incentive to losing weight"; deep cleaning and specialized facials; electrolysis; wax baths; eyelash and eyebrow tinting and eyebrow shaping; makeup lessons; face, neck, and shoulder massage; manicures, pedicures, and a wonderful Sixtus foot treatment; depilatory waxing; everything for the hair and beard; ear piercing. The Cedars salon is open from 9:00 to 5:00 Monday through Saturday, closed during the lunch hour (12:30 to 1:30) and on Sundays. In addition to the treatments that are part of your program—sauna, steam cabinet, body massage, G5 vibrating massage, peat bath hydrotherapy—and your option of extra treatments, you can also indulge yourself in a 60-minute aromatherapy massage, a 30-minute reflexology foot treatment, and sun beds.

Accommodations: Not counting the Falcon Lodge, previously described, there are 66 rooms categorized in ascending price levels as Budget (with shared WC and shower), Economy (with shower and WC), Standard (with shower and WC), Premier (with private bathroom), Split Level (with sitting room and private bathroom), Executive, Executive Deluxe, and Inglewood Suite (the priciest of the guest accommodations, excluding Falcon Lodge). All accommodations are centrally heated and are complete with telephone, color TV and radio—VCRs are chargeable extras—and orthopedic beds. A few rooms have balconies. No ground floor guestrooms. Bedboards are available for those who require or want them.

What to Bring: See USEFUL INFORMATION. Bring bathing suit(s), cover-up bathrobe for use in between treatments, casual country clothes, raincoat, and appropriate foot gear. The accent is on informality. A wide range of "all the dress/undress requirements one could need at a Health Farm" is available for men and women at Inglewood's Emma Jane Boutique, including sportswear, shoes, lingerie, toilet accessories, paperbacks, and take-home gifts. Cruisewear and clothes for other special events can be ordered on approval from the Emma Jane Boutique's main branch in Hungerford. Newspapers and magazines can be delivered to your room. Bring your own film. Only a limited number of books on health and recreation are available at Inglewood. Shops in Hungerford are well stocked with basic sundries. Laundry and dry cleaning service is available.

Documentation from Your Physician: Neither requested nor required. "We will always ask questions, and if we suspect information is withheld, we will act accordingly. Full medical staff will always be on alert," says Dr. James Walker, Medical Director.

The Use of Alcohol and Tobacco: Guests are not permitted to bring alcohol onto the premises. Wine is served on Friday and Saturday evenings in the main dining room, and on Friday (discothèque night) in the Cellar Bar. Smoking is permitted only in the Cellar Bar or in your bedroom.

Fees, Method of Payment, Insurance Coverage: From budget to luxurious suite accommodations, single occupancy rates per person for 3 days range from approximately £209 to £413; for 2 people sharing a room for the 3-day program, £374 to £660. For 7 days, single rates are £286 to £963; for 2 people sharing a room, £528 to £1540. Rates do not include fifteen percent VAT and 10 percent service charge. All prices are subject to change. A deposit is required. Ask about the cancellation policy. Cash, personal checks or travelers' checks in pounds, Visa, MasterCard, American Express, Diners Club, Barclaycard, and Access are accepted in payment. Fees are not deductible in England as a medical expense.

⤳ Ragdale Hall Health Hydro ⤳
Leicestershire

A castellated and towered neo-Georgian house, brick with white trim, Ragdale Hall occupies a 16-acre estate encompassed by farmland in Leicestershire, 90 miles northeast of London. The exterior is stately, but the interior is plain and simple rather than grand, the atmosphere decidedly casual. The carpets are indestructible-industrial, the furnishings contemporary rattan, the emphasis on comfort and convenience rather than on visual esthetics, chic, the fashionable, or the trendy. Nor is there a "nursing sister" (a registered nurse) in sight. "We are not a medical facility in any way," says Vicky Hale, a program director. "People come here for healthy relaxation, and we pamper them from the moment they arrive." Guests can have their dietetic or vegetarian or "whole food" meals served on a tray in their room at no extra cost.

Accommodating a maximum of 80 guests, Ragdale Hall caters mostly to a British clientele whose average age is 38, with a ratio of approximately 80 percent women to 20 percent men coming to lose some weight, tone up, make use of a range of body and beauty treatments, and enjoy either an energetic holiday or a relaxing vacation. You have free use of on-site bicycles, swimming pools, and an obstacle course laid out in the woodlands bordering the estate that includes rope swings for would-be Tarzans and Janes, plus extras such as coaching in the art of archery and clay pigeon shooting for which a gun is free but cartridges are not.

There are off-site local facilities for riding, golf, and squash, and pleasant country walks with mapped itineraries provided and possibilities for low-key sightseeing. Ragdale Hall is about 10 miles from Leicester, a manufacturing center, home of King Lear, with many reminders of historic associations, including a unique Roman Forum, and a 15th-century Guildhall. Nottingham, 20 minutes away, is associated with Robin Hood as well as Lord Byron, whose house, Newstead Abbey, contains rooms kept exactly as they were when the poet lived there. It has extensive surrounding gardens. Local car hire is available.

Name: Ragdale Hall Health Hydro

Mailing Address: Ragdale, near Melton Mowbray, Leicestershire, LE14 3PB, England

Telephone: (066475) 411; from the US, 011 44 (66475) 411; reservations, (066475) 458

Established: 1975

Managing Director: Martin J. Wootton

Program Directors: Victoria Hale, Jean Oliver

Owner: Leisure Development, Ltd.

Gender and Age Restrictions: Co-ed; minimum age 16. Young people of 16 to 18 must be accompanied by parents or a "responsible adult."

Season: Year-round

Length of Stay Required: Guests may arrive any day, depart any day, stay as long as they like. Arrival time after 11:30 AM and before 7:30 PM. Room availability after noontime. Your room must be vacated on departure day by 10:30 AM. If treatments are required on the day of departure after 10:30 AM, a changing room can be arranged for a fee.

Programs Offered: Nonresidential day packages are offered as well as stays up to 8 days/7 nights and more. Every stay includes free use of sauna and plunge pools, open from 8:00 AM to 8:00 PM, with hours assigned for use by men and for women; the whirlpool spa bath, open from 9:00 AM to 9:30 PM; the indoor pool, heated to 80 degrees F, with a maximum depth of 5 feet and a minimum of 4 feet, used also for supervised water exercise classes, and the heated outdoor pool, open during the summer months; and the gymnasium, which is outfitted with a rowing machine, Hydra-Fitness equipment, treadmill, free weights, dumbbells, stationary bicycles, and minitrampolines (PT bouncers). There are supervised classes in yoga, dance, and calisthenics held throughout the day, supplemented with scheduled sessions to familiarize you with the use of the gymnasium equipment. Organized runs on the obstacle course are scheduled daily, and groups are organized twice a day for supervised jogging; you can also do both on your own at any time.

All on-site recreational facilities are included, and coaching is available on request for a fee. For novice or experienced archers, there is a selection of bows, varying in strength. No experience is necessary for the clay pigeon shooting, but a steady aim and a good eye help. Cost, including a box of cartridges, is under £15. Ten bicycles may be used at any time. Tennis rackets are provided for play on the hard court. Mallets and balls for croquet, golf clubs and ball for the putting green are yours for the asking at the reception desk. Off-site squash, riding, and golf on a 9-hole course in Melton Mowbray are easily arranged for moderate fees. The reception staff can provide maps and suggest pleasant walks or selected routes for jogging on the property or through the surrounding Leicestershire countryside.

With a *2-night stay,* you receive a Swedish body massage or a G-5 vibrating massage (with or without infrared lamp heat), a facial and a Uvasun tanning treatment for your face. With a 6-night stay, you receive 5 massages or G-5 massages, 2 facials, 1 Uvasun tanning treatment for your body, and 2 Slender-tone treatments. With a 7-night stay, you receive in addition a Cleotherm Body Treatment, a relaxing, perspiration-inducing, skin-softening treat that combines aromatherapy, massage, and being cocooned between thermal blankets; or a wax bath for the same purpose and with possibly even more of a silkening effect on your skin.

After you arrive, you have a consultation with the dietitian, a beauty therapist, and a fitness therapist (if you wish to organize a fitness program for yourself). A fitness test and a body composition test (to check the ratio of lean tissue to body fat) are options available for a fee, as are individual or group counseling in stress management and relaxation techniques. You can work out a program as structured or as unstructured, as active and full or as relaxed and simple as you wish. Evening lectures, demonstrations, and a nightly video film you can view in your room on an in-house television channel are also included in every stay.

Diet and Weight Management: Ragdale Hall raises its own trout and grows some of the vegetables and herbs used for its low-fat, low-sodium, high-fiber meals. Guests have a choice of calorie levels, and calorie contents are marked on all menus. Lacto-ovo or strictly vegetarian menus are provided in addition to calorie-controlled portions that include meat or fish. The "whole food" menu offers wholesome, healthful, nutritious meals with higher calorie levels than the dietetic meals.

Breakfast is served to you in your room between 7:30 and 8:15 AM, and consists of tea or coffee, fresh orange juice or grapefruit juice, crispbread, and a portion of fruit preserves. A supplementary breakfast may be ordered for consumption either in your room or in the dining room between 7:30 and 9:30 AM. Lunch and dinner can be served in the dining room or in your room. Lunch is at midday. Dinner is early—at 5:45 or 6:45 PM. The dining room closes at 8:00 PM. However, there is 24-hour room service, and soft drinks, tea, coffee, and Bovril are served from 9:00 AM until 10:00 PM at à la carte rates in the bar.

A 750-calorie-a-day menu is recommended for dieters. Lunches are usually cold salad buffets, with a variety of meats, seafood, and cheeses offered, plus a fruit dessert. Dinner is a 3-course cooked meal, comprising a vegetable soup, an entrée such as paella (600 calories) or seafood (195 calories) or bacon and sweet corn pie (482 calories), with a low-calorie fruit mousse or soufflé for dessert, or a cheese platter—Cheddar, Brie, Camembert, Cheshire, Edam, and Stilton offered in small portions for reducers, biscuits (crackers), and crispbread. There are no provisions at Ragdale Hall for fasting.

For an extra fee, you can have a basal metabolic rate test to establish the number of calories required to maintain your heartbeat and other basic functions. The dietitian can then analyze your food intake and eating patterns and supply you with a diet sheet if necessary. Additional personal dietary advice regarding nutrition and caloric intake, long-term food regimens, and methods for preparing food are other available options.

Beauty Treatments and Welcome Indulgences: The hairdressing salon, using Vidal Sassoon products and treatments, is open from 9:00 AM to 6:00 PM 7 days a week, for conditioning, hot oil treatments, styling, and all hair care needs. Aromatherapy, acupressure, cathiodermie, Cleorderm and Cleotherm facials, ionithermie Inchaway, manicures including nail extensions and art designs, makeup and makeup instruction, pedicures, reflexology, Slendertone, depilatory waxing and full body waxing therapy comprise an alphabetic range of treatments and services offered, in addition to chiropody, figure analysis, tanning treatments, eyelash and brow dying, and eyebrow shaping. René Guinot, Clarins, De Cleor, and RoC products are used. Ragdale Hall has been licensed by Clarins to practice the Paris Method of face and body treatments developed by M. Jacques Courtin, a method only a few dozen beauty therapists in Britain are licensed to use.

Accommodations: All 49 rooms—singles, twins, 2 three-bedded rooms, studios, and suites—have private showers and loos, and all are centrally heated, provided with color TV with an in-house video channel and 24-hour switchboard-operated telephone service. If you want a bathtub in lieu of a shower, opt for the studio or suite accommodations, where fresh fruit and flowers will also be waiting for you. Suites feature a separate sitting room and, in the bedroom, a zipper-link that can transform twin beds into a double bed. Rattan furniture and bland colors—pinks, beiges, light greens—make for characterless guest-rooms, but rooms are convenient, comfortable, functional. Bedboards are available on request and will be provided free of charge. For a fee, you can have newspapers delivered with your morning tea or coffee.

What to Bring: See USEFUL INFORMATION. Bring a bathing suit for swimming and solarium; sandals and bathrobe or dressing gown for between-treatment use. Dress is informal at all times. Some guests like to dress for supper. Others prefer to have supper in their rooms on a tray. The boutique, just off the foyer, carries bathing suits, sportswear, warmup suits, and leisurewear from leading European fashion houses. It also stocks skin care and makeup products, toiletries, perfume, jewelry, watches, postcards, paperback books, gift items, and a selection of athletic footwear and sandals. The boutique is open from 9:00 AM to 6:00 PM 7 days a week. Laundry service is available for a nominal fee.

Documentation from Your Physician: A letter of approval is requested but not required. On arrival, all guests are asked to fill in and sign a questionnaire "which covers everything." A physician is on call should any emergency arise.

The Use of Alcohol and Tobacco: House wines are available. Smoking is permitted in guests' bedrooms and in the bar.

Fees, Method of Payment, Insurance Coverage: Year-round rates, including service, per night:

Single room: £77.55

Twin room: £57.75 per person

Studio: £88.55 single; £68.75 per person double

Suite: £105.05 single; £82.25 per person double

3-bedded room: £57.75 per person whether occupied by 1 or more guests

All prices are subject to change, and all rates are subject to a 15 percent VAT. A deposit is required. Ask about the cancellation policy. Payment may be made by cash, personal check if backed with a credit card, travelers' checks in pounds, or by Barclaycard, Access, American Express, or Visa.

Follow-up Assistance: Video and audio cassettes and cookbooks are available. Annual newsletters are sent to all guests.

⟡ Shrubland Hall Health Clinic ⟢
Suffolk

Shrubland Hall is the aristocrat of British spas. The family seat of the baronets of Saumarez, a distinguished English family of Norman descent, it belongs to and is lived in by Lord and Lady de Saumarez who, in order to keep the Hall intact, transformed Shrubland into the grand, romantic, and astonishingly affordable health spa it is today. It is situated in East Anglia, the eastern rounded prominence of southern England, 6 miles from Ipswich, a large thriving port on the Orwell river close to the seaside-village-studded North Sea coast, 48 miles from Cambridge, and 80 miles from London. In this part of England, Norman castles, Roman city walls, church ruins, oak trees, and roses were often painted by Constable.

Shrubland Hall is a palatial Georgian manor house. Built on one of the highest points in Suffolk, with spectacular English classical gardens laid out in the majestic Italianate style of the Villa d'Este, it is complete with a terrace staircase of 100 balustraded stairs that lead from the house to the centerpiece pool and fountain and to the loggia beyond. No other spa in England has such an impressive exterior; it was chosen, you may remember, for the opening sequence of the James Bond film *Never Say Never Again,* a scene that some claim revitalized English male spa-going. Even Agent 007 was unable to get a vodka martini here and had to be content with a shower instead of a tub bath. The low-calorie diet is surprisingly satisfying as it slims away the 5 or 10 pounds most guests come here to lose. Those guests, business- and arts-oriented, with an age range mostly from 30 to 65, frequently return.

The house contains remarkable English and French furniture, interesting paintings and prints, outstanding collections of English, Oriental, and European porcelain, and a bedroom with museum-quality hand-painted Chinese wallpaper specially designed for Queen Victoria and Prince Albert when they visited here in the mid-19th century. The room you occupy may have a recessed or a canopied bed, a fireplace, a balcony, a patio garden, and is sure to have its own writing desk with a supply of writing paper and envelopes, telephone, and television set. The loftiness of high-ceilinged rooms, parquet floors, marble and gilt breakfronts, and the regal red-carpeted staircases of a truly stately house are balanced by the comfort of down-filled chairs and sofas to sink into, fresh flowers everywhere, spacious sitting rooms, a library, and a billiard room. A house elevator takes you to the upper rooms with access to the Tower. There is a large conservatory filled with lush tropical greenery flanked by the shimmering water of a heated swimming pool. An outdoor solarium for women is designed for sunbathing in your birthday suit surrounded by thick, tall walls of yew.

The grounds merge into wild gardens and woodlands where you come upon whimsical follies such as a Japanese garden or a Russian summerhouse, but you'll also find a hairdressing and beauty salon, Nautilus equipment, two boutiques purveying the latest in exercise clothes and exercise cassettes, a sauna, Turkish bath, aromatherapy and physiotherapy rooms, and body conditioning classes taught by a superb staff trained in the Pilates system as well as by qualified gymnasts. You can have thalassotherapy-style seaweed baths here, salt rubs, a full body wax, and wonderful massages.

A maximum number of 50 guests can be accommodated in the main house; in the Russian *dacha* with 2 bedrooms, sitting room, and kitchen; in 4 single-room chalets 50 yards from the main house; and in the 6 rooms of the Old Hall, the original house that stands in the heart of the park about a 10-minute walk from the main house. Don't worry about getting to the main house in time for breakfast, for it will be served to you in your room as it is to all guests.

Guests are welcome to hire a rod from Shrubland's private fishing club and fish the 10-acre Sharmford Mere that is amply stocked with trout, or to hire well-schooled horses from Newton Hall, an excellent private riding stable nearby. Individual and group outings (maximum 12 persons) can easily be arranged for about £5 per person aboard the Lady Florence, a 50-foot motor vessel, which cruises daily from Orford Quay on the rivers Alde and Ore along a beautiful section of the "Heritage Coast" that includes the Havergate Island Bird Sanctuary.

In Ipswich, England's oldest town, with 12 medieval churches, a Tudor mansion, and 700 acres of parks that recently won top prize in the "Beautiful Britain in Bloom" competition, you'll find a fine collection of paintings by Gainsborough and Constable in Christchurch Mansion, a museum with a Roman villa display, and the Great White Horse Hotel, scene of Mr. Pickwick's memorable nocturnal adventures. The area hosts garden, music, and arts festivals galore and offers antique auctions and fairs, historic houses, museums, sports events, and quality craftware. A very reasonable local taxi service is available for these and other excursions in delight-filled Suffolk and nearby East Anglia. In Suffolk, the Aldringham Craft Market near Aldeburgh, the Bury St. Edmonds Art Gallery housed in a Grade I Robert Adam building, the remarkable collection of 19th-century buildings at Snape Maltings on the banks of the Alde river, the medieval town of Lavenham, the antique shops in Woodbridge, the race meets at Newmarket, Aldeburgh Moot Hall's Regional Museum, Clare's Ancient House Museum, the historical recreation of Tudor life at Kentwell, concerts at Snape Maltings, and the beach at Felixstowe are among many attractive possibilities near at hand for starters.

Name: Shrubland Hall Health Clinic

Mailing Address: Coddenham, near Ipswich, Suffolk, IP6 9QH, England

Telephone: (0473) 830 404; from the US, 011 44 (473) 830 404

Established: 1966

Managing Director: The Hon. Victor de Saumarez

Program Directors: A. Boag, M.D.; R. Haigh

Owners: Lord and Lady de Saumarez

Gender and Age Restrictions: Co-ed; minimum age 16

Season: Year-round except for 2 weeks over the Christmas holidays

Length of Stay Required: Minimum 7 days. Arrival Sundays and Wednesdays from 2:00 to 4:00 PM. Rooms to be vacated by 11:00 AM on departure.

Programs Offered: Emphasis is on an individual approach to guests' needs and requirements in regard to diet, nutrition education, behavior modification, physical activity, and exercise programs. When you arrive, you have a consultation with a state-qualified registered nurse, who records your weight, measurements, and medical history. You then have a consultation with Lady de Saumarez, a highly respected dietitian, followed by a medical examination by a qualified physician. Your individual regime is then worked out.

Shrubland Hall is registered as a health clinic and has 2 licensed physicians on staff, assisted by 4 state-qualified registered nurses, 4 highly qualified exercise therapists, and a registered dietitian. Nutritional counseling, behavior therapy, psychotherapy, and training in stress management and relaxation techniques as required are yours for a modest additional fee of about £15 for each consultation. Blood tests, physical performance testing, body composition analysis, electrocardiograph, and psychiatric sessions are available off-site by referral to competent specialists. Appointments for acupuncture treatments, chiropody and posture assessment, postural reeducation and remedial exercises are available. The tranquility and peaceful surroundings of Shrubland are sufficient to induce blissful relaxation for most guests, but further treatments for stress and insomnia are also offered for the same price as other medical consultations. Orthopedic treatments are offered by one of Shrubland's physicians "to restore a full and painless range of movement to spinal and other joints." Physiotherapy, when prescribed by the physician in charge, is obtainable in a department well equipped for remedial treatments known as "manipulative therapies."

Included in your daily program is a massage by a massage therapist who "does" you regularly during your stay. Aromatherapy massage for your body and face with "costly oils" is available by appointment and a marvelous "must" for most. Also included in your daily program is a "heat treatment"—Turkish bath, individual steam cabinet, or a sauna ending in a brisk salt rub and an icy cold plunge afterward. One Kneipp hydrotherapy bath, using Kneipp's plant and herbal essences and extracts, is included in your program, as is an underwater massage. You can have a soothing peat bath or a wax bath that has a truly remarkable effect on your skin, leaving it admirably smooth and supple, or a seaweed-paste, thalassotherapy-style body wrap, all pleasant extras. After your underwater massage or your session in an individual steam cabinet, you have a choice of a sitz bath or an alternating low- and high-pressure, hot and cold, hosing of your body, known as the "Guss and Blitz Guss" treatment. A gander at yourself afterward, all rosy and toned up, may be adequate compensation for the *aqua frigida* sessions of the sitz and blitz treatments, but then again. . . .

Exercise classes, some based on hatha-yoga, are held every day in the gym, which is equipped with stationary bicycles and multistationed Nautilus. Emphasis is given to correct breathing, posture, stretching, and relaxation. A Shrubland exclusive—classes in body conditioning using the Alan Herdman system of exercise based on the techniques of German osteopath Joseph Pilates. Classes are limited to 2 persons at one time, and an extra charge of £17 is made for a course of 5 lessons. They consist of exercises performed horizontally on a series of machines using springs as resistance, allowing your body to be centered and your spine aligned in positions that avoid stress on your lower back and neck. The movements, combined with deep breathing, provide maximum stretching and elongation of the muscles and eliminate the "bunched" effect caused by improper use of weights or unsupervised calisthenics.

You might like to try a faradism treatment or a Minitone facial treatment, both extras at reasonable prices. You may be happy just to swim in the heated pool, covered in winter, on the South Terrace, next to the luxuriant foliage and flowering plants in the conservatory. Equipment—rackets, clubs, mallets—can be obtained at the reception desk for playing tennis on a court located in the garden, clock golf, and croquet. You can use the solarium in the conservatory or sunbathe in a sheltered natural area down the terrace steps at the left-hand end of the swimming pool terrace. Mattresses are provided. You can coze or doze in a garden chair, or ask the porter to put up the table for table tennis in the gym. Guests who have brought their own golf clubs are welcome to play on the courses at Stowmarket and Woodbridge 12 miles away. Greens fees will run you about £11 a round, or £15 for the day.

In the evenings, there is usually a once-a-week concert of classical guitar music, a talk or a demonstration, a video program, a game of bridge or chess, or the option of a local taxi service or self-drive car rental to whisk you away to a film in Ipswich, a play, concert, or other engaging local attraction—if you have any desire to stir from Shrubland's cushioning serenity. *All outside doors are locked at 10:00 pm.* Arrangements can be made for you to be let in later but no later than 11:00!

Diet and Weight Management: Diets are prescribed for you in consultation on your arrival to meet your individual needs and requirements. For weight loss and "cleansing your system," you can fast on liquids under close supervision. If you do so, you are encouraged to steep yourself in fresh air, enjoy gentle exercise, and not to drive on your own but to let other people chauffeur you "as all reactions tend to be slower" during a fasting period. It is further recommended that all excursions and sight-seeing be postponed until you ease off on your fast during the latter part of your stay.

Whatever your diet, you are encouraged to drink a few glasses of water between meals. Fresh water drawn from Shrubland's own private-well and flavored with a slice of lemon is always available in jugs in the Light Diet Room for this purpose. All guests are also advised to have afternoon tea, preferably with sugar or honey and *not* artificial sweeteners, which is served in the Light Diet Room at 4:00 PM. For those on a light diet or a liquid fast, lunch is served at noon in the Light Diet Room. Those on less restricted diets have lunch in the main dining room at 12:45 PM and at noon on Sundays. All evening meals are served in the Light Diet Room at 6:00 PM except for dinner at 7:00 on Tuesday and Saturday for those guests whose diet includes a cooked meal on the evening before departure. Whatever food regimen you are following, breakfast will always be served in your room between 7:30 and 8:30 AM. Where and when food is served is important at Shrubland Hall. No casual wandering in or out of the dining rooms. You are asked to be on time for meals.

Although the diet of each guest is adjusted in consultation with the nutrition-ist, the general pattern of your food regimen might be as follows:

If you have opted for a strict fast, for 3 days your breakfast, lunch, and supper will consist of a thermos of hot water containing a lemon slice, accompanied by a little pot of locally produced honey. On days 4 and 5, you have fruit juice for lunch and vegetable broth for supper. On day 6, you have grapefruit for breakfast, fruit and yogurt for lunch, and a cooked meal of chicken and vegetables in the evening. On day 7, you add crispbread for breakfast and soup, salad, cheese, and biscuits (crackers) for lunch before you leave.

For those on a Light Diet, breakfast is a thermos of hot water flavored with a slice of lemon accompanied by a tiny pot of honey, slices of grapefruit, and possibly a slice of crispbread. Lunch, days 1 to 4, is a light, low-calorie salad and perhaps a portion of cottage cheese flavored with lemon, parsley and garlic.

Supper, days 1 to 4, consists of vegetable broth and a serving of 2 different kinds of fruit.

Lunch, days 5 to 7, is salad in the main dining room, where a changing variety of three high-calorie salads and 3 low-calorie salads are served, accompanied by a platter of grated and shredded raw vegetables. One level dessertspoon each of the high-calorie salads and one each of the low-calorie salads is your recommended portion. No more. You are told to chew your salad well, to eat it slowly "since digestion begins in the mouth." Safflower seed oil, fresh lemon juice, and delicious homemade mayonnaise are on the salad table and may be added to salads "in moderation." You are also allowed to have small cups of homemade soup and a serving of cheese and biscuits.

Supper, days 5 to 7, comprises vegetable broth, fruit, and yogurt. The food is primarily lacto-ovo vegetarian, high in fiber, low in fat. Salt is not used in any of the soups or salads, but Maldon Sea Salt and a grinder of black peppercorns are available. Soups are made from fresh vegetables, and no artificial seasoning or thickening is added. Bread is freshly baked daily using wheat and barley grown on the estate. Cottage cheese and yogurt are made from the milk of Shrubland's herd of Jerseys and Friesian cows. The food is presented with style and elegance, delicious. If requested, food preparation is demonstrated in the main kitchen. Cooking lessons are available.

Beauty Treatments and Welcome Indulgences: Beauticians provide facials, manicures, and pedicures. A hairdresser comes on Tuesday and Saturday by appointment for simple wash, set, and dry and heated roller hairdos. Hair coloring and cutting, permanents, and other treatments are available, as are eyelash and eyebrow tinting, eyebrow shaping, depilatory waxing treatments, faradism, Vacusage, and Minitone facial toning. The great treatments are the wax bath to silken your skin, and aromatherapy, as well as an irresistible range of creams, cosmetics, and shampoos.

Accommodations: Romantic. Comfortable. High ceilings, moldings, tall windows, pastel colors, and the use of robin's egg blue set off the charm of good antique furniture, mostly English and French. All rooms, of course, are individually furnished. Of the 28 rooms in the main house, 2 have double four-poster beds, some have twin beds, some single accommodations. All have color TV, most have fireplaces. There's excellent maid service and telephones in all rooms operated through the switchboard service open from 8:30 AM until 10:00 PM, when Shrubland closes down for the night and all outside doors are locked. Writing materials are provided. Newspapers are delivered daily. Shoes set outside your door are collected, cleaned, and returned in the morning. With the exception of 10 single rooms in the main house that share 3 toilets, all rooms have private loos. There are 4 garden rooms 50 yards from the main house for single accommodation, each comfortably and tastefully furnished, well heated, with private loo and wash basin, and large picture windows facing southwest onto lovely garden vistas. The Old Hall, a picturesque and charming historic house overlooking the park, has a double room with twin beds and adjoining shower and toilet, and 5 single rooms sharing shower and toilet facilities. The rooms are attractive and charmingly furnished, but this is a residence best for summer months until a heating system can be installed. About 200 yards from the main house is an attractive rustic timber cottage constructed in the circular style with peaky roof of a Russian *dacha,* surrounded by its own garden. There are 2 cheerfully furnished single bedrooms, a sitting room, a small kitchen, and bathroom, another charming residence best for summer occupancy. No pets are allowed in the house, but dogs can often be accommodated in nearby kennels, providing you reserve space in advance. For a choice in single rooms, you must reserve at least 6 months in advance. Otherwise, you might end up with a room without a bath.

What to Bring: See USEFUL INFORMATION. Bring warm nightwear and woolly slippers. Bring bathing suit(s) and your thong sandals for wear around the pool. Your Wellies are useful for walking after rain and for fishing. Bring sweaters, and something warm to throw over your shoulders in the evening. Bring informal, casual country clothes, and something slightly dressier for festivals and concerts. You are asked not to bring "smart clothes, i.e., evening dress," as dress for dinner is informal. A skirt, sweater and blouse, or caftan will be just fine for the ladies, and blazer and tie or turtleneck sweater will do for men. There are two boutiques on the premises well stocked with athletic wear, sundries like toothpaste and sun blocks, exercise books, cookbooks, and exercise cassettes. Magazines are supplied in the library and sitting rooms. The lending library is open from 4:00 to 10:00 PM daily, so you won't be short of general reading material. You are asked not to bring portable televisions, Walkmans, radios— "Don't bring anything noisy!" It's advisable, as always, to bring your own film.

Documentation from Your Physician: A letter of approval is requested when appropriate. A medical history and documentation of recent physical examination are requested. A medical disclaimer is required from every guest who does not wish to be examined by one of Shrubland's physicians.

The Use of Alcohol and Tobacco: Alcohol is forbidden. Smoking is strongly discouraged, but allowed in the guest's room and in the TV room and conservatory. Guests who come to Shrubland to give up smoking are given supportive encouragement.

Fees, Method of Payment, Insurance Coverage: Year-round rates per person per week, inclusive of service:

Main house:

Single room: £297 to £473

Double room: £341 per person

Single occupancy chalets or garden rooms: £341

Old Hall:

Single room: £330 or £385

Double room: £330 per person

Russian Lodge:

£330 per person for double occupancy; single occupancy rates vary

Rates depend on size, outlook, and amenities of room, and are higher for deluxe accommodations. All rates are subject to 15 percent VAT, and all prices are subject to change. Gratuities in addition to service charges are optional. A deposit is required. Ask about the cancellation policy. Payment must be made in pounds, by travelers' checks or personal check. No credit cards are accepted. Insurance coverage is claimable only for prescribed physiotherapy treatment.

Follow-up Assistance: A routine for continuing the Pilates exercises at home without the use of special equipment can be arranged. A videotape and a book about these exercises for use on leaving Shrubland are available and are sold only to guests who have learned this method either at Shrubland or at Alan Herdman's exercise studio in London. Diet sheets can be bought when you leave, and additional dietary consultations can be arranged if necessary. Shrubland's salad recipe book is available. Bread, yogurt, cottage cheese, soups, pâtés, quiches, herbs, "biscuits," cakes, preserves, chutney, dried fruits, honey, and other delectable, wholesome fare can be bought at Shrublands to enable you to continue your diet when you leave. Box lunches, if requested, can be provided.

Scotland

  Stobo Castle Health Spa
Peebleshire

"The Puritan conscience that frowns on luxury, enjoyment, or pleasure has no place at Stobo Castle," avers its slim owner Gaynor Winyard, former chairwoman of the Society of Health and Beauty Therapists of Britain and author of *A Guide for Beauty Therapists,* published by Longmans. "Come to Stobo to be pampered and cosseted, to escape from stress and strain, to be cared for, to become more conscious of your body and its potential." She and her son Stephen, a blond, bearded, cheerful young man with the athletic build and height of a basketball player, bought the property in 1975 from the Countess of Dysart's estate. Restoring and renovating this monumental early-19th-century baronial castle of stone and brick, with four crenelated towers, two courtyards, and massive porte-cochère—a building listed as Grade A for its architectural importance by the Historic Buildings Council—they opened it as a luxurious health and beauty spa for men and women in 1978.

The spa stands on 14 acres, with access to the surrounding 4000 acres of forested park and rich farmland owned by the present laird, Leopold Seymour. A minute's brisk from the Great Hall, you are gazing at swans on a loch with the calm of its waters disturbed only by the soft plop-plop of rising trout or the splash of a local fisherman's Wellington boots. The loch's overflow cascades into the waterfalls of a Japanese water garden, carefully concealed in a coniferous and broad-leafed woodland, set about with a lichened stone lantern, arching bridges, a tea house, and stepping stones across "a wee burn." In this magical combination of the mystical Orient and a Scottish wood, you may startle an owl, a rabbit, a pheasant, or a red deer as you walk along paths cushioned with pine needles toward Stobo kirk, with its Norman nave, chancel, and tower and later 17th- and 18th-century additions. (In these parts, anything built after the 16th century is often referred to as "new.")

Some 27 miles miles south of Edinburgh's airport and about 5 miles southwest of the town of Peebles, which has been a royal burgh since the 14th century—

and where the traditional Beltane Festival, the "Riding of the Marches," still takes place on the last Saturday in June—you find yourself in the heart of the Scottish Border region, close to the Tweed River, which may not be the finest salmon river in Scotland but as an all-rounder is unbeatable, with spring and autumn salmon, brown trout, and sea trout. You are close to the site of Roman camps, to the traditional burial place of the wizard Merlin, and to many stately homes. This is sparsely populated Sir Walter Scott country, pretty much unchanged through the centuries.

Many guests are just as happy to stay put at Stobo where the emphasis is on relaxation, consuming deliciously fresh, low-calorie food in the handsomely paneled dining room, sitting before the open fire in the high-ceilinged drawing room resplendent with coral-colored panels and elaborate white plasterwork, or catching up on correspondence, reading, or watching television in their own spacious, comfortable rooms, each with a fireplace set with easier-to-cope-with electric coals. Although married couples frequently visit together, the ratio of women to men is usually 4 to 1. The age range of guests runs from 16 to 95, but the average age is 40 or so. Since this is not a medical spa, most guests come here to lose 5 to 10 pounds by cutting back on calories and exercising, while enjoying an extensive array of beauty and skin care treatments in an ambience of total comfort and indulgence—if you feel like slopping in to lunch or dinner in your dressing gown, you can. "Castle Care" is the name of Stobo's brand of cosmetic products, but castle comfort is what is amply proffered to you and no more than 30 companions every tranquil hour of your pleasurable stay.

Name: Stobo Castle Health Spa

Mailing Address: Stobo Castle, Peebleshire, EH45 8NY, Scotland

Telephone: Stobo (07216) 249; from the US, 011 44 (7216) 249

Established: 1978

Managing Director: Stephen Winyard

Program Directors: Gaynor Winyard, Overall Spa Director; Pauline Mason, Spa Manager; Mark Stoll, Fitness Director; Patricia Morton, Spa Supervisor

Owner: The Winyard family

Gender and Age Restriction: Co-ed; minimum age 16

Season: Year-round

Length of Stay Required: Minimum 2 nights. Arrival time from 2:30 PM, and you should vacate your room before noon on the day of departure.

Programs Offered: You can opt for the *Health and Beauty Plan,* the *Health and Fitness Plan,* or the money-saving *Holiday Plan.* Yoga relaxation classes are included in all programs, as are stretching and warm-up exercises, aerobics, and dance classes held in the ground-floor gym room. At the entrance of the room is a harmonium for hand-played musical accompaniments when desired. At the other end of the room, there's a Gympac body-builder (simplified Nautilus-type equipment), a Tunturi stationary bicycle, a rowing machine, a recliner, a treadmill, and free weights.

Downstairs is the softly lit spa area, done in restful tones of olive green and silver, open for your use from 7:30 AM to 10:30 PM. Here are room after room of curtained cubicles for beauty and skin care treatments, a hairdressing salon, sun beds, a small cabinlike sauna, 4 individual steam cabinets in which all but your head is enclosed, changing cubicles, showers, enclosed areas for mud, paraffin, and aromatherapy treatments. A lilac-toned room has curtained cubicles for massage treatments. There is a hydrotherapy tub room. The "wet area" is a solariumlike room enclosing the heated (82 to 84 degrees F) 10- by 24-foot swimming and exercise pool, 4 feet 6 inches deep, and the hexagonal whirlpool, heated to 96 degrees F. Plans are underway to enlarge the spa area by glassing in the courtyard it abuts, so expect changes by 1990 and possibly before.

All guests may use the wet area facilities of the spa, and all have the recreational use of an outdoor tennis court and 2 bicycles, free of charge. Tennis rackets and golf clubs are also provided free of charge. There is a superb 18-hole golf course 6 miles away at Peebles, with modest greens fees. Bows and arrows are provided if you are interested in archery on an outside target lawn, or you can engage in croquet on the south lawn, badminton, or indoor table tennis. Hiking and walking trails, hill climbing, and bird-watching are extraordinarily interesting in this area of the Border country, which has evoked some of Scotland's most poignant ballads. Evening lectures on subjects allied to health, beauty, and fitness are given by Stobo's trained staff or by visiting specialists and supplemented with a chef's cooking demonstration twice a week in the castle kitchen, a delightful seminar in flower arranging, and a demonstration in self-defense. The specialty of Stobo, however, and its main focus, is the variety of skin care, face, and body treatments available.

On arrival, you are given a private consultation to check your blood pressure, medical history, weight, measurements, physical condition, and the medications you are taking in order to assess which treatments are most suitable for you and if any are not advisable. Extra treatments and spa appointments can be booked at the spa reception desk, open Monday to Saturday 9:00 AM to 5:30 PM, Sunday from 9:00 AM to 1:00 PM. It is recommended that you book requests for additional treatments prior to arrival whenever possible, and be particularly foresighted about hairdressing appointments as there is only 1 hairdresser on staff. When you arrive, you will receive a 14-page sheaf of stapled information for your guidance and explanation of all treatments offered.

On request, thorough and professional preventive medicine programs from Lifewatch, Edinburgh, can be arranged for you in Edinburgh. The *Wellwoman Program* is offered at 2 levels—with a nurse or with a general practitioner in charge of the screening. The first is designed to identify breast and pelvic disease, and tests include measurement of height, weight, and blood pressure, together with urine analysis, rubella screening, blood test, and cervical smear. The second, with the doctor, takes gynecological and medical history and provides breast and pelvic examination in addition to the above services. You will receive a written report. The *Wellman Program* is similarly offered at 2 price levels (approximately £60 and £75) for a Wellman Cardiac Report, which covers height, weight, blood pressure, urine, blood test for cholesterol, and EKG, while at the second level special attention is paid to the cardiovascular system, with a discussion of drinking, smoking, and exercise.

Diet and Weight Management: Calories per portion are indicated on a lunch and dinner menu which also offers a vegetarian dinner. Guests on a 400- to 500-calorie diet are asked to select only a main course with vegetables or salad; guests on an 800-calorie diet can make their selection from a choice of "starters" and main courses; guests on a 1000-calorie diet can choose from starters, main courses, and "sweets" (desserts); nondieters, in addition to the menu items, can have potatoes boiled in their jackets, local whole-meal bread, homemade natural yogurt with honey, and locally produced Border cheeses, which are available at each meal.

Stylishly printed on a pasteboard folder, your luncheon menu might include celery and apple soup, prawn chowder, French onion soup with cheese croutons (ranging from 55 to 80 calories); fillet of beef en croute with mushroom and brandy sauce, vegetable and nut rissoles, fillet of sole with orange and almond sauce, monkfish poached in lime juice with hazel nuts, a choice of many salads, cold fish, and meat (ranging from 195 to 250 calories). Both the regular and the vegetarian dinners might present fresh asparagus with lemon and sunflower dip, tomato and coriander soup, avocado vinaigrette, or broccoli and chive soup. A regular dinner might be a baked wood pigeon on blackcurrant coulis, salmon and limes in aspic, or supreme of chicken stuffed with prawns (all under 250 calories). Vegetarians receive such goodies as five-bean cassoulet, fettucine with walnuts and cottage cheese, sweet potatoes baked with sweet corn and cheese, or Mexican vegetable tortillas. Desserts for lunch and dinner are usually made with fruit—fresh peach with raspberry ice, fresh plum soufflé, raspberry fool, baked banana with Demarara rum, orange brandy caramel. These delectable dishes and many others are prepared by Chef Malcolm ("Mac") Browning. Meals are high in fiber, low in calories, low in fat, and low in sodium. Nondieting guests are allowed a maximum of 2 glasses of wine "per evening meal." If on a diet, you can imbibe the delicious water on tap, piped pure and sparkling clear from Stobo's own freshwater spring.

The paneled dining room, set with mahogany tables and chairs, covered with cloths at lunch, with mats at dinner, is a splendid setting for flavorful and attractively presented spa food. Breakfasts are served in your room. To be able to dress as you please, to munch away in your dressing gown or warm-up suit at every meal or to dress up when you feel like it may delight you or displease you as not seemly in such a baronial ambience as Stobo's dining room with its tapestried frieze and formal place settings, but how relaxing to have a choice! Coffee, tea, and low-calorie beverages are available throughout the day in the dining room.

Beauty Treatments and Welcome Indulgences: A dozen highly qualified skin care and beauty therapists operate hydrotherapy equipment, and will rub your body with salt, slather you with marine algae, coat you with paraffin wax, poultice you with northern Italy's renowned Battaglia mud as well as mineral-rich mud imported from Peru, biopeel your skin, and treat your face with the mild galvanic currents involved in the cathiodermie process. You can also have a therapeutic Moor Peat bath or a Thalgo seaweed bath; a reflexology foot massage; leg cover treatment for heavy or swollen legs; a 2½-hour algotherapy session, which is a super-thalassotherapy treatment; a Frigi-Thalgo wrap around a problem area; collagen and elastin facial treatments; 45 minutes of faradic muscle contracting and relaxing treatment; and massages with pulsating and nonpulsating plastic cups. Aromatherapy treatments with Stobo's own Castle Care aromatherapy oils—with more than 50 selections to choose from—are exceptional; an hour's treatment guarantees utter relaxation for approximately £25. The spa's full-service beauty salon dyes eyelashes and eyebrows, does depilatory waxing, and from Tuesday to Saturday provides a variety of hair-dressing services for men and women. Guests on the *Holiday Plan* must request these treatments on an à la carte basis.

Accommodations: There are 19 bedrooms, some on the ground floor, most on the second floor, including 7 double bedrooms with bath; 6 single guestrooms with a "vanity unit" (a mirror and basin combination) and sharing a turret bathroom with lavatory, shower, and bath; and 3 particularly handsome double bedrooms, the Elliot, Murray, and Phillipson rooms on the ground floor, as well as 2 of the original family bedrooms, the Darnley and the Montgomery. The Darnley has a WC and shower and the Montgomery has a WC and bath. Each room and private suite is centrally heated, has a radio, color television, electric top blankets, telephone, and fireplace with simulated fire, electrically controlled and providing cosy warmth. Each room and private suite has its individual decor and personality, decorated in "the English country look," a look of unstudied elegance, charm, and comfort with a mix of furniture styles and periods, nothing obviously matching, but everything going well together just as you would expect in a large country house. All rooms are truly spacious, with high ceilings, large windows, comfortable beds, sofas, and chairs. Two double rooms on the ground floor have terraces and are referred to as "the terrace twins."

A nice touch are room keys attached to long dark-green-plastic tags printed with your name in gold letters. Some of the bathrooms are equipped with enormous bathtubs that must be close to 6 feet long and wide enough to give you room to clasp your hands behind your head while bending your elbows hardly at all. Others just have showers and lavatories. The main switchboard is open daily from 8:30 AM to 10:00 PM, but there is a public telephone in the reception hall in case you are seized with the desire to make a midnight call.

All outside doors to the Castle are locked between 10:30 PM and 7:30 AM. If you want to enter or leave the building between these times, however, you can, using the main front door to leave and pressing the front doorbell when you return, taking your chances on just how long you will have to wait before the door is opened for you.

What to Bring: See USEFUL INFORMATION. Bring your most presentable terry-cloth bathrobe or dressing gown because you'll be wearing it a lot as a bathing suit cover-up and for treatments. Bring casual, comfortable country clothes for excursions and something to change into at night even though mealtime dress is optional. Bring warm socks and Wellington boots if you plan to have fun exploring the loch and the Japanese water garden (those stepping stones are slippery with moss!). Bring sweaters. A fold-up or regular raincoat is always useful in Scotland, and you'll need a scarf, hat, or cap to cover your head. You don't need to bother with an umbrella unless you're an ardent golfer. A warm lap rug is recommended if you plan to sit outside in early spring or late autumn. Bring reading and writing materials. Newspapers and periodicals are provided in the coral-paneled drawing room, but you're supposed to read them there and not take them with you to your room. The boutique has a revolving rack of health, beauty, and exercise books—that's all—but bookshops like W. H. Smith in Peebles stock marvelous reference books as well as classics and bestsellers. A small corner shelf in the boutique carries toothpaste and other vital necessities, and the exercise clothes, leisurewear, and accessories should fill in if you have forgotten anything. You can find sheepskin-lined bedroom slippers and heavy-weight cashmere shawls in Peebles shops and local woolen mills; wool and cashmere sweaters are excellent buys. Laundry can be arranged through the housekeeping department.

Documentation from Your Physician: A brief check into your medical history will be made at Stobo on your arrival, and your blood pressure will be read. If you have a cardiovascular condition, a history of thrombosis or arteriosclerosis, abnormally high or low blood pressure, congestive conditions of the lungs, skin problems, allergies, epilepsy, diabetes, are pregnant, on any medication, or have a hip relacement, these are contraindications for various treatments and should be brought to the attention of Mrs. Winyard.

The Use of Alcohol and Tobacco: No hard liquor is sold on the premises. Guests are permitted a maximum of 2 glasses of wine with dinner if not following a calorie-controlled diet. Guests are not permitted to smoke in public rooms, but they may smoke in their own rooms or outside.

Fees, Method of Payment, Insurance Coverage: Year-round rates per day:

For single accommodations: £79 to £115

For double occupancy: £51.75 (with a vanity unit on the *Holiday Plan*) to £74.25 per person

Daily fees do not include 15 percent VAT or gratuities, the latter of which is at your discretion. All shared accommodations are subject to a 25 percent discount (included in the above prices), which will run through 1988. Expect price increases of 10 percent in 1991. A deposit is required. Ask about the cancellation policy. Personal checks and travelers' checks are accepted when backed with Diners Club, American Express, Visa, Access, MasterCard, Style, Carte Bleue, or Eurocard. Fees are not deductible as a medical expense.

Follow-up Assistance: A Stobo Castle audio cassette about exercise and beauty routines is obtainable, as is *The Castle Cookbook,* Woods of Windsor and Castle Care cosmetics and the aromatherapy oils and essences Gaynor Winyard has custom-produced. Guests also receive a biennial (spring and autumn) 5-page newsletter, *Image,* well written and packed with helpful hints—even a contest with a grand prize of a weekend for two at Stobo.

France

ᘯ Centre de Thalasso-Esthétique ᘰ
de Pointe Biotherm

Deauville

Biotherm, specialists in skin care products and treatments for the face and body—firming, antiwrinkle, slimming, and relaxing—has created a sleek, chic, shimmering blue-and-white thalassotherapy–beauty care center in Deauville, that dazzling resort where life in the high season centers around the Casino. If you're looking for a feeling of Saratoga, Palm Beach, Newport, a dash of Hollywood, a splash of Atlantic City, it's all here—polo, the race meetings, regattas, parties, galas, and the environs of the *plage fleurie,* the flowered beach, with its baize-green lawns, masses of hydrangeas, elaborate swimming pool, and Bar du Soleil's outdoor tables for people-watching. And that's not all. There is tennis on 20 courts, sailing, windsurfing, golf on 2 international standard courses, an aero club where you can learn to fly, minigolf, bicycles and cars to rent, boats to charter, nightclubs, discos, and shops.

The Biotherm Center, with a special program for men, has a complete physical fitness program for both men and woman. The center's high-tech architecture and decor are immaculate, uncluttered, light, bright, and fabulous. Its 8100 square feet of space include an aqua–gym and sites for treatments such as acupuncture, massages with a variety of techniques, electrotherapy for beneficial passive exercise, electrostimulation face lifts, hot seawater therapy, lymphatic drainage, ultrasound—just about everything you can think of to streamline, remodel, tone, and firm your face and body (with 39 specific treatments for wrinkles and sagging skin alone) and fight fatigue and burnout from stress and overwork. The center also has a 6-day postnatal cure, designed to help women shape up after childbirth. No cots to rest on here—you relax instead on *repos bleu*—inflated, transparent, blue, heated water beds—under the supervision of a highly qualified and charming staff of attendants, cosmetologists, fitness instructors, and massage therapists.

Upon your arrival at the center, you are introduced to an impressive team of doctors, hydrotherapists, nutritionists, and cosmetologists who assist you in defining your problems, then advise you on a personalized program to meet your specific needs. In a package plan, you are entitled to 3 thalassotherapy treatments daily, such as a *bain bouillonnant* (whirlpool), a *douche à jet* (jet shower), *jet sous-marin* (underwater jet massage), plus 90 minutes of kinesitherapy, which could be a combination of a workout in the pool, gymnastics, and jazz dancing. *Bio tonic, bio gym,* and *bio musculant* (for muscle strengthening) exercise workouts are available in the well-equipped gym under supervision. There are daily classes in aqua-aerobics in the indoor pool, which is windowed in such a way that you feel you are swimming outdoors in an open-air pavilion. Sports are an important part of your spa program, and your regimen includes *bio footing* (jogging along the beach) plus a daily sports activity of your choice—golf, tennis, bicycling, windsurfing, riding. You have free access to the sauna, and to the Bar Bleu, where you can drink as many *boissons diététiques* (fruit and vegetable juices, tisanes, and other no-calorie or low-calorie beverages) as you desire. If you prefer an hour's time spent in beauty treatments rather than 90 minutes of physical activity, you can opt for moisturizing algae and plankton facials, massages, a *Bio-Lift* (electrotherapy that strengthens and firms your facial contours for a few hours or a few days) or a *grand soin biotherm visage* treatment, which does wonders for your face, and which men seem to enjoy as much as women do.

A body contouring treatment with Crème Contour Suractivée appears to improve the rippled effect of cellulite and tauten your skin. You can try it in one of Biotherm's special 10-day treatments at the spa and continue to use it at home. Another effective treatment is Biotherm's pressure point massage, which stimulates and energizes your skin by briefly applying pressure to 12 key energy points on your face in combination with Energie Active cream to lift your spirits and improve your appearance, a technique you can also take home with you along with an illustrated guide. The Biotherm sunblocks, sun filtering stick for your lips, conditioning after-sun balm, antiaging tanning cream, protective tanning lotion, shower gels, revitalizing gels, body lotion moisturizers, antiwrinkle treatments and cover-ups, and other products are specials you can also try and buy at the spa's enticing Blue Boutique where you can also acquire attractive bathing suits and sportswear.

Biotherm suggests you stay at the 4-star Normandy, the 4-star Royal, or the 3-star Golf hotel. At the Hôtel Normandy, one of France's finest hostelries, an architectural fantasy with apple trees and roses in its garden and a delightful swimming pool with a glass roof that can be slid shut in inclement weather, you can supplement your Biotherm diet luncheon fare with delicious and artistically presented dietetic cuisine at the Normandy's Restaurant Minceur. Fresh asparagus, topped with slices of summer squash and decorated with strips of steamed red peppers, appears like a Christmas wreath. Shrimp freshly caught that morning are steamed and presented with carrots and onions ranged like petals in a *sauce verte*. The use of cutlery with enameled handles to match placemats or tablecloths and also complement small pots of flowers accompanying each setting makes every meal a visual treat. The Royal, staid and traditional, is excellent. The outdoor swimming pool is encompassed by a patio pleasant for genteel sunning and for scarfing light meals served at tables shaded with umbrellas. Guestrooms are commodious and well-appointed. Public rooms glow with Old World elegance. The Royal has the presence of a dowager queen. The Normandy has the verve and the spirit of a light-hearted princess. The Hôtel du Golf is further out of the resort, up on a hill overlooking the town and the Baie de Seine and, of course, the 27 holes of Le Golf de Deauville, with an attractive clubhouse and an indoor practice range.

The Centre de Thalasso-Esthétique de Pointe Biotherm is open daily from 9:00 AM to 6:00 PM from January 24 to December 30. Price for a full day's program is 1078 FF. Also available are 90-minute and 2-hour programs. The Hôtel Normandy (Boulevard Cornuché; telephone 31 88 09 21; telex 170617 Centre Thalasso 38 F) charges 154 to 193 FF for dietetic dinners, which neither the Golf nor the Royal offer. Unlike the Hôtel Royal (Boulevard Cornuché; telephone 31 88 16 41; telex 170549 F) and the Hôtel du Golf (Mont Canisy; telephone 31 88 19 01; telex 170448 F), both open May to September, the Normandy is open year-round. Low season is January 23 to March 31, the month of October, and November 12 to December 19. High season is April 1 to the September 30, October 31 to November 11, December 19 to December 30. Peak season is late August, when the Grand Prix de Deauville is run, a race in which the top thoroughbreds in France compete, followed by La Coupe d'Or world championship polo match. For a minimum 3-day stay in the high season, prices for the Normandy and the Royal are 528 FF per day for single occupancy, 374 FF per person per day for double occupancy. At the Golf, you pay 473 FF for single occupancy, 319 FF per person double occupancy. When figuring costs you should add a daily supplement of 99 FF per person at the Normandy and Royal and 88 FF per person at the Golf for taxes, service, and breakfast. Combination golf and Biotherm weekends are specially priced for stays at the Hôtel du Golf for about 1100 FF, 2-night minimum.

The Normandy, Royal, and Golf hotels and the Biotherm Spa accept American Express, Carte Bleue Visa, and Diners Club credit cards. The Royal and the Normandy also accept Eurocard. A deposit is required.

The tourist information office in Deauville (Office du Tourisme de Deauville, Bôite Postale 79, Place de la Mairie, 14800 Deauville, France; telephone [31] 88 21 43, from the US, 011 33 [31] 88 21 43; telex OFITOUR 170220 F) can supply you with the names, addresses, and details of several dozen hotels and other recommended lodgings in the area to suit almost any budget.

Name: Centre de Thalasso-Esthétique de Pointe Biotherm

Mailing Address: Boulevard de la Mer, 14800 Deauville, France

Telephone: 31 98 48 11; from the US 011 33 (31) 98 48 11; telex 171772

ᴥ Institut de Thalassothérapie ᴥ de Quiberon/Hôtel Sofitel Diététique
Quiberon

Presqu'île de Quiberon, the almost-island ᴄ Quiberon, is a promontory that extends from Brittany's Côte Sauvage—a wild coast, for the most part undomesticated—to dip into the Atlantic Ocean, with the bay of Quiberon on its south-facing side, the Gulf of Morbihan on its north-facing side. Because of the Gulf Stream, a beneficent microclimate brings out summertime roses and camellias. Quiberon attracts a star-studded roster of guests to its Institut de Thalassothérapie and its 2 two-story motel-like 4-star hotels: the 113-room Thalassa and the 78-room Diététique.

What attracts this mostly French clientele, composed of celebrities, industrialists, business and professional people? The hotels are white concrete monsters on the outside and OK but not all that wonderful inside. The food at the Diététique is deliciously healthful and wholesome, but spa director Marie-José Laroche Bobet (former wife of the late Louison Bobet, France's bicycle-racing champion who founded the thalassotherapy spas at both Quiberon and Biarritz) is aware that quite a few guests sneak off to enjoy pancakes at the crêperies in the village, or skip a meal to have one instead at the Thalassa Hotel where "real" food is served.

The appeal of Quiberon's thalassotherapy institute, in spite of its commonplace lodgings, is ingrained in the verities of French philosophy, which holds that the human spirit, body, and mind cannot function up to par unless separated from time to time from the stresses of everyday life, the rigors of money-making and acquisition, overindulgence in food and alcohol, late nights, lack of exercise, and too much city-polluted air, noise, and distraction. Allied to this basic concept is the belief that all discipline—even if practiced for only a week or a fortnight annually—will strengthen your will to overcome all obstacles. Add to this the reassurance of a strong, qualified medical team supervising sophisticated and extensive facilities for health and cosmetic therapy—everything from cardiological check-ups to consultations with a cosmetic surgeon. Add to this the intuitive feeling that the sea air and marine environment are good for

you physically and psychologically—calming, restorative, invigorating, healing—good for depression, fatigue, nervousness, weight problems, cellulite
deposits, problems of circulation, respiration, aging, digestion, allergies, rheumatism, arthritis, and stress, just as Director Marie-José Laroche Bobet has said and
penned—and *voilà!* the big appeal of Quiberon and the Thalassa, for people who
want to get away from it all, rest, and get healthy, whether or not they enroll
at the Thalassotherapy Institute.

Although there are extensive beauty care facilities and many extras in the
program, your basic program takes up only alternating mornings and afternoons,
so there is ample time not just for jogging along coastal paths above a patch
of beach right by the hotel—there are several better beaches elsewhere—but also
for renting or chartering a boat for fishing or sailing, waterskiing, hiring a horse
for riding, traveling some 15 miles to the mainland to play golf at the 18-hole
course at St.-Laurent, playing tennis on all-weather courts 150 feet from the
hotels, and making excursions to remember for the rest of your life. Port
Haligruen, off to your left as you face the Atlantic, is a delightful fishing port
as well as a *port de plaisance* (pleasure port) with a sailing school. Port Maria,
the port of the peninsula, is charming, with sardine boats unloading their catch
and many romantic and adventurous boat trips possible: to Belle-Ile-en-Mer; to
the Gulf of Morbihan; up the Côte Sauvage; to the local island of Houat, where
ingredients for plankton- and seaweed-based cosmetics are taken from the ocean
to be processed, and the island of Hoedic. The island of Houat is a 60-minute
boat ride from Quiberon by ferry. Take sandwiches, or have a simple meal there
at the Hôtel des Iles. Hoedic is a 105-minute trip. Strange, elemental, Hoedic
is called the "île au flottage," because it does seem to float like a lily pad. The
island is even simpler than Houat, with stone or white-washed houses, a tiny
church, a graveyard, a signal station. Belle-Ile, an island larger in area than the
peninsula, is a 35-minute boat ride south from Quiberon to the major town and
the main port of Le Palais, with its harbor winding back into the hills, small
houses with soft, bright colors, an interesting museum, and a lighthouse close
by at Port de Goulphar where you'll find a gem of a hotel, Castel Clara. An
excellent ferry/bus tour of Belle-Ile is available and worth taking, although it
skips La Citadelle, a military fortress worth seeing at Le Palais. Small biplanes
at the island's Bangor airport are available for sight-seeing.

In October 1987, construction began on a new nonmedical spa to be called
L'Espace Hypertonic-Biobell. When in operation, it will accommodate 250
spa goers and visitors daily to its wooded site near the village of Runello in
Bangor, one of the four counties, or *communes,* of the island. Centered around
a seawater swimming pool, Hypertonic-Biobell will be devoted primarily to
beauty and healthy recreational exercise—your *esthétique*—and *sports tonique,*
such as tennis, riding, sailing, scuba diving, and golf on a 9-hole golf course.

Cosmetics with seaweed and herbal bases will be used, and the *"équipements new look"* will include saunas, solaria, cascading showers, steam rooms, and whirlpools. Its founders, a cosmetologist and an oceanographer, have international backing, with a majority of Swiss funding, for this exciting new project on an island you can explore for yourself when you are staying at Quiberon's thalassotherapy spa.

On a line almost directly west from the island's port of Le Palais is Carnac on the mainland, site of a 7-mile stretch of spectacular neolithic dolmens and menhirs, or standing stones, most about 4 feet above the meadow grass. Nearby is the golf course at Plouharnel and Carnac's thalassotherapy center by the Bay of Quiberon.

Name: Institut de Thalassotherapie de Quiberon/Hôtel Sofitel Diététique

Mailing Address: Pointe de Goulvars, Boîte-Postale 170, 56170 Quiberon, Brittany, France

Telephone: (97) 50 20 00; from the US, 011 33 (97) 50 20 00; telex 730 712

Established: 1964

Managing Director: Marie-José Laroche Bobet

Program Directors: Dr. Alain Deledique, Orthopedic Medicine; Dr. Anne Elisabeth Dumel, Rheumatology; Dr. Jean-Luc Le Guiet, Sports Medicine; Dr. Jean-Claude Gorret, Nutrition, Mesotherapy, Auriculotherapy; Dr. Guy Rossolini, General Medicine, Naturotherapy

Owners: Novotel Hotel Group

Gender and Age Restriction: None in the hotels. Co-ed; minimum age 16 in the spa.

Season: Year-round (hotels); Thalassotherapy Institute open daily except Sunday and holidays (May 1, November 1, December 25, January 1)

Length of Stay Required: 8-day/7-night minimum

Programs Offered: Having arrived, checked out your room to note the 2 bottles of mineral water in your room's minifridge that you are asked to drink every day, you put on one of the 2 white terry-cloth dressing gowns provided for you and proceed to the Thalassotherapy Institute, which connects the Thalassa and Diététique hotels, for your medical consultation, weigh-in, nutritional assessment, and scheduled treatments. Your package program includes dietetic meals; room; use of the 81-foot indoor heated swimming pool; use of the Cure de Silence, a corridorlike room lined with low white cots facing a window wall overlooking the sea, where it is suggested you rest and nap after your 4 daily seawater treatments, which take up about 2 hours during alternating mornings and afternoons; and obligatory medical consultations, their number depending on the length of your program (from 1 to 8 days, 2 consultations; 9 to 13 days, 3 consultations; 14 to 18 days, 4 consultations). No treatments are scheduled for the day you arrive so that you have time to settle in and change for dinner. The morning of the day after you arrive will probably be left free, and your treatments will be scheduled for that afternoon. The Thalassotherapy Institute is open from 8:00 AM to noon and from 2:30 to 6:30 PM daily except Sundays and holidays.

The thalassotherapy spa area is large enough to accommodate almost 600 clients a day and is usually operating fairly close to its capacity, which means you may find yourself, on occasion, with time on your hands, waiting for a class or a treatment while other *curistes* staying at other hotels in the area finish up their scheduled treatments. Most guests pass the time amiably around the spa bar where you can have hot and cold beverages (for herbal tea, the *tisanerie* at the Diététique is preferable). The spa has 3 pools, including a rehabilitation pool for accident/trauma victims, who make up about 30 percent of the clientele. The variety of showers, baths, and treatments include *jet sous-marin* (having turbo-jets of water hosed on you while you are standing waist deep in heated seawater, then jumping up and down in front of the jets before you mount a stationary bicycle while being hosed); *pédiluve* for your circulation (dunking your legs alternately into a tub filled with warm seawater, then a tub filled with icy cold seawater); the *grand douche,* or jet shower (in which you stand ungarbed at the end of a tiled corridor while an attendant trains what feels like a fire hose on you, concentrating on your thighs, bottom, upper arms, and other areas where excess fat, referred to as "cellulite," tends to concentrate); *affusions* (lying on a table with overhead showerheads sprinkling for a *"sédatif"* effect over your skin); *bain multijets* (a whirlpool with powerful underwater massage); *bain bouillonant* (an invigorating bubbling—not to be confused with bubble—bath infused with sea algae); and *application d'algues et de boues marines* (seaweed and mud packs). There is also an inhalatorium where you can inhale draughts of sea air, known as *les aérosols.* There are supervised classes for working out with weights and stationary bicycles in the gymnasium; dance and fitness classes; classes in aqua-aerobics, gymnastics, and relaxation; yoga; saunas; and à la carte massages by therapists skilled in a variety of techniques.

The ambience of the spa is one of immaculate, attentive, and somewhat slow-paced clinical efficiency. Procaine (localized anesthetic) therapy is available for treating acne, migraines, hair loss, facial lines, and wrinkles. Auriculo-therapy, a form of acupuncture using dry needles in your ears, is an available treatment for breaking a smoking habit, relieving aches and pains referred to as *douleurs,* and alleviating fatigue. An alternative method for smoking cessation is homeopathy, in which you are given capsules or pills with small quantities of nicotine to wean you from the habit. These treatments are reasonably priced for each session required. Organized jogging and bicycling tours are offered, as are fishing trips and tennis lessons on the open courts nearby and swimming lessons for those who prefer organized exercise to long walks in the brisk sea air along miles of sandy and rocky beaches. Volleyball and fencing are other available recreational activities. Some guests recline in lounge chairs on the sea-facing terrace of the Diététique to sunbathe, read, and relax, while others spend their free time off on excursions, sight-seeing, shopping, picnicking, riding horses hired from a local stable, boating, waterskiing, sailing, scuba diving, or treating themselves to an array of *soins* at the beauty salon (see Beauty Treatments). In the evenings, some guests enroll in bridge or Scrabble tournaments, play table tennis, wend their way to whichever village discothèque appeals, or flake out in their rooms to watch first-run movies on their TV-VCR sets.

Diet and Weight Management: A dietitian and nutritionist will work out calorie levels appropriate for your weight management goals. A *repas lacté,* a mixture of low-fat yogurt and low-fat white cheese that tastes rather like *crème Gervais,* may be recommended every alternate night as a substitute for regular dietetic fare if you want to lose as much as 5 or 6 pounds in a week. For a 900- to 1200-calorie-a-day regimen, seafood lovers will delight in Belon oysters fresh that morning from the Gulf of Morbihan, fresh lobsters, clams, mussels and crabs, all garnished with tiny, tender vegetables and served with crisp salads. Roast chicken and vegetables or sautéed duck liver are typical dinner fare. Desserts are usually fresh fruit sorbets, sliced fruit, a baked apple or pear. Breakfast, wonderful to have outside on a terrace above the beach or on your room's balcony facing the sea, may be a boiled egg, toast, fruit, and beverage of your choice. The Diététique's *tisanerie,* open day and evening, offers a choice of dozens of *tisanes,* or herbal teas, tart with lemon, refreshing with mint, some aromatic, a few that taste like tea flavored with cough medicine. The fun is in the sampling and experimenting and judging for yourself whether the tea is soothing, stimulating, or whatever else it is claimed to be. Fruit and vegetable juices are usually served with your meals. Guests rarely experience hunger pangs on this diet, but in an area where Brittany's famed *crêperies* offer the most delicious thin pancakes imaginable, few guests are able to resist the temptation of sampling some when they are passing through the local villages. Classes in dietetic cuisine are available from the chef de cuisine at the Diététique Hôtel.

Beauty Treatments and Welcome Indulgences: A la carte beauty care in the *esthétique* salon features 4-step facials employing algae and seaweed rich in calcium, potassium, iron, iodine, and magnesium, or concoctions good enough to eat—strawberry and mint, for example. You can try a hot algae paraffin masque for facial cleansing and skin toning; electrotherapy for the benefits of passive exercise; a medical pedicure to buff away dead skin and calluses and do away with troublesome corns and ingrown nails; or have your hair dressed in becoming ways, cut or colored. You can have bust treatments, depilatory waxing, hand and foot treatments, and treatments that seem to minimize wrinkles and lines.

The estheticians are exquisitely skilled, and the face-peeling, revitalizing, regenerating, antiwrinkle, restorative, and refining creams and gels made from products of the sea are unquestionably refreshing and pleasant to use, or have used, on your face, hands, feet, and body.

Accommodations: All 78 rooms of the Diététique and all 113 rooms of the Thalassa are sea-facing, with balconies. All rooms are equipped with radio, color TV and video channel, minibar (with minirefrigerator), telephone, and private bathroom. The furnishings and decor are functional, motel-like, with adequate seating space. All rooms, recently renovated and refurbished, are bright and airy, and face westward on the sea so that you have fine views of sunsets. Comfortable and functional though your room may be, don't expect charm, a sense of luxury, or beauty beyond the view of the sea, which should be more than adequate compensation for your room's lack of esthetic appeal.

What to Bring: See USEFUL INFORMATION. Bring bathing suits, bathing caps, rubber thong sandals. Two terry-cloth robes are provided for you for the week. There is a spa boutique where bathing wear, beachwear, and sportswear is on sale. Bring cover-ups and sweaters for walking on the beach and nonskid sneakers or other foot gear for beach walking and rock climbing. If you plan on bicycling, riding, sailing, playing golf or tennis, or fishing, bring appropriate wearing apparel, foot gear, and equipment. Masks and foils are provided for fencing. Scuba diving gear is rentable as are fishing rods and reels. Blue jeans, shirts and sweaters and windbreakers will stand you in good stead for picnicking and boating excursions. But remember that in the evenings the dress code is customarily dresses for women, jackets and ties for men. Bring film for your camera.

Documentation from Your Physician: French guests enrolled in the French Social Security system are required to bring letters from their physicians stating their requirements and specifying treatments that are and are not recommended or advisable for them. Other guests would be wise to do the same. This will aid the doctors at the Thalassotherapy Institute in establishing your program.

The Use of Alcohol and Tobacco: No smoking is permitted in the spa area. You are allowed to drink whatever is available at the spa bar unless your nutritionist or dietitian specifies beverages not recommended for your program.

Fees, Method of Payment, Insurance Coverage: The daily rate for the Thalassotherapy Institute, comprising 4 treatments and the use of the swimming pool, is 319 FF from February 9 to April 11. From April 13 through the rest of the year, the price is 336 FF. These rates do not include the 385 FF charge for obligatory medical consultations. High-season (April 11 to October 31) daily room rates for the Hôtel Diététique, including all dietetic meals:

Single occupancy: 1331 FF

Double occupancy: 2002 FF

Rates, which include taxes, are higher for deluxe accommodations and lower in the off-season. Non-sea-facing rooms and rooms at the Thalassa Hôtel are less expensive. All prices are subject to change. Extra charges for additional treatments and services not included in your program, as well as recreational options, optional lessons and classes. Food and board for dogs (not allowed in restaurants) is about 120 FF daily, and dogs are only accepted if they are kept on a leash in the establishment and the immediate surroundings.

Your reservation in the Thalassotherapy Institute must be confirmed before you make your hotel reservations, and when you do so, you should specify the name of the doctor you wish to supervise your treatment (the physicians' names are supplied to you when your receive the information packet which you should request be sent to you). A deposit is required. Ask about the cancellation policy. All payments must be made in French francs, by travelers' checks or in cash.

With a physician's letter outlining the treatments they would most benefit from, the French enrolled in their Social Security system are reimbursed for their spa treatments. Whether you can also receive partial reimbursement depends on your physician, the stipulations of your health insurance, and your physical condition.

Centre de Thalassothérapie, Boîte Postale 83, 56340 Carnac, Brittany, France; telephone (97) 52-04 44; from the US, 011 33 (97) 52-04 44
Of particular interest to budgeteers, golfers, sailing and tennis enthusiasts, inveterate sightseers, and archaeologists is Novotel's other Thalassotherapy Center, which opened in July 1978 at Carnac. About 18 miles east and slightly south of Pointe de Goulvars on the French mainland, the center at Carnac offers all the recreational diversions and excursions of Quiberon mentioned previously with the convenience of a location less than 5 miles from the 18-hole golf course at St.-Laurent, about 6 miles from the train station at Auray, and 27 miles from the airport at Lorient. Carnac is also close to La Trinité-sur-Mer, one of the largest European sailing centers.

Mile-long avenues of Neolithic standing stones, the legendary menhirs and dolmens, hewn from local granite, adopted by the Romans for religious purposes and now time-pelted with white lichen, are ranged across the moorland less than a mile from the ocean-side village, where there is a small museum, the Musée Miln-Le Rouzic, with an important collection of Roman and Neolithic artifacts. You are also right on a stretch of sandy beach, with 45 tennis courts and a good riding stable in the area. The medieval town of Vannes is 18 miles away to the south, and from the station at Auray, you can entrain for some of Brittany's most interesting locales—Quimper, Nantes, and Brest.

The Thalassotherapy Center is a long and low modern building sheltering a 25-meter heated swimming pool, 2 rehabilitation pools, massage rooms, saunas, aerosol seawater inhalation room, and extensive facilities for algae-enriched baths, bubbling baths, underwater jet water massages, jet showers, kinesthetic therapy, and lymphatic drainage. Rehabilitation gymnastics, weight-resistance training, and other mechanotherapeutic equipment are available in the gymnasium. The center is architecturally attractive inside, bright and cheerful in its employment of wood, mosaic tile, and the use of blue as a complement to lots of sunny yellow and orange, the colors of the spa bathrobes provided. Treatments focus on arthritis, rheumatism, water-retention edemas, fatty deposits referred to as "cellulite," traumas caused by accidents, and therapy for those recovering from operations.

As at Quiberon, there is a wide choice of hotels, pensions, and furnished studio apartments for accommodation, but the 3-star Tal-Ar-Mor Hôtel, Novotel-owned, is connected to the Thalassotherapy Center by a private corridor (which leads to the sunlit indoor swimming pool with windows on the beach) and is the preferred choice. Room prices for single occupancy are 429 FF a day, for double occupancy, 506 FF per person per day. For room and board, prices range from 440 to 550 FF a day. All of the Tal-Ar-Mor's 106 bright and spacious rooms have private baths, and most have radios and TV. Rooms are comfortable, and the hotel has 2 restaurants, a grill, a bar, and evening entertainment. The price of the Thalassotherapy Center and the obligatory fee for physician's consultations are about the same as at Quiberon.

◈ Institut de Thalassothérapie ◈
Louison Bobet/L'Hôtel Miramar
Biarritz

An hour by air from Paris, 6 hours by rail, 7 or 8 hours by scenic motorway, Biarritz is located in the heart of Basque territory, in southwestern France at the southern extreme of the Bay of Biscay, 25 miles from the Spanish border. The former regal retreat of Empress Eugénie, kings, dukes, and duchesses (including the Windsors), Biarritz maintains many of the buildings and traditions of an *époque de grand luxe* side by side with the modernist and futurist. You relax and revive yourself in the futurist-facaded 4-star Hotel Miramar, on a wide, sandy beach around the corner from the *phare,* the lighthouse of St. Martin, built in the 19th century to warn boats away from the outcroppings of rock along the Atlantic shoreline. Louison Bobet's fitness spa at the Miramar Hotel provides a complete health, beauty, and nutrition program, including a sumptuous filtered seawater swimming pool above the sheltered beach. You're close to the Hôtel du Palais, one of the great grand hotels of the world, and the Bellevue Casino, open daily from 4:00 PM to 2:00 AM, where you can play roulette, blackjack, or baccarat, or dance the night away at Le Baobab discothèque. You're 6 miles west of Bayonne, a large port city and commercial center—bayonets used to be made there—on the Adour River; a little over 15 miles north of the attractive fishing village resort of St.-Jean-de-Luz, with its 17th-century Quartier de la Barre and its sheltered bay ideal for novice swimmers and for getting the knack of windsurfing; and under 25 miles north of Hendaye, another attractive fishing port just across from the Spanish border. The Biarritz Golf Club can make reservations for you on 4 fine courses within 15 miles. The oldest golf course on the Continent is at Pau, 30 miles from Biarritz in the foothills of the Pyrenees. Opened in June 1987, the European International Golf Training Center in Ilbaritz-Moriscot, a short distance from the center of Biarritz, is under the direction of Dominique Dubos. It offers chipping, pitching, putting, and bunker work, technical improvements for your game, and correction of game deficiencies on 40 acres of ocean-facing golfing hazards of every type, with 14 workshops organized over a progressive circuit. Entry fee of 55 FF for 2 baskets of 40 balls; lessons, training courses available; clubhouse, bar, locker rooms. (Centre International d'Entraînement au Golf: telephone [59] 12 74 65/[59] 03 71 80.)

Tennis? The Aguiléra Tennis Club, close to the Miramar, has a dozen courts, 2 indoor, 2 lighted for night play, intensive tennis courses, and coaches available for instruction. Squash courts and lessons are available at Biarritz Milady Squash Courts. Instruction at all levels for all water sports: surfing, ski-surfing, parachute-water skiing. Several local surf shops sell and rent windsurfing boards and wet suits. Private riding lessons with certified instructors and trail rides in the neighboring Basque country are available from Biarritz Equitation Riding Center less than 3 miles from the Miramar. Deep-sea fishing, surf casting, tuna fishing, freshwater fishing inland, cruises aboard ocean-going sloops by the day or weekend, sailing lessons, 16 bowling alleys, a nearby aero club and gliding center, scuba diving, skiing, archery, and more, more, more things to do, plus rentals of bicycles, motorcycles, and 4-wheel drive vehicles for exploring the Basque country. Plus a year-round calendar of festivals, bullfights, concerts, sports events and competitions, folkloric events, firework displays. And, of course, all the swimming and beach life you like on your doorstep in the summer season. For more information, get in touch with Comité de Tourisme et des

Fêtes, "Javalquinto," Square d'Ixelles, 64200 Biarritz, France; telephone (59) 24 20 24, from the US, 011 33 (59) 24 20 24; telex 570 032.

Name: Institut de Thalassothérapie Louison Bobet/L'Hôtel Miramar

Mailing Address: 11–13 rue Louison-Bobet, Avenue de l'Impératrice, Boîte Postale 159, 64202 Biarritz Cedex, France

Telephone: (59) 41 30 00 and (59) 24 20 80 (spa); to call from the US use 011 33 prefix; telex 540831 MIRAMAR; telefax 59 24 77 20

Established: 1979

Managing Director: Daniel Broch

Program Directors: Medical staff of the Thalassotherapy Institute

Owner: Interhotels SAM

Gender and Age Restrictions: None for the Miramar; minimum age 16 for the spa

Season: Year-round for the hotel; the spa is open every day except Sundays and holidays (January 1, May 1, November 1, and December 25)

Length of Stay Required: None for the Miramar; for the spa, 6 nights minimum; recommended stay 9 to 12 days

Programs Offered: The Institut de Thalassothérapie is recommended for fitness, slimming, the relief of aches and pains, stiffness, stress-induced fatigue, reactional depression, convalescence, and infirmities brought on by rheumatic ailments or accidents. On arrival you are fully examined by a member of the expert medical staff. An individual schedule of treatments is then arranged in combination with a delicious slimming diet if desired, with plenty of time allotted for resting, walking, recreational sports and activities.

Depending on your needs, you receive 3 types of treatments. Marine Hydrotherapy includes a session in a bubbling bath *(bain bouillonnant)* in which you lie in heated seawater for a vigorous body hydromassage which relaxes your muscular tissues while it braces your capillary vessels; a session in a jet shower in which a 10-pound pressure-jet is aimed at varying spots in your body, or a gentler spray is played over your body; underwater showers and jet baths in either a whirlpool bath or a rehabilitation swimming pool for a 2-minute session focusing particularly on your spine, hips, and lower limbs; foot and hand baths; ultrasonic baths. Algotherapy, with general or localized treatments, consists of thin layers of heated seaweed applied to your skin beneath the gentle warmth of infrared rays. Physiotherapy includes Swedish, shiatsu, or "Californian" types of massage (extra charge); weight-resistance training in the gym; exercise and yoga classes; sauna; aqua-aerobics in the indoor or outdoor heated seawater pool; and lymphatic draining treatments (extra charge). From Monday through Saturday, there is supervised jogging along the beach at 9:00 AM; gym classes are held from 10:00 AM to 1:00 PM and from 3:30 to 7:30 PM, at which time the sauna is also open. The heated swimming pool is open from 10:00 AM to 8:00 PM. For resting, there is a long indoor corridor and outdoor sea-facing terrace equipped with wheeled white chaises, blue-cushioned, with adjustable headrests. A *tisanerie* serves herbal teas and light snacks.

Organized entertainment is laid on in the evenings at the hotel for spa guests: arts and crafts exhibits, dancing, travel and adventure films, fashion shows, exhibitions of folkloric and flamenco dances, *soirées musicales* (jazz, classical, blues, Spanish, pop), seminars on astrology, poetry, and history. The Miramar also has a game room set up for bridge, checkers, Scrabble, backgammon, and Ping-Pong, as well as a billiard and pool room and a dart board. A selection of video films is available from the concierge for entertainment in your room. The hotel also makes arrangements for guests who want to spend their free time learning how to play bridge or speak Spanish. Sight-seeing excursions to folkloric and fine arts museums in Bayonne can be arranged; also sight-seeing tours of Biarritz, fishing trips along the Adour River near Bayonne, helicopter flights, and excursions to local bullfights, festivals, pelote games, and various Basque celebrations.

Diet and Weight Management: Chef André Gaüzère presents a delicate and appetizing low-calorie cuisine—light sauces, flourless cakes, seafood salads, fish preparations, and other delectable specialties—at Les Pibales, the Miramar's dietetic restaurant across the swimming pool's courtyard from the main *gastronomique* restaurant. At both, you can feast on sea bream, sardines in herbs, turbot with leeks, oysters, lobster, crayfish, grills, fresh pasta, irreproachable light desserts such as fruit sorbets and fresh raspberries, enticing salads, and vegetables that sing of freshness. If you want to know the secrets of Gaüzère's preparation of *basse-calorie* dishes, his vegetable pâtés, and the miracles he achieves with a few strips of red pepper, asparagus tips, and a sauce you would swear was made from cream, you can enroll, with advance notice, in his daily hour-long cooking course, held in the Miramar's marvelous kitchen. The 5-day Monday to Friday Ecole de Cuisine Basses Calories costs 500 FF per person.

Beauty Treatments and Welcome Indulgences: The à la carte salon de beauté specializes in 5 daily sessions for the treatment of your hands, body, bust, face, and hair, as well as a relaxation package, which includes shiatsu massage, facial care, a medical pedicure, manicure, facial masque, and hairdo for a total price of 1450 FF. Lymphatic drainage, pressure-point massage, Slendertone passive exercise, and La Prairie cell therapy regeneration treatments are also offered at extra cost.

Accommodations: Most of the 122 pleasant rooms and suites are sea-facing with balconies. All rooms have private baths, telephone, and color TV with 14 channels and excellent reception, including a video channel.

What to Bring: See USEFUL INFORMATION. Bathrobes are furnished by the hotel for use in the spa. Bring bathing suits and cover-ups; dress-up clothes for evening wear, dancing, excursions. Bring rain gear, sweaters, seasonal attire. Casual elegance is the look in Biarritz, and if you find you don't have quite the right thing to wear, you can have fun shopping for it in the hotel's boutique and in neighboring shops.

Documentation from Your Physician: Unless you are French and seeking reimbursement for your treatments, this is not required, but it is useful to have on hand to facilitate your obligatory physician's consultation.

The Use of Alcohol and Tobacco: Neither alcohol nor tobacco is permitted around the pool or in the treatment rooms. No restrictions elsewhere.

Fees, Method of Payment, Insurance Coverage: Rates per person, per day—including either dietetic or regular *gastronomique* meals, 4 treatments daily, and taxes—with a minimum 6-night stay:

For single: 1153 to 1813 FF

For double: 1980 to 3300 FF for 2 people

Rates depend on the season and your accommodations—standard, superior, luxe or facing southwest. Medical fees and a daily surcharge of 150 FF per person are not included. All prices are subject to change. The price for having your dog in your room is 100 FF daily. Cats and other pets are not allowed, and your dog is not allowed in public places. A deposit is required. Ask about the cancellation policy. Payment is accepted in cash or by travelers' checks (in French francs) as well as by American Express, Diners Club, or Carte Bleue Visa.

⊘ Les Prés d'Eugénie ⊘
Eugénie-les-Bains

Once upon a time, on May 8, 1861, to be precise, Empress Eugénie, the Spanish bride of Napoleon III, officially gave her name to Les Eaux de Saint-Loubouer, hot and cold springs revered for their healing power, and from then on, the springs and the little village built around them came to be known as Eugénie-les-Bains. Eugénie's longevity—she lived to age 94—was often credited to *les bienfaits* of the waters, which are also said to be diuretic, sedative, and detoxifying if you drink them in measured doses, and excellent for obesity, rheumatism, arthritis, and urinary and intestinal maladies if you bathe in them or apply poultices of the vegeto-mineral mud to your body. Slightly radioactive, with a trace of arsenic, rich in sulphur, calcium, and sodium, the waters are constantly checked by the French Ministry of Health.

Located in the southwestern corner of France and not far from the foothills of the Pyrenees close to the Spanish border, Eugénie-les-Bains is known as the *premier village minceur de France,* the centerpiece jewel of Maison du Thermalisme and its 12-spa Châine Thermale du Soleil, an eminent Paris-based organization founded by Adrien Barthélémy in the early 1950s. *Minceur? Bien sûr. Diététique gastronomique.* No meal above 500 calories. Soufflés like cobwebs, blanquettes like clouds. Barthélémy gave his daughter Christine—who resembles portraits of Empress Eugénie—the château and park beloved by Eugénie and the old spa hotel and building to renovate. Christine married Michel Guérard. Guérard created *"grande cuisine minceur."* And voilà! Now you have Les Prés d'Eugénie, a 4-star luxe hotel harmoniously combined with a restaurant with *cuisine minceur gourmande*. Advance reservations are required at the hotel, its *gourmande* and *minceur* cuisine open not only to hotel guests but also to nonresidents.

Les Prés d'Eugénie is romantically and elegantly furnished. The three-story hotel, with projecting balconies enclosed by lacy, wooden fretwork, is mounted on an arcaded platform. Together with the connecting wing to the spa and a bridge to the renovated old château, it forms an open-ended rectangle around the stone-paved patio garden area. At night, lighting illuminates the palms, the low stone water basins, each with a spritzing fountain jet, and the garden, with its Hellenic-style sculptured goddess.

Like the hotel, the spa building, Les Thermes, is all pale, soft colors, filled with palms, orchids, wicker screens, mirrors, and radiant overhead lighting. Its exterior arcaded corridor is hung with brass-based goblet-shaped lamps for daytime decoration and evening illumination. A section with chaises curved to elevate the feet of resting curists faces the hotel's patio garden. Surrounding the hotel is a 37-acre private park filled with mimosas, plane trees, palms, magnolias, and camellias and containing a lake, meadows—those ubiquitous *prés*—clumped with peonies and irises, superb flower gardens, and the Parson's Garden, where Michel Guérard grows his fragrant culinary herbs.

You can rent a bicycle and *"brûler vos calories"* in the immediate, somewhat hilly terrain of meadows and orchards, farmhouses and old towns. Gathering mushrooms, those delicious *cèpes,* is a time-honored pastime. In Les Landes, boasting the finest and largest production of duck and goose livers in all of France, the *marchés au gras,* the markets where foie gras is bought and sold, are as much a part of the local scene as the folkloric festivals and bullfights staged in the grandstand arenas you'll find in every little town and village. Even a jaded traveler will be stunned by the loveliness of the châteaus, towers, churches, and antiquarians' wares in the old towns of Geaune and Saint-Sever, 7 and 12 miles, respectively, from the hotel.

If you're an ardent golfer, don't miss the oldest golf course in Europe in Pau, 30 miles south, built by the English in 1851. Pau is a marvelous provincial capital, famed for its flowers, its hippodrome racetrack, the collection of 16th-century tapestries housed in its castle, its magnificent views of the Pyrenees, and for being one of the major centuries-old way stations along the pilgrims' path to Saint-Jacques de Compostelle (Santiago de Compostela). At Mont-de-Marsan, 30 miles to the north, you can go canoeing or kayaking, riding, parachuting, or take a few golf lessons.

For curists and fine food aficionados, there are scads of accommodations other than Les Prés in the village and its environs—furnished rooms, studios, inns, hotels, pensions, bungalows, motels, farmhouses. The Syndicat d'Iniative (40320 Eugénie-les-Bains, Les Landes, France; telephone [58] 51 15 37, from the US, 011 33 [58] 51 15 37) can supply you with a list as well as with maps and descriptions of interesting walks and information. The Maison Rose (telephone [58] 51 19 50), a charming manor house under the aegis of the Guérards, a few minutes' walk from Les Prés, offers tastefully furnished 1-room studios and larger apartments, suitable for families with babies and children up to age 11 who can be accommodated in their parents' studios (with kitchenettes) for half-price.

Name: Les Prés d'Eugénie

Mailing Address: 40320 Eugénie-les-Bains, Les Landes, France

Telephone: Administration, (58) 51 19 01; reservations, (58) 51 19 50 (to call from the US use 011 33 prefix); telex Eugénie 540 470 F

Established: 1970

Managing Directors: Christine and Michel Guérard (hotel); La Maison du Thermalisme, Compagnie Française du Thermalisme, 32 avenue de l'Opéra, 75002 Paris, France; telephone (1)47-42-67-91; telex 210 256 F

Program Directors: Physicians and medical staff of Les Thermes d'Eugénie-les-Bains (spa facility) including kinesitherapist and dietitian

Owners: Locataire-Gérant Compagnie Française du Thermalisme, SA; Chaîne Thermale du Soleil

Gender and Age Restrictions: None

Season: The beginning of March to the beginning of December

Length of Stay Required: 7 days for *La Semaine Privée (A Week Apart)* program; shorter and longer stays can be arranged; maximum 3 weeks for the classic spa cure; an intensive accelerated 11-day cure; minimum 13-day stay at La Maison Rose

Programs Offered: The new *A Week Apart (La Semaine Privée)* program was created mostly for English-speaking spa guests interested in physical rejuvenation and slimming. Those who are interested in other hydrotherapy cures for other ailments—rheumatism, arthritis, metabolic disorders, urinary and digestive problems—are also welcome. It is essential that you reserve at least a month preferably 2 months, before your arrival—and make sure there is space in the spa before your room reservations are confirmed. The spa facilities are closed on Sundays and open on holidays provided these days do not fall on a Sunday. From the first of April to the end of October, the first three weeks of each month are often very busy. The Guérards strongly recommend that you plan to begin your cure between the 20th and 30th during these months. Arrangements require filling in a form, returning it, and waiting 3 weeks for confirmation. These exacting requirements apply to all bookings, including those at La Maison Rose. If you are French and enrolled in the Social Security system, you must reserve no more than 3 months in advance. You should cling to your spa confirmation cure receipt which entitles you to enter the spa and to deduct an advance payment of about $40 from your treatment bill.

When you arrive at the white colonial palace of Les Prés, your first morning is set aside for a compulsory consultation with the spa physician (fee about $50), followed by enrollment formalities at the Medical Secretary Service in the Thermal Center. Your prescribed treatment begins in the afternoon at 4:45. Your daily treatments are scheduled either between 9:30 AM and noon or from 4:45 PM on after a team of medical experts, including a qualified kinesitherapist and dietitian, have given you a general check-up with a computerized analysis of the results. Although the consultation is compulsory, you aren't required to have any treatments that do not appeal to you.

Among the treatments offered are a "diuretic drinking cure" (you drink measured amounts of water at specified times); high-pressure hand and foot showers; needle-spray shower; high-pressure underwater whirlpool and shower; underwater massage; hydromassaging penetrating shower; general shower with a special Eugénie spray; an experimental weightlessness mud bath, enriched with thermal plankton—white mud for a change, and refined to the consistency of a lotion. There is a sauna, also a room for gymnastic exercises and mechanotherapy (stationary bicycles, weights, other equipment). Filiform showers are said to have a "spectacular effect on cellulite," causing fat deposits to crumble. Mud poultices can be applied locally where required for various conditions. Many medical treatments are offered for specific ailments. The Saint-Loubouer and Empress springs, referred to as *L'Impératrice,* "are cool, colorless, and have a sulphurous odor and taste, and are used for cleansing and drinking waters." The waters from the spring called Christine-Marie are 102 degrees F, rich in thermal plankton, and drawn from nearly 1300 feet below the earth's surface. Their chemical composition is similar to the L'Impératrice waters but richer in trace minerals. The waters are said to be "slightly radioactive and rich in rare gases." A radio-vaporarium room is provided "for total internal and external impregnation with hot springs steam and rare gases which contribute greatly to your cure."

The park surrounding the hotel is open only to hotel guests and curists for recreational walks and strolls and *le footing,* or jogging, if you feel so inclined. The Italianate swimming pool is set about with towel-cushioned chaises you could recline on forever, a wall of boxwood at your back. With the lawn bowling green and the tennis courts, it is for the private use of hotel guests.

Guests participating in *La Semaine Privée* are offered outings to places of local interest, optional discounted car rental with Renault cars, and the promise that in an atmosphere of serenity, space, beauty, and silence they will get back in touch with their inner selves in true luxury. It's a week "where there is no one to please but yourself." If you like riding, suitable horses can be hired at a local stable. If you prefer indoor pastimes, the game room and billiard room at the hotel are at your disposal.

Diet and Weight Management: Michel Guérard, no taller than Napoleon and with facial features rather like those of actor Dudley Moore or a choirboy, and his team of 17 sous-chefs, will have you feasting on an unimaginably delicious 1200 calories a day of *cuisine minceur,* with a *gourmande cuisine* dinner of 500 calories—a true celebration—on your last gala evening. A *minceur,* slimming lunch might be a lobster salad with mangoes, roast pigeon with spicy mincemeat, millefeuille crêpes filled with apples and apricots spiced with lemon. Dinner might be cream of crab soup with tarragon, pan-fried bass with leeks and spaghetti squash, Paris Brest cake. Another entrée might be grilled salmon with crayfish, a dot of verbena-scented butter, shallots, and asparagus tips; or even a sampling of the type of entrées Guérard has marketed with Nestlé-Findus since 1976 as gourmet frozen food—like breast of chicken with figs and lemon, spiced with oranges. Guérard has won many awards as a pastry chef and a *"papa gâteau,"* and Michelin has awarded him 3 of its coveted stars, so you can expect heavenly desserts such as a pastry cornucopia of iced fruits, and marvelous mélanges of the locally grown raspberries and strawberries served in silver baskets with green and purple grapes. There are champagne goblets filled with fresh orange juice for breakfast, a hot pear soufflé to look forward to at lunch, and a petit pot de crème for your dinner dessert. Everything is served with extraordinary panache—crystal, antique silver cutlery and objects, even clear-as-crystal water served in a crystal pitcher. And to lose 5, even 8 pounds on fare like this? A miracle!

Beauty Treatments and Welcome Indulgences: There is a full-service beauty salon for hairdressing, manicures, pedicures, waxing services, and facials using the plankton-rich products developed at the Pyrenees-based spa Molitg-les-Bains (pronounced mo-leech), a fellow member of the Chaîne Thermale du Soleil.

Accommodations: Each of the hotel's 48 spacious, luxurious bedrooms and suites has not only an evocative name to conjure the sweetest of dreams—Nuages, Bois de Rose, Candide, Citronelle, Bouton d'Or—but also its own aura of distinction, its particular cachet. Each is set about with charming artifacts and art objects, furnished with marvelous flair and style through the help of local antiquarians. An attic room with the romanticism of ancient beams—and would that we all had an attic room like this—might have furniture of Shaker or Stickley simplicity; another might have wicker and brass accessories; another might offer a terrace bannered with banana fronds; or a suite might offer a sumptuous bathroom with ferns, terra-cotta busts on the marble, a pewterlike stainless steel double-basin area, and a door that leads to your own sunbathing patio with a whiff of roses and rosemary winging in from the garden. The rooms on the east side have terraces and open onto a shimmering little lake ringed with plane trees. The west side rooms have swimming pool and meadow views. All rooms have private bathrooms, some grand enough to be styled "bathing salons," and all rooms have direct dial telephone, color TV, a minirefrigerator, and a music broadcasting system. Not all rooms have terraces, balconies, patios, or original attic architecture, but all rooms and suites are charmers, luxurious, comfortable.

Accommodations at La Maison Rose include studios, and 2-roomed apartments suitable for 2, 3, or 4 persons. Second- and third-floor rooms feature showers; ground-floor rooms have tubs in ample bathrooms and miniterraces. All come with closet-style, fully equipped kitchenettes, direct dial telephone. Rooms are airy, furnished in simple, attractive contemporary style. Babies and children to age 11 can be accommodated in their parents' studio for half-price. Pets, except guide dogs, can be accommodated for half the price of children. Although it is necessary to reserve a table, guests at La Maison Rose are "always welcome" to eat in the Restaurant Michel Guérard.

What to Bring: See USEFUL INFORMATION. At Les Thermes, you are advised that nonskid bath sandals are essential for health and safety reasons to moving about during treatment. One-piece bathing suits can be bought at the Thermal Secretary Service's shop, but you may feel happier bringing your own to use in the swimming pool at Les Prés. A traditional and comfortable, woolly, warm capelike "cure robe" can be rented—advisable, because the water, mud, and spa treatments are rough on synthetic materials and can stain your own garments. The ambience is elite and discriminating. Jackets and ties for men and dresses for women are *de rigueur* at Michel Guérard's restaurant. You don't need to be reminded that the French are fashion-conscious, and you won't feel happy if you aren't dressed accordingly.

Documentation from Your Physician: Required if you are attending the spa as a curist. Advisable even if you plan on just a few treatments.

The Use of Alcohol and Tobacco: No smoking, wine, or liquor in the thermal center. No restrictions elsewhere.

Fees, Method of Payment, Insurance Coverage: High-season (April 1–May 31, June 9–June 30, July 9–August 31, September 9–October 4) rates, including all meals, use of the Thermal Center, and taxes (with the exception of a small charge for local taxes), for *La Semaine Privée:*

For 1 person/1 cure: 14,455 FF

For 2 persons/2 cures: 20,764 FF

For 2 persons/1 cure: 18,916 FF

High-season rates per night at Les Prés d'Eugénie, not including meals or 15 percent service tax:

Single room: 1067 FF

Suites for 1 or 2 persons: 1392 FF

March through November rates per night at La Maison Rose (minimum stay 13 days):

Single room for 1 person: 138 to 242 FF

Studio for 2 persons: 171 to 297 FF

2 rooms for 2, 3, or 4 persons: 319 FF

Children up to the age of 11 are accommodated in their parents' studio for half-price. Rates are not inclusive of tax and are higher for deluxe accommodations and lower in the off-season. All prices are subject to change. A deposit is required. Ask about the cancellation policy. Everyone lucky enough to be entitled to the blessings of the French Social Security system receives a 70 to 100 percent reimbursement.

⋑ Les Thermes Marins/ ⋐
Le Grand Hôtel des Thermes

Saint-Malo

Here is a winning combination of a thalassotherapy center noted for its highly skilled professionalism and a *parcours aquatonique* unique in the world, a luxurious 3-star turn-of-the-century truly grand hotel serving both traditional and low-calorie *haute cuisine,* and a setting guaranteed to excite the mind and melt the heart of even the most jaded traveler.

Just west of Mont-Saint-Michel, the Breton port of Saint-Malo in northwestern France is situated on the English Channel, on the right bank of the estuary of the Rance River. The old walled city stands on a granite islet, joined to the mainland by an ancient causeway and by an avenue bridging the inner harbor.

Besides the recreational activities of golf, riding, tennis, bicycling, sailing, coastal walks, and promenades on the ramparts on Sunday afternoon, when the entire town seems to walk there, Saint-Malo has interesting historical and fine arts museums, a marvelous fort (Fort National), as well as the forts, accessible at low tide, on the small islands of Le Grand Bey, with Chateaubriand's tomb. You can pick blackberries in September, or walk, rather than wade, on Le Petit Bey when the tide is completely out, then climb up the rocks to the ruined Vauban fort on the summit. Many hydrofoil and harbor boat trips are available, and Mont-Saint-Michel, the rocky islet famous for its medieval walls, towers, and ancient abbey, is located not far away in a bay embraced by the Gulf of Saint-Malo. The town of Saint-Servan to the south, which merged with Saint-Malo in 1967, is a charming resort area where the medieval Solidor Tower is wrapped around an international museum of Cape Horn memorabilia.

Paramé, a seaside suburb, which also merged with Saint-Malo in 1967, is the location of Les Thermes Marins and Le Grand Hôtel des Thermes, united in a pale pink palace on a promenade above the sea with a stairway down to the wide sandy beach of La Grande Plage. The interior of the 98-room four-story hotel is attractive, its rooms comfortable, pleasant, perfectly soundproofed, provided with all the amenities and with furnishings delightfully in keeping with the lovely porticoed, balconied, pillared, and cupola-ed exterior. The dining room, recently enlarged, offers you a delectable choice of *pension classique* or *basse-calorie* meals—about 1200 calories a day. You also can eat à la carte at the hotel's Le Cap Horn *restaurant gastronomique* facing the sea.

The esthétique (beauty salon) in the hotel section offers 24 face and body treatments: facials, depilatory waxing, manicures and pedicures, day or evening makeups, lash and brow dying, *gommage* (exfoliating) treatments for your back and body, lymphatic drainage for your face and body, massages, suntanning and *régénération* treatments. The *salon de coiffure* offers full-service hairdressing for men and women. Adjacent is the heated, filtered-seawater swimming pool, handsomely glass walled and ceilinged, its courtyard setting scheduled for landscaping but temporarily serving as a car park, the only off-key note in an otherwise charming orchestration.

The state-of-the-art Thalassotherapy Center comprises more than 12,000 square feet and offers a dozen treatments under the supervision of 3 physicians and a team of 20 kinesitherapists, all highly qualified, skilled, and commendable for the quality of their services. In an immaculate and attractive setting, washed in tones of cool blues, gray, and peach, facilities include massages, underwater jet massage pool, rehabilitation pool equipped with handgrips and armrests, bubbling baths and whirlpools, algae and paraffin packs, *grands jets* (a powerful stream of water directed at fatty deposits), electrotherapy for passive contracting and relaxing of your muscles, showers to stimulate your circulation, underwater shower massages (a treatment where you repose in a tub while an attendant runs a hose like a vibrator up and down your body), baths with jets of water of varying force, inhalation rooms for breathing in the beneficial negative ions of sea air, and ultrasound treatment for localized aches and pains. There is a gymnasium where supervised exercise classes in aerobics, weight-resistance exercises, calisthenics, gymnastics, and yoga are also offered.

A new steam room/Turkish bath/*hammam* was installed in 1987, at which time the *parcours aquatonique* was completed, the first of its kind, but you can count on many future imitators. This watery parcours, with 9 stations, occupies more than 600 square feet in a pool and leads you from a warm bath to a current you walk with, then a strong countercurrent you make your way against, then a whirlpool, then underwater jets, then vertical geysers and cascading showers. You can then sit on benches equipped with water jets to massage your back and feet, or lie down, Roman style, on a banquette in a Jacuzzi-style area.

Within a perimeter of 500 yards, you have a choice of a dozen 1- to 3-star hotels, with or without restaurants, and a list of furnished studio apartments, bed-and-breakfast accommodations, and hotels in other locations to accommodate all budget requirements. Le Grand Hôtel des Thermes is unquestionably the most luxurious and convenient choice, open year-round. Les Thermes Marins is open daily except Sunday, and closed from the first week in February to the beginning of January.

Rates are about 286 FF for 3 daily treatments, 330 FF for 4 treatments, plus a fee for medical consultation. For the lucky French there is the customary reimbursement from Social Security for treatments received. Hotel rates are moderate, about 440 FF a day for single accommodations, 561 FF with all diet meals included.

Name: Les Thermes Marins
Mailing Address: Grande Plage, 100 Boule-
vard Hébert, Boîte Postale 32, 35401
Saint-Malo Cedex, Brittany, France

Telephone: (99) 56 02 56; from the US, 011
33 (99) 56 02 56

◇ Royal Club Evian/ ◇
L'Institut Mieux-Vivre
Evian-les-Bains

The Royal Club Evian, a wonderful 4-star deluxe establishment now under the management of The Leading Hotels of the World, is backed by the alpine slopes of snow-crowned Mont Blanc and blessed by a climate Marcel Proust extolled as enchanting. From an altitude of 1500 feet, the hotel overlooks the southern shore of Lake Geneva (Lac Léman) and is directly across from Switzerland's Lausanne, linked to it by the old-fashioned joy of a 35-minute crossing on a pristine lake steamer. The small town of Evian-les-Bains on Lake Geneva (winter population 5000, summer population 20,000) is a 15-minute walk or 5-minute minibus ride from the hotel. It is the site of the immaculately maintained *fin-de-siècle* thermal establishment, where you will find four larger-than-life marble caryatids, underneath each a miniature lion's head spouting the famous water from La Source. The good-tasting water, one of the world's most popular table waters, mildly alkaline (78 mg of calcium and 24 mg of magnesium per liter—less than 10 percent of the USRDA for both minerals) is, according to the French spa annual, beneficial for kidney troubles, gout, migraine, insomnia, metabolic imbalances, rheumatism, arthritis, digestive problems, hypertension, general well-being, and bodily chemical balance and is served at all meals in the hotel. For years, fashion magazines have recommended that women spray Evian water on their faces to fix their makeup and to impart a soft and misty glow, and a spray is available at the spa.

The stately six-story Belle Époque hotel has 200 guestrooms, each with a balcony for admiring superb views of the lake or the hotel's 28-acre park estate filled with venerable chestnut trees, topiary boxwood, gardens of carnations and begonias. Well-fed deer browse in the park and in a large enclosed area in front of the hotel. There are rooms for games, reading, and bridge as well as an auditorium and a top floor of conference, seminar, and committee rooms. There are boutiques, a hairdressing salon, a heated outdoor pool, and, on the ground floor of the west wing, the totally private Institut Mieux-Vivre devoted to individualized spa and beauty treatments for face and body as well as the special

Cure Biologique, which incorporates many of the latest European concepts in revitalization and rejuvenation.

The circular, tent-ceilinged *Rotonde,* a gourmet *restaurant diététique* exclusively reserved for those on slimming diets, is one of 5 restaurants serving delectable meals. Although your diet breakfast is served to you in your room, don't deprive yourself of the pleasure of having tea, coffee, or other refreshment served to you on the terrace fronting the lake, one of several sunny *terrasses* from which you can gaze out at the white sails dotting the lake or view guests disporting themselves in the pool, watch the bicyclists setting off for a botany ramble, the hikers in pursuit of mountain views, nannies escorting their young charges to the children's play center, and joggers heading for the 20-station parcours vita track.

On the hotel property there is an archery field, tennis courts, the golf course, putting greens, and a pitch and putt range. Other attractions of a sophisticated, lovely, elegant lake resort are there for you at Evian and nearby—sailing, boating, windsurfing, music and flower festivals, a beach and the harbor promenade, as well as steamer boat rides on Lake Geneva. The hotel and the town share the hotel-owned casino, with air-conditioned gaming rooms, piano bar, restaurant, disco, and entertainment. Lit up at night like a ship at sea, it is a dazzling spectacle visible for miles around.

The Geneva-Cointrin International Airport is 30 miles from Evian, within easy reach by bus, taxi, hired car, or helicopter—the hotel has its own heliport—and that alpine chopper ride is a treat in itself. The only problem you are likely to come across in this Eden-like watering spot is its pricing system. Seasonal price changes, varying prices for lake or park views and differently-sized rooms, supplements, single and double rates, all to be tabulated with program fees, require a calculator and mathematical wizardry to compute.

Name: Royal Club Evian

Mailing Address: 74500 Evian-les-Bains, France

Telephone: (50) 75 14 00; from the US, 011 33 (50) 75 14 00; telex Casiroy 385 759; also through offices of The Leading Hotels of the World; in the US, (800) 223-6800; in New York City and State, (212) 838-3110, call collect. In France, toll-free 19 05 90 84 44. In Great Britain, 0800 181 123. Telefax 50 75 38 40

Established: 1904

Managing Director: Robert Lassalle

Program Directors: Institut Mieux-Vivre/

Better Living Program: Corinne Palomba; *Dietetic Program:* Michelle Berthevas, Nutritionist; *Biological Cure:* Dr. François-Louis Dauvilaire; *Golf,* Julian Moller; *Tennis and Relaxation Program,* Thierry Clement

Owner: Pierre Taittinger

Gender and Age Restrictions: None for the hotel. For *Spa, Dietetic,* and *Biological Cure* programs: co-ed, minimum age 18. For nonmedical sports programs: co-ed, minimum age 12

Season: Early February to mid-December

Length of Stay Required: For package programs, 6 days or more: Sunday evening orientation, Monday to Sunday morning. On request, special arrangements can be made for you to start your 6-day program off schedule, but there are no spa treatments on Sunday.

Programs Offered: The *Mieux-Vivre/Better Living Program, Super Better Living for Ladies, Super Better Living for Men, Dietetic Program, Biological Cure Program, Beauty Program, Facial Program, Cellular Treatment Program, Golf Program,* and *Tennis and Relaxation Program* are intended to be mixed and matched. You are encouraged to take and combine as much as you want from each of these programs. Additional programs include a *School Tennis Program* for boys and girls aged 9 to 15 and a special *Music Program* during the International Springtime Music Festival. All package programs include room, private bath, and balcony; Continental breakfast served in your room; a choice among 4 restaurants and a poolside barbecue for fixed-price dinners; guaranteed access free of charge to tennis courts, 18-hole golf course, pitch-and-putt area, putting greens, golf clubhouse, and tennis clubhouse; use of the heated swimming pool, archery range, and jogging itinerary on the 20-station parcours vita track; musical gymnastic session, gymnasium, and sauna; and complimentary minibus shuttle service from the hotel to the golf course, casino, harbor, and town. Those selecting the *Dietetic Program* eat in La Rotonde (at extra cost). Activities, detailed daily in a bulletin delivered with your breakfast, include organized countryside walks, Alpine flora-and-fauna discovery rambles, treks in Landrovers and other excursions, evening programs and demonstrations relative to health, beauty, cooking and nutrition, fashion, and similar topics.

Each participant is scheduled for an individual program, with treatments alternating mornings one day, afternoons the next. Before starting your program, you are required to have a medical checkup at the hotel. (*The fees for this cursory examination are not included in the program,* and, as is the law in France, the examining physician's fee is payable directly to the physician and not disclosed in advance to the hotel. The fee usually does exceed $100.) At 7:30 PM Sunday evening, there is a welcoming reception and orientation in a polyglot whirl of French, English, German, and Italian (Japanese, Arabic, and other languages by arrangement). Each morning, there is a jogging itinerary on the parcours vita track under the surveillance of an instructor, or a session of calisthenics with lively musical accompaniment, or a group stretching session. Then you check into the spa for your whirlpool bath with essential oils added to the water for aromatherapy; your seawater hydromassage bath (thalassotherapy), your algae or seaweed bath, your Swiss shower of alternating hot and cold jets of water or a spray shower; your hydrogymnastics (aqua-aerobics accompanied by jet-stream underwater treatment), and "ozone and oxygen" baths. In the *Better Living Program,* you receive 3 daily sessions chosen as the best suited for you from hydrotherapy, hydrogymnastics, and ozone and oxygen bath. With the *Super Better Living for Ladies,* you receive 4 treatments a day chosen from ozone and oxygen baths, a perspiration-inducing wrap, lymphatic drainage by acupressure therapy, seaweed wraps, ionization, "exitomotor" (a form of passive exercise with electrically induced contraction and relaxation of your muscles), hydrogymnastic and hydrotherapy sessions as detailed above, and 3 massages by physical therapists who massage your body on a table beneath multiple shower jets. Women receive specific exercises for firming thighs and buttocks. Men receive specific exercises for firming their abdomens.

There is a small elevator in the hotel reserved for spa guests, which takes you directly from your floor to the spa to spare you from traipsing through the hotel lobby in your dressing gown. In the morning (or afternoon, depending on when your treatments are scheduled), those participating in the spa program put on their bathing suits and the terry robes supplied in their rooms and go directly to the spa, where they check their room keys at a convenient desk near the spa's elevator. After treatments in the spa, you are given a hot towel to wrap around yourself, a soothing Oriental practice. For facials and other treatments *not* involving water, you are covered with a sheet and a cozy down comforter— bliss! The *Dietetic Program,* comprising 500 calories a meal, or 1500 daily calories, can be combined with other programs but is considered insufficient to support golf and tennis activities in addition to the spa's regimen of daily exercise. See Diet and Weight Management.

The *Beauty Program* promises cell therapy "based" on the work of Nobel Prize–winning scientists Watson, Crick, and Carrel. This program promises "spectacular results on the vascularization of the face, the improvement of the 'grain' of the skin and the attenuation of wrinkles, thanks to the complete absence of toxic or allergic phenomena." You receive a daily "application of fresh cells" plus 1 "royal" facial treatment using queen bees' honey cream, 1 biopeeling, 1 facial with aromatic oils, a manicure and pedicure/foot treatment, and 3 multijet water massages by a kinesitherapeutist/massage therapist. On completion of the program, you are given all the treatment products you have used to take home and continue your beauty regime. There is also a less expensive beauty program involving facials and hand and feet care.

The *Biological Cure Program* is presented as a "medical program" and said to be "an original approach to regaining tip-top physical shape by combining the physique with the psychic. Based on the synergy of advanced therapeutics, the Biological Cure gives surprising results for many ailments and makes you years younger." Under the supervision of Dr. François-Louis Dauvilaire, your "clinical" and "homeopathic" symptoms and samples of your blood are tested and the results computerized so that your "fields of disturbance" can be treated. The late Dr. Anna Aslan's procaine therapy is offered. For more than 30 years, miracles of rejuvenation and regeneration have been attributed to procaine, a substance similar to brand-name Novocaine, injected intravenously or intramuscularly. (In the US, dentists now use Xylocaine for numbing pain.) In this program, you can be massaged with essential fragrant oils of plants and flowers in aromatherapy treatments, be bathed in plant essences in "phytotherapy" treatments. Neuraltherapy, homeopathy, hyperoxygenation, and other therapeutic techniques for treating your "disturbance fields" are offered, including lasers, short-pulsed waves, magnetic fluxes, and electrical fields. Also available are treatments for wrinkles by means of collagen, DNA, and placenta; the use of placental implants; treatment of "varices" (what we think of as varicose veins); treatments for slackness of the skin and of the breasts and for hair loss. The price of the *Biological Cure Program* is based on the treatments needed once your blood serum has been analyzed. French law requires that you settle all fees directly with the medical consultants as well as the fees and costs of whatever laboratory work is involved. *Alors, ça va.*

The *Golf Program* is recommended for both beginners and skilled players. The American methods of the National Golf Foundation are adapted to every level of individual requirements. You have unlimited no-charge access to the 18-hole golf course, the pitch and putt range, and the putting greens at any time, and are supplied with lightweight canvas golf bags with wheels and a pull handle, clubs, and practice balls for use during this program. Demonstrations, films, and videotapes are shown for your edification. Coaching and individual lessons are offered at extra charge. You can sit around beneath sun umbrellas on a terrace outside the golf clubhouse where you can enjoy light meals from the Chalet du Golf, a less expensive diversion for most than battening upon the provender in the pro shop. Special muscular warm-up exercises for golf players are given at the beginning of the program, and competitions are staged at the end.

The *Tennis and Relaxation Program* also initiates you to the skills of archery (toxophily) and golf in an afternoon devoted to each. You also get to go on a mountain foothill excursion in a Landrover and spend an afternoon on the vast and lovely lake. You have unlimited access to the 6 Greenset tennis courts, 3 of which are lit for night play, and the practice backboard (training wall, as it is called). If it rains, there are covered courts nearby, for which transport and programs are provided. You get 2 hours of actual tennis play every morning, with a maximum of 4 trainees per court, and are also offered films, demonstrations, and videotapes of tennis play. You can relax and have a snack at umbrella-ed tables outside the Royal Tennis Club. Tennis professionals are courtside to coach you and give you individual instruction at extra cost.

In the *Total Tennis* and *School Tennis* programs, the focus is all on tennis. With the *Tennis and Relaxation Program,* exercise and jogging with a lead instructor on the parcours vita track are included daily, plus 2 afternoons a week at the Institut Mieux-Vivre for a session of group stretching and a session of hydrogymnastics in the outdoor heated pool.

The carpeted gymnasium is known as the *salle de musculation,* or "fit room." Exercise classes are given there, and it contains a Vitatrain Lifecycle and weight lifting equipment. The daily exercise schedule includes jogging at 8:30 AM, stretching at 9:00 AM and 3:00 PM, gymnastics/calisthenics to music at 11:30 AM, classes at noon and 3:30 PM for women to firm thighs and buttocks and for men to strengthen their abdominal muscles, and a Keep Fit class at 6:00 PM. On Sunday, only jogging, musical gym, and stretching are scheduled in the morning. In addition, you can join volleyball games or play pétanque (French lawn bowls) at no extra charge. For extra fees, you can rent bicycles, spend a morning riding, sailing, windsurfing, water skiing, or sail boarding. Check costs first, since they may be expensive. Ask the hotel concierge for details. There is a well-equipped playground for children not far from the hotel, with swings, slides, turnabout, and more.

Diet and Weight Management: Director Robert Lassalle won his chevrons aboard the French Line's *Liberté,* in luxury hotels, and at the Shah of Iran's court before being awarded the distinction of master chef. He directs the Royal's restaurant complex with "faultless authority," according to Gault-Millau, France's foremost critics of international cuisine. Chef André Crispino also receives enthusiastic commendation from these honest and sharply witty critics for his creations. The *Dietetic Program* includes a personal consultation with the dietitian/nutritionist. Instead of a Continental breakfast, you get a diet breakfast served in your room and you have lunch and dinner in La Rotonde. The circular dining room, swathed in prettily printed green-and-white floral fabric, which peaks to form an airy, tented ceiling, is set with small round tables for double or single occupancy. If you prefer, you can eat alone, or join other guests at the *table d'hôte.* During the week, a cooking demonstration is given by Chef Crispino in the hotel's huge and fascinating kitchens. You also receive printed information about changing your eating habits when you get home.

Your 1500-calorie-a-day intake, its nutritional excellence scrupulously tabulated by nutritionist and dietitian Michelle Berthevas, is served on Limoges porcelain. Starters for lunch might be shrimp cocktail, vegetable pizza à la Provençale, fruit cocktail, seafood cocktail, or lobster, followed by a choice of meat or fish as an entrée, such a grilled sole or veal with a trio of vegetable custards, or salmon or grilled tournedos with tiny fresh vegetables. Desserts might include a chocolate Bavarian cream or a cream cheese and herb scented mousse, goat cheese or a brandied pear, fresh pear custard or a pistachio parfait. Your dinners begin with choices such as consommé, white mushrooms with sorrel, oysters, clams, a gratin of pears and mushrooms, and shrimp bisque. For entrées, you might have grilled lotte fish or lamb with tarragon, mixed grill or a poached fish with capers. Desserts might be a choice of low-calorie fresh cheese, delicious fresh cherries, or a *tarte fine* of exotic fruit. Everything is exquisitely presented, delicately flavored, and delectable. Special diets can be accommodated. (Even though you pay extra for diet meals, and coffee for breakfast is included in the price of the meal, lunch and dinner coffee is not included. If you order a demitasse, there's a 16 FF charge.) Average weight loss on this 1500-calorie lovely fare? A couple of kilos, or about 5 pounds.

Beauty Treatments and Welcome Indulgences: See *Beauty Program* under Programs Offered. The hotel has a beauty salon for hair and nail care and wax depilation. Welcome indulgences? Just about everything you need is available.

Accommodations: Comfortable, elegant, twin-bedded rooms with carpets, draperies, and bedspreads predominantly peach with tender green accents, include a writing desk, often a chaise longue, always a room balcony, and central heating but not air-conditioning for which there is no need with all that lovely lake and mountain air. Beds are covered with heavenly soft down comforters. All rooms have direct-dial telephone service, a minibar (small refrigerator-cooler), and a television with six color channels including one in German and one in Italian and one with English programs, plus four radio stations to tune in on. Rooms come in "standard" sizes and "residential," a term that simply means larger-than-standard; and suites on request.

What to Bring: See USEFUL INFORMATION. White terry-cloth bathrobes are provided. Make sure to bring at least 2 bathing suits, since most treatments involve water. Bring appropriate wear for sports you intend to participate in. On the archery field, sports clothes are subtly dressier, as they are on the golf course, where women generally wear short skirts, culottes, top, and over-sweater or cardigan. More guests wear tennis whites than color-splashed outfits. Leisure-wear is resort wear, simple, well-cut, conservative attire. Men wear business suits or dinner jackets at the Casino. Women wear long-sleeved dinner dress; bare-armed, short, decolleté cocktail/evening dresses; evening skirts and tops. The casual daytime chic, with accent on the chic—women generally wear "natural" eye makeup even on the parcours track—gives way to casual elegance in the evenings. Bring rain gear. Bring light- and medium-weight sweaters during the summer months and your woolies and thermal underwear for early spring and fall. *N.B.* Casual sports clothes may be worn for lunch in La Rotonde, but *please*, no jogging suits or sweats or leotards. At night, in La Rotonde, men wear jackets or blazers, and women wear dresses, tunic-pajamas, or tops and skirts. Laundry and dry cleaning are returned the same day.

Documentation from Your Physician: Neither requested nor required, but useful to have as a reference. If you arrive Sunday evening, you will be examined the next morning by a physician with whom an appointment will have been made when you made your reservation for the *Mieux-Vivre/Better Living Program.* To repeat for emphasis, French law requires that all medical treatments be paid for separately and not charged to your hotel bill.

The Use of Alcohol and Tobacco: At your discretion or at the discretion of the personnel in charge. Naturally, Evian water is the preferred beverage, stocked in your room's minibar, set before you at table, available at the clubhouses.

Fees, Method of Payment, Insurance Coverage: The room rates below, given in French francs (FF), include all meals, city taxes, and service charges per person and per room and 18.6 percent VAT surcharge for *6-day/7-night program.* They do not include program prices.

High-season (July 20–August 20) rates range from 6930 FF for double accommodation with a park view to 12,936 FF for single accommodation in a double room with a lake view.

Medium-season (July 1–July 19) rates range from 6930 FF for double accommodation with a park view to 9779 FF for single accommodation in a double room with a lake view.

Low-season (April 1–June 30; September 1–October 31; and slightly less rest of year) rates range from 5544 FF for double accommodation with a park view to 8363 FF for single accommodation in a double room with a lake view.

Children ages 5 to 15 are accommodated free of charge in parents' room. Tariff for your household pet is 121 FF per day, not including feeding. Rates for "residential guestrooms" (larger rooms) are slightly higher. Half board, full board, and room-only prices can also be arranged by adding a supplement of 55 to 605 FF to your room price, depending on the season.

To determine your total cost, you must also add the program price. The following rates are for 6 days (per diem rates—which are substantially more than package prices—if you stay beyond 6 days are in parentheses):

Dietic Program: 539 FF (99 FF per day)

Better Living Program: 1254 FF (209 FF per day)

Super Better Living Program: 1914 FF (319 FF per day)

Beauty Program: 3201 FF

Golf Program: 154 FF

Tennis and Relaxation Program: 1540 FF

The price of the *Biological Cure Program,* as previously mentioned, depends on the individual treatments selected once your blood serum has been analyzed and your clinical symptoms have been computerized. A deposit is required. Ask about the cancellation policy. Payment is accepted in cash, travelers' checks, and by American Express, Diners Club, Eurocard, Carte Bleue Visa, and JCB credit cards.

Follow-up Assistance: Take-home skin care products.

ᘓ Additional ᘓᗆ
Thalassotherapy Centers in France

The following offer weight loss *(amaigrissement),* slimming, and toning treatments as well as dietetic meals at recommended hotels nearby. All have medical supervision. Prices are for the program only and not for hotel board and lodging unless otherwise specified. To telephone from the US use the prefix 011 33 before the numbers given here.

Centre de Thalassothérapie de la Baule, 28 Boulevard de l'Océan, 44500 La Baule, France; telephone: 40 24 30 97
Price for 6-day fitness regimen: 1345 FF
Beautiful beach, aerobic and body-building classes, 2 golf courses nearby

Centre de Balneothérapie et de Thalassothérapie, 3, rue de Bône, 06400 Cannes, France; telephone: 93 38 57 05
Price for 4 daily treatments (about 2 hours): 264 FF
Specializing in massages, renewal of energy

Institut de Thalassothérapie "Thalacap," Place de la Falaise, 34300 Cap d'Agde, France, telephone: 67 26 14 80
Price for 4 daily treatments: 314 FF in high season (late spring and summertime), 292 FF in low season
Brand new with ultramodern equipment, free use of swimming pool, sauna, solarium; 62 tennis courts

Centre de Thalassothérapie de Dieppe, Arcades du Casino, 76900 Dieppe, France; telephone: 35 84 28 67
Price for 12-day weight loss and toning regimen: 2310 FF
Excellent program, pleasant and cordial ambience

Centre de Cure "Profils"/Hotel Meridien, 1, Promenade-des-Anglais, 06000 Nice, France; telephone: 93 87 73 37
Price for a 6-day residential slimming and toning program: 4510 FF
Up-to-date toning and weight reduction program with excellent beauty treatments and hotel accommodation

Centre de Thalassothérapie "Thermes Marins," Plage de Trestraou, Boîte Postale 50, 22700 Perros-Guirec, France; telephone: 96 23 28 97
Price for a 6-day sojourn: from 1650 FF
Right on the beach, with good fitness and beauty services, pleasant staff

Neptune Institut de Thalassothérapie, Boîte Postale 10, 77740 Sainte-Marie-de-Ré, France; telephone: 46 30 21 22
Daily rate: 275 FF
Combined with residential stay at 3-star Atalante Mapotel (telephone: 46 30 22 44): from 4290 FF a week
Open year-round, weight treatments, dietetic meals, fitness and beauty services in a peaceful and relaxing setting on the island of Ré off the Atlantic coast, near La Rochelle; an ideal getaway retreat

Institut de Thalassothérapie "Thalamer," Front de Mer, Boîte Postale 214, 62520 Le Touquet, France; telephone: 21 05 10 67
Daily rate: from 286 FF
On the beach, many recreational activities, baby-sitting available for children of new mothers seeking postnatal care

Institut de Thalassothérapie de Marina-Baie-des-Agnes, "Marina Health Center," Boîte Postale 11, 06270 Villeneuve-Loubet, France; telephone: 93 73 55 07
Price per week: 1991 FF
Toning, weight loss, antistress treatments

Germany

✑ Wiesbaden ✑
Hotel Nassauer Hof
Schwarzer Bock Hotel
Aukamm Hotel Wiesbaden

An enchanting way to arrive at Wiesbaden is by a Rhine steamer cruise, sailing past the massive Biebrich Castle, former home of the Dukes of Nassau, or by train, but many people zip from the Frankfurt Rhein-Main Airport, Germany's major gateway, in a 20- to 25-minute drive or subway ride to this scenic spa town. Wiesbaden, at an altitude of 328 feet (100 meters), is renowned for its 26 brine springs, said to be particularly good for rheumatism, obesity, and catarrh, and for just about anything else that might be a stress-induced problem. Of equal renown is its sumptuous, Edwardian, Palladian-style, domed Kurhaus, all 19th-century glass, bronze, gilt, marble, paintings, and chandeliers, as well as its vast bathing facilities and steam rooms, not to mention the casino and the spa gardens, where summer concerts and garden festivals are held with fountain and flowers illuminated and fireworks showering overhead. The May festival is spectacular. Wiesbaden, the provincial capital of Hesse, also boasts the magnificent Hessian State Theater, a *fin de siècle* masterpiece, with three separate houses for opera, operettas, plays, ballet, and musicals; museums; a zoo and pheasantry; and fine shopping along the Wilhelmstrasse, the boulevard that links the inner city with the spa area. Taunusstrasse, around to the left of the Nassauer Hof, is the longest antiques shopping street anyone could wish for. For additional exercise, there are riding stables, sign-posted walks and "keep fit" gymnastic trails, tennis, golf, squash, badminton, ice-skating, hiking tours, and many possible excursions.

You enter the Kurhaus through an Ionic-columned portico bearing the inscription *Aqui Mattiacis* to be dazzled by the splendor and ornate decoration of the domed ceiling. Casino at the left. Assembly rooms and concert halls to your right. After paying an entrance fee, you can be steamed, showered, bathed, slathered with saline mud, and hydrotherapied to your heart's content in the most gorgeous surroundings imaginable. At the nearby municipal Emperor Friedrichbad, also elaborate and gorgeous, treatments include supervised gymnastics, weight-resistance training, underwater therapy massage, sitz baths. The 100-foot-long Turkish bath, used on alternate days by men and women, the former Royal bath with its own sitting room, and the resting rooms are a curist's and a sightseer's delight.

If you follow Parkstrasse, which would be more or less at a right angle with Wilhelmstrasse if the State Theater didn't intervene, it's about a 10-minute drive to the turnoff at Aukamm Allee where the "new" thermal baths are. These include indoor and open-air freshwater pools heated for wintertime swimming pleasure while snow is lying all around, massage rooms, solaria, saunas, a gymnasium, and a fully equipped diagnostic center with a staggering range of facilities for testing your heart, muscles, reflexes, and prescribing appropriate therapy. Balneology, electrotherapy passive exercise, hydrotherapy, mechantherapy, Kneipp baths, *und so weiter.* Treatments are medically supervised by an army of friendly physicians who specialize in stress reduction, fitness, cardiology, and ailments of every sort relating to your *gezundheit.*

For accommodations, you have an attractive choice. Right across from the gambling casino, the Kurhaus gardens, the State Opera and Theater, is the Hotel Nassauer Hof, a 5-star grand hotel, a member of The Leading Hotels of the World and Preferred Hotels Worldwide. *Hof* as a suffix means that the hotel once provided a walled courtyard where travelers could rest safely while passing from stronghold to stronghold. In the summer of 1979, it opened its Die Ente vom Lehel (The Duck from Lehel) restaurant, featuring the light and low-caloried cuisine of one of Germany's top young chefs, Hessian-born Hans-Peter Wodarz. Wodarz's superb fare combines the *haute, grande,* and *nouvelle cuisines* of France with the cookery of his native Hesse. The Duck restaurant is the hotel's formal dining area, with a balcony and a lower level seating arrangement, glazed chocolate-brown walls, and a pale round illuminated ceiling well. Between your fish and meat course, Wodarz's speciality of abstract fruit and vegetable purées is served on octagonal, black-bordered, gold-edged bone china as sorbets to cleanse the palate. Herr Wodarz refers to these delights as "dialogues." Duck is almost always on the menu, with Bordeaux sauce, or minted apple sauce and ovals of duck liver pâté fanned with Belgian endive, or served in thin slices with julienned vegetables. You can expect grated potato pancakes and apple pancakes, salmon, trout, venison, chicken in Riesling sauce, rolled loin of veal with herbs, salads with blanched white asparagus (seldom green), almond sauces garnishing sorbets, delicious wood (wild) strawberries. The Duck restaurant can provide you with a feast of slimming fare, as can the small, charming Bistro with only 8 tables, each with a watchful duck ornament and a different array of flowers against a background of shelves filled with cookbooks and ivory, wood, ceramic, and silver ducks from many countries and periods, a visual feast to balance the culinary delights. An adjacent gourmet boutique offers pâté, salads, shellfish, cookbooks, and food magazines.

The 150 double rooms, 38 single rooms, 20 suites, and 1 presidential suite all come with private bath, radio, TV with video channel, minibar, and direct dial telephone. Your spacious bathroom is equipped with scales, a built-in hair drier, and a lighted magnifying mirror. The minirefrigerator in your room is useful for storing the complimentary fruit and bottle of wine chilled in an ice bucket, which await you with flowers when you arrive, as well as salads and seafood from the gourmet boutique or other edibles to save calories and money. Since the hotel dates back in part to 1819, with constant renovation and additions through the years, many rooms have air-conditioning, but some do not. Many have balconies. Some rooms may have 19th-century paneling on the walls. Other rooms may be completely contemporary. All are luxurious, attractive, light, bright, spacious, and airy, with interior furnishings coordinated in a pleasing, restful style with detailed attention to comforts. Higher priced suites are truly *luxe*.

The hotel has its own thermal bathing pool built in 1985, fed by its own spring, and heated to 90 degrees F (32 degrees C). The octagonal pool-solarium is set about with white chaises and chairs padded in sunny yellow, and the complex includes saunas, a fitness room with weights and other equipment, saunas, and quiet rooms where you can enjoy skillful massages in a variety of techniques. The pool bar serves light meals and freshly squeezed fruit juices and offers a superb view over Wiesbaden. There is a full-service hairdressing salon on the premises where you can also have pedicures, manicures, and facials. Courtesy transport from and to the Frankfurt International Airport is provided by the hotel on request. Travelers' checks, but not personal ones, are accepted in payment, as well as Visa, MasterCard, American Express, Diners Club, and some European credit cards.

Name: Hotel Nassauer Hof

Mailing Address: Kaiser-Friedrich-Platz 3-4, D-6200 Wiesbaden, West Germany

Telephone: (06121) 1330; from the US, 011 49 (6121) 1330; telex 4 186 847

Established: 1819 (as Hotel Nassau); fitness center/sauna/thermal pool 1985

Managing Director: Karl Nueser (Nüser)

Owners: Nassauer Hof GMBH; Stinnes Corporation AG

Gender and Age Restrictions: None

Season: Year-round

Length of Stay Required: No minimum

Rates: Year-round rates per night, not including meals or tax: single room—DM 265 to 345; double room—DM 395 to 450. Rates are higher for deluxe accommodations. All rates are subject to change and a tax. There is no charge for children up to 10 years sharing their parents' room.

Another choice in the area, close to the Wilhelmstrasse and the Kurhaus, is the handsome, classic, elegant 4-star Schwarzer Bock Hotel, with indoor pool, exercise room, sauna, solarium, thermal tub baths, and other health spa facilities including massage therapists. The hotel dates back 500 years and is decorated with antiques, museum-quality objets d'art, and priceless 15th-century wood carvings, with the classic, tasteful atmosphere extending to its new wing as well. There are 250 guestrooms, with private bath or shower. Minimum rooms are a tad small, but each has 2 washbasins in its bathroom. Each room has color TV, minibar, radio, and telephone. The fifth-floor roof garden with restaurant grill, the Chinese tearoom, and the formal French restaurant, Le Capricorne, can accommodate all tastes and calorie levels required.

Name: Schwarzer Bock Hotel

Mailing Address: 12 Kranplatz, D-6200 Wiesbaden, West Germany

Telephone: (06121) 1550; from the US, 011 49 (6121) 1550; for reservations in the US, Utell International Reservations: (800) 223-9868 or (800) 448-8355

Established: 15th century, updated

Managing Director: H. D. Grube

Gender and Age Restrictions: None

Season: Year-round

Length of Stay Required: No minimum

Rates: Year-round rates per night, not including meals or tax: single room—DM 248; double room—DM 336. Rates are higher for deluxe accommodations. All rates are subject to change and a tax.

You can also stay at a 5-star modern deluxe hotel next to the diagnostic clinic. The Aukamm Hotel Wiesbaden has 160 comfortable, balconied rooms with private baths and 12 suites, a Japanese and a Continental restaurant, a cosy beer *stube* with live music, and a nightclub. You can have massages and a raft of beauty treatments at the hotel, enroll in a fitness program, and hike or jog to your heart's content on trails laid out in the spa gardens. MasterCard, Visa, American Express, Diners Club, and Carte Blanche credit cards are accepted.

Name: Aukamm Hotel Wiesbaden

Mailing Address: Aukamm Allee 31, D-6200 Wiesbaden, West Germany

Telephone: (06121) 5760; from the US, 011 49 (6121) 5760; telex 4186 283 AUK D

Rates: Single room, DM 330 (approximately) per day, not including taxes and meals

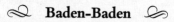

Baden-Baden

Lancaster Beauty Farm/ Brenner's Park-Hotel

Baden-Baden, 23 miles southwest of Karlsruhe, at an altitude of 600 feet, is Germany's most famous spa, a showplace, and the indestructible reigning queen of Europe's spas. Beautiful and glamorous, it is set in the dark woodlands and bosomy hills of the Black Forest (better known here as the Schwartzwald). The crystal-clear Oos (pronounced oh's) River (well, rivulet), divides the town proper on its right bank from the pleasure grounds and resort area for visitors on its left bank. Old World charm, elegance, luxury, service, the art of living well, and the romance of a golden past are as carefully preserved in Baden-Baden as the treasured trove of more than 300 different kinds of exotic trees you'll find along the Lichtentaler Allee, where horse-drawn carriages spank along in stately style in the warm weather, horse-drawn sleighs in the winter, and the tour buses are shunted out of sight through a tunnel far below ground.

Some 2000 years ago, the Romans discovered the Aquae Aurelia, more than 20 thermal springs, heavy with sodium chloride, all radioactive, their ionized mineral water bubbling up from a depth of 6500 feet. They are the hottest springs in Europe—Hell Spring is 155 degrees F. In the early part of the 3rd century, Emperor Caracalla laid out the pattern for therapeutic baths whose designs and graffiti can still be seen in the catacombs beneath the Romerplatz. Today, the neo-Renaissance Friedrichsbad, the "old" Roman-Irish baths built between 1869 and 1877, with towering dome, gilded coffered ceilings, decorative tile vaultings of pastoral fantasies, and marble pools, and the "new" Caracalla Baths added to the Augustabad (The Baths of Augustus), built in the 1960s, flank the ruins of the original Roman baths. Not far away are the Corinthian columns of the Trinkhalle (Pumproom), circa 1840, replete with water nymphs and nymphets sculptured in the gables, frescoes romanticizing the past, and an impressive 100-yard-long hall where not only the water cure is dispensed, but also a grape juice drinking cure in the spring and the autumn.

During the Belle Epoque, Baden-Baden was the most fashionable resort in the world. Everyone who was anyone stayed here to play with gold and silver chips in the Pompadour Salon of the casino, Germany's oldest and largest; to go to the theater; to hear the opera and the spa orchestra; to attend the Spring Meeting (May–June) or Grand Race Week (August–September) at the flat and steeplechase track, one of the oldest leading international tracks in the world, 7 miles northwest of Baden-Baden at the Rennplatz-Iffezheim; and, of course, to take the cure for whatever was ailing them, known as the *Entschlackungskur,* for relaxation, or what is now known as stress-reduction. Kings and queens, writers ranging from Mark Twain to Dostoevsky, great musicians such as Johannes Brahms, who composed a symphony while he was taking the waters, princes, princesses, pretty ladies, the old rich and the new rich all came here. Baden-Baden was socially big stuff then. Nothing much is changed except for contemporary improvements.

In German, *Bad* (pronounced bahd to rhyme with your beautiful bod) means bath and, like its plural form *Baden,* by extension has come to mean a watering place or *spa* (from the eponymous thermal springs' place name Spau, in Germany). Baden was officially renamed Baden-Baden in 1900 to distinguish it from other places of the name (far less elegant) in Austria and Switzerland.

To many, Baden-Baden is synonomous with Brenner's Park-Hotel, which opened in 1914 on the Lichtentaler Allee. A member of The Leading Hotels of the World and world famous for its high standards of quality, it is situated in a sylvan grove with a terraced stream and fountain, and, for indoor pleasure, has a classic Roman-style swimming pool with heated marble benches. It is so sought after that a 3- to 4-week limit-of-stay is established for all visitors. Brenner's Park-Hotel is superbly managed by Richard Schmitz, who sees to it that your every whim is catered to and every comfort provided. There are flowers, chocolates, and wine for you when you arrive. Linen mats are spread beside your bed so that your feet never need to touch the immaculately vacuumed rug or Persian carpet. Your toast is kept warm with a quilted jacket. If you requested an extra soft pillow last time you visited, you'll be sure to receive one automatically the next time you visit. Your questions can be answered in English, French, German, Arabic, Japanese, Italian, or Spanish. For other languages, request in advance an interpreter's assistance.

And now Brenner's Park-Hotel is combined with the Lancaster Beauty Farm, which offers a weekly program to restore your body and beauty. A 1000-calorie diet you would swear was 2500 calories is provided by that chef-wizard of Oos, Albert Kellner. Plus which, a complete medical check-up is possible in the Schwarzwaldklinik in the adjoining Villa Stephanie. The clinic, specializing in internal problems, has its own kitchen managed by a staff of trained dietitians.

The hotel can help you arrange half-day and full-day excursions to the Black Forest (antique and cuckoo clock museum, glass-blowing factory, and a living museum of old-time farmhouses with antique household furniture and farming tools); the Rhine Valley for a ride in a historical steam train to various little villages; the baroque Castle Favorite, with a view of a fascinating collection of faience, china, glass, and antique furniture; Strasbourg, 47 miles away, with its cathedral and medieval houses, and Colmar with its world-famous Grunewald altar piece; or the Alsatian wine route, with visits to the wine villages, wine cellars, and wine-tasting ceremonies. You can take a trip on a Rhine riverboat from Greffern to Strasbourg with dinner, music, dancing on board, a late afternoon and evening treat; or spend a morning or afternoon taking in the medieval, Renaissance, Gothic, and Belle Epoque architectural wonders of Baden-Baden.

There is nearby tennis, golf, fishing, and riding, but what everyone seems to like to do best in Baden-Baden, in addition to swimming as recreational exercise, is to walk, shop, explore, and hike.

Name: Lancaster Beauty Farm, Brenner's Park-Hotel; Schwarzwaldklinik, Villa Stephanie

Mailing Address: Brenner's Park-Hotel, An der Lichtentaler Allee, Schillerstrasse 6, D-7570 Baden-Baden, Germany

Telephone: Hotel: (07221) 3530; from the US, 011 49 (7221) 3530; telefax (07221) 353 353; telex 0781 261; Lancaster Beauty Farm: (07221) 31457; from the US, 011 49 (7221) 31457; telex 0781 261

Established: 1982 (Lancaster Beauty Farm)

Managing Director: Richard Schmitz, Managing Director, Hotel and Spa; Claudia Maria Melms, M.D., Medical Director, Schwarzwaldklinik (Black Forest Clinic), Villa Stephanie

Program Director: Director of Lancaster Beauty Farm unknown at press time

Owner: Rudolf August Oetker

Gender and Age Restrictions: None at hotel; co-ed, minimum age 16 at Lancaster Beauty Farm

Season: Year-round. No *Beauty Week Programs* at Lancaster Farm during 2 weeks over Christmas and New Year's, usually December 18 to January 1, or during Grand Race Week, which takes place at varying dates in August and early September. At that time, Lancaster Beauty Farm treatments on an à la carte basis only.

Length of Stay Required: For *Beauty Day* and *Beauty Week Programs,* 1, 2, 6, or 7 days required. For *Beauty Week,* arrival after 2:00 PM Sunday, departure up to 12:00 PM the following Sunday.

Programs Offered: Your program includes full board (diet on request), welcome cocktail, farewell gala dinner, accommodations at differing rates; a health checkup at the Schwarzwaldklinik; Lancaster Beauty Farm face and body beauty treatments Monday through Friday; daily physical exercise; daily aqua-aerobic exercise/swimming; city sight-seeing tour, excursion to the Black Forest with lunch, visit to the Friedrichsbad Roman-Irish baths establishment; hairdressing appointment for shampoo and set or blow-dry.

You begin your stay at the Lancaster Farm Beauty Clinic at 10:00 AM Monday morning, when the director is on hand to welcome you and explain the finer points of her *Ganzheitskosmetik* program (cosmetics aiming at beautifying all parts of your body). After you have been weighed and measured, a careful analysis of your skin is made and your final schedule, Monday through Friday, is put together. Early in your program, you check in to the Schwarzwaldklinik in the adjoining Villa Stephanie for a check-up, which begins with an examination by an internist, followed by chest X rays, an electrocardiograph before and after exercise, a functional test of your lungs, a complete laboratory examination of your blood and urine, plus a final examination and advice at the end of your program. The medical clinic specializes in preventive medicine and offers treatment, diagnosis, and therapy by a team of 10 physicians with visiting consultants.

In the course of the *5-day treatment program,* you get a complete daily face-neck-shoulders treatment adjusted to your skin's needs and problems; 2 skin-sloughing brush massages with body packs; 3 facials and 2 face lymph drainage treatments to reduce puffiness, including decolleté masques (face-neck-shoulders); 2 body massages; a cosmetic manicure and a medical pedicure (which takes care of corns, bunions, ingrown toenails, calluses, and dry skin as well as shaping up problem-free tootsies, with polish applied only as an option). There is an individual makeup consultation and advice preceding a makeup application and an after-treatment for dyeing your eyebrows and lashes at no extra charge. Available at extra charge are other treatments (see Beauty Treatments). On the last day of your program, you are given an individual chart on which the cosmetician assigned to you during your program has listed all the beauty products (for men as well as women) you are advised to make use of at home, with a detailed makeup chart for day and evening and recommended use with wardrobe colors.

The prescribed exercise programs start as early as 8:00 AM. One of the 6 water exercise classes included in your week's program is held in the Pompeiian-red-walled, columned, high-ceilinged, light, bright, and airy indoor swimming pool room with heated marble benches. Its end wall is windowed floor to ceiling to give you an outlook onto the hotel park. Your daily fitness class meets, weather permitting, in the hotel's heavenly park, or in the fitness room designated for exercise classes. Individual gym and yoga classes at additional cost can be arranged.

Your program includes 1 afternoon's sauna treatment at the hotel and, to repeat for emphasis, a city sight-seeing tour and Black Forest excursion and a trip to Friedrichsbad. However, you might want to check out Friedrichsbad and its Roman-Irish baths on your own. For under $15, this 190-minute experience in grand neo-Renaissance, classical sumptuosity begins with a shower, 2 saunas, and a soap and brush massage, all just to be sure you are clean, followed by eucalyptus-scented steam baths, whirlpools, bathing pools, freshwater pool, and an obligatory 30-minute rest, wrapped in sheets and blankets. The new Caracalla Baths include water and floor gymnastic sessions under the supervision of expert physiotherapists, mud packs, whirlpools, 7 indoor and outdoor swimming pools and therapeutic baths, massage jets, solariums, inhalatorium, fountains, and a coeducational, *nudity-required* sauna playground area of 2100 square feet, with heated whirlpools, showers, cold water sprays, massage rooms, rest areas, open-air terrace, solaria, and a bar selling refreshments. Heaven to some, a Hierony-mous Bosch-like hell to inhibited, shy types. At Friedrichsbad, nudity is of the same-gender variety, and the trip to Friedrichsbad included in your program is optional.

If this is not enough daily exercise for you, ask the concierge to fix up riding indoors at the Reithalle for you, or outdoors with suitable mounts provided by the Reitbahn, both along Lichtentaler Allee; or get you teed up at the Golfplatz close by (rental class available) or the minigolf (Kleingolfplatz), where bowls are available free of charge for lawn bowling or boccie/pétanque. In season, cross-country skiing is possible. There's outdoor swimming in a heated outdoor pool and lawns for sunbathing. The list of footpaths, rocky ledges, and shelter houses for hikers in the area is as long as a pikestaff. Wildlife game enclosures and waterfall gardens, of which the Italianate Paradise and the art nouveau Gönneranlage are particularly recommended, let you get in all the walking pleasure you require, beside jogging or walking around the hotel grounds.

Those who prefer quieter, more sedentary pleasures or night-life entertainment are lavishly provided for. You're only a few minutes away from the fabulous casino, housed in classic splendor; the hotel has its own *Kunsthalle* (art gallery) and the concierge can direct you to numerous private art galleries as well. The Haus des Kurgastes, formerly part of the Stephanie Hotel, is next door, with rooms furnished for table tennis, bridge, chess, billiards, piano playing, reading, or writing. Open daily, it also has a television room. There is music and nightly dancing at the hotel. And if you want to float about in the clouds, the concierge can arrange for you to go up in a balloon for aerial views. Chamber music and classical music concerts, theater, and opera are also part of the scene, as well as the spectator delights of the May–June Iffezheim race meeting.

Diet and Weight Management: The Lancaster Beauty Farm reducing diet is based on the exquisite *nouvelle cuisine* of neighboring France with fresh, regional produce. No egg-white omelettes here. The diet consists of 40 percent complex carbohydrates, 30 percent protein, and 30 percent fat. You can have your regular or diet breakfast in your bedroom or in the smaller rustically decorated Schwarzwald-Stube, where the ambience requires less formal dressing than the main hotel restaurant. On 1000 delicious calories a day, your breakfast might be coffee or tea and orange juice, dietetic yogurt, *Knackenbrot* (a rye flour crisp biscuit), and melon or raspberries you forgot could taste so good. A midmorning thirst-quencher of fresh vegetable juice tides you over nicely until lunch, which could be a frilly green salad, 2 grilled tournedos of beef garnished with 2 stalks of blanched Belgian asparagus, 5 peapods, 3 tender carrots, and melon for dessert. Or it could be something equally satisfying, such as turtle soup, guinea fowl with mushrooms, French *petits pois,* and a fresh fruit sorbet or lemon cream for dessert. For dinner, you might have a small but delightful sirloin served with fluffy rice, or grilled scampi and a crisp watercress salad, with champagne sorbet, fresh strawberries, or stewed cherries for dessert. A master chef since 1974, Bavarian-born Albert Kellner is pleased to let you have a look at the hotel kitchen one evening in your program, and will reveal one of his original Brenner's Park-Hotel recipes or answer a few questions about diet and nutrition. You'll shed 2 to 5 pounds with no tummy rumblings on his fare. *Guten appetit!*

Beauty Treatments and Welcome Indulgences: Available for extra charge at Lancaster Beauty Farm's pink-of-perfection salon are total and partial body massage, leg waxing, bust treatments, body and partial lymph drainage, reflexology massage, back treatments, "cellulite treatments to loosen up fatty deposits on your thighs and derrière," a moisturing, refining special-ingredient ampoule added to your facial, and more, more, more.

Accommodations: Your choices in the *Beauty Week Program* include a single room with shower/bath and toilet, a double room with bath and toilet, connecting bedrooms with shared bath, a double room with bath and toilet, and a sitting room styled a salon, a suite, or a Royal suite with butler service included. You'll find wine, chocolates, and flowers waiting for you, and a minibar with refrigerator. A silent valet for your clothes, sachets, long-handled shoehorns, a purse-sized sewing kit, plus the usual 5-star complimentary bath and cosmetic goodies with which each of the 100 rooms (158 beds) is supplied. Guest rooms were freshly renovated and decorated in 1988.

Rooms have floor-to-ceiling French doors opening onto terraces with striped awnings to roll up or roll down depending on how you feel about sun or shade; writing desks; down pillows and comforters; contemporary or antique-style furniture; bathrooms that are spacious; and color TV transmitted at its best thanks to the Südwestfunk TV station complex located a few miles away. All the amenities are provided along with courtesy, service, and efficiency as welcome as the pink roses that grace your breakfast tray and the linen mat changed daily for you to step on when you get out of bed. Attention to details, substantial comfort and convenience, space, and service with a smile are what you can expect and count on.

What to Bring: See USEFUL INFORMATION. Except for attractively coordinated exercise wear for gym and yoga classes, and bathing suits, everyone appears well dressed in classic, conservative ensembles morning, noon, and at night when many gentlemen and their ladies stroll off to the casino in "black-tie" regalia. The look in general is posh, well-heeled, conservative, elegant, classic, and correctly *sportif* for golf, hiking, riding, tennis, shooting, skiing. An Adolfo or Chanel suit—or reasonable facsimiles thereof—would get most women nicely through the day. Women will feel comfortably dressed in summertime with a silk dress and coordinated cardigan. For evening, an ankle-length dinner dress would be appropriate for concerts, theater, dining, and the casino. At the casino, however, you'll see a lot of bare shoulders and jewelry, both real and fake-that-looks-real, displayed. For men, Prince Philip, Prince Charles, and Ralph Lauren advertisements are good fashion images to bear in mind. Rain gear—your Burberry raincoat, please, or "good" rain gear as opposed to plastic slip-ons—and in wintertime fur coats and fur hats should be on your packing list. A terry-cloth dressing gown for wear during your Lancaster Beauty Farm treatments is ready and waiting in your room closet. Bring half the clothes you think you'll need and twice as much money. Shopping, 15 minutes from the hotel, is irresistible.

Documentation from Your Physician: None is requested or required, as you will be given a comprehensive check-up. However, a medical history and documentation of recent physical examination are helpful to have on hand for your own guidance and that of the physicians at the Schwarzwaldklinik.

Fees, Method of Payment, Insurance Coverage: High-season (May 1–June 25, August 28–October 29) rates for the *Beauty Week*—including VAT, service, visitor's tax, all meals, and standard accommodations:

For a double: DM 2972 to DM 3118 per person

For a single: DM 1587 to DM 2355

The price depends upon your selection of accommodations and whether you want to have all your meals at the hotel or only breakfast, breakfast and dinner, or breakfast and lunch. Rates are higher for deluxe accommodations and lower in the off-season. All prices are subject to change. You will be charged DM 60 a day to keep your dog in a basket in your room. (Dogs are not allowed in public rooms.)

During the Iffezheim race meeting weeks, there is an additional 20 percent charge for rooms. During the times when Lancaster Farm is only open on an à la carte basis, a Beauty week costs DM 550, with extra charge for additional treatments.

A deposit may or may not be required. Ask about the cancellation policy. Personal checks, travelers' checks, and Diners Club, American Express, and major European credit cards are accepted in payment.

Italy

✑ Abano Terme ✒
Montegrotto Terme
Battaglia

In the Euganean foothills 10 miles from Padua, Abano is accessible by the Rome-Florence-Bologna-Padua-Venice rail service and has extensive motorbus connections. Padua is a boat ride (in season) from Venice along the Brenta Canal for a look at Palladian architecture at its best.

Abano dates back to the days of Claudius and Tiberius when the Abano mud and water were a magnet for Roman matrons in search of skin and "firming" treatments. Abano's waters—with high saline levels, high levels of bromine, iodine, and lithium, and 2.28 millimicrocuries of radioactivity—are hyperthermal, with temperatures that reach 188.6 F (87 degrees C). Albano's renowned black muds are radioactive and of vegeto-mineral composition.

Some people prefer the simpler, quieter, and more pastoral setting of Montegrotto, where the waters are iodic-bromine-saline and hyperthermal, reaching temperatures of 197.6 F or 92 degrees C but are said not to be radioactive. Open year-round, both Abano and Montegrotto offer concerts, dances, opera, art and craft exhibits, evening entertainment, golf, tennis, minigolf, riding, swimming, and clay pigeon shooting.

At nearby Battaglia, on the Venice-Bologna rail line, the waters are saline-bromine-iodic and hyperthermal, reach temperatures of 168.8 F or 76 degrees C, and are said to be radioactive. Just what the composition of the famous Battaglia mud is remains a mystery, but its reputation for being the "finest" and the "best" mud in the world—for both therapeutic treatments (for rheumatism, arthritis, and the aftereffects of traumas) and cosmetic purposes such as skin softening and sleekening—continues undiminished.

In Abano, you can stay at the superior first-class Hotel Bristol Buja (Via Monteortone 2,35031 Abano Terme, Padua/Padova, Italy; telephone [049] 669 390, from the US, 011 39 [49] 669 390; telex 430210 **BRIABA I**), situated in a large park and garden. It has 3 swimming pools, indoors and outdoors, tennis courts, a physician in residence, and an array of thermal cures and beauty treatments, plus a courtesy association with the Golf Club Euganeo. The Bristol Buja, with 152 rooms, charges from 34,650 to 63,800 lire (L) for its single accommodations; and from 53,350 to 87,450 L for its double rooms, without meals. The deluxe and luxurious Sheraton Orologio Hotel, with a neo-Hellenic, classical facade which dates back to 1776, offers 2 open-air swimming pools and 1 covered pool, tennis courts, an extensive treatment center for massages, mud packs and mud baths, ozonized thermal baths, lymphatic draining, inhalation, firming and "lifting" facials, in addition to supervised exercises and jogging in its parklike setting. Golf nearby at the Club Euganeo. Prices for the 5-star Sheraton Orologio (Viale delle Terme, 66, Abano Terme, Padua/Padova, Italy; telephone [049] 669 502, from the US, 011 39 [49] 669 502) with 165 guest bedrooms and bath, range from 79,200 to 16,170 L for single accommodation; from 114,400 to 25,740 L for double accommodation, without meals. The dining rooms at both hotels serve excellent fresh vegetables, fruits, meats, salads, and homemade pastas.

✑ Ischia ✑

The island of Ischia is on the western side of the Bay of Naples, about 90 minutes by car-ferry from Naples, about an hour by motor launch or steamer, 30 minutes by hyrdrofoil, or a 20-minute-or-so whirl away by helicopter for the 17-mile trip. Ischia is four times the size of Capri, 23 miles to the southeast. Its vineyards sloping down to its cliffs, its pine woods, orchards of lemons, oranges, and groves of silvery olives, its chestnut woods and the intense sapphiric blue of the water lapping its 21 coastal miles of bays, peninsulas, and promontories are scenically ravishing. The highest point of the island is the slumbering volcano Mount Epomeo (788 meters, 2600 feet), an hour's leisurely climb through olive groves and vineyards. It's worth the climb for the 60-mile panoramic view of the Tyrrhenian coast, Naples, Vesuvius, Sorrento, and Capri. Make the hike before dawn from the village of Fontana to see the lights of the Bay of Naples and the lights of the fishing boats extinguished one by one as the sun comes up and Mount Epomeo casts a shadow over the sea. Great exercise, romantic, memorable.

Ischia's main tourist attractions are its spas: thermal centers at Porto d'Ischia, Forio d'Ischia, Casamicciola, the Olmitello spring, and Lacco Ameno. The baths at Lacco Ameno were rebuilt in 1951 on the site of Greco-Roman baths, by the late publisher and film producer Angelo Rizzoli, who promoted the building of luxurious new hotels and *ecco!* Ischia's emergence as a major health retreat/spa resort. It's also a popular seaside holiday resort for mothers, nannies, and babies in July and August when the *motocicli,* 3-wheeled motorcycle taxis with a canopy at the back to shade 2 customers, are out in force, and the horse-drawn carriages ply their trade, and the harbor is filled with yachts of rich Neapolitans holidaying with their families.

The waters at Porto d'Ischia are available at the baths of Antiche Terme Communali, Grande Albergo delle Terme e Nuove Terme Communali, Terme Felix, Terme Continentale, Terme Parco Verde, and Stabilmento Termale Militare. They contain bromine and iodine salts and come from 2 radioactive springs, Fornello and Fontana, cited by the Italian State Tourist Department (ENIT) as having "Radioactivity at 120 U.M." and temperatures of 129 to 149 degrees F (54 to 65 degrees C). The waters are used for baths, mud baths, steam baths, inhalations, and internal irrigation at the municipally run establishments where "cures" are offered for arthritis, rheumatism, aftereffects of traumas, gynecological ailments, and sterility. The waters are said also to be good for bronchial troubles, the skin, the gums, and the teeth.

The lively port area is the most popular center, with its thermal swimming pool, sports arena, movie houses, nightclubs, dancing spots and discos, tennis courts, beaches and bathing establishments, waterskiing, scuba diving, and spear fishing. One can stay here in villas, apartments, pensions, and first-, second-, and third-class hotels. The 4 leading hostelries are the Grand Hotel Punta Molino in the curve of the bay facing the Aragonian Castle, with its small, private beach, pretty gardens, and good swimming pool; the Excelsior, with its private bathing beach and pool; the Moresco, a Moorish-style construction on the beach with attractive gardens and ambience and 56 rooms with balconies or terraces, plus swimming pool; and the Jolly, with 220 functional, comfortable rooms and a pool that's covered and heated for the colder months.

At Forio d'Ischia, in the center of the west coast, the thermal sodium-sulphate-chloride springs (113 degrees F, 45 degrees C) have a radioactivity count of 17 millimicrocuries at both the Terme Castaldo and Giardini Poseidon (Gardens of Poseidon). A seductive and secluded location favored by artists, Giardini Poseidon is a new spa built over the old thermal baths. A 15-minute walk from the village of Forio, you'll also find the Temple of Venus, constructed by the Greeks, on the beach with outdoor pools and streams that flow between miniature islands of plants and flowers. The Santa Caterina is the best of the local hotel and pension accommodations in this lovely pleasure spot, where the underwater fishing is splendid and the beach inviting and beautiful.

At Casamicciola Terme, on the north side of the island, is another sea-front spa. Thermal sodium-chloride waters of unspecified radioactivity levels, from the Gurgitello (154.4 F, 68 degrees C) and the Rita (161.6 F, 72 degrees C), supply various spa establishments as well as the 65-room Hotel Elma. The Elma is surrounded by its own parklike gardens encompassing a large swimming pool, tennis court, and thermal bath area, and has resident physicians and nurses. The rooms all have sea views. The attractions here are the beach, water sports, clay pigeon shooting, cinemas, places for dancing, and the battlemented Castello with its fireworks displays on feast days.

"Radioactive power" is said to influence the "therapeutic drinking cure" of Olmitello's alkaline bicarbonated waters, taken for various intestinal problems, uric acid and liver problems, and obesity, at a spa area by the Maronti beach where as yet there are no first-class accommodations.

For those who come to Ischia for the "cure" as well as *la dolce vita,* the major attraction is the Baths of Lacco Ameno where, 5 miles from the port area, you'll find a fabulous pink, white, and yellow complex of 3 hotels—the Regina Isabella, the Reginella, and, perched on a hill above, the Royal Sporting. The Regina Isabella baths are housed in a handsome Pompeiian-red building enhanced with an impressive white-pillared portico and a white-columned arcade adjoining the prestigious hotel, which features 118 rooms with bath, and an elegant old-world atmosphere, including linen sheets, a decor of spectacular blue-and-white tiled walls, hairdressing salon and barbershop. The hotel's seawater swimming pool is sited above the bay, and another swimming pool is charmingly set in a shady grove of pines and flowering shrubs with an islet of plants and trees in its center. Its glorious indoor-outdoor terrace dining-room (jackets and ties required for dinner) serves *prima classe* gourmet fare. A buffet lunch for swimmers, sunbathers, and the casually dressed is dispensed daily on the adjoining Sporting Terrace. The complex of the Regina Isabella, the Royal Sporting, and the Reginella hotels with their own private beach and swimming pools and a bayside location, with fishing boats and launches at the ready for excursions, is complemented by a miniature golf course, bowling alley, tennis courts, and thermal pools for the use of guests at a sports center, plus a cinema-theater where musical entertainment is also staged. (Piazza Santa Restituta, 80076 Lacco Ameno, Isola d'Ischia, Italy; telephone [081] 99 43 22, from the US, 011 39 [81] 99 43 22; telex 710120 Isabel I)

Guests at all three hotels have access to the main treatment centers, Terme Regina Isabella e Santa Restituta at the Regina Isabella and another at the Reginella. Of the 6 thermal alkaline-sodium-chloride-bicarbonate waters (116.6 to 150.8 degrees F, 47 to 66 degrees C) supplying the baths, the Santa Restituta spring has the highest radioactivity—1386 millimicrocuries—with the Greek spring rated average in radioactivity, and the "old" Santa Restituta spring, the Regina Isabella, Sorgente Fangharie, and Romana reported to have slight to very slight radioactivity. The waters of Lacco Ameno, alkaline with sodium chloride and bicarbonates, are "highly radioactive" and are used for hot sand baths, thermal baths, mud baths, inhalations, and gynecological irrigations for a wide variety of problems including gout, obesity, endocrine malfunction, respiratory ailments, hardening of the skin, and facial and neck wrinkles.

The traditional 3-week stay is recommended as ideal for 15 to 18 sessions of treatment with 3 or 4 days of rest at intervals in between treatments, but 1-week programs are also offered at the luxe Regina Isabella and other hotels in the spa complex. The programs are medically oriented, with physical check-ups and heart rate and blood pressure testing done before and during treatments under the constant supervision of resident physicians. Lacco Ameno spa treatments include radioactive mineral baths, whirlpools, underwater shower massage, total or partial mud baths followed by massage and rest, sand baths with sand applied hot and dry after lengthy contact with radioactive mineral water, high-pressure showers, inhalation treatment, filiform showers of radioactive water, kinesitherapy and electrotherapy for passive exercise, lymphatic drainage, body massages, and cosmetic facial treatments. Exercise classes are also available.

ℚ Montecatini Terme ℚ
Grand Hotel e La Pace

Montecatini is a legendary spa town of 9 different thermal springs and some 800 hotels, from pensions to palaces, which house more than 150,000 visitors who come here annually to drink the waters and to bathe in them and their muds. It is situated in the heart of Tuscany, in the Val di Nievole, about 8 miles from Pistoia, the chief town of the province, and 24 miles from Florence, the regional capital. A red-roofed town of gray, ocher, and white buildings, it is surrounded by Apennine hills all around, dotted with castellos, and has 300 square miles of luxuriant woods, parks, and gardens, which keep things cool in the summer.

The season is from the beginning of April until the last week in October, when the Grand Hotel e La Pace, which international visitors simply call "La Patch-eh," is open. Conceived in the latter part of the 19th century, the Grand Hotel, one of the most renowned in Italy, was declared a national landmark in 1975. Elaborately decorated with mosaics, frescoes, columns, and Carrara marble, with all of its 170 guestrooms and suites individually furnished with Belle Epoque–style antiques and/or reproductions harmonious with the period, the hotel is set in a large parklike garden, piney, palmy, and pink with flowers, and enclosed with a tall cast-iron fence which encompasses its free-form heated pool area and clay tennis courts.

The Grand Hotel e La Pace and the pavilions of the various *terme* (thermal baths) are in classical style, with pale stone columns tapered as they are at the Parthenon, statuary, balustrades, fountains, pools, caryatids, mosaics, marble inlaid in complex designs to dazzle and delight you, and orchestras playing soft classical music all day long. The *terme* are situated in parks, which used to belong to the Medici and which vary in ambience, style, and the chemical properties, temperatures, radioactivity, and designated curative powers of their alkaline-sulphate-salt springs. The springs are classified as "weak": Rinfresco (78 degrees F, radioactivity 2.7 millimicrocuries), Tettucio (76 degrees F, radioactivity 26.5 millimicrocuries); "medium": Regina; and "strong": Torretta, Tamerici, Leopoldina, Giulia. First-class centers include the Tettucio, Excelsior, Tamerici, Torretta-Rinfresco, and Regina. For baths and mud baths, the Leopoldine Baths are locally recommended; the Excelsior for inhalatory treatment; the Istituto Termale Grocco for physical treatment. La Salute and Bagni Redi are classified as second-class centers. The Excelsior, with most of its facilities indoors, and favored for autumnal and winter visits, is located on the Viale Verdi, the main pedestrian promenade. Tettuccio, the grandest and most elaborate structure of all, also located on the Viale Verdi, is a neo-Greek temple, with piazzas, gardens, fountains, cafés, bistros, shops, a bank, and a post office, as well as its centerpiece mosaic marble counter where you receive the prescribed dosage of water in your calibrated spa glass. The water "works" quickly, and you relieve yourself of its purgative effect in one of the 1600 immaculate white *gabbinetti* (literally, "cabinets," or toilets) in the spa, then drink the next prescribed dose if you are on a "cure" program, operative at the Tettucio since the 14th century.

Besides the drinking cures, said to be particularly beneficial for the liver, many other treatments are available in the *terme:* cardiological examinations, inhalational treatments, massages, gymnastics, saunas, ozonized baths, cosmetic algae treatments, and fangotherapy, or mud body-packs applied and allowed to dry for about 20 minutes until the heated mud cools, then washed away in a hot bath followed by a relaxing massage.

One is then free to stroll around town, sightsee, shop, sit in one of the innumerable cafés sipping coffee, and listen to the gentle music of a small orchestra before it's time for dinner. A pleasant afternoon can be spent by taking the funicular (cog train) up the hill of Montecatini Alto for a view of the plain and a panorama of Pistoia, Prato, and Florence, enjoying the hilltop cafés, then coming back down to town again. A trip to Lucca, an enchanting medieval town, or to Pistoia are other rewarding possibilities for afternoon excursions. Or you can amuse yourself at the racetrack, play tennis or golf, use the outdoor swimming pools, go on walks, or try pigeon shooting in September.

A *1-week Beauty and Relaxation Program* is now offered at the sumptuous Grand Hotel e La Pace, which includes 7 nights' accommodation, 3 low-calorie meals daily, a welcome cocktail reception, a complimentary fruit basket in your spacious room, free use of the hotel's outdoor heated swimming pool and tennis courts, and a daily spa treatment. You meet first with Dr. Sirio Stefanelli, the hotel's resident physician, and with Dr. Tommei, the program's nutritionist, to receive your personalized health plan, individualized diet, and schedule of exercise and medical advice. Your spa treatments include an underwater massage, a loofah scrub and hydrotherapy, and fangotherapy. Some of your treatments are scheduled at the hotel, others at the Leopoldine Baths. Treatments given at the hotel to familiarize you with the skin care products formulated by Princess Marcella Borghese include an antiwrinkle and anti-aging fango facial, an aromatherapy massage with a compelling fragrance called Giardini di Montecatini (the gardens of Montecatini), and other delightful beauty services such as a hydro- and manual massage. Hairdressing and other Borghese beauty treatments are available à la carte. Four physiotherapists are on hand to supervise your scheduled exercise in the hotel's gymnasium, equipped with rowing machine, stationary bicycle, and other apparati, and your use of the hotel's sauna.

Chef Mario Melani prepares meals at whatever calorie level you desire or require. These are served to you in your room to enjoy on your private terrace, or poolside in the garden, or in the dining room. Slivers of veal, beef, breast of chicken, seafood, fish, delicious vegetables, fruit, homemade pasta, salads served with a dressing of olive oil, lemon juice, and pepper, sorbets and other frozen desserts are all beautifully prepared, garnished, and presented.

Your charming bedroom and marble bathroom are each equipped with a direct dial telephone; your room has color TV, a minirefrigerator, air-conditioning, heating, and a vase filled with roses or other flowers from the hotel garden. Your week's program includes complimentary transportation from and to the Pisa airport. Price for this package is 2,695,000 L.

Regular room rates for single occupancy are 220,000 to 242,000 L per night; 308,000 to 407,000 L for a double room and breakfast; 407,000 L for single occupancy of a junior suite, or 517,000 L for double occupancy; not including the 1980 L per person per day city tax.

Name: Grand Hotel e La Pace
Mailing Address: Via Della Torretta 1/A, 51016 Montecatini Terme, Italy
Telephone: (0572) 75801; from the US, 011 39 (572) 75801; for information and reservations in the US, (212) 838-7874

(The Leading Hotels of the World) in New York State or (800) 223-6800 outside of New York
Managing Director: Gino Degli Innocenti
Owner: Ricardo Pucci

Spain

❦ Hotel Byblos Andaluz y Talasoterapia ❧
Louison Bobet/Mijas Talaso Palace
Costa del Sol

For spa connoisseurs ready to spring for the ultimate luxe, Hotel Byblos Andaluz y Talasoterapia Louison Bobet/Mijas Talaso Palace is *the* Spa in Spain, a unique Spanish spa under French direction with an international clientele. A 25-minute drive from Málaga Airport on the Costa del Sol—rightly named, this Mediterranean resort area averages 330 sunny days a year—the Byblos Andaluz is set high in the hills near the little village of Mijas. It is surrounded by 2 magnificent 18-hole golf courses designed by Robert Trent Jones, with the first tee of both courses just a few minutes' walk from the hotel. A member of Preferred Hotels Worldwide, this recently built Andalusian palace cost $22 million to create. The heart of the hotel is an authentic Andalusian garden with cypress and citrus trees, fragrant vines, and flowers. Tiled roofs, arcaded balconies, exterior walls white as confectioner's sugar, patios with pools and fountains set with ornamental tiles, gardens, the best of regional decorative handcrafts and contemporary design, wonderful swimming pools and plenty of terraces and umbrella-ed tables around them for sunning and casual meals, wonderful spa installations including a new thalassotherapy center, 144 guestrooms and suites that are perfection for comfort, style, luxury, and convenience—few resort spa hotels can offer so many pleasures, so many seductive excursion and recreation possibilities in such a luxurious and pleasure-filled environment. Service is attentive and efficient.

You have a choice of à la carte elegance in a restaurant where French *haute cuisine* is presented on Limoges; or a wood-beamed charmer where Andalusian and dietetic fare is presented on Rosenthal china; or you can enjoy both kinds of fresh, natural food in this delightful regional ambience either indoors or out on the terrace.

There's on-site golf, tennis, swimming; easily accessible off-site riding, hiking, hill climbing, and mountaineering. Boating and watersport facilities are available at Puerto Banus in sea-front Marbella. For those traveling with children there are 2 aquaparks (amusement parks with lots of get-wet fun rides) in the hills beyond the protective privacy of the golf courses.

Sight-seeing? Mijas, a nearby village dating back to 600 BC, an arts and crafts center, with a bull ring, a donkey taxi service for negotiating narrow alleyways and hilly streets, and the lovely Hermitage of the Virgen de la Peña, is an obvious choice. Another pleasant excursion is Málaga, 18 miles away, the provincial capital, with museums, shops, bull ring, cathedral, and marvelous castle overlooking the sea. You can whisk off 90 miles to Granada to see the Alhambra, palace, chapel, and gardens, or make the 150-mile trip to Seville and Cordoba to take in the cathedral, palatial Moorish Alcazar, Mosque, Jewish quarter, Roman bridge, and satisfy your urge for Cordovan leather from its source. Ronda, 50 miles away, is an offbeat excursion, scenically breathtaking, and visiting the white villages in the hills is a treat admirably suited for vacationers who have time to steep themselves in atmosphere. Transport is simple with a plethora of rental cars, taxis, and tourist bus excursions to choose from.

Name: Hotel Byblos Andaluz y Talasoterapia Louison Bobet/Mijas Talaso Palace

Mailing Address: Mijas Golf, Apt. 138, Fuengirola, Málaga, Spain

Telephone: (52) 473050; (52) 460250; telex 79713 BYAN-E; telefax (52) 476783; in the US: for information (800) 628 8929, reservations (800) 323-7500

Established: 1986

Managing Directors: Pierre Aron, Director General (hotel); Claire Debrand and Françoise Bobet, Spa Directors of Mijas Talaso Palace

Program Directors: Claire Debrand; Françoise Bobet; Sanchez Almeida

Owner: Golf Palalto, SA.

Gender and Age Restrictions: None in hotel; minimum age 16 for spa

Season: Year-round

Length of Stay Required: 6 days/7 nights minimum for spa

Programs Offered: The program is permissive, nondemanding, unstructured with options. Its focus is to conserve good health and to ameliorate or eliminate the aftereffects of trauma and rheumatism-related ailments and problems relating to stress, such as nervous fatigue, anxiety, and weight loss or gain. Treatments, which center around hydrotherapy, algotherapy, thalassotherapy, and massage and include the benefits of heated seawater and mineral-rich seaweed imported from France's Brittany coast, are offered in the 23,225-square-foot Mijas Talaso Palace adjacent to the hotel. Massage and treatment rooms in this pink sandstone Andalusian spa open out onto gardens perfumed with jasmine, honeysuckle, and the fragrance of lemon trees in a low-walled garden. Constantly replenished seawater, piped from the sea 4 miles away, filtered and heated, supplemented with fresh algae extracts imported from France, fills 3 indoor swimming pools and whirlpools, jets from surface and underwater nozzles for toning water massages, alternates hot and cold in foot and hand baths.

Dr. Sanchez Almeida, a specialist in thalassotherapy, supervises a staff of 20 health professionals, qualified hydrotherapists, massage therapists, and kinesitherapists. Treatments include massage-table and underwater massage; jet pool aerobic exercises; cavitation/marine ultrasonics (alternation of ultrasonic frequency in water); and aromatherapy in whirlpools supplemented with algae and essential oils. Algotherapy, or application of algae with the heat therapy of infrared light as a sedative for pain and a muscle relaxer, is another popular treatment. The spa also encompasses saunas, relaxation rooms for stretching out on cots, a rehabilitation room, a large body-building, general training gymnasium with Nautilus weight-resistance equipment and stationary bicycles, and a *tisanerie,* or refreshment bar, supplying various dietetic drinks made from fruit and vegetable juices and herbal extracts.

In addition to the spa installations, the hotel offers 2 open-air, unheated, freshwater swimming pools; a jogging/running track; 5 tennis courts at extra charge, 2 of which are "fast" and 3 "hard" clay, 2 floodlit for night play (rental rackets and balls as well as lessons available); a practice golf range 300 yards from the hotel, with lessons available; and two 18-hole, par 72 golf courses (greens fees are modest, and golf clubs can be rented). Riding facilities are nearby for lessons or longer rides for more experienced equestrians. Aerobic classes are available and there is a wealth of trails for walking, hiking, hill climbing, and mountaineering, with the added attraction of caves to explore and ancient Roman potsherds to look for.

All spa clients are given a medical examination by a physician before their spa treatments are scheduled, and an examination at the end of their visit. All spa treatments are included in your spa package for the experiencing.

Diet and Weight Management: After a consultation with a physician and a nutritionist, clients are assigned an individually prescribed 1000-calorie daily food regimen. A 200-calorie breakfast is served in your room for you to enjoy on your balcony; 400-calorie lunches and 400-calorie dinners are served under the supervision of a nutrition specialist in the dietetic restaurant, El Andaluz, or outdoors on the terrace. You can also enjoy regular meals, alternating or substituting for your dietetic meals, of delicious regional fare.

Diet lunch might be a vegetable quiche with tomato sauce, turbot stew with a saffron-flavored sauce in a *courgette* (squash) base, and thinly sliced fruits; or a cream of cucumber sauce with prawns, thinly sliced breast of duck with candied turnips, and fruit salad drenched with orange juice. Dinner might be a fresh garden salad with vegetable juice dressing, an assortment of sliced meats garlanded with mushrooms, and fruit yogurt; or a cream soup of spring vegetables, grilled fillet of sea bream with fennel, and fresh pineapple.

Nutritionists are always on hand at mealtimes to advise you on cooking techniques, choice of food, and menus. All dietetic meals are low in sugar, fat, and sodium and high in fiber. Caffeine-free beverages are optional. Lacto-ovo or strictly vegetarian meals are available, and kosher diets, as well as other diets for medical reasons, can be accommodated.

An unusual presentation of French *haute cuisine* featuring fresh Andalusian ingredients is served at the hotel's elegant à la carte restaurant, Le Nailhac. Reducers, weight maintainers, those with jaded appetites, and those who wish to gain a pound or so can make judicious selections among this restaurant's specialties.

Beauty Treatments and Welcome Indulgences: The Jacques Dessange Beauty Salon at the hotel and a hairdressing salon provide full service for men's and women's hair, nails, and skin, including biopeeling wraps, which slough off dead skin and reveal your fresh skin smooth as satin. Estheticians trained in France and Spain are skilled in facials, makeup, and all the niceties of beauty and grooming.

Accommodations: Few of the 144 rooms and luxurious suites are alike. All the beds are approximately 6 feet square, but some may be canopied and others set in columned recesses. Styles of decoration are Roman, Arabic, Andalusian, and rustic. The Byblos Andaluz is decidedly not just another hotel. Colors used are mostly in sunny tones of lemon, peach, rose, and orange set off with shining brass table and chair frames, sparkling glass tabletops, and fresh flowers. All rooms have telephones, color TV, double doors, air-conditioning, a safe, a minibar, a radio, tile floors, attractive Spanish rugs, plenty of mirrors, excellent lighting, and glorious bathrooms decorated with ceramic tiles and provided with a telephone and a hairdryer. A chambermaid inquires when you arrive which type of soap you would prefer to have your bathroom stocked with. All rooms have a terrace, a balcony, a garden view, or a panoramic view with a sense of space fanning out on all sides. Many of the terraces are so private that they are perfect for nude sunbathing.

What to Bring: See USEFUL INFORMATION. White terry-cloth dressing gowns are provided for you. Laundry service is swift and impeccable. Bring bathing suits and rubber thong sandals for spa and around-the-pool wear. Bring tennis and golf shoes, if you plan on playing. The dress code is definitely dressy or formal when you dine in Le Nailhac. Elegant resort wear is the style most guests adopt when they are staying here. You can pick up rope-soled espadrilles in Mijas. The ground floor shopping arcade between the spa and the hotel includes a drug store and boutiques offering ready-to-wear fashion, accessories, gifts, jewelry,

Spanish leather and suede goods, sundries, reading and writing materials, newspapers, and camera film.

Documentation from Your Physician: A letter of approval, medical history, and documentation of recent physical examination are requested. You will be examined by a physician at the spa.

The Use of Alcohol and Tobacco: No alcoholic beverages are allowed at the spa center, and smoking there is not permitted. Elsewhere on the premises, you are free to do as you please.

Fees, Method of Payment, Insurance Coverage: Year-round rates per night, including service, in pesetas:

For single occupancy in a minisuite: 49,500 pts

For double occupancy in a minisuite: 38,500 pts per person

For total package price, multiply by the number of nights desired (minimum 7)

Rates are higher for deluxe accommodations and lower for twin rooms. All prices are subject to change, and all rates are subject to 12 percent VAT. A deposit is required. Ask about the cancellation policy. Personal checks are not accepted. Travelers' checks, cash in pesetas, Visa, MasterCard, American Express, and Diners Club credit cards are accepted. Check with your physician to see if fees may be tax-deductible in whole or in part under the headings of medical expenses or health institute fees.

Other Foreign Spas

Australia

There are more than 100 mineral springs in Australia around which spas have developed, none of which the authors have visited. Of a dozen or so health care and weight loss centers, most easily accessible by air, about 6 miles from the Coolingatta Airport (an hour's flying time from Sydney) is the 14-room Camp Eden (Currumbin Creek Road, Currumbin Valley, Gold Coast, Queensland, Australia 4221; telephone [075] 33 03 33, from the US, 011 61 [75] 33 03 33), a health-care center with weight loss as its major objective. Located about 8 miles inland, Camp Eden offers a strictly controlled program for men and women. No alcohol, no smoking, Pritikin diet only. One week minimum stay for $1540, which includes all meals, comfortable accommodation, and an exercise program. Write for further information.

Located 90 minutes' driving time north of Cairns on the northeastern coast of Queensland, near Port Douglas and about a mile inland from the Pacific Ocean, is a 200-acre rare tropical fruit farm run by Diane Cilento. Half its acreage is rain forest. The other 100 acres are planted with rambutans, papayas, zapotes, sapodillas, lichees, pineapples, bananas, kiwis, tamarillos, carambolas, mangoes, persimmons, and passion fruit, all organically grown with the approval of Australia's Rare Tropical Fruit Board, of which Cilento is a member. The farm, which includes ducks, horses, goats, an apiary, two rivers for fishing, and many water holes for swimming, is called Karnak. Since 1977, Diane Cilento, a fair-haired actress whose Shakespearean performances in British theater spanned astonishing arpeggios, has also operated an alternative lifestyle center here, an esoteric study movement. "Not an institution," she says, "but a course in transformation."

People don't just come here to lose weight. "They come to discover their real selves," says Cilento. "Personal individuation is what we're all about." She prefers to accept no more than 20 guests, who are accommodated in 4 houses and usually take their meals together in the main house. Participants in the program learn to make bread, and everyone "has a go" at preparing meals, which consist only of produce from the farm—fruit, vegetables, fish, goats' milk, honey, eggs, poultry. Drinking and smoking are discouraged, but not prohibited.

Truckdrivers, professors, potters, "anyone who feels riveted into a pattern" can come to Karnak. There they can "decondition themselves and find out who they really are, sort things out for themselves," Cilento says. Partipants study together, read what they write to each other, attend informal lectures, and engage in creative projects of their own choosing. Some build stairs. Some build fountains. All work outside, gardening, doing carpentry, working with the animals. Each year the program varies in its focus. One year, the emphasis may be on Tai Chi, another, on yoga. Jungian philosophy may be studied, or the works of Ibn Arabi, the teacher of the teacher of the 13th-century Sufi (mystic) Persian poet Jalal ad-Din ar-Rumi. The program is co-ed, minimum age 18. Cilento, a scholar of philosophy, a translator of Arabic into English, and a world traveler before she settled in Australia, observes that changes in the participants are often "quick and dramatic." She offers a 10-day program for $385 to familiarize guests with the transformation course, and an 8-month course for $4950 for those seeking an intensive lifestyle change. For further information: Diane Cilento, Karnak via Mossman, Queensland, Australia 4873; telephone (070) 988 194, from the US, 011 61 (70) 988 194.

People's Republic of China

Name: Beijing Combined Traditional Chinese and Western Medical Research and Therapy for Obesity Center

Mailing Address: Garrison Hospital, Zao Ying Road, Chao Yang District, Beijing, People's Republic of China

Telephone: The country code is 86; the city number is 1; the internal number for Beijing is 816—not written in Chinese with parentheses—so the telephone number as you would dial it directly from the US is 011 86 1 816-595631, extension 433. *N.B.* Some telephone numbers in Beijing have five numbers, some six, seven, or eight.

Directors: Wei (last name) Bei-Hai, telephone 816-446621, extension 226; Jia (last name) Bao-Peng, telephone 816-550460; Wang (last name) Wen-Yuan, telephone 816-595631, extension 361.

This obesity research clinic opened in October 1987 after citing a finding that 18 percent of a sample of Beijing children and 30 percent of a sample of Beijing adults were overweight. Affiliated with the People's Liberation Army Garrison Hospital, the center has developed diets and medical treatments for obesity. It is open to the public year-round, Monday through Saturday, from 8:00 to 11:00 AM. Inquiries concerning prices and treatments are welcomed and may be addressed to the directors.

Finland

Now that there has been a renaissance of spa treatment in Finland, you can enjoy the pleasure of letting your excess pressures, pounds, and inches disappear in Finn air. Most of the spas are located in southern Finland, close to the Gulf of Finland or to the Gulf of Bothnia. Based in modern hotels with up-to-date specialized equipment, staffed by trained doctors and nurses, the spas are mostly residential establishments that provide various kinds of health baths, physical therapy, and nature treatments, often in areas where local waters and mud are believed to have healing and curative properties. Beauty treatments are usually also offered. You can come with a program for diet and exercise prepared by your own doctor, or you can be examined by the physician attached to the spa who will tailor a program to suit your specific needs and requirements. Or you can come for a restful or recreation-filled holiday with the added advantage of personalized treatments designed for you by a well-qualified spa staff in a peaceful site of scenic beauty.

Saunas are found all over the world, but they are never quite the same as they are in the country of their origin. In Finland there are well over a million of these wood-lined rooms with benches and heaters topped with heat-retaining stones onto which water is thrown to vaporize. Light beating with soft, fragrant birch twigs leaves your skin smooth and supple. In winter, hardy Finns cool off by dipping through a hole into an iced-over lake or river, but you don't have to do that. Spas have showers and heated swimming pools. Of the many spas, among the best are Haikko Health Spa in Porvoo on the Gulf of Finland, former playground of the Russian Czars, a year-round spa and convention center hotel that belongs to the international Best Western chain of hotels; and the Naantali Spa, rebuilt in 1984 to combine a traditional yet contemporary spa atmosphere devoted to relaxation, rehabilitation, and rejuvenation with holiday enjoyment in a lovely archipelago setting by the Gulf of Bothnia, which separates Finland from Sweden, close to Turku. Colorful 18th-century wooden houses in a romantic living museum are next door to the spa, and a celebrated chamber music festival takes place here in June.

Major credit cards—American Express, Visa, MasterCard, and Diners Club—are generally accepted. Finnish and Swedish are the official languages, but English is widely spoken. During the summer months, dress for days in the 70s. A raincoat and sweater are always advisable to have on hand. For more information about Finland and the attractions of the following spas, contact the Finnish Tourist Board, 655 Third Avenue, New York, New York 10017; telephone (212) 370-5540; or Finn Air, which offers special Finnish spa package flights.

∾ Haikko Manor Hotel Health Spa ∾

In a 24-acre park, a compound of open lawn, small lake, flowering shrubs, and evergreen forest, by the shoreline waters of the Gulf of Finland close to Porvoo, lies this majestic, pillared, romantic manor house hotel, its history dating back to the 14th century when it was a monastery for the Dominican Black Friars. Burned, razed, and rebuilt, the manor was the early-20th-century pleasure palace for members of the Russian Imperial Court. In 1966, its 28 double rooms and 2 suites were renovated in Victorian style, but including handsome bathrooms, air-conditioning, central heating, room telephones, minibar refrigerators, color television, and comfortable beds. In 1974, separate Congress Center and health spa buildings were completed, and in 1983, the Congress Center was expanded to include larger conference, theater, and lecture areas; 102 double rooms, 54 single rooms, and 2 suites, all furnished in contemporary style; coffee shop, breakfast room, lounge, and nightclub. Dining facilities in the manor house were increased to seat 450 guests plus 200 more in summer at its umbrella-ed terrace restaurant.

Organized indoor and outdoor activities are scheduled every day of the week—cruises, excursions, fishing picnics, exhibitions, contests, children's entertainment, games, and sports. In summer there is an open-air tiled swimming pool, tennis, dance pavilion, volleyball, a daily lawn barbecue, boats and boards available to rent for sailing and windsurfing, hiking and walking trails. In winter there is ice-skating, ice fishing, ice hockey, sleighriding, cross-country and downhill skiing, tobogganing, and curling, with all equipment except skates available for reasonable rental.

The completely modern health spa promises a 3-kilo or 6.6-pound drop in weight during a 7-day program if you "loyally abide by the directions." The spa offers a full program of health and beauty treatments, including a window-walled, indoor, filtered-seawater swimming and exercise pool; vigorous group exercise programs; massage; 3 saunas; solarium; herbal, carbonated, and effervescent baths; parafango treatments; facials and other face, hand, nail, hair, feet, and body treatments. In the land where the sauna was invented, where there is a sauna for every four people, the log sauna on Haikko's beach may be one of the more idyllic, with its cabin lounge and open hearth in front of which guests often gather to grill sausages after a plunge in the Gulf.

Porvoo, a 600-year-old town with a population of 20,000, is 4 miles away from Haikko. With its row of red riverside warehouses, museum home of national poet Johan Ludvig Runeberg, the Edelfelt-Vallgren Museum of fine art, Hunting Museum, summertime flower market, harbor, cobbled lanes, the rare coin collection and library housed in the Borgå Gymnasium (high school), an endearing doll collection at #14 Jokikatu, and nearby Ruskis bird sanctuary, Porvoo is a charmer, a town beloved by artists and poets, and the site of one of Finland's largest book publishing firms, Werner Söderström. About 6 miles from Porvoo, there is the Postimäki Open-Air Museum in the village of Ilola.

Name: Haikko Manor Hotel Health Spa

Mailing Address: SF 06400 Porvoo 40, Finland

Telephone: (9) 15 153 133, from the US, 011 358 15 153 133; telex 1734 hahot sf

Established: 1974

Managing Directors: Kaarina Kalliokoski, Health Spa Manager; Pekka Sahenkari, Hotel Manager; Keimo Ollila, Conference Manager

Program Director: Kaarina Kalliokoski

Owner: Point Hotels/Best Western Hotels

Gender and Age Restrictions: None in hotel; co-ed, minimum age 16 for spa

Season: Year-round

Length of Stay Required: 5- to 10-day holiday packages (Christmas, sports holidays, Easter, summer vacation), 7-day Health Spa package plan; shorter or longer stays by arrangement

Programs Offered: Spa programs are individually designed to suit your needs, desires, and requirements. Before treatments are recommended, your blood pressure, breathing, and lung volume are tested. Available à la carte treatments include manual and water-pressure massage; warm clay packing of your body to relax and improve blood circulation and as a treatment for joint and muscle problems; paraffin packing for hands, feet, and body; herbal baths "to ease respiration, nourish dry skin, reinvigorate peripheral blood circulation and metabolism"; carbonated baths to "lower blood pressure, improve metabolism and peripheral blood circulation"; bubblebaths (whirlpool) for stimulating blood circulation; ultrasound, and infrared treatments for muscle and joint inflammation and aching muscles; neck and lumbar stretching; individual therapeutic gymnastics; group gymnastics; aqua-exercise in the indoor pool; physiotherapy; relaxation exercises; and yoga. Health lectures in the evenings are given in English, German, Finnish, and Swedish.

No treatments or beauty services are available on Sundays. Otherwise, the spa's staff of health, fitness, medical, and beauty professionals are on hand at all times to supervise, attend, and monitor you. You have a choice of male or female massage therapists, co-ed or single-sex swimming exercise classes. The gymnasium and training hall are well equipped. Table tennis, board games, and a library are available at no charge, but there is a small hourly fee for use of the billiard room. In winter, downhill and cross-country ski boots and skis are available for rent as is winter fishing tackle; no charge for curling, ice hockey, or skating (no skate rentals available). Free use of saunas and outdoor and indoor swimming pool. Summer rentals available for sailboats, canoes, windsurfing.

Diet and Weight Management: Guests lose up to a pound a day during their spa program of exercise and diet, which is an attractive mix of freshly caught fish, vegetables, fruit, and crispbread for the most part.

Beauty Treatments and Welcome Indulgences: The services of the hairdressing salon and of the esthetitians who do manicures, pedicures, facials, and masques for face, hands, and feet are excellent. Body massages are superb.

Accommodations: Manor house accommodations in the 19th-century style are charming and spacious, comfortably furnished, every room with air-conditioning, central heating, room television, telephone, minibar refrigerator, and large bathroom. Accommodations in the Congress and spa building are smaller, furnished in contemporary style, with all conveniences. The manor house accommodations comprise 28 double rooms and 2 suites. The Congress and spa building accommodations comprise 102 doubles, 54 singles, and 2 suites. Of 184 guestrooms, 166 have showers, 18 have baths, 111 have minibar refrigerators.

What to Bring: See USEFUL INFORMATION. In summer, bring clothing suitable for temperatures in the 70s. Bring bathing suit(s), bathrobes or cover-ups for walking to and from your accommodations to the outdoor swimming pool and for indoors in between treatments and salon services. Casual sportswear, blue jeans, sweaters, shirts, and jackets are fine for daytime outdoor sports other than tennis or squash, but for mealtimes and evening wear, dresses for women, jackets and ties for men are customary.

Documentation from Your Physician: Neither requested nor required, but useful to have on hand if you have a medical problem.

The Use of Alcohol and Tobacco: A glass or two of wine may be allowed in your daily spa diet if your calorie requirements do not prohibit its consumption. Smoking is discouraged.

Fees, Method of Payment, Insurance Coverage: Single rooms run from 585 to 730 Finnish marks (Fmk); doubles from 730 to 875 Fmk.

⌾ Naantali Spa ⌾

A brief car-ferry trip from Sweden and close to Finnish train and plane transport, seaside Naantali is a spa devoted entirely to relaxation, rehabilitation, and holiday enjoyment in full cooperation with the Turku University Hospital and the Finnish National Rehabilitation Center. Counting 3 physicians specializing in rehabilitation and cardiovascular and internal diseases, physiotherapists, specialized registered nurses, massage therapists, fitness trainers, cosmetologists, and attendants, the spa has a total of 45 health professionals on staff. It attracts men and women of all ages and levels of fitness. Housed in a four-story balconied building—peach stucco with rose-red roofing—with a Russo-European institutional look that appears part airport terminal, part sanitarium, part hotel, Naantali Spa is no Alvar Aalto master architectural design, that's for sure, but the interior is all sparkling light and spacious. Immaculate, comfortable, and functional accommodations are found in all 93 rooms of contemporary design, each with telephone, television, private shower, and bathroom. Room service is a happy surprise.

Naantali Spa has large elevators to accommodate wheelchairs and wheeled transportation of bedridden patients to treatments; an entire floor, as well as tables in the restaurants, reserved for nonsmokers; and all rooms already or easily equipped with helping aids for the handicapped. Naantali Spa is open Christmas and New Year's.

The spa has 2 restaurants and a café serving delicious Finnish specialties, and offers dancing at night. There is a well-equipped gymnasium, swimming and fishing on its own beach, and the attractive Nunnalahti beach less than a mile away, as well as the popular rocks of Kuparivuori for sunbathing and swimming a bit further on. Roller skates, bicycles for 1 and tandems for 2, sailboats, motorboats, canoes, and windsurfing boards are available for rent. Riding, tennis, concerts, children's entertainments, and park chess can all be found at Kaivopuisto, the park by the celebrated Convent church, less than a mile away by the yacht harbor center of Naantali.

Naantali, one of the oldest towns in Finland, grew up in the 15th century around a Birgittine convent at the Valley of Grace, where both nuns and monks knitted socks with such expertise that knitted socks became an export handcraft for centuries. Handmade dolls, called "Tokka-Lotta," with finely knit clothing, are present-day souvenirs of this small (10,000 population) resort town, as are the scrumptious ginger biscuits sold at Café Antonius, a popular gathering place. The Naantali Music Festival is held in the middle of summer when nights are at their longest. Kailo, an attractive recreation center, has an open-air theater, picnic areas, beaches, saunas, tennis, and boating. Kultaranta, the summer residence of the president of the Republic of Finland, on Luonnonmaa Island, connected by a bridge with Naantali, is celebrated for its roses and garden park, open to the public during the summer months every Friday from 6:00 to 8:00 PM; and for its manor houses and Käkölä, a manor-house museum, a fascination of old-time household objects, with unusual items made of knotty wood on sale.

The Viking Line operates car-ferry boat service twice a day from Naantali via Mariehamm Island in the Gulf of Bothnia to Kapellskär, just north of Sweden's Stockholm. There is also a daily noontime waterbus connection with Turku, about 8 miles inland, reachable also by bus and train. A university town, with a population of 162,000, Turku is Finland at its finest, with many museums, a fabled castle, a botanical garden, market halls, artisan buildings, and other attractions. Cruises among the islands of the Gulf of Bothnia's archipelago between Finland and Sweden are easily arranged.

Name: Naantali Spa
Mailing Address: Kalevanniemi, SF-21100 Naantali, Finland
Telephone: (9) 21 85711; from the US, 011 358 21 85711; telex 62314 ruish sf
Established: 1984
Managing Director: Martsi Lindfors
Owner: Rehabilitation Group, National Rehabilitation Center, Turku, Finland
Gender and Age Restrictions: None
Season: Year-round

Length of Stay Required: 1 day to 4 weeks; *2-day Recreational Weekend; 3-day Music Festival; 5-day Beauty Holiday; 5-day Stress Reduction Program; 5-* and *7-day Christmas packages; 1-day New Year's package; 7-, 15-,* and *30-day Spa Programs;* plus programs individually tailored for back and rheumatism problems (both of these programs begin on Sunday)

Programs Offered: Medical, recreational, and beauty facilities are available. The 3 physicians and 2 registered nurses on staff specialize in muscular and locomotor disturbances and injuries, postparalytic rehabilitation, circulatory problems, multiple sclerosis and other traumas, respiratory, cardiovascular, and rheumatic ailments. Physiotherapists and fitness instructors supervise fitness and relaxation training, therapeutic gymnastics and massage, thermal treatments, shortwave therapy, electrogalvanic baths and stimulation, movement treatment, and stretching. A team of therapists is specialized in hydrotherapy, underwater massage and calisthenics, herbal and remedial baths, thermal exchange and electrogalvanic baths. Other instructors supervise fitness and motion gymnastics, light athletics, games, and leisure-time activities.

Among treatments offered are a doctor's examination, laboratory measurements, injections, ergometry test, mammography (screening and clinical tests), individual and group medically indicated exercises, infrared heat and ice treatments, and ultrasonic heat treatments. All treatments meet with the approval of the Public Health Act and are licensed by the Finnish Bureau of Medicine.

Recreational activities that can be enjoyed individually or in groups include swimming in the various indoor pools or outdoors in the private beach area, surfing, and waterskiing. A variety of ball games are scheduled outdoors in summer, indoors in winter. Hiking, walking, boating, wintertime skiing, and sight-seeing tours are other planned activities. A Finnish sauna, Turkish bath, hot-water Roman pools, Jacuzzi, massages, and loofah scrubs are available in the spa department.

All package programs include breakfast and lunch *or* dinner or, for an additional charge, full board; free use of sauna and pools; and guided and well-supervised morning exercise classes on weekdays. With the *7-day Spa Program,* you also receive 2 mud treatments, 1 hay pack treatment, 2 fragrant herbal baths, 1 water massage, and two 30-minute body massages. A *5-day Beauty Holiday,* which begins on Sunday, gives you 1 algae treatment and light massage, a facial, a foot treatment, a hand treatment, and 2 solarium sessions. The *5-day Stress Reduction Program,* which begins on Sunday, provides 2 stress group sessions, 2 hydrotherapy or electrogalvanic baths, 2 fitness group sessions, and 1 60-minute full body massage. The *3-day Music Festival program* includes a water massage, a mud treatment, a herbal bath, and a 30-minute body massage. Guests with rheumatism and back problems receive a doctor's examination followed by a personalized course of instructions for treatments and recreation.

Diet and Weight Management: Weight loss, vegetarian, and other special diets are offered. Rye, wheat, and barley bread; chanterellelike mushrooms; venison, elk meat, reindeer meat; crayfish in season; Karelian pastries made from rye flour and filled with hard-boiled egg, potato, or rice; a marvelous variety of berries—tart lingonberries reminiscent of cranberries, blueberries, Arctic brambleberries somewhat like huckleberries, Arctic cloudberries, pearly and yellow, somewhat like raspberries in flavor—all are staples of the Finnish diet likely to be included in a weight loss regimen. Since only lunch *or* dinner is included in your program without extra charge, you are on your own to select diet-appropriate foods at the other meal, which you can take at either of the spa's 2 restaurants or in the café, which serves light snacks, or at any of the cafés and restaurants in Naantali. A nutritionist at the spa will advise you about foods suitable for inclusion in a calorie-controlled diet. Organized weight management courses make effective use of fresh fruits and berries; carrots, rutabaga, and other seasonal vegetables; fish, chicken, and lean meat in tempting smorgasbord buffets for weight loss, and guide you in portion control in the spa's restaurant, which serves both dieters and nondieters.

Beauty Treatments and Welcome Indulgences: Hand, foot, and facial treatments are expertly performed by skilled cosmetologists. For reasonable prices, you can be mulched with black mud and hay pack treatments to emerge feeling like a tree in springtime. There is an on-site hairdresser. Loofah scrubs, known as water and brush massages, are modestly priced and leave your skin smooth and glowing. Heated paraffin body waxing and mud packs, inducing perspiration and relaxation, leave your skin soft, smooth, and radiant and are also reasonably priced. The algae treatment, similar to thalassotherapy treatments elsewhere in the world, is pleasant. A facial can be almost as expensive as a clinical mammography test, but the results are worth the $75 tab. Although you haven't lived until you have had a Finnish sauna in the country of its origin, all the body and hydrotherapy treatments offered at Naantali are recommended for their excellence.

Accommodations: Of the 93 double rooms furnished in contemporary, functional style, each equipped with telephone, television, shower, and WC, some come with balconies. All are or can be specially equipped for handicapped persons and are comfortable and convenient as well for guests without disabilities. Two suites are available, each with its own private balcony. If you are a nonsmoker, ask for accommodations on the nonsmoking floor.

What to Bring: See USEFUL INFORMATION. Bring bathing suit(s) and cover-up. In July, the warmest month, the minimum temperature recorded in the Turku area is 52 degrees F and the maximum is 72 degrees F; in February, the coldest month, the minimum is 12 degrees F and the maximum, 26 degrees F. Dress warmly, and be sure to bring appropriate seasonal dress. Summertime rain in Finland is less than in Great Britain, the Netherlands, and Belgium, but November is usually a month of clouds, mist, and rain. A lined trenchcoat or raincoat is always useful. Jackets and ties are *de rigueur* for men at evening meals in the spa's restaurants. Save room in your suitcase for Finnish-made sweaters and athletic gear you'll be sure to want to buy.

Documentation from Your Physician: A letter of approval is neither requested nor required. Medical testing can be done at the spa. A medical history and documentation of recent physical examination are requested if you have a medical problem.

The Use of Alcohol and Tobacco: Wine and spirits are available. A no-smoking guestroom floor, and no-smoking sections in the restaurants are provided. Unless prohibited for medical reasons, whether you drink or smoke is an individual concern.

Fees, Insurance Coverage: Year-round rates, including breakfast, lunch *or* dinner, service, and tax, are quoted in Finnish marks:

For *7-day Spa Holiday:* 3760 Fmk single, 2850 Fmk per person double.

For *spa day:* 480 Fmk single, 360 Fmk per person double. Additional days, 460 Fmk single, 330 Fmk per person double

For *5-day Beauty Holiday:* 2930 Fmk single, 2280 Fmk per person double

For *5-day Stress Reduction:* 2735 Fmk single, 2085 Fmk per person double

For *3-day Music Festival:* 1370 Fmk per person single, 1760 Fmk per person double

For *2-day Recreational Weekend:* 960 Fmk single, 470 Fmk per person double

There is no charge for children under 4 years of age sharing accommodations with parents in the same room, and a 50 percent reduction for children ages 4 to 14 sharing parents' accommodations. Rates are higher for deluxe accommodations, and all prices are subject to change. The only gratuities expected are for the porters and doormen who get a taxi for you; other gratuities at your discretion. A deposit is required. Ask about the cancellation policy. Medically required physiotherapy treatments are refundable in Finland under the Finnish health insurance system and may also be refundable under other health insurance policies, or tax-deductible as medical expenses.

Israel

There are three major health- and beauty-oriented spa vacation areas in Israel: the Sea of Galilee and the resort town of Tiberias, where coins struck at the time of the Emperor Trajan, about 100 AD, show Hygeia, goddess of health, astride a rock at the source of hot springs praised by the legendary King Solomon, as well as by Herod and Pliny, for their bathing pleasure and healing virtues; the region of the Dead Sea; and the Daniel Hotel and Spa at Herzliya on the Mediterranean, 9 miles north of Tel Aviv.

Galilee is the hilly area of northern Israel, bordered by Syria on the northeast and Lebanon on the northwest, between the Golan Heights in the east and the mountains in the west, and its sea is really a freshwater lake, some 660 feet below sea level, roughly half as wide as its 14-mile length. Its waters teem with sardines, carp, perch, *bourri* (grey mullet), and tilapia (better known as St. Peter's fish, for it was in the mouth of this fish that St. Peter found the shekel [*shequel*] with which to pay his taxes). Its waters also teem year-round with sailboats, swimmers, windsurfers, water- and paraskiers. The district of Galilee includes the subdistrict of Akko, the Crusaders' Acre, north of Haifa, with remains of the old knights' halls and an excellent beach; Nazareth (Nazerat), childhood home of Jesus; Zefat (Safed), pronounced svaht, center of Jewish mysticism in the Middle Ages and one of the four holy cities of Israel; and Tiberias, a lush and fertile subtropical area. The misty violet of jacarandas is everywhere in season, licorice grows wild, bannered groves of bananas and date palms flourish, and on the terraced hillsides, mulberry trees, olive groves, grapes, and citrus fruits grow in profusion.

At Tiberias's restaurants along its Promenade on the western lakeside bank, the ingredients of a typical delicious Middle Eastern meal are also what is generally available throughout Israel: tahini, a paste or sauce of ground sesame seeds; hummus, a paste of ground chickpeas, tahini, olive oil, and spices; grilled fish, chicken, and lamb; salads with a dressing made of olive oil, garlic, parsley, lemon juice, and a tad of vinegar; eggplant in every conceivable guise from ratatouille to sliced, baked, stuffed, and fried; tomatoes; melon, strawberries, grapes, bananas, citrus fruit, and other fruit in season; pastries steeped in honey and chopped walnuts layered between philo dough baked to a crisp, or pastries like rugelach made with heavier dough and filled with whipped cream, custard, or preserves. If you skip the pastry desserts and watch your portions, the food is a reducer's delight—tasty, healthful, light, satisfying. In Tiberias, from November to March, the average maximum temperature is around 70 degrees F. The rains of November through February are interspersed with days of brilliant sunshine, and the weather allows for year-round bathing in the Sea of Galilee. April to October, as in the rest of Israel, is virtually rainless.

The Tiberias Hot Springs Health Center (P.O. Box 22, Tiberias 14100, Israel; telephone [067] 91967, from the US, 011 972 [67] 91967) on the western shore of the Sea of Galilee, is about a 3-hour drive from Tel Aviv (84 miles, 135 kilometers) by way of Haifa (43 miles, 70 kilometers), and takes about the same time from Jerusalem (94 miles, 152 kilometers), motoring via Jericho northward along the barren, arid wasteland along the western bank of the Jordan River. A nonresidential establishment, specializing in the treatment of arthritic, rheumatic, respiratory, muscular, and gynecological disorders for an average yearly clientele of 30,000, as well as catering to 200,000 guests who visit here for rest and relaxation, the Tiberias Hot Springs Health Center is open Saturday to Thursday from 8:00 AM to 4:00 PM; Fridays from 8:00 AM to 1:00 PM. It is set in 15 acres of waterfront parkland, bordered by the larger Hammat National Park, which offers peaceful walks among excavated 3rd-century bathhouses, the ruins of ancient synagogues with mosaics as ravishing as those in Ravenna, trees and plants that are a sanctuary for local and migrant birds.

The center is staffed with highly trained physicians, hydrotherapists, fitness instructors, and massage therapists. Its health and recreation facilities include treatment pools and baths heated to between 97 and 102 degrees F, thermal swimming pools between 90 and 97 degrees F, and individual tubs for carbon dioxide baths, underwater massage, and hydrotherapy; electrohydrotherapeutic baths for treatment of the entire body or specific limbs; Scotch/Swiss/Vichy showers for alternating hot and cold water treatments; pools for physiotherapy; a solarium with ultraviolet and infrared treatment facilities; an exercise gymnasium and classes for gymnastics and calisthenics; ultrasonic treatments; and "dry" physiotherapy treatment rooms. You can also enjoy loofah scrubs here and mud packs with piloma, the natural mud, smooth, gray, soft, and plastic as butter, found on the banks of the Jordan south of the Sea of Galilee. Like the mud (fango) from Italy's Battaglia, piloma mud packs, applied at a temperature of 118 degrees F, retain their initial heat for a long time to exert thermal and biological action in depth. Massages, physiotherapy, and other services at the spa are priced at bargain rates. Before entering the hot baths, all guests are examined by a physician. Guests are requested and advised to bring detailed medical reports relevant to their health or medical problems, such as current electrocardiograms, X rays, blood counts, and blood pressure. There is a restaurant here plus a self-service café.

If you would prefer a more recreational ambience for hydrotherapy, head for Hammat Gader Thermal Gardens (Mobile Post South, 12480 Ramat Hagolan; telephone [067] 51039, from the US, 011 972 [67] 51039). Some 11 miles southeast of the Sea of Galilee in the Yarmuk Valley, this resort park is open Saturday to Thursday, 8:00 AM to 4:00 PM; Fridays from 8:00 AM to 1:00 PM. You can soak, warm, and relax in mineral-rich pools with temperatures varying from 82 to 127 degrees F, surrounded by palm trees and gardens. Hydrojets provide a dozen underwater body massage installations, and shower and dressing room facilities are located at the water's edge. The park is the site of 2000-year old baths, the second largest in the Roman Empire after those in Naples. First excavated in 1932, they are now being renovated, with the marvelous cooling and heating system that provided hot, warm, and cold baths restored to working order. You can also visit three ancient synagogues, a Roman theater, a wildlife area with roaming deer and gazelles, and an alligator park to remind you that the Romans liked man vs. alligator wrestling spectacles. There is a self-service restaurant, and 2 buffets to appease your hunger after a dip in the thermal waters.

Where to stay:

· The Ganai Hamat Hotel (P.O. Box 22, 14100 Tiberias; telephone [067] 92890, from the US, 011 972 [67] 92890; telex 6674 GAMAT) less than 2 miles south of town on the lake road, is a 4-star hotel that features its own beach, 2 tennis courts, swimming pool, and special rates at the Hammat Tiberias (the Tiberias Hot Springs Spa) next to it where the water steams at 140 degrees F, just as it did in Biblical times. High-season rates for a double room and bath: single occupancy about $100, double occupancy $135; low season $55 and $75; not including 15 percent service charge but including breakfast. Fully air-conditioned and heated, private bathroom and room telephone, radio.

· The Galei Kinnereth (Kaplan Avenue, 14100 Tiberias; telephone [067] 922331-8, from the US, 011 972 [67] 922331-8; telex 6655) fully air-conditioned and heated, private bathroom, radio and telephone in each room, also has a swimming pool, private beach, and its own boating club with sailboat, motorboat, rowboat, 4 windsurfers, and waterskiing boat; also a beauty parlor. A 5-star hotel, its high-season rates are $100 to $120 for single occupancy of a double room and bath, $135 to $150 double occupancy; low season, $80 to $90, $100 to $120.

·A score of other hotels, hillside and lakeshore, as well as kibbutz inns and holiday villages offer every type of accommodation, but those who can afford it would do well to spring for the Sheraton's luxury 5-star Tiberias Plaza (P.O. Box 375, 14103 Tiberias; telephone [067] 92244, from the US, 011 972 [67] 92244; telex 6663), fully air-conditioned and heated; private bathroom, radio, telephone, and color TV in each room; in-house video movies 14 hours a day; beauty parlor; swimming pool; several restaurants; health club; water-skiing club; and every Wednesday, leaving from the hotel, a good-exercise, guided walking tour. Prices $100 to $120 for single occupancy of a double room, $120 to $135 for double occupancy in the high season; low season $80 to $100, $110 to $120. All rates include breakfast but not the 15 percent service charge.

The Kinneret Sailing Company (telephone [067] 21831,51007) leaves Tiberias daily at 10:30 AM for Kibbutz Ein Gev across the lake, a holiday village on the eastern shore, with gardens, beach, and 83 rooms, air-conditioned and heated, private bathroom and kitchenette in each room, and good restaurant, and returns at 12:15 PM, with additional trips in the summer. The Minus 200 round-the-lake bus service (telephone [067] 20474) leaves Tiberias every 2 hours, beginning at 8:30 AM until the last bus at 3:15 PM for a 21-stop tour.

For adventurous types interested in old synagogues and contemporary art, or in soaking up atmosphere after soaking in thermal mineral spring water, a visit to Zefat (Safed), an ancient town on the edge of Galilee with a spectacular site on the top of a mountain, is an excursion possibility less than an hour's drive north from Tiberias. In winter, don't go, because it can be windy, cold, and even snowbound, but when it's hallucinatingly hot in desert areas in the summertime, it's very pleasant here. The artists' quarter in the lower section of town contains the Rimon Inn (telephone [069] 30665-6, from the US, 011 972 [69] 30665-6; telex 6611), a 4-star twinkler, with 34 delightful rooms in a garden setting, all rooms with private bath, telephone, radio, many rooms with balcony or patio; partially air-conditioned; video films; terraced garden with swimming pool. High-season rates about $90 for double occupancy; $55 in low season; breakfast included but not the 15 percent service charge. The food is good and the inn is surrounded with the picturesque showrooms of Israeli artists who, during the summer, have permanent exhibitions of their work on sale.

The Dead Sea area is said to be at the forefront of the Israeli spa scene, particularly for those with psoriasis and those who wish to be lulled into a state of health and equilibrium, or would like a base for visiting Masada fortress, the ruins of Jericho, or the caves of Qumran, where the Dead Sea scrolls were discovered in 1947. The Dead Sea is the lowest spot on earth, 1312 feet below sea level, an area of 386 square miles, divided into southern and northern basins. It has the greatest mineral concentration of any body of water in the world—33 percent, as compared with 3 percent for the Atlantic. You are kept afloat effortlessly in the water. The dry, oxygen-rich air—10 percent more than at the Mediterranean sea level—the high barometric pressure, and the high rate of evaporation create a mineral haze, making sunburn rare, yet allowing for the penetration of the longer ultraviolet rays responsible for tanning, not burning. Due to the high concentration of bromide in the Dead Sea's water, the haze it gives off contains large quantities of bromine (a potentially toxic component of many sedatives). King Herod (73–4 BC) who built Masada in the Judean hills overlooking the Dead Sea, is said to have used the waters for his ailments, and for centuries the Bedouins of the Negev and Sinai deserts have praised the health-giving properties of the Dead Sea's waters and climate, claimed by many doctors to be helpful for psoriasis, eczema, muscle and joint diseases, emphysema, and sinusitis as well as for physical rehabilitation.

Cleopatra is reported to have used the thermo-mineral springs for cosmetic purposes, and to have bathed in the dark, algae-rich mud from alluvial deposits near Ein Gedi, an oasis dating back to 3000 BC on the western shores of the Dead Sea. This is the present site of Kibbutz Ein Gedi Spa (86910 Dead Sea, Israel; telephone [057] 84757, from the US, 011 972 [57] 84757; telex 5364) at Hamme Mazor, where guests have unrestricted use of the natural therapeutic mud with no extra charge at the private beach on the property. The kibbutz spa has 6 indoor sulphur pools, 2 for women only, 2 for men only, and 2 for mixed bathing, all at a natural temperature of 102 degrees F, in an air-conditioned building where there is a vegetarian restaurant as well as areas for relaxing. There are 50 guest cottages, each with air-conditioning, private bathroom, color TV and radio; a swimming pool and minigolf. Cafeteria-style meals are provided. The spa facility is adjacent to the sea, a 5-minute shuttle-bus ride away. Rates are about $50 a person a day with 2 meals and about $55 with 3 meals. The Ein Gedi Nature Preserve, terrain which evoked the Song of Songs, is a short walk from the main entrance of the kibbutz and contains a fine assortment of unusual trees, waterfalls, birds, and wildlife, including ibex and hyrax (rock badgers).

To the south, at Hamme Zohar, also on the western banks of the Dead Sea, the 5-star Moriah Dead Sea Spa Hotel (86930 Dead Sea, Israel; telephone [057] 84221, from US, 011 972 [57] 84221; telex 5284) has a heated indoor swimming pool containing mineral-rich Dead Sea water to float or bathe in and heated alluvial mud for fango therapy treatments to improve your circulation, relieve arthritic pain, and silken your skin. An evaluation by a staff physician for a small fee is required for this therapy. The spa hotel offers a *beauty package* with dietetic meals if desired and 3 spa activities daily, with choices of hydrotherapy, loofah scrub, facials, fangotherapy, seaweed wraps, manicure, pedicure, and massage. Buffet breakfast features cheese; lunch is either a dairy lunch or a buffet of cold meats and salads; dinner features a hot entrée of chicken, veal, or lamb. All rooms are fully air-conditioned and heated, each with a private bathroom, color TV, radio, and telephone. There's an outdoor freshwater swimming pool, a tennis court, private Dead Sea beach, and live rock music at night. Prices at the spa hotel are $108 to $127 for a double room in the high season, or $79 to $91 for single occupancy; regular rates are $97 to $110 for a double room, or $73 to $79 for single occupancy; breakfast is included but not the 15 percent service charge.

The 4-star Moriah Gardens Hotel has *14-* and *21-day programs* for the treatment of arthritis and psoriasis. The Moriah Gardens Hotel is about 20 percent less than the Moriah Dead Sea Spa Hotel. Count on a 60-minute drive from Jerusalem, 3 hours from Tel Aviv.

◇ The Daniel Hotel Health and Beauty Spa ◇

". . . And among them all was found none like Daniel" (Dan. 1:19). This is the Biblical slogan of The Daniel Hotel Health and Beauty Spa, on the shores of the Mediterranean, a 6-mile, 10-kilometer zip by car north of Tel Aviv. There are 350 deluxe rooms and suites and conference and banqueting facilities for 800 guests. With its own synagogue, extensive shopping arcade, a galleried indoor heated swimming pool with mosaic columns and eaves three stories underground and rimmed with Astroturf, the Daniel's Health and Beauty Spa enjoys the most sumptuous setting—a veritable "celebration of splendor," claims its owner—of all Israeli spas. Children's activity programs are available. Babysitting on request.

Name: The Daniel Hotel Health and Beauty Spa

Mailing Address: Herzliya-on-Sea, Israel 46769

Telephone: (052) 544-444; from the US, 011 972 (52) 544-444; telex 341812 IL

Established: hotel, 1975; spa, 1984

Managing Directors: Ezra Gazita, Operational Director of the Spa; Anat Begerano, Administrative Manager of the Spa

Program Directors: Ezra Gazita, Anat Begerano

Owner: Leon Tamman, owner of the International Generics (IG) Hotels

Gender and Age Restrictions: None in hotel; co-ed, minimum age 16 in spa; no one under 16 allowed in the indoor pool

Season: Year-round

Length of Stay Required: 1 night; *4-* and *7-night spa packages* available, also longer

Programs Offered: All guests have free use of the heated indoor pool and outdoor pool, sauna, Turkish steam room, 3 Jacuzzis, 8-station Nautilus, fitness room, 2 tennis courts, gymnasium with stationary bicycles, rowing machine, free weights. Spa guests receive a blood pressure check by a registered nurse; a consultation with a registered dietitian; and a consultation with the resident physician. Exercise classes include yoga, stretch, calisthenics, aerobics, jazz dancing, and aerobic pool exercise.

You receive a daily 30-minute massage—classic Swedish, shiatsu, Oriental, relaxation, G-5 vibrating electric, or acupressure; daily inhalation therapy of "pure simulated mountain air" (eucalyptus vapor); and a choice of à la carte services and treatments to be included on alternate days of your spa program, an option that varies with the time of year and the rate of exchange when you make your reservation. Available are treatments such as underwater massage, a spa bath with Dead Sea water, Swiss shower and Scotch hose, an oil and steam panthermal steam cabinet session, an aromatic spa bath, and mud packs of heated Dead Sea alluvial mud. The spa has a staff of 40 fitness instructors, massage therapists, and cosmetologists, and about the same number of guests are generally enrolled in spa programs. Exercise classes are limited to a dozen or less participants. Supervised jogging and health walks supplement your exercise program. If you tire of lolling in the Jacuzzi encased in a splendid mosaic shell, you can walk on the beach or swim in the Mediterranean, swim in the outdoor pool or sun in a lounge chair on the poolside deck. Plans are under way for an organized water sports program.

Diet and Weight Management: A daily choice of dietetic meals providing a total of 500 or 1000 calories is offered in calorie-controlled portions. After a personal consultation, the nutritionist advises you on what and how much to eat. Spa guests are served breakfast and dinner at the Danieli, the bougainvillea-arbored Italian balcony restaurant with a view of the sea. No meat is served. You have a dinner of soup, fish, and vegetables, fruit for dessert. Lunch, served at the spa's health bar, includes salads, fruits, vegetables, and a variety of freshly baked bread. There is 24-hour room service; a poolside restaurant for al fresco snacks, meals, barbecues, and light drinks; a Polynesian restaurant, Bali Hai, which features hula dancers and Kosher food; Cleopatra's Tent restaurant, which features belly dancers and other Middle Eastern folkloric entertainment; as well as 6 bars for guests who are not concerned about weight loss and wish to supplement their diet fare with à la carte meals and snacks. Except for room service and special requests, Kosher dietary laws are observed at all restaurants.

Beauty Treatments and Welcome Indulgences: In addition to the massages and baths, beauty services include a variety of facials, skin analysis and review, makeup instruction, eyebrow arch or wax, manicures, pedicures, hairdressing services, depilatory waxing, loofah scrubs, suntanning, and aromatherapy massages. To be able to enjoy treatments with the fabled Dead Sea water and Dead Sea mud on the shores of the Mediterranean is a welcome indulgence. The treatment rooms for massages, the hairdressing salon, and the hydrotherapy section of the spa are mirrored and sumptuously appointed. The services of the massage therapists and cosmetologists are excellent. Equipment is first-class.

Accommodations: Five-star hotel accommodations, fully air-conditioned and heated, all rooms with private bath and shower, color TV, radio, telephone, in-house video channels (2) for films, balconies, and sea views. Condominium apartments and suites with kitchenettes are available.

What to Bring: See USEFUL INFORMATION. Terry-cloth robes and warm-up suits are provided. Bring bathing suits and a cover-up for beach wear. From April to October, pack lightweight suits, slacks, and sport shirts for men; plenty of light cotton wear for women, including summertime dinner dresses and light sweaters or a light knitted coat or wrap for evening outings along the beach. Sunglasses and a sun hat are musts. From November to March, bring a warm coat, sweaters, rain gear. Jackets and ties are worn by men in the evenings at the hotel restaurants. Women generally dress up in the evenings. The shopping arcade has a selection of clothing and accessories as well as gift items and Israeli handcrafts.

Documentation from Your Physician: Neither requested nor required.

The Use of Alcohol and Tobacco: No restrictions

Fees, Method of Payment, Insurance Coverage: High-season (March, April, mid-July through August 31, and late September through early October) rates:

For *7-night program:*
For a double room: $1150 per person
For single occupancy: $1500

Rates are higher for deluxe accommodations and lower in the off-season. All prices are subject to change, and all rates are subject to a 15 percent service charge. A deposit is required. Ask about cancellation policy. All major credit cards are accepted. The spa plan is not medically tax-deductible.

◕ The Sans Souci Hotel Club & Spa ◔
("Charlie's Spa")

The Sans Souci Hotel Club and its spa, whimsically named for a green turtle resident in its own mineral spring grotto, is located on a 12-acre promontory of tropical gardens on Jamaica's north coast, with its own private white sand beach fronting the turquoise waters and coral reefs of Little Bay. The 5-star hotel complex of Caribbean architecture, four-storied, oleander-pink, each room with its private balcony, is charming and romantic, with picturesque gazebos in the gardens and a bona fide mineral spring swimming pool as well as a freshwater one. The hotel has 72 rooms and suites. The spa accepts no more than 20 guests, who can do as much or as little as they please. The hotel's Casanova Restaurant is ranked among the best in the Caribbean. Directors and management are super-professional. Chris Silkwood, who earned her laurels as president and executive director of the Phoenix Fitness Resort in Houston, Texas (see AMERICAN SPAS: WEST), created the spa, supervised its installation and fitness and beauty services. Kenneth S. Kennedy, who trained at the Plaza Athenée in Paris, Suvretta House in St. Moritz, and with Cunard Shipping and Hilton International, is overall managing director.

Sans Souci is 2 miles east of the town of Ocho Rios, where you can arrange shopping tours, deep-sea fishing expeditions, paraskiing, waterskiing, and boat charters. A raft ride on the Rio Grande River is a pleasant way to observe the richness of Jamaica's variety of tropical vegetation and bird life, as you can also do at the 20-acre Carinosa Gardens, where waterfalls and pools are interlaced with tropical gardens, a wonderful walk-in aviary, and a "seaquarium." Hummingbirds are a specialty of Jamaica, from tiny iridescent green ones to the doctor birds that whir past with flowing black streamer tails, making this a bird-watcher's delight. Jamaica is also heaven for shell collectors and orchid lovers. A highlight tour of Ocho Rios and Dunn's River Falls is included in your program; also a weekly cocktail party. Rental cars can be hired from over 50 firms. Unmetered taxis are available, as are numerous companies specializing in sight-seeing tours. The Sans Souci club secretary can make all the arrangements.

There is marvelous swimming on site at the spa in its mineral pool or snorkeling in the bay, as well as on-site tennis and croquet. You can play golf with complimentary greens fees at the Upton Country Club close by, and in the evenings, at the Sans Souci, there's dancing on a marble pavilion with the stars above, a piano bar, and a weekly folkloric performance.

Name: The Sans Souci Hotel Club & Spa ("Charlie's Spa")

Mailing Address: Box 103, Ocho Rios, Jamaica, West Indies

Telephone: (809) 974-2353/4; (809) 974-2535; for reservations (Elegant Resorts of Jamaica) in US and Canada, (800) 237-3237; from the Miami area (305) 666-3566; telex 381 7496

Established: Hotel, circa 1930s, renovated and refurbished 1984–86; spa, 1987

Managing Director: Werner Dietl

Program Director: Susan Brewster, Spa and Fitness Director

Owner: Maurice W. Facey, Chairman of Pan-Jamaican Investment Trust, Ltd.

Gender and Age Restrictions: None in hotel; co-ed, minimum age 16 for spa

Season: Year-round

Length of Stay Required: 7 days/6 nights for spa program; check in 3:00 PM Sunday, check out following Saturday by noon

Programs Offered: The program is structured, but you are free to go off sight-seeing or to laze on the beach or swim or snorkel, as you wish. Monday through Friday at 10:30 AM, spa orientation and a tour of the facilities convenes in the hotel lobby, where you can make the acquaintance of Sir Walter Raleigh, a handsome caged macaw, before you wend your way across the bridge at palm-tree-top level to the Charlie's Spa office to schedule your beauty and body treatments and exercise classes. After an initial consultation with Hilary Coley, the fitness director, you are assigned a personal fitness counselor to guide you through the program and advise you. You also have an individual consultation with Jerard Resnick, the resident nutritionist and consultant chef, to determine which calorie level of meals you prefer or whether you would prefer to alternate diet meals with à la carte provender. Included in your spa package are: 6 hour-long massages, or 5 hour-long massages and a special body treatment; 2 facials; a manicure and a pedicure; a hairdo, styling, and makeup; use of the mineral swimming pool and hot mineral water whirlpool tub; 3 daily exercise classes and use of gym equipment. Exercise classes include toning, stretching, low-impact aerobics, yoga, and water exercise held in the spa's mineral spring-fed swimming pool, which is set like a gem in a semicircular foundation raised above the beach, its water continually replenished. Recently tested by spa analyst Dr. Hans Gockel of

Germany, who determined that they "rivaled those of the great spas of Europe," the waters have been reputed for centuries to have curative and healing power. You'll meet the 3 fitness instructors as well as Charlie, the resident green turtle, the spa's mascot namesake, who has enjoyed the sustenance of his own mineral-fed grotto for some 20 years, dining on lobster. You'll be shown the hot mineral water whirlpool bath in which you can soak and relax; the sauna; and the gymnasium equipped with 6-station Universal circuit training weight equipment, 2 stationary bicycles, a rowing machine, and free weights. You'll meet the 4 estheticians and massage therapists who will minister to your needs in a pavilion overlooking the sea. Outside the pavilion, on the patio above the beach, is a giant chessboard with 2-foot-tall chess pieces carved from lignum vitae, Jamaica's national tree.

Recreational facilities include a freshwater outdoor swimming pool in addition to the spa's mineral-spring-fed pool; 4 Laykold tennis courts (2 lighted for night play); 2 manicured croquet lawns; free equipment provided for snorkeling off the private white sand beach, for windsurfing, and for hoisting a sail on a sunfish craft; complimentary privileges at the Upton Country Club's golf course nearby, where golf clubs can be rented; guest membership at the St. Ann Polo Club where, if you play, a match can be arranged with advance notification or, if you time things right, you can watch a match on Saturday afternoons. Scuba diving is available for an extra fee. Parasailing and jet skiing, deemed too noisy to disturb the serenity of Little Bay and Sans Souci's private beach, are available in the main bay of Ocho Rios, where you can also hire fishing boats for deep-sea fishing and charter sailboats or motor vessels for tours around and about the island.

Diet and Weight Management: Nutritionist Jerard Resnick, a graduate of the Culinary Institute of America, suggests a daily diet of 1000 to 1200 calories. If there are fewer than 5 guests enrolled in the spa program, you have breakfast served in your room. When there are more than 5 guests there's a buffet breakfast in the Casanova Restaurant, awarded 11 gold medals by the Jamaica Cultural Development Commission for its New Caribbean cuisine, seafood, chicken dishes, appetizers, soups, and pastries. Casanova is also known for its Italian preparations created by Arrigo Cipriani of Harry's Bar when the restaurant first opened in 1970, and carried forward to the present.

Calorie counts for low-calorie offerings appear on every menu along with the regular specialties. Spa specials, such as yogurt chicken, fresh dorado filet, pasta primavera, and rock lobster salad with island vegetables—eggplant, cauliflower, spinach, pumpkin, carrots, tomatoes, peas, beans, and plantain—are supplemented with a largesse of fruit. Freshly caught Jamaican rock lobsters, grouper, and blue fish with a squeeze of a lime plucked from a nearby tree are samples of low-calorie treats served. All guests receive a complimentary basket of fruit—mangoes, finger bananas, pineapples, star apples, apples and pears and grapes from Mandeville Highland Orchards, as delicious as any you have ever eaten, and ugli fruit, a hybrid grapefruit, surprisingly good—and all the fresh fruit juices, as well as all the bar cocktails and French house wine you care to drink, free of charge. Soursop sorbet is a spa dessert to make your taste buds sing. Coconut ice cream with fresh coconut and fruit sauce is a high-calorie treat few can resist. Still, even supplementing spa meals with à la carte goodies, guests manage to trim off pounds and inches.

Afternoon tea is served at the Casanova, and there is also all-day dining at the Blue Marlin Beach bar. You have a choice of dinnertime hours, either 7:00 PM or 8:45 PM, in the Casanova restaurant.

Beauty Treatments and Welcome Indulgences: To lie on a massage table and look out on a turquoise and sapphire sea, listen to the soft sibilance of the waves and perhaps catch a glimpse of a humming bird is a treat in itself. The serenity, quiet, and beauty of the spa and the comforts of the hotel are a welcome indulgence as is the outdoor environment in which exercise classes are led. Other treatments include facials, manicures, pedicures, and hairdressing services.

Accommodations: Sans Souci is a 5-star hotel, with 72 first-class rooms and suites, each with its own private balcony overlooking Little Bay and the sparkling Caribbean; all rooms are air-conditioned and also equipped with ceiling fans if you prefer natural cool and sea breezes lilting in through your room's windows or balcony door; light, airy, Island-style room decor, everything crisp, clean, with pale and bright flower colors as accents; double and twin beds, good reading lights, room telephones; no room radios or television but satellite hook-up television in the hotel lounge; all rooms with tiled bathrooms, immaculately clean.

What to Bring: See USEFUL INFORMATION. You receive a pink-and-white-striped seersucker bathrobe and beige tote bag with Charlie-the-Turtle logo in burgundy and green—not just for use in the spa, but to take home with you. Bring bathing suits, sun block, and sun glasses. Although the white sand beach is raked and cleaned daily, and the shallow water cleared of sea urchins—those spiky little devils—lightweight sneakers are recommended for wading out in the water above thigh level, and definitely for walking on coral reefs. Bring shoes for walking and for negotiating the slippery rocks of Dunn's River Falls if you feel like climbing up them. Bring year-round summer resort wear for winter temperatures that average in the 70s, summer temperatures that climb to 95 degrees F. At Ocho Rios, you have the benefit of cool sea breezes, which at night can mean you'll be happy with a shawl, serape, poncho, lightweight knitted coat, sweater, *something* to keep you warm if you're walking on the beach or sitting out on your balcony. Everything is daytime-casual, white for tennis or bright cottons for beachwear or leisuretime. In the evenings, everyone changes into jackets and ties and informal, designer-type dinner wear—caftans, pajamas and tunics, floaty, cool-colored dresses or comfortably sleek ones, clothes to show off tanned shoulders, arms, and legs. Some men feel comfortable in the Southampton uniform of navy blue blazer and white trousers at night; others sport the sockless-with-loafers, bright-or-pastel-trousered Palm Beach look. Bring sweaters, shorts, light cottons, and layer for comfort. There is a spa boutique, and the laundry service is rapid and reliable for your cotton clothing.

Documentation from Your Physician: Neither requested nor required. There is no resident physician, but a local physician is on call.

The Use of Alcohol and Tobacco: No restriction on the use of alcohol, unless you are on a weight loss regime, in which case it is suggested, but not required, that you substitute iced tea, coffee, or fresh fruit juices for high-calorie liquor. Smoking is not prohibited.

Fees, Method of Payment, Insurance Coverage: High-season (December 21 to April 15) rates (in Jamaican dollars) for *7-day/6-night packages,* including tax and gratuities:

For one-bedroom suite:

$2560 single ($376 per extra night)
$1733 per person double ($238 per person per extra night)
$1523 per person triple ($203 per person per extra night)

For double room:

$2297 single ($330 per extra night)
$1600 per person double ($215 per person per extra night)

Summer rates are about 20 percent less. Special rates for children under 12. All prices are subject to change. Full payment is required in advance in travelers' checks or by American Express, Visa, or MasterCard. Ask about the cancellation policy.

The Jamaican dollar is the only legal currency accepted for extra meals and purchases and can be bought at the hotel or at the airport exchange booths. No medical insurance tax deductions are possible.

Japan

In Japan, there are over 10,000 thermal mineral springs, more than in any other country in the world, and over 2000 hot spring, or *onsen,* resorts. Some of these are located in isolated mountain villages. Others are large pleasure resorts served by Western-style or Japanese-style hotels, the traditional *ryokans* (inns).

Ryokans are uncluttered, spartan to Western eyes. Your *tatami* (straw mat) room comes with low tables, translucent *shoji* screens, which usually slide open to an appealing vista, as airy an environment as a birdcage to some, and forlorn as a dungeon to others who prefer a canopied four-poster to a *futon* (cotton or down quilt) placed on the floor for sleeping. Luxury-level *ryokans* may feature lacquer furnishings inlaid with mother-of-pearl, a *kokatsu* (a table with a heat lamp and quilted padding like a tea cosy to keep the heat from escaping), heated toilet seats, and other niceties. In some, you can rent a television set for little more than $1 a day. In all, you are provided with a *yukata* (sleeping kimono) of cotton for summertime wear or lined with wool for winter use, slippers for walking inside, and *geta,* or rectangular, elevated wooden clogs 2 to 4 inches high, with a strap for your toes, for outdoor walking.

At some spa locations, massage and acupuncture treatments are available. Relief from ailments is promised through soaking, warming, and relaxing in your own private high-sided, vatlike bathtub, or by taking *o-furo,* a steaming soak in a wooden or stone pool brimming with mineral water in a public bathhouse. One of Japan's deeply rooted traditions is mixed male and female nude bathing, in the steam bath, but many *ryokans* have separate facilities.

Beppu is a seaport on the southern main island of Kyushu, in the prefecture of Oita. Its scenic valleys and hills proffer a variety of natural spring baths, from steaming hot mineral water spouting from more than 4000 openings—some spurting up smack in the center of town—to the muddy, bubbling oozing of a fumarole's "hellpond," some vermilion, some deep blue, said to stimulate a clear complexion and to heal arthritis, bronchitis, and circulatory problems with a week's daily 30-minute treatments. This therapy is experienced outdoors, so that while you let the hot mud slurp around you—the less you move, the more heat you can stand, and the longer you can endure lolling about in it—you can look upward at lush and undulating green hills in the distance and admire the charm close up of a wooden bridge garlanded with seasonal flowers. The bridge leads to the bathhouse where you use buckets of water and soap to cleanse yourself of your mud coating before you slide into the communal bath. (For all communal baths, you always soap yourself and rinse off several times before you are considered clean enough to get in.)

Less messy, but just as therapeutic, said to promote active circulation and to help sufferers of gastrointestinal ailments, neuralgia, and rheumatism, are the natural hot sand baths at one of Beppu's oldest establishments, which first opened for serious sand bathers in 1879. The sand, rich in sulphur, is layered above a hot spring and heated to a hotsy-totsy temperature of 140 degrees F, both by the hot water rising through the sand and by the steam the water releases to vaporize in the air. An attendant buries you up to your neck in heated sand for a short stint while your body is treated by the underground spring below as well as by a hot mineral spring after-bath.

The giant Suginoi Hotel has 508 Japanese-style rooms, 89 Western-style rooms, all with private baths, and is the most expensive; for 2 meals, tax, and service, from 17,600 to 29,700 yen (Y) per person per night. The Hanabishi, the Bokai, the Seifu, and the Shiragiku also have both Japanese-style and Western-style accommodations with private baths, from 12,100 to 27,500 Y per person per night. And there are other accommodations, all Japanese-style or a mix, from 3 minutes by car to 30 minutes by bus from the station, that are also rated first class by the Japan Ryokan Association, from 8,800 to 22,000 Y. Dozens less expensive and not in the deluxe category are recommended for seasoned travelers. Most helpful in Beppu is the Foreign Tourist Information Service, with English-speaking operators: telephone (0977) 23 1119; from the US, 011 81 (977) 23 1119.

Noboribetsu Onsen, on the island of Hokkaido, is a spa resort located in a narrow valley among wooded mountains. A sanctuary for brown bears on the top of nearby Mt. Kuma and a close-by village of Ainu folk is of interest to most visitors. It is noted for its Valley of Hell, a huge indentation in the earth from which various types of sulphuric, salt, and mineral waters and muds spout, gurgle, and steam for the health and relaxation of its patrons. For both Japanese-style and Western-style accommodations, the top hotel is the 264-room Noboritbetsu Grand Hotel (154, Noboritbetsu-Onsen, Noboritbetsu City 059-05;

telephone [01438] 4 2101, from the US, 011 81 [1438] 4 2101). Prices per person range from 18,700 to 27,500 Y per night.

Spa areas of particular appeal to Westerners include Nikko, in the Tochigi Prefecture northeast of Tokyo; Kusatsu, in the Gumma Prefecture northwest of Tokyo; Hakone, just to the south of Tokyo in the Kanagawa Prefecture; Katsuura and Shirahama in the Wakayama Prefecture convenient to Nara and Osaka; Arima in Hyogo Precture convenient to Kyoto; Dogo, in the Ehime Prefecture, convenient to Nara and Osaka; and Unzen in Nagasaki Prefecture on the tip of the island of Kyushu opposite to Oita. Nikko is located by Lake Yunoko in Nikko National Park. You get a great view of Mt. Fuji in the Hakone area. At Katsuura, the Nachi waterfall is a 25-minute bus ride away, and you can cruise around the Kino-Matsushima islets. Kusatsu is located near a notable ski resort on the flanks of Mt. Shirane. Zao Onsen in Yamagata Prefecture in the northern highlands is also located near a ski resort, with choice deluxe accommodations as well as venerable *ryokans* comprising thatch-roofed buildings connected to each other, allowing them to share hot sulphur springs that pour out of the mountainside into steaming pools in each inn, often reachable from open verandas. In some, time-worn green and black stone baths for communal bathing are kept constantly brimming by cool, warm, and hot water spouts you can stand under like showers. A large room with an entry foyer–lanai set with a wicker table, chairs, and a toilet—the location of privies in country *ryokan* architecture may involve walks through labyrinthine corridors, so this placement is considered a luxury—may cost $110 per person per night, including a Japanese breakfast and a 14-course dinner.

Your best bet for a first Japanese spa experience might be Atami, a scenic resort perched on the slopes of an extinct volcano overlooking Sagami Bay, about 55 minutes south of Tokyo by Kodama Express to JR Atami Station. Popular since the 18th century, when Japan's shoguns made their ceremonial way down the Tokkaido Road to Atami's waters—rich in calcium, magnesium, and other minerals said to be good for relieving bronchitis, constipation, eczema, and indigestion and aiding relaxation and relief of anxiety—Atami, often referred to as Japan's Riviera—minus beach—is a favorite spot for lovers, honeymooners, and company-sponsored parties and outings. Atami hosts over 350 hotels, *ryokans,* and pensions, most with natural hot-spring mineral baths.

Horai Ryokan (750-6, Izuyama, Atami City 413; telephone [0557] 8-05151, from the US, 011 81 [557] 8-5151), 7 minutes by bus from Atami Station, is a classic *ryokan* of traditional tea-house architecture, owned and operated for four generations by the Furutani family. It is one of Japan's finest inns, and its prices of 36,300 to 55,000 Y per person per night, with breakfast and lunch or dinner included, as well as service and taxes, may seem as steep as the hillside trek to it from the waterside setting of its bathhouse, but Atami Sekitei, with more than twice as many rooms, and a 15-minute-longer bus ride from the station, also with only luxury-style Japanese accommodations, is pricier.

For Horai's standard charge of about $350, you are accommodated in a suite of tatami rooms (only 17 suites in all) with a splendid view of the bay. Your breakfast is included—a traditional meal, exquisitely presented, of soup, rice, steamed spinach and cabbage, and a slice of fresh pineapple or other fruit. Your 10- to 14-course Japanese *haute cuisine* dinner—*kaiseki*—an artful and complex seduction of your palate, turns out to be—surprise!—low in calories, high in fiber, low in fat, delicious, and filling. Your dinner presentation varies daily and with each season, but generally includes buckwheat noodles, a stuffed persimmon, sashimi, and a local fish called *aji*. You might begin with sweet, hot sake (rice wine) and a bed of iced oysters, or a lacquerware bowl filled with a fragrant broth made from local wildflowers, or a jellied consommé spiced with fresh horseradish. Charbroiled Hokkaido salmon steak is a specialty, as is a spicy cabbage dish, and *yakitori,* chicken broiled with scallions with a pungent rice wine and ginger sauce. Fresh fruits cut and carved in charming ways are offered for dessert as an alternative to the more traditional ending of clear broth or rice and pickles. Your meals are served to you in your room by a smiling *nesan* (maid) whose job is to see that you are comfortable and have whatever it is you require.

The amenities of a true *ryokan* do not include a restaurant or a dining room. If you are attuned to American spa resort hotels, with planned activities, playgrounds, gymnasiums, and tutors, you may be bewildered by the Japanese penchant for solitude and seclusion, but in Japan, solitude is considered to be a status symbol, and nowhere better to be enjoyed in Atami than at Horai. Trained in shiatsu and other forms of massage, licensed masseurs and masseuses are available by appointment to come to your room to relax and tone your body. Each of the 17 suites at the Horai is equipped with a square cypress-wood bathtub for you to steam in up to your chin, perhaps for half an hour before dinner. But to miss the communal co-ed bathhouse is to bypass the grand passion of the Japanese—immersion in water so hot as to be barely tolerable, keeping still so that the hot water does not hurt, a sacramental ritual of regeneration. You'll also miss the exercise of negotiating the steep covered walkway down to the ancient-style bathhouse, with slots and joints instead of nails and screws holding its cypress roofbeams together above the granite tub brimming with water kept at a temperature of 108 degrees F. Your wooden *geta* make the trek down and up the stone steps an excellent exercise for your leg and foot muscles. Yoshi Furutani, the proprietor's wife, and Yukimasa Kinjo, the assistant manager, explain that guests do not come to Horai for the stair-climbing exercise, or for the healthy diet, but for the therapeutic qualities of the water, the view, the peace, the solitude.

For more information about Japanese spas: Japanese National Tourist Organization, 630 Fifth Avenue, New York, New York 10019; telephone (212) 757-5640.

Mexico

⚘ Rancho La Puerta ⚘

Rancho La Puerta, or the Ranch, as it is known by its fans, was first envisioned by Deborah Szekely, who later founded the Golden Door (see AMERICAN SPAS: WEST COAST). As she stood in the shadows of Mount Cuchuma, regarded by local Indians as a sacred healing center, she dreamed of creating a rustic, holistic health spa retreat in this inspiring land of the Sierra Madres, blue skies, and meadows blooming with manzanitas, sage, camphor, cactus, and flowers.

Rancho La Puerta is dedicated to fitness, recreation, a modified vegetarian diet, a stress-free environment, and therapies and treatments performed by a skilled and caring staff in a setting of 150 lavishly landscaped acres with organically cultivated, pesticide-free vineyards, orchards, vegetable and flower gardens, and apiaries.

Approximately a 3-hour drive from Los Angeles, 40 miles southeast of San Diego, and 3 miles south of the border in Tecate, the ranch's property encompasses rolling country in the foothills of Baja at an altitude of 1800 feet. The dry, fogless, smogless climate (341 sunny days) is cooled with year-round breezes, bracing in winter, equable-to-agreeably-hot-but-not-humid in summer. Some of the Ranch's buildings are built of native stone, others are of white stucco construction, most with terra-cotta tiled floors and beamed ceilings. Your rooms are filled with Mexican rugs, mirrors, candelabra, and other whimsical and decorative Mexican folk-art objects. Villa suites and studios have their own complex of bright, fragrant gardens, plus a pool and sauna just a 5-minute brisk walk away from the older accommodations. In the villas, if you feel like relaxing you can arrange for a Continental breakfast to be served poolside to you in summer and in your cozy, fire-lit room in winter.

No one can pinpoint for certain the mystical, magical moments you will experience at Rancho La Puerta, but there will be many appeals to the senses: the aromatic fragrance of rosemary, pine, juniper, and camomile Kneipp herbal wraps, which Szekely was the first to bring to the US; the pungency of eucalyptus and sage on a morning hike; the scents of roses and night-blooming jasmine growing by your window; the sound of donkeys braying and roosters crowing when you awaken; the emerald whir of a hummingbird; hot pink flowers garlanding a grey boulder; cottontail rabbits by the dozens. The camaraderie among guests during their shared week is well known to have developed into rewarding and enduring friendships. Families, including teenagers and grandparents, sometimes small children, frequent the Ranch for holiday get-togethers. Ages of guests generally range between 30 and 60, with a large percentage of guests escaping from a hectic business life. The Ranch is also a favorite of writers and publishing executives from both coasts. Since people with serious health or weight problems are not accepted, you'll find most guests fairly fit on arrival, some eager to lose 10 to 20 pounds in longer stays. Rancho La Puerta appeals to people who appreciate being treated as responsible grown-ups, allowed to do their own thing at their own pace, and motivated to bring what they have learned home with them. With no deadlines to meet, no telephones, radios, or television in the rooms, most guests steep themselves in the Ranch's total environment devoted to fitness. A small selection of Mexican artifacts, hand-picked on annual buying trips by Golden Door/Rancho La Puerta executives, is available at the spa's Mercado (boutique) and in the Women's Health Center. Some guests travel outside the Ranch with their own car, share a ride in the car of a fellow guest, or hire a taxi to have a look at Tijuana, the largest city on the peninsula, 30 minutes distant, or explore Tecate, a few minutes away. Driving to Ensenada, 1 hour south of the border, along the scenic coastal route is a highly recommended excursion.

Name: Rancho La Puerta

Mailing Address: P.O. Box 2548, Escondido, California 92025 (for reservations, business correspondence, and information). Address for visitors at the Ranch is P.O. Box 69, Tecate, California 92080. (The spa is in Mexico. The town of Tecate straddles both the American and the Mexican sides of the border.)

Telephone: (619) 744-4222 for reservations and information; (800) 443-7565; in Mexico, to leave messages for guests (706) 654-1155

Established: 1940

Managing Director: Jose Manuel Jasso

Program Directors: Phyllis Pilgrim, Fitness Director

Owner: Deborah Szekely

Gender and Age Restrictions: Co-ed. Those who exceed their desirable weight by 35 percent or more, who have difficulty walking or seeing, or who have other serious health problems are not accepted. The 1st week in March and 2 weeks in October (variable) are reserved exclusively for couples. Although there are no child-care facilities, families are welcome. The recommended minimum age for children is 14, but younger ones are accepted if accompanied by a nanny or other child-care companion.

Season: Year-round
Length of Stay Required: 8 days/7 nights, Saturday through Saturday. Occasion-

ally, if space is available, shorter stays are possible.

Programs Offered: At orientation, in the administration building, you are given a map so that you can see where your hacienda, ranchera, villa, or villa studio accommodation is in relation to the swimming pools, tennis courts, gyms, pavilions, men's and women's vapor saunas, hot tubs, the 2½-mile jogging track in the vineyard, the new weight training gym, volleyball court and game court, men's and women's health centers, beauty salon, laundry room, recreation center, craft and lecture hall, dining room, the well-stocked Mercado (boutique), the irresistibly eclectic library, and the gazebo where you can sip fruit juice, chat with chums, or laze in a hammock. After checking out a schedule of over 30 classes and activities offered continuously from dawn until dusk, the rest is up to you. You can do as much or as little, as strenuously or as gently as you want. There are always members of the fitness staff on hand to give you help or recommendations on the type of program to follow geared to your physical capabilities and personal goals. To balance your day and enhance results, it is suggested that you choose at least one session daily from each of these categories:

- Cardiovascular Workouts–Aerobics—circuit training, hiking, walking, running, lap swimming;

- Strengthening/Toning Anaerobic—yoga, water exercise, modified kinetic toning, men's fitness, kinetic toning, body contouring, "Bottom Line" exercises, and Absolutely Abdominals (contracting four—upper, bottom, central, and diagonal—"abs" in quick order, an exercise some guests complain is abominably difficult);

- Stretch and Flexibility exercises;

- plus Relaxation—time for yourself, which you can use in the hot tub, sauna, pool, hammock, playing billiards or the piano in the recreation center, or just flaking out in a lounge chair;

- plus Rewards—for a moderate fee to which you can treat yourself, facials, herbal wraps, massages, hairstyling, scalp treatment, manicure, pedicure.

Classes last 45 minutes with 15-minute intervals in between for you to pace yourself from place to place. You can speed walk, take a nature or garden hike, climb to the peak of Mount Cuchuma, take a class in painting on silk or pottery, learn how to folk dance, catch up on your reading. You can load up your breakfast tray and eat in your quarters listening to music (bring your own cassettes). No regimentation. In the evenings, you also have a choice. You may watch an Academy Award–winning VHS film, take in a humorous or informative lecture or audio-visual slide presentation by a guest speaker, enjoy munching popcorn while you play Bingo and maybe win a charming Mexican memento as a prize, or sneak off to a bar in Tecate for a salty margarita, an *antojito* (an appetizer, a "small whim"), or the larger whim of a Mexican meal. It's up to you. And if you feel you do need pointers and experience in stress management, you can learn practical relaxation techniques through the Inner Journey course and yoga classes. Phyllis Pilgrim and other members of the fitness staff under her direction will coach you in "Happy Feet" therapy, which is guaranteed to revitalize the tiredest of tootsies. Everything is attuned to your taking it home, to your going back to the real world and developing realistic ways to integrate the things you have learned, maintaining a fitness routine and eating healthily.

Maximum Number of Guests: 150

Full-Time Health Professionals on Staff: 15, plus 15 masseuses, 5 masseurs, 7 manicurist-pedicurists, 7 hairstylists, 6 facialists, 2 herbal wrap therapists. All the massage and beauty therapists are trained by Golden Door experts. No medical doctors or nurses are on staff, but all the fitness staff members are trained in CPR. In the event of an unexpected emergency, guests can be flown to Mercy Hospital and Medical Center, San Diego.

Diet and Weight Management: Fresh natural foods are emphasized. Cornucopias of fresh fruit spill over in abundance on sideboards in the handsome balconied dining room, which is in a Mexican Colonial–style building constructed in 1986, with a huge fireplace, fascinating aviary of colorful Mexican songbirds ensconced between kitchen and dining room, and a broad outdoor patio for breakfasting and lunching if you like in the shade of grapevines adorning the *ramada* over your head. Sit-down dinners are served at your choice of candle-lit tables seating 2 to 12 people. The low-sodium, low-cholesterol, lacto-ovo vegetarian diet offers fish or shellfish—red snapper, shrimp, sometimes lobster or other choices—twice a week plus turkey or chicken on holidays; specializes in wonderful dark bread baked with flour stone-ground on the property, acidophilus milk, organic honey supplied by large double hives from La Puerta's own apiary, organic vegetables and fruit grown in the ranch's extensive private gardens and orchards. Caloric levels of food are chalked up on a blackboard, and you are responsible for keeping track of your own portion amounts. The suggested diet of 1000 daily calories for women, 1200 daily calories for men is deliciously prepared. The Ranch's menu offers a breakfast corn polenta; a luncheon dill and tomato soup, mushroom-corn-spinach loaf, and fresh pineapple sherbet; and desserts like vanilla and cinnamon flan or mango and papaya slices swirled with mint leaves and nasturtium blossoms for dinner. When served as authentic Mexican cuisine or adapted, Tex-Mex dishes bear little resemblance to the so-called south-of-the-border fare often served elsewhere across the nation. The chef will tell you how you can bring the ranch's cuisine home with you. Cooking demonstrations as well as nutritional counseling and lectures are available. Of the guests who sign up for the weight loss program, over 50 percent lose a minimum of 3 pounds a week. Many lose more.

Exercise and Physical Therapy Facilities: New in 1987 was the splendid Azteca weight-training gymnasium with $100,000 of Camstar equipment, Bosch and Monark stationary bicycles, Trotter treadmills, free weights, and rowing machines. Olmeca, Tolteca, Pine Tree, and Cuchuma are the romantic names of other aerobic gymnasia, with sliding doors kept closed in cold weather that are replaced with screens in hot weather. You can also do your exercises beneath a *ramada* at the Vineyard Gym. A heated hydrotherapy pool, 2 unheated pools with adjacent Jacuzzis, and a lap-swimming pool are positioned so that wherever you are housed a pool is nearby. The Men's Health Center and the recently completely Women's Health Center feature additional Jacuzzis as well as massage rooms. Men's and women's vapor saunas are quartered in separate buildings.

Opportunities for Recreational Exercise: Guests can use any of the 4 swimming pools (another is currently planned), 6 concrete tennis courts lighted for night play, the 2½-mile jogging track, and "miles and miles" of mountain and meadow hiking trails as well as miles of walking area in the garden and landscaped surroundings.

Beauty Treatments and Welcome Indulgences: Not included in the weekly price but available at moderate fees are massages, facials, herbal wraps, hairstyling and scalp treatments, manicures, pedicures. A packet of 6 treatments (5 massages, 1 facial, or 1 herbal wrap or scalp treatment) is available for $121; individual treatments are similarly bargain-priced. The "Happy Feet" exercise-massage therapy is included in your package price and is taught so that you can do-it-yourself at home.

Accommodations: Rancheras (studio bedroom and bathroom), Haciendas (living room, fireplace, 1 or 2 bedrooms, and a bathroom), Villa Studios (new in 1985, with living room, fireplace, bedroom in alcove, and bath), and Villa Suites (living room, dining area, kitchenette, fireplace, 2 bedrooms, 1 or 2 baths) are individually decorated with hand-woven rugs and other attractive Mexican folk-art objects. Beamed ceilings confer a "rustic" look, but sunken bathtubs in some of the Villa accommodations supplement the simple country look with the style of a Spanish grandee. In the cold season, you are supplied with electric blankets and firewood; in hot weather, electric fans. All accommodations have a choice of porches, patios, patio gardens, sun decks, and a decor of serape and rebozo colors—hot pink, yellow, red, orange, fuchsia—guaranteed to lighten and brighten one's mental outlook on the spot. Public telephones but no room telephones and no television in the rooms as an aid to getting away from it all and refreshing your spirit. If you would like to share a Hacienda, Villa Studio, or Villa Suite with another same-gender single, the management will try to pair you up with a compatible fellow guest on request when you make your reservation.

What to Bring: See USEFUL INFORMATION. Women wear warm-ups or sweat shirt and pants combinations at breakfast and lunch, or a skirt and shirt slipped over leotards. Men generally wear T-shirts and shorts and warm-up gear. In the evenings, guests wear informal sportswear, so bring pants or skirts, shirts and blouses, and simple long skirts or caftans. Leotards and tights, warm-up suits, and T-shirts with the Rancho La Puerta logo are sold on-site in the boutique. Although safety deposit boxes are available, leave your good jewelry at home: the spa is not responsible for losses. Bring film for your camera. The library has a fascinating selection of books—reference, fiction, and nonfiction. There is an on-site dispensary for sundries, and if you need something that is not available, the staff will try to obtain it for you through the Ranch's offices in San Diego.

N.B. A Tourist Card, required for Mexican Immigration, issued without charge by a Mexican consulate, will be supplied to you by Rancho La Puerta's reservation office. You should keep your tourist copy of this, which you must relinquish at the border gate when leaving Mexico. Along with your Mexican Tourist Card, you will need proof of US citizenship: a valid US passport, naturalization papers, birth certificate, or certificate of voter's registration. Non-US citizens visiting America should present passports.

Documentation from Your Physician: Neither requested nor required, but guests are asked to undertake a physical examination before arriving if they are not used to an active physical schedule. If you are in doubt of acceptance, write to the offices of Rancho La Puerta in San Diego, and they will reply promptly.

The Use of Alcohol and Tobacco: Alcohol is neither served nor sold on the ranch property. The use of tobacco is discouraged. Guests who smoke are asked to do so outdoors, near their accommodations, or, when eating, only outside on the patio.

Fees, Method of Payment, Insurance Coverage: Year-round rates for the 8-day/7-night program:

For single: $1250

For double: $1000 per person (Rancheras)

Rates are higher for deluxe accommodations. All prices are subject to change, and all rates include Mexico's I.V.A. tax. Children age 6 and under are accommodated without charge; ages 7 to 14 are charged $600 a week. (You are responsible, remember, for providing your own baby-sitter or child-care companion.) A deposit is required. Ask about the cancellation policy. Payment is only by personal check or travelers' check. Neither cash nor credit cards are accepted. Tips are often given by guests to room maids, kitchen staff, masseuses and luggage boys. The amounts are what you would give as gratuities in the US. Fees are not usually tax-deductible, but check with your physician and insurance carrier.

Follow-up Assistance: Cassettes and cookbooks are available. A guest questionnaire is placed in each room for guests to complete at the end of their stay, and all comments are read. Everything in the program at the Ranch—food, exercises, new ways of thinking and being—is an idea thoughtfully conceived to be taken home by you as an enduring going-away present.

Medical Weight Loss Programs

The Aerobics Center
Texas

The Aerobics Center is a 30-acre, parklike complex in north Dallas considered by many health professionals to be one of the world's leaders in the study of the medical value of exercise as well as a provider of expertise in preventive medicine. The Aerobics Center, comprising the Cooper Clinic, the Aerobics Activity Center, the Institute for Aerobics Research, and the Aerobics Center Guest Lodges, realizes the dream of Dr. Kenneth H. Cooper, its founder and director and the man who has done so much to persuade Americans to improve their bodies' ability to use oxygen efficiently through exercises such as running, swimming, bicycling, and walking. The author of *Aerobics, Aerobics for Women* (written with his wife), *The New Aerobics, The Aerobics Way, Running without Fear,* and *The Aerobics Program for Total Well-Being,* Dr. Cooper advanced the concept that the key to fitness and good health lay in "a strong heart, lungs, and blood vessels." His program consists of calorie restriction, nutritional counseling, regular exercise, and a series of condensed "wellness seminars." "The results," says Dr. Cooper, are "equally as impressive as those documented with the Pritikin program . . ." with a diet "less restrictive," "more palatable," and "much easier to follow." The emphasis is on individual attention and counseling, and the Institute for Aerobics Research utilizes the largest and only known exercise data base on record in combination with "an objective measure of fitness—the treadmill stress test."

The facilities, housed in colonial-style pillared buildings neatly set on well-manicured grounds, are handsomely maintained. The Center attracts participants who may need to lose from 0 to 100 pounds; 60 percent married, 50 percent male, 25 percent couples, 25 percent women on their own. Their ages range from 19 to 75, with an average age of 48. Most are business-oriented, with many young and middle-aged professionals.

Group outings include visiting the Dallas Museum of Art, the John F. Kennedy Memorial, the South Fork Ranch (home of the TV "Dallas" Ewings), shopping, going to movies, and picnicking at Bachman Lake. Time for these excursions is available in the evenings and during weekends. You have the option of using the center's limousine service, taxi, bus, or rental car, or you can ask to share rides with other participants or staff. In addition to the attractions within a 15-mile radius of Dallas, you also have access, within a 30-mile radius, to attractions in Forth Worth—the Six Flags Over Texas Amusement Park, Amon Carter Museum of Western Art, Kimbell Art Museum, and Fort Worth Museum of Science and Industry, which includes the Omni Theater, a 3-story theater with a 180-degree curved viewing screen.

Name: The Aerobics Center In-Residence Programs/The Aerobics Center

Mailing Address: 12230 Preston Road, Dallas, Texas 75230

Telephone: (214) 386-0306; (800) 527-0362; The Aerobics Activity Center: (214) 233-4832; The Cooper Clinic: (214) 239-7223

Established: The Aerobics Center, 1970; The Aerobics Center Guest Lodge, 1983; Guest Lodge II completed 1987

Managing Directors: Roy E. Vartabedian, D. H. Sc., M.P.H. Director, In-Residence and Community Wellness Programs

Program Director: Roy E. Vartabedian

Owner: Kenneth H. Cooper, M.D., M.P.H., Preventive Health Medicine

Number of Full-Time Health Professionals on Staff: 4, plus 15 who rotate through the programs

Accreditation of Professional Staff Members:
Roy E. Vartabedian, D. H. Sc., M.P.H., Director, In-Residence and Community Wellness Program, is a preventive care specialist. Ava S. Bursau, M.S., Exercise Physiologist, Assistant to Director of In-Residence Programs, is a member of the American College of Sports Medicine and the Association for Fitness in Business. Kathleen S. Duran, R.D., Nutritionist in the In-Residence Programs, has a B.S. in Home Economics and a B.S. in Nutrition and Dietetics. The overall director is Kenneth H. Cooper, M.D., M.P.H., Preventive Medicine.

Gender and Restrictions: Co-ed; minimum age 18

Season: Year-round, except for national holidays

Length of Stay Required: 4 days, 7 days, or 13 days

Programs Offered: The *Aerobics Wellness Weekend* (from 3:00 PM to 10:00 PM check-in Wednesday to 1:00 PM Sunday) and the 7- or 13-day *Aerobics Programs for Total Well-Being* emphasize weight loss, physical activity, stress management, diet, nutrition and exercise education programs, behavior modification, preventive and therapeutic medicine, smoking cessation, and total well-being in a supportive live-in environment. All programs include both individual one-on-one supervision and counseling and supervised group exercise classes.

Orientation for the *Aerobics Wellness Weekend* and for the *Aerobics Programs for Total Well-being* begins with a 3:00 PM check-in at Guest Lodge I or II, a review of required preparation for medical testing to be conducted the following day at the Cooper Clinic, an interview with one of the program's physicians, dinner on your own, and from 7:00 to 8:30 PM, welcome, introduction to, and overview of the program by Roy E. Vartabedian.

All programs begin with a Type II Comprehensive Preventive Medical Examination, a 6-hour head-to-toe physical to measure cardiovascular fitness and screen for risk factors and problems. The examination (which also can be done as a nonresidential service) includes recording your medical history; a physical examination of your cardiopulmonary system; a clinical analysis questionnaire to determine your personality type and susceptibility to stress; dental, oral, and pharyngeal examination, including an examination of your vocal cords; 2 maximal-performance treadmill exercise tests with 12-to-15-lead EKG monitoring, resting EKG, and blood pressure measurements during exercise and recovery; underwater weighing and skin-fold-thickness measurements to determine your body's fat-to-lean ratio; 2 blood specimens drawn for 24 different tests, including high- and low-density-lipoprotein (HDL and LDL) cholesterol; a computerized nutritional analysis and evaluation and personal nutrition prescription; a hearing test; vision and glaucoma tests; pulmonary function tests; urinalysis; chest X ray; proctosigmoidoscopy for clients over the age of 40; measurement by Cybex equipment of the force and speed of your muscle contractions, to test your strength and flexibility; mammography; and a 20-page writeup of your test results, a 30-minute discussion of them with a physician, and another 30-minute discussion during the first week of your 7- or 13-day *Aerobics Programs for Total Well-Being*. At the completion of the 7-day and 13-day programs, you are evaluated again with the treadmill stress test, a complete blood workup, and your weight, blood pressure, and body circumference measurements recorded for comparison. (Additional medical tests, beyond those included in your program, are extra.)

The goals for the *Aerobics Programs for Total Well-Being* are to "introduce you to a new way of life and to teach you the necessary skills to maintain your new lifestyle. Results include improved ability to cope with stress; a decrease in weight, cholesterol, triglycerides, glucose, and blood pressure; and increased HDL cholesterol and treadmill time." Each of the program's days include 4 exercise sessions (walking/jogging, treadmill, stationary bicycling, swimming, tennis, racquetball, toning/flexibility classes, pool exercise classes); and access to the Aerobic Center's and Activity Center's indoor/outdoor running/jogging tracks, swimming pools, tennis courts, racquetball courts, steam room, sauna, whirlpool, and Nautilus equipment. With lectures and group demonstration of techniques such as positive mental imagery, simple biofeedback, progressive muscle relaxation, and "tapping into your relaxation response," you learn about the physiological responses of your body to stress and the mechanisms for managing it, along with risk-factor reduction for coronary heart disease, diabetes, hypertension, and cancer. In addition, an average 3 lectures daily offered by each of the programs cover topics concerned with nutrition, medical test results, motivation, behavior modification, and smoking cessation.

You are monitored for all medications and medication adjustments during the programs, and exercise physiologists and dietitians can monitor your exercise and diet programs as a further safety measure. Each of the programs includes at least 1 Healthy Dining Out experience at the Colonnade Restaurant, which is also open to the public, to school you in choosing low-fat, low-calorie foods. On the 13-day program, you get treated to 2 such meals, and also attend a breadmaking class and a cooking class in the demonstration kitchen. Each program includes a Shopping Smart class to educate you in wise food shopping.

Participants in all programs receive a weight training demonstration, a copy of Dr. Cooper's book *The Aerobics Program for Total Well-Being,* plus a 350-page comprehensive workbook and an Aerobics Center T-shirt. For all programs, you are encouraged to bring your spouse or a friend along with you either as a participant in the program or as a nonparticipant. It is recommended that all participants attend all of the meetings and participate in the total program, which is structured to keep you busy from 7:00 AM to 7:00 PM, with some unstructured time and options available during the day, in the evenings, and on weekends. Relative to your initial physical level, each of the programs is "demanding for each participant"—that is, you are asked "to improve."

Maximum Number of Participants: Guest Lodge I can accommodate 80 guests; the new Guest Lodge II can accommodate 44 guests. Each Aerobics Program is limited to 20 to 25 participants in order to maintain individual attention and counseling.

Diet and Weight Management: The recommended daily food menus (1000 calories for women, 1200 calories for men) are low in fat, sodium reduced (2000 to 3000 mg a day), low in cholesterol (less than 300 mg a day), high in fiber, and 60 percent complex carbohydrates, 20 percent protein. Except for the evening(s) when you dine at the Colonnade Restaurant at Guest Lodge II to practice your new eating habits, you gather around 8 tables in Guest Lodge II's demonstration kitchen not only for hands-on instruction but for all your meals.

The fare is plain, simple, and wholesome. For breakfast you might have cold or hot cereal or a couple of whole-wheat pancakes served with hot blueberry topping, a wedge of cantaloupe, or sliced bananas served with low-fat milk, and decaf tea or coffee; for lunch, grilled chicken breast, a medley of vegetables, and a bran muffin; for dinner, fish, broccoli, and fruit gelatin. Caffeine-free beverages only are served. Multivitamin and calcium supplements are given. Lacto–ovo and strict vegetarian diets, special diets for medical reasons, and Kosher meals can be arranged. All programs aim to teach participants how to cook healthy fare, shop for it, order it from restaurant menus, and to make it a lifetime habit for general health improvement and fitness levels. Those who have an ideal body weight can use the diet as a baseline and add fruits, vegetables, and grains to 1500 and 1800 calories or more if desired.

Combined with aerobics exercise, the weight loss is up to 5 pounds a week on the 1000- to 1200-calorie level. Additional nutritional counseling appointments can be arranged. Those interested in weight reduction may also participate for an additional fee in the P.E.P. (Positive Eating Program) at which weekly sessions teach nutrition, behavioral modification of eating habits, and physical fitness. Individual or group classes are available. A Nutrition Heart Class, part of the regular *Cardiac Rehabilitation Program,* is taught by a staff nutritionist and can be attended if you wish.

Exercise and Physical Therapy Facilities: The gymnasium area is 15,000 square feet. It includes a regulation-size basketball court marked so that it can also be used for volleyball. There is a 3000-square-foot weight-training area located in the balcony, which includes 11 pieces of Nautilus equipment, free weights, isokinetic machines, a 16-station Universal Gym, and 6 individual pieces of Universal Gym equipment; a 3-lane indoor track with 14-15-16 laps to the mile and an automatic timer that blinks lights around the inside of the track so that you can set the pace you want to run or walk; a $\frac{1}{16}$th mile banked indoor jogging track; a cardiovascular fitness room equipped with Pacer treadmills, stationary bicycles, Schwinn Air-Dyne bicycles, Versa–Climber machine, and rowing machine. Included in the facility are 4 racquetball/handball courts and a "wet area"—sauna, steam room, and whirlpool. Men's and women's locker room facilities are high-tech functional and immaculate.

For outdoor exercise, you've got 3 outdoor walking/jogging tracks on Tartan-surface lighted tracks of ¼, ½, and 1 mile each, which wind around the 30-acre estate; 2 heated outdoor 6-lane, 25-yard lap pools; 4 outdoor lighted Laycold tennis courts and an automatic ball machine. If you're a resident Dallas member of the AAC, you and your family can benefit from all sorts of leagues, tournaments, special events, seminars, and activities for children, including fun runs and regular Bible studies.

Opportunities for Recreational Exercise: Guests can enjoy hiking and walking trails; 2 outdoor heated swimming pools (lessons extra); and 4 tennis courts, lighted for night play (lessons extra). Racquetball is also available (lessons extra). Those wishing to venture beyond the center can find roller-skating at Bachman Lake, Dallas, 10 miles distant (rental skates available). Box lunches are provided for these activities when they are part of the scheduled program.

Beauty Treatments and Welcome Indulgences: A 30-minute massage on the *Weekend Program,* 2 on the *7-day program,* 4 on the *13-day program.* More, if desired, at extra charge. Hairdressing and beauty salon on site, services included in the fees for longer stays.

Accommodations: Guest Lodge I (40 rooms, including 8 suites) and Guest Lodge II (22 rooms and 4 suites) are classified as twin 4-star hotels. They are Colonial in style, with Henredon reproduction French provincial and 19th-century English furnishings and a salmon and lake-blue decor. Opt for Guest Lodge II if you want the convenience of the Colonnade Restaurant and the program's demonstration kitchen on the ground floor. Guestrooms have comfortable queen- and king-sized four-poster beds; 3 telephones (bedside, desk, and bathroom), cable television, air-conditioning, and room balcony or porch. Suites include refrigerator, cassette stereo, Dr. Cooper's cassette tapes, television sets in the bedroom and living room area, conference table, and large desk. Rooms are available for single or double occupancy. Standard room includes bathtub, shower, and hair dryer (lighted make-up mirror in suites). Laundry facilities include complimentary service for exercise clothes, coin-operated machines, and outside laundry and dry-cleaning service. Complimentary copies of the *Dallas Morning News* and the *Wall Street Journal* delivered daily.

What to Bring: See USEFUL INFORMATION. For Colonnade Restaurant dining, you'll need semicasual clothes. For men, no ties are necessary, but jackets are required. Bring a watch with a sweep second hand or a digital readout of seconds to measure your pulse rate during exercise. Women should bring a sleeveless or short-sleeved blouse that opens down the front for medical examinations. Underwire bras are not recommended. *N.B.* Shoes appropriate for tennis, racquetball, volleyball, or basketball must have nonblack soles to avoid marking up courts. Shops at the Aerobics Center Guest Lodges and the Aerobics Activity Center sell T-shirts, shorts, jackets, robes, bathing caps, and all types of exercise shoes and clothing. Within a mile, there is a large shopping mall and stores that sell sporting equipment and sundries.

Documentation from Your Physician: It is recommended that you bring with you copies of any relevant medical records for your Cooper Clinic appointment, including records of a recent or ongoing medical problem. All participants are given a thorough medical evaluation at the onset of the program and receive permission from the Aerobics Center's physicians to participate unless otherwise indicated by a personal physician. Clients with severe chest pain or other evidence of existing heart disease or other serious illnesses will be referred to other facilities and may be admitted to the program at a later date or not at all.

The Use of Alcohol and Tobacco: No alcohol or tobacco is permitted in the programs. Those who are not eager to quit smoking at the time they enter the program are asked to refrain from smoking during the program. Guestrooms need to be chemically cleaned to remove smoking odor if smoking occurs in the room. You are not billed for this procedure, so let your conscience be your guide!

Fees, Method of Payment, Insurance Coverage:

For 4-day *Wellness Weekend:* $1595 single, $1495 per person double

For 7-day *Aerobics Program for Total Well-Being:* $2795 single, $2595 per person double

For 13-day *Aerobics Program for Total Well-Being:* $3995 single, $3595 per person double

Rates are higher for deluxe accommodations. All prices are subject to change, and all rates are subject to a 13 percent state tax on room cost and 8 percent tax on food costs. Personal checks, travelers' checks, Visa, MasterCard, and American Express are accepted in payment. At the completion of your program, the Cooper Clinic will itemize your medical charges and mail the paperwork to you for your insurance company if you indicate that you desire this service when completing your Cooper Clinic Medical History form. Medical fees not covered by your insurance policy may be deductible from your income tax, as well as other program and travel expenses.

Follow-up Assistance: Video teaching tapes, Dr. Cooper's books and cassettes, cookbooks, the 350-page program workbook, and a 320-page textbook are included in the program for continued learning. *Controlling Cholesterol* (Bantam), a recent book by Dr. Cooper, is particularly recommended. A follow-up telephone call is made a month after the completion of the program, and a monthly subscription to the *Aerobics Center Newsletter* is included, as well as a quarterly In-Residence program newsletter featuring participants' updates. Two annual *Alumni Wellness Weekends* are available to participants who opt for refresher courses. Special discounts are available for refresher 7-day and 13-day programs.

◈ The Charleston Retreat ◈
at the Weight Management Center
South Carolina

At The Charleston Retreat Weight Management Center (WMC), it is considered that the total of a person's lifestyle habits determines the degree of weight control success. It follows that at The Charleston Retreat a sensible, healthy food plan is promoted and taught that is not restrictive, faddish, or short term. Part of the Medical University of South Carolina's Department of Psychiatry, The Charleston Retreat program emphasizes behavioral change. The academic setting of the program provides access to the rich resources (internal medicine, nutrition, dietetics, exercise physiology) available through the university.

Apart from the 28-day program provided for out-of-towners, The Charleston Retreat offers people who live in the Charleston area lifestyle change programs, worksite programs tailored to the employees of specific businesses, and a program that combines the lifestyle change plan with a *very-low-calorie (VLC)* phase to promote more rapid weight loss initially.

The Charleston Retreat staff includes behavioral specialists who have been active in clinical work and research in health-related problems of overweight for more than 10 years. Mental attitude is considered as important in the treatment as the more commonly emphasized behavioral concepts.

The program is targeted toward adults of all ages for whom excess weight represents a health risk, individuals at least 20 to 30 pounds overweight. Participants represent a diversity of professional and personal interests and come from all over the United States and Canada.

Located on the Medical University of South Carolina campus, the facility includes group meeting rooms of various sizes, an exercise room, a demonstration kitchen/dining room, and a waiting/lounge area. A private dining room in the university hospital, directly across the street, is reserved for the exclusive use of center participants for daily meals.

One of the appeals of The Charleston Retreat is its location in the historic coastal city of Charleston. As part of its weekly schedule, the Retreat arranges group walking tours of downtown Charleston, beach and park outings, and tours of Charleston's legendary gardens and plantations. If you prefer to go on your own, reduced rates from several car rental agencies are available. The bus service to historic downtown stops across the street from the Weight Management Center, and there's no problem about taxi service. There's also an air-conditioned downtown area Dash trolley (25 cents, 10 cents for seniors) you'll love. The highly acclaimed Spoleto Festival U.S.A., a dazzling and comprehensive arts festival, is held each May to June in Charleston, but you can enjoy music year-round performed by the Charleston Symphony, see plays with well-known casts at the Dock Street Theater, and take in the ballets performed by Charleston's sprightly ballet company. You can drive in horse-drawn carriages along cobbled streets past block after block of charming old houses, stroll along quiet streets and mews, browse among art galleries, antiquarian book shops, and antique shops, or visit the open-air City Market, which dates back to 1841.

Charleston is an outdoor town. Golf and tennis can be played year-round, and from April to the beginning of October, ocean swimming, sunning, and seashelling on wide, sandy beaches 20 minutes away from city center by car are among the most relaxing ways to spend an afternoon. Fishing equipment can be rented, boats for sailing and fishing can easily be chartered. If you don't want to strike out on your own, there are harbor tours, house tours, church tours, walking tours, horse-drawn carriage tours, city tours.

Charleston's Visitors and Convention Bureau can send you the Charleston Area Visitors Guide with all the information you will want to look at before you arrive (see Accommodations). This is an important item to put on your Must Do list, because your choice of accommodation is up to you, and it helps to know beforehand which areas appeal to you most or will give you most convenient access to the Retreat.

Name: The Charleston Retreat at the Weight Management Center

Mailing Address: Department of Psychiatry and Behavioral Sciences, Medical University of South Carolina, 171 Ashley Avenue, Charleston, South Carolina 29425

Telephone: (803) 792-2273; (800) 553-7489

Established: 1974

Program Director: Patrick M. O'Neil, Ph.D.

Owner: Medical University of South Carolina

Number of Full-Time Health Professionals on Staff: 8 full-time faculty positions with The Charleston Retreat's Weight Management Center. The Center also utilizes on a part-time basis faculty members who are general internists and cardiologists.

Accreditation of Professional Staff Members: Patrick M. O'Neil, Ph.D., Director, is associate professor of psychiatry and behavioral sciences at Medical University of South Carolina (MUSC). He has been associated with the Center since

1977. He is a licensed clinical psychologist.

Robert J. Malcolm, M.D., is associate professor in the departments of Family Medicine and of Psychiatry and Behavioral Sciences, MUSC, and Chief Medical Consultant to the Weight Management Center. He is certified by the American Board of Psychiatry and Neurology and the American Board of Family Practice. Hal S. Currey, B.S., is Administrative Director and Behavioral Consultant to the Center.

Gender and Age Restrictions: Co-ed; minimum age 18

Season: Closed from Thanksgiving until New Year's Day

Length of Stay Required: 28 days

Programs Offered: An intensive 4-week program is offered to out-of-towners, who live in accommodations of their choice off-campus. Extensive orientation materials are sent to you prior to your arrival, including forms that enable you to keep detailed eating records for 2 weeks before the start of the program. The first 4 days of the program are devoted primarily to assessment, which includes a complete medical examination, measurement of behavioral and cognitive patterns, dietary assessment, and determination of your exercise capacity. The medical examination includes a complete medical history and physical examination at the Medical Center's University Diagnostic Center, extensive laboratory studies, resting EKG, treadmill EKG (when appropriate), and health risk appraisal. Your physical capacity is determined by means of standard bicycle or treadmill tests. Additional doctor's appointments can be scheduled if needed.

The behavioral examination includes an evaluation of the way you view your overweight condition, with your self-appraisal of success, your manner of coping with setbacks, and your levels of anxiety or depression. A specific meal plan suited to your estimated calorie requirements is created for you by the dietitian. Upon completion of the program, you receive individually planned menus for follow-up.

Approximately 45 hours are spent in classes with center instructors to help you develop effective lifestyle changes to manage your calorie intake during the program and (more important) at home after completion of the program. Individual consultations are used to provide feedback from assessment, work on unique individual problems, provide necessary support, and develop systematic maintenance plans.

An exercise specialist is also available to supervise aerobic and recreational exercise activities each day, including a scenic early morning walk of a mile.

Maximum Number of Participants: Flexible

Diet and Weight Management: Calorie levels are prescribed jointly by a physician and a registered dietitian. The center provides a diet low in saturated fat, cholesterol, and sodium and high in fiber. Upon special request, lacto-ovo vegetarians may be accommodated as well as menus modified upon a physician's recommendation. Caffeine-free beverages are optional.

You learn how to choose and prepare meals that will help you in long-term weight management. You participate in cooking demonstrations. For practical experience, the classroom shifts from the demonstration kitchen to the grocery store to local restaurants to outdoor picnics, and to Charleston's evening social events. In each of these settings, you acquire and rehearse weight management strategies.

Daily meals are proffered in a small private dining room in the MUSC hospital building across from The Charleston Retreat facility. The freshest of Charleston's produce is featured. A typical regimen of 1200 daily calories might include buttermilk pancakes with blueberry sauce for breakfast, seasonal fruit, decaffeinated or regular coffee or tea, and skim milk. Lunch could be grilled tuna salad or shrimp and rice salad, whole-wheat rolls, low-fat frozen yogurt or kiwi sorbet for dessert, and a choice of tea, coffee, skimmed milk, or dietetic beverages. Dinner might be the fresh fish "catch of the day" or chicken with capers and mushrooms, a medley of carrots and snowpeas or other steamed vegetables such as broccoli or green beans, a stuffed potato, spinach salad, and imaginative desserts: honeydew-grape sorbet, orange chiffon whip, orange and banana ambrosia, blueberry cheesecake, melon with ginger. Fruit "milk shakes" or "smoothies" and low-fat crackers are provided for afternoon snacks.

Exercise Facilities: The Charleston Retreat has an exercise room on-site, which contains stationary bicycles and rowing machines. You can use other facilities, including a 25-meter indoor swimming pool, indoor walking/jogging track, bicycle ergometers, and weight machines, during designated times.

Opportunities for Recreational Exercise: Possibilities in the downtown area include bicycling (bicycles can be rented), tennis (bring your own racket), swimming, and walking tours. Planned and optional excursions to several nearby parks and gardens offer an array of nature walks, plus bicycling, canoeing, and swimming. Charleston's fine beaches and rivers offer boating, water-skiing, windsurfing, beach walks, seashelling, ocean swimming, kite flying, beach volleyball, and fishing. The center plans other activities such as bowling and dancing.

Beauty Treatments and Welcome Indulgences: Salons are available a mile from the center.

Accommodations: A wide variety of housing options is available in the Charleston area. Lodging rates vary during the tourist season, which runs from March through June for in-town and from June through August for beach accommodations. The Charleston Retreat Center's participants may be able to take advantage of special monthly rates. Choices include hotels, motor inns, carriage house inns in historic Charleston, efficiency apartments, bed and breakfast facilities, beach rentals, and, for those arriving by boat, marina slips. Rooms and apartments for rent are also listed in the classified sections of the *Charleston News and Courier* and the *Charleston Evening Post.* The Sunday edition is available by mail. Send your request to the newspaper at P.O. Box 758, Charleston, South Carolina 24902. An excellent visitor's guide to the Charleston area can be obtained from the Charleston Trident Convention and Visitors' Bureau, P.O. Box 975, Charleston, South Carolina 24902; telephone (803) 723-7641.

What to Bring: See USEFUL INFORMATION. Bring comfortable, casual clothing, warm-up suits, shorts, slacks, bathing suits, cover-ups, and beach sandals. Warmer clothing is needed for the winter months. Good walking or running shoes are a necessity. Bring a digital watch, tote bags, pedometer (if you have one), camera, your Walkman, rain gear, health insurance claim forms, and any necessary prescription medication. In general, dress is casual but bring appropriate attire for evening occasions. Expect midday highs of 89 degrees F in August and 63 degrees F in February. The center does not provide any athletic equipment, but in most cases such equipment can be rented. A book and stationery store close by is stocked with instructional and recreational reading materials, writing paper, newspapers, magazines, and many other items.

Documentation from Your Physician: Strongly encouraged but not required.

The Use of Alcohol and Tobacco: Alcohol is not part of the allotted daily calories. Smoking is restricted to specific locations.

Fees, Method of Payment, Insurance Coverage: For 28-day program: $2950. The center accepts cash, personal checks, travelers' checks, Visa, and MasterCard. Insurance coverage varies widely depending on the insurer, the insurance plan, and your medical condition. You are provided with an itemized statement listing specific services rendered by the center with appropriate fee and procedure code for each, as well as the diagnosis. The Charleston Retreat will help you file claims for reimbursement. Participants are encouraged to obtain from their physicians, when appropriate, a written recommendation that they lose weight for the amelioration of one or more specific weight-related medical problems. This letter should accompany claims and requests for preauthorization.

Follow-up Assistance: Follow-up telephone consultations are held on a regular basis. An alumni newsletter is published to keep you in touch with the center and to bring you timely weight control tips and up-to-date information about health-related topics. If you wish, you can be referred to a reputable weight control program near your home. Currently, monthly alumni meetings are offered for all local weight management clients. Brief intensive programs (2 to 7 days) are planned for out-of-town alumni at a reduced rate.

❧ Cormillot Clinic ❧
Argentina

If you or your spouse are suffering from anorexia, bulimia, or overweight, want to get away, like art, music, theater, and the sophisticated cosmopolitan life, and wouldn't mind learning or speaking a little Spanish, it's as simple as ABC— Argentina, Buenos Aires, and the Clinica Cormillot, or Cormillot Clinic, pronounced cor-me-shot in Spanish, cormy-lot in English.

You can be an outpatient and stay at a hotel for a couple of weeks—the most expensive in town is the Sheraton, $110 a day. Most of the other "best" hotels are in the $33-a-day range. Plan to check in at the clinic at least 5 times a week for $17 a visit. You can be an inpatient and spend $55 a day for a semiprivate room, daily meals, an exercise program, and both individual and group counseling. English-speaking counselors are available.

Alberto Cormillot, owner, founder, and director of the clinic, born in 1938, is currently Minister of Social Action in Buenos Aires. Once overweight himself, Cormillot, trim, fit for decades, and a dynamo of energy, has welded a staff of health professionals from a variety of disciplines into an enthusiastic and effective team for the treatment of eating disorders, alcoholism, and various addictions at his clinic.

Buenos Aires, the second largest city in the southern hemisphere and the eighth largest in the world, is an impressive port city, with attractive beaches, parks, and gardens. Public transportation is abundant at astonishing Old World nickel, dime, and quarter prices, with buses and underground trains and inexpensive taxis. Driving a car yourself in Buenos Aires is recommended only to the most intrepid foreigner. Arranged tours are excellent and recommended.

The clinic is in the western part of town in the Palermo neightborhood, 10 blocks south of the American Embassy near the Rio de la Plata, and right by the Palermo Parks with their magnificent avenues and a layout similar to the Bois de Boulogne in Paris. The parks include the Hipodromo Argentino, a fabulous trio of racetracks (sand) where the Argentine Triple Crown is run. Next to the Hipodromo are the National Polo Fields flanked by ivy-covered grandstands, a few blocks north of the turn-of-the-century zoo with the oldest carousel in South America. To get your bearings, hire a *mateo,* a horse-drawn carriage, from a rank by the zoo, and enjoy a 20-minute clip-clop pleasure tour for a pittance.

You can shop at the Recoleta, the chic residential and shopping center. Buenos Aires is *the* town for leather and silver and jewelry. Telmo is the street for antiques you won't find in North America and the site for a don't-miss wonderful fair, Saturday and Sunday afternoons. Fine arts galleries and museums of every type abound. You can commission a *fileteadore* to paint anything you want *on* anything you want—you'll find one of these artists of *filete* painting in the San Telmo Fair. If inflated prices have got you jibbering and juddering with frustration, you'll be happy to know that in Buenos Aires you can get your hair shampooed for $1, ride in a taxi for 30¢, and buy local furs, such as Patagonian fox, otter, skunk, and guanaco, as well as silver, jewelry, and antiques at prices that will save you the price of your airfare and more. And lose weight and get healthy at the same time.

Name: Clinica Cormillot

Mailing Address: Cuba 3684, Buenos Aires, Argentina C.P. 1429

Telephone: (701) 6080/3482/2822 and (70) 7939/2518/6193/3804 (Buenos Aires has both 6- and 7-digit numbers); from the US, 011 54 1 70 6193

Established: 1962

Manager: Monika Cormillot

Program Director: Alberto E. J. Cormillot, M.D.

Owner: Alberto E. J. Cormillot, M.D.

Number of Full-Time Health Professionals on Staff: 15 full time (2 internists, 1 psychiatrist, 2 psychologists, 3 nurses, 3 nurse assistants, 2 nutritionists, 1 physical training instructor, 1 occupational therapist) and 30 part time

Accreditation of Professional Staff Members: Alberto E. J. Cormillot, M.D., Director of the Clinica Cormillot since 1967, is a member of the North American Association for the Study of Obesity, the American College of Sports Medicine, and the New York Academy of Sciences. All of the professional staff are appropriately licensed and accredited in Argentina.

Gender and Age Restrictions: None; general age range 15 to 50

Season: Year-round

Length of Stay Required: 15-day minimum

Program: At this 4-story, 40-room clinic, the atmosphere is friendly, courteous, low-key, and highly professional. Many of the staff speak English fluently, and if you have a Spanish-English dictionary, you can have fun deciphering what the sensible, cartoon-illustrated reading material the clinic dispenses is all about. If you're here to lose weight, the program deals with diet, nutrition education, behavior modification, and physical activity. Having sent in your pretreatment information, on admission you are given an orientation session, a psycho-physical evaluation, an evaluation of the nature and severity of your weight problem, a dietary analysis, and an appraisal of your physical fitness. If necessary, you may also be referred to one or more specialists (cardiologist, psychiatrist, orthopedic surgeon) for additional consultations.

The Cormillot Clinic views obesity as having a metabolic component (probably genetically determined), which, at the present time, is not susceptible to direct treatment. However, eating habits can be worked on. The clinic's treatment program helps you make the necessary changes in behavior and attitude through intensive behavior therapy, confrontation with reassurance, and guided increases in physical activity. General education and individual counseling on diet and nutrition are provided.

Once ensconced in your hospital room—white, brown, and orange is about as much as can be said about the decor, but everything scrupulously clean and orderly—you may feel the atmosphere is more like college than a hospital. There are rules and schedules, but you're also meeting with professors (physicians) and going to classes (nutrition counseling, behavior therapy, body image disorders group, assertiveness training), viewing educational films, and making use of the clinic's gym facilities as well as outside exercise facilities. You have classes in yoga, and classes in cooking in the clinic's demonstration kitchen. You receive training in stress management and optional obesity-relevant psychotherapy by staff psychiatrists or psychologists. You receive individual counseling and group sessions, which involve play acting and family sessions for some. Exercise activities are scheduled daily, both in the clinic and outside: workouts on stationary bicycles and treadmills in the clinic's gym, and swimming and walking/jogging in the Palermo Park area. Outpatients also have the option of joining in the exercise component of the program. You can go to the theater at night, and you have a few hours of free time every afternoon to get acquainted with Buenos Aires' many and varied attractions.

Maximum Number of Participants: 40 inpatients

Diet and Weight Management: Depending on the severity of overweight, a daily caloric intake of from 400 to 1200 calories is prescribed and, if necessary, diet supplements of vitamins and minerals. In a 15-day period, the average weight loss is 15 pounds. You eat your meals in one of 2 dining rooms, each seating 20, for smokers and nonsmokers. Breakfast consists of coffee or tea served with a portion of skimmed milk; a pear, apple, or other fruit; and ricotta or low-fat cheese. At lunch and dinner, you can expect vegetable soup or clear broth; chicken or fish; soy beans or brown rice; green beans, carrots, zucchini, or parsley onions; a salad of carrots or coleslaw; ricotta or low-fat cheese; and a gelatine dessert. Water, Diet Coke, and flavored low-calorie drinks are served throughout the day. Meals are high in fiber and low in fat content; the use of salt to season food as you wish is allowed.

Exercise and Physical Therapy Facilities: The clinic's gymnasium is equipped with stationary bicycles, treadmills, and heart-rate and EKG monitoring equipment. An outdoor swimming pool is situated nearby. Massage ($8.00 for 30 minutes, $15.00 for an hour) and heat treatments are available.

Opportunities for Recreational Exercise: Use of nearby tennis courts and swimming pool can be arranged.

Beauty Treatments and Welcome Indulgences: Available half a block away is a hairdressing establishment—$1 for a shampoo and $2 for a haircut. Manicures and pedicures in Buenos Aires are sensational. Depilatory waxing is usually available at other nearby establishments. Monika Cormillot can recommend the best places for facials and any other services you might like. Makeup classes are included in the program.

Accommodations: All rooms are air-conditioned, with a bedside telephone you and your roommate share. No private room television, as this is not allowed by the government, but there is a television lounge. Rooms are equipped with piped-in music. If your roommate wants to listen and you don't, no problem—just bring your Walkman. Some rooms have private bathrooms with a shower but no bathtub. There are 2-bedded and 3-bedded rooms. If you insist on a private room, you probably can have one if you pay a double fee, $110 a day. Naturally, there is maid service daily. Laundry facilities are in the clinic, but you can also pay a maid to take care of this for you.

What to Bring: See USEFUL INFORMATION. Buenos Aires is a high-fashion town, but wear casual clothes for frequenting Palermo Park, for jogging and walking, rowing on the lake, going to the zoo and the San Telmo Fair. Bring walking/jogging shoes, good-looking warmups and exercise clothes, bathing suits and cover-ups, and, if you want to play, your tennis gear and golf shoes. Seasons are the reverse of those in the northern hemisphere: Christmas is warm, the Fourth of July is cool. By all means, bring your Walkman and tape player for music and/or recording the seminars that interest you, but leave your good jewelry at home. Bring an English-Spanish dictionary and phrase book.

Documentation Approval from Your Physician: A letter of approval is not requested but appreciated.

The Use of Alcohol and Tobacco: Use of alcohol is not permitted. There is a program for alcoholism at the clinic. Smoking is not allowed in the medical offices or during the clinics's therapeutic activities. Although the use of tobacco is discouraged, smoking is permitted in designated areas. A smoking cessation course is available.

Fees, Method of Payment, Insurance Coverage: For each of 15 inpatient days, $55 a day covers virtually all services and activities. Optional services for which there is an extra charge include psychotherapy, consultations with certain specialists, and body massage. Personal checks are accepted. Travelers' checks and credit cards are not accepted. You are urged to contact your own insurance carriers to determine whether any or all of the services provided by the Cormillot Clinic are reimbursable. The clinic will cooperate by providing you with documentation of the services rendered during the inpatient treatment period together with the itemized charges.

Follow-up Assistance: "Graduates" are encouraged to return to the clinic periodically for "booster" treatments. After you leave the clinic, you receive follow-up telephone calls and letters. The clinic has videotapes and audio cassettes on weight control issues for sale. Cookbooks and other "lifestyle" books concerned with the problem of overweight can also be purchased at the clinic.

⟡ Durham, North Carolina, ⟡ Diet Capital of the World

Durham, North Carolina, has gained a reputation as the Diet Capital of the world. This city with a population of 105,000 annually attracts some 2000 people from out of state to its four major weight loss and fitness programs—Kempner Clinic/Rice Diet, Structure House, Duke University's Preventive Approach to Cardiovascular Disease (DUPAC), and Duke University Diet and Fitness Center—where they shed a combined average yearly total of 50 tons of excess weight. Once known as a market town for textiles, tobacco, and cigarettes, where James Buchanan Duke, tobacco magnate and philanthropist, reigned like a benevolent king, Durham became linked with diets in the 1940s, when Dr. Walter Kempner, a Duke University medical researcher and physician, discovered that a diet of rice, fruit, and sugar not only helped patients suffering from severe kidney disease, diabetes, heart disease, and hypertension, but also promoted fast, dramatic weight loss. The attendant publicity prompted Duke University's psychologists and physicians to experiment with alternative and more moderate approaches to weight loss and the treatment of severe overweight, which led to the development of today's major programs.

Although the majority who come to Durham have 40 or more pounds to drop, people of all ages, many in their 20s and 30s, also come here to lose 20 pounds or less that they have been unsuccessful in whittling off elsewhere. Too self-conscious to risk appearing in a bathing suit or be seen dancing at home, reducers do so with impunity in Durham. Formalized in their commitment to lose weight, they come to the Imperial Inn's weekly Tuesday dance (which they affectionately dub the Crisco Disco) and the Hotel Europa's weekly Thursday dieters' disco and splash through the aqua-aerobics sessions some of the programs offer. They also enjoy "aerobic shopping"; wearing warm-ups and sporting pedometers, motivated dieters walk the malls, including the sprightly collection of specialty shops housed in restored tobacco warehouses in downtown's Brightleaf Square. Although each of the five programs has a different philosophy and emphasis, none provides beauty or grooming treatments, but all encourage walking as part of their therapy.

Durham is not only eminently walkable, but the town and its environs are inviting with recreational attractions, including free and frequent university-sponsored literary events, lectures, and art museum exhibits, plus an active Art Council's eclectic schedule of weekly exhibits and things to see and do. The inspiring American Dance Festival takes place in late May, early June. Nightclubs provide comedy entertainment. Free films are shown evenings at Duke's Institute of the Arts' Bryan Center. The university's centerpiece Gothic cathedral, with a 50-bell carillon and a splendid 5000-pipe organ, provides free concerts of organ works. The 55-acre Sarah Duke Memorial Gardens, with lily ponds and statuary, vie for walking pleasure with the North Carolina Museum of Life and Science, a 78-acre wonderland with extensive exhibits of prehistoric lore, including life-sized dinosaur models, a wildlife sanctuary with nature trails, a zoo, and a mile of narrow-gauge railroad to transport the weary. Durham has many health clubs, bowling alleys, 9 recreation centers, 2 racquetball clubs, 14 softball fields, 72 public tennis courts with many lit for night play, 4 riding stables, 6 public golf courses with rental clubs available, rental bicycles, and rental canoes. Not more than 15 minutes from the center of town, the Eno River, meandering through Durham County between banks wooded with towering oaks and tulip poplars in 1600 acres of water-oriented wilderness, is one of Durham's favorite recreational areas for rafting, canoeing, and hiking. Duke Forest, an 8300-acre tract of woodland with hiking and walking trails, is less than 10 minutes away.

For those with their own cars, Chapel Hill, 11 miles to the west, and Raleigh, the state capital, 20 miles south, have much to offer in an area abounding with state parks and lakes offering rental boats and water sports. Rental cars are useful for excursions and explorations and give you more leeway in your choice of accommodations.

Accommodations: Although three of the programs offer their own on-site, off-site, and within-a-minute's-walk accommodations (see below), lodging for the participants in all programs is optional, a matter of preference, convenience, and bank account. Weekly prices for accommodations run from $75 to $350, and this pays for a variety of furnished rooms, motels, condominium apartments, inns, hotels, and residential suites. Furnished rooms in private houses are listed in the Sunday classified sections of the *Durham Morning Herald* and the *Durham Sun.* A map of the city, information about accommodations and car rentals, and a sample of the *Lean Times Digest,* a monthly periodical for Durham's dieters, are available on request from the Greater Durham Chamber of Commerce, 201 North Roxboro Street, P.O. Box 3829, Durham, North Carolina 27702; telephone (919) 682-2133.

Duke University Diet and Fitness Center is across the street from the 112 residential suites ($45 a day) of Duke Towers (telephone [919] 687-4444), available to participants in all the programs. Suites comprise living room, kitchen, bedroom with 2 double beds, bathroom, 2 remote-control TV sets with HBO and cable, a radio, 2 telephones (with charge for hookup). Facilities include wake alarm, maid service (additional charge), a coin-operated laundry, men's and women's hairdressers in the building, an outdoor pool (not heated), a covered walking track, garden patio, and free chauffeured limousine transport to the airport on your departure. Structure House offers on-campus 1- and 2-bedroom apartments, 60 in all, with no price difference for larger accommodations, which include fully equipped kitchen, bathroom, TV with HBO, washer/dryer, telephone, linens, and once-a-week maid service (additional service available for $12 daily). Cost for 4 weeks, $1175; weekly cost, $295. Structure House's downtown apartments, 2 miles away, include washer/dryer, TV with HBO, telephone, linens, kitchenette, bathroom, sitting room, and bedroom with double or twin beds. Special rates have been arranged with a local rental car agency for transportation. Apartment rates: $675 for 4 weeks; $175 weekly; $25 daily.

What to Bring: See USEFUL INFORMATION. Bring bathing suits and cover-ups and thong sandals or flip-flops for wear around the swimming pool. Bring exercise clothes, slacks or trousers, shirts and tops for walking and recreational sports. You'll want to wear loose, casual, comfortable clothes during your program and for guided walks and shopping. Bring rain gear and seasonably warm clothing for the colder months. Sweaters and a jackets should be brought for all-season wear, as mornings and evenings can be cool. Bring appropriate clothes (a little dressier and more festive) if you plan on attending concerts, theater, and the weekly dances. If you have smaller sizes of exercise clothes and casual wear, bring them along. If not, you'll have plenty of opportunities to shop for small-sized clothing in Durham. A duffel bag/tote bag for your exercise clothes and bathing gear is essential, and you may need an extra one for your tape recorder and cassettes if you plan to record some of the seminars and talks. Film, sundries, reading material, and athletic gear are all available in Durham's shopping malls.

Duke University Diet and Fitness Center
Durham

Duke University Diet and Fitness Center is one of the more effective weight control programs in the United States. Its connection with the Duke University Medical Center is apparent in its medical approach to individually programmed weight management and in its team of physicians, nurses, clinical psychologists, dietitians, and exercise physiologists who are all skilled specialists. The treatment program offers medically supervised weight loss through nutrition education, diet therapy, planned exercise, and behavior modification.

In the program, participants usually lose substantial amounts of weight, depending on the severity of their overweight, and continue to lose weight at home until their goal weight is reached. Duke University Diet and Fitness Center reports that 70 percent of 300 former participants taking part in a research study maintained their original weight loss over a 3-year period. Director of the center's program Dr. Michael Hamilton whimsically compares participation in the program to being a "musician practicing on scales for the concert which takes place when you get back home."

The facility's one-story, 25,000-square-foot rectangular brick building may look like an elementary school, but make no mistake about it, you're treated like a grown-up here. The program emphasizes support and guidance, not denial or hardship, with the philosophy that self-management through understanding is the way you can help yourself best in an atmosphere of trust and acceptance. You receive top-notch schooling in medical, behavioral, nutritional, and fitness aspects of weight loss and all the tools you need to identify and change destructive habits and behavior. (You are required to keep a diary of your "structured eating" and planned activities.) You also have access to an excellent nutrition manual, a loose-leaf, 3-ring, vinyl-bound book that discusses many aspects of food, its nutritional components, dietary recommendations, weight loss, grocery shopping, recipe modification, nutritional labeling, meals away from home, travel guidelines, holiday eating, indulging without bulging, and more.

Duke University Diet and Fitness Center, as its name implies, also gives strong emphasis to exercise. Along with a gym and a heated indoor 25-meter swimming pool, the center also houses a kitchen, dining room, lounge and game room, classrooms, and a medical clinic. In addition, it offers massages ($45), image counseling (extra), a family support program (extra), medical referrals for diabetes management, a preventive and therapeutic program for osteoporosis, a pulmonary rehabilitation program, and help with filing insurance claims. It is located across the street from deluxe accommodations at the Duke Towers as well as near the university's continuing education short courses and cultural and sports activities.

Name: Duke University Diet and Fitness Center

Mailing Address: 804 West Trinity Avenue, Durham, North Carolina 27701

Telephone: (919) 684-6331

Established: 1971

Administrative Manager: Jonathan I. Carmel, M.P.H., R.D.

Program Director: Michael A. Hamilton, M.D., M.P.H.

Owner: Duke University Medical Center

Number of Full-Time Health Professionals on Staff: 8 full time, 3 part time, including a cardiologist

Accreditation of Professional Staff Members: Michael A. Hamilton, M.D., M.P.H., Program Director, board certified in Internal Medicine and Family Medicine, assistant professor in the Department of Community and Family Medicine of the Duke University Medical Center; Phillis Byrd, L.P.N.; Ronette L. Kolotkin, Ph.D. (Clinical Psychology), Behavioral Director, registered psychologist, clinical assistant professor in the departments of Psychiatry and of Community and Family Medicine of the Duke University Medical Center; Dominic Moore, M.S., Exercise Physiology; Diane Cogburn, R.D., M.P.H.

Gender and Age Restrictions: Co-ed; ages 18 to 75 (76 to 80 on approval of physician)

Season: Year-round

Length of Stay Required: New patients: 2- and 4-week programs, beginning Monday at 8:00 AM. Return patients: minimum stay 1 week.

Programs Offered: Your first several days are devoted to assessments by the medical, behavioral, nutritional, and fitness staff, reviewing these findings with the staff, and discussing ways of attaining your health goals. Services available from the medical component include primary medical care during the course of the program, counseling on preventive health behavior, and help in planning for your medical needs when you return home.

Through group discussions, workshops, and seminars, you enhance your awareness of eating and exercise patterns and the relationship of these patterns to your personality traits and lifestyle. Individual therapy is available upon request (at additional cost).

Nutrition education and "at-the-table training" are used to help you develop healthier eating patterns. The wonders of delectable low-calorie food preparation and cooking are demonstrated for an hour each week, with 6 hours of cooking classes during your third week in the program, and are supplemented with off-site restaurant experience, shopping for foods in local markets, and lectures and seminars to provide you with the nutritional knowledge and awareness that serve as the foundation for sensible eating.

Great emphasis is placed on enhanced fitness through exercise. You are given an exercise prescription (that can be continued at home) based on the results of a treadmill test. There is an outdoor running track and a large east-facing gym, which can be used for volleyball, badminton, and basketball and which is equipped with a Universal weight-resistance machine, free weights, and 12 Air-Dyne stationary bicycles; a 25-meter swimming pool, heated to 81 degrees, is located in the western section of the building.

As pointed out in DFC's excellent quarterly newsletter, one idea strongly promoted at DFC is that *you* are personally responsible for your success in the program. DFC provides the roadmap for change, but you are in the driver's seat and go at your own pace.

After your first week, family members and close friends are encouraged to participate in a support program that allows them to eat meals and participate in all cooking demonstrations, lectures, and discussion. They may use the exercise facility provided they go through a cardiac screening by DFC medical personnel, $40.

Diet and Weight Management: The DFC diet provides as little as 750 calories a day, but your intake depends on your needs. Calorie levels are prescribed by a registered dietitian. The diet not only promotes weight loss but is helpful in blood pressure control, cholesterol control, and the management of certain intestinal disorders. Menus are far from draconian, and offer portions of tandoori chicken, sirloin steak, shrimp, eggplant Parmesan, and spinach omelette à la Florentine. For breakfast you might have half an English muffin, a 3-eggwhite omelette, and ½ a cup of vegetables; for lunch, 1 cup of tabouli and fruit for dessert; for dinner, 6 ounces of crispy chicken with ½ cup of parsley carrots, ½ cup of coleslaw, and ½ cup of fruit jello. Menus can be modified to accommodate vegetarians, those with allergies, and those requiring Kosher food.

Maximum Number of Participants: 120; 70 is average

Documentation from Your Physician: Requested but not required. The preadmission telephone screening process effectively identifies those who would not benefit from the program because of health reasons.

The Use of Alcohol and Tobacco: Alcohol is not allowed on the premises, and smoking is not permitted inside the DFC facility.

Fees, Method of Payment, Insurance Coverage: The 4-week program costs $3300, exclusive of housing but including admission fee, treadmill, standard lab fee, program fee, and meal fee. The weekly support program for family member or friend costs $354. A 2-week program costs $2600. A 50-minute session of therapeutic massage—Swedish, deep muscle, sports massage, acupressure—is extra. Other physical therapy is available for an extra fee through the Duke University Medical Center. Fees are payable on the admittance date. Payment can be made with cash, personal check, travelers' checks, Visa, MasterCard, or American Express. Participants who return to the program within 3 years pay a reduced fee depending on the duration of the intervening time. Beyond 3 years, you are treated as a new participant except that your admission fee is $450 rather than $700.

In many instances, particularly when obesity-related health conditions like hypertension or diabetes are involved, the services provided by the Duke University DFC are reimbursable by health insurers. However, prospective participants are cautioned that insurance companies vary considerably in their reimbursement practices.

Follow-up Assistance: The Duke University Diet and Fitness Center sends a quarterly newsletter containing excellent counseling, fitness, nutrition, and recipe modification advice. The DFC *Nutrition Manual* ($29) is encyclopedic and an enhancement to an intelligent reader's reference library.A Duke University Diet and Fitness recipe book ($15) is also available. In early 1990, Ballantine will publish *The Duke University Diet and Fitness Program.*

Structure House

Durham

On the tenth anniversary of Structure House, its founder and owner, Gerard J. Musante, a clinical psychologist, and his wife, Rita, celebrated by opening a new facility, Structure House Village, a "life-extension community" located on a 21-acre estate on the outskirts of town. A well-planned "campus" of 9 neat little white houses and a Life Extension Center, Structure House Village boasts a handsome indoor lap and exercise pool; a gymnasium; Nautilus weight-training and massage rooms; medical offices; outdoor walking and jogging trails; an outdoor swimming pool; and a white-porticoed, new brick, three-story main building.

Clients, whose ages generally range from 30 to 50, come here to lose from 20 to 200 pounds and to learn how to develop order out of their "unstructured" eating and living habits. Some suffer from weight- and lifestyle-related illnesses, including hypertension, diabetes, and heart problems. Others have mobility problems for which Structure House provides elevators and ramps. Many of the participants are business or professional people.

Name: Structure House

Mailing Address: 3017 Pickett Road, Durham, North Carolina 27705

Telephone: (919) 688-7379

Established: 1977

Program Director: Gerard J. Musante, Ph.D., A.B.P.P.

Owner: Gerard J. Musante

Number of Full-Time Health Professionals on Staff: 13, 9 more are part-time

Accreditation of Professional Staff Members: Gerard J. Musante, Ph.D., director of the program, is a clinical psychologist and a diplomate in clinical psychology who received his postdoctoral training at the Behavior Therapy Institute of Temple University Medical School in Philadelphia. Stephen Hirsch, M.D., and Sigrid Nelius, M.D., serve as attending physicians and medical consultants.

Gender and Age Restrictions: None, but supervisory or recreational facilities for children accompanying a parent are not available.

Season: Year-round

Length of Stay Required: 1-week minimum; average stay, 4 to 6 weeks; new group begins each Monday at 8:00 AM

Programs: Musante advocates treating overweight as a psychological as well as a physiological problem. His concern is not *what* people eat as much as it is *why* they overeat, or indulge in "unstructured" eating; *why* they use food as a reward, a treat, a way of allaying fear, calming anger, relieving boredom and depression, lifting spirits, munching away loneliness, or, literally, stomaching a lack of self-esteem.

A psychological evaluation is made after an initial consultation with Dr. Musante, and you then participate in group sessions focused on weight management, assertiveness training sessions in lifestyle change, and stress management workshops. Group and individual psychotherapy ($65 to $85) an hour are available as needed. You are also given in-depth information about weight-related problems such as body image, depression, environmental control, and life and time management.

Health education begins with a physician's evaluation of your medical records. If a further medical evaluation is required, laboratory tests and/or an exercise stress test may be obtained ($100 to $200). Depending on your health status, instruction is given in cardiac risk prevention and blood pressure/glucose self-monitoring. Appointments with medical specialists can be arranged as needed. An effective smoking cessation program is offered ($100).

In workshops and with demonstrations, you receive dietary reeducation in such subjects as restaurant dining, sodium and cholesterol control, weight loss and plateaus, recipe alteration for low-calorie cooking, vegetarian diets, and portion sizes.

Structure House participants keep food and activity diaries, which are reviewed with the staff, to help them identify "antecedents"—specific events, situations, times, emotions, or feelings that systematically precede overeating—in order to learn why and when they turn to food. They are urged to have a "bank" of rewards that don't involve food—shopping, a massage ($50 extra), exercise—and to condition themselves to realize that it's easier to say no to an empty refrigerator than it is to a full one.

Exercise training begins with fitness testing and a prescription for your individualized conditioning program to promote strengthening, flexibility, and relaxation. A variety of stretch, warm-up, calisthenics, and low-impact aerobics classes are supplemented with workshops and demonstrations on the benefits of exercise, exercise misconceptions, fitness, and related topics. Activities include walking, "aerobic shopping," jogging, stationary bicycling, Nautilus weight-resistance training, and instruction in the use of free weights and trampoline. The sumptuous indoor pool is large enough for laps, perimeter water walking, and energetic pool volleyball games as well as aqua-aerobics and "aerobic" swimming. An aquatics instructor is also available for private swimming lessons ($12 for a half-hour lesson). Rather than go off-site for entertainment, SH participants are encouraged to take part in co-ed group sports activities such as water volleyball, softball, indoor volleyball, or basketball. *N.B.* If you aren't medically cleared for aerobic exercise, substitute warm-up, cool-down, and stretching exercises are designed for you.

The *Family Support Program,* a 5-day family participation program, is offered Monday through Friday to enable a family member to get a sense of the Structure House experience and philosophy. The program is designed to give a comprehensive overview of the program. SH suggests that your final week is the most appropriate time to have your nearest and dearest participate in the *Family Support Program,* which costs $310 per week. Meals, materials, workshops, exercise, and family therapy counseling are included in the price.

New in 1988, 1-week and 2-week intensive *Executive Institute Programs,* which emphasize stress management, are also available.

Diet and Weight Management: You eat all your meals in the Structure House dining rooms. Menus, changed every week on a 4-week cycle, consist of low-sodium, low-cholesterol, plain ordinary foods (POF) and decaffeinated beverages.

You are asked to stay on a preplanned menu of 650 to 700 calories for the first 2 weeks of your visit; in your third week you may choose a few alternate menu selections. After you have been at Structure House for 6 weeks, you increase your calorie intake to 1000 calories. Your week's menu, sunshine-yellow for 700-calorie diets, true blue for 1000-calorie diets, is given to you on a large sheet of construction paper with tear-off chits, or meal tickets, on which you record your name, the number of calories you have downed, and alternates you have chosen. Breakfast on a 700-calorie regime might be an eggwhite and cheese omelet, an apple and ½ toasted bagel. Lunch could be a grilled cheese sandwich (diet bread and Lite-Line cheese), 2 broccoli spears, ½ cup of summer squash, and ½ cup of beets. Dinner could be 3 ounces of baked chicken with lemon garlic and parsley, ½ cup of wild rice, 1 cup of peas, and ½ cup of chilled mixed vegetables. Meatloaf, beefburger, stuffed zucchini Florentine, roast beef sandwiches, and hot turkey sandwiches are offered, in small portions, and served with diet bread, diet mayonnaise, diet gravy, diet dressing, diet syrup, diet drinks such as Kool-Aid, and diet cheese. The Wednesday salad bar offers bacon bits, olives, chopped eggs, cottage cheese, grated cheddar cheese, tomatoes, onion, carrots, celery, croutons, ham, tuna, turkey, shredded cabbage, green pepper, cucumber, and more. Hanukkah, Christmas, New Year's Eve, Valentine's Day, Easter, and the Fourth of July are big events at Structure House, where staff and participants join together to celebrate. For Rosh Hashannah, there is a candlelight dinner of baked chicken with garlic, baked sweet potato half, carrots, and salad. Halloween is costumed fun and frolic and a dinner of chicken in orange sauce, glazed carrots, asparagus spears, and a pumpkin muffin.

Maximum Number of Participants: 140 to 150

Documentation from Your Physician: A letter of approval is requested but not required. A medical report from your personal physician is requested to avoid duplication of medical expenses and to assure continuity of care. In the absence of such a report, if warranted by the presence of a medical problem or risk factor, you will be given an appointment with Structure House's consulting physician.

The Use of Alcohol and Tobacco: Alcoholic beverages are neither served nor allowed in the dining rooms. Although smoking is discouraged, and a smoking cessation course is offered, smoking is permitted in a smokers' dining area and outdoors.

Fees, Method of Payment, Insurance Coverage: Rates range from $1500 for the 1-week program, to $6260 for the 8-week program, inclusive of housing and most other costs. Program fees are due during the first week. Payment may be by cash, check, travelers' checks, Visa, or MasterCard.

Follow-up Assistance: Rates are lowered for graduates who return for anywhere from 2 days to many months, and for them no advance reservation is required. "Update" newsletters are sent to former participants every 2 months. In addition to these informative well-written bulletins, letters, diaries, and cards are sent to encourage graduates to maintain their improved eating and exercise habits. Graduates are encouraged to keep daily diaries and send them regularly to Structure House for review by their personal therapist. Structure House has a mail-order line that offers cassettes on various aspects of weight control; low-calorie, low-cholesterol cookbooks; diet condiments, salad dressings, food and bathroom scales, portion cups, logo sweatshirts, and other items, also obtainable on site.

Kempner Clinic (Rice Diet)
Durham

In the 1940s, Dr. Walter Kempner, then an assistant professor of medicine at Duke University's School of Medicine, developed the "Rice Diet" for the treatment of kidney disease, high blood pressure, and vascular disease. As a side effect, the diet promotes fast, sometimes dramatic weight loss.

Uncomplicated as its regimen of unsalted rice, fruits high in carbohydrates, and limited amounts of fruit juice, tea, or decaffeinated black coffee may appear, the Rice Diet is not a simple "do-it-yourself" regime. In addition, the diet is monotonous, as monotonous as the sound of a ticking clock. Not disagreeable, just boring. An exercise in eating to achieve certain health goals but not associating food with pleasure, the diet is a real test of character. Sometimes medical, or more rarely psychological, factors necessitate small additions, such as vegetables, to the diet of certain patients. "But it's about 6 months before you see a sliver of breast of chicken," said one "ricer" who lost 40 pounds in her first 6 weeks there.

The program allows you plenty of free time to do anything you please—except go off the diet.

Name: Kempner Clinic (Rice Diet)

Mailing Address: Box 3099, Duke University Medical Center, Durham, North Carolina 27710

Telephone: (919) 286-2243

Established: 1939

Program Directors: Walter Kempner, M.D.; Barbara C. Newborg, M.D.

Owner: Duke University Medical Center

Maximum Number of Participants: Approximately 250

Number of Full-Time Health Professionals on Staff: 7

Accreditation of Professional Staff Members: Walter Kempner, M.D., Founder and Medical Director, professor emeritus of medicine at the Duke University School of Medicine; Barbara C. Newborg, M.D., associate professor of medicine at the Duke University Medical Center; Robert A. Rosati, M.D., associate professor of medicine at the Duke University Medical Center; John Robert Horn, Physician Associate–Certified; Carol Blessing-Feussner, Physician Associate–Certified; Norma J. Neal, R.N., Duke University Medical Center

Gender and Age Restrictions: None; at physician's discretion, children and teenagers occasionally admitted accompanied by parents or guardians

Season: Year-round

Length of Stay Required: Patients are encouraged to stay until any diseases or abnormal findings have resolved or are under control and a normal weight has been achieved. The length of treatment ranges from a few weeks to months, occasionally to more than a year.

Programs Offered: You report to Dr. Kempner's Clinic, a satellite facility of Duke University Medical Center, at 1821 Green Street, for initial consultation and testing. For daily weight and blood pressure measurements and discussions with physicians or "patient counselors" or both, you check in at the Rice House, 111 North Magnum Street. You eat only at the Rice House, where your 3 daily meals are served to you in accordance with your dietary prescriptions. You are constantly encouraged to keep on the regimen by physicians and counselors, and also by your fellow "ricers," who all gather round when results of sodium chloride tests of your urine are published and posted in the Rice House (with low, successful values circled in red). The peer pressure is equally apparent as you compare cumulative weight loss.

An individualized exercise regime is prescribed for you. The prescription takes into account age, sex, exercise history, history of any disabilities, and the results of a resting or exercise electrocardiogram, or both.

In addition to your frequent contacts with physicians and counselors, you are required to attend at least 1 lecture a week dealing with some subject relating to diet and health. In the program, the health hazards of obesity and a diet high in fats, salt, and protein are continually emphasized.

Diet and Weight Management: The initial diet prescribed for most (the "basic rice/reduction diet") is 400 to 800 calories a day. Of these calories, 90 to 95

percent are carbohydrates, taken as rice and fruit. The diet is also low in salt, protein, fat, and cholesterol. As your condition improves, nonleguminous vegetables may be added to the diet and subsequently, for most, small amounts of chicken or fish.

Maximum Number of Participants: Approximately 250

Documentation from Your Physician: Previous medical records are helpful. All patients receive a comprehensive evaluation in the Kempner Clinic prior to beginning the diet.

The Use of Alcohol and Tobacco: Alcohol is forbidden; smoking is discouraged. No smoking is allowed in the Rice House.

Fees, Method of Payment, Insurance Coverage: The initial medical evaluation and history, physical examination, X ray, and laboratory testing will run you about $900 to $1200. The treatment phase—rice/reduction diet, associated monitoring, counseling, and education—is about $1200 a month. Follow-up visits are appreciably less expensive. Personal checks, travelers' checks, and money orders are accepted. Credit cards are not accepted. You receive itemized statements that you can submit to your insurance carrier for reimbursement. The extent of your reimbursement depends on your medical diagnosis and the nature of your health insurance policy. *N.B.* Your fees do not cover the cost of lodging, which may range from $75 to $350 a week (see introductory material on Durham).

Follow-up Assistance: Patients are advised to return for periodic examinations and further treatment as necessary. Telephone or mail follow-up of new patients has been recently instituted.

DUPAC

Durham

Duke University's Preventive Approach to Cardiology (DUPAC) was founded in 1976 by Dr. Andrew G. Wallace, then chief of the Division of Cardiology, Duke University Medical Center, to improve the cardiovascular fitness level of patients through exercise training. At present, the program's expanded purpose is to improve the quality of life for individuals already suffering from coronary heart disease (CHD); to prevent diseases of the circulatory system in apparently healthy individuals; and to increase scientific knowledge through research in preventive cardiology. DUPAC's treatment program focuses on seven CHD "risk factors" that are potentially controllable: cigarette smoking, high blood cholesterol, mismanagement of life stress, physical inactivity, obesity, diabetes, and high blood pressure. The DUPAC approach helps those with one or more CHD risk factors to change unhealthy lifestyles.

Name: DUPAC (Duke University's Preventive Approach to Cardiology)

Mailing Address: Box 3022, Duke University Medical Center, Durham, North Carolina 27710

Telephone: (919) 681-6974

Established: 1976

Managing Director: Pamela B. Morris, M.D., Medical Director; Dorothy Efland, Patient Relations

Owner: Duke University Medical Center

Number of Full-Time Health Professionals on Staff: Approximately 60, of whom 45 are full-time

Accreditation of Professional Staff Members: Pamela B. Morris, M.D., Medical Director, Associate in Medicine (Cardiology) at the Duke University Medical Center, board certified in Internal Medicine (all other health professionals associated with the DUPAC program possess the credentials appropriate to their roles)

Gender and Age Restrictions: Co-ed; minimum age 16

Season: Year-round

Length of Stay Required: Treatment lasts a minimum of 4 weeks. Individuals may be advised to remain in the program for longer periods.

Programs Offered: When you join DUPAC your health status is evaluated, with special attention paid to your fitness level and risk factors for coronary heart disease. Testing includes a history and physical examination by a DUPAC physician, blood studies, an electrocardiogram and exercise stress test, determination of body fat content and desirable body weight, a dietary assessment, and a psychological profile. A multidisciplinary program is then designed for you, which can include exercise, dietary modification, medication changes, stress management training, and education in nutrition and other subjects.

Participants attend group exercise sessions at the DUPAC facility at least 3 days a week. The exercises, which include stationary bicycle riding, arm ergometry, floor exercises, track walking with warm-up and cool-down, weight-resistance Nautilus training, stretching, aerobics, walking and jogging either on the track or on trails, and aqua-aerobics in the swimming pool, are supervised by physicians' assistants, nurses, and exercise physiologists. You work out at your own pace and keep daily records of your heart rate responses during various exercises.

The nutrition program is supervised by 2 registered dietitians who plan all meals prepared by the DUPAC chef. You eat 3 meals a day at DUPAC, 5 days a week. Weekend meals are provided by the Duke University Diet and Fitness Center. DUPAC's diet conforms strictly to the criteria of the American Heart Association, which calls for a low-sodium, low-cholesterol, low-total-fat, and low-saturated-fat intake. If you are overweight, you are given a low-calorie version of the DUPAC diet so that you lose excess body fat while improving your cardiovascular fitness. Cooking classes, field trips to supermarkets to check out food labeling and to restaurants to practice selecting appropriate meals, and individual and group dietary counseling are offered. Diet, exercise, and educational programs are designed specifically for those with hypertension and diabetes.

Counseling, biofeedback, relaxation training, and group therapy are employed in the stress management component of the program to help participants gain control over such self-damaging behavior traits as excessive impatience, compulsive perfectionism, and inability to relax.

A smoking cessation program is available through professionally guided group and individual services.

Maximum Number of Participants: No maximum figure has been determined. There are now 700 to 800 people participating in various components of the program.

Documentation from Your Physician: Requested but not required. DUPAC acts as a consultant to your regular physician or specialist. On admission to the program, you are examined by a physician who is a member of DUPAC's professional staff. Every effort is made to avoid duplicating laboratory studies or tests recently performed by your physician.

The Use of Alcohol and Tobacco: Neither are permitted in the facility.

Fees, Method of Payment, Insurance Coverage: Fees for the initial medical and fitness evaluation, which includes professional fees, laboratory studies, stress, EKG, and any other indicated tests or consultations, range from $500 to $700. Weekly cost for meals is $125, for exercise regimen, $180. Fees for outpatient treatment vary, depending on the nature of the treatment required. For specific information, call Dorothy Efland at DUPAC. Cash, money orders, and personal checks are accepted. Credit cards are not accepted. You are responsible for contacting your insurance carrier to clarify policies that govern insurance payments.

Follow-up Assistance: DUPAC operates an "At Home" program, which is coordinated by a staff member. Through this program, you are periodically contacted by letter and telephone and asked about your current status. In this way, the coordinator can obtain follow-up information and provide psychological support and guidance. At the same time, the coordinator can determine whether you want or require further evaluation or treatment at DUPAC.

Green Mountain at Fox Run
Vermont

Ladies, brace yourselves for the minimum fortnight's training session or the more customary 4-week session at Green Mountain at Fox Run, which is a mind-body experience that requires total commitment and determination to change your eating habits and to make the effort to exercise. No nonsense. No frills. You bring your own towels, washcloths, and shampoo. You make your own bed if you can't stand seeing it unmade. Once a week, a maid changes the sheets, vacuums the teal-blue, pink-dotted carpet, dusts the contemporary furniture, and scours the bathroom, but that's about as much service as you'll get. You do your own laundry, or deliver, pick up, and pay for your laundry being done in the neighboring town of Ludlow. You wait on yourself in the dining room and, after you've eaten, you clatter your plates into a bin to be washed, one of the few tasks you don't have to do for yourself.

You don't come to Green Mountain at Fox Run to be pampered or prettified. The ambience is that of an all-women's college cum Olympics training camp. You come here to learn how to take charge of your life, to shed weight and learn how to maintain your new weight, to transform your feelings of physical phhhtness to a lifetime of fitness. You walk, jog, hike, and swim here year-round as you usually can at home. A plus in the winter months is expert training in cross-country skiing.

Most of the women who come to Green Mountain at Fox Run—and they come here from every state and from 20 foreign countries—are professionals who make their living with their minds, often at the expense of their bodies. They come here to get away from stress, and to learn how to deal with stress and their weight problems. Some have little to lose and some may need to lose as many as 100 pounds or more. Classroom lectures concerned with nutritional and behavioral awareness, stress management, and exercise physiology are a required element of the program, as is training in body conditioning and aerobic exercise. The program operates as a group concept, but if a participant has a special need it will be dealt with. You may choose among differing outings or activity classes, but you aren't allowed to spend time flaked out doing nothing until your scheduled day is over.

What makes this highly structured program bearable to sybaritic, sedentary souls? It helps if you keep in mind that participants in this program not only achieve weight loss but are claimed to be about 50 percent above the national average in maintaining their new weight. It also helps if you are a nature lover.

Even if you aren't, it's difficult not to become one in the environs of the Green Mountain National Forest.

In comparison with the dazzling seasonal beauty of GMFR's 26-acre private estate, the contemporary facade of the white-trimmed, barn-red lodge where you live and take your classes looks like an unremarkable example of institutional-bland architecture. The compensating advantage is that its interior furnishings are a comfortable, unpretentious vantage point from which you can look out upon the vistas and horizons of some of central Vermont's finest cross-country and downhill skiing territory.

The 9-hole (soon to be 18 holes) Fox Run Golf and Cross-Country Ski Touring Center spreads beneath you, and about a quarter of a mile away you can see the Okemo Mountain family ski area with several lifts, including a beginner lift, downhill trails suitable for varying degrees of expertise, a base lodge, ski school, ski shop, ice-skating, several inns and condominium-unit hotels, and specialty shops. About 20 minutes away in Sherburne, off U.S. Route 4, is the less staid Killington downhill and cross-country ski resort. Other sightseeing possibilities? Calvin Coolidge's birthplace in Plymouth, where you can watch cows being milked and cheese being made, summer stock performances at the Weston playhouse, and Woodstock, a rich-cream New England village, often called one of the loveliest villages in America, with many of its buildings listed in the National Register of Historic Places.

Shopping? In and around Manchester, a 30-minute car jaunt, designer discount outlets are a bargain hunter's delight. Closer by, in Ludlow, 1½ miles from GMFR's doorstep, and scattered throughout its surrounds, antique shops offer amusing curiosities and collectibles, sometimes a few real treasures.

There is no taxi service available, but it is likely, if not guaranteed, that those with cars will ask those without to share an excursion, or drive to Ludlow to catch an evening movie.

Name: Green Mountain at Fox Run

Mailing Address: Box 164, Fox Lane, Ludlow, Vermont 05149

Telephone: (802) 228-8885

Established: 1973

Managing Directors: Thelma J. Wayler, M.S., R.D.; Alan H. Wayler, Ph.D.

Owner: Thelma J. Wayler

Number of Full-Time Health Professionals on Staff: 8 to 12

Accreditation of Professional Staff Members: Full-time professional staff includes an academically trained nutrition scientist (Ph.D.), an expert in health behavior (Dr. H. Sci.), 2 registered dietitians with M.S. degrees in nutrition, 2 exercise physiologists (B.S. and M.S.), and a behaviorial therapist (M.S.). David F. Cross, M.D., is Physician in Charge.

Gender and Age Restrictions: Women only, 18 to 80

Season: Year-round.

Length of Stay Required: 2-, 4-, 8-, or 12-week sessions

Programs Offered: Weight management as it relates to health and fitness is the core program. Medically supervised and demanding, the program provides educational courses in nutrition, exercise physiology, behavioral awareness, and stress management to repattern your styles of eating, activity, and self-imaging; and prescribes plenty of exercise, including swimming, NordicTrack and training with light free weights to enhance muscular tone and flexibility, jazz and aerobic dance, bicycling, and cross-country skiing and snow-shoeing in winter. Depending on the weather and your preferences, you can also play tennis, golf, downhill ski, and ice-skate. The program is recommended as effective by many physicians in the field of weight management and by a top executive at Weight Watchers.

Outside speakers' seminars, group and individual counseling, cardiovascular fitness training, and training in lifestyle repatterning take up the hours not filled with physical activity. From 7:00 PM on, your time is your own unless there is a guest seminar to attend. Some women watch television in the living room. Others may gather in the Buttery, where there is another television set, an upright piano, and a wood-burning stove. On Sundays, except for obligatory meal attendance, you are free to do as you please.

Maximum Number of Participants: 65

Diet and Weight Management: Directly opposed to the deprivation approach of most weight loss diets, Thelma Wayler believes you can eat anything you want if you learn to eat moderately and with reasonable judgment about what you eat. No fixed, faddish, or fanatic formula. Skipping meals is definitely not permitted, even on Sunday, your "free" day. When you first arrive, you line up to be given preweighed food, a visual conditioner and an eye-opener to some of what a "moderate portion" is. Then you graduate to self-service at a buffet, or help yourself from platters set on your group's table. Toward the end of your stay, you go to local restaurants to practice choosing foods low in sodium, sugar, fat, cholesterol, and calories. Classwork also trains you to eat moderate portions of food such as turkey, fish, skinless chicken, salads, vegetables, and fresh fruit. You are, however, allowed to nibble on cheese pizza, ice cream, pasta, peanuts, and pancakes. You can eat the same as a thin person might, promises Thelma Wayler, just less of it.

The basic philosophy, The Option, means that you can eat anything you want, but if you're trying to lose weight, you must be aware of the choices you make, take responsibility for them, and move away from the all-or-nothing mentality of dieting. The meals you eat comprise an average of 1000 to 1200 calories a day, are light but not drastically restricted, and are well balanced, with particular attention to low sodium, fat, and cholesterol. Lacto-vegetarian preferences can be accommodated. The dining room, carpeted in navy blue with a pattern as festive as confetti, is large, airy, and with a mountain outlook to be seen through its tall window wall.

Exercise and Physical Therapy Facilities: Indoors, there are 4 exercise rooms with 8 stationary bicycles, sets of free weights, and a NordicTrack simulated cross-country skiing machine. Outdoors, there is a level walk/jog/running track of ¹⁄₁₀ mile circumference and a stainless steel-lined swimming pool beneath a bubble dome that can be opened in warm weather. There are future plans for the construction of a new building to house an indoor swimming pool and additional rooms for exercising and classes. There are daily water exercise and swimming classes, 60-minute daily sessions of low-impact aerobic exercise, jazz dancing and stretch classes, and a daily class in body-building, with free weights no heavier than a cantaloupe to hold in each hand, the exercise instructor jokes, to emphasise the point that there is nothing here that you can't do at home without buying expensive equipment.

Opportunities for Recreational Exercise: There are 2 clay Har-tru courts on site in a clearing in the woods aromatic with evergreens. Rackets and balls are provided. Guests have the use of 8 single-gear and 3- to 5-gear bicycles, and many hiking and walking trails through the old and rounded Green Mountains, forests of pine, beech, birch, and maple. If you've never played "nerf ball," an indoor racquet sport, you'll have fun playing it here. You can play golf at the Fox Run Golf and Cross-Country Ski Touring Center adjacent to the GMFR property (greens fees and rental equipment extra). In the winter, you can try snow-shoeing (GMFR has a dozen pairs for use by its clients). Cross-country skiing is available at Fox Run Golf and Cross-Country Ski Touring Center where you'll find a comfortable lounge with a fireplace for après-ski, lunches served, and a bar. Skating and downhill skiing are available at Okemo Mountain and Killington.

Beauty Treatments and Welcome Indulgences: There are hairdressing shops in nearby Ludlow where you can also have your nails manicured.

Accommodations: All single and double bedrooms are in one wing of the main lodge. There are also duplexes (translated: gallery lofts) for 4 occupants. Freshly renovated in 1986–87, the pricier accommodations feature polka-dotted maroon wall-to-wall carpeting, pinkish cream-colored walls, matching quilted flower-patterned bluish-lavender bedspreads and curtains, and blond oak furniture. Given a choice in the bilevel duplexes, opt for the lower level accommodations. If the ladies up top get the benefit of extra stair climbing and can literally look down on you except when they are safely tucked in their beds, you will have the benefit of the unit's bathroom on your level. Each single, double, and duplex unit has its own private bathroom. There are public telephones, but there are neither telephones nor television sets in the bedrooms.

What to Bring: See USEFUL INFORMATION. The atmosphere is country casual. You may change, but you do not dress up for supper. Wear whatever you feel comfortable in for traveling and excursions. If you do forget any basic sports gear, GMFR's activewear dispensary stocks most seasonal items. Cassettes and reading material about health, fitness, and nutrition are for sale at GMFR. *N.B.* Remember to bring towels, shampoo, and washcloths. Bring Woolite and detergent. You'll find it a lot easier and a time-saver to wash and dry your clothes in GMFR's laundry room rather that to lug them into Ludlow and carry them back from the laundry and dry cleaner there. Tennis rackets and balls are provided. Rental golf clubs, cross-country skis, boots, poles and bindings, skates, and downhill equipment are available.

Documentation from Your Physician: Requested but not required. If you arrive without a letter of approval from your physician, medical history, and the results of a recent physical examination, you will be asked to sign a medical release form. (See Fees.)

The Use of Alcohol and Tobacco: No alcoholic beverages are allowed on the premises. Smoking is allowed in certain designated areas.

Fees, Method of Payment, Insurance Coverage: All-inclusive fees:

  2-week session: $3200 single, $2600 per person, double occupancy $2900 bi-level accommodation

  4-week session: $5500 single, $4100 per person double occupancy, $4800 bi-level accommodation

No additional fees to pay for services, activities, taxes, or gratuities. Payment is accepted in cash or by personal check, travelers' checks, MasterCard, or Visa. Tuition may be tax-deductible under "Health Institute Fees" if you are referred by your personal physician for treatment of hypertension or other weight-related problems. If medical care or special evaluation is necessary, referral will be made by GMFR's staff physician. Health insurance forms consistent with eligibility will be completed with the assistance of the GMFR staff.

Follow-up Assistance: Six newsletters are sent annually to alumnae with news of GMFR and its clients and helpful suggestions for building health goals into your environment, menu planning, recipes, handling stress, and maintaining exercise routines. GMFR body-conditioning and relaxation tapes are available. An exercise videocassette is anticipated by pub date.

⤳ Hilton Head Health Institute ⤳
South Carolina

The programs and activities of Hilton Head Health Institute promote improved physical and mental fitness—plus a reduction of weight-related medical risk factors such as high blood pressure, high blood cholesterol, and diabetes—through structured group seminars monitored by a team of health professionals and by individual consultations in a supportive environment. A maximum of 40 participants (accompanied, if they wish, by their spouses and/or friends) enroll either in HHHI's 12- or 26-day *Health and Weight Control Program* to learn basic skills of behavior modification and methods of self-management to maintain a healthy lifestyle and cardiovascular fitness. Participants familiarize themselves with the low-fat, low-calorie food regimen for weight reduction and weight maintenance. The diet is designed "not merely to help you lose weight, but also to enable you to change your body chemistry so that weight control becomes easier."

Hilton Head Island, connected to the mainland of South Carolina by a double-span bridge with an entrance close to Bluffton, is shaped like a high-topped tennis shoe, with its sole in the Atlantic, its toe pointed south. About 12 miles long and 5 miles wide, the island is a planned resort area well known for the annual tournaments at Harbour Town Golf Links, Sea Pines Plantation; the 605-acre Sea Pines Forest Preserve (alligators, wading birds, bobcats, raccoons, cormorants, pelicans, interesting flora including palmetto palms); and 12 miles of gently sloping beach. Savannah, Georgia, is 1 hour's drive away; Charleston, South Carolina, 2 hours.

The Hilton Head Health Institute is located in Shipyard Plantation in the ball of the island's foot, with access to Shipyard Racquet Club's tennis courts, 27-hole golf course, and lagoons for rod fishing/angling. Participants have use of 20 of Shipyard Plantation's 100 condo single- and double-story 2- and 3-bedroom cottages. Country-style, tin-roofed, silvery-gray the color of Spanish moss, the cottages have wooden latticed-screen front and back porches and latticed crawl spaces beneath the porches and bear a resemblance to Cape Cod cottages. But once you get inside, the ambience is corporate executive, reproduction-traditional in a clean-as-a-whistle, shipshape arrangement, crisp, functional, and comfortable. Accommodations may be private or shared. They're a mile from the hard-packed sand of a wide stretch of Atlantic beach that's fun to bicycle to and on, ideal for wonderful walks.

Most of the participants in the program are married and between 35 and 55 years of age, although ages range from 18 to 85. The majority need to lose 40 pounds or more and frequently have health problems related to obesity. Many less seriously overweight people also attend. Couples are encouraged to attend together. For an additional charge, you can rent an extra bedroom or cottage to accommodate your children, who are accepted as long as a suitable caretaker accompanies them, or rent space for a friend or friends.

Name: Hilton Head Health Institute

Mailing Address: P.O. Box 7138, Hilton Head Island, South Carolina 29938-7138

Telephone: (803) 785-7292; (800) 292-2440

Established: 1977

Program Directors: Peter M. Miller, Ph.D., Executive Director; Howard J. Rankin, Ph.D., Clinical Director; Robert P. Wright, M.A.T., Operations Director; Anne Vieira, Office Manager

Owner: Peter M. Miller

Number of Full Time Health Professionals on Staff: 4

Accreditation of Professional Staff Members: Roger Sargent, Ph.D. (Biology and Nutrition), Nutritional Consultant; Howard J. Rankin, Ph.D. (Clinical Psychology), Clinical Director; Robert P. Wright, M.A.T. (Health Education), Operations Director; Hunter Goss, B.S. (Physical Education), Fitness Coordinator

Gender and Age Restrictions: Co-ed; minimum age 18

Season: Year-round except for 2 weeks at Christmas

Length of Stay Required: 12 days for the *Executive Stamina Program;* 26 days for the *Health and Weight Control Program.* Arrival time Sunday between 3:00 and 5:00 PM.

Programs Offered: The 12- and 26-day *Health and Weight Control Programs* start with a medical evaluation that includes a physical examination, laboratory tests, and an exercise stress test. You meet with a physician, a psychologist, and a health educator to establish individual medical, behavioral, nutritional, and physical fitness goals. Individual progress is carefully monitored throughout the program. You attend workshops and seminars on weight control and metabolism, health promotion and disease prevention, nutrition, physical fitness, stress and time management, and craving control. You also take part in a closely supervised exercise program that comprises aerobic walks, low-impact aerobics, weight training, and calisthenics. Behavior modification training is provided to change health-threatening habits such as smoking, a sedentary lifestyle, overconsumption of unhealthful foods, and excessive reliance on alcohol and certain medications. You receive instruction in stress management and relaxation techniques to help with stress-related problems such as lack of energy, insomnia, moodiness, inability to concentrate, erratic and/or binge eating, and excessive smoking and/or drinking.

The 12-day program offers a basic introduction to the program and provides over 45 hours of instruction on the above-mentioned topics.

The 26-day program provides additional instruction and information to help break old habits, lose more weight, develop and practice new routines, reduce cholesterol levels, lower blood pressure, become a better self-manager, and relax.

Participants in the *Health and Weight Control Program,* which focuses on nutrition education, physical activity, and behavior modification, receive a medical screening that includes a physical examination, a review of your medical history, laboratory tests (including thyroid and lipid profiles), and either a regular electrocardiogram or an exercise stress test. The results of the test are discussed with a physician. Initial and follow-up consultations plus group sessions are also scheduled with the health educator and the fitness instructors to help define individual goals for exercise, nutrition, and behavioral change.

In their 26-day stay, participants are provided with 44 hours of instructor-led exercise classes—warm-ups, stretching, mind-body coordination, calisthenics, aerobic exercise; 10 hours of nutrition discussions and demonstrations, from food measurement to herbal cookery; 21 hours of seminars, teaching, and workshops in behavior modification and stress management, for a total of 75 hours of teaching and practical experience provided within a daily routine of meals, exercises, and classes to change destructive eating habits. Specialized behavioral training is offered for bulimics and persons who want to stop smoking.

Maximum Number of Participants: 40 participants is the maximum, but there is no limit to the number of accompanying but nonparticipating spouses, friends, and children as long as caretakers for the children are provided and accommodations are available; and additional fees for extra persons are paid.

Diet and Weight Management: Thomas P. Miller, trained in nutritional cooking at the Culinary Institute of America in Hyde Park, New York, has been head chef at the institute since 1983. The Hilton Head Metabolism Diet, described with recipes in Dr. Peter Miller's book of the same name, is rich in complex carbohydrates (vegetables, fruits, cereals, grains, legumes, and tubers) and dietary fiber and low in fat, sodium, and cholesterol. Three regular meals a day are served at the institute's dining room. Although your cottage accommodations are equipped with kitchens, these are primarily for your "metabo-meals" and for the convenience and use of spouses and friends. The metabo-meal, to be eaten either in the afternoon or in the evening, may consist of banana bread, oat-bran muffins, popcorn, or a variety of seasonal fruit.

The diet consists of two phases: (1) Monday through Friday, 800 calories a day; (2) Saturday and Sunday, 1100 calories a day. Guidelines for gradually increasing calories to maintenance levels are provided. If needed, your caloric intake can be raised. The emphasis is on simple, low-calorie foods such as berries, lettuce, melon, skim milk, bananas, cereal, and pasta. Fish, Rock Cornish hen and other poultry, and lean meats like veal are included. Low-fat versions of mayonnaise, margarine, yogurt, and cheese are utilized. Only caffeine-free beverages are provided, but caffeine-containing drinks are sanctioned if you want to buy them for personal consumption. Kosher and vegetarian (strict or lacto-ovo) diets are not provided.

The Institute's diet plans conform to guidelines of the American Heart Association and the American Diabetes Association. You are taught the principles of healthful eating in small group seminars. You also learn how to prepare nutritionally prudent meals.

A typical daily 800-calorie menu is a breakfast of ¾ cup of cereal low in sugar content with ½ cup skim milk; ½ piece of orange, banana, pear, apple, grapefruit, or peach; and coffee or tea with sugar substitute and a dash of skim milk if desired. Lunch might be a whole tomato stuffed with chicken salad. Dinner, 6 to 8 ounces of broiled fish or shrimp, 1 medium ear of corn on the cob, a small tossed salad with 2 tablespoons of diet dressing, and a whole peach sliced and topped with 1 ounce of plain or vanilla yogurt. Plus a metabo-meal of 6 raw carrot sticks, 6 celery sticks, 6 radishes, and 6 cauliflower florettes with vegetable dip. On 1100-calorie fare, the extra calories are made up of additional complex carbohydrates such as vegetables, pasta, and cereals.

Exercise and Physical Therapy Facilities: The Institute has a heated, semienclosed outdoor swimming pool (kickboards provided) and a gym equipped with stationary bicycles, treadmills, rowing machine, rebounder, and Nautilus-type weight machine. A sauna is also available. Arrangements for off-site massages can be made. Three 20-minute "thermal" walks—so called because they are scheduled after each meal to burn up calories—are scheduled daily, as are a 45- to 60-minute period of low-impact aerobics and walking, and a 45-minute exercise period for calisthenics or a workout with hand weights.

Opportunities for Recreational Exercise: During your free time, you are encouraged to exercise in whatever ways seem most agreeable to you. The Institute has 2 dozen rental bicycles (wide-seated, with coaster brakes, no gears, high handle bars). You can pedal on 13 miles of bike trails, or to the beach a mile away where you can bicycle on the hard-packed sand, or to many shops within a mile. You can walk, hike, or jog along nature trails through pine and live oaks, bird-watch in 3 nature preserves, hire a suitable horse from one of the 3 excellent equestrian centers on the island, water-ski, windsurf, fish in a nearby lagoon or avail yourself of the charter fishing fleet (rental equipment also available), rent a sailboat, take a sight-seeing or sunset cruise, paddle a canoe, or just stroll around Windmill Harbor to ogle the nautical neighborhood and unique lock system designed to operate like that of the Panama Canal, or go through the lock by rental charter. Box lunches can be provided by the Institute for picnickers. You can bowl strikes and spares at the commercial bowling alley or score birdies at the Shipyard's 27-hole golf course, where the greens fees and golf cart rental are $50 from March to May, $45 in summer and winter months, and both lessons and rental clubs are available. There are 14 clay courts (8 lighted for night play), and 6 hard-surface courts at the Shipyard Racquet Club (rental rackets available) and 2 racquetball courts at the institute (racquets and balls provided).

Beauty Treatments and Welcome Indulgences: Off-site hairdressing salons and barbershops also offer facials, manicures, pedicures, and a variety of other services. Most participants find the facilities at the nearby Marriott's Hilton Head Resort Hotel convenient and satisfactory.

Accommodations: A score of one- or two-story, 2-bedroom or 3-bedroom, uniformly furnished condominium cottages are provided with maid service once a week, or more often at an additional charge. Each unit has a fully equipped kitchen, including dishwasher, washing machine and drier, dining area seating 4 to 6 persons, and living room attractively furnished with sofa, wing chairs, a coffee table, sofa end tables for lamps, dining area chairs, television set (VCR hookup is possible), and telephone. The decor is usually in tones of brown, peach, or blue. Bedrooms are furnished with bed, bureau, nightstand, lamp, and chair. You either share a cottage with one or two other guests, with each of you enjoying your own private bedroom and bathroom (with bathtub and shower) or take an entire cottage at additional cost. All cottages are air-conditioned and have pleasant front and back porches with woods, lagoon, and golf course views.

What to Bring: See USEFUL INFORMATION. Bring bathing suit(s) and cover-ups. Bring a lightweight raincoat, warm sweaters for evening beach walks, dressier clothing for optional excursions to Charleston, Savannah, or for local theater performances. The atmosphere at HHHI is casual and informal. Shorts and T-shirts are fine for summertime, sweatsuits for cooler months. You are asked to bring an alarm clock or clock radio, a flashlight for winter months, postage stamps and writing paper for your personal correspondence, a spiral notebook for class notes, a supply of pens or pencils for writing notes, reading material for your own pleasure, and a watch with a sweep second hand as an exercise timer. You can bring your Walkman and portable radio, TV, or cassette player. There is no activewear shop at the Institute. Newspapers, magazines, sundries, stationery, athletic shoes, sportswear, and sunglasses are all available at Wexford Village and shopping centers within a mile-and-a-half bicycling or walking distance.

Documentation from Your Physician: Requested but not required. All participants undergo medical screening upon arrival.

The Use of Alcohol and Tobacco: Alcoholic beverages are not allowed. No smoking is permitted on the institute's premises. Smoking is allowed outside and in your room.

Fees, Method of Payment, Insurance Coverage: Year-round rates:

For 26-day *Health and Weight Control Program:* $4200

For 12-day Health and Weight Control Program $2700

These fees include a private bedroom and bath in a shared villa, all meals, a medical screening, a supervised exercise program, lectures, and professional consultation.

Accompanying spouses and friends are responsible for their own food supplies and are *not* invited to share meals with participants in the Institute's dining room. Rates are higher for private cottages. All prices are subject to change. Gratuities for the kitchen staff and maids are gratefully received but are not obligatory. Personal checks, travelers' checks, and cash are accepted but not credit cards. Ask about the cancellation policy. Since the program is medically supervised, fees are often covered by health insurance upon recommendation of the client's physician.

Follow-up Assistance: These include optional purchases of video teaching tapes, cassettes, six books on health and lifestyle change including *The Hilton Head Metabolism Diet,* by Dr. Miller, pedometers and weights for at-home use, as well as complimentary compilations of the institute's favored recipes, such as Fish Parmesan and Crab Sauce. All participants receive a quarterly newsletter, and individual follow-up letters are also sent at 1-, 3-, 6-, 9-, and 12-month intervals. As a by-product of the Institute's programs, seminars are offered to associations, corporations, and organizations throughout the United States as well as to conference groups meeting on Hilton Head Island. The seminars, which can range from an hour to 3 days, encompass such topics as health, fitness, stress, and time management. To forestall backsliding and to consolidate habit changes, 7-day and 14-day refresher or "graduate" courses are offered at a reduced rate every month.

✑ Pritikin Longevity Centers ✑
California, Pennsylvania, Florida

Nathan Pritikin, the eponymous founder of the Pritikin Longevity Centers, tried hard to change the eating habits of Americans. The *esprit de corps* that exists among Pritikin graduates is as remarkable as that of networking members of Alcoholics Anonymous. The ambience at Pritikin Longevity Centers is an inspiring mix, part evangelical revival meeting, part out-of-town business conference, casual, clubby, sympathetic, supportive.

About two-thirds of all Pritikin participants are men, but since they are urged to bring their wives or companions to participate in learning and share the programs with them, your first impression is that program groups are divided equally between men and women. There is a strong sense of people united with singular determination in a single cause. Their enthusiasm is long-lived. More than 50 percent of the participants have more than 10 pounds to lose. Some have as many as 200 pounds to lose. Although you'll find participants in their 20s and 80s, the average age range is between 35 and 55. Many graduates claim that Pritikin saved their lives, made heart surgery unnecessary, rid them of health problems, and greatly relieved their diabetes, hypertension, heart disease, obesity.

The Pritikin Center at Santa Monica, California, was the first founded and is the center where the program is least tinged by extramural influence. The Pritikin Center at Downingtown, Pennsylvania, deep in the heart of a former Quaker stronghold, now shares its sleeping quarters with Mickey Rooney's Tabas Hotel and offers aqua-aerobics in both indoor and outdoor pools. Many participants welcome this as a respite from all the indoor treadmill, rowing machine, and stationary bicycle exercise that is the major athletic pursuit at the Santa Monica facility, where the Pacific is to look at but not to swim in. At both sites, you will find first-rate medical facilities, well-trained health professionals, and the regimen of diet and exercise created by founder Nathan Pritikin religiously observed. The licensed Pritikin Center in Florida, now based in Miami, offers the same regimen of diet and exercise, monitored by a fine medical staff aided by other health professionals, but its administrative staff has yet to acquire the reputation for a high degree of efficiency and service that is maintained by its parent centers in Santa Monica and Downingtown.

Your orientation tour at the Santa Monica Center may remind you of your first day at college or boarding school. Your room, of course, is considerably more luxurious now than it was then, but the instructional atmosphere is pervasive. The proximity of the ocean beach for walking at both the Santa Monica Center and the Miami Center seems to decrease the desire of most

Pritikin participants to seek further diversions, but at the Santa Monica Center you can find rental shops for bicycles and roller skates, visit Marina del Rey, America's largest small-craft harbor, or hike and picnic in the Santa Monica Mountains. The Los Angeles Museum of Contemporary Art and the Los Angeles County Museum of Art are a taxi ride away.

At the Downington Center, in farmland country, you can hop into the center's van and drive off to Chadd's Ford to the Brandywine River Museum, which houses a splendid collection of paintings by Andrew and Jamie Wyeth, and end the afternoon at Longwood Gardens. Some participants prefer to head for Atlantic City for a fling in the casinos where they can virtuously maintain their eating regimens at The Sands, The Golden Nugget, Bally's, and Harrah's, all of which serve Pritikin fare in their dining rooms. After a talk and film show about Amish and Mennonite history, usually shown at the center on the first Thursday of every month, you may be interested in touring Amish country on your own to see the legendary enclaves of Blue Balls, Intercourse, and Paradise, as well as displays of scissor-cut artwork, covered bridges, and hex signs painted on big red barns. By far the most popular excursion, however, is to the neighboring King of Prussia Court Plaza, America's largest shopping mall. If your wallet and foot-soles aren't totally exhausted by hours of aerobic shopping, you can press on to Reading, where manufacturers' discount warehouses abound.

Name: Pritikin Longevity Centers

Mailing Address: 1910 Ocean Front Walk, Santa Monica, California 90405; 975 East Lincoln Highway, Downingtown, Pennsylvania 19335; another center, at the Flamingo Hotel, authorized to use the Pritikin regimen, is located at 5875 Collins Avenue, Miami Beach, Florida 33140

Telephone: California center: (213) 450-5433, (800) 421-9911 outside CA, (800) 421-0981 within CA; Pennsylvania center: (215) 873-0123, (800) 344-8243 outside PA, (800) 342-2080 within PA; Florida center: (305) 866-2237 (center), (305) 865-8645 (hotel), (800) 327-4914

Established: 1976 in California; 1982 in Pennsylvania

Executive Directors: Amy Fates, California; Lawrence Berman, Pennsylvania

Program Directors: John Hall, California; Steve Billone, Pennsylvania

Owner: Corporately owned, principally by members of the Pritikin family, widow Ilene and sons Robert and Kenneth

Number of Full-Time Health Professionals on Staff: 40 at Santa Monica plus 15 part-time; 15 at Downingtown plus 4 part-time

Accreditation of Professional Staff Members: Monroe B. Rosenthal, M.D., Medical Director, Internal Medicine/Endocrinology and Diabetes; Fred Weisman, M.D., Internal Medicine; Tom Anderson, Ed.D. (Physical Education), Director of Exercise. The Research Foundation is headed by R. James Barnard, Ph.D., research cardiologist, professor in the departments of Kinesiology and

Medicine and Surgery of the University of California at Los Angeles.

The Pritikin Centers in Pennsylvania and in Florida each have 15 health professionals with similar qualifications and accreditation. In Pennsylvania, John Tumola, M.D., Cardiology, is the Medical Director.

In Florida, Robert Bauer, M.D., and David E. Lehr, M.D., are senior staff physicians.

Gender and Age Restrictions: Co-ed; minimum age 16

Season: Year-round

Length of Stay Required: 7, 13 or 26 days

Programs Offered: Healthy people who want to lose weight can enroll in either the 13-day or 26-day program. Overweight people with advanced health problems, such as heart disease or diabetes, are eligible only for enrollment in the 26-day day program in order "to receive the complete medical supervision needed for their health condition." Everyone is encouraged to bring along a companion or a spouse. The programs, highly structured and challenging, are among the world's most expensive. Their primary focus is to "help restore to normal function those who suffer from symptoms, pain, or disability from degenerative diseases, atherosclerosis (hardening of the arteries), angina, claudication (leg circulation problems), stroke, diabetes, obesity, arthritis, gout."

The program revolves around the Pritikin diet, exercise, and an intense educational program about nutrition and stress management as a way to a new, healthy life.

For people with mild weight problems, mild diabetes (on oral medication only), or hypertension, or for people who are basically healthy and simply want a solid education in the Pritikin lifestyle or optimum care by a personal physician, there are two 13-day programs: the *Cardiovascular Exercise Evaluation Program* (CEEP), and the *Comprehensive Medical Management Program* (CMMP). The CEEP includes a risk factor evaluation history and physical examination; 2 physician visits; 2 blood chemistry panels, including cholesterol and triglyceride levels; and a treadmill exercise tolerance test to determine the safest and most effective program for your heart and to assign you to a group exercise class in which your classmates will have the same endurance level you have. The CMMP includes a physician's review of medical records; 3 physician's visits; 2 blood chemistry panels, including your cholesterol and triglyceride levels; an exercise tolerance test and exercise prescription; and a physician-supervised therapeutic exercise class. Additional medical services requested or required are extra. These programs are implemented with a nutrition education program, daily cooking school classes and demonstrations, stress management workshops, and daily exercise classes.

The instructional material designed to help you with your lifestyle changes ranges from prevention and control of high blood pressure to relaxation training to composition of foods to control of out-of-control eating habits to a plan of action for continuing good health habits at home. In addition to the educational courses, you can also audit practical and helpful group or individual counseling sessions about stopping smoking, controlling compulsive overeating, and cutting down on alcohol.

With the development and advent of nationwide Centers for the Pritikin Learning Experience—nonresidential centers open during the day and in the evening where you can check in for a month's course of similar educational programs—Pritikin grads can take a refresher course, and those who can't afford the residential Pritikin programs can receive solid knowledge of nutrition and its relationship to the human body as well as everything they want to know about their bodies, cholesterol, exercise, fitness, and all aspects of good health. Centers are open in Arizona, California, Colorado, New York, and Texas, and more are planned by publication date.

Maximum Number of Participants: 150 at the Santa Monica facility; approximately 60 at Downingtown; approximately 72 at Miami

Diet and Weight Management: The Pritikin diet is about 80 percent complex carbohydrates—fresh fruits, fresh vegetables, whole grains—7 to 8 percent fat, and 12 to 13 percent protein. At least twice a week, lean animal protein—chicken, turkey, or fish—is served in small portions (a generous garnish would be a positive way of describing them), and moderate amounts of skim milk are served or used in food preparation. When your triglyceride and cholesterol levels have stabilized at acceptable levels, your maintenance diet shifts to 75 percent complex carbohydrates, 15 percent protein, and 10 percent fat. Cholesterol intake is kept at 100 mg or less per day. No salt, no sugar, no caffeine, no alcohol.

Thousands of participants in the program attest to the miraculous and lifesaving virtues of the diet; others claim it is impossible to follow, monotonous, tasteless, boring, and fanatical. Participants seldom voice complaints about feeling hungry on this regimen, however. Many people easily adjust to the food served, which is listed on the menu with its correlating Pritikin cookbook page, number of calories, and equivalent exchanges in complex carbohydrates, vegetables, dairy products, fruit, and animal protein, as a method for keeping to your prescribed caloric allotment.

There are classes designed for permanent weight control that change your attitude about diets and about all the food you didn't think you could live without. Steak? Who wants to eat a dead animal? Cheesecake? A mound of disgusting fat that can clog your arteries, yuck! You are shown in the demonstration kitchen how to make fast, simple Pritikin meals, and can practice cooking and preparation during the daily cooking lessons. By the end of the program, you will have learned from cooking classes and lectures, and unlimited consultations with registered dietitians if you wish, how to adapt any recipe to Pritikin, how to shop in grocery and health food stores, quick and easy ways to cook vegetables, how to cook one morning for the entire week, how to snack nutritiously, how to order a healthful breakfast in a coffee shop, fast-food Pritikin style, how to take Pritikin to the office—brown-bagging your lunch or eating out, entertaining à la Pritikin, how to order Pritikin-style at a restaurant, and much else.

Given this age of convenience package foods, one of the former problems with the Pritikin diet was that nearly everything is cooked from scratch. There were a lot of balkers and backsliders. Now, for people who don't have the time or the inclination to prepare and cook many meals, there are, in addition to bottled Pritikin salad dressings and sauces, packaged rice and tinned soups and frozen packaged products of Pritikin Quick Cuisine, new in 1988.

Weight loss is considered a beneficial side effect of the Pritikin program, which promotes a new way of life for most participants. The average weight loss in 26 days is 13 pounds for men, 8 to 12 pounds for women. Within a 6-month period, the majority of clients adhering to the diet and exercise regimen drop an additional 25 to 60 pounds and are said to keep it off. For maximum weight loss, if you have no illnesses and just want to tone up or lose weight safely and sanely, you can supplement your exercise regimen—of stretching and toning warm-ups, walking laps, treadmill walking, jogging or cool-down exercises, yoga classes, exercises for a healthy back—with classes in aerobic dance, muscle conditioning, and other high-endurance classes for high-fitness individuals.

Exercise and Physical Therapy Facilities: In the California center's 5000-square-foot gymnasium, there are Lifecycle, Aire-Dyne, and Tunturi stationary bicycles, treadmills, rowing machines with and without ergometric monitoring, stations for heart rate/EKG monitoring, and telemetry stations to track and visually screen individual heart rates. The center at Downingtown has similar equipment, as does the Florida franchise. There are 2 swimming pools, indoor, and outdoor, both heated, for laps and for aqua-aerobics at the Pennsylvania center; 1 outdoor pool, heated, at the Florida Pritikin Center; no pools at the California center. Body massages are available, moderately priced, at all three facilities.

Opportunities for Recreational Exercise: At all centers, there are opportunities for walks, picnics, and excursions (admission extra), for which Pritikin brown-bag lunches are provided free of charge. Car rentals and taxi service are available. At the Santa Monica facility, you can bicycle on paths parallel to the beach adjacent to the hotel, or roller-skate. At the Miami center, you can play golf and tennis at nearby locations; clubs and rackets can be rented. At the Downingtown center, riding, except in winter, is possible, with a stable located across the road; reasonable rates. There is a 40-lane bowling alley adjacent to the center, with a free pass for a set of 3 games for Pritikin guests; bowling shoes can be rented. Free tennis is available at the 4 indoor, wooden-surfaced courts of the Tabas Hotel whose facility is shared by the Downingtown Pritikin Center, and at 4 outdoor, macadam-surfaced courts; rackets require a refundable deposit, balls are free. Tennis and tennis lessons are available across the way at the Brandywine Inn, where 3 indoor wooden-surfaced courts and 6 outdoor cement-surfaced courts are available nights and weekends; racket and ball rental for a pittance. Also at Brandywine Inn, an 18-hole golf course with clubs and balls for modest rental fees. Mac's Lighted Driving Range across the road from the Tabas Hotel offers day and evening golf practice for a modest fee, and a free bucket of balls to Pritikin guests. Pool swimming at the Miami and Downingtown Centers. Beaches at the Miami and Santa Monica Centers.

Beauty Treatments and Welcome Indulgences: Body massages at reasonable hourly rates offered at all three centers. Hairdressing establishments and beauty salons are within accessible range of all three centers.

Accommodations: Standard hotel accommodations, all rooms with television, air-conditioning, private bathroom, room telephone, and daily maid service. Larger rooms or suites are available. In Miami, the decor is peach, green, and beige. In Santa Monica, the predominating colors are in shades of blue, violet, and beige, with white accents. In Downingtown, the blue and burgundy decor is accented with white furniture. At the Santa Monica center, your sleeping quarters, furnished in a functional contemporary style, are on the fifth and sixth floors of a six-story bracket-shaped hotel building originally constructed in the 1920s. At the Miami center, your sleeping quarters are located in a standard hotel. At Downingtown, the center's sleeping quarters are in their own separate space in Mickey Rooney's Tabas Hotel, reachable through the main hotel lobby, up a flight of stairs. The Hotel, a large, square, four-storied brick building, is furnished in Hollywood-style French Provincial. Standard rooms at Downingtown are furnished with 2 queen-sized beds, suites with a king-sized bed and a bathroom with a shower but no bathtub. Coin-operated laundry machines are available at all three facilities, as well as one-day outside laundry service.

What to Bring: See USEFUL INFORMATION. The Pritikin sports boutiques carry only polo shirts, T-shirts, sweat shirts, sweatsuits, warm-up suits, socks, headbands, and portable Pritikin health-food products (salad dressings, sauces, soups, packaged rice). Dress is warm-up suit-casual at all the centers; sports clothes, shirts, sweaters, whatever is easy, comfortable. Bring bathing suits and beach wear because you won't find any replacements in the sports boutiques. Jackets and ties are optional for men. You are encouraged to bring your Walkman, reading and writing materials, film. Since there are no hairdressing facilities on the premises, women would do well to tuck in a few extra head scarves or turbans. Strongly recommended by the Pritikin staff: bring a watch with a sweep second hand for your exercise classes.

Documentation from Your Physician: A letter of approval is required, as are a medical history and records of a physical examination within the past 4 months. Ask your physician to send the center a copy of your most recent medical examination; copies of any medical tests taken within the past 2 years, particularly those related to your cardiovascular system, such as blood chemistry panels, exercise tolerance tests, and angiogram results. You cannot be accepted into the program until Pritikin physicians have reviewed and approved your medical records. Spouse/companions must also send medical records. All participants need to be ambulatory and able to provide for their own personal needs. If, upon review of your medical records, you are not accepted, Pritikin physicians will telephone you and discuss alternatives, and your $500 to $1000 deposit will be fully refunded. If you are accepted, you will receive a confirmation letter from the Center.

The Use of Alcohol and Tobacco: Neither is permitted in the buildings or in your rooms.

Fees, Method of Payment, Insurance Coverage (Prices slightly lower in Miami and Downingtown facilities):

For *7-day program:* single occupancy, $2967; double occupancy, you pay full price, your spouse/companion pays about $700 without medical services and exercise classes, while sharing your room, eating the same meals, attending all lectures; about $1200 if enrolled in the *Cardiovascular Exercise Evaluation Program;* and 50 percent of the slightly more expensive *Comprehensive Medical Management Program.*

For *13-day program:* single occupancy, $5500; double occupancy, you pay full price, your spouse/companion pays about $1500 without medical services and exercise classes, while sharing your room, eating the same meals, and attending all lectures; about $2500 if enrolled in the *Cardiovascular Exercise Evalua-*

tion Program; and 50 percent of the slightly more expensive *Comprehensive Medical Management Program.*

For *26-day program:* single occupancy, $9000; double occupancy, you pay full price, your companion pays about 50 percent less if enrolled in the program; if your companion wishes only to share your room, eat with you, and attend all lectures, the fee is about 75 percent less.

Rates are higher for deluxe accommodations, and prices may vary with room size and view. All prices are subject to change. Personal checks, travelers' checks, and cash are accepted as payment for fees. Additional small charges, such as bills for laundry sent out, can be paid by credit card. Depending on your diagnosis and your personal insurance carrier, fees may be partially or wholly reimbursable. The medical director and staff will help with medical insurance forms.

Baby-sitting services, summertime only, are available at Downingtown; they urge you not only to bring your spouse and child, but also to bring along your dog or cat to be housed in the excellent kennels nearby.

Follow-up Assistance: Graduate sessions are offered at reduced rates. Every graduate receives a monthly newsletter, *The Center Post,* providing details of group meetings held by alumni and activities at "satellite centers." Video teaching tapes, cassettes for exercise and relaxation, cookbooks, and instructional books are available for sale on the premises. Best-selling titles include *The Pritikin Permanent Weight Loss Manual, The Pritikin Program for Diet and Exercise,* and *The Pritikin Promise,* all by Nathan Pritikin. An alumna or alumnus of Pritikin can call an 800 number to find the nearest support group in her or his area. Holiday refresher programs at considerably reduced fees are offered to alumni/ alumnae at both the Santa Monica and Downingtown facilities.

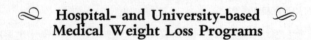 Hospital- and University-based Medical Weight Loss Programs

CENTER FOR NUTRITIONAL RESEARCH,
NEW ENGLAND DEACONESS HOSPITAL

Mailing Address: 110 Francis Street, Suite 1C, Boston, Massachusetts 02215
Telephone: (617) 732-9295
Established: 1973
Program Director: George Blackburn,

M.D., Ph.D.
Owner: CNR Corp.
Gender and Age Restrictions: Co-ed; minimum age 18
Length of Stay Required: The program con-

sists of three phases: evaluation (1–2 weeks), comprehensive treatment (26 weeks), and maintenance (9 months).
Fees: $300 for evaluation phase; $115 per week for comprehensive treatment phase; and $25 per session for maintenance phase.

The Center for Nutritional Research helps you achieve and maintain medically significant weight loss through 5 different diets (liquid and nonliquid), group behavior modification training, and nutrition and exercise counseling.

DIET MANAGEMENT AND EATING DISORDERS PROGRAM OF GEORGETOWN UNIVERSITY

Mailing Address: 3800 Reservoir Road, N.W., Washington, D.C. 20007
Telephone: (202) 687-8128
Established: 1976
Program Director: Aaron Altschul, Ph.D.
Owner: Georgetown University School of Medicine
Gender and Age Restrictions: Co-ed; minimum age 17
Length of Stay Required: Flexible, as determined by client and counselor
Fees: $65 for each counseling session

Clinical psychologists and social workers run individual and group sessions that combine the disciplines of medicine, psychiatry, biochemistry-nutrition, and psychological counseling for the treatment of excess weight, bulimia, and anorexia nervosa.

DIET MODIFICATION CLINIC, BAYLOR COLLEGE OF MEDICINE

Mailing Address: Methodist Hospital, 6550 Fannin, SM 120 3, Houston, Texas 77030
Telephone: (713) 798-4150
Established: 1975
Program Director: Lynne Scott, M.A., R.D./L.D.
Owner: Methodist Hospital and Baylor College of Medicine
Gender and Age Restrictions: Co-ed; ages 17 to 70
Length of Stay Required: 2 hours a week until desired weight loss is reached, then 4 to 6 weeks' attendance during "refeeding program" and requested attendance for a year for weight stabilization and maintenance
Fees: $365 for the orientation-evaluation phase; $240 per month for the therapeutic phase; and $120 per month for the maintenance phase

The Diet Modification Clinic program revolves around a "protein-sparing modified fast" and incorporates medical, nutritional, and psychological components. Weekly nutrition and behavior modification classes are required.

EATING DISORDERS TREATMENT PROGRAM,
C. F. MENNINGER MEMORIAL HOSPITAL

Mailing Address: Box 829, Topeka, Kansas 66601

Telephone: (913) 273-7500, ext. 5310

Established: 1983

Program Director: C. A. Barnhill, M.D.

Owner: C. F. Menninger Memorial Hospital

Gender and Age Restrictions: Co-ed; minimum age 13

Length of Stay Required: 4 weeks, but you may stay longer

Fees: From $100 per day (outpatient) to $500 per day (inpatient)

Inpatient and outpatient programs focus on rapid control of the problem coordinated with psychiatric assessment and treatment to help you examine the issues underlying your symptoms and develop a healthier lifestyle and proper eating habits.

HEART-HEALTH PROMOTION, INC.

Mailing Address: 122 East 64th Street, New York, New York 10021

Telephone: (212) 980-1273, 3960

Established: 1987

Program Directors: S. Robert Levine, M.D., Medical Director; Stephen C. Josephson, Ph.D., Clinical Director

Owners: S. Robert Levine, M.D., and Stephen C. Josephson, Ph.D.

Gender and Age Restrictions: Co-ed; minimum age 18

Length of Stay Required: Nonresidential programs are generally 10 to 12 weeks in duration but are flexible according to need and goals.

Fees: Because programs are individualized, fees vary depending on services rendered.

Heart-Health Promotion (HHP) is a biobehavioral approach to healthy lifestyle management including control of cardiovascular risk factors (smoking, high cholesterol, hypertension), weight control, and stress and anxiety reduction. Treatment includes individual and/or group counseling, biofeedback and relaxation training, hypnosis, and programmed exercise.

METABOLIC NUTRITION PROGRAM

Mailing Address: 77 Scripps Drive, Suite 100, Sacramento, California 95825

Telephone: (916) 922-3438

Established: 1984

Program Director: William G. Cushard, Jr.,

M.D.

Owner: William G. Cushard, Jr., M.D.

Gender and Age Restrictions: Co-ed; minimum age 18

Length of Stay Required: Program operates

in 4-week cycles; participation continues until goal weight achieved

Fees: $185 for initial exam; $450 for the diet portion of each 4-week cycle; $330

for 8 weeks of the weight management phase; and $360 for 6 months of the maintenance phase

The Metabolic Nutrition Program uses a liquid-formula diet and group behavior therapy sessions to help clients lose weight rapidly and avoid weight regain.

THE METHODIST HOSPITAL WEIGHT CONTROL PROGRAM
(SID W. RICHARDSON INSTITUTE FOR PREVENTIVE MEDICINE)

Mailing Address: 6565 Fannin, MS S 400 Houston, Texas 77030

Telephone: (713) 790-6450, 790-3000

Established: 1977

Program Director: Molly Gee, M.Ed., R.D.

Owner: The Methodist Hospital

Gender and Age Restrictions: Co-ed; minimum age 17

Length of Stay Required: 8 weeks minimum

Fees: $320 for *Weight Control Program;* $85 for *Exercise Component*

The *Weight Control Program* and *Weight Control-Exercise Program* teach you to lose weight by following a flexible, well-balanced, calorically restricted "food exchange system" and by modifying inappropriate eating habits through group therapy. The length of the program is determined by the needs of the client.

OBESITY PROGRAM, NUTRITION CLINIC,
UNIVERSITY OF ALABAMA AT BIRMINGHAM

Mailing Address: Department of Nutrition Sciences, University of Alabama at Birmingham, University Station, Birmingham, Alabama 35294

Telephone: (205) 934-5112

Established: 1976

Program Director: Roland L. Weinsier, M.D., Dr. P.H.

Owner: University of Alabama at Birmingham

Gender and Age Restrictions: Co-ed; minimum age 16

Length of Stay Required: 16 visits over a 22-week period, followed by individualized scheduling

Fees: $27 for preliminary visit; $595 for 16 visits

The Obesity Program emphasizes the Time-Calorie Displacement (TCD) approach: an increased intake of high-fiber and other calorically dilute foods that provide for total nutritional needs without supplementation, complemented by nutrition education and counseling, physical activity training, behavior modification, and psychological support.

PHYSICIANS' WEIGHT REDUCTION CENTER

Mailing Address: 2001 Santa Monica Boulevard, Suite 380 West, Santa Monica, California 90404 (Programs are operated at three additional locations in the Greater Los Angeles area.)
Telephone Number: (213) 829-0221
Established: 1978
Program Director: Morton H. Maxwell, M.D.
Owner: Western Institute for Health

Maintenance
Gender and Age Restrictions: Co-ed; ages 16 to 70
Length of Stay Required: Dependent on amount of desired weight loss
Fees: $110 for medical evaluation; $290 every 4 weeks for weight loss phase; and $290 per 6 months for maintenance phase

The Physicians' Weight Reduction Center uses a variety of liquid diet formulas and nutrition education/behavior modification classes to tailor the weight management program to the individual. Classes are didactic and empirical in nature rather than psychologically oriented. The program is highly structured and demanding.

SCHOOL FOR WEIGHT MANAGEMENT, FITNESS INSTITUTE, LDS HOSPITAL

Mailing Address: 325 Eighth Avenue and C Street, Salt Lake City, Utah 84143
Telephone: (801) 321-1396
Established: 1975
Program Director: Timothy Butler, M.S., C.E.S.
Owner: Intermountain Health Care

Gender and Age Restrictions: Co-ed; 18 and over
Length of Stay Required: Flexible, depending on individual needs. Average participation is 6 months.
Fees: $198 for 18 weeks of weekly weight management classes.

The School for Weight Management offers a long-term approach to lifestyle modification that helps develop the self-management skills required to regulate eating and exercise habits. You receive group training in nutrition and stress management, physical fitness, communication skills, and techniques to enhance your self-image.

UNIVERSITY OF MINNESOTA PROGRAM IN WEIGHT MANAGEMENT AND RESEARCH

Mailing Address: Box 291, University of Minnesota Hospital and Clinic, East River Road, Minneapolis, Minnesota 55455

Telephone: (612) 624-6468
Program Director: Katherine Williams, R.N.
Owner: University of Minnesota

Gender and Age Restrictions: Co–ed; ages 18 to 65
Length of Stay Required: Dependent on amount of desired weight loss
Fees: $275 monthly

The program comprises a protein-sparing modified fast, behavioral modification, nutrition evaluation and education, exercise instruction, and fitness monitoring. A cost-free, 52-week maintenance plan follows the program.

WEIGHT CONTROL UNIT, OBESITY RESEARCH CENTER, ST. LUKE'S–ROOSEVELT HOSPITAL CENTER

Mailing Address: 411 West 114th Street, Suite 3D, New York, New York 10025
Telephone: (212) 523-3570
Established: 1977
Program Director: Steven B. Heymsfield, M.D.
Owner: St. Luke's-Roosevelt Hospital Center
Gender and Age Restrictions: Co–ed; minimum age 18
Length of Stay Required: Evaluation phase, 4 weeks; treatment phase, 12 to 20 weeks; advanced treatment phase on a monthly basis
Fees: $525 for the evaluation phase including physical examination and $180 per month for the treatment phase. Prices for the advanced treatment phase depend on the number and type of therapy chosen.

The major emphasis of the Weight Control Unit program is to help you acquire self-awareness and learn how to control eating behavior through group behavioral therapy. The program focuses on food management rather than food avoidance.

WEIGHT MANAGEMENT PROGRAM, DEPARTMENT OF FOOD & NUTRITIONAL SERVICES, YALE NEW HAVEN HOSPITAL

Mailing Address: 20 York Street, DCB, New Haven, Connecticut 06504
Telephone: (203) 785-2422
Established: 1985
Program Director: Michele Fairchild, M.A., R.D.
Owner: Yale New Haven Hospital, Food and Nutritional Services
Gender and Age Restrictions: Co–ed; minimum age 21
Length of Stay Required: Weekly visits for 10 weeks
Fees: $175 for 10 weeks

The Weight Management Program emphasizes the use of a nutritionally adequate calorie-reduced diet (a "food exchange system") together with increased exercise and group therapy to induce weight loss at a prudent rate (1 or 2 pounds a week).

WEIGHT REDUCTION PROGRAM, OBESITY RESEARCH GROUP, UNIVERSITY OF PENNSYLVANIA

Mailing Address: 133 South 36th Street, Suite 507, Philadelphia, Pennsylvania 19104

Telephone: (215) 898-7314

Established: 1957

Program Directors: Albert J. Stunkard, M.D., Director; Thomas A. Wadden, Ph.D., Clinical Director; Kelly D. Brownell, Ph.D., Research Director

Owner: University of Pennsylvania

Gender and Age Restrictions: Co-ed; ages 21 to 65

Length of Stay Required: Most treatment is weekly for 26 weeks, with a one-year monthly follow-up

Fees: $200 for initial evaluation, plus $25 per weekly group session during the treatment stage and $25 per weekly group session during maintenance stage

The Weight Reduction Program, which accepts you only if you can be treated in connection with a research project, helps you lose weight and resolve the psychological problems that accompany a weight problem through group treatment. The treatment includes nutrition education, behavior therapy, and exercise counseling.

National
Weight
Loss Programs

Since about 60 million men and women in the US think of themselves as overweight, 45 percent of the adult population are potential targets for products and services related to weight control. This has given rise to a large and, for the most part, unregulated weight control industry.

The continued ability of national weight control programs to maintain a constituency suggests that they fill a genuine need. Large national programs have the advantage of being able to afford the consulting services of highly respected experts in the various fields of medicine, nutrition, and behavioral science related to the treatment of excess weight, which in turn enables them to keep up with advances in therapy and to render responsible treatment.

On the other side of the coin, national programs may be locked into the use of gimmicks that have a marketing rather than a therapeutic value. Quality control is another major concern. As programs continue to be replicated in various parts of the country, whether by franchise or by direct ownership, strong safeguards have to be set up to ensure that the quality of the program is not in any way compromised. Fortunately, most national weight control programs appear to be aware of the need to maintain quality control over their satellites.

Unlike medically directed programs, which are restricted to the treatment of the severely overweight, the nonmedical national programs do not provide medical monitoring and are willing to accept mildly or moderately (as well as severely) overweight participants.

DIET CENTER, INC.

Headquarters Mailing Address: 220 South Second West, Rexburg, Idaho 83440

Telephone: (208) 356-9381; check your local white pages for local number

Established: 1970

Program Directors: Sybil Ferguson, President and Founder; Charlene Moore, M.S., R.D., Executive Nutritionist; Lester J. Petersen, M.D., Medical Director

Owner: American Health Companies, Inc.

Target Clientele: Participants are 25 to 54 years old and need to lose 40 or more pounds

Fees: Based on the number of pounds needed to lose

The Diet Center program is designed "to guide overweight and obese individuals through all necessary stages of weight loss and to teach them how to maintain ideal weight permanently." During the first 2-day conditioning phase, you are put on a 1200- to 1500-calorie diet and take 8 tablets a day of the Diet Center Supplement. During the 6-week reducing phase, you visit a Diet Center 6 days a week for weigh-ins and private counseling for monitoring and motivation reinforcement, and join a group for once-a-week instruction in nutrition, behavior modification, and a screening of Image One, a 10-part video series on nutrition information. The reducing phase is followed by a 3-week stabilization phase (6 weigh-ins and counseling visits and video viewing), during which a wider variety of foods in greater quantities is gradually introduced into the diet, while use of the "supplement" continues. The maintenance phase, up to 52 weeks, includes weekly weigh-ins, counseling visits, and 10 classes on nutrition and behavior modification.

THE HMR COMPLEMENT 100 PROGRAM

Headquarters Mailing Address: Health Management Resources, 59 Temple Place, Suite 704, Boston, Massachusetts 02111-1307

Telephone: (617) 357-9876

Established: 1979

President: Lawrence Stifler, Ph.D.

Owner: Employee-owned

Gender and Age Restrictions: Co-ed; minimum age 18; adolescents accepted at medical discretion

Length of Stay Required: Dependent on amount of weight to be lost

Fees: $42 a week for dietary supplement until weight loss is achieved, plus $65 a week for medical visits and group education; $55 a month for 18-month maintenance phase after weight loss

HMR treats "high-risk" obesity (individuals who are 20 percent or more above ideal weight) with a liquid formula diet, medical tests, and educational-behavioral group treatment.

NUTRI/SYSTEM, INC.

Headquarters Mailing Address: 3901 Commerce Avenue, Willow Grove, Pennsylvania 19090
Telephone: (215) 784-5600
Established: 1971
National Medical Director: Stuart H. Shapiro, M.D.
Owners: A. Donald McCulloch; Reef C. Ivey II, Albert J. Dimarco; John E. Sylvester

Fees: Fees vary from client to client and from center to center. Initial program fees (which rarely exceed $400) depend on how much you want to lose and the length of time you stay in the program. Cost of a week's supply of food packets (all you need with the exception of fresh vegetables and skim milk) is about $50.

In Nutri/System's program, your personal statistics are entered into a computer to determine ideal weight, goal weight, projected weekly weight loss, and projected time estimated to reach goal weight. You fill out a questionnaire that determines your personal obstacles to losing weight, see a nurse, who takes a medical and dieting history and dispenses vitamins and mineral supplements, and buy the first week's allotment of food packages. You then enter the weight-loss phase and return each week to the center for a 30-minute health behavior class, for a nursing visit, to receive vitamin and mineral supplements, and to receive food order forms for food purchases. After weight loss, maintenance visits at weekly intervals continue with nursing appointments and health behavior classes.

Nutri/System's new Flavor Set-Point Weight Loss Program is based on findings suggesting that overweight people have a higher flavor set-point than normal weight individuals. Low-calorie foods designed to be rich in flavor and "flavor enhancers" (spicy, buttery, and sweet) are available.

THE OPTIFAST PROGRAM/SANDOZ NUTRITION CORPORATION

Headquarters Mailing Address: 5320 Twenty-Third Street, Minneapolis, Minnesota 55440
Telephone: (612) 925-2100 (corporate office); (800) 328-5392 (local programs)
Established: 1971
Program Director: James B. Parsons, Executive Director

Owner: Sandoz Nutrition Corporation
Target Clientele: Participants are at least 18 years old and 30 percent, or 50 pounds, over ideal body weight
Fees: $2500 to $3000 for a 26-week program, including 15 weeks supply of diet formula

Individuals who enroll in Optifast programs are likely to be suffering from weight-related health problems such as high blood pressure, diabetes (Type II), or elevated blood cholesterol and/or triglyceride levels. A specially trained physician monitors patient progress.

The program has four phases: During Phase I, which lasts for 12 weeks or more, you take the 420-calorie or the 800-calorie Optifast formula and eat no solid food. Phase II of the program, called "refeeding," involves the gradual re-introduction of solid food over a 6-week period. Phase III is a 7-week weight stabilization period, which prepares you for Phase IV, lifetime maintenance. Throughout all phases of the program, you attend individual and group sessions, which address behavioral control of food intake, nutrition education, and exercise.

OVEREATERS ANONYMOUS

Headquarters Mailing Address: P.O. Box 92870, Los Angeles, California 90009
Telephone: (213) 542-8363 for corporate headquarters and World Service; check your local white pages for local number
Owner: Not-for-profit corporation
Target Clientele: Participants are all ages.
Fees: None. The organization is self-supporting through contributions of local membership. Most local groups "pass the basket" at meetings to cover the cost of the meeting place, reading material, and other expenses. Outside donations are not accepted.

Overeaters Anonymous views compulsive overeating as an addiction, a problem to be treated on physical, emotional, and spiritual levels, an illness that can be arrested but not cured. OA's 12-step program, patterned after that of Alcoholics Anonymous, complements medical care, and its members are referred to their physicians for medical guidance and approval of a food plan. OA urges its members to abstain from *over*-eating, one day at a time, and cautions them that although the program is simple, it isn't easy.

SLIMMING MAGAZINE CLUBS LIMITED

Headquarters Mailing Address: 7 Kendrick Mews, London SW7 3HG, England
Telephone: (01) 225-1711; from the US, 011 44 (1) 225-1711
Established: 1971
Program Directors: Elizabeth Evans, Ph.D., Chief Nutritionist; John Yudkin, Ph.D., Chief Consultant
Owner: Argus Press Holding PLC
Target Clientele: Members, aged 25 to 34, need to lose from 7 pounds upward.
Fees: £4.00 to join; £2.60 per week for attendance

The program consists of weekly group meetings, designed to provide information, inspiration, group support, and motivation for those who wish to lose weight, conducted by thoroughly trained group leaders. The meeting consists of a confidential weigh-in, when encouragement is given to each member, a talk, followed by discussion of weight control issues. The 21 diets available are low in fat and salt, high in dietary fiber, and provide at least 1000 calories a day.

TOPS CLUB, INC.

Headquarters Mailing Address: 4575 South Fifth Street, P.O. Box 07360, Milwaukee, Wisconsin 53207
Telephone: (414) 482-4620
Established: 1948
Director, Obesity and Metabolic Research Programs: Ronald K. Kalkoff, M.D.

Fees: $12 annually for the first 2 years and $10 annually thereafter; 5- to 7-day Getaway Retreats range from $135 to $200

TOPS (Take Off Pounds Sensibly) is a noncommercial, nonprofit international network of support groups that employ group dynamics, competition, and recognition to motivate the overweight to achieve and maintain weight loss.

Members meet weekly in local self-directed chapters, where meetings consist of a weigh-in followed by a program of motivation and positive reinforcement. All TOPS members are told to see their own physicians for weight goals and dietary regimens. Members can follow a manual on nutrition with diets at three calorie levels if their doctors approve.

TOPS offers retreats throughout Canada and the US to provide members with a quiet setting and 5 to 7 days of low-calorie meals in a supportive and nurturing environment at bargain prices.

UNITED WEIGHT CONTROL CORPORATION

Headquarters Mailing Address: 425 West 59th Street, New York, New York 10019
Telephone: (212) 956-8922
Established: 1985
Program Directors: Theodore B. Van Itallie, M.D., Chief Medical Advisor; Dawn Schiffhauer, R.D., Vice President; Jonathon Landow, Associate Corporate Medical Director
Other Sites: Brooklyn, Long Island, New Jersey, and Philadelphia
Owner: United Weight Control Corporation
Target Clientele: Co-ed; minimum age 18
Fees: $250 for initial evaluation; $380 for

4 weekly visits; $50 weekly for formula diet and supplement; $350 for 6 months of maintenance, plus $150 rebate towards next 6 months with 75 percent attendance

The canon of United Weight Control Corporation is quality of weight loss rather than quantity or speed of weight loss. The standard is achieved by individualizing calorie prescriptions to your activity level and body mass index to assure weight loss of at least 75 percent fat and no more than 25 percent of lean body mass. UWCC takes your new body composition into account as weight is lost and changes your diet accordingly every 2 weeks until your desired goal weight is reached. To guard against too rapid weight loss, calories are added to meals if you exceed the prescribed rate of weight loss.

WEIGH TO LIVE SYSTEM

Headquarters Mailing Address: 2311 205th Street, Suite 103, Torrance, California 90501
Telephone: (213) 533-0221, (800) 554-LIVE
Established: 1982
Medical Consultant: George A. Bray, M.D.
President: A.Y. Dahlman, Ph.D.
Target Clientele: Co-ed; minimum age 18
Fees: $125–$150 per week

After examination and analysis of personal problems of excess weight, you are assigned one of three rapid weight loss alternatives: a "protein-sparing" diet, a formula diet, or a choice of menu plans. Vitamins, minerals, and electrolytes necessary for proper nutrition are supplied in supplement form for all alternatives. A liquid formula to aid in weight maintenance and weight management is available as a meal substitute for prescribed use in individual dietary regimens. You participate in a minimum of 16 weekly 90-minute sessions, which are supplemented by ongoing individual monitoring, physician monitoring, and laboratory studies. The program furnishes monthly reports on your progress to your physician, supplies a planning guide, and helps to develop individual exercise regimens based on individual energy requirements.

WEIGHT CONTROL FOR LIFE!

Headquarters Mailing Address: Nunn, Newton & Associates, 4034 First Avenue, San Diego, California 92103
Telephone: (619) 298-9542
Established: 1985
President: R. Gregory Nunn, Ph.D.
Owner: R. Gregory Nunn and Karen S. Newton
Target Clientele: Moderately to significantly overweight men and women who do not have medical problems limiting participation
Fees: $2000 to $3000 for 25 weeks and 18 months for maintenance

The Weight Control for Life! (WCFL!) program integrates behavior change principles, nutrition education, stress management, and physical activity with weight loss induced by adherence to a very-low-calorie formula diet. The program is divided into four phases. During Phase I, Assessment, your medical status is evaluated by a staff physician, and a "personal body assessment" is made. If you have no medical problems limiting participation, you begin Phase II, Weight Loss, during which you attend weekly 2-hour classes and start on a very-low-calorie (VLC) formula diet, which consists of drinking 5 packets a day of the powdered formula. You are evaluated weekly by a medical staff member during this 25-week phase. Solid foods constituting one meal a day may be added to the formula regimen. Phase III, Pre-Maintenance Workshops, consist of self-management workshops that provide practice with menu planning and analysis, portion control, and food/nutrition skills. You are required to attend at least 3 nutrition workshops and 2 self-management workshops before entering Phase IV, Weight Maintenance, a series of classes over a 12- to 18-month period designed to help you maintain your new weight.

WEIGHT NO MORE/AMERICAN INSTITUTE FOR PREVENTIVE MEDICINE

Headquarters Mailing Address: 19111 West 10 Mile Road, Suite 101, Southfield, Michigan 48075

Telephone: (313) 352-7666; (800) 345-2476

Established: 1983

Director: Elaine Frank, R.D., Nutrition Services

Owner and President: Donald R. Powell, Ph.D.

Target Clientele: Participants are 25 to 70 years old and 5 to 75 pounds overweight.

Fees: $160 for one-year membership

The American Institute for Preventive Medicine (AIPM) provides lifestyle, self-help, and communication programs. The Weight No More System (the lifestyle program) is a ten-session course that makes you aware of eating behaviors and helps you cope with the changes necessary to avoid regaining weight. Exercise counseling and training in relaxation techniques are included as part of the behavior therapy component.

The program does not provide food products, and the diets you follow are individually tailored and moderate rather than drastic in their restriction of calories. The program's emphasis is on nutrition education and behavior change rather than on the treatment of obesity-related medical problems.

WEIGHT WATCHERS INTERNATIONAL, INC.

Headquarters Mailing Address: 500 North Broadway, Jericho, New York 11753-2196

Telephone: (516) 939-0400; (800) 333-3000 for chapter near you; (718) 229-1090 in New York

Established: 1963

President: Charles N. Berger

Owner: H. J. Heinz, Inc.

Target Clientele: Participants are 25 to 54 years old with up to 300 pounds to lose.

Fees: Vary slightly from state to state. New York rates: $18 registration, $8 a week thereafter and $7 for seniors (in most areas).

The objective of the Weight Watchers program is to provide overweight individuals with a safe, healthy, and effective weight loss program reinforced by weekly meetings to promote positive attitudes and actions. The recommended food plan conforms to guidelines for cholesterol, fat, and sugar control set forth by the American Heart Association and the American Cancer Society. The recommended exercise plan meets the guidelines for effective weight loss programs established by the American College of Sports Medicine.

After losing weight, you are taught the Weight Watchers maintenance plan for a 6-week period to stabilize your weight, after which you become a lifetime member, which entitles you to free lifetime attendance at meetings as long as you maintain your weight.

Useful
Information

DO YOU HAVE
TOO MUCH BODY FAT?

Because many weight control programs have a "target clientele"—the severely obese, the moderately overweight, or the mildly overweight—you need to know to what degree you're overfat.

Finding out how overfat you are is important for another reason too: your extra fat may be more of a health risk than you realize. Being even moderately overweight increases your risk of developing high blood pressure, diabetes, elevated blood cholesterol levels, gout in men, breast and uterine cancer in women, and premature heart disease, and may shorten your life span.

OVERWEIGHT VERSUS OVERFAT

It's important at this point to clarify the terms "overweight" and "overfat." Overweight simply refers to a body weight for height in excess of some standard, such as the Metropolitan Life Insurance Weight Table we're all so familiar with. But being overweight doesn't necessarily indicate that you're at a higher risk for developing heart disease or other conditions. It's being overfat—having a too high percentage of body fat in relation to lean mass—that constitutes a health risk. And it's not only how much fat you have that's a health factor; where you carry that extra padding counts too. Fat deposited in some body areas—such as the upper abdomen—seems to be more hazardous than fat deposited in hips and thighs.

Body fat, then, is a marker that really counts when it comes to rating your physical condition and assessing your weight goals. That's why many health facilities, spas, and hospital-sponsored diet clinics like to test how much of your weight is made of fat before starting you on a weight control program. You are likely to encounter four body fat tests at a health facility. The two newest, total body electrical conductivity (TOBEC) and bioelectrical impedance analysis (BIA), involve painless "electrical" procedures. With TOBEC, for instance, you simply lie down fully dressed on a stretcherlike tray that is then pulled through a cylindrical electrical coil. The test—which takes about 90 seconds to perform—is based on the principle that lean tissue is more conductive of electrical energy than fat.

Another way to get a body fat reading is with the underwater weight test. The test is simple, but memorable. You crouch on a scale placed at the bottom of a large tank of warm water, duck your head underwater, and exhale all the air in your lungs. At this time your weight is taken. Then, by comparing your underwater weight with your on-land weight, a computer can quickly estimate what your percentage of body fat is.

Some facilities also rely on skin-fold tests. The thickness of the loose skin, usually around your upper arm, is measured using a specially designed caliper. These measurements are then used to calculate percentage of body fat.

You can estimate whether your body fat is too high once you know your body mass index (BMI), a measure that takes into account not only weight but also exact height. Here's an accurate way to figure out your BMI:

1. Find out your weight in kilograms (divide the pounds by 2.2).
2. Obtain your height in meters squared (multiply your height in inches by .0254, then multiply that number by itself).
3. Now simply divide step 1 by step 2, and you have your BMI.

After you have determined your BMI, you can easily identify the category it falls into by using the chart below.

	Body Mass Index
Mild overweight	*25–27.9*
Moderate overweight	*28–31.9*
Severe overweight	*32–41.9*
Morbid obesity	*42–*

AIM FOR FAT LOSS

Since how much body fat you have and its distribution are what really determine whether your extra weight is unhealthy, you should drop "fat" pounds when you begin your weight loss regime. But how will you know if you're losing the right proportion of fat to lean? It's hard to be sure, but if you lose weight too fast—that is, more than 2 to 3.5 pounds a week, unless you're extremely overweight—chances are you'll be depleting too much lean tissue. In other words, your body will start to break down its own muscle and organ tissue in order to meet its energy needs. And that can be harmful, leading to weakness, fatigue, depression, dry skin, brittle nails, hair loss, and a constant feeling of being cold. In extreme cases, it can even make your heart vulnerable to abrupt disturbances of rate and rhythm—upsets that on rare occasions can cause sudden death. If you lose pounds gradually, on the other hand, you'll not only be sure to lose stubborn "fat" pounds, you'll protect yourself from suffering unnecessary health-endangering side effects.

DIETS, DRUGS, & DEVICES:
WHAT WORKS, WHAT DOESN'T

Below is a look at what's known and what isn't, what's considered right and what's considered wrong about all of the currently popular major weight loss methods. Keeping these assessments in mind will help you avoid the gimmicks and find a sane, reliable program for permanent weight loss.

DIETS AND DRUGS

Low-Carbohydrate/High-Protein Diets   These diets are based on the mistaken belief that only calories from carbohydrates are fattening, and they make no provision for the development of sensible eating habits once your weight is lost. In fact, some people crave carbohydrates so intensely after the diet that they not only regain the weight lost but add a few extra pounds besides. In addition, these diets can produce an acid condition in the blood known as ketosis, a state that can cause nausea, malaise, and in extreme cases, severe dehydration. Low-carbohydrate/high-protein regimes can make you susceptible to attacks of gout and leave you perilously shortchanged in a variety of vitamins and minerals. Because these diets are likely to be high in saturated fat and cholesterol, they can raise your blood cholesterol level and may even (if used for prolonged periods) increase the risk of various cancers, particularly colon and breast cancer.

Liquid Formula Diets   Formula diets have some advantages. First, they tend to suppress your hunger, and their monotony rarely tempts you to overindulge. The best ones are both nutritionally well balanced and low in calories, and since they don't require much preparation, they help keep you out of the kitchen and away from the temptation of regular food.

   The disadvantages of long-term use include restrictions on your social life (making it awkward to eat out) and the lack of provision for control over your later intake of regular food. There are risks too, especially for people who self-prescribe these diets, of a variety of unpleasant symptoms and even death.

Still, many weight reduction programs find formula diets effective in helping severely obese patients get started losing weight. A reliable program will stick by your side and include lots of psychological support and nutritional counseling once you start to eat solid foods to make it more likely you don't regain the weight lost on liquids.

Food-combining Diets   These diets are founded on the bizarre theory that eating the right combination of food helps unlock fat from the body. Fruit usually plays a prominent role in these plans. None of these diets have any scientific support, nor is there any scientific evidence indicating that people who lose weight on food-combining regimes keep it off. What's more, diarrhea and dehydration are a risk on these diets, which generally don't provide an adequate range and quantity of essential nutrients. Finally, because you can eat as much as you want of the "right combinations" of food, these diets actually reinforce compulsive, binge eating behavior.

High-Fiber Diet Aids   The term "fiber" refers to a complex mixture of plant materials that can't be broken down by the digestive juices of the human intestinal tract. Fiber-rich foods—whole grains, fruits, and vegetables—tend to be filling, since some fiber constituents absorb water and increase in bulk as they pass through your digestive system; some even seem to reduce slightly the amount of calories you absorb from other foods you eat. A number of over-the-counter fiber products are now being promoted as appetite suppressants. There is little evidence that these commercial products are particularly effective in promoting weight reduction by themselves, but they may be useful in helping you stick to a calorie-reduced diet. If not overeaten, they appear to be harmless.

Near Fasting   Partly to prevent discouragement, regimes of under 600 calories a day are designed to help the severely obese lose a large amount of weight quickly. Long-term diets this spare can be dangerous: careful weekly monitoring of blood chemistry as well as heart function is required, which is why a prolonged near fast should be conducted only under strict medical supervision. It should always include extensive, ongoing diet counseling, behavior modification training, and education to ensure that you learn and maintain good eating habits once the low-calorie diet ends.

Low-Fat Diet, Education, and Exercise Plans   This three-tiered approach is fast becoming the cornerstone of more and more responsible weight control programs and spas. The first element, a low-fat diet, has respectable health credentials. Diets reduced in total fat are likely to lower blood cholesterol levels and may lessen your risk of developing premature coronary heart disease. Since low-fat diets emphasize vegetables and fruits as well as leanly prepared pastas, potatoes, grains, and beans, they're naturally low in calories. On a low-fat diet, you get a larger volume of food for your calories, which helps you feel satisfied and full. The educational element is part nutrition awareness and part behavior therapy. Some major aspects of a behavioral calorie management program are self-monitoring, control of food-related stimuli, portion control, self-image restructuring, and self-reward. The last component is exercise, which is becoming an integral part of more weight control programs.

The positive aspects of this three-tiered approach are many: it's sensibly paced, nutritionally sound, easily adaptable for everyday eating, and flexible for long-term use. The negatives are that it doesn't melt pounds off quickly and that it requires considerable hard work.

Weight Loss Drugs   Treating weight problems with the help of drugs is a controversial practice for three reasons. First, both prescription and over-the-counter appetite suppressants are associated with a wide range of negative side effects. Secondly, abuse of these drugs is believed to be common. Finally, although a few studies suggest that appetite suppressing drugs can increase the rate of weight loss by about ½ pound a week, most of the drugs are not recommended for longer than 3 months maximum. That means the most a drug might do is shake loose 6 extra pounds. And not surprisingly, many people regain those pounds when drug therapy stops.

Still, drug treatment may be justified in a few special circumstances. Obese patients who have become stalled in a weight control program, for example, can sometimes renew their momentum by short-term use of an appetite suppressant.

MECHANICAL AND SURGICAL OPTIONS

The Garren-Edwards Balloon   This device is based on the premise that when your stomach feels full, you eat less. The balloon is inserted through your mouth into your stomach via a long, flexible fiberoptic tube, usually while you're under light sedation. The balloon is then inflated to about 2×3 inches, whereupon it self-seals and starts to float in your upper stomach. The balloon can be left in your stomach for up to 4 months, after which it's punctured and withdrawn by your doctor.

How safe and effective is this balloon? It can inflict harm: some patients treated with the balloon have experienced gastric ulcers, others have suffered from tears in their esophagus, and others have had intestinal blockages (caused by a deflated balloon). There has also been one report of a death. As far as effectiveness is concerned, the preliminary results of several controlled studies showed no benefit of the balloon versus sham insertion. At best, the balloon may help you restrict your caloric intake temporarily, but it's certainly no long-term solution for weight maintenance.

Major Surgery An even more radical approach to weight loss involves operations that reduce the size of your stomach (commonly called "stomach stapling") or that interfere with your digestion and absorption of foods. Because surgery is risky—there's a small chance of death in the postoperative period and a 25 percent chance of acute or chronic complications—surgery is generally reserved for people who are 100 pounds overweight or at least double their desirable body weight, who have failed at serious attempts to lose weight by more conservative means, and whose obesity is causing them grave health and psychosocial problems.

If you think you might qualify for obesity surgery, you should contact an accredited surgeon who specializes in this type of operation and is on the staff of a hospital (usually one affiliated with a medical school) equipped to handle obesity surgery. It's also important to talk to a number of patients who have already undergone such an operation and who have lived with the results for a number of years. That way you'll be sure you're comfortable with the long-term consequences.

Liposuction More along cosmetic lines, this surgical technique is designed to "vacuum out" localized deposits of bulging fat, usually on your arms, thighs, or ankles, under your chin, and over your knees. The surgeon makes incisions less than an inch long near the sites to be vacuumed, inserts a hollow metal rod under the skin, and repeatedly pokes the fat deposits. This manipulation breaks the fatty tissue into small fragments, which are then sucked out. The technique leaves virtually no scar.

The procedure is expensive and the results achieved will not necessarily resemble the pretreatment fantasy. What's more, older women whose skin has lost resilience are not optimal candidates for liposuction (in fact, some surgeons have limited the operation to women under 40). Liposuction is not without its dangers, either. Occasionally, it leads to excessive blood loss, serious infection, and death.

The procedure may be done in a doctor's office or a hospital. Since any doctor is free to perform liposuction, but not all are qualified and experienced in it, be sure to consult an accredited plastic surgeon who has had extensive experience with the method.

ASK QUESTIONS

Because new weight loss methods appear every day, it's important to ask questions, both before you choose a program and whenever you don't fully understand the rationale of a program's prescription. As a general rule, be wary of any plan that stresses one type of food over most others; of those that exclude exercise; of those that promise huge weight losses in a short time (unless you have a very serious weight problem and are working closely with an M.D.); of those that don't seem to have a well-thought-out game plan for maintaining your loss; and of those that bandy about lots of scientifically inappropriate catchwords like enzymes, amino acids, assimilation, and immunology. Unfortunately, anything that claims to require no serious effort on your part is probably a gimmick.

WHAT TO BRING

For directives about clothes to wear in the evening or after class programs, and for all the information about which exercise clothes may be provided and/or special requirements, see the What to Bring section in each spa entry.

Medicinal and Health Items and Grooming/Beauty and Feminine Hygeniene Articles   Stow these in a zippered, waterproof bag and carry them in your hand luggage. Don't forget Band-Aids, tweezers, nail scissors, foil-wrapped towelettes, body lotion, and cosmetics. Be sure also to hand-carry your medical records and the letter from your physician, if required.

Prescriptions   Bring photocopies of all your prescriptions. This is an absolute must if you are traveling outside of the US and need to get the prescription accurately refilled, and as proof sometimes requested by customs inspectors.

Eyewear

- Contact lenses. Consult your doctor about wearing hard or soft lenses for sports activities.
- Sunglasses. Be sure to buy sunglasses with a tag stating how much UV radiation they block (75–90 percent is preferable); and bring a couple of pairs with you. Choose gray, brown, green, or amber lenses to reduce the intensity of light.
- Goggles. If you plan on skiing or swimming, well-fitting goggles reduce the risk of eye problems and are a blessing to have with you.

• Eye protectors. For squash and racquetball, you need shatterproof, wraparound goggles, and shatterproof protectors if you wear glasses. The open kind with an empty frame are not recommended. Regular eyeglasses, even those with "shatterproof" lenses, are no protection. Bicyclists would do well to heed this warning also.

Sun-Block and Sunscreen Products   Don't assume they will be available at your destination; bring plenty with you. Use a sunscreen with the highest possible sun protection factor (SPF), usually 15 or higher.

Insect Repellent   To keep biting insects at bay, insect repellent containing N-diethyl-meta-tolumide ("Deet" for short) in a spray container (not recommended if you wear contacts) or in less bulky squeeze bottles or sticks is a highly recommended packable. Avon's Skin So Soft bath oil, available in a spray pump bottle, is a recommended insect repellent for sensitive skins. To order, call (800) 445-AVON.

Antihistamine/Nasal Decongestant   These are not just for head colds or sniffle fighting, but in case you come across unexpected ragweed, or other allergy-activators.

Adapter Kits   These are necessary for any electrical plug-in gear if you are traveling to spas outside the US. Cordless appliances are a lot more convenient.

Underwear   It's better to wear loose, comfortable underwear that does not chafe or bind and reward yourself with new underwear after you have shed pounds and inches. For exercise, underwear made with Orlon or polypropylene synthetic material is recommended, because these materials wick moisture away from the skin and provide warmth. Ladies, if you're planning on aerobics, exercising, or jogging, a sports bra to minimize bouncing and to provide support and comfort is recommended. The latest in sports bras are colorful tops designed as outerwear but with built-in breast support. These are best-suited to small-breasted women. More voluptuous types would do better with regular sports bras.

Sleepwear   Terry-cloth bathrobes may be bulky to pack, but they are wonderfully practical as bathing suit cover-ups. Rubber thong slippers may double as bedroom slippers and around-the-pool footwear. A lightweight sweatsuit does double duty as practical, convenient, comfortable sleepwear, and can be used in place of a terry robe if your packing room is limited. Some spas provide robes, so check first.

Athletic Footwear

- For walking, shoes should be lightweight and have a rigid shank for support, rubber heels to absorb shock, and extra support around the heel. Classic casual footwear or loafers work as well on level country lanes as they do on sidewalks and cobbled streets and are comfortable for traveling.

- For running, choose running shoes that are lightweight, with a durable, deeply patterned outer sole, a thick heel wedge to tilt the body forward, and a firm, shock-absorbent midsole and breathable upper. Running shoes should bend at the ball of the foot.

- Tennis-type shoes—heavier and stiffer than running shoes—are good for any activity that primarily involves side-to-side movement. They have a reinforcement under the toes for stop-and-go action and a herring-bone outer sole. For hard courts, nubbed or patterned polyurethane soles are recommended. For clay courts, choose rubber soles with a flat or open tread.

- Aerobics shoes for multidirectional, high-stress movement combine the features of running and tennis-type shoes. You can get away with using tennis-type shoes in aerobics classes, but not running shoes.

- For bicycling, you need a shoe with a stiff sole that spreads the pressure of the pedal across the length of your foot. Cycling shoes should be comfortable for walking, have plenty of toe room, and be soft and well ventilated on the uppers. Soles should have grooves to help grip the pedals.

- For riding, if you don't have proper jodhpur boots or cowboy boots, you must have a boot or a shoe with a heel to keep your foot from slipping through the stirrups. Sneakers or sandals are neither safe nor comfortable for riding.

- If you do a lot of cross-country skiing, you may want to heft your own boots, bindings, skis, and poles with you. If you don't, rental shops can take care of your needs.

- For light hiking on smooth trails, you should bring low-cut trail shoes that weigh only a bit more than running shoes but provide better support. Ankle-high boots are best for hiking on rough, steep trails or in wet weather. The lightest boots are made of canvas reinforced with leather. Slightly heavier, but offering better support and durability, are the suede veldtschoon-type boots, or boots with all-leather uppers. The sturdiest, most dependable boots have a treaded outer sole of hard rubber, an innersole and one or more midsoles for cushioning and strength, a heel counter for stability, and a padded tongue to protect your instep. When shopping for athletic shoes, keep in mind that a well-fitting shoe never needs to be broken in. If shoes don't feel comfortable when you try them on, keep looking. Remember that your feet will expand as much as half a size during activity, so shop at the end of the day, when your feet are largest. To be sure of a good fit, take along a pair of socks you plan to wear for your sport as well as inserts (orthotics) if you use them. *N.B.* Many bootmakers size their women's boots on a scaled-down version of a man's foot, which usually results in poor-fitting boots, because women tend to have higher arches and narrower heels in relation to the front of their feet.

Socks   Bring lots of them. You should change your socks at least once a day and after each workout. Socks should fit your foot well, with enough room to wiggle your toes but not so much that they wrinkle or fold when you put your shoes on. Runners and joggers should remember that cotton and wool socks lock in heat and sweat and that socks made with Orlon and polypropylene wick the sweat away from your toes and thus help to prevent blisters and infections. Best for hiking: light polypropylene liners with outer wool socks.

Headgear and Gloves

- For ski resorts and cold weather activities, bear in mind that a great deal of body heat is lost through the hands and head, and bring gloves and a hood/cap with ear flaps made of wool, cashmere, fur, or polypropylene, or lined with these materials, and a waterproof shell. For hot weather, a white cotton hat with a brim will shade your eyes and help keep your hair from frizzing.

- For riding, you are advised to wear a special hard hat, preferably of molded fiberglass covered with cloth, with a narrow inflexible brim that will protect your face if you take a fall. The best hats have thick padding around the inner perimeter, as well as webbing or netting to create some space between the crown of the hat and the top of the head.

- For bicycling, a hard-shelled cycling helmet, sometimes vented, fully enclosed on top, with a polystyrene foam liner inside, is recommended.

- For swimming in chlorinated pools, remember to bring your bathing cap.

CLOTHES YOU'LL NEED FOR ACTIVE SPORTS

Before you even flex a muscle to think about what to take, *think layering*. The key to smart wintertime dressing is the three-part system of layering. The first layer absorbs perspiration, the second provides warmth, the third shields you from wind and rain. It's particularly important to dress in layers for downhill skiing; speeding downhill subjects you to a windchill factor, and the ride back to the top may be fr-e-e-e-zing. Think multipurpose sporting gear, such as jackets with canvas shells and inner jackets or vests that can be zipped together to make a pocketed parka with a detachable hood. In summertime, layering provides fine tuning—a layer or two can be removed to lower body temperature during active exercise. You should bring a light backpack to hold clothes you plan to put on or cast off.

Not so long ago you had to wear wool and cotton for warmth and absorbency during exercise, but today you can take advantage of the new generation of innovative synthetics. These include polypropylene, breathable waterproof materials such as polytetrafluorethylene (PTFE—brand names include Gamex and Gore-Tex), and lightweight insulative materials such as Thinsulate and Thermolite, which provide warmth without heavy weight and bulkiness and are generally less expensive than their natural goose or duck down counterparts.

Some spas provide exercise clothes but spa issue gear may not always fit the way your own clothes do and may not always be as becoming as your own clothes. Just because a spa provides shorts, warm-ups, T-shirts, leotards, whatever, doesn't mean you are not free to bring your own—with a few exceptions duly noted in individual spa write-ups. If you take your own exercise clothes:

Men need sweats, shorts, T-shirts, sweaters and trousers, bathing suits.

Women need sweats, shorts, T-shirts, sweaters, leotards, cotton tights (stirrup and/or footed type), tops, and bathing suits.

ITEMS YOU'LL BE HAPPY YOU BROUGHT

Walkman and cassettes

Camera and film

Field glasses

Spiral notebook and pens

Scotch tape

Five or six extra passport photographs, in case you need a ski lift identification card, a driver's license, a visa

Tape measure, gauged to both inches and centimeters

Travel alarm clock

Sewing kit with plenty of needles and safety pins

Cold water detergent

Bottle opener, corkscrew, and collapsible cup

Writing paper, envelopes, stamps

Reading material

Pedometer

Small, battery-lit magnifying glass for reading maps

Phrase books or pocket dictionaries

Wristbands, headbands, leg warmers

One of the most important clothing items women will need at most spas is a wraparound skirt or pareu, a smock-type dress, a long T-shirt, lightweight sweats or jump suit or similar cover-up to slip over shorts or leotards before going in for lunch or into lounge areas. Men generally exchange shorts for jeans or chinos, and put on a clean shirt or pullover. At resort spas, guests are expected to wear sportswear for breakfast and lunch, and to observe whatever dress code is operative for evening dining. For summertime in European spas, which tend to be more formal than American spas, you might want to add to your list of essentials a zip-front jumpsuit; cotton knit cardigans, pullovers, and tunics; a pair of flannel trousers and a doubleknit blazer; 2-piece cotton dresses for beach or poolside; a pair of cotton stirrup or straight pants and matching zip jackets and inner shell.

EVERYTHING ELSE LIST

Unless you are traveling with the entourage of a rock star, travel only with what you are prepared to heft all by your lonesome, in and out of your car, in and out of train stations, in and out of airports, even in and out of hotels. Don't disable yourself with backaches, shoulder strain, or low back strain caused by improper lifting of heavy luggage, or the imaginary chimpanzee arm syndrome of carrying it. Unless you are a stevedore by trade, use wheeled luggage or a pullcart. Finally, go with enough room in your luggage to hold the additional purchases you will probably be tempted to make.

N.B. Spa management personnel everywhere recommend that you leave your real jewelery at home and request that you do not bring food or alcoholic beverages with you.

GLOSSARY

acupressure   See MASSAGE.

adipose tissue   Fat cells held together in a supporting framework of connective tissue. A normal constituent of the body, it acts as a cushion and storage place for energy in the form of fat to be drawn upon in response to body needs.

aerobic exercise   Movements fully supported by oxygen delivered to the working muscles by the blood circulation. Examples of aerobic activity include walking, ballroom dancing, and steady, slow jogging. In contrast to aerobic activity, *anaerobic exercise* involves muscular work that is not fully supported by the oxygen available from the circulating blood. Activities like weight lifting, body building, and sprinting (100-yard dash) have a large anaerobic component. Aerobic simply means "in the presence of oxygen." See also LOW-IMPACT AEROBICS.

aerobic shopping   Brisk walking in shopping malls, large spaces heated in winter, and air-conditioned in summer, where there is no traffic, where the surface is smooth and conducive to walking, and where there are no fears about safety or traffic. You can feel virtuous if you stop to buy something. Your purchases can serve as *exercise weights*.

anaerobic exercise   See AEROBIC EXERCISE.

aqua-aerobics   An exercise workout in a swimming pool utilizing the natural resistance of water to strengthen and tone the muscles. Also called *aquacize*. See also AEROBIC EXERCISE.

aromatherapy   Facial or body massage with herbal, floral, and resinous scented oils. From ancient times, various fragrances have been associated with the power to dispel aches and pains, wake you up, cheer you up, settle you down, and clear your sinuses. Pine, roses, lavender, camomile, and dozens of other choices are available.

behavior modification   A weight control approach based on the premise that overeating and inactivity are habits that can be replaced by new, more desirable eating and exercise habits. See also COGNITIVE TRAINING.

bioelectrical impedance analysis (BIA)   A noninvasive method of measuring body water based on the conductance of an electrical current injected into the body by means of electrodes (used to establish electrical contact with a nonmetallic surface) clamped (usually) to wrist and ankle. Also called *electrical impedance measurement.*

blood pressure   The pressure exerted by the blood on the walls of the body's arteries. *Systolic* blood pressure is the blood pressure while the heart is contracting and pumping out blood. *Diastolic* blood pressure is the blood pressure while the heart is expanding and filling with blood.

body composition   The percentage of various body components such as fat, lean body mass, total body water, extracellular water, and intracellular water that make up your total weight.

body image   An individual's perception of his or her own body in such terms as size, shape, thinness, fatness, and degree of attractiveness.

body mass index (BMI)   A measure of body weight adjusted for height. See Do You Have Too Much Body Fat? earlier in this part for how BMI is calculated.

body scrub   See LOOFAH.

calorie (kilocalorie or kcal)   The amount of heat needed to increase the temperature of a kilogram (2.2 pounds) of water by 1 degree centigrade, from 15 to 16 degrees centigrade. Most commonly, the energy content of foods and the energy expended by the body to maintain life processes and perform muscular work are expressed in calories. In this use, calories are the heat equivalent of stored or expended energy.

carbohydrate   A class of foods whose main function is to supply energy. When a food containing carbohydrate is eaten and digested, most of it is turned into the simplest carbohydrate unit, glucose, which enters the blood stream to be used as one of the body's major fuels. Dietary carbohydrates may be classified as *simple* or *complex.* Examples of simple carbohydrates include sugars found in syrups, honey, refined sugar, fruits, soft drinks, and milk. Foods rich in complex carbohydrates include potatoes, breads, cereals, pasta, rice, and some vegetables.

cardiovascular   Pertaining to the heart and blood vessels. Common cardiovascular conditions include coronary heart disease, arteriosclerosis, hypertension, stroke, and cerebrovascular diseases.

cardiovascular fitness   The ability of the heart (a muscle) and blood vessels to meet the demands of physical exertion. Fitness is relative; one must always ask "Fit for what?" Someone who is fit to play tennis may not be fit for cross-country skiing or mountain climbing. Thus, different levels of fitness are achieved by different kinds of physical training. Cardiovascular fitness can be determined with considerable precision in the laboratory by the use of one or more tests of "maximal aerobic power." Maximal aerobic power ($\dot{V}o_{2max}$) is the highest oxygen uptake a given individual can achieve while performing a standardized exercise, like running on a motorized treadmill.

cathiodermie   An electric machine using both galvanic and high-frequency currents that are claimed to deep-cleanse and revitalize your skin and oxygenate its outer tissue layer.

cellulite   A nonscientific term used by some cosmeticians and beauticians to describe a pebbly or uneven surface of the skin of the hips, thighs, or buttocks of women, associated with increased deposits of fat in those areas. The notion that this condition is pathological and caused by a "toxin" of some sort is without scientific foundation.

cholesterol   A waxy substance that the body uses in the transport of fats and to make certain hormones. The body can manufacture what little cholesterol it needs. The cholesterol that circulates in the blood plasma is present primarily in complex molecules called *low-density lipoproteins (LDL),* which are used to transport fat to cells in the body that either store it or use it as a fuel. There is a strong relationship between the blood plasma level of LDL cholesterol and risk of developing disease of the heart and blood vessels. About one-quarter of the cholesterol in the blood plasma of adults is carried in *high-density lipoproteins (HDL).* HDL may serve the function of removing excess cholesterol from tissues. Whatever the case, the risk of heart and blood vessel disease declines as HDL cholesterol increases. Cholesterol is also in foods of animal origin such as meat, poultry, some seafood, and dairy products. Egg yolks and organ meats are very high in cholesterol. Foods of plant origin such as fruits, vegetables, grains, cereals, nuts, and seeds contain no cholesterol.

circuit weight training   Weight lifting for a total body fitness program. On a circuit, you put yourself through a series of training stations, stopping only briefly between each exercise to keep your heart rate within an acceptable range throughout the circuit.

cognitive training   In weight control programs, the replacing of negative or defeatist thinking with positive attitudes to help those trying to lose weight to stick to their program.

complete protein   See PROTEIN.

complex carbohydrate   See CARBOHYDRATE.

cool-down exercises   Movements at the conclusion of your exercise session to give your body a chance to ease out of the routine while your pulse rate returns to normal.

cross-country ski machine   Total body exerciser. Standing on short "skis," your legs move back and forth while your arms alternate pulling on a cable suspended in front or on poles attached at the machine's base. Burns calories at an amazing rate while utilizing nearly every muscle.

depilatory waxing   See WAXING.

diastolic blood pressure   See BLOOD PRESSURE.

dietary fiber   A number of chemically different components of plant cell walls and cell contents that are not broken down by the digestive enzymes in the human gastrointestinal tract. Some types of fiber help move food more rapidly through the body, aid in bowel regularity, and promote a healthy digestive tract. Certain types of fiber can also effect a modest lowering of blood cholesterol levels. Fibers are found in a wide range of foods, including fruits, vegetables, grains, cereals, nuts, seeds, and legumes (dried beans and peas). Only foods from plant sources contain fiber.

diuretic   A medicine that promotes the loss of salt, water, and other constituents from the body via the urine. Diuretics are used in the treatment of high blood pressure and certain types of *edema*.

edema   Swelling of a part or parts of the body (for example, the feet or ankles) due to abnormal retention of water in certain body tissues.

elastics   See RUBBER-BAND WORKOUTS.

electrical impedance measurement   See BIOELECTRICAL IMPEDANCE ANALYSIS.

electrocardiogram   A graphic, systematic record of the electrical currents produced by the heart. Often referred to as EKG or ECG.

ergometer   A built-in digital timer and workload indicator to enable you to measure your performance in a given time. These instruments can help you avoid overexertion at the start, and measure your improvement on a continuing basis.

exercise weights   Small weights gripped in your hand, strapped or Velcroed to your wrist, or worn across your chest while working out to add to the impact of exercise routines, build upper body muscles, and intensify workouts.

exercourse   See PARCOURS/PARCOURSE

fango therapy   Mineralized mud, which can be heated and placed on various parts of your body as a poultice, or on your face as a masque, effective as a muscle relaxant and skin cleanser, and recognized for the "silkening," "softening" effect it has for up to a week or more on your skin. Also called *mud packs.* RADIOACTIVITY is present in the mud at several spas. Pregnant women and women in their reproductive years should not risk possible genetic mutation by avoidable exposure to radioactivity.

faradism   Electric muscle stimulators used to tone muscles through low-level electricity conducted through contact pads attached to the body for "passive exercise," often used for treatment of certain medical conditions such as bursitis, running injuries, broken limbs, muscle spasms, and muscle atrophy from disuse. *Should not be used by pregnant women, people with heart problems, including those who wear pacemakers, or people with cancer or epilepsy.* Also called *slendertone.*

fast   To abstain from food. Also, to eat sparingly or abstain from some foods. A *supplemented fast,* or very-low-calorie diet, consists of small amounts of regular foods and extra vitamins and minerals, or of a liquid "formula" diet that is nutritionally adequate except for its content of calories. A *protein-sparing modified fast (PSMF),* another term for a very-low-calorie diet, is usually limited to lean meats, poultry, and fish (supplemented with vitamins and minerals), which in aggregate provide 600 to 800 calories a day.

fat   An organic nutrient that provides the most concentrated source of calories available; that is, 9 calories per gram. *Saturated fat,* which is usually of animal origin, tends to raise blood cholesterol levels. It is solid or semisolid at room temperature. Examples include lard, butter, hydrogenated vegetable shortening, palm oil, and coconut oil. *Monounsaturated fat* may reduce blood cholesterol levels. Examples include olive oil, peanut oil, and avocados. *Polyunsaturated fat,* usually of plant or fish origin, also tends to lower blood cholesterol levels. These fats are liquid at room temperature. Examples include safflower, corn, sunflower, soybean, and cottonseed oils.

The terms *saturated, monounsaturated,* and *polyunsaturated* refer to the predominance in a fat or oil of fatty acids whose carbon bonds are saturated in varying degrees with hydrogen atoms. A polyunsaturated fat is rich in fatty acids that are highly unsaturated (containing more than 1 double bond). A monounsaturated fat is rich in fatty acids that contain only 1 double bond. Saturated fatty acids, with no double bonds, have their full complement of hydrogen atoms.

fiber   See DIETARY FIBER.

fitness evaluation   A test for your aerobic capacity, flexibility, and strength under the direction of an exercise specialist, usually in order to design an individual exercise program to meet your needs and capacities.

formula diet   A liquid food used in the treatment of overweight people, varying in calorie content but often supplying in the range of 420 to 800 calories a day. Formulas are usually designed to be nutritionally adequate except for calorie content. Some formulas require supplementation with potassium, calcium, magnesium, and other nutrients.

free weights   Dumbbells. Lifting them allows you to isolate and tone specific muscle groups.

gastric   Refers to the stomach.

gastric balloon   See Diets, Drugs, and Devices earlier in this part. Also called *gastric bubble*.

high-density lipoprotein cholesterol   See CHOLESTEROL.

holistic   Health care that focuses on your whole self—mental, physical, emotional, and spiritual.

hydrostatic weighing   Underwater weight test. See Do You Have Too Much Body Fat? earlier in this part.

hydrotherapy   An underwater massage given in a multijet tub to stimulate circulation while toning your skin.

hypertension   High blood pressure, which may eventually lead to blood vessel damage and increased heart size.

hypoglycemia   Low blood sugar.

ideal weight   Strictly speaking, this confusing expression refers to the tables of "ideal weights" published by the Metropolitan Life Insurance Company in 1942–43. In 1959, Metropolitan Life replaced the ideal-weight tables with new "desirable-weight" tables. In 1983, the desirable-weight tables were, in turn, replaced by "The 1983 Metropolitan Life Tables" based on more recent mortality statistics. Although "ideal weight" is an outdated term, it continues to be used (improperly) to refer to the desirable weights for height determined by Metropolitan Life in 1959 or associated with the greatest longevity in the 1983 tables.

infrared treatment   A heat treatment to aid in muscular relaxation and increased blood circulation.

inhalation room   A wood-paneled room filled with hot vapors and/or steam from seawater, mineral water, or thermal water, sometimes augmented with pine, eucalyptus, and other oils for relieving respiratory congestion and enjoying the pleasures of *aromatherapy*.

isometric exercise   Movements in which opposing muscles are so contracted that there is little shortening of the muscles but a great increase in the tension of the muscles involved. For example, attempting to lift a weight that is too heavy to move will result in increasing the tension of certain muscles without muscle shortening. See also ISOTONIC EXERCISE.

isotonic exercise   Movements that involve muscle contraction with shortening. Exercises like tennis, running, and golf are isotonic. See also ISOMETRIC EXERCISE.

ketosis   The accumulation in the body of ketone bodies, generally associated with a low carbohydrate intake and commonly observed in cases of starvation, prolonged ingestion of low-calorie, low-carbohydrate diets, and poorly controlled insulin-dependent (Type I) diabetes.

Kneipp bath/therapy/treatment   The use of herbal bath oils, eucalyptus, lavender, rosemary, meadow blossom, spruce, pine, juniper, camomile, and hops to comfort body and mind as a component of treatment originated in the 19th century by Sebastian Kneipp, a German clergyman.

lacto-ovo   Latin for milk and eggs, generally used in connection with a vegetarian diet that is extended with the same.

lipids   A general term for fats and fatlike substances. Lipids include fats, cholesterol, lecithins, phospholipids, and similar substances that are generally insoluble in water.

liposuction   See Diets, Drugs, and Devices earlier in this part.

liquid-protein diet   A term originally used to describe the type of very-low-calorie liquid diet associated with the deaths of some 58 obese dieters in 1977 and 1978. The diets consisted of heavily flavored gelatin or collagen hydrolysates (predigested from such animal sources as skin and hooves of cattle). These protein products, even when supplemented with the amino acid tryptophan, proved to be nutritionally inadequate.

loofah   A body scrub with vegetable husk combined with salt, honey, almond oil, or other items to rid your body of old, dead, flaky skin, increase circulation, and soften and smooth your skin.

low-density lipoprotein cholesterol   See CHOLESTEROL.

low-impact aerobics   Exercise that substitutes side-to-side marching or gliding movements for the jumping, hopping, jogging movements of conventional aerobic exercises without subjecting your body to excessive stress. One foot is almost always kept on the floor, and your body is kept closer to the floor than in conventional aerobics, with the body's pressure against the floor used to create resistance and condition muscles. See also AEROBIC EXERCISE.

lymphatic drainage   The removal of lymph, a body fluid devoid of red blood cells that bathes and contributes nourishment to the body's tissues. Normally, lymph is drained by changes in the body's position and by the pumping action of nearby muscles. In otherwise healthy people who are physically very inactive and whose muscle tone is greatly diminished, excess fluid may accumulate in the lowest parts of the body such as the feet, ankles, or the small of the back. Large accumulations of fat under the skin can also cause mechanical interference with lymphatic drainage, with resulting *edema*. Impaired lymphatic drainage in sedentary but otherwise healthy persons is best treated by increasing physical activity, muscle strengthening exercises, and, when appropriate, calorie restriction to reduce the size of the fat deposits. Massage of the involved areas may provide temporary relief.

massage   A wonderful antidote to stress and muscle tension. It doesn't, as myth would have it, rub away weight, but it will rub away fatigue, inducing relaxation. *Swedish massage,* the most familiar technique, uses oils to reduce friction and lubricate your skin, and employs long full strokes, along with kneading and pounding motions. *Acupressure* and *shiatsu massage* are Oriental techniques in which fingers are pressed along defined paths on your body to release *chi,* or trapped energy. *Rolfing* is deep tissue massage. Touch ranges from firm to intense to the point of bearable pain. The amount of verbal interaction and client participation depends on the individual practitioner. Tensions blocking freedom of movement are released through systematic balancing of muscles and connective tissue around the vertical pull of gravity. *Trager massage* is "a release of psycho-physiological patterns that block free-flowing movement. Structural and functional improvements occur spontaneously as a result of sensory repatterning in your mind, as your body is rhythmically moved by the practitioner, producing deep relaxation and release of mental and physical stresses." There is minimal verbal communication between you and the practitioner. *Reflexology* is a foot massage in which pressure points on your feet and toes that correspond to other parts and organs of your body are stimulated. It is one of the great massages for relaxation and stress reduction.

metabolism   All the biochemical activities that occur in living organisms, which, in aggregate, sustain life and support function.

monounsaturated fat   See FAT.

mud packs   See FANGO THERAPY.

natural foods   Although no formal or legal definition exists, the term is generally used to describe foods that have not been processed or refined and do not contain additives or other artificial ingredients. "Natural" foods are not necessarily more nutritious or safer to eat than processed foods available in the supermarkets.

nutrients   Substances derived from foods that are necessary for the functioning of the human body, including proteins, carbohydrates, fats, vitamins, and minerals. Nutrients are used by the body in three ways: to permit growth and repair of its tissues, to furnish energy and heat, and to regulate body processes.

obesity A bodily condition marked by excessive fat in adipose tissue. Obesity is often defined as being present in an individual who is 20 percent above the "optimal weight" for height and sex in standard height-weight tables. See Do You Have Too Much Body Fat? earlier in this part.

orthion treatment A 3-dimension mechanical treatment with traction modes for soothing reflexive relaxation and stimulation of your body and relief of aches, pains, and muscle spasm.

overweight Usually defined as 20 percent or more above "desirable weight," using the midpoint of the range for persons of medium frame size in the Metropolitan Life Insurance Company height and weight tables (1959 or 1983).

ozonized baths A tub of thermal water or seawater with a system of jets that provide streams of ozonized bubbles, used for relaxation and stimulation of circulation and as an aid for the relief of minor aches and pains.

paraffin masque/mask Wax applied to smooth and soften your skin temporarily, often used in combination with volcanic ash or fango (see FANGO THERAPY) for a therapeutic and cosmetic effect.

paraffin wax bath Warm paraffin wax applied to your body. The liquid wax coats your skin and, as it solidifies, forms a vacuum that causes any dirt in the pores to be drawn out, removes dead skin, and induces a loss of body fluid in the form of perspiration. The deep heat created by this treatment helps to relieve stress and promote relaxation.

parcours/parcourse A path or trail with exercise stations along the way provided with instructions and equipment for sit-ups, pull-ups, chin-ups, and a variety of other "obstacles" that are fun and challenging. Also called *vitacourse* and *exercourse* and written as two words, *par cours(e)*

polarity therapy A relaxation experience to "remove blocks in the flow of life energy systems through gentle manipulations and holding/contact techniques."

polyunsaturated fat See FAT.

protein An essential foodstuff required for growth and repair of body tissues. Chicken, fish, lean meat, cheese, eggs, and peanut butter are good sources of protein. *Complete proteins* contain all of the essential amino acids in significant amounts and in the proportions necessary to maintain life and to support growth. *Incomplete proteins* lack certain amino acids that are essential to maintain life and support growth.

protein-sparing Referring to the ability of a diet or a medication to reduce the rate at which the body loses protein from its lean tissues (such as muscles and organs). More body protein is lost by individuals who fast than by those who adhere to a protein-sparing diet.

protein-sparing modified fast See FAST.

radioactivity The spontaneous nuclear disintegration of certain elements, accompanied by the emission of radiation in the form of particles or rays. Exposure to radioactivity should be controlled, in order to protect the present generation from somatic effects and future generations from genetic effects. Pregnant women especially should avoid radiation. Never drink radioactive water.

rebounder A miniature trampoline.

recommended daily (or dietary) allowances (RDA) Amounts of nutrients recommended by the Food and Nutrition Board of the National Academy of Sciences National Research Council as adequate for the maintenance of good nutrition in practically all healthy persons in the United States.

reflexology See MASSAGE.

rolfing See MASSAGE.

rubber-band workouts Giant rubber bands used for resistance techniques in calisthenics. Also called *elastics*.

salt rub A massage with warm almond or avocado oil mixed with sea salt to remove dead skin and lubricate your skin. Also called *salt glow, salt glo*.

saturated fat See FAT.

sauna A wood-lined room heated with dry heat up to 210 degrees F. Wooden benches are provided for reclining on towels you bring with you. One purpose is to make you sweat out "toxins." Follow with a cool shower.

Scotch hose Alternating horizontal jets of hot and cold water for invigorating and toning treatments.

shiatsu See MASSAGE.

simple carbohydrate See CARBOHYDRATE.

sitz bath Immersion of buttocks in small tubs of water, alternating from hot to cold, while soaking feet in water alternating from cold to hot, a treatment considered good for the circulation.

slendertone See FARADISM.

StairMaster. A stair-climbing machine. See VERSA-CLIMBER.

supplemented fast See FAST.

Swedish massage   See MASSAGE.

Swiss shower   Alternating hot and cold vertical jets as an invigorating and toning shower.

systolic blood pressure   See BLOOD PRESSURE.

Tai Chi   An ancient discipline that integrates body coordination with mental awareness. Smooth, flowing movements are blended with meditation and relaxation.

thalassotherapy   Seawater baths and seaweed wraps for therapeutic effect. *Thalasso* is the Greek word for sea.

thermal wrap   A procedure claimed to eliminate "toxins" from your body through perspiration and promote muscle relaxation in which your body is wrapped in hot, wet linen sheets infused with herbal essences, and then covered with a blanket or plastic sheet to retain the heat. A cool compress is applied to your forehead. If you are claustrophobic and don't want to be completely swaddled, you can ask that your arms and hands be left outside your Egyptian mummy–like wrapping.

total body electrical conductivity (TOBEC)   A rapid and convenient method for measuring body composition. It is based on the principle that electrical energy is conducted better by the body's fat-free mass (including muscle and other lean tissues) than by fat.

Trager massage   See MASSAGE.

triglyceride   Chemical name for neutral fat, a concentrated calorie source found in varying amounts in most foods. In the blood, triglycerides circulate as a component of lipoprotein molecules, which also contain cholesterol and other lipids.

underwater weight test   See Do You Have Too Much Body Fat? earlier in this part.

Versa-Climber   A ladder-type machine with moving rungs to simulate stair climbing for cardiovascular workouts.

vitacourse   See PARCOURS/PARCOURSE.

warm-up exercises   Movements to get your blood flowing and your pulse rate going and help you ease into the regular portion of your exercise program, loosening and readying your muscles and making them less prone to injury.

waxing   Removal of facial, leg, arm, or bikini area hair by a trained specialist who applies wax to the area desired. When wax is removed, hair is removed. Slight ouch, but leaves area smoother and removes hair longer than shaving. Also called *depilatory waxing*.

wellness   A term used by some health workers to describe disease prevention–health promotion activities.

yoga   An ancient discipline to promote relaxation and increase inner awareness and flexibility through deep breathing techniques and movements.

yo-yo syndrome   A repetitive pattern of weight loss followed by a rapid regain of weight, frequently in excess of the amount originally lost.

INDEX

ABOUT THE AUTHORS

Theodore B. Van Itallie, M.D., is a Professor Emeritus of Medicine at Columbia University's College of Physicians and Surgeons and founder of the Obesity Research Center at St. Luke's/Roosevelt Hospital in New York City. He has received a number of national awards for his achievements in medical research and for contributions to national health programs.

Leila Hadley, a writer living in New York City, is the author of *Fielding's Europe with Children* and other books and articles.